PLE
BY 1
TUL

FIN
MAXI

Frequent flyers.

British Airways offers regular scheduled
services from the UK to Tunis.
Ask your travel agent or British Airways
Travel Shop for further details or
call us direct on 0345 222111.

BRITISH AIRWAYS

Tunisia
Handbook
with Libya

Anne & Keith McLachlan

Footprint Handbooks

Upon the night of parting
Within the desert deep
Beneath the soft acacia
How sweet it is to sleep

Shaikh Sa'adi, Gulestan

Footprint Handbooks

6 Riverside Court, Lower Bristol Road
Bath BA2 3DZ England
T 01225 469141 F 01225 469461
E mail handbooks@footprint.cix.co.uk
www.fooprint-handbooks.co.uk

ISBN 0 900751 91 6 ISSN 1363-7487
CIP DATA: A catalogue record for this book is
available from the British Library

In North America, published by

PASSPORT BOOKS
a division of *NTC Publishing Group*

4255 West Touhy Avenue, Lincolnwood
(Chicago), Illinois 60646-1975, USA
T 847 679 5500 F 847 679 24941
E mail NTCPUB2@AOL.COM

ISBN 0-8442-4867-3
Library of Congress Catalog Card
Number: 96-72521
Passport Books and colophon are registered
trademarks of NTC Publishing group

©Footprint Handbooks Limited
1st Edition
January 1997

First published in 1993 as part of *North African
Handbook* by Trade & Travel Publications Ltd

Cover design by Newell and Sorrell; cover
photography by Dave Saunders, TRIP/Helene
Rogers and Matthew Kneale

Production: Design by Mytton Williams;
Typesetting by Jo Morgan, Ann Griffiths and
Melanie Mason-Fayon; Maps by Sebastian
Ballard, Kevin Feeney and Aldous George;
Charts by Lindsay Dawson; Original line
drawings by Geoff Moss; Proofread by Rod
Gray and David Cotterell.

Printed and bound in Great Britain by
Clays Ltd., Bungay, Suffolk

The authors

Anne McLachlan

Anne McLachlan is an avid traveller with a long experience of Tunisia and its varied regions. She had visited Tunisia for many years on a regular basis to check on the detailed changes that occur in hotels, travel facilities and political atmosphere. She also manages a team of international co-researchers who up-date the text of the *Handbook* both from sources in Tunisia and elsewhere.

In the last year, she has made extensive field visits to SW Tunisia and the Sahel, Tunis and Cap Bon, and the deep SE of the country to bring the latest information for the readers of this *Handbook*. New and improved site plans of the principal ancient sites have been prepared for this first edition of the *Tunisia Handbook* after visits to key sites for visitors.

Keith McLachlan

Keith McLachlan is a professional observer and traveller of many years standing in Tunisia and Libya, first visited in 1958 and 1959, respectively, and since kept in touch with through residence there and regular visits. He has extensive experience of trans-Saharan travel in Libya and has also in the last year traversed much of the northern sections of the Sahara in Tunisia and elsewhere in North Africa. In recent months he has completed extended visits to the important sites for antiquities and sight-seeing in central and southern Tunisia.

He is professor emeritus at the School of Oriental and African Studies and a consultant on Tunisia, Libyan and North African affairs which keeps him abreast of travel and change in the region and thus able to provide the reader with up-to-date information on the region of the *Tunisia Handbook* and on the quirks of travel in the two countries.

Keith McLachlan began his research career in Libya and Tunisia in the 1950s has for many years acted as a consultant to Libyan government agencies and major international companies on economic, border and oil affairs.

Introduction and hints

TUNISIA IS North Africa's jewel in the traveller's crown – compact, intriguingly exotic and infinitely varied in scenery and landscape. The *Tunisia Handbook* provides a comprehensive guide to travel, with an up-to-date and extended review of all the current and background information that the visitor might need. Libya, little known but rich in antiquities, is also covered in this *Handbook* in a depth available nowhere else in the literature.

Tunisia brings together all that is best in North Africa. It has warm weather for almost all of the year yet is cultivated and green over much of its central and northern areas. Furthermore, in the Saharan south, a concentrated range of marvelously varied desert landscapes that include one of the world's largest salt lakes, sand dunes, rugged mountains and seemingly infinite space are waiting to be explored. It is not surprising that Tunisia has produced many of the contemporary Arab poets with a strong lyrical tradition given its contrasting pastoral scenes and peoples!

The Tunisians themselves have given North Africa its most sustained economic miracle, with rising living standards, an export-oriented manufacturing industry and a modern, thriving agriculture. A symbol of Tunisia's long success with farming is the olive tree, which is found in vast numbers, some in serried rows, in the vast Sahel Plain of the centre east and others in antique mountain groves which have existed since the Roman invasion. Tunisia is making a name as a modest but growing oil and gas exporter whilst effectively maintaining its wonderfully unspoilt desert environment in the south. Even the phosphate mining area of Gafsa contributes its bit to the diversity of adventures offered to the visitor with a rail journey on the *Red Lizard*, a narrow gauge line through the moonscape territory in the southwest hills.

Tunisia's population is made of people from mixed origins. There is still a strong element of Berber roots to be found – a continuity through at least 3,000 years – and the Berber language is spoken by the inhabitants of remote mountain villages in many parts of the country. Even troglodyte houses, set into the earth, can be found together with *ghorfas*, traditional arch-roofed rural dwellings perched on hill tops. The Berbers are known for their great sense of hospitality and good humour. Arab tribes are of course well represented in Tunisia and have given Tunisia its national language and its religion – Islam. City life is a compound of both Arab and Berber cultures with a spice provided by the long contact with Mediterranean cultural traditions, particularly French and Italian. Tunis and the major cities are thus a combination of the best of the oriental bazaar and the well planned modern European-style residential and shopping quarters. The capital, Tunis, has one of the world's most captivating and rich bazaars, still throbs with life and teems with an enormous variety of goods which will entrance the visitor from abroad. Architecturally old Tunis, the medina with its mosques, great houses and souqs is unrivalled as an example of mediaeval Islamic town-building.

Tunisia offers some of the best and sandiest beaches on the southern Mediterranean. Here at its fine purpose-built resorts such as Port El-Kantaoui and Hammamet peace, sun, water sports and some wonderful golf/tennis facilities are to be found. In total contrast, opportunities exist for unrestricted individual travel in the north and interior of the country by train, bus and car to discover a different Tunisia of hills and forests. In southern Tunisia a new and expanding itinerary is there for those who want to battle with the sand tracks and harsh terrain of the great Chotts and desert in four-wheel-drive vehicles.

Libya is another country – an ethnic twin of Tunisia but totally different in every dimension. Libya is of enormous surface area with a variety of desert landscapes to delight the most seasoned connoisseur. It is an underrated and under-travelled country. This *Handbook* tells you how to take advantage of its wonderful and truly unmatched wealth of Greek built above all Roman ruins, of which the magnificence of Leptis Magna and the artfulness of Sabrata are merely a small sample.

How to go

DOCUMENTS

Passports

All foreign tourists are recommended to have a passport that is valid for the whole of the period of stay. This avoids unnecessary contact with the bureaucracy. Depending on origin of passport some countries require visas. Details are given in each country section.

Special permits

Certain zones, particularly adjacent to borders and in areas of conflict haverestricted access and travel there is permitted only with military approval. Details of sensitive areas are given in the relevant country section.

Identity & membership cards

If you are in full-time education you will be entitled to an International Student Identity Card (ISIC), which is distributed by student travel offices and travel agencies in 77 countries. The ISIC gives you special prices on all forms of transport (air, sea, rail etc) and access to a variety of other concessions and services. Contact ISIC, Box 9048, 1000 Copenhagen, Denmark, T (+45) 33939303.

HEALTH

See main section, page 453

MONEY

Travellers' cheques

TCs can be honoured in most banks and *bureaux de change*. US$ are the easiest to exchange particularly if they are well-known like Visa, Thomas Cook or American Express. There is always a transaction charge so it is a balance between using high value cheques and paying one charge and carrying extra cash or using lower value cheques and paying more charges. A small amount of cash, again in US$, is useful in an emergency.

Some countries have a fixed exchange rate – wherever the transaction is carried out. Other countries have a varied exchange rate and, to a greater or lesser degree, a black market. See the appropriate country sections and be sure you know what you are doing before you get involved.

WHAT TO TAKE

Travellers tend to take more than they need though requirements vary with the destination and the type of travel that is to be undertaken. Laundry services are generally cheap and speedy. A travelpack, a hybrid backpack/suitcase, rather than a rigid suitcase, covers most eventualities and survives bus boot, roof rack and plane/ship hold travel with ease. Serious trekkers will need a framed backpack.

Exchange rates (20 January 1997)

	US$	£	Ffr	DM	Ptas
Libya	0.35	0.59	0.07	0.22	0.003
Tunisia	1.01	1.70	0.19	0.63	0.008

Clothing of light cotton or cotton/polyester with a a woollen sweater for evenings, more northern regions, higher altitudes and the clear desert nights. Comfortable shoes with socks as feet may swell in hot weather. Modest dress for women including (see page 12) a sunhat and headscarf.

Checklist:

Air cushions for hard seating
Earplugs
Eye mask
Insect repellent and/or mosquito net, electric mosquito mats, coils
Neck pillow
International driving licence
Photocopies of essential documents
Plastic bags
Short wave radio
Spare passport photographs
Sun hat
Sun protection cream
Sunglasses
Swiss Army knife
Tissues/toilet paper
Torch
Umbrella (excellent protection from sun and unfriendly dogs)
Wipes (*Damp Ones*, *Baby Wipes*)
Zip-lock bags

Those intending to stay in budget-accommodation might also include:
Cotton sheet sleeping bag
Money belt
Padlock (for hotel room and pack)
Soap
Student card
Towel
Toilet paper
Universal bath plug

Health kit

Antiacid tablets
Anti-diarrhoea tablets
Anti-malaria tablets
Anti-infective ointment
Condoms
Contraceptives
Dusting powder for feet

First aid kit and disposable needles
Flea powder
Sachets of rehydration salts
Tampons
Travel sickness pills
Water sterilizing tablets

GETTING THERE

AIR

It is possible to fly direct to several destinations within Tunisia from Europe, from the Middle East and most adjacent African countries. Libya is currently suffering a UN embargo on international flights. More details are given in the *Information for travellers* sections. General airline restrictions apply with regard to luggage weight allowances before surcharge; normally 30 kg for first class and 20 kg for business and economy class. An understanding of the term 'limited' with regard to amount of hand luggage varies greatly. The major destinations are the national capitals and, particularly in Tunisia, the tourist airports. The scheduled flying times from London are Libya 3 hrs (but now only to Djerba 3 hrs or Cairo $4\frac{1}{2}$ hrs) and Tunis $2\frac{1}{2}$ hrs. Package tours which frequently offer cheaper flight-only deals generally operate smaller planes which take longer.

Discounts

It is possible to obtain significantly cheaper tickets by avoiding school vacation times, by flying at night, by shopping around and by booking early to obtain one of the quota of discounted fares. Group discounts apply in many instances.

Airline security

International airlines vary in their arrangements and requirements for security over electrical items such as radios, tape recorders and lap-top computers (as does the interest of the customs officials on arrival and departure). Check in advance if you can, carry the items in your hand luggage for convenience and have

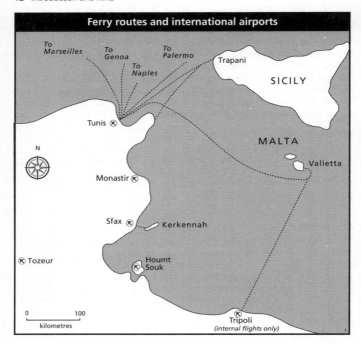

Ferry routes and international airports

them wrapped for safety but available for inspection. Note that internal airlines often have different rules from the international carriers.

Note

This *Handbook* outlines further details on air links to and from Tunisia, arrival and departure regulations, airport taxes, customs regulations and security arrangements for air travel in the relevant *Information for travellers* section.

SEA

Ferries Numerous ferries operate across the Mediterranean carrying both vehicles and foot passengers. Prices vary according to the season. Details are given in the country sections along with entry points by land.

ON ARRIVAL

APPEARANCE

There is a natural prejudice in all countries against travellers who ignore personal hygiene and have a generally unkempt appearance. Observation of the local people will show, where they can afford it, their attention to cleanliness and neatness. The men attend the office in suits with a white shirt and tie or a newly pressed native garment and the women beneath their veil are very well dressed. All persons other than manual workers will be fully dressed. Scantily clad visitors, other than round the hotel pool, show insufficient consideration for their host country. In a hot climate it is eminently sensible and certainly more comfortable to copy the locals and cover the body.

BARGAINING

Bargaining is expected in the bazaars. Start lower than you would expect to pay, be polite and good humoured, enjoy the experience and if the final price doesn't suit – walk away. There are plenty more shops. Once you have gained confidence, try it on the taxi drivers and when negotiating a room, see box page 13.

BEGGARS

Beggars are a fact of life. It is unlikely that they will be too persistent. Have a few very small coins ready. You will be unable to help many and your donation will most probably be passed on to the syndicate organizer!

CONFIDENCE TRICKSTERS

The most common 'threat' to tourists is found where people are on the move, at ports and railway and bus stations, selling 'antiques', 'gems', offering extremely favourable currency exchange rates and spinning 'hard luck' stories. Confidence tricksters are, by definition, extremely convincing and persuasive. Be warned – if the offer seems too good to be true that is probably what it is.

COURTESY

Politeness is always appreciated. You will notice a great deal of hand shaking, kissing, clapping on backs on arrival and departure from a group. There is no need to follow this to the extreme but handshakes, smiles and thank yous go a long way. Be patient and friendly but firm when bargaining for items and avoid displays of anger. Be very careful never to criticize as officials, waiters and taxi drivers can understand more than you think. See page 24 on how to deal with the bureaucracy. **However** when it comes to getting onto public transport, forget it all and be ready to push.

DRUGS

Ignore **all** offers of drugs. It is more than likely that the 'pusher', if successful, will report you to the police.

FIREARMS

Firearms including hunting guns may not be taken into the countries covered in this *Handbook* without prior permission.

MOSQUES

Visitors to mosques (where permitted)

The bazaar and bargaining

An enduring characteristic of bazaars, especially those in Tunisia, is their use of pricing through bargaining for every transaction, however large or small. Bargaining has evinced rather polarized views from economists. On the one hand bargaining is seen as a function of the efficiency of the bazaar. Each business transaction is done with the finest of margins so that prices are very sensitive.

Other contrary opinions are not lacking which maintain that, far from being efficient, bazaar transactions maximize profits for the seller per article sold rather than maximizing potential total profit flows. Bazaars thus act as a brake on the expansion of commerce as a whole. They also rely on the ability of the seller to exploit the absence of quality controls, trade mark conventions and other types of consumer protection. In these situations, the seller treats each transaction as an opportunity to cheat the customer. Bazaars are, in this view, places where the buyer much be doubly wary since short measure, adulteration of goods and falsification of provenance of goods for the benefit of the seller is normal. By definition this system can operate only in countries with minimal regulatory regimes and where consumer information is unorganized, mainly therefore, in the Third World.

and other religious buildings will normally be expected to remove their shoes and cover-all garments will be available for hire to enable the required standard of dress to be met.

PERSONAL SECURITY

Travellers in Tunisia or Libya are unlikely to experience threats to personal security. On the contrary, followers of Islam are expected to honour the stranger in their midst. However basic common sense is needed for the protection of personal property, money and papers. Use hotel safes for valuable items as hotel rooms cannot be regarded as secure and when travelling, carry valuables as close to the body as possible, and where convenient, in more than one place. External pockets on bags and clothing should never be used for carrying valuables. Bag snatching and pick pocketing is more common in crowded tourist areas. It is obviously unwise to lay temptation in the way of a man whose annual income is less than the cost of your return airfare. **NB** It is wise to keep a record of your passport number, TCs number and air ticket number somewhere separate from the actual items.

POLICE

Report any incident which involves you or your possessions. An insurance claim of any size will require the backing of a police report. If involvement with the police is more serious, for instance a driving accident, remain calm, read the section on how to deal with the bureaucracy (see page 24) and contact the nearest consular office without delay.

TIPPING

Tipping in Tunisia and Libya is a way of life – everyone expects a coin for services rendered or supposed. Many get no real wage and rely on tips. In hotels and restaurants the service has probably been included so a tip to the waiter is an optional extra. It does no harm to round up the taxi fare, and a handful of small coins eases the way.

WOMEN TRAVELLING ALONE

Women face greater difficulties than men or couples. Young Muslim women rarely travel without the protection of a male or older female, hence a single Western woman is regarded as strange and is supposed to be of easy virtue – a view perpetuated by Hollywood. To minimise the pestering that will certainly occur, dress modestly, the less bare flesh the better (see page 19), steadfastly ignore rude and suggestive comments directed at you but aimed at boosting the caller's ego, avoid any behaviour which would aggravate the situation, and keep a sense of humour. Single men often attract greater attention from customs officials and are more liable to receive unwelcome propositions.

WHERE TO STAY

HOTELS

There is a very wide range of accommodation in North Africa. In the major cities and the popular tourist resorts, the top quality hotel chains are represented. The best offer top class accommodation with the full range of personal and business facilities while the cheapest are spartan and most frequently sordid. Availability of accommodation for visitors varies from country to country. While Tunisia is organized in this respect, the traveller in Libya will experience greater problems in finding a place to lay his head. The peak season when there is greatest pressure on accommodation varies on the country and the latitude and the relevant country section gives details.

Prices for the top class hotels are on a par with prices in Europe while medium range hotels are generally cheaper in comparison. In almost every case, the advertised room price, that charged to the individual traveller, is higher than that paid by the package tourist and it may be worth bargaining. The six categories used in this *Handbook* are graded as accurately as possible by cost converted to American dollars. Our hotel price range is based on a double room with bath/shower in high season and includes any relevant taxes and service charges but no meals. Normally the following facilities will be available and are therefore not repeated in the descriptions.

Abbreviations in the listings: a/c = air conditioning, T = telephone, Tx = Telex, F = Facsimile. Bath denotes bath and/or shower.

AL   US$75+ This is an international class luxury hotel as found in the capital, large cities and major tourist centres. Good management ensures that all facilities for business and leisure travellers are of the highest international standard.

A   US$75 An international hotel with choice of restaurants, coffee shop, shops, bank, travel agent, swimming pool, some business facilities, some sports facilities, air conditioned rooms with WC, bath/shower, TV, phone, mini-bar, daily clean linen.

B   US$60-75 Offers most of the facilities in **A** but without the luxury, reduced number of restaurants, smaller rooms, limited range of shops and sport. Offers pool and air conditioned rooms with WC, shower/bath.

C   US$40-60 These are the best medium range hotels found in the smaller towns and less popular areas of larger cities. Usually comfortable, bank, shop, pool. Best rooms have air conditioning, own bath/shower and WC.

D   US$20-40 Might be the best you can find in a small town. Best rooms may have own WC and bath/shower. Depending on management will have room service and choice of cuisine in restaurant.

E   US$10-20 Simple provision. Perhaps fan cooler. May not have restaurant. Shared WC and showers with hot water (when available).

F   under US$10 Very basic, shared toilet facilities, variable in cleanliness, noise, often in dubious locations.

Ungraded hotels – too primitive to reach the standard of **F** – but may be cleaner and more interesting than **F**.

CAMPING

Provision varies. It is permitted at certain hostels; enlightened countries have both government and private sites, often with guards; beach camping depends on location and/or gaining permission. Often the difference between a cheap hotel and paying for a campsite is minimal. Assess the security of any site you choose and where possible ask permission to avoid any unpleasantness.

YOUTH HOSTELS

These are found in Tunisia and Libya as part of the International Youth Hostel Federation. They differ according to location and size, provide a common room, sleeping provision in dormitories, a self-catering kitchen and often budget meals. There is no maximum age limit, persons under 15 should be accompanied by an adult and in some hostels only male guests are accepted. Permission is necessary to stay more than 3 days in one hostel. Most hostels are open 1000-1200 and 1700-2200. Prices are given in the country sections.

FOOD AND DRINK

FOOD

Restaurants Given the variations in price of food on any menu our restaurants are divided where possible into three simple grades – ◆◆◆ expensive, ◆◆ average and ◆ cheap. Bearing in mind the suggestions in the Health section (page 456) on food best avoided in uncertain conditions, a wide choice still remains. Forget the stories of sheep's eyes and enjoy the selection of filling, spicy and slightly unusual meals. For the less adventurous, Western style food (other than pork) can be found in most hotels.

DRINK

The most common drink is tea without milk, in a small glass, probably with mint. Coffee is generally available too. Bottled soft fizzy drinks are found even in small settlements and are safer than water. *Alcohol* is officially forbidden in Libya but in Tunisia beer and local wine is sold. Where available imported wine and spirits are very expensive. *Bottled water* is an essential part of every traveller's baggage.

WATER

Be prepared for shortage or restriction of water, never regard tap water safe to drink. Bottled water is cheap and easily available. See Health, page 456.

GETTING AROUND

AIR

Domestic airlines link the main towns and run to published but infinitely variable schedules. Safety records vary. Don't use internal airlines in Libya for this reason. See country sections for times and availability.

ROAD

Conditions vary from excellent dual carriageways to rural roads and unnerving one-vehicle wide and farflung roads which are a rough, unsurfaced *piste*. Problems can include blockage by snow in winter, floods in spring and sand at any time.

Buses, the main mode and cheapest means of transport, link nearly all the towns. Air-conditioned coaches connect the biggest cities and keep more strictly to the timetable. Smaller private vehicles require greater patience and often work on the 'leave when full' principle. Book in advance wherever possible. Orderly queues become a jostling mass when the bus arrives. Inner city buses are usually dirty and crowded and getting off can be more difficult than getting on. Sorting out the routes and the fares makes taking a taxi a better option.

Taxis The larger, long distance taxis are good value, sometimes following routes not covered by service buses and almost always more frequent. They run on the 'leave when full' principle and for more space or a quicker departure the unoccupied seats can be purchased. In general these taxis are 25% more expensive than the bus. Inner city taxis are smaller, colour coded, may have a working meter, and can also be shared.

CAR HIRE

Cars can be hired, with varying degrees of difficulty. They are not cheap and the condition of the vehicles often leaves much to be desired. The problems of driving your own or a hired car are two fold – other drivers and pedestrians.

HITCHHIKING

This is really only a consideration in outlying places not served by the very cheap public transport. Here, eventually, a place on a truck or lorry will be available, for which a charge is made.

TRAIN

Rail networks are limited, are slow and generally more expensive than the alternative – the bus. First class is always more comfortable; offering air-conditioning and sometimes sleeping accommodation. Cheaper carriages can be crowded and none too clean. Train travel offers the advantage of views available only from the track.

COMMUNICATIONS

LANGUAGE

While Arabic is the official language in all the countries of North Africa, many people have as their first language one of the many dialects. French is widely spoken in Tunisia and in all tourist areas some English or French will be understood. See Language for Travel, page 447 for a simple vocabulary.

SHORT WAVE RADIO GUIDE

The BBC World Service (London) broadcasts throughout the region. Frequencies are shown in the accompanying table.

Radio frequencies			
Country	**KHz**	**Transmission times (GMT)**	
		Summer	**Winter**
Tunisia	17705	0900-1615	0700-1615
	15070	0700-2315	0700-2030
	12095	1500-2315	1500-2315
Libya	21470	0430-1615	0430-1615
	17640	0800-1515	0800-1515
	15070	0600-2030	0600-2030
	12095	0400-0730	0400-0730
	12095	1600-2215	1600-2030

Horizons

The people of North Africa principally follow Islam, which is similar to Judaism and Christianity in its philosophical content and Muslims recognise that these three revealed religions (religions of the book *Ahl Al-Kitab*) have a common basis. Even so, there are considerable differences in ritual, public observance of religious customs and the role of religion in daily life. When travelling through Islamic countries it as well to be aware that this is the case. The Islamic revivalist movement has in recent years become strongly represented in North African countries.

Travel, tourism and foreign workers are common throughout the region so that the sight of outsiders is not unusual. Tourists attract particular hostility, however. They are seen as voyeuristic, short-term and unblushingly alien. Tourists have become associated with the evils of modern life – loose morals, provocative dress, mindless materialism and degenerate/Western cultural standards. In many cases these perceptions are entirely justified and bring a sense of infringed Islamic values among many local people, most of whom are conservative in bent. Feelings are made worse by apparent differences in wealth between local peoples whose per head income ranges from US$6,800 in Libya to US$1,780 in Tunisia and foreign tourists living on an average of US$17,500 per head in the industrialized states. Tourists, whose way of life for a few weeks a year is dedicated to conspicuous consumption, attract dislike and envy. Muslims might wonder why a way of life in Islam, seen as superior to all other forms of faith, gives poor material rewards vis-à-vis the hordes of infidels who come as tourists.

The areas where sensitivity can best be shown are:

The dress code

Daily dress for most North Africans is governed by considerations of climate and weather. Other than labourers in the open, the universal reaction is to cover up against heat or cold. The classic case is Libya, where the traditional dress, the *barakan*, is a successor of the Roman toga made up of 5 or more metres length by 2m width of woven wool material which wraps round the head and body. For males, therefore, other than the lowest of manual workers, full dress is normal. Men breaching this code will either be young and regarded as of low social status or very rich and westernized. When visiting mosques (where this is allowed), *medressa* or other shrines/tombs/ religious libraries, men wear full and normally magnificently washed and ironed traditional formal wear. In the office, men will be traditionally dressed or in Western suits/shirt sleeves. The higher the grade of office, the more likely the Western suit. At home people relax in loose *jallabah*. North Africans will be less constrained on the beach where Ber-

The practice of Islam: living by the Prophet

Islam is an Arabic word meaning 'submission to God'. As Muslims often point out, it is not just a religion but a total way of life. The main Islamic scripture is the Koran or Quran, the name being taken from the Arabic *al-qur'an* or 'the recitation'. The Koran is divided into 114 *sura*, or 'units'. Most scholars are agreed that the Koran was partially written by the Prophet Mohammad. In addition to the Koran there are the hadiths, from the Arabic word *hadith* meaning 'story', which tell of the Prophet's life and works. These represent the second most important body of scriptures.

The practice of Islam is based upon five central tenets, known as the Pillars of Islam: Shahada (profession of faith), Salat (worship), Zakat (charity), *saum* (fasting) and Haj (pilgrimage). The mosque is the centre of religious activity. The two most important mosque officials are the *imam* – or leader – and the *khatib* or preacher – who delivers the Friday sermon.

The **Shahada** is the confession, and lies at the core of any Muslim's faith. It involves reciting, sincerely, two statements: 'There is no god, but God', and 'Mohammad is the Messenger [Prophet] of God'. A Muslim will do this at every **Salat**. This is the prayer ritual which is performed five times a day, including sunrise, midday and sunset. There is also the important Friday noon worship. The Salat is performed by a Muslim bowing and then prostrating himself in the direction of Mecca (Arabic *qibla*). In hotel rooms throughout the Muslim world there is nearly always a little arrow, painted on the ceiling – or sometimes inside a wardrobe – indicating the direction of Mecca and labelled qibla. The faithful are called to worship by a mosque official. Beforehand, a worshipper must wash to ensure ritual purity. The Friday midday service is performed in the mosque and includes a sermon given by the *khatib*.

A third essential element of Islam is **Zakat** – charity or alms-giving. A Muslim is supposed to give up his 'surplus' (according to the Koran); through time this took on the form of a tax levied according to the wealth of the family. Good Muslims are expected to contribute a tithe to the Muslim community.

The fourth pillar of Islam is **saum** or fasting. The daytime month-long fast of Ramadan is a time of contemplation, worship and piety – the Islamic equivalent of Lent. Muslims are expected to read one-thirtieth of the Koran each night. Muslims who are ill or on a journey have dispensation from fasting, but otherwise they are only permitted to eat during the night until "so much of the dawn appears that a white thread can be distinguished from a black one".

The **Haj** or Pilgrimage to the holy city of Mecca in Saudi Arabia is required of all Muslims once in their lifetime if they can afford to make the journey and are physically able to. It is restricted to a certain time of the year, beginning on the 8th day of the Muslim month of Dhu-l-Hijja. Men who have been on the Haj are given the title *Haji*, and women *Hajjah*.

The Koran also advises on a number of other practices and customs, in particular the prohibitions on usury, the eating of pork, the taking of alcohol, and gambling.

The application of the Islamic dress code varies across North Africa. It is least used in the larger towns and more closely followed in the rural areas.

Adhan – the call to prayer

This is know as the *adhan* and is performed by the *muezzin* who calls the faithful to prayer, originally by the strength of his own voice from near the top of the minaret but today, taking advantage of technological advances, it is probably a recording timed to operate at a particular hour. Listening to the first call to prayer just before the sun begins to rise is an unforgettable memory of Tunisia.

There is no fixed tune, perhaps tune is too definite a description, but in Egypt there is one particular rhythm used all over the country for the *adhan*. The traditional Sunni *adhan* consists of seven phrases, with two additional ones for the morning prayer. There are some variations which the well-tuned ear will pick up.

1. *Allahu Akbar* (Allah is most great) is intoned four times. This phrase is called *al takbir*.
2. *Ashhadu anna la ilah ill'-Allah* (I testify that there is no god besides Allah) is intoned twice.
3. *Ashhadu anna Muhammadan rasul Allah* (I testify that Muhammad is the apostle of Allah) is intoned twice. This and the preceeding phrase are called the *shihada*, a confession of faith.
4. *Hayya 'ala 'l-salah*, (Come to prayer) is intoned twice.
5. *Hayya 'ala'l-falah*, (Come to salvation) is intoned twice. This and the preceeding phrase are called *tathwib*.
6. *Allahu Akbar* is intoned twice.
7. *La ilah ill'Allah* (There is no god besides Allah) is intoned once.

The two additions to the morning prayer are: *Al-salatu khayr min al-nawm* (Prayer is better than sleep) which intoned twice between the fifth and sixth phrases, and *Al-salatu wa'l-salam 'alayka ya rasul Allah* (Benediction and peace upon you, Oh Apostle of Allah) intoned after the seventh phrase.

muda shorts and swimming trunks are the norm, especially in the Maghreb states.

For women the dress code is more important than for men. Quite apart from dress being tell-tale of social status among the ladies of tribal/regional origin, decorum and religious sentiment dictates full covering of body, arms and legs. The veil is increasingly common for women moving in public as a reflection of growing Islamic revivalist views. There are many women who do not conform, including those with modern attitudes towards female emancipation, professional women trained abroad and, remarkably, many Berber women or women with genuinely nomadic or semi-nomadic lives such as the Touareg. The religious minorities – Jews in Morocco for example – do not wear the veil.

Jewellery (see page 48) is another major symbol in women's dress especially heavy gold necklaces (see the Dar Cherait Museum at Tozeur in Tunisia for an excellent set of displays of women's dress (see page 277).

The role of dress within Islamic and social codes is clearly a crucial matter for the people of North Africa. While some latitude in dress is given to foreigners, good guests are expected to conform to the broad lines of the practice of the house. Thus, except on the beach or 'at home' in the hotel (assuming it is a tourist rather than local establishment), modesty in dress pays off. This means jeans or slacks for men rather than shorts together with a shirt or tee-shirt. In Islamic places such as mosques or *medressa*, hire *jallabah* at the door. For women, modesty is slightly more de-

Fundamentalism in Tunisia

Islam has been marked over the course of history by the emergence of rigorous revivalist movements. Most have sought a return of the faithful to the fundamentals of Islam – the basic doctrines of the Prophet Mohammed – uncluttered by the interpretations of later Islamic jurists and commentators. Behind the movements was generally the idea that Muslim people should go back to the simple basics of their religion. Some, like the Wahhabi movement in Saudi Arabia were puritan in concept, demanding plain lives and an adherence to the tenets of Islam in all daily aspects of life. Others, imposed a rigorous schedule of ritual in prayer and avoidance of the 'unclean' in public life. A good example of this type of reformist tendency was the Senusi Movement in North Africa which in the period from the close of the 19th century to 1969 created an educational, commercial and religious society.

Until recent times the fundamentalist movements inside Islam arose from a desire to cleanse the religion of unnecessary ideology and to make all the Islamic community observe the basic pillars of the Islamic religion – prayer, belief and righteous actions on a consistent and demonstrable basis. In the last one hundred years there has been a growing tendency in the Islamic world for revivalist movements to be reactions to political, military and cultural setbacks experienced at the hands of the western industrialised world. The aim of the reformers has been to make good the disadvantage and backwardness of the Muslim states in contrast with the powerful countries of Europe, America and the Far East. The matter is varied and complex, depending on the particular cases involved but the clear linkage between an increasingly dominant Western culture and economy and the growth of reactive Islamic movements is inescapable. The Muslim Brotherhood was an early form of revivalist movement of this kind. Founded by an Egyptian school teacher, Has al-Banna in 1928, it initially tried to take Islam back to its it roots and therefore to its perceived strengths but was later taken over by extremists who used its organisation for political ends. The development

manding. In public wear comfortable clothes that at least cover the greater part of the legs and arms. If the opportunity arises to visit a mosque or *medersa* open to tourists such as the Grand Mosque in Kairouan, *jallabah* and slippers are available for hire at the doors. Elsewhere full covering of arms and legs and a head scarf is necessary. Offend against the dress code – and most Western tourists in this area do to a greater or lesser extent – and risk antagonism and alienation from the local people who are increasingly fundamentalist in their Islamic beliefs and observances.

Forbidden places

Do not enter mosques is not a Moslem unless clearly invited to do so. Also do not enter mosques during a service. In other places dedicated to religious purposes behave with decorum – refrain from shouting, unseemly laughter and take photographs only when permitted. Outsiders have spent much time and ingenuity in penetrating Islam's holiest shrines. In North Africa this is not worth the effort since the most interesting sites are open to visitors in any case. People who are clearly non-Muslim will be turned away by door keepers from places where they are not wanted. Those who try to slip past the guardians should be sure they can talk their way out of trouble!

Good manners

Islam has its codes of other practices and taboos but few will affect the visitor un-of the Muslim Brotherhood as a clandestine political group and the harnessing of religious fervour to political objectives, including the assassination of political enemies, set the pattern for most later movements of the kind and has its Islamist emulators in Tunisia.

The Islamic scene in Tunisia is unique since nowhere in the Middle East and North Africa has secularisation of the laws affecting official and private life gone further, largely thanks to the liberalising activities of the former President, Habib Bouguiba. The *Personal Status Code* has given women in particular immense freedom of economic opportunity and, with the 1992 legislation on family rights, enables women to have custody of children, protection against violence in the home, and guaranteed rights to a passport. The scale of female emancipation is such that any real threat to it from Islamist forces is resisted strongly by an increasingly urban, educated and economically active female population, whose position is in great contrast to its sisters in Algeria and Libya, for example. It is estimated that women now occupy a quarter of all employment, 35% of industrial jobs and 22% of serviced activities in addition to managing one in ten farms. Their role is crucial to economic success in national and family budgets. What is more, Tunisian women are well aware of their new-found economic importance.

At the level of the State, there has been a combination of repression of the Islamists and continuing social reform. The Islamist parties such as El Nahda and trade unions with radical policies have had a hard time in recent years, to the extent that Amnesty International has condemned a number of government actions against dissidents. Short, however, of a major change of regime favouring the Islamists in Algeria, the Ben Ali administration in Tunisia has drawn most of the future sting of its own Islamist movement and has enough of a popular mandate in its secular social and political programmes to survive the fundamentalist challenge.

---

less he or she gains entry to local families or organisations at a social level. A few rules are worth observing in any case by all non-Muslims when in company with Muslim friends. (i) Do not use your left hand for eating since it is ritually unclean. If knives and forks are provided, then both hands can be used. (ii) Do not accept or ask for alcohol unless your host clearly intends to imbibe. (iii) If eating in traditional style from a common dish, use your right hand only and keep your feet tucked under your body away from the food. (iv) Never offer pork or its derivatives to a Muslim visitor. Buy *hallal* meat killed in accordance with Muslim ritual and/or provide a non-meat dish. Do not provide alcoholic drink.

Religious festivals and holidays

The Islamic year (Hejra/Hijra/Hegira) is based on 12 lunar months which are 29 or 30 days long depending on the sighting of the new moon. The lengths of the months vary therefore from year to year and from country to country depending on its position and the time at sunset. Each year is also 10 or 11 days shorter than the Gregorian calendar. The Islamic holidays are based on this Hejarian calendar and determining their position is possible only to within a few days.

Ramadan is a month of fasting (see below). The important festivals which are public holidays (with many variations in spelling) are *Ras el Am*, the Islamic New Year; *Eïd al-Fitr* (also called Aïd es

Seghir), the celebration at the end of Ramadan; Eïd al-Adha (also called Aïd el Kebir), the celebration of Abraham's willingness to sacrifice his son and coinciding with the culmination of the Haj in Mecca; *Mouloud*, the birthday of the Prophet Mohammad.

The Muslims consider Friday to be their Sabbath and services in the mosques on this day are more important and better attended. Holy days and feast days are taken very seriously. The 'day of rest' is Sunday, a legacy from colonial times. Most shops, except those in tourist areas, are closed on that day. The main exception is tourism where all systems remain operative other than in Libya. Holy days and feast days are taken seriously throughout the North African region.

Approximate dates for 1997:

12 Jan	Beginning of Ramadan
8 Feb	End of Ramadan
17-18 Apr	Festival of Sacrifice
7 May	Islamic New Year (Anno Hegira 1418)
16 Jul	Prophet's Birthday

Ramadan, the 9th month of the Muslim calendar, is a month of fasting for Muslims. The faithful abstain from eating between dawn and sunset for the period until an official end is declared to the fast and the start of the festival of the Eïd Al-Fitr. During the fast, especially if the weather is difficult or there are political problems affecting the Arab world, people can be depressed or irritable. The pace of activity in official offices slows down markedly. Travellers have to manage in these conditions by leaving even more time to achieve their aims and being even more patient than usual. If you have a choice, stay out of North Africa during Ramadan and the Eïd Al-Fitr. Travel, services and the atmosphere are all better at other times of year. Travel facilities immediately before and immediately after Ramadan are often very congested since families like to be together especially for the Eïd Al-Fitr.

BUREAUCRACY AND THE POLICE

North Africa is Islamic in religion, oriental in civilization and despotic in political tradition. Travellers will not be put off by these 'facts of life'. It is important, though, to adapt to the local ethos and to learn to live with it wherever you are.

There are a number of quite clear rules in handling situations in these areas:

Avoid trouble The main areas of difficulty affect relations with the bureaucrats, police and other officials. To avoid trouble bear in mind:

(i) Documents: do not lose your passport and ensure that all travel documents are in order. Passports are lost but they are also traded for cash/drugs and officials can be very unsympathetic. Long and often expensive delays can occur while documents are replaced, especially in Libya where there is no diplomatic help for US, British, Venezuelan and several other nationals. Keep all forms such as landing cards and currency documents together with bank receipts for foreign exchange transactions.

(ii) Prices: understand what prices are being asked for taxis, meals and hotels. Do not accept 'favours', like 'free lunches' they do not exist. In Tunisia for example, shop owners will attempt to give you gifts. At best these are used as a lever to get you buy other items expensively or can lead to disputes over alleged non-payment for goods. It is also a matter of discretion how you handle friendly relations with locals who invite you home for a meal/visit. In Libya, only hospitality will be involved. In Tunisia in particular, commercial or other motives might arise in the form of pressure to buy a carpet, to deal in drugs or to pledge help for a visa to Europe. Be genial but firm in these situations. Or use local ways out – promise to look at the matter *ba'd bokhra enshallah*, ie later!

(iii) Drugs: do not get involved in buying and selling drugs. It is an offence in all the countries in this *Handbook* to handle drugs. Penalties can be severe including jail sentences in dismal prison conditions.

(iv) Politics: keep clear of all political activities. Nothing is so sensitive in North Africa as opposition to the régimes. By all means keep an interest in local politics but do not become embroiled as a partisan. The *mokharbarat* (secret services) in North Africa are singularly unforgiving and unbridled in taking action against political dissent.

(v) Black Market: make use of black market currency only when it is private and safe. Some countries such as Libya have tight laws against currency smuggling and illegal dealing.

(vi) Driving: keep to driving regulations and have an appropriate international licence. Bear in mind that the incidence of traffic accidents in North Africa is high and that personal rescue in the event of an accident can be protracted and not necessarily expert.

(vii) Antiquities: trading in antiquities is everywhere illegal. Most items for sale such as 'Roman lamps' and ancient coins are fakes. Real artifacts are expensive and trading in them can lead to confiscation and/or imprisonment.

Keep cool Remain patient and calm whatever the provocation. Redress against officials is next to impossible. Keep the matter from becoming serious by giving no grounds for offence to officials. Be genial and low key. Aggression and raised voices do little to help. Where you feel you are right, be smilingly persistent but not to the point of a break down in relations.

Caveat Emptor – the art of bargaining

Haggling is a normal business practice in Tunisia and Libya, though far more in the former than in its eastern neighbour, where there is a certain directness to commercial transactions in staple commodities rather than confrontation over price, except notably for tourist items such as handicraft goods.

Modern economists might feel that bargaining is a way of covering up high-price salesmanship within a commercial system that is designed to exploit the lack of legal protection for the consumer. Even so, haggling over prices is the norm and is run as an art form, with great skills involved. Bargaining can be great fun to watch between a clever buyer and an experienced seller but it is less entertaining when a less than artful buyer such as a foreign traveller considers what he/she has paid after the game is over! There is great potential for the tourist to be heavily ripped off. Most dealers recognize the wealth and gullibility of travellers and start their offers at an exorbitant price. The dealer then appears to drop his price by a fair margin but remains at a final level well above the real local price of the goods.

To protect yourself in this situation be relaxed in your approach. Talk at length to the dealer and take as much time as you can afford inspecting the goods and feeling out the last price the seller will accept. Do not belittle or mock the dealer – take the matter seriously but do not show commitment to any particular item you are bargaining for by being prepared to walk away empty handed. Never feel that you are getting the better of the dealer or feel sorry for him. He will not sell without making a very good profit! Also it is better to try several shops if you are buying an expensive item such as a carpet or jewellery. This will give a sense of the price range. Walking away – regretfully of course – from the dealer normally brings the price down rapidly but not always. Do not change money in the same shop where you make your purchases, since this will be expensive.

Get help Getting help can often be cheap or free. Start off with agencies used to foreigners, namely travel agents, airline offices and hotels. They will have met your problem before and might offer an instant or at least painless solution on the basis of past experience. They will know the local system and how it works. They act as free translators. Friends who are either locals or who live locally can act as translators and helpers. They will often have networks of family and acquaintances to break through the bureaucratic logjams. Last, and only last, turn to your embassy or consulate. Embassies are there principally to serve the needs of the home country and the host government, not the demands of travellers, though they have ultimate responsibility for official travel documents and, at their own discretion, for repatriation in cases of distress. Treat embassy and consular officials calmly and fairly. They have different priorities and do not necessarily feel themselves to be servants for travellers in trouble.

INTERNAL SECURITY

Risks are not necessarily higher in North Africa than in other parts of the 'developing world' but they do exist. Any traveller who intends to be travelling in North Africa for a protracted period should check with his/her national authorities on the advisability of visiting the area. In the UK, the relevant Foreign and Commonwealth Office T 0171 2333000 desk will give you the latest assessment from their embassies overseas. If you are deeply concerned, where possible phone your national embassy direct and ask for the press/information officer. Otherwise, take an interest in trends in the countries you intend to visit before leaving home. Some newspapers can be very helpful in this area notably the *Financial Times*, *Le Monde*, and the *International Herald Tribune*.

TUNISIA

Tunisia is wracked by many of the problems – transition from an established highly centralized and increasingly unrepresentative régime to new structures which have a stamp of democratic legitimacy but at a time when Islamic revivalism is deeply affecting society. The current régime has established itself, though at the expense of becoming more hardline against the Islamic groups. It is in control of the fundamentalists to a large extent and seems to have been accepted fairly widely by the population at large. The government's economic difficulties are substantial but are being handled well, assisted by acting as a gateway to Libya during that country's international isolation. The government has repaired its relations with the USA and Europe in the wake of the Gulf Crisis and is experiencing a return of its important tourist trade. Overall, Tunisia seems to have survived a difficult few years and has remained for the most part a pleasant, mannerly and cultured society with a fair prospect for political stability. The future is inevitably slightly uncertain, however, since changes in adjacent states could adversely affect Tunisia. For the traveller, Tunisia is not immediately threatening, since the Tunisians generally recognize their dependence for jobs and income on tourism and will be most unlikely to attack foreigners.

LIBYA

Libya is a political oddity. In a general sense there are few domestic risks to the stability of the régime. There is negligible organized political opposition. Colonel Ghadhafi has a certain populist appeal which should not be underestimated. The security services and Colonel Ghadhafi's bodyguard battalions are relatively very powerful. The main risks in Libya are that Colonel Ghadhafi, who is the undisputed and sole centre of power, is removed by natural or other means or that there is a palace coup d'état. The Libyan state is so bound with personalities and so weak in national institutions that change could bring comparative anarchy for a period.

The main risks for foreigners are from capricious alterations in Libyan government policies on visas, internal movements and taxation on foreigners. Decisions are taken overnight by the ruling personalities and implemented without due notification to the public. A second area of risk is the actions of foreign governments against Libya. Libya is believed in some Western countries to be involved in state terrorism. The Lockerbie incident is currently at the centre of attention but other issues of a similar kind also exist. The bombing of Tripoli by the USA in 1986 was not notified in advance while the cessation of international air traffic in 1992 was. Measures of this latter kind are more of an inconvenience to travellers than an absolute block. But the tensions that go with failures in diplomatic relations mean that foreign visitors should be highly sensitive to personal risks. Care

in taking photographs and asking questions needs to be doubled in Libya. Some European governments and the US administration advise their nationals to take care when visiting Libya but the realities on the ground suggest that travellers are suffering no problems other than those arising through the UN embargo on air transport to/from Libya.

What to do if unrest occurs

It is wise in circumstances of political uncertainty for a foreigner to be very discreet:

1. Stay in your hostel or hotel.
2. If the telephones are working, get in touch with your embassy or consulate so that your location is known.
3. Conserve any rations you might have.
4. Do not join in any action by locals. Your motives could be misunderstood.
5. Make contact in your hostel or hotel with other foreigners so that you can form a mutual-assistance group.
6. Listen carefully to the advice given by local hostel or hotel officials.

The History of North Africa

The Sahara began to dessicate some 10,000 years ago and divided the Caucasoid populations of North Africa from the Negroid populations of W and Equatorial Africa. The original agricultural mode of production which had been the basis of settlement there was gradually replaced by nomadic pastoralism which, by around 4000 BC, had become the preserve of two groups, the Libyan-Berbers in the E part and the ancestors of the modern Touareg in the W. North African populations, all classified as part of the Hamito-Semitic group which stretched E into Arabia, soon became sub-divided into the Berbers in the W, the Egyptians in the E.

GREEKS AND PHOENICIANS

The North African coastal area became the arena for competition between those Mediterranean civilizations which had acquired a naval capacity – the Greeks and the Phoenicians. Indeed, this became the future pattern and resulted in the history of the region being described in the terms of its conquerers.

We do know, however, that the Greek and Phoenician settlements on the coast provoked a response from the nomadic communities of the desert – the Garamantes around the Fezzan in Libya, the Nigritae around Tuwat in modern Algeria and the Pharusii who were located in the Western Sahara. These communities appear to have specialized in warfare based on charioteering and they began to raid the new coastal settlements. At the same time, they also controlled trans-Saharan commerce – one of the major reasons why the Phoenicians, at least, were so interested in North Africa. As a result, they also engaged in trade with the new coastal communities, particularly those created by the Phoenicians.

The Greeks had begun to colonize the Egyptian and eastern Libyan coastline as part of their attempt to control Egyptian maritime trade. Cyrene, the first of five Greek colonies in Cyrenaica in Libya, was founded about 625 BC and, a little earlier, three Phoenician colonies were created in western Libya, on the coast of what is today Tripolitania – hence the name – in order to exploit new commercial opportunities, for the Phoenicians were first-and-foremost traders. More important, however, was the major Phoenician settlement at Carthage, on the coast of northern Tunisia, close to the modern capital of Tunis, which was founded in 814 BC, in order to control access to Sicily.

Greeks and Phoenicians competed for control of the coastal areas in Libya and eventually created an uneasy division of the region between themselves. The Greeks took over Egypt after the creation of the Ptolemaic Kingdom on the death of Alexander the Great in 323 BC and incorporated Cyrenaica into the new kingdom. The Phoenicians, by now being harried in their original Lebanese home base of Tyre by the Assyrians and Persians, created a new and powerful maritime commercial empire based on Carthage, with outlying colonies to the W, right round to the Atlantic coast at Lixus (Larache).

THE ROMAN EMPIRE

Control of North Africa passed on once again, this time to the rapidly expanding city-state of Rome. Control of the Ptole-

Important historical sites

N

SICILY

Bulla Regia
Tunis
Dougga
Carthage

Thuburbo
Majus

ALGERIA

Maktar
Kairouan

Sufetula
El Djem

MALTA

*Mediterranean
Sea*

TUNISIA

0   100
kilometres

Tripoli

Sabrata

LIBYA

Leptis
Magna

maic Kingdom of Egypt passed to Rome because of Roman interest in its agricultural produce and Egypt became a province of Rome in 30 BC. Cyrenaica had become a Roman province in 74 BC. Conflict with Carthage had begun much earlier because of its interest in Sicily which, for Rome, was of vital strategic importance. Although Carthage was expelled from Sicily in 201 BC, Rome still feared Carthaginian power and the city was eventually razed to the ground in 146 BC, after 3 years of warfare. The fertile plains around the city, a hinterland which had been its agricultural base and part of the Carthaginian Empire, were then converted into the Roman province of Africa.

The difficult problem of border security for Roman administrators was solved by creating the *limes*, a border region along the desert edge which was settled with former legionaries as a militarized agriculturalist population. Thus, although the border region was permeable to trade, resistance to tribal incursion could be rapidly mobilized from the resident population, while regular forces were brought to the scene. The limes spread W from Egypt as far as the Moroccan Atlantic coast. In S Tunisia, the limes were reinforced by a ditch – the *fossia regia*.

By the beginning of the Christian era, North Africa had been organized into four Roman provinces: Proconsular Africa, Numidia, Mauritania Caesariana and Mauritania Tingitania. It had also become a major source of food for Rome and a major centre of Roman culture as the sedentary Berber populations themselves were Romanised. North Africa

Chronology of Tunisian history

Date	Event
circa 1100 BC	Phoenician city of Utica is founded.
814 BC	Carthage founded by Queen Dido of Tyre.
264-241 BC	First Punic War (Carthage versus Rome). Loss of Sicilian, Sardinian and Corsican trading towns by Carthaginians.
219 BC	Second Punic War begins.
218 BC	Hannibal invades Italy.
205 BC	Carthaginians defeated in Iberia.
202 BC	Hannibal defeated by Roman general Scipio.
201 BC	End of Second Punic War.
149-146 BC	Third and final Punic War. Carthage is destroyed by Romans.
47-46	BC Roman military campaign in North Africa.
29 BC	Establishment of Pro-Consular Africa and the reconstruction of a settlement at the site of Carthage.
29 BC-225 AD	Rapid growth of Roman territorial control in Tunisia with colonization and thriving agrarian and trading economy.
235 AD	End of rule of the Severus Emperors.
238 AD	Revolt by Thysdrus (of El Djem) and weakening of imperial control of Tunisia.
439 AD	Carthage captured by the Vandals. Disruption and decay of city life.
534 AD	Tunisia taken by Byzantine Empire. Christian religious buildings become important part of the urban architectural heritage.
647 AD	Islamic conquest reaches Tunisia.
670 AD	Founding of Islamic city of Kairouan by Aqba ibn Naffi.
671 AD	Founding of the Great Mosque at Kairouan, developed by succeeding Aghlabites.
800-909	ADAghlabid dynasty with capital at Kairouan later moved to Mahdia.
909-973 AD	Fatimid dynasty. Shi'ite Islam in ascendant.
973 AD	Fatimids conquer Egypt and leave Tunis in hands Berber Zirid dynasty.
1041 AD	Invasion of North Africa by the Arab Beni Hilal tribe.
1051 AD	Tunisia under Beni Hilal domination.

had, in short, ceased to be culturally part of Africa and was, instead, now part of the Mediterranean world. In addition to the commercial and cultural interpenetration of North Africa and Rome, this cultural interaction was intensified by two other factors. First, the region had long been in contact with Greek culture and, indeed, through the Phoenicians, with the culture of the Levant. Secondly, as a result of the destruction of the kingdom of Judea in 70 AD, large numbers of Jews migrated into North Africa and Judaism intermixed with Berber culture to a significant extent, as contemporary Jewish traditions in Tunisia make clear.

CHRISTIAN NORTH AFRICA

North African Christianity became the major focus of the development of Christian doctrine. The Coptic Church became the major proponent of Monophysitism after the Council of Chalcedon in 451 AD; Donatism dominated Numidia; and Tunisia was the home of the greatest of the early Christian fathers, St Augustine. At the same time, official Christianity in Egypt – the Melkite Church – combined with the Coptic Church to convert areas to the S

1159 AD	Tunisia under Almohads rule from Morocco.
1228 AD	Hafsid dynasty makes Tunisia independent first as a Governorate, then as a kingdom with Tunis as capital. Known as a period of great prosperity and age of cultural splendour.
1534	Hafsids deposed by pirate chiefs Barbarossa and Kheireddine.
1535	Spanish conquest by Charles V.
1574	Ottoman Turks take Tunis.
1590	Revolt of the Janisseries, Dey becomes governor.
1631	Beys of Tunis take the title of *Pasha*.
1705	Hussein Ben Ali Bey seizes power as hereditary Pasha of Tunis.
1837-1855	Ahmad Bey. Abolished slavery and introduced modern industry into Tunisia.
1869	France enforces control over Tunisian financial affairs for European creditors of Bey.
1881	Treaty of Bardo, following invasion by French army from Algeria, ratifies a permanent French interest in the running of Tunisian foreign and defence affairs.
1883	Convention of La Marsa gives French rights effectively to manage the government of Tunisia.
1920	Start of an organised Tunisian independence movement with founding of the Destour Party.
1934	Activists break from Destour Party to form the Neo-Destour Party under leadership of Habib Bourguiba.
1942-43	Axis control in Tunisia with Bey collaborating with Germans.
1943	Moncef Bey deposed by French.
1945-49	Habib Bourguiba in exile organizing campaign for Tunisian independence.
1946	Trade Union founded.
1956	France grants independence to Tunisia.
1957	Habib Bourguiba made first President of the new Republic of Tunisia.
1963	Final withdrawal of French troops from Bizerte military base.
1987	President Bourguiba is deposed in bloodless coup d'état by Zine El-Abidine Ben Ali who became second president.

of Egypt to Christianity.

Political evolution, however, did not mirror the growth of Christian influence. In the 5th century, as the Roman Empire crumbled, North Africa was invaded by a Teutonic tribe based in Spain, the Vandals, who by 429 AD, had conquered as far as E Cyrenaica.

Byzantine control, of Tunisia at least, was restored by the Emperor Justinian and his general, Belisarius, in 533 AD. However it was unpopular, not least because of the onerous taxation system necessary to cover Byzantium's heavy military expenditure as it tried to confront the Sassanids in Asia as well as maintain its position in the Mediterranean. Hence when, a little more than a century later, Byzantine rule in Africa was threatened by the expansion of Islam, there was little enthusiasm to support its continuation in northern Africa.

THE ISLAMIC PERIOD

In 642 AD, 10 years after the death of the Prophet Mohammad, Arab armies, acting as the vanguard of Islam, conquered Egypt. To secure his conquest, the Arab commander, Amr bin al-As, immediately decided to move W into Cyrenaica where the local Berber population submitted to the new invaders. Despite a constant pattern of disturbance, the Arab conquerers of Egypt and their successors did not ignore the potential of the region to the S. Nubia was invaded in 641-42 AD and again 10 years later. Arab merchants and, later, bedouin tribes from Arabia were able to move freely throughout the S. However, until 665 AD, no real attempt was actually made to complete the conquest, largely because of internal problems within the new world of Islam. Then, after two feints SW towards the Fezzan, an army under Aqba ibn Naffi conquered Tunisia and set up the first Arab centre there at Kairouan in 670 AD. 4 years later, the Arabs in Kairouan were able to persuade Kusayla, the leader of the Berber confederation which spread right across Tunisia and modern Algeria as far as the Oued Muluwiya in Morocco, to convert to Islam. Shortly afterwards, Aqba ibn Naffi, in a famous expeditionary raid to scout the unsubmitted areas to the W, swept across North Africa along the northern edge of the Sahara desert as far as the Atlantic coast of Morocco, into the land of the Sanhadja Berbers who dominated the major Western trans-Saharan trade routes.

These early conquests were ephemeral, being based on two mistaken assumptions. The first was that the new conquerers could afford to ignore the isolated Byzantine garrisons along the North African coast, because they would eventually collapse due to their isolation. The Byzantine navy, in fact, supplied them by sea. The second was that the Ommayyad Arab commanders and administrators now imposed on North Africa ignored the promises of equality of treatment given to Berber converts and thus encouraged a major rebellion, led by Kusayla. Arab control of Kairouan was lost and the Arab conquest of the Maghreb had to be undertaken again.

The first Arab move was against Kusayla, who was killed in 688 or 689 AD. Then after a further delay caused, once again, by unrest in the Levant, a new army moved northwards against Byzantine centres in Carthage and Bizerte, where the last remaining garrison was defeated in 690 AD. The Arab conquest came up against determined Berber resistance, this time in the Algerian Aurés where the core of the Berber Zenata confederation was led by al-Kahina, a Judaized or Christianised Berber priestess. Once again the Arabs retreated to Cyrenaica, returning to the attack only in 693 AD. In 697 AD, al-Kahina was killed and her forces defeated in a battle at Tubna in the Aurés which marked the start of a permanent Arab presence in North Africa.

The city of Tunis was founded to prevent further Byzantine encroachment at neighbouring Carthage and, under Musa bin Nusayr, Arab armies swept westwards to conquer Tanger in 704 AD. There they came to terms with the sole remaining Byzantine governor in North Africa, Julian of Ceuta, a Christian potentate who paid tribute to the new Muslim governor of neighbouring Tanger, Ziyad bin Tariq, in order to be confirmed in his post. 7 years later, Ziyad, with help from Julian who had maintained links with the Visigoth rulers of Spain, organized the Muslim invasion of the Iberian peninsula, starting at Gibraltar. By 732 AD, Muslim forces had conquered virtually all of Spain and Portugal and had even crossed the Pyrenees. The Muslim advance was stopped at or near to Poitiers by Charles Martel and, although, for the next 4 years, large parts of Provence were ravaged by marauding Muslim armies, the Muslim presence in Europe effectively ceased at the Pyrenees.

THE EARLY ISLAMIC PERIOD

Despite their victory, the Ommayyads soon became very unpopular in North Africa where the egalitarian and revolutionary doctrines of the *kharejite* movement – that the caliphate should be elective, that a caliph who failed to uphold Islamic principle could be dismissed by the Muslim community and that sin automatically disqualified those involved from being considered to be Muslims – began to take root. Southern missionaries arrived in Kairouan in 719 AD and, within 30 years, the Berbers had become such enthusiastic supporters that they launched a rebellion against the Ommayyads at Tanger in 739-40 AD.

Although the rebellion was crushed, *kharajism* survived and, given the difficulties facing the Ommayyads in the Middle East where they were threatened by a new opposition, North Africa was left to its own devices. Ibadi kharajism gained the upper hand in Tripolitania and Sufri kharajism became dominant in southern Tunisia, while the core of Tunisia was left in the hands of the Fihrids, an Ommayyad Arab military caste now effectively abandoned by the Ommayyad caliphate in Damascus. The Ibadis eventually expanded their control throughout Tunisia and forced the Sufris westwards in 758 AD.

In 750 AD, the Ommayyad caliphate was destroyed by the Abbasids who rejected Ommayyad ideas of Arab superiority and supported the early Shi'a schismatic movement against the Sunni Muslim majority. 8 years later, the new Abbasid caliphate reconquered the old Arab province of *Ifriquiya* (modern Tunisia), but was unable to extend its authority further westward. In any case, the Abbasids did not have the resources to maintain a close control on such far-flung provinces and, by 800 AD, the Abbasid caliph in Baghdad, Harun al-Rashid allowed his governor in Ifriquiya, Ibrahim bin al-Aghlab, virtual autonomy. In effect, therefore, the Aghlabites became an independent dynasty in Tunisia until their downfall in 909 AD. The Aghlabites brought prosperity and high culture to Tunisia and, in 827 AD, began the Muslim conquest of Sicily.

The Aghlabites had to share North Africa with three other separate political authorities. After being expelled from Tripolitania, the Ibadis set up a separate state under Ibn Rustam at Tahert in central Algeria, which maintained close links with the Ibadi centre of Basra in southern Iraq. The Sufri Berbers of the Beni Midrar established their own state, based on their control of trans-Saharan trade, at Sijilmassa in southern Morocco.

THE GREAT DYNASTIES AND THEIR SUCCESSORS

The failure of the Abbasid caliphate to retain control of North Africa paved the way for a series of local dynasties to take control.

(1) **The Fatimids** The first of the great dynasties that was to determine the future of North Africa did not, however, originate inside the region. Instead it used North Africa as a stepping stone towards its ambitions of taking over the Muslim world and imposing its own variant of Shi'ite Islam. North Africa, because of its radical and egalitarian Islamic traditions, appears to have been the ideal starting point. The group concerned were the Isma'ilis who split off from the main body of Shi'ite Muslims in 765 AD.

The Fatimids took control over what had been Aghlabid Ifriquiya, founding a new capital at Mahdia in 912 AD. Fatimid attention was concentrated on Egypt and, in 913-14 AD, a Fatimid army temporarily occupied Alexandria. The Fatimids also developed a naval force and their conquest of Sicily in the mid-10th century provided them with a very useful base for attacks on Egypt.

After suppressing a kharejite-Sunni rebellion in Ifriquiya between 943 AD and 947 AD, the Fatimids were ready to plan the final conquest of Egypt. This took place in 969 AD when the Fatimid general, Jawhar, finally subdued the country. The Fatimids moved their capital to Egypt, where they founded a new urban centre, al-Qahira (from which the modern name, Cairo, is derived) next to the old Roman fortress of Babylon and the original Arab settlement of Fustat.

The Fatimids' main concern was to take control of the Middle East. This meant that Fatimid interest in North Africa would wane and leave an autonomous Emirate there which continued to recognize the authority of the Fatimids, although it abandoned support for Shi'iteq Islamic doctrine. See box, page 30.

(2) The Hilalian invasions Despite Fatimid concerns in the Middle East, the caliph in Cairo decided to return North Africa to Fatimid control. Lacking the means to do this himself, he used instead two tribes recently displaced from Syria and at that time residing in the Nile Delta – the Beni Sulaim and the Beni Hilal – as his troops. The invasions took place slowly over a period of around 50 years, starting in 1050 or 1051 AD, and probably involved no more than 50,000 individuals.

The Beni Sulaim settled in Cyrenaica, although, 2 centuries later, factions of the tribe also moved westwards towards Tripolitania and Tunisia. The Beni Hilal continued westwards, defeating and destroying the Zirids in a major battle close to Gabés in 1052.

The Hilalian invasions were a major and cataclysmic event in North Africa's history. They destroyed organized political power in the region and ensured the break up of the political link between Muslim North Africa and the Middle East. They also damaged the trading economy of the region. There was a major cultural development too for the Hilalian invasions, more than any other event, ensured that Arabic eventually became the majority language of the region.

(3) The Almoravids The power vacuum left in the wake of the Hilalian invasions was filled by religious revival-

ism amongst the Lamtuna tribe, under the influence of a religious scholar, Abdullah ibn Yasin. He transformed the lackadaisical religious observance into a dynamic, inspiring, fully integrated and committed Islamic community. He called his new community the *dar al-murabitun* – the House of the people of the *ribat* (the Muslim equivalent of a monastic retreat, dedicated to preparation for *jihad*), now corrupted to 'Almoravid'.

Religious committment spurred them on. Ibn Yasin was succeeded by Yusuf Ibn Tashfin who led the Almoravids to victory over most of western North Africa as far as Algiers and over the southern half of Spain between 1060 AD and the end of the century. The Almoravids managed, however, to offend established religious leaders and the *Sufi* orders (mystical religious orders) of North Africa by their religious intolerance and rigidity. They also failed to check Christian expansionism in Spain. As a result, when a major rebellion against their authority began close to their capital of Marrakech in 1125 AD, it was not long before they were overthrown.

(4) The Almohads The Almohads (from *al-muwahhidun* – the unitarians) also began as a religious revivalist movement, this time amongst the Masmouda Berbers of the High Atlas close to Marrakech. They were inspired by a religious leader from the Hargha tribe of the Masmouda, located in the Anti-Atlas mountains, Muhammad ibn Tumart, who was born in 1080 AD. He studied in Spain and the Middle East before returning to Morocco, where he sought support for a revivalist movement designed to purify Islamic doctrine and practice.

The Almohads were organized on a tribal basis and, when Ibn Tumart died in 1130 AD, the most capable tribal leader, Abd al-Mumin, took over. In 1145 AD Abd al-Mumin crushed the

Almoravids and, 2 years later, occupied the two leading cities of Fes and Marrakech, the latter of which became the Almohad capital.

The Almohads first moved against the Christian *Reconquista* in Spain, where they held the Christian advance towards Granada and Sevilla, although the ruler of Murcia managed to remain independent until 1172 AD. The more important move was against the growing threat of the Normans in the central Mediterranean. By 1160 AD, the Almohads had expelled the Normans from North Africa and had united the region under a single political authority.

The Almohad state was sapped by its essentially tribal political structure. In 1207 in Ifriqiya, the son of the Almohad governor, Abu Hafs Umar, a close associate of Ibn Tumart, created an independent Hafsid state which governed Tunisia until the Ottoman occupation in the 16th century. In a similar fashion, control of the Central Maghreb devolved on the Beni Zayyan clan of the Beni Abd al-Wad in 1233 AD.

(5) The successor states The disappearance of the Almohads brought the era of the great unifying North African dynasties to an end. Thereafter power would reflect the division of the region, rather than its unity. There would also be a change in direction and influence, for now Christianity and Europe would increasingly dominate the North African horizon, as would the Mediterranean as a zone of conflict. Yet the experience of the Fatimids, the Hilalian invasions, the Almoravids and the Almohads did leave an important monument behind.

The Hafsids The new Hafsid state saw itself as the legitimate successor to the Almohads and its ruler as caliph. The claim was widely accepted, even in the Middle East, because the foundation of the Hafsid state coincided with the Mongol invasions which destroyed Baghdad

and the last vestiges of the Abbasid caliphate in 1250 AD. But in reality, the Hafsid state lacked the social and political cohesion of its predecessor. Thus its long history was marked by the constant interplay of internal conflict between different members of the Hafsid family and with Arab and other tribal leaders who sought supreme power. Like the Marinid state, it also had to integrate increasing numbers of Muslims and Jews emigrating from al-Andalus.

It had to deal with an ever greater Christian threat. This came in two forms: direct aggression, such as the 8th crusade, led by the French King Louis IX, which besieged Tunis unsuccessfully in 1270 AD, and commercial penetration. In the early part of the 13th century, the great Italian trading cities of Pisa, Genoa and Venice, together with the French of Provence, obtained trading and residence rights in Ifriqiya. The most important example of commercial penetration came from Aragón. The Aragonese had created a major trading empire in the Western Mediterranean and, after 1246 AD, Aragón had an ambassador in Tunis, the Hafsid capital. This was followed by mercantile representation after 1253 AD. After Aragón annexed Sicily in 1282 AD, this commercial hegemony was backed by military dominance as well.

By 1318 AD Aragonese influence was on the wane and Hafsid fortunes revived. The Hafsid state was, nonetheless, a Mediterranean state rather than one with its attention directed towards Africa or the Middle East. Its finances increasingly depended on piracy. By the end of the 15th century Hafsid influence had declined once again. Spain, the new threat to the Mediterranean Muslim world, annexed Tripoli in Libya and Bejaïa in Western Algeria in 1510 AD, as the first move in a widening penetration into the Maghreb. The Hafsids lingered on until 1574 AD, when the Ottoman Turks destroyed their state.

THE OTTOMANS IN NORTH AFRICA

The arrival of the Ottomans in North Africa was the last invasion of the region before the colonial period began in the 19th century.

THE OTTOMAN OCCUPATION

The Ottoman occupation of North Africa was a by-product of Ottoman-Venetian competition for control of the Mediterranean, itself part of the boundless expansionism of the Ottomans once they had conquered Constantinople in 1453. The Ottoman attack was 2-pronged, involving their newly acquired maritime power to establish a foothold and then backing it up with the janissary, land based forces that formed the empire's troops. The decrepit Mamluk Dynasty in Egypt fell to the Ottomans in 1517 and a new, centralized Ottoman administration was established there.

Ottoman interests were soon at-

The Hafsid Sultans and Tunisia's twilight age

In the early 13th century Tunisia was amalgamated in the Almohad empire of Ifriquiya with Tunis as its capital, see page 37. The Governor of Tunis, Mohammed Ibn Ali Hafs, declared independence in 1207 and under the rule of his successor, Abu Zakariya Yahia I, full political autonomy from the Almohads in Marrakech was achieved. While the Hafsid sovereigns were adept at maintaining the integrity of their lands, thwarting a crusading attack on Tunis by the French King Louis in 1270, the Hafsid empire was not distinguished as a golden age. By 1277 the country became subject to disputes over the succession and was only saved by Abul Abbas Ahmad (1370-94) and his successor Abu Faris Abdelaziz (1395-1434) who put down a series of regional revolts against rule from Tunis.

The expansion of European colonial and maritime power, particularly in Spain, put great pressure on Tunis, which suffered both political and military eclipse in the years 1490-1526.

Between 1526-1574 Tunis was fought over by Turks, Spanish and Austrians not to mention local pirate chiefs. By that time in any case the intense rivalry of the Spanish and Ottoman empires led to the overthrow of the Hafsids and the incorporation of Tunis into the Ottoman domains after the fall of Tunis to Sinan Pasha in 1574. Thus ended a rule noted for its artistic, scientific and literary banality.

The Hafsid rulers:

Mohammed Idn Ali Hafs	1207-1221 AD
Abu Zakariya Yahia I	1228-1249
Al-Mustansir	1249-1277
Abu Zakariya Yahia II	1277-1279
Abu Ishaq Ibrahim I	1279-1283
Abu Hafs Omari	1284-1295
Abu Abdallah Mohammed II	1295-1309
Abu Yahia Zakariya I	1311-1317
Abu Yahia Abu Bakr	1318-1346
Abu Ishaq Ibrahim I	1350-1369
Abul Abbas Ahmad	1370-1394
Abu Faris Abdelaziz	1394-1434
Abu Amar Othman	1435-1488
Abu Yahia Zakariya II	1489-1494
Abu Abdallah Mohammed V	1494-1526

tracted westward and a maritime campaign was launched on the North African coastline. It was carried out mainly by privateers, attracted both by the religious confrontation between Christian powers in Southern Europe and Islam in North Africa and by the growing practice of corsairing. In the wake of the *Reconquista* in 1492, Spain began to prepare for a veritable crusade against North Africa. 2 years later Spain and Portugal, with Papal blessing, divided their future spheres of influence in North Africa between them and, 3 years later, the Spanish occupation began with the conquest of Melilla.

The Ottoman moves on North Africa were precipitated by the privateering activities of the Barbarossa brothers, Uruj and Khayr al-Din. The Ottomans eventually occupied Tunis permanently in 1574. Before this, however, they had gained a hold over Libya. Khayr al-Din Barbarossa occupied Tajura, on the coast close to Tripoli, in 1531 and was consequently able to threaten the precarious hold of the Knights of the Order of St John of Jerusalem on Tripoli itself. They had just occupied Tripoli and Malta at the request of Charles V of Spain, but were forced out of Tripoli altogether by the Ottomans in 1551. For 270 years North Africa, except for Morocco, was an Ottoman preserve.

THE BARBARY REGENCIES

Direct control from Istanbul did not last long. The North African coastline was divided into a series of administrative units, with power divided among the *bashas*, sent from Istanbul, the *deys* who were in charge of the permanent janissary garrisons and, in Algiers at least, the *taifa*, the captains of the corsairing privateers that continued to operate.

Tripoli

At the beginning of the 18th century, the final formal links with Istanbul were broken. In 1711 a dynasty was founded in Tripoli by Ahmad Karamanli, who seized power in the temporary absence of the Ottoman governor and then massacred the leaders of the janissaries. The new autonomous government eventually controlled Tripolitania and the coastal regions of Cyrenaica. After a tussle for influence in Tripoli between Britain and France, the Ottoman Empire reoccupied the Regency of Tripoli and ejected the Karamanlis in 1835.

Tunis

Once the Spaniards had been driven out of Tunisia and the remnants of the Hafsid Dynasty had been eliminated, the Ottoman commander, Sinan Pasha, organized an administration similar to that in Algiers. By 1591, a system of janissary leadership through the *dey* was imposed on the Ottoman-appointed *basha* but rural administration was entrusted to another official, the *bey*, a post which soon rivalled the power of the *dey*. In 1702 the two offices were combined. After defeating an attempt by the Regency of Algiers to conquer Tunisia in 1705, Hussein Ben Ali became *bey* and initiated the Husseinid Dynasty that ruled Tunisia until 1957. Following his accession to power, Tunisia effectively became independent of Istanbul and was known as the Regency of Tunis.

By the 19th century, the rule of the *bey* had become corrupt and remote. European interference in Tunisian affairs had became more intrusive resulting in a growing European population which enjoyed extra-territorial rights under the 'Capitulations' system, and European consuls who became ever more powerful. Domestic unrest increased and in 1860, the *bey*, in desperation, granted Tunisians the Arab world's first constitution, the *Destour*. By 1868 the economic crisis had worsened and European powers insisted on a debt commission being instituted to handle Tunisia's finances in order to ensure repayment.

In 1878, the Congress of Berlin decided that Tunisia should fall under French influence. Then, in 1881, on the grounds that the Khroumir border tribe had been raiding into French-controlled Algeria, France invaded Tunisia and, in a rapid campaign, took control of the country.

COLONIALISM IN NORTH AFRICA

The colonial experience throughout North Africa took many different forms. It involved four European states: Britain after WW2, in part of Libya; Italy in Libya up to WW2, together with residual interests in Tunisia; Spain in northern Morocco and in the Sahara desert to the S of the country; and France, which controlled Tunisia, Algeria and most of Morocco, as well as the southern part of Libya after WW2. Colonialism took different forms, as well. In Algeria and Libya full colonial occupation was instituted, with a degree of integration into the administration and political structures of the metropolitan power. In Tunisia and Morocco, a form of protectorate was instituted whereby the colonial power was present as a tutor, with the object of modernising political structures and the economy before restoring full Independence.

THE COLONIAL PERIOD IN LIBYA

The reimposition of Ottoman rule in Libya in 1835 marked an end to the corsairing economy of the Regency of Tripoli. Ottoman control was never fully applied throughout the country.

The Sanusi Order, which was named after its Algerian founder, Sayyid Muhammad bin Ali al-Sanusi was an Islamic revivalist movement. It chose the Sahara for its arena and settled amongst the Cyrenaican tribes, where it was welcomed for its piousness and for its ability to arbitrate tribal disputes. Later on, the Order also coordinated tribal resistance throughout the Sahara to French colonial penetration. The Order also began to control the eastern trade routes across the Sahara and, as a result, effectively became, an autonomous government of the central Saharan region. In Cyrenaica its power was so great that, outside the major urban settlements such as Benghazi, the Ottomans accepted it as the de facto government and a Turkish-Sanusi condominium developed.

The Ottoman administration in Tripoli had to cope with continuing European pressure, particularly from Italy and Malta. British and French influence led to the end of the slave trade towards the end of the 19th century, while the economy of Tripoli became increasingly integrated into the global economy of the Mediterranean region. By the start of the 20th century Italy's intention to colonize Tripolitania, Cyrenaica and the Fezzan became clear.

Fighting broke out between tribes backed by dissident Ottoman officers and the Italian army. The outbreak of WWI allowed the Ottoman Empire to provide military aid to the resistance and eventually a peace agreement was signed between Italy and the Sanusi at Akrama in Apr 1917. In 1922, with the Fascists in power, Italy again decided to occupy Libya. The second Italo-Sanusi war was between the Italians and the bedouin of Cyrenaica, for resistance in Tripolitania and the Fezzan was quickly broken. The ferocious struggle continued to 1930 when the last remnants of resistance were wiped out and Italy finally occupied the vast Libyan desert hinterland.

The Fascist victory was short-lived, for the Italian army was forced out of Libya during WW2 and British military administrations took over in Cyrenaica and Tripolitania with the French in Fezzan. Under the Italians, Libya had acquired the basic elements of a communications infrastructure and some modernisation of the economy. It had also acquired a 50,000 strong Italian settler population, a substantial portion of whom remained until they were expelled by the Ghadhafi régime in 1970.

The situation of Libya posed problems. By the end of WW2 it had acquired strategic significance for Britain and, after the Cold War began, for the USA as well. Britain had promised Cyrenaica that Italian control would never be restored. A series of proposals were made including Soviet Union trusteeship over Libya and the Bevin-Sforza Plan, whereby Britain would take a mandate for Cyrenaica, Italy for Tripolitania and France for the Fezzan for a period of 10 years, after which the country would be granted Independence. These were clearly unacceptable to the Libyans themselves, and the whole issue was dropped in the lap of the newly created United Nations in 1949.

The United Nations' special commissioner was able to convince all the Libyan factions that the only solution was a federal monarchy, bringing the provinces of Cyrenaica, Tripolitania and the Fezzan together under the Sanusi monarchy of Sayyid Idris. In Dec 1951, the independent kingdom of Libya came into being.

COLONIALISM IN THE MAGHREB

Tunisia

In the immediate aftermath of the installation of the French Protectorate, Tunisian resistance was confined to tribal groups in the S of the country. Opposition to colonial occupation gradually began to gather strength reflecting popular opposition to the growing and predominantly Italian European settler colony in Tunisia, a colony totalling around 100,000 people and controlling some 800,000 ha of Tunisia's best agricultural land.

The opposition was led by a young, French-trained lawyer, Habib Bourguiba, who wanted a far more radical approach towards the French presence. In 1934, Habib Bourguiba took over the movement, now renamed the neo-Destour. French reaction to this radicalisation was very repressive until WW2 when Tunisia was eventually occupied by Allied forces. In the wake of the war, it became clear that some concessions to nationalist sentiment would have to be made.

Before this was done, France tried to enforce its position in Tunisia by requiring the Bey to accept the idea of 'co-sovereignty', whereby France would gain permanent rights to Tunisian territory. Following this attempt by France in 1950 to gain a firmer foothold inside North Africa, the nationalist movement under Habib Bourguiba took on the characteristics of a mass movement. As a result, Habib Bourguiba was able to negotiate autonomy for Tunisia in 1955 and in 1956, when Morocco was granted Independence, Tunisia soon followed suit.

For the history of the region after Independence, see Tunisia, page 68; and Libya, page 369).

Tunisian Museums

Tunisia has a very rich and diversified archaeological history. The museums throughout the country have on display some of the richest artifacts ranging from Punic and Roman times to the present day. There are over 40 museums under the management of the Institut National du Patrimoine and another 15 managed by a number of official and private institutions. Exhibits are housed in old palaces (Bardo, Raccada), in forts (Monastir), government buildings (Sfax), purpose-built mansions (Dar Chefait, Tozeur) and on Punic/Roman sites (Kerkouane, Dougga).

Wildlife

The area covered by the book divides itself into two climatic regions, the Mediterranean and the Desert, with transitional areas between the two extremes. Within these zones, however, is a wide variety of habitats. The Mediterranean coastline is varied, rugged inaccessible cliffs, smooth sandy bays. Coastal wetlands include deltas, salt marsh and estuaries, while inland lakes and reservoirs provide freshwater sites. The *maquis* and the *garrigue* contrast with the agricultural areas, while mountain ranges such as the Atlas provide their own climate, delaying flowering and shortening seasons. Even the desert areas provide contrasts with the sands (*erg*), gravels (*reg*) and rock (*hammada*) interspersed with the occasional oasis.

Many of the habitats mentioned above are under threat, either from pollution, urbanisation, desertification or advanced farming techniques. Fortunately, in some countries such as Tunisia, the conservation movement is gaining pace and many National Parks and Nature Reserves have been created and programmes of environmental education set up.

In both the Mediterranean and Desert regions, wildlife faces the problem of adapting to drought and the accompanying heat. The periods without rain may vary from 4 months on the shores of the Mediterranean to several years in some parts of the Sahara. Plants and animals have, therefore, evolved numerous methods of coping with drought and water loss. Some plants have extensive root systems; others have hard, shiny leaves or an oily surface to reduce water loss through transpiration. Plants such as the *broom* have small, sparse leaves, relying on stems and thorns to attract sunlight and produce food. Animals such as the *addax* and *gazelle* obtain all their moisture requirements from vegetation and never need to drink. Where rain is a rare occurrence, plants and animals have developed a short life cycle combined with years of dormancy. When rain does arrive, the desert can burst into life, with plants seeding, flowering and dispersing within a few weeks or even days. Rain will also stimulate eggs to hatch which have lain dormant for years. Many animals in the desert areas are nocturnal, taking advantage of the cooler night temperatures, their tracks and footprints revealed in the morning. Another adaption is provided by the *sandfish*, which is a type of skink (lizard) which 'swims' through the sand in the cooler depths during the day. Perhaps the most remarkable example of adaption is shown by the *camel* (see box, page 315). Apart from its spreading feet which enable it to walk on sand, the camel is able to adjust its body temperature to prevent sweating, reduce urination fluid loss and store body fat to provide food for up to 6 months.

MAMMALS

Mammals have a difficult existence throughout the area, due to human disturbance and the fact that many of the species are not well adapted to drought. Many have, therefore, become nocturnal and their presence may only be indicated by droppings and tracks. Some mammals common in northern Europe can, nevertheless, be seen in the Mediterranean environments and these include *fox*, *rabbit*, *hare*, Red, Fallow and Roe *deer* and at least three species of *hedgehog*. Despite widespread hunting, *wild boar* are common wherever there is enough cover in deciduous woodlands. *Hyenas* and *jackals* still thrive in many areas but the attractive *fennec*, whilst still fairly common in Tunisia is frequently illegally trapped. Typical woodland species include the *red squirrel* (the grey variety from North America has not been introduced), *garden dormouse*, which readily hibernates in houses, *pine* and *beech martens* and the *polecat*. The cat family, once common, is now rare, but the *lynx* hangs on in some areas. The *leopard*, formerly common, is now extremely rare, but is occasionally seen in some isolated regions, to the panic of local people. There are at least three species of *gazelle* in North Africa, the Dorcas Gazelle preferring the steppes, the Mountain Gazelle inhabiting locations over 2,000m especially where there is juniper forest, and the Desert Gazelle locating in the *reg* of the northern Sahara. The latter is often hunted by horse or vehicle, its only defence being its speed. There are over 30 species of *bat* in the area, all but one – the Egyptian Fruit Bat – being insectivorous. Recent ringing has shown that bats will migrate according to the season and to exploit changing food sources. Many species of bat have declined disastrously in recent years due to the increased use of insecticides and disturbance of roosting sites. Desert rodents include the large-eyed *sand rat*, the *gerbil* and the *jerboa*. Many, sadly, find themselves in pet shops.

REPTILES AND AMPHIBIANS

Tortoises are widespread in North Africa. The best distributed is *Hermanns tortoise* which can reach a maximum size of 30 cm. *Pond terrapins* are small fresh water tortoises and can be found in all the Mediterranean habitats. Both tortoises and terrapins are unfortunately taken in large numbers for the pet trade. There are over thirty species of lizard in the area, the most common being the *wall lizard*, which often lives close to houses. *Sand racers* are frequently seen on coastal dunes, while *sand fish* and *sand swimmers* take advantage of deep sand to avoid predators and find cooler temperatures in the desert *reg*. The *ocellated lizard* is impressive in size, growing to 20 cm. *Geckoes* are plump, soft-skinned, nocturnal lizards with adhesive pads on their toes and are frequently noted near houses. The *chameleon* is a reptile with a prehensile tail and a long sticky tongue for catching insects. Although basically green, it can change colour to match its surroundings. *Snakes* are essentially legless lizards. There are some thirty species in the Mediterranean areas alone, but only the viperine types are dangerous. These can be identified by their triangular heads, short plump bodies and zig-zag markings. The *horned viper* lies just below the surface of sand, with its horns projecting, waiting for prey. *Sand boas* stay underground most of the time, while other species twine themselves around the branches of trees. Most snakes will instinctively avoid contact with human beings and will only strike if disturbed or threatened. For what to do if you are bitten by a snake (see page 458).

MARINE LIFE

The Mediterranean is a land-locked sea and it is only in the extreme W that there is any significant tidal range. Without strong tides and currents bringing nutrients, the Mediterranean is somewhat impoverished in terms of marine life. Fish and shell fish, nevertheless, have figured prominently in the diet of the coastal people for centuries, with *sardines*, *anchovies*, *mullet*, *sole*, *squid* and *prawns* being particularly popular. *Tuna* and *swordfish* are also widely caught. Over-fishing, leading to the depletion of stocks, has become increasingly problematic.

BUTTERFLIES AND MOTHS

Because of the lack of vegetation on which to lay eggs, butterflies are scarce in the steppe and desert areas. The Mediterranean fringe, in contrast, are often rich in species, some quite exotic. The life cycle – mating, egg production, caterpillar, pupa, butterfly – can be swift, with some species having three cycles in 1 year. Some of the butterflies are large and colourful, such as the *swallowtail* and the *two-tailed pasha*. The most common butterflies in the early spring are the *painted ladies*, which migrate from North Africa northwards, often reaching as far as Britain. More familiar species include the *Moroccan orange tip*, *festoon*, *Cleopatra* and *clouded yellow*. Moths are also widely represented, but as they are largely nocturnal they are rarely seen. Day flying moths include the *Burnet* and *hummingbird hawk moths*. The largest moth of the area is the *giant peacock moth*, with a wingspan of up to 15 cm.

BIRDS

Neither the Mediterranean nor the desert areas is particularly rich in resident bird species, but both can be swollen temporarily by birds on passage. Four categories of birds may be noted. Firstly, there are the **resident** birds which are found throughout the year, such as the *crested lark* and the *Sardinian warbler*. Secondly, there are the **summer visitors**, such as the *swift* and *swallow*, which spend the winter months S of the Equator. **Winter visitors**, on the other hand, breed in northern Europe but come S to escape the worst of the winter and include many varieties of wader and wildfowl. **Passage migrants** fly through the area northwards in spring and then return southwards in increased numbers after breeding in the autumn. Small birds tend to migrate on a broad front, often crossing the desert and the Mediterranean Sea without stopping. Such migrants include the *whitethroat*, plus less common species such as the *nightjar* and *wryneck*. Larger birds, including *eagles*, *storks* and *vultures*, must adopt a different

strategy, as they depend on soaring, rather than sustained flight. As they rely on thermals created over land, they must opt for short sea crossings. One route uses the narrow Straits of Gibraltar, while the more easterly route follows the Nile Valley, Turkey and the Bosphorus. A third, lesser-used, route runs via Tunisia, Malta and Sicily, where birds run the gauntlet of the guns of so-called 'sportsmen'.

Within North Africa there is a number of typical habitats each with its own assemblage of birds. The Mediterranean itself has a poor selection of sea birds, although the rare *Audouins gull* always excites 'twitchers'. Oceanic birds such as *gannets* and *shearwaters*, however, enter the Mediterranean during the winter. Wetland areas, such as Lake Ichkeul in Tunisia (see page 182) contain numerous varieties of the heron family such as the *night heron* and *squacco heron*, while *spoonbill*, *ibis* and both *little* and *cattle egrets* are common.

Flamingoes breed in a number of locations when conditions are right. Waders such as the *avocet* and *black winged stilt* are also typical wetland birds. The wetland species are augmented in the winter by a vast collection of wildfowl. Resident ducks, however, are confined to specialities such as the *white-headed duck*, *marbled teal* and *ferruginous duck*. On roadsides, the *crested lark* is frequently seen, while overhead wires often contain *corn buntings*, with their jangling song, and the colonial *bee-eaters*. Mountain areas are ideal for searching out raptors. There are numerous varieties of *eagle*, including *Bonelli's*, *booted*, *short toed* and *golden*. Of the *vultures*, the *griffon* is the most widely encountered. The *black kite* is more catholic in its choice of habitat, but the *Montagu's harrier* prefers open farmland.

The desert and steppe areas have their own specialist resident birds which have developed survival strategies. Raptors include the *long-legged buzzard* and the *lanner*, which prefer mountain areas.

Among the ground-habitat birds are the *Houbura bustard* and the *cream coloured courser*. *Dupont's lark* is also reluctant to fly, except during its spectacular court-ship display. The *trumpeter finch* is frequently seen at oases, while the insectivorous *desert wheatear* is a typical bird of the *erg* and *reg* regions.

We are grateful to Rowland Mead for providing us with this information.

Travel and Survival in the Desert

TRAVELLERS AND THE NATURE OF DESERTS

For those travellers staying in well regulated accommodation in good hotels, the realities of the desert can be disguised for as long as electricity and pure water supplies are sustained. Much of the information in the following section can thus be ignored, though not with total impunity. Trips into the desert even by the most careful of tour operators carry some of the hazards and a knowledge of good practice might be as helpful on the beach or tourist bus as for the full-blooded desert voyager.

There is a contemporary belief that the problems of living and travelling in deserts have been solved. Much improved technology in transport together with apparent ease of access to desert areas has encouraged these comfortable ideas. The very simplicity of the problems of deserts, lack of water and high temperatures, make them easy to underestimate. In reality, deserts have not changed and problems still arise when travelling in them, albeit with less regularity than 20 or so years ago. One aspect of the desert remains unchanged – mistakes and misfortune can too easily be fatal.

Desert topography is varied. Excellent books such as Allan JA & Warren A (1993) *Deserts: a conservation atlas*, Mitchell Beazley, show the origins and constant development of desert scenery.

In North Africa, desert and semi-desert is the largest single surface area and so has an importance for travellers rarely met with elsewhere. Its principal features and their effects on transport are best understood before they are met on the ground. The great *ergs* or sandseas comprise mobile dunes and shifting surface sands over vast areas. Small mobile *barkhans*, which are crescent shaped, can often be driven round on firm terrain but the larger transverse and longitudinal dunes can form large surfaces with thick ridges of soft sand. They constantly change their shape as the wind works across them. While not impassible, they can be crossed only slowly and with difficulty. The major sand seas such as those at Calanscio, Murzuq, and Brak should be treated as no-go areas for all but fully equipped and locally supported expeditions. Similar conclusions apply to the extensive outcrops of rocky desert as exemplified by the Jabal As-Sawda in Libya. The *oued* beds which penetrate much of the Sahara, *serirs* and gravel plains provide good access for all-terrain vehicles.

The main characteristic of the desert is its **aridity**. Aridity is calculable and those navigating deserts are advised to understand the term so that the element of risk can be appraised and managed with safety. CW Thornthwaite's aridity index shows water deficiency relative to water need for a given area. There is a gradient from N to S throughout the region, of rising temperatures, diminishing rainfall and worsening aridity. Aridity of the desert is thus very variable, ranging from the Mediterranean sub-tropical fringe to a semi-arid belt to the S and a fully arid desert interior. In basic terms, the further S you are the more dangerous the environment. Do not assume that conditions on the coast properly prepare you for the deep S. The Sahara is also very varied in its topography, climate and natural difficulties posed for the traveller. Rapid tran-

sition from rough stone terrain to sand sea to salt flat has to be expected and catered for.

For practical purposes, aridity means **no moisture and very high temperatures**. The world's highest temperatures are experienced in the Sahara – over 55°C. Averages in the S desert run in summer at more than 50°C in the shade at midday. In full sun very much higher figures are reached. High temperatures are not the only difficulty. Each day has a large range of temperature, often of more than 20°C, with nights being intensely cold, sometimes below freezing. In winter, air temperatures can be very low despite the heat of the sun and temperatures drop very rapidly either when the sun goes down or when there is movement from sunlight to shade, say in a deep gorge or a cave.

Increasing aridity means greater **difficulty in water availability**. Scientists define the problem in terms of water deficits. North Africa as a whole and the deep Sahara in particular are very serious water deficit areas. Surface waters are lacking almost everywhere. Underground water is scarce and often available only at great depths. Occasional natural see pages of water give rise to oases and/or palmeries. They are, however, rare. Since water is the key to sustaining life in deserts, travellers have always to assume that they must be self-sufficient or navigate from one known water source to another.

Isolation is another feature of the Sahara. Travellers' tales tend to make light of the matter, hinting that bedouin Arabs will emerge from the dunes even in the most obscure corner of the desert. This is probably true of the semi-desert and some inland *wadi* basins but not a correct assumption on which to build a journey in the greater part of the Sahara. Population numbers in the desert are very low, only one person per 20 km sq in Al-Kufrah in SE Libya, for example, and most of these are concentrated in small oasis centres. Black top road systems are gradually being extended into and through the Sahara but they represent a few straggling lines across areas for the most part without fixed and maintained highways. The very fact that oil exploration has been so intense in the Sahara has meant that the surface of the desert is criss-crossed with innumerable tracks, making identification of all routes other than black top roads extremely difficult. Once off the main roads, travellers can part from their escorts and find no fixed topography to get them back on course. Vanishing individuals and vehicles in the Sahara are too frequent to be a joke. To offset this problem read on.

The most acute difficulty with off-road emergencies is finding the means of raising assistance because of isolation. Normal preventative action is to ensure that your travel programme is known in advance by some individual or an institution to whom regular check-in is made from points on the route. Failure to contact should automatically raise the alarm. Two vehicles are essential and often obviate the worst problems of break-down and the matter of isolation. Radio communication from your vehicle is an expensive but useful aid if things go wrong.

Bear in mind the enormous distances involved in bringing help even where the location of an incident in the desert is known. Heavy rescue equipment and/or paramedical assistance will probably be 500 km or more distant. Specialist transport for the rescuers is often not instantly available, assuming that local telecommunications systems work and local administrators see fit to help.

LIVING WITH THE CLIMATE

Living with desert environments is not difficult but it does take discipline and adherence to sensible routines at all times. It is an observed fact that health problems in hot and isolated locations take on a greater seriousness for those involved than they would in temperate climates. It is still common practice with Western oil companies and other commercial organizations regularly engaged at desert sites to fly ill or injured persons home as a first measure in the knowledge that most will recover more rapidly without the psychological and environmental pressures of a desert site. Most health risks in the desert are avoidable. The rules, evolved over many years, are simple and easy to follow:

1. **Allow time to acclimatise** to full desert conditions. Conserve your energy at first rather than acting as if you were still in a temperate climatic régime. Most people take a week or more to adjust to heat conditions in the deep Sahara.

2. **Stay out of direct sunlight** whenever possible, especially once the sun is high. Whenever you can, do what the locals do, move from shade to shade.

3. **Wear clothes to protect your skin** from the sun, particularly your head and neck. Use a high Sun Protection Factor (SPF) cream, preferably as high as SPF15 (94%) to minimize the effects of Ultraviolet-B. Footwear is a matter of choice though many of those from the temperate parts of the world will find strong, light but well ventilated boots ideal for keeping sand, sun, venomous livestock and thorns off the feet. Slip on boots are best of all since they are convenient if visiting Arab encampments/housing/religious sites, where shoes are not worn.

4. **Drink good quality water** regularly and fully. It is estimated that 10-15 litres per day are needed by a healthy person to avoid water deficiency in desert conditions, even if there is no actual feeling of thirst. The majority of ailments arising in the desert relate to water deficiency and so it is worth the small effort

of regular drinking of water. Too much alcoholic drink has the opposite effect in most cases and is not, unfortunately, a substitute for water!

5. Be prepared for cold nights by having some warm clothes to hand.

6. Stay in your quarters or vehicle if there is a **sand storm**.

7. Refrain from eating dubious foods. Deserts and stomach upsets have a habit of going hand in hand – 'gyppy-tummy' and 'Tripoli-trots' give a taste of the problem! Choose hot cooked meals in preference to cold meats and tired salads. Peel all fruit and uncooked fresh vegetables. Do not eat 'native' milk-based items or drink untreated water unless you are absolutely sure of its good quality.

8. Sleep off the ground if you can. There are very few natural dangers in the desert but scorpions, spiders and snakes are found (but are rarely fatal) and are best avoided.

TRANSPORT AND COMMON SENSE IN THE DESERT

The key to safe travel in desert regions is reliable and well equipped transport. Most travellers will simply use local bus and taxi services. For the motorist, motorcyclist or pedal cyclist there are ground rules which, if followed, will help to reduce risks. In normal circumstances travellers will remain on black top roads and for this need only a well prepared 2WD vehicle. Choose a machine which is known for its reliability and for which spares can be easily obtained. Across the whole of North Africa only Peugeot and Mercedes are found with adequate spares and servicing facilities. If you have a different type of car/truck, make sure that you take spares with you or have the means of getting spares sent out. Bear in mind that transport of spares to and from Libya might be tediously long. Petrol/benzene/gas is everywhere available though diesel is equally well distributed

except in the smallest of southern settlements. 4WD transport is useful even for the traveller who normally remains on the black top highway. Emergencies, diversions and unscheduled visits to off the road sites become less of a problem with all-terrain vehicles. Off the road, 4WD is essential, normally with two vehicles travelling together. A great variety of 4WD vehicles are in use in the region, with Toyota and Land Rover probably found most widely.

All vehicles going into the S areas of North Africa should have basic equipment as follows:

1. Full tool kit; vehicle maintenance handbook and supplementary tools such as clamps, files, wire, spare parts kit supplied by car manufacturer, jump leads.

2. Spare tyre/s, battery driven tyre pump, tyre levers, tyre repair kit, hydraulic jack, jack handle extension, base plate for jack.

3. Spare fuel can/s, spare water container/s, cool bags.

For those going off the black top roads other items to include are:

4. Foot tyre pump, heavy duty hydraulic or air jack, power winch, sand channels, safety rockets, comprehensive first aid kit, radio-telephone where permitted.

5. Emergency rations kit/s, matches, Benghazi burner (see page 47).

6. Maps, compasses, latest road information, long term weather forecast, guides to navigation by sun and stars.

Driving in the desert is an acquired skill. Basic rules are simple but crucial.

1. If you can get a local guide who perhaps wants a lift to your precise destination, use him.

2. Set out early in the morning after first light, rest during the heat of the day and use the cool of the evening for further travel.

3. Never attempt to travel at night or when there is a sandstorm brewing or in progress.

4. Always travel with at least two vehicles which should remain in close visual-contact.

Other general hints include not speeding across open flat desert in case the going changes without warning and your vehicle beds deeply into soft sand or a gully. Well maintained corrugated road surfaces can be taken at modest pace but rocky surfaces should be treated with great care to prevent undue wear on tyres. Sand seas are a challenge for drivers but need a cautious approach – ensure that your navigation lines are clear so that weaving between dunes does not disorientate the navigator. Especially in windy conditions, sight lines can vanish, leaving crews with little knowledge of where they are. Cresting dunes from dip slope to scarp needs care that the vehicle does not either bog down or overturn. Keep off salt flats after rain and floods especially in the winter and spring when water tables can rise and make the going hazardous in soft mud. Even when on marked and maintained tracks beware of approaching traffic. One of the editor's friend's car was hit by the only vehicle which passed him that day on a 500 km drive in S Libya!

EMERGENCIES

The desert tends to expose the slightest flaw in personnel and vehicles. Emergency situations are therefore to be expected and planned for. There is no better security than making the schedule of your journey known in advance to friends or embassy/consulate officials who will actively check on your arrival at stated points. Breakdowns and multiple punctures are the most frequent problem. On the highway the likelihood is always that a passing motorist will give assistance, or a lift to the nearest control post or village. In these situations it is best simply to remain with your vehicle until help arrives making sure that your are clear of the road and that you are protected from other traffic by a warning triangle and/or rocks on the road to rear and front.

Off the road, breakdowns, punctures and bogging down in soft sand are the main difficulties. If you have left your travel programme at your last stop you will already have a fall back position in case of severe problems. If you cannot make a repair or extricate yourself, remain with your vehicle in all circumstances. Unless you can clearly see a settlement (not a mirage) stay where you are with water, food and shelter. The second vehicle can be used to search for help but only after defining the precise location of the incident. In the case of getting lost, halt, conserve fuel while you attempt to get a bearing on either the topography or the planets/stars and work out a traverse to bring you back to a known line such as a highway, mountain ridge or coastline. If that fails, take up as prominent a position as possible for being spotted from the air. Build a fire to use if and when y ou hear air activity in your vicinity. Attempt to find a local source of water by digging in the nearest wadi bed, collecting dew from the air at night. If you have fuel to spare it can be used with great care both as a means of attracting attention and a way of boiling untreated water. A *Benghazi burner*, two crude metal cones welded together to give a water jacket and space for a fire in the centre can achieve this latter purpose. As ever in North Africa, be patient and conserve your energy.

Jewellery and dress

JEWELLERY

North Africa today boasts a distinctive culture whose abundance of styles of dress and adornment almost defies description. The dynamic history of the region has produced imaginative traditionial designs mixed with foreign elements leading to a range of decoration few regions in the world can rival. Influences from the Phoenicians, Greeks and Romans, Arabs and Andalusians have each contributed subtly to the immense range of jewellery found in this part of the world.

Although some urban dwellers have adopted Western attitudes to dress and decoration, at times of festivals and especially for marriage ceremonies, traditional dress and elaborate jewellery that has changed little since the Middle Ages is still worn. The increase of tourism, while in some cases destroying traditional values, is in fact promoting and preserving crafts, especially jewellery making, by providing an eager and lucrative market for ornaments that was rapidly declining. Unfortunately, with the changes of cultural values, changes in fashion and style also occur and large quantities of old, exquisite silver jewellery have been destroyed to provide raw materials for new pieces.

Throughout the region there is a division of tastes and wealth between towns where gold is favoured and the countryside where silver predominates.

Basically, traditional styles continue to be popular and, especially in the Maghreb, jewellery tends to become more traditional the further S one goes. A general shift can be discerned away from silver towards gold which is now believed to be a better investment.

Despite a whole field of inspiration being forbidden to Muslim jewellers, that of the human form, they developed the art of decorating jewellery in ways that eventually merged to become a distinctive 'Islamic' style. Using floral (arabesque), animal, geometric and calligraphic motifs fashioned on gold and silver with precious and semi-precious gems, coral and pearls they worked their magic.

According to Islamic law, silver is the only pure metal recommended by the Prophet Mohammad. For the majority of Muslims this sanction is felt to apply

Braclets from the Maghreb

only to men who do not, as a rule, wear any jewellery other than a silver wedding ring or seal ring.

Every town has its own jewellery *souq* with larger centres providing a greater range of jewellery. There is almost always a distinction between the goldsmiths and the silversmiths and there are also shops, which produce jewellery in brass or gold plate on brass for the cheap end of the market.

Jewellers also sell silver items in the cheaper end of the tourist market which is very popular as 'ethnic' jewellery. Gold and silver jewellery is usually sold by weight and, although there might be an additional charge for more intricate craftmanship, this means the buyer must judge quality very carefully.

The **earring** is by far the most popular and convenient ornament throughout the region. It appears in an infinite variety of styles with the crescent moon shape being the most common. This is closely followed by the **bracelet** or **bangle** which is also very much part of a woman's everyday wardrobe.

Most of the jewellery is worn both as an **adornment** and as an indication of social status or rank. It generally has some symbolic meaning or acts as a charm. Jewellery is usually steeped in tradition and is often received in rites of passage like puberty, betrothal and marriage. In Tunisia, women receive most of their jewellery upon marriage. This is usually regarded as their sole property and is security against personal disaster.

Many of the **symbols** recurrent in such jewellery have meanings or qualities which are thought to be imparted to the wearer. Most of the discs appearing in the jewellery represent the *moon* which is considered to be the embodiment of perfect beauty and femininity. The greatest compliment is to liken a woman to the full moon. Both the moon and the fish are considered as *fertility symbols*. The cresent is the symbol of

One of the many styles of Khamsa or Hand of Fatima

North African anklets or *Khul-Khal* (always worn in pairs)

Islam but its use actually predates Islam. It is the most common symbol throughout the region and acquires greater Islamic significance with the additon of a *star* inside. Other symbols frequently seen are the *palm* and the *moving lizard* both of which signify life and the *snake* which signifies respect.

Amulets are thought to give the wearer protection from the unknown, calamities and threats. They are also reckoned to be curative and to have power over human concerns such as longevity, health, wealth, sex and luck. Women and childen wear amulets more frequently as their resistance to evil is considered to be weaker than that of a man.

The most popular amulets are the *Hirz*, the Eye which has always had mystical connotations and the *Khamsa* or hand. The *Hirz* is a silver box containing verses of the Koran. The *Khamsa* is by far the most widespread of the amulets. It comes in a multitude of sizes and designs of a stylized hand and is one of the most common components of jewellery in the region. This hand represents the 'Hand of Fatima', Mohammad's favourite daughter. Koranic inscriptions also form a large section of favoured pendants and are usually executed in gold and also heavily encrusted with diamonds and other precious stones.

Coins or *mahboub* form the basis of most of the traditional jewellery, seen in the spectacular festival and marriage ensembles worn in the Mahgreb. Each area, village or tribe has its own unique and extraordinary dress of which jewellery, be it hundreds of coins or huge amber beads, forms a fundamental part.

Among the more interesting items are **anklets** called *khul khal*, worn in pairs and found in a great variety of styles. They are mostly of gold or solid silver and may be patterned or fringed with tiny bells. Fine examples are expensive due to their weight. They are losing popularity among the younger genera-

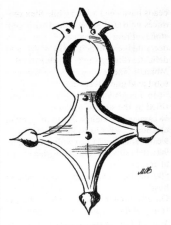

Agades Cross

tion as they are cumbersome to wear with shoes and because of their undertones of subservience and slavery.

Characteristic **Libyan** jewellery is gold plated silver though both silver and gold are common. The predominant motif, a tiny version of the *'Hand of Fatima'*, appears on every piece. In **Tunisia** and other countries of the Maghreb, look out for *fibulae* and *pectorals* used to secure women's capes. They occur in various styles and are usually of silver, sometimes inlaid with coral. Saharan tribes like the Touareg have jewellery which is generally made of leather and engraved silver. The most well known *Touareg* piece is the *Agades Cross (tanaghilit)* which comes in many variations of the basic style.

Today the main jewellery bazaars are *Souq al-Mushir* in Tripoli (page 379) and *Souq el-Birka* in Tunis, (page 112). Souq el Birka is well known for it gold jewellery, either simple or inlaid with gems in both traditional and modern forms. In Nabeul craftsmen produce silver for the rural women, Moknine provides solid silver jewellery to which coral and glass beads have been added while Sfax produces gold and silver inlaid with gem stones. From Djerba comes the richly decorated enamelled solid silver and delicate filigree silver while Mahdia, Monastir and Sousse are know for their solid gold and silver work.

In Tunisia authentic jewellery is certified by the state as follows:

18 carat gold is stamped with the symbol of a horse's head or a ram's head.

9 carat gold is stamped with a scorpion.

900/1000 silver is stamped with a bunch of grapes.

800/1000 silver is stamped with a human head.

On all jewellery there ought to be the stamp of the maker and of the state.

Marie-Claire Bakker contributed the text and illustrations for this section.

DRESS

First time visitors to the countries of North Africa will be fascinated by the variety and colour of the garments worn as 'everyday' wear. This section, contributed by Jennifer Scarce, Curator of Eastern Cultures, National Museums of Scotland, sketches in the background and attempts an explanation of what is being worn and why.

The dress traditions of North Africa are striking and colourful evidence of a rich cultural heritage. Here, as in all societies, dress is a powerful form of cultural expression, a visual symbol which reveals a wealth of information about the wearer. Dress also reflects historical evolution and the cumulative effects of religious, ethnic and geographical factors on a society.

It is hardly surprising that the many influences which have shaped North African history have produced an equally diverse dress culture in which elements from antiquity, the Islamic world and Europe are found. The heritage from earlier times is a rich blending of decorative motifs and drapery. Carthaginian material culture drew upon local tradtions of colourful geometric ornament, which is still seen in Berber clothing and textiles. Greek and Roman fashions have survived in the striking dress of the inhabitants of the deserts and mountains of Libya and Tunisia where draped and folded garments are fastened with elaborate jewelled pins (see Jewellery page 48) and buckles. The Arabs introduced a different dress tradition, influenced by the styles of Egypt and Syria. Here the main features were loose flowing robes and cloaks, wrapped turbans and headcovering which combined a graceful line, comfort and modest concealment. The establishment of Islamic cities encouraged a diverse range of professions and occupations – civil and religious authorities, merchants, craftsmen – all with their distinctive dress. Within cities such as Tunis specialist trades in textiles, leather and jewellery supported dress production. Widening political and commercial relations stimulated new elements in dress. Jewish and Muslim immigrants from Andalucía in the 15th century introduced styles influenced by Spanish tradition which survived in the full-skirted tight-waisted dresses of Jewish women.

The Ottoman Turks introduced another feature into city dress, in the form of jackets, trousers and robes of flamboyant cut and lavishly embroidered decoration. Finally European fashion, with emphasis on tailored suits and dresses entered the scene.

One of the more rewarding pleasures of a visit to North Africa is the opportunity to see the intricate pattern of mixed dress styles which reflect an adjustment to economic and social change.

The widest range is seen in urban environments where European styles mingle with interpretations of local dress and the clothing of regional migrants. Men have adopted European dress in varying degrees. The wardrobes

Ksa or Barakan

is based on a flexible combination of loose flowing garments and wraps which gives considerable scope for individuality. One of the most versatile garments is the *jallabah*, an ankle length robe with long straight sleeves and a neat pointed hood, made in fabrics ranging from fine wool and cotton in dark and light colours to rough plain and striped homespun yarn. Elegant versions in white may be beautifully cut and sewn and edged with plaited silk braid. A modern casual version has short sleeves and a V-shaped neck and is made of poly-cotton fabric in a range of plain colours. Professional men may change from a suit into a *jallabah* at home, while working class men may wear a plain or striped *jallabah* in the street over European shirt and trousers.

The more traditional interpretation of dress can be seen in the medinas. Here the *jallabah* is worn with the hood folded at the the back or pulled up and draped over the head. In the past a fez or turban was worn under the hood and a white cotton high-necked shirt with long sleeves and loose white trousers gathered just below the knee were worn under the *jallabah*. In Tunisia trousers of a more exaggerated voluminous style were worn as a result of Ottoman Turkish influence.

A handsome and dignified garment worn by high ranking state and religious officials is the *caftan*, another long robe with very wide sleeves and a round neck. The cut and detail, such as the use of very fine braid around the neck and sleeves and along the seams, are more formal than those of the *jallabah*. The modern *caftan* has narrower sleeves and is worn in public by men of an older and more conservative generation.

Traditional dress may be completed with the addition of drapery. Examples include the *selham* or *burnous*, a wide semicircular cloak with a pointed hood and the *ksa*, or *barakan* a length of heavy white woollen cloth which is skilfully

of civil servants, professional and business men include well-cut sober coloured European suits, which are worn with toning shirts, ties and smart shoes. Seasonal variations include fabrics of lighter weight and colour and short-sleeved shirts and 'safari' jackets. Casual versions of this dress code, including open-necked shirts, are seen in more modest levels of urban society. Blue jeans, blouson jackets, T shirts and trainers may be worn equally by manual workers and students.

Men's city dress alternates between European and local garments according to taste and situation. Traditional dress folded and wrapped around the head and body in a style resembling that of the classical Roman toga.

Headcoverings are a revealing indication of status and personal choice. A close fitting red wool felt pillbox cap, a *fez* or *chechia*, was normally worn alone or neatly wrapped with a turban length. Such caps were a major product of the souk of Tunis and were widely exported. Currently they are seen more often on older men both in traditional and European dress.

Footwear is a distinctive product of North Africa's longstanding leather industry. Shoes usually in bright yellow or white, are made of fine leather. They are close fitting, have a long pointed toe and are worn with the back folded under at the heel.

Women's town dress is also a mixture of traditional and modern European forms and depends on wealth, status and personal taste. In the larger cities where women are employed in business and professions, European clothes are worn, cleverly accessorised with scarves and jewellery. Longer skirts and long-sleeved blouses are worn, being a more modest form of European dress.

Traditional dress is remarkably enduring especially in the cities among women of all classes. The most important garments are the *caftan* and *jallabah* of the same basic cut and shape as those for men. The *caftan*, as worn in the past by wealthy women, was a sumptuous garment of exaggerated proportions made of rich velvet or brocaded silk embroidered with intricate designs in gold thread. The modern *caftan* is usually made of brightly coloured and patterned light-weight fabric and edged with plaited braid. The shape is simple and unstructured with a deep slit at each side from waist to hem. Variations can be found in texture and colour of fabric, changes in proportions of sleeves and length of side slits. The *caftan* in its

many variations is always worn as indoor dress and can suit all occasions. Traditionally it is worn as an everyday garment belted over a long underskirt. A light shawl may be draped around the neck and the hair tied up with a patterned scarf. Women who normally wear European dress to work often change into a *caftan* at home. Very chic versions of the *caftan*, combined with modern hairstyles and accessories, are worn as evening wear at private and official functions.

Outdoor dress varies in Tunisia and offers different solutions to the traditional requirements of modesty and concealment. The Tunisian outdoor dress is less structured and may be worn over European clothes. Here the basic garment is the *sifsari*, a length of white fabric which is folded in half and secured around the waist. The top half is then pulled up over the head and draped according to the required degree of facial concealment.

While the balance between contrasting dress codes is subject to subtle changes of emphasis in everyday life, the rituals of *marriage* still require a conspicuous display of traditional dress, jewellery and cosmetics for both bride and female guests. Wedding ceremonies

Traditional Tunisian headgear - a dark red chechia of felt

can still be very traditional and here the bride, robed in layers of magnificent brocaded garments and shawls and adorned with a gold crown hung with strings of pearls and with intricate patterns drawn with henna on her hands, is transformed into a splendid icon.

Regional dress, though less varied than in the past, is a striking visual record of the complex ethnic patterns and harsh living conditions of the rural areas. The tradition of the Berber tribes both settled and nomadic, is still retained in their handsome and brilliantly coloured draped garments. Extremes of heat and cold mean that adjustable layers of loose clothing and protective headgear such as a swathed turban or a straw hat are essential.

In rural areas the men's hooded *jallabah* is the most common, usually of homespun wool in unbeached white, blue or beige and brown stripes. It may be worn over another *jallabah*. Head coverings may be a closefitting knitted cap, a loosely wrapped white turban, or a tall pointed hat with a wide flat brim plaited from reeds, palm fibre or dried grass. Berber men used to drape a *haik*, a heavy cloak in coarse plain or striped wool, over their garments. In the S, the Touareg men still wear brilliant blue robes and conceal their heads and faces with turbans and veils as an extreme precaution against the sun, wind and sand.

Women's dress is considerably more varied and depends on a combination of colourful drapes. The basic garment of the Berber women is an *izar*, a long straight piece of cotton or wool in a series of colours ranging from white or black through to vivid reds, purples and yellows. The *izar*, worn over a *caftan,* is folded in half to envelope the body and is fastened at the shoulders with heavy silver pins or brooches. (See Jewellery, page 48). It can then be further draped, belted and adorned according to local usage. Striped woollen cloaks may be worn over the *izar*. Large turbans bound with cords and scarves, elaborately plaited and coiled hair, and much chunky silver jewellery traditionally complete this form of dress.

In tourist areas doormen, porters and waiters are garbed in white *jallabah* and scarlet *fez*, watersellers in traditional dress and gaily decorated broad-brimmed hats roam the streets, displays of Berber dancing are arranged and tourists are encouraged to purchase 'local garments' and participate in versions of local festivals. The souks in these resorts are festooned with *caftans* and leather slippers.

At another level, North Africa's impressive cultural heritage is taken very seriously and many museums have displays of traditional dress which can be enjoyed by both local and foreign visitors (see Dar Cherait Museum, Tozeur, page 277).

Writing to us

Many people write to us - with corrections, new information, or simply comments. If you want to let us know something, we would be delighted to hear from you. Please give us as precise information as possible, quoting the edition and page number of the Handbook you are using and send as early in the year as you can. Your help will be greatly appreciated, especially by other travellers. In return we will send you details about our special guidebook offer.

For hotels and restaurants, please let us know:

- each establishment's name, address, phone and fax number
- number of rooms, whether a/c or air-cooled, attached (clean?) bathroom
- location - how far from the station or bus stand, or distance (walking time) from a prominent landmark
- if it's not already on one of our maps, can you place it?
- your comments - either good or bad - as to why it is distinctive
- tariff cards
- local transport used

For places of interest:

- location
- entry, camera charge
- access - by whatever means of transport is most approriate, eg time of main buses or trains to and from the site, journey time, fare
- facilities - nearby drinks stalls, restaurants, for the disabled
- any problems, eg steep climb, wildlife, unofficial guides
- opening hours
- site guides

Tunisia

FOR the travellerTunisiaoffers a gentle introduction to North Africa being very Western in character. French is widely spoken. It offers endless reliable sunshine, beautiful beaches, inspiring mountain ranges, palm-fringed oases and in the south, wide expanses of sandy desert. It contains many spectacular Roman monuments, a wide range of Islamic architecture and unusual underground dwellings.

Tunisia is small, by far the smallest country in North Africa, equal in area to that of England and Wales or half of Italy. Thus the variety of geographical and historical sights as well as the opportunities to relax or be entertained are all easily accessible. There are 1,600 km of coast for the sun-bather and the windsurfer, 330 km facing the north and the major part facing east to the central Mediterranean Sea.Tunisia lying between 30°N and 38°N and 9°E and 12°E extends the furthest north of all the African countries.

BASICS

OFFICIAL NAME al-Jumhuriyah at-Tunisiyah (Republic of Tunisia).

NATIONAL FLAG Red with a white circle in the centre, bearing a crescent moon and a five point star in red.

OFFICIAL LANGUAGE Arabic.

OFFICIAL RELIGION Islam.

INDICATORS *Population*: 8.9 million. *Urban*: 53%. *Religion*: Sunni Muslim 99.4%, Christian 0.3%, Jewish 0.1%. *Birth rate*: 24 per 1,000. *Death rate*: 6 per 1,000. *Life expectancy*: 67/69. *GNP per capita*: US$1,780.

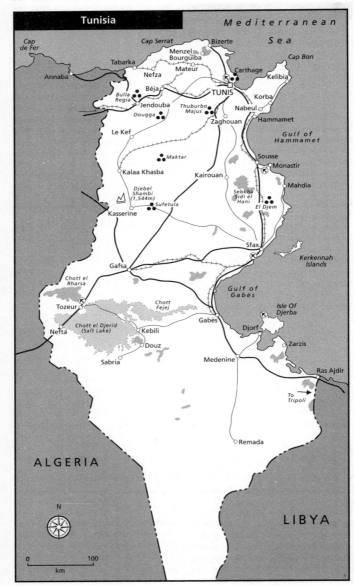

THE LAND

GEOGRAPHY

The Republic of Tunisia has a surface area of 163,610 sq km. It measures 750 km from N to S and averages 150 km from W to E. The Gulf of Tunis is included in the northern coastal (330 km) zone while to the S, forming part of the E facing coast (1,270 km), are the Gulfs of Hammamet and Gabès, the latter lying between the islands of Djerba in the S and Kerkennah in the N.

Borders

Tunisia has a long land border with Algeria, with a multiplicity of crossing points. It has a short land border with Libya, the crossing point at Ras Jedir being well used at present. The Tunisia/Libya offshore boundary dispute over the Bouri oilfield in the Gulf of Gabès was arbitrated in favour of Libya. Tunisia and Libya are, however, contemplating joint development of other oilfields lying across their offshore boundary. The creation of the United Maghreb Association has made other potential border disputes with neighbours less likely in the short term. Travel between UMA states also helps all UMA and other Arab travellers and tends to make it slightly easier for non-Arab tourists to get through border crossings in Tunisia and other N African countries.

Main regions

Traditionally, Tunisians relate to their tribal or hometown areas which often do not coincide with the country's physical regions. The Tunis metropolitan area is regarded as the principal region, with the Medjerda valley, the Sahel, the interior plateau and the S also being differentiated.

Three physical regions can be distinguished. **Northern Tunisia** is the economically dominant area. In the extreme N forming a rugged coastline – an extension of the mainly sandstone Algerian Atlas – rises a distinctive range known as the Northern Tell. In places these uplands with altitudes exceeding 1,000m are covered with cork oak and pine. The S flanks of the Tell in the Béja region are lower, more open and more fertile. To the E are the rich alluvial plains around Bizerte. The Oued Medjerda, Tunisia's only major perennial flow, cuts a wide fertile valley to the S of these ranges flowing NE to enter the sea in the Gulf of Tunis. This is the major agricultural region noted particularly for cereals. Further S, aligned SW-NE, is an extension of the higher, broader and mainly limestone Saharan Atlas. This forms the distinctive Dorsal/High Tell region with its harsher climate and sparser vegetation. The Dorsal range, which boasts Tunisia's highest point, Djebel Shambi at 1,544m, ends in the NE at the peninsula of Cap Bon. This peninsula is Tunisia's richest region, with a mild climate, fertile soils and a dense population.

Central Tunisia is a lower central plateau of semi-arid steppe land. Its harsh environment renders the area bleak and barren, especially in the W. Only the lower, E steppe offers opportunities for stock raising and cereal cultivation. The Sahel, a low-lying and flat westward extension of the coastal plain, has seasonal salt lakes and sandy soils with a widespread, dense cover of olive groves which are supported by light rainfall, heavy dews and the tempering influence of the Mediterranean Sea.

Southern Tunisia, lying S of the steppes and stretching from the Algerian border to the sea, is an area of low-lying salt lakes or *chotts*, some below sea level, which are flooded during the winter and which dry to give extensive seasonal salt flats. Other depressions, where the water table is exposed or very close to the surface, produce the spectacular green oases of date palms. The depressions in the

N and the level summits of the Djebel Dahar to the E give way S to the sand dunes and rocky wastes of the Great Eastern Erg, the Sahara.

Relief/altitude

Tunisia is a country of low relief, less than 1% of the land being over 1,000m and more than 65% being under 350m. The highest land lies to the N and W.

Rivers

The only major river in Tunisia is the Oued Medjerda, which runs in the N from the Souq Ahras area in Algeria to the Gulf of Tunis. It has been heavily engineered for irrigation purposes and carries only a moderate flow in its easterly reaches. Elsewhere the streams are short *oueds* which often drain internally into seasonal salt lakes, the largest complex being in the Chott el Djerid, S of Gafsa. *Oueds* in spate are dangerous and in recent years heavy floods in the S have carried away whole villages. Travellers should not attempt to cross *oueds* in flood and should certainly not camp in stream beds.

CLIMATE

The climate of the N region is archetypically Mediterranean in character with hot dry summers and warm, wet, westerly winds in winter. To the S the influences of the Sahara increase and the aridity of the landscape intensifies. Rainfall is irregular and decreases progressively to the S with annual averages ranging from 1,000 mm in N regions to 200-400 mm on the central plateau and less than 200 mm in the S. Rainfall, nowhere reliable, is most regular in the N. There was heavy rainfall in 1995/96 winter season, suggesting the start of a run of wetter years. Humidity is generally low, especially away from the coast and towards the S. High temperatures and high relative humidity are an unpleasant combination, especially in Jun-Jul.

The prevailing wind is from the W, though in summer NE winds also occur. A fierce, hot sirocco-type wind from the

Sahara, the *ghibli*, takes temperatures into the mid 40°C range, relative humidity to 10% and has serious effects on human and plant life. Temperatures are influenced by proximity to the coast. Average temperatures increase to the S and extremes of temperature between day and night occur in the desert. For the visitor, summers can be hot by day and over warm at night on the coast and unbearably hot (45°C) by day and surprisingly cool (10°C) by night inland. Winters are pleasantly mild in the N in the lowlands but temperatures fall quickly with altitude giving snow-blocked passes, while high daytime desert temperatures plummet at night making it 'too cold to sleep'.

The natural vegetation and farm crops are strongly influenced by the climate. The cork oak and pine forests of the wetter cooler N give way to thin pastures and esparto grass cover and eventually to desert in the S where the oases, supplied by natural springs, contrast sharply with the surrounding barren sands.

FLORA AND FAUNA

The variety and quantity of vegetation is controlled by climatic conditions. Cork oaks clothe the mountain slopes in the N, esparto grass covers vast areas of the plains further S while the separate oases offer a wide selection. In spring the semi-desert in bloom is a sight to behold. The number of large wild mammals is declining but wild boar still roam in the cork forests of the N and gazelle bound across the scrub land in the S.

Lake Ichkeul and the surrounding reed beds in the N and the temporary lakes in the S provide resting places for migratory birds such as storks and flamingoes, bee eaters and hoopoes. There are many birds of prey at all times of the year. Other less attractive creatures such as snakes which are rarely seen, and scorpions, also to be treated with great respect, are natives of Tunisia. See page 40, section on wildlife of North Africa.

Main archaeological sites of Tunisia

Roman name in capital letters
Modern name in italics

Mediterranean Sea

HIPPO-DIARRHYTUS
Bizerte

UTICA
Utique

THABRACA
Tabarka

MATERA
Mateur

KARTHAGO
Carthage

CLUPEA
Kelibia

VAGA
Béja

TUNES
Tunis

BULLA REGIA

CINCARI
Testour

UTHINA
Oudna

NEAPOLIS
Nabeul

N

THIGNICA
Ain Tounga

SIMITHU
Chemtou

THUGGA
Dougga

THUBURBO
MAJUS

ZIQUA
Zaghouan

PUPPUT
Hammamet

MUSTI

SICCA-VENERIA
Le Kef

ALTHIBUROS
Medeina

MACTARIS
Maktar

HADRUMETUM
Sousse

KAIROUAN

Uzitta

AMMAEDARA
Haidra

MAHDIA

SUFETULA
Sbeitla

THYSDRUS
El Djem

CILLIUM
Kasserine

ACHOLLA
Botria

THELEPTE

TAPARURA
Sfax

THAENAE
Thyna

CAPSA
Gafsa

TACAPAE
Gabès

TRITONIS LACUS
Chott el Djerid

GIGTHIS
Bou Ghrara

0   40
kilometres

7

Scorpions – the original sting in the tail

Scorpions really deserve a better press. They are fascinating creatures, provided they no not lurk in your shoe or shelter in your clothes.

Scorpions are not insects. They belong to the class Arachnida as do spiders and daddy longlegs. There are about 750 different kinds of scorpions. The average size is a cosy 6 cms but the largest, *Pandinus imperator*, the black Emperor scorpion of West Africa, is a terrifying 20 cm long. The good news is that only a few are really dangerous. The bad news is that some of these are found in North Africa.

They really are remarkable creatures with the ability to endure the hottest desert climates, revive after being frozen in ice, and survive for over a year without food or water. They have a remarkable resistance to nuclear radiation, a characteristic yet to be proved of great use.

Scorpions are nocturnal. They shelter during the heat of the day and to keep cool wave their legs in the air. They feed on insects and spiders, grasping their prey with their large claw-like pincers, tearing it apart and sucking the juices. Larger scorpions can devour lizards and small mammals.

Their shiny appearance is due to an impervious wax coating over their hard outer shell which protects them from any water loss. They have very small eyes and depend on their better developed senses of touch and smell. The sensitive bristles on the legs point in all directions and pick up vibrations of movements of potential prey or enemies. This sensitivity gives them ample warning to avoid being seen by heavy-footed humans.

The oft reported 'courtship dance' before mating is merely repeated instinctive actions. The grasping of claws and the jerky 'dance' movements from side to side are a prelude to copulation during which the male produces spermatozoa in a drop of sticky fluid to which the female is led so that they may enter her body. The male departs speedily after the 'dance' to avoid being attacked and devoured.

Scorpions bear live young. After hatching, the young crawl on to the female's back and are carried there for two or three weeks until their first moult. They gradually drop off after that time and have to fend for themselves.

Most scorpions retreat rather than attack. They sting in self-defence. The sting is a hard spine and the poison is made in the swelling at the base. The sole of the bare foot, not surprisingly, is most often the site of a sting, and the advice in the section on Health (see page 254) is not to be ignored. The African **fat-tailed**

scorpion (we do not recommend measuring the size) is described as aggressive and quick-tempered. It is responsible for most of the reported stings to humans and most of the human fatalities in North Africa. The beautifully named *Buthus occitanus*, the small **Mediterranean yellow scorpion** and *Leirus quinquestriatus*, the **African golden scorpion**, also have neurotoxic stings that can be fatal.

AGRICULTURE

Land use

This is recorded as arable and orchards 31%, meadow and pasture 20%, forest and woodland 4% and non agricultural 45%. Yields are generally low as a consequence of the unreliable precipitation, small dispersed plots of land, outdated methods of farming and lack of investment by absentee landlords. Due to poor investment in vital water supplies, 75% of farm output comes from non-irrigated plots.

Land tenure

Currently nearly 65% of Tunisia's farms are under 10 ha, 31% are between 10 and 50 ha and only 5% are over 50 ha. Few farmers own their land, most is owned by absentee landlords. Tenants rarely have legal protection. The farms, already too small to be economically viable due to division for inheritance, are made up of geographically separate plots often some distance apart. A government move to consolidate plots through land reform was not popular. Some 220 co-operative farms exist, mainly in the northern region and are mainly concerned with cereal growing.

Potential

The economic potential of Tunisia is considerable. There are large areas that could be brought under irrigation. Improved land tenure would also benefit farm output. Even in the Medjerda Valley the modern irrigation schemes are not fully and effectively used because of poor rural leadership and lack of incentives for farmers. Tunisia is rich in natural resources – phosphates, iron, zinc and lead – all of which offer the basis for further industrialization. The full extent of the country's petroleum resources is not yet known but good yields of both oil and natural gas are already contributing to foreign exchange earnings, while the country's position as a transit zone for an increasing volume of natural gas moving by pipeline from Algeria to Italy is an added bonus. Tourism has continuing potential for improvement, not just in the desert S where current efforts are concentrated, but in rehabilitation of the coastal areas of mass tourism, where age and poor management can be corrected to the advantage of the country's foreign exchange earnings. As with other states of N Africa, the potential will only be revealed if political stability can be maintained.

CULTURE

ETHNIC ORIGINS

Tunisia is populated over the fertile plains and valleys by mainly Arab stock of the Beni Hilal and Beni Sulaim. As much as 98% of the population is Arab. The original Berber population and mixed Berber-Arab groups are found in the remoter inland areas and in the hills of the S. Pure Berber stock accounts for a mere 1% of the total population and are found in the Matmata region. There is a 3% residual element of the European colonists, of which more than half is French and the remainder Italian in origin. After Arabic, French is an important second language in the larger towns. Orthodox Islam is the main religion but revivalist Islam is increasingly prevalent among younger Tunisians.

The traveller's guide to Tunisian tribal areas

Modern governments are slightly embarrassed by ethnic, linguistic and cultural variations in their populations. Tribalism hints at social backwardness and lack of national political cohesion. Yet local area names, the names of *oueds* and *djebels* and the foundation stones of all social activities spring from tribal roots. The traveller who knows some tribal background will be better equipped to understand Tunisian society and to understand some of the local problems.

The original inhabitants of Tunisia were **Berbers**. Berber kinships lines were divided into two major parts – Branes and Maghdes, with the former, broken into 10

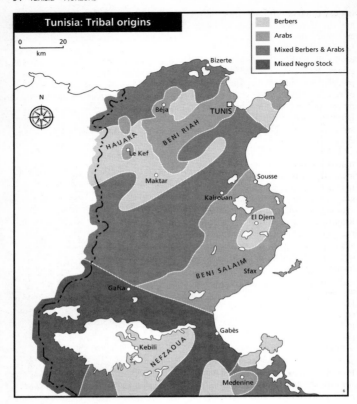

Tunisia: Tribal origins

Berbers
Arabs
Mixed Berbers & Arabs
Mixed Negro Stock

great families, being the most numerous. The Berbers in southern Tunisia are in part descended from the once large and influential Hauara tribe of the Branes group. Relicts of the Luata tribe are to be found as the Nefzaoua in the area S of Gabès and Gafsa (see page 290). The Zenata of the Maghdes tribe probably moved to Tunisia after the Arab invasions. They were joined by Arab raiding groups during the course of the Moslem conquest, which effectively began in 670 AD after the foundation of Kairouan. The Hilalian invasion of the 11th century, however, put an end to all Berber

political power. The country's ethnic mix has gradually altered to give a population which ranges from a few 100,000 pure Berber people through large groups of Arabized Berbers and Berberized Arabs to some small numbers of true Arab stock. The process was not one of homogenization and slight differences in tribal origin are still important in establishing social status and legitimacy.

Berber centres are to be found in places of refuge, distant from the fertile zones or tucked away in hilly redoubts. Medjez el-Bab, the High Tell, the El Djem region, the Djebel Nefusa range (an extension of this range from Libya) and the Monts des Ksour by Tataouine are among the key Berber areas, where families still look upon themselves as essentially Berber. The Berbers are to an extent themselves divided by anthropologists into three main groups – those of central Tunisia, those of the central mountain zone and those of the Isle of Djerba – each of which tends to have separate lineages and somewhat different physical characteristics.

The traveller is never far from a remnant Berber-speaking community either located in the Ksour villages, which were in origin fortified granaries managed by groups who were semi-nomadic or transhumant pastoralists, or in long-established settlements, where families were permanent urban residents. There are also many places which are Berber archaeological sites or carry Berber place-names.

If you are in northern Tunisia there are Berber sites near Medjez el-Bab at Hidous, Toukabeur and Chaouach, located in the hills N of the Medjez el-Bab to Tébourba road in the Medjerda Valley (see page 172).

Within striking distance of Cap Bon and the seaside resorts such as Sousse, Hammamet and Nabeul are the Berber sites at Djeradou, Hergla, Zriba and Takrouna. Djeradou is readily accessible by a good road (C35) from the coastal highway at Bou Ficha and is a pleasant spot still occupied by Berber families. The site at Zriba, set in the hills at 735m to the W of the C133 road is spectacular but unoccupied at the present day. Takrouna, near to Enfida is well worth the slight deviation from the coast road (see page 223).

Out of the way but a marvellous example of a working Berber village is La Kesra located N of the Kairouan to Maktar road (see page 247).

For those with their own transport or in safari vehicles in SW Tunisia there is a cluster of Berber villages close to the Algerian border, Chebika, Midès and Tamerza – now abandoned by their inhabitants for more spacious and convenient accommodation nearby. These villages lie on the round trip between Metlaoui and Tozeur on the C201. They have small oases and ruined houses, some used as coffee shops as at the spring at Midès (see page 282).

There are two Berber sites just off the P14 E of Gafsa, Bou Omran and Senned, 10 km S of Senned Gare (see page 275). They give opportunity to break up an otherwise long ride between Gafsa and the coast. Both settlements are occupied.

In the S the Berber villages of the Djebel Matmata include Matmata itself, Zeraoua, Temezret and Techine. While the physical structures of Zeraoua are still in good condition, it has been abandoned by its population. Matmata and Techine are very attractive sites and thus well visited by tourist groups. Some underground troglodyte houses are kept going for the tourists to look at and even stay overnight in. Access to this area is via the C107 from Gabès (see page 307).

In the Monts des Ksour some six Berber sites – Ghoumrassen, Guermessa, Chenini, Douirat, Beni Barka and Ksar Zohra – can be found in an arc in the Djebel Nefusa near Foum Tatouine on the P19 out of Medenine. The most scenic spot is Chenini at an altitude of 575m and some 20 km W on a minor road from Foum Tatouine. Chenini is important in being a surviving Zenet community with a *ksar* of some antiquity (12th century). The original community was troglodytic like its sister settlements in Libya. The residents still speak Berber and retain their oral traditions and social customs.

Djerba is a major Berber centre and, given the turbulent history of the island, an amazing survival. There are four main Berber sites – Ajim, Sedouikech, Guellala and Mellita, each with important traditional buildings such as mosques, maraboutic tombs and fine houses. Many features of "North African" architecture, domes, doorways and minarets, were influenced by their Berber past so that it is well worth while looking carefully at the vernacular architecture of those Berber villages that continue to exist, especially ones like Sedouikech, that are still lived in.

The **Arabs** brought an end to the sophistication of the Romano-Berber urban culture. Bedouin ethos of the tent and the desert became dominant from the 7th century and was given great strength through the Hilalian invasions of the 11th century. Although it is no longer accepted wisdom that the Arabs brought a sudden end to civilization in Tunisia, it is clear that great damage was done by the elevation of the nomadic herder over the settled farmer. Water sources were neglected and the cultivated margin retreated. Berbers withdrew to the hills with their farming knowledge and agricultural techniques to leave the rich plains to the Arabs.

The Arabs in North Africa are still profoundly tribal in social organization and family affiliation. Until the Hilalian invasions of the 11th century there was little mass Arab settlement in North Africa. In 1051 the Hilalians, comprising four great family confederations – the al-Atbeg, Beni Riah, Beni Zoghba and al-Ma'aqel – came to the area and in 3 years took every major city in Libya and Tunisia. The Zoghba tribe took over Gabès and the Riah tribe overran Kairouan. The Beni Hilal was later followed by the Beni Sulaim who tended to push them W or S as they advanced from Egypt. The Beni Sulaim were made up of two large divisions – the Beni 'Auf and the Debbab, most at one time represented in Tunisia. The most Arabized sections of the country are the Sahel of Sousse and the low steppe on its W rim together with the Medjerda valley. Additionally, tribes made up of the descendants of the Prophet Mohammed or *Sherif* and the descendants of holy men

marabouts are to be found throughout the country.

Most tribes are now and have for some years been sedentary, whilst retaining their social connections through the extended family and tribal system. The only nomadic Tunisian tribes are the Marazig, maraboutic semi-nomads of Nefzaoua in S Tunisia and the Oulad Ayar of Maktar in the central Tunisian steppe.

POPULATION DENSITY

Tunisia's estimated population in 1995 was 8.9 million, growing at a rate of slightly over 2.25% annually in Tunis and 2.2% in the central and eastern regions. The population distribution is biased heavily towards the N and the coasts. Greater Tunis now includes almost 2 million people. The capital, the Medjerda Valley and the coastal strip as far S as Sfax account for over 60% of the population. Kairouan province with 0.5 million and Gafsa with 0.25 million people are the only important population centres away from the N and E coasts. Migration from the land to the towns is increasing. Population densities in Tunis run at 2,000/sq km against less than 10 in the deserts of the S. Tunisia has a youthful population with some 37% under 15 years of age.

QUALITY OF LIFE

Tunisia is attempting to improve the quality of its labour force and its educational system is struggling to lift standards. By 1995 approximately 67% of the population over 15 was literate (79% of males and 55% of females). Tunis has centres of academic excellence in its university institutes of higher studies.

Income/head is calculated at US$1,780. This is gradually improving but only erratically. Slumps in tourism, trade and remittance income from workers abroad have depressed levels in recent years. There is great variation in income levels between the better off people in Tunis and the poor semi-nomads

Sporting Tunisians

The young male Tunisian's leisure time is devoted to cards and the *chicha* pipe at the café, raising canaries, and above all, to endless discussions about *Koura* (football). Summer is the time for a *takwira* (a kick around) on the beach, while on winter Sunday afternoons the streets are empty as the men go off to the stadium. Two Tunis-Medina based teams dominate the football scene: the Club Africain (red and white strip) of Bab Jedid, and the EST (Espérance Sportive de Tunisie) or Taraji in Arabic (red and gold strip) of Bab Souika. The passions aroused are as intense as for the racing factions of ancient Rome, the exploits of the young players like Hédi Berrikhissa and Ayyadi Hamrouni on everyone's lips.

Modern Tunisian football's finest hour was the 1978 Argentina World Cup when a team led by Abdel Magid Chettali (The Magician) and Sadok Sassi Attouga won a 3-1 victory over Mexico and held West Germany to a 0-0 draw. Other past heroes of Tunisia's number one sport include Club Africain's Tahar 'Boy' Chaïbi and Tarak Dhab (The Strategist).

More recently, the 1995 African Football Confederation Cup was won by the Sousse club Etoile Sportive du Sahel. In 1994, Tunisia hosted the Coupe d'Afrique des Nations (only to be ignominiously knocked out by Mali). However, Jan 1996 saw Tunisia in the finals of the same cup, beaten 2-0 by South Africa.

In 1995, at national level, the Etoile won both the championship and cup (2-1 against Olympique de Béja). The regional clubs are prospering – particularly Taraji Zarzia and Gafsa, while the EST has had a run of poor seasons. The other main Tunis team, Stade Tunisien (red and green strip) are on the way up. Thousands fill the streets after a major victory and politicians and others squabble furiously to preside a top football club.

In other team sports, Tunisia is strong in basketball, volleyball and handball. The men's volleyball team went to the Atlanta Olympics and the women's team El Hilal does well in volleyball and handball. Tunisian women regularly win African and Arab swimming titles with top swimmers like Faten Ghattas and Sendra el Gharbi.

But Tunisia's greatest sporting legend is undoubtedly runner Mohammed Gammoudi, who struck gold in the 5,000m (14'05") in Mexico in 1968. He also won silver in Tokyo (1964) in the 10,000m and at Munich (1972) in the 5,000m.

However, apart from *koura* the most popular sports are really Oriental martial arts, bodybuilding (*beauté de corps!*) and boxing. Every town has its share of private karaté and taekwando clubs and salles de culture physique. In international boxing, two legends have been forged: the Kairouan-born (1958) Kamel Bouali, who took the WBO super featherweight title (59 kg) in Dec 1989 against the Puertorican Rivera and light heavyweight Taoufik Balbouli (born La Soukra 1959), Arab champion in Iraq 1980, and holder of a total of 26 victories out of 27 professional fights. French-based Balbouli's finest hour was on 25 March 1989 when he won the World Championship in Casablanca against the American Daniels.

The present government, with its emphasis on youth, is keen to promote sport – witness the new sports halls springing up across the country. The key piece of this infrastructure will be the Cité Sportive in the S Tunis suburb of Radés, especially built for the Mediterranean Games of 2001, to be hosted by Tunisia.

of the deserts. The labour force is diversified including, among others, 23.0% in farming, 1.6% in mining, 17.9% in manufacturing industry and 12.5% in construction. Under-employment and unemployment remain a problem and many Tunisians emigrate to Libya or Europe for work.

HISTORY SINCE INDEPENDENCE

For the history of this region before Tunisia gained Independence see The History of N Africa, page 28. For information on the Desert Campaign of WW2, see page 324.

Tunisia's Independence from the French Protectorate administration was achieved on 20 Mar 1956. The transformation from self-government to Independence was managed by **Habib Bourguiba**, head of Tunisia's national liberation movement, the **Neo-Destour**, and later president. The new state had three basic, interconnected problems to resolve: its relations with France, the crucial issue of economic development, and its future political structures.

Relations with France began badly. In 1958 French aircraft bombed the Tunisian border village of Sakiet Sidi Youssef, apparently in retaliation for Tunisian support for Algerian Independence. In response, Tunisia demanded that French forces should abandon the naval base in Bizerte granted at NATO request. French refusal led to fighting and over a thousand Tunisians died before France withdrew.

In 1959 land belonging to European (mainly French) settlers in Tunisia was expropriated. The French left, taking their capital, a development which had an adverse effect on the Tunisian economy. Subsequently relations with France normalized and Tunisia became noted for its cautious, pro-western attitudes in international diplomacy, President Bourguiba becoming a well-known independent voice in Arab affairs.

Economy After Independence the Tunisian Government concentrated on state-directed economic development, the collectivization of agriculture and government control of major industrial enterprises. By 1969, popular resistance and economic stagnation convinced the president of this policy's failure and a free market economy was instituted.

One consequence of this was a growing disparity between rich and poor which, by the 1980s, caused a rift between the governing **Destourian Socialist Party** on the one hand and the **UGTT**, formerly part of the Destourian Socialist Party, on the other. Severe riots during a general strike in Jan 1978 ushered in a period of social tension. Countrywide riots followed in Jan 1984 when the IMF, concerned over Tunisia's growing foreign debt, insisted the government remove food subsidies. A programme was introduced in 1987 to revive the economy, together with a wide-ranging programme of privatization. Tunisia, with Europe its major market, faces the negative implications of the new Single European Market.

Social and political affairs The need for economic development had social and political effects. Firstly, as part of the process of modernization and development, monogamy was introduced into the legal code. Then, in 1963, President Bourguiba attempted to abolish fasting during Ramadan in the interests of economic efficiency. Popular resistance undermined this initiative but, overall, Tunisia underwent a process of secularization and social modernization during the first two decades of Independence.

Secondly Bourguiba introduced a single-party system, in which his now renamed Destourian Socialist Party became the sole official party. The Communist Party was banned, re-emerging in the early 1980s, and leading members of the UGTT which, after the Jan 1978 'Black Thursday' riots found itself in opposition to government throughout the 1980s, were frequently imprisoned.

Islamic fundamentalism became a significant political movement in the early 1970s. By the 1980s its influence was widespread through Tunisian society. An organized Islamicist political movement, the **Mouvement de Tendence Islamique** (MTI), appeared. Though initially tolerated it was soon seen as a major threat and its leaders were imprisoned, while its frustrated supporters turned to urban violence in response.

The collapse of the Bourguiba régime

The repression of the MTI was symbolic of events in Tunisia during the 1980s. As economic difficulties increased so, too, did the alienation of the Bourguiba régime from the population at large. The promise of political liberalization was replaced by repression and Tunisia acquired an unhappy reputation over human rights abuses. In foreign affairs Tunisia and Libya, but for a brief period in 1974, have not seen eye to eye. A friendship treaty with Algeria, conversely, worsened relations with both Libya and Morocco.

After 1984 President Habib Bourguiba began increasingly to interfere with government, relying on a small group of advisers, particularly **Zine El-Abidine Ben Ali**, whom he appointed Interior Minister in 1986 and Premier in 1987. Within a week of being appointed, the new premier seized power in a 'legal' palace coup – legal because constitutional niceties were observed – and President Habib Bourguiba, then in his eighties, was declared mentally incompetent to discharge his duties.

Tunisia today The removal of President Habib Bourguiba reduced political and social tension, whereas the execution of the MTI leadership, which he had demanded and which had precipitated the coup, would have led to serious unrest. The new president proposed political liberalization with a multi-party system. Political prisoners were released, new political parties were permitted and political consensus was sought around a National Charter. Economic reform was pushed ahead and foreign confidence in Tunisia was restored. However the new régime could not bring itself to legalize

President Zine El Abidene Ben Ali – Tunisian Head of State

In Nov 1987 a bloodless coup d'état brought Zine El Abidene Ben Ali to power as President of Tunisia, replacing the aging Habib Bourguiba. President Ben Ali was trained in electronics as a military man at the Saint-Cyr Military Academy in France. His rise to authority was early. He became a member of Bourguiba's cabinet in 1977 as Minister of National Defence. His control over the Interior Ministry gave him unique access to management of the State and a springboard to the presidency. On the political front Ben Ali became a member of the Politbureau of the Parti Socialiste Destourien in 1986 and its head in 1987.

President Ali Ben has followed a policy of total resistence to the Islamists and repression of opposition groups. In 1994 the president was re-elected to office with no less than 99% of the votes cast while his party took all the seats in the elections to the legislature. The permitted political opposition was given 19 seats in the legislature as an act of grace by Ben Ali but critics of the régime note that the government acts effectively on an autocratic basis.

President Ben Ali has genuine popular support and, once the Islamist threat seems dimmer, he might move Tunisia more towards a democratic structure of government, assisted in this by the country's tightening economic and diplomatic contacts with the EU.

Why do souqs survive?

The survival of the souq/bazaar system calls for an explanation. Why do the souqs in some countries of North Africa flourish while in other countries this is not the case? Part of the explanation is straightforward. Governments in Tunisia, with few exceptions, have left the merchants of the souq to undertake most of their traditional trading functions unhindered. This seems to indicate a first principle for the survival of the bazaar, that it be left to operate a generally unrestricted trading network. The opposite view is also true, that the bazaar system will not survive the socialization/nationalization of trade as the example of Tunisia's neighbour Libya so recently proved with the total demise of the Tripoli souq in the 1970s.

It appears that immature economies are much more favourable to the bazaar than modernized economic systems. The bazaar must stay at the apex of the commercial hierarchy, unchallenged by modern high-tech businesses. In traditional society, the bazaar is an important source of informal lending to both rural and urban enterprises or to individuals. Non-Muslim bazaar merchants were not of course impeded by the taboo within Islam on taking interest on loans made to third parties. In Tunisia and Libya before 1948 (the foundation of Israel), the Jewish merchants of the souq undertook this important task of funding investment and providing short term credits.

It might be hazarded that bazaar economies thrive best where there are, as in Tunisia, Morocco and Egypt, generally low average incomes, say, of US$1,500 per year or less. In such societies the structure of demand is oriented towards survival, with foodstuffs, traditional clothing and textiles and locally manufactured material objects in demand rather than modern consumer durables. Where there is least direct government involvement in trade and nationalization of trade has been avoided, souqs show the strongest continuity.

Closely associated with the basic structure of supply and demand, bazaars survive best when they have long-standing local manufacturing industries based within them. The more individual and highly prized the goods manufactured, the more competitive the individual or national bazaars will be. In Tunisia, well crafted copper, tile and textiles give commodities of distinction and commercial strength to the souq. The operation of a healthy tourist industry also assists the bazaar to keep its traditional influence and prosperity.

It might also be concluded that, economic factors aside, those societies which still have a vibrant bazaar culture, with all its human colour, noise and bustle are far richer than those who have, in the process of 'modernization', lost their traditional central markets.

the Islamicist movements, thus thwarting full political liberalization. In legislative elections in 1994 the majority of seats was won by the **Rassemblement Constitutionnel Démocratique**, demonstrating its reluctance to abandon power, although allowing five permitted opposition parties a minor role in the Assembly.

President Ben Ali is being forced back on policies similar to those of his predecessor. The major domestic crisis, the relationship between government and the Islamicist movement, became increasingly bitter in the 1990s. Tunisia's future social and political scene will, however, depend largely on successful economic reforms and on improvements in its relationships with its N African and European neighbours. In Feb 1989

Tunisia joined neighbouring states in the **Maghreb Arab Union**. Within the wider Muslim world, Tunisia was increasingly isolated for its opposition to the UN-authorized war to force Iraq out of Kuwait in 1991. In recent years Tunisia has mended its political fences with the Gulf States and the moderate Arab governments.

MODERN TUNISIA

GOVERNMENT

The republic

Tunisia is a republic headed by a president with a 5-year term and considerable powers over the armed forces and the cabinet. The current president is Zine El-Abidine Ben Ali who constitutionally unseated Habib Bourguiba, Tunisia's president since Independence, in 1987. Ben Ali is a former army general and diplomat, chosen to change and protect the ruling party. There is an executive cabinet appointed by the president reporting to a single 141-member, 5-year elected legislative chamber. All Tunisians over 20 years of age are eligible to vote in elections. The socialist Democratic Constitutional Rally party has ruled since Independence (see History, page 68) under various names. Some secular, but generally innocuous, political opposition is permitted but radical Islamic groups are vigorously suppressed.

Domestic policy

Central government policies are concerned with maintaining political stability in a climate of contained Islamic revivalism. The cabinet's last major reshuffle in Oct 1991, leant towards the hard line in attitudes towards the fundamentalist Islamic groups. The government is also greatly concerned with keeping the economy developing to cope with a growing population and the pressures of worldwide recession.

Foreign policy

In foreign policy Tunisia has moved towards a slightly more Arab stance. Tunis was, until recently, the site of the PLO headquarters, and the Arab League has offices there. Tunisia is seeking better relations with its Maghreb allies but also needs US and European aid together with foreign visitors for its principal industry, tourism. Moderation thus tends to dominate foreign relations.

Regional government

This is through 23 *wilayat* (governorates) and sub-districts, while regional political representation is managed through delegations which have access to the higher levels of central government.

ECONOMY

Tunisia has a more diversified economy than surrounding countries. Its modest endowment with oil has been an advantage in providing funding for non-oil development but has never been sufficient to encourage reliance on petroleum. There is, nevertheless, deep vulnerability to external economic pressures including the vagaries of international trade, foreign aid flows, variation in tourist numbers and access to the EU bloc for Tunisia's trade and labour. A youthful and fairly fast-growing population creates an added need for economic growth.

Agriculture

Is the basis of the economy, employs 23% of the labour force and produces about

Gross domestic product 1994		
	Value (TD000,000)	Share (%)
Agriculture	2,070.4	13.0
Mining	698.3	4.4
Manufacturing	2,827.5	17.7
Construction	647.8	4.1
Electricity/gas/utilities	293.4	1.8
Transport/communications	1,267.2	8.0
Trade	4,355.0	27.3
Other services	3,768.0	23.7
Total	15,928.2	100.0
Source: *Encyclopaedia Britannica*		

Tunisia – the economic miracle

The Tunisian government needs an economic miracle for political reasons. Clear improvements in personal incomes will perhaps persuade the majority of Tunisians that President Ben Ali and his colleagues are a better choice than the opposing Islamists. There have been great steps forward in the state of the economy and in living standards of most ordinary people – Tunisia is a model for developing economies in this respect. In the last decade Tunisian national income per head rose steadily by almost 2% each year – itself a major success against the generally falling incomes in surrounding countries. The quality of life has also gone up by significant steps, with Tunisians (Libyans in brackets) living for an average of 67 years (62) for men and 69 (67) for women. Education in Tunisia is dealt with seriously and literacy is 68% (64). Tunisians even have a better diet than those who live in oil-rich Libya.

A reward for the government's economic success was the special link with the EU agreed in 1995 under which Tunisia will join a free trade zone with the EU over a 12-year period. Tunisia is already making economic reforms to take advantage of the new relationship with the EU – improving productivity, diversifying the export base and deregulating the marketplace. Agriculture, though still important as an employer is falling as a sector of importance, accounting for only 13% of GDP now against 15% 10 years earlier. Manufacturing, meanwhile, is now almost 18% of the nation's output, one of the highest degrees of industrialization in North Africa, which enables no less than one in five of the labour force to be employed in this modern activity. Trade, mainly in private hands, has expanded to more than 27% of GDP. In all respects, therefore, Tunisia is a maturing economy – increasingly losing its third world characteristics.

Tunisia is fortunate in possessing some oil and gas, with more reserves expected to be discovered. Production of oil and natural gas exceed domestic demand but, as a whole, petroleum is only 9% of the value of all exports and does not dominate the economy in the way that is the case in nearby Libya and Algeria. The principal foreign investor in Tunisia is none the less British Gas, which spent some US$650mn bringing into production the Miskar oil field and exploring

18% by value of all national output. Chief crops are cereals, citrus fruit, olives, dates and grapes. Approximately 20% of the value of agricultural production comes from cereals. Olive oil is an important export accounting for 4% of the total but suffers heavy competition from Spain and Italy in the main European market. The Sahel is a monoculture of olives over much of its area. Irrigation is vital to ensure reliable cropping but large areas of the country with low rainfall lack provision of supplementary water supplies. Fishing and sponge gathering are important in the coastal ports, notably in the Gulf of Gabès. Fishing provides about 6% of the country's food supply with a catch

of 84,000 tonnes/annum. Tuna fishing is declining as stocks in the Mediterranean dwindle. Esparto grass is collected to export for paper making and the oak forests of the N provide timber and cork.

Industry

Tunisia remains a large producer and exporter of phosphates with annual production running at some 5.5 million tonnes/annum from the Gafsa region. The main mines are at Djebel Mdilla, Redeyef, Metlaoui, and Phillippe Thomas. Phosphate and its products of phosphoric acid and fertilizer provide about 5% of all exports. Industrialization based on phosphates is developing slowly with plants to

for other sources of petroleum in recent years. A gas-fired power station will be built by French and British companies at Radès, close to Tunis, in association with British Gas. Kuwaiti interests in refining and petrochemicals on the Gulf of Gabès remain while the well established trans-Mediterranean pipeline from Algeria through Tunisia to Southern Europe continues to prosper.

Farming is still at the heart of the Tunisian economy outside the Tunis conurbation. Rainfall was excellent in the winter of 1995/96 and underlined the importance to rural and small town Tunisians of the produce of the land. Agriculture is thriving thanks to modernization of farming techniques, improved use of water resources, rural electrification and privatization of state held lands. Olive oil is the main crop still on one third of the farmland carrying 55 million trees. The tourist industry provides a continuing high value market for farmers and wine producers alike. Long term difficulties have still to be faced – EU controls on farm imports, variable rainfall and the small, often uneconomic, size of farm.

Tunisia's economic miracle has come most of all from manufacturing. In 1995 industry expanded quickly (7%) and provided almost 45% of exports by value. Textile manufacture in association with W European companies, mainly German, Belgian and Italian, is important and employs a quarter of a million persons.

Tourism is a key foreign exchange earner (20%) for Tunisia and provides a strong level of employment. The upmarket hotels are still among the best in North Africa but the smaller hotels are suffering from lack of investment and there is a need for refurbishment in many areas not to mention an injection of imaginative development of entertainment for foreign visitors. Only the growth poles of desert travel are visibly thriving.

The special link between Tunisia and the EU has set an ambitious target for the country in the field of economy over the next 12 years. One miracle – the expansion of the last 5 years – is apparently not enough for the government and a new leap forward is planned. The authorities will need to show real progress in incomes and living conditions to make the regime's political aims, including the repression of the Islamist movement, acceptable.

produce superphosphates and sulphuric acid. Other mineral resources being worked include lead and zinc at Laghouat and Djebel Hallouf and iron at Djerissa.

Manufacturing

Tunisia has made remarkable steps in effective industrialization, most of it small scale and private sector. Manufacturing now accounts for 18% of the work force and 17% of national production. The main products, principally from the N are cement, flour, steel, textiles, and beverages. The textile industry is most remarkable with piece-goods being made up in Tunisia for re-export back to manu-facturers in Western Europe. In recent years this trade has provided 30% of Tunisia's total export earnings. There is a long established handicraft industry which has benefited through the tourist trade. Nabeul pottery, Kairouan carpets, decorative ironwork, leather goods, regional brass and hand-crafted textile wares are all world famous and find a steady market among tourists.

Energy

Tunisia's oil industry by no means compares with that of Libya or Algeria, with proved reserves of only 1,700 million barrels of crude oil (0.2% of the world total) and production of approximately 98,000

The Tunisian film industry: bold new cinema?

Back in the Fifties, the ingredients for a good Arab film were a {dose of kitsch} lots of sentimentality and plenty of singing under the stars on the banks of the Nile. Things changed with the return home in the 1970s of young European-trained directors, and films by Tunisian directors have won a number of international prizes – the most recent international success was Moufida Tlatli's 1994 *Les Silences du Palais*, a maid's eye view of a Tunis aristocratic home in the mid-1950s.

Independent Tunisia set up its first film laboratories, the SATPEC, in 1967. However, it was President Bourguiba's wife's nephew, the flamboyant Tarak Ben Ammar, who got Tunisia on the international directors' circuit. In the ex-president's home town of Monastir, he set up a studio complex where Polanski filmed part of *Pirates* and (curiously) a number of films figuring Christ were made, including *Life of Brian* and Zeffirelli's *Jesus of Nazareth*. A further stimulus to the nascent Tunisian film industry was the creation of the Carthage Film Festival in 1966, which provides a bi-annual meeting point for the African and Arab film industries.

In the mid-1970s a few Tunisian films were taken on by international distribution companies, including Naceur Ktari's **Les Ambassadeurs** (1976), a sharp critique of the conditions of migrant workers in Europe, and Rida Behi's sardonic look at the side effects of tourism, **Le Soleil des Hyènes** (1977).

In the 1980s a new generation of local film makers and production companies like Carthage Film and International Monastir Film reached maturity, putting the experience gained on international productions to good use. A series of highly individual films gained the respect of the local public, among them Nacer Khemir's aesthetic reworkings of the theme of lost Andalucía (**Les baliseurs du désert** (1984) and **Le Collier perdu de la colombe** (1991)) and Mahmoud Ben Mahmoud's **Traversées**).

At the end of the decade, producer Ahmed Attia's Cinétéléfilm came up with three highly successful art house films: **L'Homme de cendres** in 1986, **Les Sabots en or** in 1989 (both by Nouri Bouzid), and Férid Boughedir's **Halfaouine** in 1990.

barrels/day with natural gas output of 277 million cubic metres/annum. Production comes from the El Borma field in the S, Sbeitla field in the S Atlas and the Itayem fields close to Sfax, all of which feed to a refinery and export complex at Sekhira. The Ashtart field offshore in the Gulf of Gabès is also productive and recent discoveries have been made both offshore and in the Cap Bon areas. It is hoped that oilfields lying across the offshore boundary line with Libya will eventually be exploited jointly. Crude and products sales account for 10% of exports.

Miskar gas field in the Gulf of Gabès was brought on stream by British Gas in 1995 enabling Tunisia to export more oil and to use less Algerian gas.

Tourism

Is a major employer and foreign exchange earner. Considerable investment in new hotels has come partially from abroad. The number of tourists rose from a mere 56,000 in 1961 to 4 million in 1995. Receipts from tourism are estimated annually at US$1,114mn. The industry is developing from bases in Tunis/Sidi Bou Said along the E coast/Sahel to the S where desert tours are of increasing popularity and serve to spread the benefits of foreign tourists. Tunisians are aware of the negative social effects of tourism and deal fairly and sensibly with foreigners so that the country retains a good name and visitors return. Efforts are being made to

With 500,000 entries, Halfaouine, a loving and sometimes whimsical portrayal of growing up in Tunis in the 1960s beat all the records for a film in Tunisia. The sensitive treatment of sexuality and the separation of the sexes in the still codefied world of an old part of the city ensured the film's success.

For its bold treatment of prostitution, the effects of child abuse and the relations between the Muslim and Jewish communities, Bouzid's **L'Homme de cendres** was condemned by more than one critic. (Tolerance and the coexistence of different communities is central to Mahmoud Ben Mahmoud's symbolic **Chichkhan** and Férid Boughedir's 1996 film **TGM**.) Bouzid's **Les Sabots en or** grew out of his experience as a political prisoner in the 1970s. The subject matter, imprisonment and the effects of torture, drew in the audiences, and the public clearly wanted more. In his third film, **Bezness**, Bouzid went on to attack 'sexual tourism' and the forthcoming **Une fille de bonne famille** will tackle that old chestnut, marital breakdown.

Tunis seems unlikely to become the Hollywood of the Mediterranean. For many years, Tunisian cinema came somewhere between the private Moroccan film industry and the state-dominated Algerian industry. It is not easy producing for a market of only 8 million people, and in the early 1990s co-productions between European TV stations such as Channel 4 and Tunisian companies dominated. Will the production of the *films d'auteur* which have made Tunisia's name on the international festival circuit continue? Various forms of French government funding directed at African cinema can no longer be taken for granted, and the American way of life is clearly on its way (70% of films shown on the Tunisian pay channel Canal Plus Horizons are US produced) and the capital's cinemas specialize in Hindi melodramas, soft porn and Jean-Claude Van Damme. Art house films need ideas, and what passes for an original idea in Tunisia is often a cliché elsewhere. Tunisia's films please the local public and seduce festival juries. Whether the laws of international distribution will allow them to reach a wider audience is another question.

provide high class hotels in the main coastal resorts to attract higher spending tourists, especially from Germany and France. Depression in Western Europe and political problems in Tunisia have tended in recent years to depress tourist numbers.

Trends

Economic trends have not favoured Tunisia recently. Rainfall has been irregular, falling for short periods unfavourable to farming but causing severe damage through flooding especially in 1995. The world depression has reduced the flow of foreign tourists and led to falling oil prices. The coming of the EU single market has adversely hit the Tunisian export trade, approximately 70% (1994: 78%) of which has traditionally gone to Western European states. Fewer Tunisian workers, who annually sent back US$560mn in 1991 are now being accepted in Europe. The problem was clearly seen in the balance of merchandise trade where the deficit stood at US$1,504mn in 1994. Membership of the United Maghreb Association (UMA), has so far failed to open up markets for Tunisia other than for migrant labour, though access to Libya has improved trade in recent years and – encouraged Libyan tourism.

Gross National Domestic Product has run at about US$15,332mn/annum. Tunisia has an increasing foreign

Economic indicators

	1992	1993	1994
Exports (TD mn)	3,567	3,803	4,696
Imports (TD mn)	5,689	6,213	6,647
Balance of trade (TD mn)	-1,726	-1,999	-1,504
Inflation index (1985=100)	113.8	118.7	124.7
Foreign debt (US$ mn)	8,500	7,627	...

Sources: IMF, EIU, *Encyclopaedia Britannica*

debt, which stood at US$7,627mn by 1993 and has since worsened. Imports regularly outstrip exports in value and rising imports for defence and security are adding to the deficit. Inflation, officially put at 5% annually, is rather higher in Tunis and other urban centres. Expenditures in a roughly balanced state budget ran at TD5,663mn in 1992, of which the main areas were education, health, security, defence and agriculture.

Tunisian textiles

The textile industry in Tunisia has ancient roots. Dyeing silk and wool for carpets and textiles in a traditional form goes on to the present day in places as far apart as Djerba and Kairouan. Caftans are manufactured, lace items and a range of embroidered cloths for table and personal adornment. The height of Tunisian textile work is seen in womens' wedding dresses like those on show at the Dar Cheriat Museum in Tozeur (see page 277). Old fashioned materials can still be bought at bazaar shops in the souqs and holiday shopping boutiques but the country is now more famous for its modern textile manufacturing. In 1994, 43% of all exports worth TD1,640mn were textiles and accessories. In 1995 this value increased to TD2,030mn. Much of the textile industry undertakes semi-finishing of labour intensive parts of the clothes producing cycle, re-exporting items back to the main factories in Western Europe for finishing. Much of the larger scale textile plant in Tunisia is owned by joint ventures between Tunisian and European partners in 1996 worth a total of US$93mn.

Tunis

T HE HISTORY of the city, so close to Carthage, goes back to Punic times but it was not until the Arab invasion in the 7th century and the final destruction of Carthage that the city of Tunis flourished. The medina grew in importance with the Great Mosque Ez-Zitouna, the intellectual and religious centre, as its heart. The souqs, commercial and crafts centres, developed around the Mosque. Tunis then became the second city in Afriqiya (a province of the Arab Empire) after Kairouan.

Pop 1,200,000; *Alt* 3m.

ACCESS Air The airport is situated 7 km outside the city. To reach the centre either take bus No 35 (cost TD0.75) that stops on Ave Habib Bourguiba by Tunis Air. The airport bus normally runs every 30 mins day and night, but from 2400 to 0600 there is only one every hour. Cost 600 mills. Otherwise take a taxi – this should not cost more than TD3, with baggage may be more. Beware of the unofficial taxis without meters. If you can't wait for an official one, be sure to agree on the price before getting in. **Train** The main train station is very central, just three streets S of Ave Habib Bourguiba, between Ave de Carthage and the medina. Cross the rather soulless square, Place de Barcelone and keep going. The metro station is convenient, to the left. The suburban station TGM is 1 km away at the port end of Ave Habib Bourguiba. **Road** There are two bus stations. Buses from Algeria and places S arrive at Place Mongi Bali by the main train station. Buses from the N arrive at Bab Saadoun. Bus No 3 will take you to the town centre from here. The main louage

terminus is 500m to the S of the train station but louages from Sousse, Medenine, Tozeur and Tataouine drop passengers by the medina walls 200m W of the train station and louages from Sfax at the station itself. From the port trains run every 10-15 mins to the TGM station and taxis are available to the town centre.

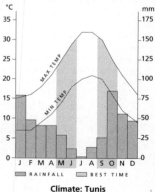

Climate: Tunis

CLIMATE

The climate is typically Mediterranean, but with a slight wind from the sea. The hottest season is obviously summer while the period from Nov to Feb is mild and sometimes rainy. The best seasons for a visit are late spring and autumn.

HISTORY

The Aghlabites

For a short time Tunis became the capital of the Aghlabites (894-905). The anarchy and destruction which typified North Africa in the late 8th century was ended in 800 AD when Ibrahim Ibn Al-Aghlab was made the ruler of Ifriqiya based in Tunis. He came from the lands of the central Caliphate and had been a successful governor for the Abbasid Caliphs in Baghdad. His brief was to manage Abbasid possessions in North Africa without relying on Baghdad for financial support. In practice, the grant of Ifriqiya gave the Aghlabites the status of a local dynasty.

Ibrahim Ibn Al-Aghlab began his reign by imposing peace on the turbulent Berber and Arab tribes of Tunisia. There was a great deal of opposition, not least from the vested interests of the Islamic jurists in Tunis and Kairouan and the Arab garrisons in the main towns who had grown slack and oppressive. In a short time, regional groups were put down and order restored.

Ibrahim Ibn Al-Aghlab's successors kept up the peace and there began a period of considerable artistic and architectural development. Under Abu Ibrahim Ahmad (856-863 AD) the great mosque in Tunis was restored. In water storage and irrigation the Aghlabites were active, the large storage pounds at Kairouan were their work and retain their name. The pools were fed by springs 36 km to the W and used a first pond to settle out impurities before moving water into elaborate and ornate long term storage pools (see page 243). The city of Raccada (page 245) was the work of the Aghlabites, built as a fortress with additional palaces, water pools, mosques and housing areas.

The Aghlabites retained independence from Baghdad but eventually fell to the conversion to Shi'ism of the Berber Katama tribes and the emergence of the Fatimid state. The Aghlabite contribution to Tunisian technology and welfare was considerable, bringing art and techniques of architecture from the eastern Caliphate to mix with Mediterranean and local traditions.

Hafsid Dynasty (1230-1574)

It was under the rule of the **Hafsid Dynasty** (1230-1574) that Tunis blossomed, with more than 100,000 inhabitants within its walls. The geographer and philosopher Ibn Khaldoun (1232-1406) was born during this period in Tunis when the intellectual and cultural importance of the city was at its peak.

Perhaps one of the most influential sources of thinking in modern archaeology, **Ibn Khaldun** (Abu Zayyed Abdelrahman Ibn Khaldun) was born in 1332 in Tunis. He served as a high official in the administrations in Morocco, Muslim Spain and Algeria, where, at the age of 43 he began writing his introduction to history – the *Moqaddimah*. He developed a segmentary analysis of Muslim society in which he saw a cycle of rise and fall of dynasties. In simplified form, he proposed that strong tribes from the interior would seize power from the sedentary powers of the cities and inject life and inventiveness into society before becoming gradually weakened by the stresses of urban politics and the temptations of the flesh pots of the city. Meanwhile, the tribal areas would once again throw up a vigorous tribal group, first to challenge and then finally take over the cities, deposing the former ruling family. The mechanics of social and political change and the causes for them outlined by Ibn Khaldun became the first serious secular

Pirates of Barbary

🌊 The pirates of Barbary occupy a notable place in the annals of Mediterranean life and history. The pirates of Morocco were slightly less well known than the famous names such as Dragut and Barbarossa who sailed out of Algiers and Tunis. Barbarossa (red beard) was a Turk and pirate leader in the 16th century. He waged war against the Portuguese and Spanish merchant fleets and eventually in 1533 became admiral-in-chief of the Ottoman Empire. Meanwhile the great pirate Dragut settled on the island of Djerba in 1550. In the period 1530-1570 the Turkish pirates preyed on the Christian merchant men travelling in the Mediterranean, took slaves at will and brought southern European commerce almost to a standstill. Their audacity knew no bounds despite punitive expeditions from Spain and Naples to Djerba. It was not until the Spanish and their allies liberated Malta (where Dragut was killed) in 1565 and the final coup de grace of the Turkish fleet at Lapanto in 1571 that the worst of piracy in Barbary was ended.

Not that the Barbary pirates were eliminated. Even Tripoli in the days of the Karamanli pashas and their corsair ships attracted reprisals from the USA. Tunisia was a leading state in Barbary and was important for piracy in the 17th-19th centuries. The pirates lived off the commercial shipping moving across the Mediterranean Sea. It was an easy prey – largely unarmed – and justified by the Muslim corsairs on grounds that the traders were infidels and thus fair game.

European consuls in the Barbary states did their best to deter attacks on their nation's shipping and to arrange the freeing of prisoners. Some European countries paid off the pirates to leave their shipping to pass safely, while the naval powers such as Great Britain were willing to condone piracy provided that its own vessels were unmolested. When the system failed, the British and French bombarded the ports in question, not always with the results expected.

In the 19th century as slavery was brought under control and the Europeans took strong measures against the local rulers in North Africa, piracy was ended. The French occupation of Algiers in 1830 being particularly effective.

interpretation of history and society. It is the modern anthropologist's 'segmentary theory', a much contested tool of contemporary sociology.

Ibn Khaldun was also a great travel and gazetteer-writer and is known more usually as among the truly outstanding Arab Geographers rather than as an anthropologist. He is known to have crossed via Egypt and his beloved Cairo to Mecca and Damascus, during the siege of which Ibn Khaldun met Timur (Timurlane the Great) in 1400. Ibn Khaldun spent some of his latter working years in Cairo and moved finally to Tunis where he died in 1406.

Ibn Khaldun is associated with end of a golden age of thought and innovation in the Muslim world when new crops, cultivation practices and the arts reached their zenith. Sadly, his ideas of social evolution only reached Europe in the 19th century and full recognition of his immense intellectual gifts only fully absorbed by the West in the 20th century. It is ironic that in an increasingly hardline Islamic world at the end of the 20th century Ibn Khaldun is, as a non-religious theorist, much under-considered even in the Arab countries.

Period of turbulence

Between 1534 and 1574 the town went through a period of turbulence. First attacked by Kherredine Pasha, better known as the pirate **Barbarossa**, from Turkey, then captured by the Algerians

Conserving historic Tunis

👣 The days when architects and politicians considered the medinas, the old cities of Tunisia, as being fit only for demolition are long gone. Today in Tunisia there is recognition that the medinas contain the secrets of a vanishing way of life, that the courtyard houses and the simple beauty of a *mesjed*, a 'parish' mosque are fragile – even though here today, they could all too easily be gone tomorrow.

The movement for conserving old Tunis only really got going in the late 1960s. Modernist development projects were on the drawing boards – particularly unsophisticated was a sycophantic project to continue the principal artery of the 19th century *ville basse* across the medina to the kasbah. Fortunately, this sabre stroke across the old city was avoided as intellectuals, architects and local politicians got together in what was to become the Association Sauvegarde de la Medina de Tunis. Architecture and planning offices were created in a restored palace, the Dar Lasram, and the new, enthusiastic, multi-disciplinary team was helped by UNESCO, in the early 1970s heavily involved with the conservation of Carthage.

The Medina of Tunis is particularly interesting for the variety of its urban fabric. Surrounding the central Ez-Zitouna Mosque, founded late in the 7th century, is a dense network of covered souqs, still very active today. The residential areas are composed of courtyard houses, the life of each family being organized around a central space open to the sky. The square minarets of the Malekite mosques and the elegant pointed minarets of the Hanefite mosques give the medina a characteristic silhouette. Domes mark public baths and mausolea. The ramparts have almost totally disappeared, replaced by apartment buildings in the neo-classical and eclectic styles, and in the kasbah area by a fine set of turn of the century buildings, representing the height of the *style arabisant* in Tunisia. The Bab Souika area, renewed in the 1980s, contains some interesting work by contemporary architects.

In the late 1960s, the Hafsia, the former Jewish quarter or *hara*, was perhaps the most decayed area. Renovation had started in the 1930s with a series of low rise apartment blocks which stood in contrast to the surrounding dense fabric of courtyard houses. The real innovation came in 1972-73 with the first reconstructions: the aim was to integrate new building into the existing urban fabric. In 1983, this first phase of the Hafsia received an Agha Khan award for Islamic Architecture. The second phase of rebuilding in the 1980s was a real integrated urban renewal project involving the City Council, the ASM, the ARRU (Urban Renewal Agency) and the World Bank. The process of clearing up the worst of the medina's slum housing was launched at Presidential initiative in late 1991, with hundreds of families being rehoused in new homes in the western suburbs.

Old medina buildings need special care, a task made tricky by a multitude of problems: a rising water table and associated damp, speculation in recuperated building materials – notably marble and *zellij* (ceramic tiles), the problem of 'operating' on buildings with many party walls in areas of tricky vehicle access. And of course there is the issue of appropriate reuse.

The Palais Kheïreddine, a 19th century mansion close to the Hafsia, has long been ripe for restoration. This seems set to become a home for the Musée de la Ville de Tunis. Once the project is completed the high ceilings of the great reception rooms will provide superb exhibition space in an area of the medina which has become the city's *quartier culturel*, especially lively during Ramadan when there are concerts in the restored *medersa*.

Urban conservation activity has expanded to include the *ville nouvelle*. The listing of the Art Nouveau municipal theatre in 1992 marked the beginning of a new awareness of recent architecture in Tunis.

The key to furthering conservation in historic Tunis will of course be the creation of a secteur sauvegardé, a conservation area based on detailed land use plans. Drawn up under the terms of the 1992 National Heritage Code, this will protect not only the buildings of great historic importance, but also the accompanying architecture significant for the character of both streets and city.

For although there will inevitably be much demolition and reconstruction, the medina of Tunis must keep its "ordinary architectures", restore façades without stereotyping, preserve the remaining traditional trades despite the pressure from the rag trade, in short, renew with sensitivity and in such a way that living conditions, notably those of the least privileged groups, are enhanced.

Further information The Association Sauvegarde de la Medina can be contacted at Dar Lasram, 24 rue du Tribunal, 1006 Tunis.

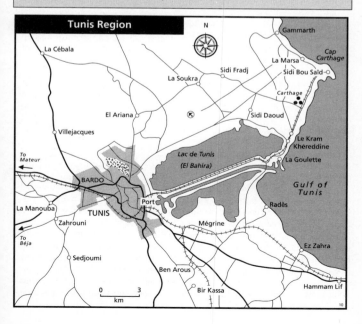

and subsequently by Don Juan of Austria. It was only with the Turkish invasion, in 1574, that a period of calm returned. The influx of 80,000 Moors from Spain at the start of the 17th century gave a renewed vitality to the city and its surroundings. Craftsmen trained in techniques unknown in Tunis made their appearance, including the makers of the important *chechias* (little red hats that were exported throughout the Mediterranean for over three centuries) (see pages 94 and 48).

Husseinid Dynasty

The Husseinid Dynasty lasted until the French colonization in 1881, but not without internal rivalries and chronic clashes with the Algerians over supremacy in the Maghreb region. This period was highly prolific in terms of the construction of palaces, *medressa* and mosques and greatly contributed to the shaping of the old medina as we know it today. It was also a period of military reform.

In the early 19th century, the beys (as the rulers of Tunisia were called) did their best to keep up with the changes taking place on the northern side of the Mediterranean. The dangers facing the country became all the more apparent after the occupation of Algiers by France in 1830 and the increasing competition between the colonial powers. Efforts to establish a modern army began under Hammouda Pasha, but ran into two major obstacles: the difficulty of abolishing once and for all the Janissaries (the corps of turbulent Turkish troops) and the problem of local military service.

Ahmed Bey (1837-55) was the founder of the modern Tunisian army based on the Ottoman model. Keen on all things military, he headed the army under his father Mustapha Bey's short reign (1835-37). He was very close to the troops, which enabled him to see where changes were needed. On coming to power in 1837, he implemented a number of reforms: the move from a small army of Turks and Zouaves to a larger professional army was accomplished. In 1840, the Bardo military academy was opened. By the end of the first decade of Ahmed's reign, a *nizami* or regular army with a strength of 27,000 men had been created. There were seven infantry regiments, and a Tunisian expeditionary force was participating in the Crimean War (1855-56) at the time of Ahmed's death in 1855.

Unfortunately, this ambitious military innovation programme put severe pressure on the state finances. Mohammed Bey (1855-9) inherited a delicate situation, and was obliged to cut military expenditure and reduce troop numbers to 5,000, the strict minimum for the maintenance of security. He also dispensed with the French military advisers called in by Ahmed Bey. The gemstones from the military decorations were sold, and all the barracks, except the one at Sousse, were abandoned.

The 1860s were a difficult decade for Tunisia: the doubling of the poll tax in 1864 led to a rebellion which was fiercely suppressed; there followed drought, a cholera epidemic in 1865 and typhus in 1868. Burdened with debts, the country was reduced to a state of misery which the reforming minister Kheïreddine was to find difficult to overcome. The general depression was of course reflected in the situation of the country's armed forces. The Bardo military academy was disbanded, the supply factories closed, and the number of soldiers (and their salaries) reduced. By 1881, the year of the French invasion, the army counted only 754 officers of various ranks and 1,725 soldiers.

The French

With the arrival of the French, large urban works were undertaken, giving rise to the new town built between the medina and the lake, with Ave de la Marine (today Ave Habib Bourguiba) as its central point linking the city to the sea. The ville nouvelle became the centre of the modern town giving it a distinctly European air. (See History of North Africa, page 28.)

WW2 and after

Tunis was occupied by the Germans for 6 months during WW2. Today it is a modern city and the centre of all the country's activities. Since Independence the population has increased dramatically from 400,000 to 1,200,000 resulting in overcrowding and the need for constant expansion. The city holds an interesting mixture of European and North African cultures, although in the ville nouvelle life has definitely been influenced by Europe, but enter the medina and you will be in another world. Indeed the medina is a good place to start your journey.

Tunis – the town

The town is situated on the shores of a lake linked to the sea at La Goulette. The new city, with Ave Habib Bourguiba as its centre, is laid out in a quasi-geometric fashion. The medina, in contrast, is full of small, confusing, winding streets. The medina is no longer walled, as the French replaced the old walls with large boulevards all around the old city. However, no cars can penetrate into the medina, making a welcome change from the overcrowded and noisy streets of the new town. La Goulette, the link between the sea and the lake, is the first of the coastal resorts and is linked to Tunis by train (the TGM) and road, both of which cross the lake over a causeway. The train goes on to the other coastal resorts of Sidi Bou Saïd, La Marsa and Gammarth, the smarter suburbs of Tunis full of luxurious villas. The first pleasant beaches are also situated here, and on summer weekends La Marsa is full of day-trippers from Tunis.

STREET NAMES

After independence in 1956, the main streets were renamed to efface the protectoral presence. Main avenues became the Ave **Habib Bourguiba**, while other chief streets received the names of various party activists, among them **Farhat Hached** (union leader assassinated by the Main Rouge terrorist organization in 1952), **Mongi Slim** (Tunisia's first am-

bassador to the UN) and **Taïeb Mehiri** (chiefly remembered for piloting the demolition of the summer palace of La Marsa and many other monuments symbolizing the Husseïnite Dynasty). Dates are also popular for street naming: **9 avril 1934** (nationalist uprising), **18 janvier 1952** (mass arrests of Destour and communist party leaders), and **7 novembre 1987** (prime minister Ben Ali becomes President of the Republic, president Bourguiba being declared medically unfit for the job).

Many streets are named after historic figures, here given in roughly chronological order:

Amilcar (290-229 BC) – commander of the Carthaginian forces in the First Punic War against Rome. Accompanied by his young son **Hannibal**, campaigned in Spain where he established a new state with the help of his son-in-law **Asdrubal**.

Hannibal (c. 247-183 BC) – after crossing the Alps into Italy, failed to take Rome. Defeated by Roman general Scipio and Berber king Massinissa in 202 at Zama. Died in exile in Bithynia (part of modern Turkey). Now a national figure featuring on the new 5 dinar note.

Jugurtha (160-104 BC) – grandson of Massinissa, entrusted with western Numidia by the Romans – with whom he clashed as he sought to restore his grandfather's kingdom. Fought Rome for 7 years. Died of poison in Rome.

Ibn El Jazzar (b. 895 in Kairouan) – physician, author of a medical treatise, the Viatica, translated into Hebrew, Greek and Latin, widely studied in Europe in the 16th century. Died leaving a large fortune.

Sidi Mehrez (953-1025) – mystic and patron saint of Tunis, defender of orthodox Malekite Islam against Shi'ite attacks. Founded the Hara (today's Hafsia) quarter for the Jews and Bab Carthagena for the Christians. Tunis was rebuilt under his leadership after destruction during the Hilalian invasions.

Restored by president Bourguiba, Sidi Mehrez' shrine in the Bab Souika district is still the object of much female devotion.

Sidi Belhassen ech-Chedly (c. 1195-1258) – another mystic, of Moroccan origin, whose tomb high above the Jellaz cemetery is still the object of much veneration by the Tunisois.

Ibn Batouta – 12th century traveller who set out from Morocco in 1352 on a journey of exploration to the sub-Saharan Africa, then economically important to the Marinid sultanate. The account of his travels was written down by the sultan Abu Inan's scribes.

Ibn Khaldoun (b. 1332 Tunis-d. 1406 Cairo) – Tunis born historian who was to rise to become top Malekite cadhi (judge) under mamluk sultan Barkouk of Egypt. Main works: El Mukaddima and Kitab El-'Ibar. Knew North African politics and tribal life intimately, and considered tribalism as central to political life in the Maghreb, based on his observations of the rise and fall of Berber groupings who founded city-based states only to be corrupted by the comforts of urban life and replaced by other more valorous groups. For portrait, see the blue 10 dinar note (see page 78).

Aziza Othmana (1606-1669) – learned princess, wife of Mourad Bey. Devoted much of her fortune and energy to charitable works.

General Kheïreddine (1822-1890) – Circassian mamlouk, came to Tunis aged 17 to the court of the modernizing Ahmed Bey. A reformist who believed that cultural borrowing could be restricted to certain areas and that Islamic society could be rejuvenated from within, retaining its beliefs and values intact. Prime mover behind the fundamental law of 1857 entitled the Pledge of Security, by which the bey committed himself to the principle of the inviolability of persons and property and equality of all before the law, and the constitution of 1860. Highly conscious of French ambi-

tions in Tunisia, ironically he became prime minister in 1873 thanks to French intrigue. Founded the Sadiki College in 1875, the first Tunisian school to have a modern curriculum. Resigned in 1877 and held ministerial posts in Istanbul where he died. Now figures on the red and mauve 20 dinar banknote.

Charles Nicolle (b. Rouen 1866-1936) – head of the Institut Pasteur in Tunis where he discovered the typhus virus. Nobel Prize for Medicine in 1928.

Abdel Aziz Thaâlabi (1874-1944) – founder of the Parti libéral constitutionnel tunisien. Exiled 1924-1937, then headed the original Destour party until his death. Author of *La Tunisie martyre* (1920).

Ali Bach Hamba (1876-1918) – nationalist leader. Inspired by the Young Turks, founded the Jeunes Tunisiens party in 1907.

Moncef Bey (1881-1948) – 18th Husseïnite ruler, came to the throne 19 June 1943 with his country under German occupation. Adopted a policy of reinforcing Tunisian presence in the government, and appointed nationalist ministers. After the Axis defeat in Tunisia in 1943, deposed and deported to France where he died. His cousin the aged and harmless Amine Bey was given the throne, seen as a usurper by the majority of his people. Moncef Bey came to be considered as a martyr, and a generation of baby boys were named Moncef in tribute. Buried in the Jellaz cemetery with the people and not in the royal mausoleum in the Médina.

Mahmoud Materi (b. 1897) – orphan. Sadiki College and medical studies in France. Journalist and Destour party activist who worked tirelessly for Tunisian independence.

Habib Thameur (1909-1949) – another nationalist doctor trained in France. Died in a plane accident in Pakistan. Author of *Voici la Tunisie*.

PLACES OF INTEREST

VILLE NOUVELLE

The Ville Nouvelle with few specific things to see, is the centre of the city's life. Walk in the late afternoon on Ave Habib Bourguiba and the surrounding streets to see the city coming to life and the cafés filling up. Drink at the *Café de Paris* and watch people go by. Here you will find shops selling European newspapers (generally only a day late). The parks are pleasant all the year round (see Parks, page 105). Most of the monuments are in the old part of town.

THE BARDO NATIONAL MUSEUM

Officially known as **The Alaoui National Museum**, it lies 3 km to the W of town, T 513842. Take bus No 3 from the TGM station or Place du 7 Novembre, Ave Habib Bourguiba and Ave de Paris.

This museum, considered to be the most important in the Maghreb, is clearly signed once in the Bardo area of town, entrance on rue Mongi Slim, W border of park. The no-entry sign on the big iron gates is obviously ignored by all and cars with blue tourist plates and huge buses are parked there. Some park outside on the road. Walk in past the guarded National Assembly building. The museum is very crowded especially early morning when it opens as tour groups 'do' this first. During the day the heat builds up and the upstairs rooms can be very uncomfortable. Purchase tickets to right of main door, entrance TD3 and photography TD1, open summer 0830-1730 and winter 0930-1630, closed Mon, toilets. The shop has very little information, guide books are rare. In the building take note of your position and route as there are no *sortie* signs until the exit is reached, making a quick departure in an emergency very difficult.

The **museum** situated in a park, is set in a former Bey's palace. This historical monument from the mid-19th century is a masterpiece of Spanish-Moorish architecture. Its many attractive features include its actual proportions, its decorated wooden and stucco ceilings, and the walls covered with ornamental tiles. The exhibits illustrate the main civilizations that developed in Tunisia and the museum is noted for its vast collection of mosaics which give a picture of the daily life, pastimes and beliefs of the Roman populations in Africa. The extensive collection is best attempted in more than one visit. Plan shows recommended route with indication of main rooms and important features worth noting, place of origin of artifacts indicated in brackets.

Ground floor

Go through the **Entrance hall**, ticket office and shop to the **Prehistory** section, a collection of flint blades, bones, costume ornaments and engraved stones from the Acheulean, Mousterian, Ibero-Moorish, Capsian and Neolithic eras.

The **Punic** rooms have 1st century, small terracotta statue of the god Baal-Hammon (Thinissut, Cap Bon); a 4th century group of three divinities, Pluto, Demeter and Kore (carrying a piglet); 4th century stele of Priest and Child (Carthage), the child being carried ready for sacrifice. In the second room is a collection of masks made of glass paste or pottery generally placed in tombs with expressions designed to frighten evil spirits; personal decorations, necklaces, etc, and a Punic tomb reconstruction in a smaller adjoining room with arrangement of funeral objects (Cap Bon).

Libyc exhibits include bas-reliefs showing gods; funeral monuments with bilingual inscriptions in Libyc/Punic or Libyc/Latin. The **Sarcophagus corridor** has two 2nd century marble sarcophagi, one representing the nine Muses (Porto Farina), the other the four seasons; 3rd century Roman funeral effigy of a Romano/African citizen (Borj el Amri) and

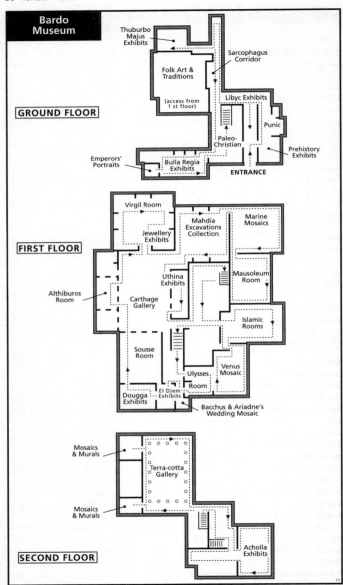

Bardo Museum

GROUND FLOOR

Thuburbo Majus Exhibits

Sarcophagus Corridor

Folk Art & Traditions

(access from 1st floor)

Libyc Exhibits

Punic

Paleo-Christian

Prehistory Exhibits

Emperors' Portraits

Bulla Regia Exhibits

ENTRANCE

FIRST FLOOR

Virgil Room

Jewellery Exhibits

Mahdia Excavations Collection

Marine Mosaics

Althiburos Room

Uthina Exhibits

Mausoleum Room

Carthage Gallery

Islamic Rooms

Sousse Room

Ulysses Room

Venus Mosaic

Dougga Exhibits

El Djem Exhibits

Bacchus & Ariadne's Wedding Mosaic

SECOND FLOOR

Mosaics & Murals

Terra-cotta Gallery

Mosaics & Murals

Acholla Exhibits

the Boglio stele, also 3rd century Roman, from a series dedicated to Saturn.

The **Thuburbo Majus** corridor and room have inscriptions, statues, marble wall panels, geometric and floral mosaics; a small bas-relief representing Maenads from 1st century while the **Paleo-Christian** corridor and room display a collection of tomb mosaics and church pavements. See particularly the 4th century 'Ecclesia Mater' tomb mosaic (Tabarka) showing the section of a church with candles on the altar; tomb mosaic with two figures and seven crowns inscribed with the names of the seven martyrs; limestone font (Gightis) in centre of room; tiles showing Biblical scenes.

In the **Bulla Regia** room from the Temple of Apollo, 2nd century BC, stands a very languid god (Bulla Regia). A gallery of portraits of Roman emperors completes the ground floor rooms.

On a staircase leading to the first floor is a series of mosaics 4th-6th centuries from funeral monuments of the Christian era (Tabarka), some giving age and occupation of the deceased; a statue of Apollo (Carthage).

First floor

The **Ulysses** room is named after the famous Ulysses mosaic (Dougga) on display here. He is depicted bound to the ship's mast to prevent him following the sirens, on the right, playing musical instruments. Ulysses' companions have stopped their ears with wax (not visible) and are looking in the opposite direction to avoid the same fate.

Other mosaics include the very large late 3rd/early 4th century (Utica) Neptune and Amphitrite in a chariot drawn by sea horses with two nereids seated on sea tigers, with three boats each with a bejewelled lady surrounded by cupids; the self crowning of a semi nude/bejewelled Venus 4th century (Carthage); Marsyas the satyr and Apollo making music while Minerva looks on (judges?)

and the surrounds depict the four seasons, 3rd century (El Djem). At one end of the room is a fountain (Thuburbo Majus), normally found in the largest room in a villa, has the head of Oceanus depicted on the exterior and the interior decorated with nereids and sea monsters.

In the corridor is **Bacchus and Ariadne's** wedding mosaic from the 4th century (Thuburbo Majus).

The **El Djem** room holds intricate *xenia* (still life) mosaics related to food and hospitality (such as men playing dice), animals (fish, duck) and musical instruments often found in dining rooms of wealthy villa owners, from 3rd century; a 3rd century mosaic – hunting, horses, hounds and a hiding hare; on the floor Bacchus rides his triumphal chariot drawn by tigers lead by Pan.

In the **Dougga** room (don't miss the magnificent painted ceiling) are two ancient models of the city, one of the Square of the Capital and the other of the theatre. On the walls and floor are mosaics (La Chebba, Carthage and Thuburbo Majus). Neptune, placed centrally, is magnificent in his chariot with hunting and seasonal agricultural scenes around, 2nd century (La Chebba, Sfax). Opposite are three dark skinned giants working the forge of Vulcan, found in the Cyclops' thermae, 4th century (Dougga); also Cup bearers serving guests (Dougga).

The huge **Sousse** room houses a large collection of mosaics from Sousse, Carthage and Tabarka; the head and feet of a colossal statue of Jupiter (Thuburbo Majus); Punic, Greek and Roman lamps, ceramics (El Aouja near Kairouan); on the floor a 3rd century mosaic of Neptune surrounded by sea creatures (Sousse); "Lord Julius" mosaic early 5th century (Carthage) – the life of Julius, a wealthy personage – a central imposing villa and pictures of the cycle of the seasons and rural life; three big pavings from apses from private villas (Tabarka) probably of the same age as the Carthage mosaic; mosaics illustrating a circus 3rd century (Carthage) and chariot races 6th century (Gafsa).

An imposing gallery, colonnade and high ornamented ceiling houses sculpture, mainly from **Carthage**. In the centre is an altar dedicated to the "Gens Augusta" with bas-reliefs on all four sides dated between 1st century AD and 1st century BC; on the floor are two famous 3rd century mosaic pavements (Uthina/Oudhna), the first of Bacchus surrounded by cupids among the vines and a second showing agricultural activities and hunting scenes. There are statues of Roman gods and an imposing statue of Emperor Hadrian.

To the side in the **Althiburos** room are mosaics (Althiburos and Carthage), on the floor a 4th century mosaic of Roman boats, all correctly titled, also a 4th century banqueting scene with guests seated on benches rather than reclining on couches; a mosaic of hunting scenes, a temple containing Apollo and Diana and a crane being sacrificed 5th-7th centuries AD (Carthage-Salammbo) indicating a survival of pagan practices into the Christian era.

The **Virgil** room is octagonal with a magnificent dome of carved plaster work. Here the 3rd century mosaic showing a seated Virgil in meditation between the muses of history and tragedy (Sousse) is the only portrait of the poet; in the centre of the floor the 3rd century mosaic has medallions with the signs of the zodiac surrounding godheads of the days of the week (Bir Chana near Zaghouan).

The ornamentation in the **Jewellery** room is mainly Punic, some from as long ago as the 7th century BC, mainly from Carthage but also Utica and Kerkouane. There are matching necklaces and earrings of tiny ceramic/ivory figures/objects, rings, seals etc, solid gold jewellery and gold plate on bronze.

The excavations from **Mahdia** were discovered by sponge divers early this century, the cargo of a Greek ship which sank off the Tunisian coast. The display includes Helenistic bronze and marble furniture, pieces of the wrecked ship, and marble statues of Aphrodite 2nd-1st century BC which look a little worse for wear after their long immersion.

Marine mosaics are sections of a huge mosaic of a seascape including dolphins, nereids and sea monsters (Carthage) while central in the **Mausoleum** room is displayed a mausoleum of a Carthaginian with carved reliefs on all four sides. On the walls are mosaics, in particular one of animals' heads (Thuburbo Majus).

The **Uthina (Oudhna)** room, originally the dining room, has many mosaics of hunting or mythology. Of particular interest are *emblemata* made from tiny tesserae embedded in terracotta. Two here show the remains of a meal. Also a large paving of a headless Orpheus with his lyre charming the wild animals.

At this point it is necessary to go downstairs to see the **Folk art and traditions room** before ascending to view the **Islamic rooms** situated in the smaller, older (1831) building set around a patio. The huge hall displays artifacts from the 9th-13th centuries, musical instruments, weapons, household objects; jewellery in particular gold necklaces, bracelets and earrings; traditional costumes, furniture; parchments, manuscripts, verses of the Koran, most of the documents from the great mosque of Kairouan, in particular pages from the Blue Koran; *tiraz* fabrics with Koranic inscriptions; astralobes, sundials and compasses; ceramics.

The last room on this floor has 4th century paving of an apse called Hunting the Wild Boar, showing three stages of the hunt; **Venus** being crowned by two female centaurs; a splendid peacock with a spread tail.

The main staircase leads to the **2nd floor** where the **gallery** overlooking the

Grandeur and decadence of the Beys of Tunis

🦶 "A visit to His Highness Ali, Bey of Tunis" wrote Herbert Vivian in 1899," is like a visit to an extinct volcano". After the declaration of the French Protectorate in 1883, the beys, as the kings of Tunisia were called, slipped into a comfortable bourgeois existence. Dividing their time between new Italianate palaces in La Marsa and the other pleasant suburbs of Tunis, they lost contact with their subjects and the demands of the pro-independence groups.

The beylical court had not always been as comfortable. Hussein Ben Ali, the founder of the Husseinid Dynasty (which provided Tunisia with eighteen rulers between 1705 and 1957) was a military man who rose to power defending Tunisia from the Turks of Algiers. Years of strife followed before the dynasty was firmly established.

Under Ali II (1759-82) and Hammouda Pasha (1782-1814), the Husseinids were at the height of their powers, benefiting latterly from Europe's involvement in the Napoleonic Wars. They built a strong position, mediating between the subsistence economy of tradition Tunisia and the expanding trade of Europe.

Colourful ceremonial reigned at the palace of the Bardo. A visitor in the 1830s, Sir Grenville Temple, glimpsed the life of the court: "Under the archway, and forming a rich and animated foreground, are seen groups of splendidly capari-soned horses, awaiting the return of their masters from the audience chamber: on the opposite side from another court rises a wild flight of steps almost covered by seated Arabs, wrapped in the graceful and classic folds of their sefsars and burnooses, patiently waiting to be ushered into the hall of justice". All visitors, foreign diplomats as well, were expected to kiss the bey's hand.

Off limits to almost all visitors, however, was the harem. Writing in the 1850s, Henri Dunant put the number of women in the harem at the La Marsa palace at over a thousand. The door to the harem was guarded by two armed eunuchs and "never does any one of the princesses appear in public, in accordance with the usage of oriental courts". The wives of the beys were Christians converted to Islam, Turkish or (more rarely) native Tunisian women.

The European wives were often originally slaves. Lella Jeanette, mother of Ahmed Bey (1837-1855), was a slave girl of Sardinian origin, taken in a raid in 1798. Her son was a decisive ruler, acclaimed at home and abroad, who abolished slavery and attempted to introduce modern industry into Tunisia. Unfortunately for the dynasty, the rulers who succeeded him were dominated by scheming ministers bent on enriching themselves rather than their country.

One bey stands out in the 20th century. Moncef Bey (1942-43) already had the reputation of a prince close to the people when he came to the throne. With Tunisia under German occupation, he called in nationalist ministers and attempted to strengthen Tunisia's political power. To no avail – after the defeat of the Axis in North Africa, Moncef Bey was accused of collaboration, was deported, and the throne was handed to his cousin the kindly, if ineffectual, Lamine Bey, soon considered as a usurper. Moncef died in exile in France in 1948, but was buried among his people in the Jellez cemetery in Tunis. His funeral was the occasion for great demonstrations, the legend of "Moncef, the martyr bey" was born.

Lamine Bey, in the circumstances, was unable to benefit from any of this popular feeling. He was easily outmanoeuvred by the nationalist leader, the wily Habib Bourguiba and the Husseinite crown was abolished, unmourned, on 27 July 1957.

A Café society?

In everyday Islam in the Maghreb, the *zaouia* or saint's shrine provided a focus point linking social life and religious expression alongside the austere Malekite rites of the mosque.

Brought to North Africa with the Ottoman conquest, much criticized but never forbidden, coffee was originally a luxury drink consumed by mystics and notables at holy shrines. The *Café M'rabet* in the Medina of Tunis still contains a saintly tomb or two, suitably bedecked with flags, and the old entrance to the *zaouia*-mosque of Sidi Bou Saïd was through the café.

The traditional Tunisian café with its rush mats was referred to as the *café maure* by 19th century travellers, in contrast to the modern cafés and bistros of the new European quarters. The Tunis intelligentsia would meet at the *Café de Paris* or the *Rotonde* by the cinema *Colisée*. Independence and the rural exodus brought a change of atmosphere: today's city centre café is a male preserve – the seats have gone, you drink and smoke leaning on a high table or counter. Other more 'local' type cafés give men somewhere to watch the international football and indulge in marathon card games with much gusto and mock disputes.

Tea is the other great Tunisian drink, so much part of local custom that it is hard to imagine that the beverage only arrived around 1910, and was a source of great concern to the government. Dupuy, writing in an official publication of 1939, talks of "the scourge of *théisme*", which "is a serious cause of impoverishment, ...the cause of late nights, leading to brawls and physical decline, for tea, mixed with mint, becomes most harmful". Today tea is practically the national drink, and few Tunisians can digest their lunch without the regulation *kas tay* (glass of tea).

Alcohol, in contrast, is still a cause of late night brawls. City centre bars are packed, blokey and hard-drinking (summer hours 1500-2200, winter 1300-2000). You order a crate of Celtia beer and put it under the table – no sophistication here. One or two bars still maintain a certain Fifties aura: the *Café Marius* on Place Barcelone must have one of the biggest collections of ashtrays in the world, lovingly displayed in glass cases, the Xuereb family's Tantonville on rue de Yougoslavie serves the best *kémia* (tapas type snacks).

The Nineties' phenomenon, however, is the return of the water pipe or *chicha*. Until recently *chicha*-smoking was an old man's habit although the young might have a go on a night out to that temple of nostalgia, the *Café des Nattes* in Sidi Bou Saïd. Now *chicha* cafés are everywhere, all tricked out with ceramic tiles and fretwork wooden tables. Football players open them on retirement, gold mines for later life. In the *chicha* café, the air is thick with the distinctive smell of *mu'assal* (honey) tobacco smoke. TD1.3 gets you a pipe with *mu'assal* tobacco, looking like so much treacled tobacco with a hot coal on top; a *chicha* with a full ration of stronger *jrak* tobacco costs TD2.

The *chicha* café is the place to meet after work – the real fanatics bring their own mouthpiece, as tuberculosis is apparently on the increase thanks to insufficient washing of the pipe. A word of warning, however. Tobacco is the ONLY substance smoked in *chichas*. Other substances get you landed in gaol in Tunisia – the penalties are very severe. Long gone are the days of the *Café du Phare* at Sidi Bou Saïd where the *takerlia* could smoke their *takrouri* and gaze out over the wine dark sea to the distant isles of Zembra and Zembretta.

Tunisian cafés: the key drinks

café turc/*kahwa bi-zazwa* – Turkish coffee
capucin – express with a little milk (noisette in France)
crème directe – strong milky coffee for a kick start in the morning
express – small black coffee
express allongé – dilute version of the above
filtre – black urn-brewed coffee (best avoided)
shtar – half filtre, half milk (poorer cafés only)
thé infusion – tea with a tea bag
thé *ahmar* – strong, sticky brew
thé akhdha/*thé vert* – strong, green tea, in its mint version
thé bil-bunduk and *thé billouz* – upmarket versions of green tea, respectively with pine nuts and almonds floating in the glass
tronjiya – herbal, verbena tea (for fragile stomach days)
gazouze – fizzy drinks: all the international standards, plus....
boga – Tunisian lemonade
boga cidra – pretty dreadful brown carob base drink
eau plate – still water (main brands Safia, Melliti and Sabrine)
eau gazeuse – fizzy water (main brand red label Garci)
jus *d'orange* – orange juice, delicious, made with sweet Cap Bon oranges, unique to Tunisia
lait de poule – banana or pear milk shake blended with a raw egg (pâtisseries only)

And finally, to get the waiter's attention: *ya chef* or *ya ma'lem* or even *min fadhlik* (please)

Favourite cafés
Sidi Bou Saïd
the *Café des Nattes*, its famous staircase painted by Paul Klee, for a sprawl on the rush mats while sipping a *thé aux pignons* on a winter evening, and the *Café Sidi Chaâbane*, with marvellous views across the Bay of Tunis from its terraces.
Medina of Tunis
the *Café de la rue Sidi Ben Arous* (chez Kamel) – time off for a *chicha* in an ancient street under the great mass of the Zitouna minaret. Also, *chez Mnouchi*: a door in the wall at the intersection of Souq el Leffa and Souq el Kebabjiya takes you into a courtyard café with wonderful tile panels.
Bizerte
Café Le Pacha, and other cafés around the old harbour of Bizerte.
El Fahs
after a roam round the ruins of Thuburbo Majus, a visit to the *Café Abou Nawas*, a masterpiece of kitsch.
Le Kef
Café de la Source, for a quiet *chicha* under the trees.
Mahdia
Café de la place du Caire, situated on possibly the prettiest square anywhere in an old town in Tunisia
Medina of Sfax
Café Diwan, up in the Borj el-Rasas tower, ramparts of Sfax.

Carthage room contains terracotta statuettes of protective gods such as Venus and Mercury from temples and tombs. Here also are objects from necropoli of the 1st-3rd centuries, glasses, bowls, dishes from tombs, funeral urns and statuettes. Don't miss the surgeons kit with lancets, scalpels and forceps.

The corridors and rooms around the stairhead have yet more mosaics, 4th century depicting Theseus slaying the Minotaur in a large maze of brown on cream, while the border depicts the walls and gates of a city (Thuburbo Majus); two mosaics on the theme of animal sports with a haloed Bacchus (El Djem) and a 4th century example from Thelepte/Feriana; a 2nd century paving (Thuburbo Majus), depicts a meditating poet seated on a column shaft, a mosaic in praise of intellect. In a separate room is a 3rd century Diana the Huntress on a deer, the medallions portray animals of the hunt, boars, gazelle etc (Thuburbo Majus); and Venus on a rock, 3rd century (Utica).

The items in the **Acholla** room (N of Sfax) were collected from private houses, large fragments from the Trajan thermae representing groin vault decoration; two panels of identical background showing busts of the four seasons and *xenia* with baskets of fruit; and two T-shaped mosaics (the blank sides being hidden by benches) one of *xenia* with birds and animals and the other relating to the Labours of Hercules. The final item, a fountain, is decorated with shoals of fish.

Leaving the Bardo – if you are now looking for somewhere nearby to have a coffee or a meal while you digest what you have seen – sorry. There is a nearby pizzeria, crowded to the doors at lunchtime and only a few stools by the counter but nothing else fit to enter in the vicinity.

The Medina

The **Medina** of Tunis was founded 13 centuries ago on the narrow strip of land between the Sebkha Es Sedjoumi and Lac de Tunis. This was a very good site for trade. With its typical layout and interesting architectural styles it has been designated by UNESCO as part of mankind's cultural heritage. It can be divided roughly into two equal pieces along rue de la Kasbah which stretches from Bab Bhar to Place du Governement. Most places of interest lie to the S side, the northern region being mainly residential and artisan workshops, metalwork, carpentry, printers. The mosque and many other monuments here are not open to the public. The admission times of those which are accessible are given in the text. **NB** It is important to dress correctly when visiting a mosque. The following route visits the areas of interest within the medina.

Best buys

Souvenir shopping in the souqs of Tunisia can be a tiresome business, especially if you're on a rushed visit to one of the medinas on a hot summer morning. For the would-be souq shopper, the following is a list of possible presents available in the medina of Tunis. Prices are as for late summer 1996 and include the 21% VAT. So in descending order of price, fifteen or so best buys:

1 **A bordeaux red wool bakhnoug** (flat weave veil) with fine white cotton embroidery (1.4m x 2.4m) from the Hanout Arabe, rue de la Zitouna – TD220 (particularly fine examples cost much more).

2 **A hamal or tent carpet** in sober ochres and reds (3m x 1m) from Youssef Gacem, intersection of Souq el-Attarine and Souq et-Trouk – TD200.

3 **Length of woven cloth from Mahdia** in *harir el-louh* silk, from Youssef Gacem, 1m x 1.4m – around TD130.

4 **Raw silk gentleman's waistcoat or** *farmla* (to order) from Tahar the Tailor

What a welcome

Romans were very anxious to ward off the evil eye (see box Talisman, page 281) to the extent of incorporating 'good' symbols at their doorway to offer greater protection. The mosaic from Sousse shows a phallus crudely designed into the shape of a fish (a good omen) set between two pubic triangles. This was the mosaic at the threshold of the main entrance of a Roman villa and now in the museum at Sousse. It is unlikely that villas in Tunis today would have such a welcome on the mat.

on the Souq des Femmes, behind the Great Mosque – TD130 (similar model in linen *kamariya*) at TD85.

5 **Mechtia** (cream wool carpet with black geometric designs) from El Jem, 2m x 1m – TD100.

6 **Heavy silver necklace** by Kate Daoud from the Hanout Arabe – TD90.

7 A high quality glass *chicha* (hubble-bubble pipe) – up to TD60.

8 **Handpainted ceramic tile panel** (20 tiles) from *Mille et un caprices* pottery shop on rue de la Zitouna – TD30. For that special Tunisian bathroom look.

9 **Engraved brass plate**, diameter 45 cm, price depending on the thickness of the metal from around TD18 (light model) to TD28 (heavy model).

10 **Blown glass vases, handpainted** with various designs, from Hamed Mnouchi, Souq el-Leffa – TD10 to TD20.

11 **Thick black belt** from Salah El Aroussi, leatherworker, 59 Souq es-Sakkagine – TD15; medium sized leather rucksack also about TD15, dinky size rucksack TD10.

12 **Casserole pots with wild boar shaped handles**, made by rural ladies in northern Tunisia, from the Hanout Arabe – TD10-16.

13 **Shallow oval bowl**, in traditional blues and greens, around TD10; modèle berbère (slightly better painting on tan ground) – TD12.

14 **A dead scorpion** crudely glued to a piece of cardboard in a glass box, around TD6, if you really must.

15 **A garn or goat's horn pipe** (the wonderful squeaking noise is sure to delight), TD6 or TD12 for the double version.

And finally, in the under TD5 range: **a sequinned stuffed fish** to bring you good luck (Souq el-Attarine) or **handpainted tea glasses** (TD3 per glass, from Mnouchi, Souq el-Leffa); plaited **alfa grass fishes** (TD2 from the Hanout Arabe). More from Souq el-Attarine: 250 ml of **eau de rose** (TD2.5); **Ned el-Haramayn** (Two Shrines Incense sticks) TD1; tiny fragile **Egyptian glass perfume bottle** (TD5) or 9 gm of **jasmine oil** (TD2).

Walking tour

Start from Place de la Victoire, inside **Bab Bhar** by the British Embassy. This is one of the original gateways, standing in isolation as the enclosing walls have long since disappeared. Walk up rue Jamaa Zitouna which is the centre for tourist shops selling a mixture of goods from all around Tunisia, but the best deals are not to be had here. Going up the street, the **Bibliothèque Nationale** is on the right and straight ahead is the **Great Mosque Ez-Zitouna**. Round the mosque to the right is the **Souq el Attarine**, which specializes in perfumes. The mosque is the centre of the medina and the old city expanded and developed around it, the most noble merchants being situated closer to the mosque (as for example the perfume sellers in the Souq el Attarine) whereas the less noble trades such as the dyers were relegated to the areas nearer the walls. Although today the souq sells a wider range of goods it is still possible to buy here incense and concentrates of perfume essences very cheaply.

The **Tourbet Aziza Othmana** lies behind the souq up a small street. Follow the N side of the Great Mosque to its entrance by the minaret then turn right towards the **Hammouda Pasha Mosque** and rue de la Kasbah.

Turn W (left) up rue de la Kasbah through one of the oldest souqs in the medina specializing in the round red felt *chechias*, the traditional men's headwear originally Andalusian but more likely associated with older Morocco (see page 82), to the **Sidi Youssef Mosque**, the Place du Governement, on three sides of this are government/ministry buildings (no photographs allowed) and a pleasant tiled pedestrian precinct with trees down the centre and another entrance to the medina. Continuing the tour turn back into the medina and take the narrow street to the right, rue Sidi Ben Ziad to the **Dar el Bey**. Keep this building on your right and walk ahead to the Souq el Leffa, a small covered street, specializing in carpets, though these can be bought more cheaply in Kairouan. Some of the carpet shops here have terraces with impressive views over the medina but walking through three storeys of carpets and not buying takes some nerve.

Continue down the Souq el Leffa to the back of the Great Mosque and go right between this and the **Medersa**

Mouradia along the Souq des Femmes. A little street, the Souq des Orfèvres, on the right at the start of the Souq des Femmes sells lovely jewellery. A detour to the right at Souq el Kachachine leads first to the **Dar Hussein** and then the **Dar el Haddad**.

Souq des Femmes becomes rue Tourbet el Bey. Follow this until you come to **Torbet el Bey**. Turn left in front of the building and right down its E side and turn left into rue Sidi Kassem which has the **Dar Ben Abdallah** palace on the right and further down on the left on the corner of rue de Teinturiers is the **Mosque des Teinturiers**. The **Dar Othman** stands opposite.

Dar Ben Abdallah Palace is off rue des Teinturiers along rue Sidi Kassem. The museum is located in a most beautiful traditional late 18th/early 19th century Tunisian mansion. The **Museum of Popular Arts and Traditions**, T 256195, is housed here. The building, with its sculptured and painted wood, its carved plaster work and marble tiles is as interesting as the collection it holds. The museum is organized around the central courtyard. The exhibits retrace traditional life throughout the 19th and 20th century in the medina showing everyday scenes covering everything from housekeeping skills to cooking implements, clothes and furniture. In the *hammam* (bath) there is an interesting map of the medina indicating the location of all the Moorish *hammam* throughout the old city. A very well kept and presented museum. Open daily 0930-1630 except Sun. Entrance TD1.

On either side along the rue des Teinturiers are small streets with dyers working using techniques that have hardly changed throughout the centuries. Go down one of these streets and take a close look. The dyers are accustomed to tourists 'peeping in' but it is better not to take pictures too conspicuously. Follow the rue des Teinturiers, which becomes the Souq el Belat, back towards the rue

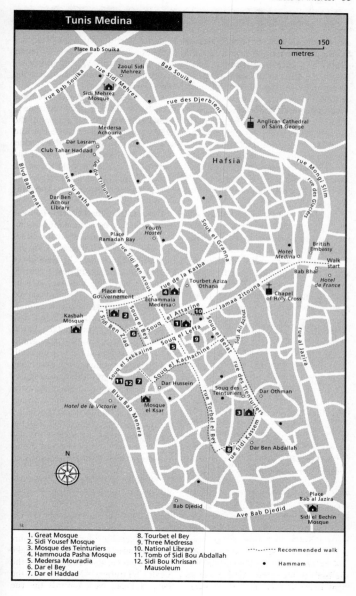

Tunis Medina

Place Bab Souika

rue Bab Souika

Bab Souika

Zaoul Sidi
Mehrez

rue Sidi Mehrez

Sidi Mehrez
Mosque

rue des Djerbiens

Anglican Cathedral
of Saint George

Medersa
Achouria

Hafsia

Dar Lasram

Club Tahar Haddad

rue du Tribunal

rue Mongi Slim

rue des Glacier

rue du Pasha

Blvd Bab Benat

Dar Ben
Achour
Library

Place
Ramadan Bay

Youth
Hostel

Souk el Granna

Hotel
Medina

British
Embassy

rue Sidi Ben Arous

Walk
start

rue de la Kasba

Tourbet Aziza
Othana

Bab Bhar

Hotel
de France

Place du
Gouvernement

Echammaia
Medersa

Souq el Attarine

Souq el Bey

Souq el Leffa

Jamaa Zitouna

Chapel
of Holy Cross

Kasbah
Mosque

Souq el Belat

Sidi Ali Azouz

Souq el Sekkajine

Souq el Kachachine

Dar Hussein

Dar Othman

Souq des
Teinturiers

rue des Teinturiers

rue al Jazira

Hotel de la Victorie

Mosque
el Ksar

rue Torbet el Bey

rue Sidi Kassem

Dar Ben Abdallah

Blvd Bab Menara

N

Bab Djedid

Ave Bab Djedid

Place
Bab al Jazira

Sidi el Bechin
Mosque

0   150
metres

1. Great Mosque
2. Sidi Yousef Mosque
3. Mosque des Teinturiers
4. Hammouda Pasha Mosque
5. Medersa Mouradia
6. Dar el Bey
7. Dar el Haddad

8. Tourbet el Bey
9. Three Medressa
10. National Library
11. Tomb of Sidi Bou Abdallah
12. Sidi Bou Khrissan
   Mausoleum

-------- Recommended walk

•   Hammam

The Zaouia

The *zaouia* is an important part of the architectural heritage of North Africa. It originated as the name of a small or local mosque but became associated with the spread of sufi orders in the area from the 13th century. It comprises a set of structures to provide a prayer room, a classroom for the teaching of the Koran and accommodation for guests. *Zaouias* were set up by holy men (marabouts) whose shrine often makes up part of the site, with a surrounding cemetery. In some cases the *zaouias* developed into monastic establishments with strong attachment to a particular sufi school of mystical Islam.

The Senussi of Libya in the 19th and 20th centuries showed that the teaching tradition of the sufi brotherhood survived and flourished until recently using *zaouias* as centres for religion, education and administration.

In Tunisia, the occurrence of *zaouia* is widespread in both Tunis and the smaller population centres. The old medina of Tunis is reputed to have over 30 *zaouias* of which that of Sidi Ali Azouz on the street of the same name is worth a visit.

Jamma Zitouna, passing on the left, on the corner of rue du Trésor, a small mosque with a beautiful 14th century minaret.

At the street after this mosque turn left to the **Three Medressa Complex** which includes **Medersa Slimania**, **Medersa Bachia** and **Medersa of the Palm Tree**.

Medina – Northern Sector

The sector known as **El Hafsia**, once a Jewish enclave, has been totally rebuilt while maintaining the traditional appearance.

The Library, **Dar Ben Achour**, 52 rue du Pasha, is located in what was once a private house, having over 5,000 books, mostly in Arabic, concerning the history and culture of Tunis medina and its people. Another private house **Dar Lasam** provides accommodation for The Association de Sauvegarde de la Medina, location 24 rue du Tribunal, T 563618. Its main purpose is to maintain all aspects of life within the medina. It won the Aga Khan architectural prize for 1995 for the Hafsia project. In the stables here is the **Club Culturel Tahar Haddad**.

Maison des Poets, opposite Dar Lasram, is a poetry study centre, with rooms of the central courtyard used for study or reading presentations.

Further N are the **Medersa Mouradia** and the **Sidi Mehrez Mosque**.

Now you have seen the main sights it is time to wander in the small streets and perhaps find areas not frequented by tourists towards the Bab al Jazira, along the rue des Teinturiers, or towards Bab Souika to the N. It is interesting to look at the different houses and perhaps peep inside. The exterior of the houses are generally quite similar and do not give any idea of the hidden splendour. All the houses have large wooden doors, simply decorated with nails. The rooms are generally organized around a central courtyard with no external windows in order to ensure privacy. The houses are generally quite large as the entire family lives there, including married sons. Each house has its own well.

NATIONAL MONUMENTS

The **Bibliothèque Nationale**, 20 Souq el Attarine, on rue Jamaa Zitouna is a very beautiful building with a spacious courtyard. It was originally built as a barracks in 1813 by Hammouda Husseinid and has now been converted into the National Library. Through the open doorway it is possible to see a magnificent chandelier hanging in the vestibule. Beyond is a large rectangular room surrounded by galleries which open on to large rooms. There are three study rooms, one in which handwritten documents are kept only for postgraduate study, one general study room for undergraduates and room with periodicals dating back to the late 19th century. While most documents are in Arabic there are a number in French and Italian. Access is restricted to serious students. Open 0800-2000 every day except Sun.

Dar Ben Abdallah, rue Ben Abdallah, off rue Sidi Kassem, a small sign points the way, built in 1796, houses the **Centre of Popular Arts and Traditions** where the collection of objects recreates bourgeois life in Tunis in the 19th century. There is a selection of gold embroidered/jewel encrusted costumes and unusually fine everyday objects. The palace itself is built round a central courtyard paved with marble, with a central fountain (not functioning at present). Note the ceramic tile decoration and white plaster work on the arches between the pillars. The exhibits are in what were the family rooms leading off the courtyard (ground floor only). There are descriptions in Arabic and French with dates of the period costumes. Not to be missed is the museum annex, left of the main entrance, showing kitchen utensils, saddles and various items of daily life at that time.

Look out here for a very useful map which pinpoints all the *hammams* in the medina. Open 0930-1630 except Mon, entrance including photography TD2.5.

Dar el Bey, Place du Gouvernement. Built in 1795 this old royal guesthouse has been converted since Independence into the Ministry of the Interior. The guards here, adorned in a striking livery with peaked cap, cloak and lots of gold braid, are unarmed. It is an interesting building, particularly with regard to its Andalusian influences.

Dar el Haddad, Impasse de l'Artillerie. Built in the 16th century it is one of the oldest palaces in the medina and was once owned by a rich Andalusian, Said El Haddad El Andalousi. Over time it has been inhabited by many different families and left to fall into decay. It was bought by the city of Tunis in 1966 and declared a National Monument.

Dar Hussein, Place du Château. Built by Ismail Kahia (1758-1781) this is a beautiful mansion which was used by the French as their army headquarters while in Tunisia. With the coming of Independence it became the **National Art and Archaeology Institute** and houses beautiful manuscripts of the Koran, glassware from Kairouan and ceramics from Rakkada as well as valuable objects from other Islamic countries.

Dar Lasram which houses the Association de Sauvegarde de la Medina was once the home of a rich landowner. The requirements for his personal use were brought into the town and stored, any excess was sold in the local markets. The building has been completely restored and clearly demonstrated the descending order of grandeur from the personal apartments at the top of the building through anterooms where visitors were received or made to wait, guest rooms, offices and down to servants' quarters and kitchens at road level with stables underneath. The private rooms of the original owner are large and beautifully decorated. The walls are tiled and the upper walls and arches have white plasterwork in stalactite design while the wooden ceilings are painted with abstract designs in the Italian style. Quality and amount of decoration decrease on the way down. The stables, with their vaulted ceilings now renovated and unrendered displaying the intricate brickwork both here and on the supporting pillars is used by the Club Culturel Tahar Hadded. Entrance is possible into Dar Lasram by making a request at reception to see the various architectural models of the medina redevelopment.

Dar Lasram (Tunis Medina)

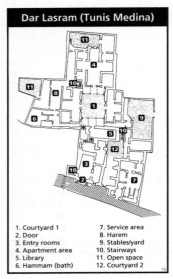

1. Courtyard 1	7. Service area
2. Door	8. Harem
3. Entry rooms	9. Stables/yard
4. Apartment area	10. Stairways
5. Library	11. Open space
6. Hammam (bath)	12. Courtyard 2

There was always a great deal of inertia in the architectural style/practices and building techniques in Tunisia aided by the Ottoman imperial practice of adopting local building types without change. In consequence there were great similarities in the lay-out and construction of large public and private buildings. Substantial private houses belonging to great families and powerful individuals were never exactly the same but did contain strong elements of continuity. All houses such as Dar Lasram had a central courtyard or *waset al-dar* (1) with perhaps a columned area, fountain, water basin and even trees which was reached indirectly through an angled corridor from the street. The house entrance was usually via a studded door (2) to a lobby or pair of small rooms (3), designed to ensure that no-one from the street could either view or easily enter the inner courtyard or rooms. Around the central courtyard were clustered all the principal rooms, including in large houses a *bait bel kebu* (4), a set of family rooms set around a main living space or an area to give family privacy from visitors. These groups of rooms had a small courtyard and may be seen as the successors to the peristyles of Romano-Greek houses in North Africa or to the Perso-Ottoman *haivans*. Libraries (5) were important in the houses of public figures, while some great houses had internal *hammam* (6) or bath areas. Naturally, there was a large staff and housing for it (7) in establishments of this kind to service the kitchen, the daily needs of the resident family and the transport/guard functions necessary for a public figure. The harem (8) was kept distant from the public rooms and often near the baths. Kitchens, stores, water well/storage, stables (9) and accommodation for servants took up considerable space (7). Tunisian great houses of the 18th and 19th centuries rarely had a developed upper storey, though roof areas were accessed by stairways (10) and used for laundry, the drying of fruits and for water gathering for the cistern below. Open space within the house was often generous in scale (11 and 12).

In lower class dwellings this same formula was repeated but on a smaller scale and without the baths and libraries. Many Tunisian houses at the present day are laid out on the *bait bel kebu* formula with an offset entry system just like the older Islamic houses.

Dar Othman Othman Dey 1544-1610 used the spoils of his piracy to build this beautiful palace at a distance from the kasbah, the Janissaries and other unrest. The palace looks out on to rue M'Bazaa. The majestic façade of black and white marble has a huge door surmounted by two carved lintels separated by a pointed arch of alternate coloured arch stones. The entrance hall, about 7m x 7m has patterned ceramic tiles on the walls with recessed arches decorated with delicately carved plasterwork. The wooden ceiling has a 12 sided recess, and the painted scroll-like pattern, now dark with age, resembles that in the *Dar Lasram*. The inner courtyard, through and to the right is for administration. It runs between two lines of horseshoe arches with black and white arch stones (like the outer doorway).

Great Mosque Ez-Zitouna (The Olive Tree), rue Jamaa Zitouna is the largest and most venerable mosque in Tunis, attributed to Hassan Ibn Noamene and considered to have been built in 732 but some reports date it back to the foundation of the Islamic city in 698. It was completely rebuilt by the Aghlabid Emir Ibrahim bin Ahmed in 856-863. The 44m high minaret was placed there in 1834 and is said to have been inspired by the minaret on the Kasbah mosque. All of the 184 columns and capitals surrounding the courtyard were brought from buildings in Carthage, giving an interesting architectural ensemble. The prayer room too has antique columns and a finely sculpted stucco ceiling, unfortunately, though, this part cannot be visited. There is a library in the wing of the building to the E of the prayer room. It was founded by Sultan Abou Othman in 1450. Courtyard open to non-Muslims from 0930-1200 all year, closed Fri and Sun, entrance TD3. Students with card free.

Medersa Mouradia College built in cloth market by Mourad II, son of Hammouda Pasha, in 1673. The huge studded door in a wide marble surround leads into a paved courtyard. Upstairs are the

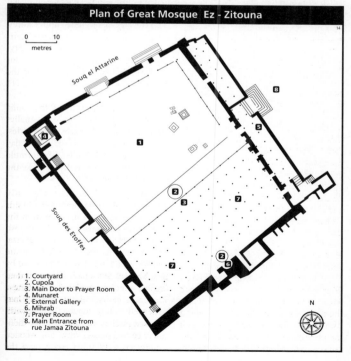

Plan of Great Mosque Ez - Zitouna

0   10
metres

Souq el Attarine

Souq des Etoffes

1. Courtyard
2. Cupola
3. Main Door to Prayer Room
4. Munaret
5. External Gallery
6. Mihrab
7. Prayer Room
8. Main Entrance from rue Jamaa Zitouna

N

old narrow-doored students' rooms and prayer chamber. Young apprentices learn their crafts here today. Open 0930-1630 except Sun, entrance TD3.

At the opposite end of the scale is a mosque situated on Ave de France in the arcade, 50m on the left approaching the medina entrance at Bab Bhar. Most people would walk straight by. It has no name but is called by those who use it the **Mosque de Magasin Generale** as it is adjacent to the shop. It is hidden away in the corner, has no minaret as it forms part of the main building of the arcade but behind the wrought iron railing and gateway the front of the mosque is visible. White marble steps rise up on left and right to the door and a delight of decorated patterned ceramic tiles illustrate a large container from which 'grows' trailing and entwining stylized flowers and leaves.

Mosque des Teinturiers (Dyers), rue des Teinturiers. Built by Hussein Ben Ali Tourki, the founder of the Husseinid dynasty, in 1716. No expenses seemed to have been spared, the ceramics coming from Turkey and the marble from Italy. Clearly influenced by the Sidi Youssef mosque with its octagonal minaret, it nevertheless has the novelty of sharing the central courtyard with a *medersa*.

Mosque el Fatah was built in 1985 on Ave de la Liberté, 100m N of Place de la République. It is a fine modern building facing on to the street, having a large, open inner courtyard with a marble floor, clearly visible to the passer-by. The entrance is surmounted by three beautifully tiled cupolas. The hexagonal minaret is very plain and very smart, buff brickwork up to a collar of black and white zig-zag patterned tiles. The top of the minaret has an open canopy surmounted by a hexagonal cupola with a dome.

Mosque of the Kasbah was built inside the walls of the kasbah during 1231-32. The square minaret is a striking copy of the Koutoubia in Marrakech and the Giralda in Seville. The four sides are

Mosque des Teinturiers – The Minaret

decorated with ornate white diamond shapes on a beige background. The prayer room is divided into 9 bays by 7 aisles, beneath this is a basement containing huge water tanks. The new town is to be built opposite the Mosque of the Kasbah. Plans show that the stonework of the new building will reflect that of the Kasbah Mosque.

Sidi Bou Khrissan Mausoleum, 12 rue Ben Mahmoud. The hemispherical domed building which contains the tombs of the Beni-Khourassan stands on an imposing square base with four large supporting pillars.

Sidi Youssef Mosque is in Souq el Bey, just behind Place du Gouvernement. An interesting mosque built in the 17th century by the Turks for the local Turkish merchants. It was architecturally innovative because it was the first mosque to have an octagonal minaret, setting the

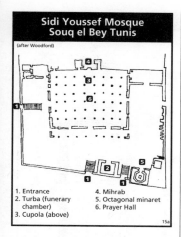

Sidi Youssef Mosque
Souq el Bey Tunis
(after Woodford)

1. Entrance
2. Turba (funerary chamber)
3. Cupola (above)
4. Mihrab
5. Octagonal minaret
6. Prayer Hall

15a

side. There is a door at each end of the market. That to the N on the side of Souq el Attarine has impressive columns.

Three Medressa These contain students' cells opening onto three sides of the courtyard with the mosque on the fourth side. The cloister round courtyard of **Medersa of the Palm Tree** (1714) is supported by horseshoe arches on stone columns with Turkish capitals. This surrounds a garden but the palm tree no longer exists. Black marble columns with white marble capitals support the arches in **Medersa Bachia** (1752). A stone fountain is incorporated in the design. The building is now a school for apprentice craftsmen. **Medersa Slimania** (1754) was built by Ali Pasha in memory of his son Suleimane who was poisoned by his brother. The entrance and courtyard are very beautiful and decorated with wonderful ceramics. It has now been converted into a cultural centre. Open 0930-1630 all year, closed Sun, entrance TD3.

Zaouia Sidi Abdel Kader The original *zaouia* was destroyed in the 1980s during restructuring works. The new *zaouia* completed in 1993, under the auspices of Association Sauvegarde de la Medina de Tunis, was made to fit into the existing tiny space – some 170 sq m. It is described as being designed with "Aghlabid inspiration". Enter up steps into the hall with eight columns. To the right is the prayer hall (dome over), the largest room in the building. The dark wooden doors are relieved with small panes of

style for many future Turkish mosques. The octagonal minaret was introduced to differentiate between Hanafi and Maliki mosques.

Souq el Attarine Traditionally each perfume has a particular significance. For example, orange will be used at weddings. Although today this souq sells a wider range of goods, it is still possible to buy concentrates or perfume essences very cheaply. Other items for sale include candles and attractive quilted baskets, traditional containers for presents from the fiancé to his future bride. Note the intricate carvings found on the wooden counters and shelves which indicate the wealth of this souq.

Souq el Birka at the S end of Souq el Bey was built in the early 17th century (1610-1637) and is now occupied by the Jeweller's guild. It is almost square with a central dome. The wooden block used for the auction of slaves used to stand in the centre, while purchasers sat on surrounding benches.

Souq el Kumach (cloth) lies to the W side of the Great Mosque. Two rows of stone columns divide the souq into a wider central lane for traffic and pedestrians with the shops located on each

Dome of Zaouia of Sidi Abdel Kader

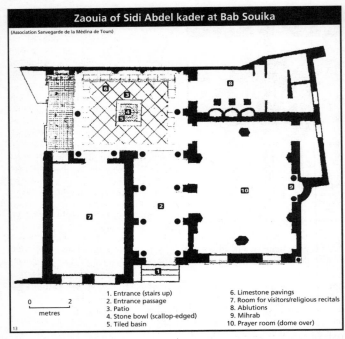

Zaouia of Sidi Abdel kader at Bab Souika

(Association Sanvegarde de la Médina de Tours)

0   2
metres

13

1. Entrance (stairs up)
2. Entrance passage
3. Patio
4. Stone bowl (scallop-edged)
5. Tiled basin
6. Limestone pavings
7. Room for visitors/religious recitals
8. Ablutions
9. Mihrab
10. Prayer room (dome over)

coloured glass (orange and green), 12 to each door. The mihrab in the far wall is decorated with orange and green ceramic tiles and the arch which has a scallop shell design is white. At the end of the hall is the small patio, floored with local limestone. In the centre is a scalloped-edge stone basin complete with small fountain. This has a tiled surround. From the patio is a room for visitors and religious recitals. The final room in the far corner is the ablutions. The white segmented dome on a hexagonal base is a new landmark in the N part of the medina.

Tourbet Aziza Othmana is at 9 Impasse Ech-Chammaia, off rue El Jelloud which leads towards the Great Mosque coming from rue de la Kasbah. Built c 1655, this is the tomb of the princess renowned for her generosity. Before dying she let her slaves go free and established a fund for a hospital, for poor girls who could not afford to marry and to provide fresh flowers for her tomb every day. Today the Tourbet is a private house and cannot be visited.

Tourbet and Mosque of Hammouda Pasha, rue Sidi Ben Arrous. The style of the mosque, built c 1655, shows a strong Italian influence, which is not surprising as Hammouda Pasha's father was Italian and converted to Islam in order to promote his career. The style is highly original and at the time was very innovative. This mosque influenced the style of the Habib Bourguiba Mosque in Monastir.

Tourbet el Bey, rue Tourbet el Bey. Built by Ali Pasha II (1758-1782), this mausoleum houses the tombs of the members of the royal family. Over the centuries, it

His tomb soon became an object of veneration and he had such prestige that some of the last Hafsid princes asked to be buried near it. Later the area became a focus for Moors following their expulsion from Spain in 1607. At that time the *zaouia* underwent significant changes at the hands of Abel Goyth al-Qachash, who repaired the damage suffered by the monument during the Hispano-Turkish wars and significantly extended the site by adding the current courtyard and the rooms which surround it. The beautiful inscription situated inside the mausoleum marks the location of Sidi Kassem's tomb and recounting his virtues dates from this time.

More recently, in the 18th century, the building was completely renovated by Hussein Ben Ali, a mosque was built in the SE of the site and the whole tomb was covered externally and internally with the decoration which is still visible today. At the same time its structure was significantly reinforced.

During the present century, the *zaouia* gradually became neglected, leading to the ruin and destruction of a large part of the courtyard and the dete-

Hammouda Pasha Mosque –
The Minaret

has been extended many times with little regard to the overall harmony. It is now the largest monument of its kind in Tunis. The most prominent style is Italian and it is interesting to note the domes covered in green, scale shaped tiles. The previous leaders of the dynasty had been buried in the Tourbet Sidi Kassem, rue Sidi Kassem. An interesting building which can normally be visited 0930-1600 except Sun, entrance TD3.

Zaouia Sidi Kassem el-Ziliji is situated overlooking the Sedjoumi salt flats in the far W of the medina, built around Sidi Kassem's tomb. Originally a gate of the same name stood here too. Sidi Kassem, an Andalusian, came to Tunis at the end of the 15th century and was very popular both for his piety and for bringing the Hispano-Moorish art of glazed tile-making to the city.

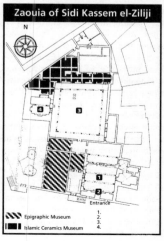

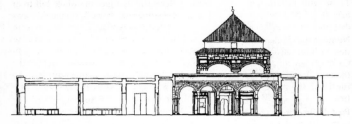

Zaouia of Sidi Kassem el-Ziliji
Looking north across the courtyard towards the museum

rioration of all the decoration. In 1976, in response to a call from UNESCO and the Tunisian Ministry of Culture to save the Medina of Tunis, the Cultural Relations Department of the Spanish Foreign Office decided to collaborate economically and technically in the restoration of the *zaouia*. Significant work was initiated which has made it possible for the monument to be restored to its earlier beauty and enchantment. As a result of this Hispano-Tunisian collaboration, the porticos in the courtyard have been reconstructed, the tiled roof of the mausoleum has been reinforced and the decorative elements have been restored. At the same time a detailed analysis of the building has been carried out in order to clarify its history and evolution.

Simultaneously in the outbuildings around the *zaouia* an **Epigraphic Museum** has been set up, as well as a **Museum of Tunisian Islamic Ceramics**. In the first of these museums numerous inscriptions, primarily funereal in origin, have been collected. Some of these come from the cemetery around the *zaouia*. In two of the rooms there is an exhibition on the evolution of the Arabic epigraph.

Around the courtyard in the **Museum of Islamic Ceramics** the whole of the development of Tunisian ceramics is displayed, demonstrating examples from modern Berber ceramics back to their precedents in the 9th century. The intention of this ceramic display is to make a worthy homage to the figure of Sidi Kassem el-Zeliji who introduced the Hispano-muslim tradition of tile making to this Tunisian land. The monument was reopened in Nov 1979 and has become once again a permanent expression of the survival of Hispano-Tunisian cultural relations.

OTHER PLACES OF INTEREST

Galerie Yahia is positioned between ONAT and the Tourist Office on Ave Mohammed V. It is a large single room exhibiting early 20th century black and white photographic enlargements of mosques and sights of Tunis. They are not annotated but some have titles. The photograph of Ave Habib Bourguiba with only one car on the road and few pedestrians shows how circumstances have changed. Well worth a visit, open 0900-1600 every day, entrance free.

Exhibition Rooms of the **Ministry of Information** are in a large white building on Ave Habib Bourguiba, to the right facing the cathedral. Although the name is only written in Arabic it is easily recognized by the large poster size photographs of Tunisian scenes in its windows. Despite the name, there is no information to be obtained and exhibitions are few and far between.

The Palais de Congress, a government building S of Kennedy Park, hosts official meetings and international events.

Those with imagination might recognize it as the 'shell shaped' building described in tourist brochures.

Numismatic Museum has an exhibition of Tunisian coins dating back to Carthaginian times. This is located in the entrance hall of the Central Bank, rue Hedi Nouira, T 254000, entrance free.

Postal Museum Here exhibitions relate to the history of the Tunisian postal system. There are many displays of old postage stamps and some very interesting collections on view. Located on the corner of rue Gamel Abdel Nasser and rue d'Angleterre, entrance free.

Military Museum, Musee de la Rose, Manouba, T 520220.

BEACHES

Tunis has no beaches itself, being separated from the sea by the Buheira or Lac de Tunis, a brackish lagoon home to cormorants and flamingoes in the winter. A causeway links to Tunis to the northern coastal suburbs and their beaches. Once the source of appalling odours in the summer, the northern half of the lagoon has been cleaned and reduced in size by the creation of polders to provide land for a vast new housing area on the airport road. The southern half of the lake continues to be polluted by industry and the port. There are beaches nearby. The coast N from La Goulette is just one long beach. The preferred beaches tend to be further along at La Marsa and Gammarth. It is easy to reach them by taking the TGM to La Marsa which is probably better but gets crowded at weekends.

PARKS

Belvédère Park is to the N of the city. To get there take the bus No 5 from Place de l'Indépendence and get off at Place Pasteur or Metro line No 2 from Place de Barcelona to Palestine station. It is then a short walk to this very large park which is pleasantly cool in summer. Park Belvédère occupies the whole hill from the summit of which are splendid views over Tunis, the most interesting being to the SE towards Korbous and Cap Bon. The park is extensive, covered with shrubs and brush intermingling with the untrimmed grass. Through this are two roads open to traffic and numerous narrow paths for pedestrians. The area is patrolled by mounted police. It takes about 30 mins to walk to the summit, so it is better to take a taxi to the top and walk down calling in at the *koubba* on the way. This is in an enclosed area with grass and trees but a call will bring the caretaker who, for a tip, will show you round. The view from the terrace towards Cap Bon is well worth the tip. The building was constructed in Turkish style by the Bey of Tunis in 1789, as a retreat from his daughter. It consists of a large room surmounted by a magnificent dome decorated with exquisitely carved plaster work. The diamond shaped spaces in the plaster decoration are filled with coloured glass, all different colours, which make different patterns as the sun shines through. Cushions cover the benches and carpets cover the floor. Off this room is an alcove, reminiscent of a small throne room. The building, inside and out, is decorated with patterned ceramic tiles.

At the foot of the hill, within the park, off Ave Taieb Mehirir is the entrance to the **Zoological garden**. By the entrance is a café. Adjacent is a small lake complete with water fowl and three fountains. There are toilets just 50m to the left after entering the zoo. This is a well established zoo, the only one we can recommend in Tunisia. Entrance TD3, children under 9 TD1, photographs TD1, open 0900-1800 (ticket office closes 1700), closed Mon. The zoo covers a large area and houses a full range of birds and animals but no aquaria or indoor displays. The information is given in Arabic and French. There is nothing to prevent anyone standing in close proximity to the cages and careful

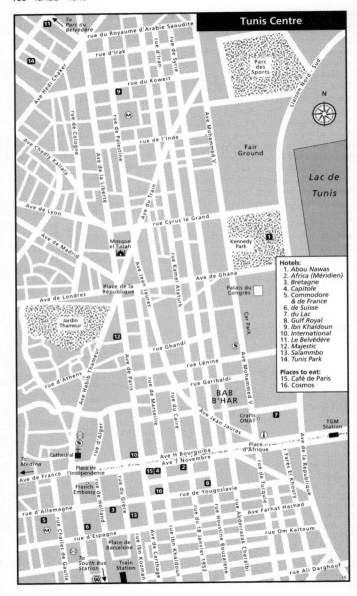

Tunis Centre

To Parc du Belvédère
rue du Royaume d'Arabie Saoudite
rue d'Irak
rue de Syrie
rue d'Iran
rue du Koweit
rue de l'Inde
Ave Hedi Chaker
rue de Cologne
rue de Palestine
Ave de la Liberté
Ave Chedly Kallala
Ave de Lyon
Ave du Train
Ave Mohammed V
Parc des Sports
Liaison Nord-Sud
Fair Ground
N
Lac de Tunis
rue Cyrus le Grand
Ave de Madrid
Mosque el Fatah
rue Kamel Ataturk
Kennedy Park
Ave de Ghana
Ave de Londres
Place de la République
Palais du Congrès
Jardin Thameur
Ave Habib Thameur
Ave Jean Jaures
Car Park
rue Ghandi
rue Lénine
rue d'Athens
Ave de Paris
rue Garibaldi
rue de Marseille
rue du Caire
BAB B'HAR
Ave Mohammed V
Ave d'Alger
Ave Jean Jaures
Crafts ONAT
TGM Station
Cathedral
To Medina
Ave de France
Place de l'Indépendance
Ave H Bourguiba
Ave 7 Novembre
Place d'Afrique
Ave de la République
French Embassy
rue du Grèce
rue de Holland
rue de Yougoslavie
Cosmos
rue de Turquie
Fares El Khoury
Ave Farhat Hached
rue d'Allemagne
Ave de Carthage
rue d'Espagne
Place de Barcelone
Charles de Gaulle
rue Ibn Kozman
To South Bus Station
Train Station
rue Ibn Khaldoun
Ave de 18 Janvier 1952
rue Houssine Bouzaiene
rue Abderrazak Cheraibi
rue Om Kaltoum
rue Ali Darghouf

Hotels:
1. *Abou Nawas*
2. *Africa (Méridien)*
3. *Bretagne*
4. *Capitole*
5. *Commodore & de France*
6. *de Suisse*
7. *du Lac*
8. *Gulf Royal*
9. *Ibn Khaldoun*
10. *International*
11. *Le Belvédère*
12. *Majestic*
13. *Salammbo*
14. *Tunis Park*

Places to eat:
15. *Café de Paris*
16. *Cosmos*

control of children is necessary at all times, for their own safety. The **Museum of Contemporary Tunisian Art**, previously in this park, by the zoo, has been closed.

Jardin Thameur, in the centre of town, is attractive, well used and consequently crowded. It provides a quiet area amidst all the bustle of the town. It has three wide parallel paths leading from the E end (Ave Habib Thameur) to a circular path round a large round water basin. Between the paths are grassed areas with flower and shrubs. Bench seats are provided every 15m or so, many of them shaded by trees.

Kennedy Park has become *Hotel Abou Nawas* and only a small strip of garden (100m x 50m) with some bench seats, a few palms and a flower bed remains adjacent to the Ave Mohammed V.

The park in **Place de Barcelone** in front of the station is not very pleasant to while away the time waiting for a train as it has no trees, just bench seats and a grass border, but to the SW of the station is Place Mongi Bali, a small square with cobbles, and flower beds around a bust of Mongi Bali on a plinth. Here there are plenty of seats, shaded by trees.

LOCAL INFORMATION

Price guide

Hotels:

AL	over US$75	**D**	US$20-40
A	US$75	**E**	US$10-20
B	US$60-75	**F**	under US$10
C	US$40-60		

Places to eat:

◆◆◆	expensive	◆◆	average
◆	cheap		

In town Around the ville nouvelle and Ave Habib Bourguiba towards the medina you will find most of the cheap hotels, the shopping streets and the post office. On Ave Habib Bourguiba are branches of most main banks and the large travel agencies and the tourist information office. To the S you will find the train station and the main bus and louages station for the S of the country.

● **Accommodation**

Few of the cheaper hotels in the centre of Tunis have any character, and some prefer to cater for Tunisians rather than foreign travellers. Consider staying in pleasanter surroundings in Sidi Bou Saïd and visiting Tunis using the TGM.

AL *Abou Nawas*, Park Kennedy, Ave Mohammed V, T 350355, F 352882, no description necessary, it has everything. This is **the** best hotel in Tunis; **AL** *Africa Méridien Hotel*, 50 Ave Habib Bourguiba, T 347477, F 347432, 170 rm, a/c, 3 restaurants, 3 bars, movie theatre, pool, hairdresser, car rental, conference facilities, automatic cash dispensers for Visa and Mastercard holders. Other 5-star hotels are **Hilton**, Ave de la Ligue Arabe, T 782800; *El Hana International*, 49 Ave Habib Bourguiba, T 331144; *Oriental Palace*, Ave Jean Jaurès, T 348846.

A *Hotel des Ambassadeurs*, rue Hedi Chaker, T 288011, rooms facing the Belvédère Park, a/c, restaurant; **A** *International Hotel*, 49 Ave Habib Bourguiba, T 254855, 228 rm, central, good restaurants; **A** *Mechtel Hotel*, T 783200, Ave Taieb Mehiri, Belvédère Park, 450 rm, pool, light sleepers should beware of taking rooms on the upper floors on the nightclub side of the hotel.

B *Hotel Gulf Royal*, Ave de la Yougoslavie, T 342422, expensive, poor value for money; **B** *Hotel Ibn Khaldoun*, rue de Palestine, by the Marché Lafayette, T 783211, good, a/c, restaurant, organized entertainment; **B** *Hotel Le Belvédère*, rues des Etats-Unis, T 783133, quiet, close to the Belvédère Park, a/c, restaurant, easily the nicest of the business hotels, willing, pleasant.

C *Hotel du Lac*, Ave Habib Bourguiba, central, T 258322, restaurant, 208 rm all a/c; **C** *Hotel Excel*, 35 Ave Habib Bourguiba, T 355088, F 341929, central position, TV, no breakfast; **C** *Hotel St. George*, 16 rue de Cologne, behind Ave de la Liberté, T 282937, 36 rm, 26 with bath, very good, clean hotel, a/c, restaurant, parking available; **C** *Hotel Tej*, 14 rue Lt. Aziz Tej, T 344899, clean, overpriced, a/c.

D *Hotel Carlton*, 31 Ave Habib Bourguiba, T 258167, clean, 40 rm with bath, a/c, slightly noisy position on main road, currently undergoing refurbishment; **D** *Hotel Dar Masmoudi*, 18 rue du Maroc, off rue d'Algerie, T 342428, very close to medina, very quiet, most rm with bath; **D** *Hotel de Suisse*, 5 rue de Suisse, T 243821, 23 rm, most with bath, clean, quiet, parking; **D** *Hotel Maison Dorée*, 6 rue de Hollande, just off Ave de la Yougoslavie behind the French Embassy, T 240632, has seen better days, good condition, spotlessly clean, good service, quite quiet, 54 rm with bath, breakfast incl, restaurant; **D** *Hotel Majestic*, Ave de Paris, T 242848, old-fashioned, 100 rm, 40 with a/c, large terrace, central, restaurant; **D** *Hotel Ritza*, 35 Ave Thameur, T 245428, close to the Thameur park, 30 rm, communal shower; **D** *Hotel Transatlantique*, 106 Ave de Yougoslavie, T 240680, relatively quiet for a central hotel, most rm with bath, breakfast incl; **D** *Tunis Park Hotel*, 7 rue de Damas off Ave Taieb Mehiri by the Belvédère Park, T 286696, 28 rm, good, very quiet, restaurant.

E *Hotel de France*, 8 rue Mustapha M'Barek, T 245876, very close to the *Hotel Commodore* and the medina, clean, 49 rm with bath, good value; **E** *Hotel Medina*, 1 Place de la Victoire, T 255056, close to Bab Bhar and the British Embassy, TD12 double rm with shower, 25 rm, clean, tidy and basic, shared toilets, the café/restaurant forms the front lower part of the hotel facing the square; **E** *Hotel Salammbo*, 6 rue de Grèce, off Ave Habib Bourguiba, T 337498, clean hotel, 52 rm, most with bath.

F *Gare Hotel*, rue de Gare, rec; **F** *Hotel Cirta*, 42 Ave Charles de Gaulle, T 241582, communal pay showers, very cheap; **F** *Hotel Commodore*, 17 rue d'Allemagne opp the central market, T 244941, clean, quiet hotel just by the entrance to the medina, 48 rm, most have bath, no breakfast, very cheap; **F** *Hotel Continental*, 5 rue de Marseille, T 259834, very quiet and cheap, communal shower; **F** *Hotel Crystal*, Ave de Carthage, quiet, clean, communal shower; **F** *Hotel de Bretagne*, 7 Ave de Grèce, T 242146, 25 rm, quite clean and quiet; **F** *Hotel de l'Agriculture*, 25 Ave Charles de Gaulle, T 246394, opp *Hotel Cirta*, very quiet situation, clean; **F** *Hotel de la Victoire*, 7 Bab el Menara, T 26, 20 rm (those on front are noisy), communal shower, clean, best of this category; **F** *Hotel Des Amis*, 7 rue Monastir, T 565653, a short walk down Souq Sidi Mahares, leading from Bab Souika, only TD6 for a double rm with no breakfast, 24 rm, shared bath and toilet, beds on iron frames, clean, basic, this and *Hotel Sfax* are in the medina, and are for the adventurous seeking authenticity – or those wanting very cheap accommodation; **F** *Hotel Rex*, 65 rue de Yougoslavie, T 257397, 29 rm, communal pay shower, rather depressing; **F** *Hotel Sfax*, 5 rue de l'Or, T 260275, a short way down Souq Sidi Mahares, leading from Bab Souika, TD5, 4 double

rm, no breakfast, 12 rm, communal toilet, no bathroom, use nearby *hammam*, iron bed frames, very basic; **F** *Nouvelle Hotel*, T 243379, 3 Place Mongi Bali, next to the station, could be cleaner, communal showers, noisy.

Youth hostels: Tunisian Youth Hostel Association, 10 rue Ali Bach Hamba, 1000 Tunis, T 353227. 1) Radès, 10 km SW of Tunis, T 483631, 120 beds, meals provided, take the train from the main station, a 10-min walk from Radès station; 2) In the medina, 25 rue Saida Ajoula, T 567850, 70 beds, 500m from Place du Gouvernement la kasbah, 1.5 km from central station; 3) *Centre d'hébergement Jelili ez Zahra*, Oued Meliane Ezzahara, BP1140, T 481547, 72 beds, kitchen, meals provided, take bus No 26A from Place Barcelone; 4) Possibility of staying in the Bardo University campus in the summer, contact T 784241, rue du Mali, Tunis.

Camping: *Le Moulin Bleu*, Hammam Plage, 20 km S of Tunis.

● **Places to eat**

NB it is better not to eat fish on Mon as the fresh fish market is closed on Sun.

◆◆◆ *Bagdad*, Ave Habib Bourguiba, very good Tunisian food, rec; *Chez Nous*, rue de Marseille, French cooking with some Tunisian specialities, alcohol; *Chez Slah*, 14 rue Pierre de Coubertin, T 258588, perhaps the best restaurant in Tunis, highly rec but the bill will be large, good idea to book; *Cosmos*, rue Ibn Khaldoun, very good food, especially the fish, service slow; *Dar el Jeld*, 5 rue Dar el Jeld in the medina, off Place du Gouvernement, T 260916, very good traditional Tunisian cooking set in an old house, a great night out with entertainment provided most evenings, closed Sun, booking rec; *Essaraya*, 6 rue Ben Mahmoud, T 560310, awarded the 3 forks de luxe grade; *L'Astragle*, 17 Ave Charles Nicolles, T 890455, awarded 3 forks de luxe grade; *L'Etable*, Ave Habib Bourguiba, nr Place de l'Afrique, Tunisian specialities, alcohol; *Le Poisson Doré*, rue Ibn Khaldoun, specializes in seafood; *La Trattoria*, 44 Ave Habib Bourguiba, beside *Africa Hotel*.

◆◆ *Cafè Zitouna*, Jamaa Zitouna in medina, Tunisian food served amid beautiful tiled decorations; *Gaston*, 73 rue de Yougoslavie; *La Mama*, rue de Marseille, mixture of French, Italian and traditional Tunisian cooking, alcohol; *Le Privé*, rue de l'Arabie Saoudite, T 891633; *Le Regent*, 16 rue de Lieutenant Aziz Tel.

◆ *Abdelaziz Elleuch*, 6 rue de Cair,

T 257701, couscous and fish; *Cafè Africa*, beside *Africa Hotel* for mint tea and an opportunity to watch the crowds; *Café de Paris*, corner of Ave Habib Bourguiba and Ave de Carthage, the only pavement café on Ave Habib Bourguiba, has an inner seating area with bar and a few tables on the pavement for surveying the scene; *Le Carcassonne*, Ave de Carthage, very clean, cheap and good; *Le Roi d'Espagne*, rue de Lénine, off rue de France, good food in a very simple setting, alcohol; *Le Prince*, Place de Barcelone, opp the train station, self-service, clean, cheap, very good typical Tunisian food; *Restaurant Novelty*, rue de Paris, self-service, very good, a warm welcome, cheap food, no alcohol, try the *coucha*; *Restaurant Zitouna*, Ave de Carthage/rue d'Espagne, Turkish food, no alcohol.

● **Banks & money changers**
American Express, c/o Carthage Tour, 59 Ave Habib Bourguiba, T 254820, open 0800-1900, Sun 0900-1200; **BIAT**, Ave Habib Bourguiba (American Express); **BT**; **STB**, Ave Habib Bourguiba, by the *Africa Hotel*, open daily 0700-1900, has automatic cash dispenser for Visa and Mastercard holders; **UBCI**, Ave Habib Bourguiba.

● **Embassies & consulates**
Algeria, 136 Ave de la Liberté, T 280082; **Canada** (and Australian affairs), 3 rue Didon, T 286577; **Egypt**, 16 rue Essayouti, T 230004; **France**, Place de l'Indépendance, T 245700; **Germany**, 18 Ave Challaye, T 281246; **Italy**, rue de Russie, T 361811 (open 0930-1130); **Ivory Coast**, 6 rue Ibn Charaf, T 283878; **Jordan**, 4 rue Didon, T 288401; **Libya**, 48 bis rue du 1 Juin, T 283936; **Morocco**, 39 rue du 1 Juin, T 288063; **Netherlands**, 6 rue Meycen, T 287455; **Norway**, 7 Ave Habib Bourguiba, T 245933; **Senegal**, 122 Ave de la Liberté, T 282393; **Sweden**, 87 Ave Taïeb Mehri, T 283433; **Switzerland**, 10 rue ech-Chenkiti, 1002 Belvédère, T 795957; **UK**, 5 Place de la Victoire, T 245100; **USA**, 144 Ave de la Liberté, T 282566.

● **Entertainment**
Art Galleries: Club Tahar Haddad, 20 rue du Tribunal, in the medina, T 561275; **Galerie Alyssa**, 3 Ave Casablanca, Bardo, T 223107; **Galerie Blel**, 70 Ave d'Afrique, El Menzah, T 231044; **Galerie des Arts**, 42 Centre Jamil, El Menzah, T 234947.

Clubs: The International World Travellers Club (CIVG) for people who have visited more than 50 countries, 26 Ave Habib Bourguiba, T 383266.

Discotheques/Nightclubs: Tunis is far from being a clubber's destination, and the main *boîtes de nuit* are situated in the upmarket northern suburbs. *La Plaza*, 22 rue du Maroc, La Marsa, T 743577, F 742554, has a clientèle eager to demonstrate its money; a drink by the pool can be pleasant in the early evening. The nicest of the banlieue nord clubs, *La Barraka*, housed in a converted barn down a track on the La Marsa/Sidi Bou Saïd road, is a long established Tunis institution; the ageing sound system does its best to keep up the required level of decibels, the club is packed in the summer. In Gammarth, *La Tour Blanche* has a club which changes its name every few years – the current appellation is *Cyklone*. The fashionable place for a pre-club drink is at the snooty *Sindbad* piano bar – right on the beach at Gammarth, just along from the *Cyklone* and next to the restaurant *Les Ombrelles*. Of the hotels on the Raoued strip, the best clubs are *Le Queen* at the *Hotel Karim* and Tunis' largest club, *Maxximum*.

Really keen clubbers, however, will head for Hammamet (*Manhattan* or the *Ranch Club*) or *La Maracana* in Sousse, just 2 hrs down the motorway. In Tunis-Capital itself, the *Hotel Mechtel* has a nightclub on the top floor, and occasional jazz evenings in the winter at *El Teatro*, a mini-theatre housed in the same complex.

Hammams: Turkish baths, are an institution in Tunisia. Everybody goes there once a week. It is a revitalizing experience and well worth a visit. The morning is reserved for men and the afternoon (until 1800 after which the men can return) for women. Rue du Maroc, next to *Hotel Dar Masmoudi*, rue de Marseille, level with No 42, just off Ave Habib Bourguiba. There are also many older ones in the medina (see map 92) and a few on rue du Pasha.

Music: Ennejma Ezzahra Palace was the palace of Baron d'Erlanger constructed between 1912 and 1922 on the hill in Sidi Bou Saïd. He was a painter and a musician. It is now the **Centre for Arab and Mediterranean Music**, open summer 0900-1200 and 1600-1900, winter 0900-1200 and 1400-1700. Here is housed the most complete collection of Tunisian musical instruments. **International Festival of Carthage** held Jul and Aug in the reconstructed amphitheatre, entertainment by world famous stars.

The Hammam

Despite all the changes of recent years, the Tunisian way of life is standing up well to the onslaught of consumer culture. People know how to take their time, meals in the home are superb, and the traditional *hammam* or Turkish bath is still popular.

A ritual purification of the body is essential before Muslims can perform prayers, and in the days before bathrooms, the 'major ablutions' were generally done at the *hammam*. Segregation of the sexes is of course the rule at the *hammam*: some establishments are open only for women, others only for men, while others have a shift system (mornings and evenings for the men, all afternoon for women). In the old days, the *hammam*, along with the local *zaouia* or saint's shrine, was an important place for women to gather and socialize, and even pick out a potential wife for a son.

A visit will cost between TD2 to TD6, depending on whether you have a massage and how generously you tip. In the older parts of the cities, the *hammam* is easily recognisable by the characteristic colours of its door: red and green picked out in white. A passage leads into a large changing room cum post-bath rest area, equipped with masonry benches for lounging on and (sometimes) small wooden lockers. Here you undress under a towel. The traditional striped foutas or cotton towels which used to be worn in the *hammam* were banned in 1994 in the capital "for reasons of hygiene", so *hammam* gear today is football or beach shorts for men and knickers for women. If you're going to have a massage/scrub down, you take a jeton at the cash desk, where shampoo can also be bought.

Next step is to proceed to the hot room. 5-10 mins with your feet in a bucket of hot water will see you sweating nicely, and you can then move back to the raised area where the masseurs are at work. After the expert removal of large quantities of dead skin, you go into one of the small cabins or *mathara* to finish washing. (Before doing this, catch the person bringing in dry towels, so that they can bring yours to you when you're in the *mathara*.) For women, in addition to a scrub and a wash, there may be the pleasures of an epilation with *sokar*, an interesting mix of caramelized sugar and lemon. Men can undergo a *taksira*, which although it involves much pulling and stretching of the limbs, ultimately leaves you feeling pretty good. And remember, allow plenty of time to cool down reclining in the changing area before you dress and leave the *hammam*.

Theatre: Municipal Theatre, Ave Habib Bourguiba, T 860888.

● **Hospitals & medical services**
Chemists: all night, 43 Ave Habib Bourguiba, opp *Africa Hotel*; 20 Ave de la Liberté, by Ave de Madrid; 44 Ave Bab Djedid.
Hospitals: *Hôpital Principal Aziza Othmana*, Place du Gouvernement, T 633655; *Hôpital Ariana*, T 713266; *Hôpital Charles Nicolle*, T 663000; *Hôpital Habib Thameur*, T 491600; *Hôpital Rabta*, T 662276; *Institute Pasteur*, T 680539; *SOS Ambulance*, T 341250; *SOS Médecins*, T 341250.

● **Places of worship**
Catholic: Cathedral on Ave Habib Bourguiba, T 247290, services in French Sat 1830 and Sun 1100 and in Italian Sun at 0900; also St Jeanne d'Arc, 1 rue de Jerusalem, T 287213, Sat 1830 and Sun 1000; Foyer Familial, rue du Parc, Radès, T 245444, Sun at 1000; 1 rue des Vergers, 2000 Le Bardo, Khaznadar, T 514850, Sun at 0900.

● **Post & telecommuncations**
Area code: 01.

Key words for a visit to the hammam

bayt es-skhoun – the hot room
doukana – raised platform covered in mats for relaxing on after washing
harza – masseuse
fouta – traditional striped *hammam* towel
kessa – rough hair glove
kobkab – wooden clogs worn in the *hammam*
maksoura – smaller, more comfortable changing area off the main room
souak – natural woody toothpaste sticks
tassa – formerly copper bowl for ladling water over the body. Today likely to be a large tomato paste can
tayyeb – masseur
tfel – perfumed clay base shampoo (women only)

Recommended hammams Tunisians have their favourite local *hammams*, so the following list is just by way of an indication.

In Tunis

Hammam Sahib et-Tabi'a – constructed in the early 19th century by the then Lord of the Seal as part of a complex including the neighbouring mosque, Souq and zaouia. Easily the most spectacular – the *hammam* scenes in Férid Boughedir's 'coming of age in Tunis' movie *Halfaouine* were filmed there. Situated 5 mins' walk from Bab Souika in the Médina. Men mornings and evenings, women in the afternoon.
Hammam Kachachine – central Médina, rue des Libraires, 2 mins from the Great Mosque. Men only, closes early around 1500.
Hammam Sidi Bel Ghith – close to Bab Jedid. Vaguely Art Deco. Men only. Stays open late.
For women only, there are good *hammams* on the rue des Femmes, just off Blvd Bab Menara and in the central Médina at rue de la Noria, close to the place du Tribunal and Dar Lasram.

In Sidi Bou Saïd

Hammam Sidi Bou Saïd – in the street opposite the Magasin Général, lower village. Modern – glorified bathroom.

In Kairouan

Hammam Sabra – next to the hotel of the same name, close to the tourist office by Bab Ech-Chouhada. Immaculately clean. Men only, closes around 1600.

Post Office: main PTT rue Charles de Gaulle, open Mon-Thur 0730-1230 and 1700-1900, Fri-Sat 0730-1330, Sun 0900-1100. A 24-hour telephone centre is off rue Gamal Abdul Nasser.

● **Shopping**

Bookshops: there are many bookshops in rue de France, but most books are in Arabic or French. The only English books can be found in the *Africa Hotel* and they are generally not very good. If you read Arabic or French go to Librairie Clairefontaine, 4 rue d'Alger. There is also an interesting book shop, Librarie Alif, which often puts on small exhibitions at 3 rue de Hollande (behind the French Embassy).

Hairdressers: women seeking an unstructured natural look as per Toni and Guy may have a little trouble finding a suitable hairdresser. Tunisian women like perms, blonde streaks and big hair. The following addresses may be of use: *Coiffeur pour hommes*, rue Gamal Abdel Nasser, nr telephone office; *Chantal* at Carthage (T 275676), in the Touta supermarket complex, is chic; *Donna* in La Souqra is the leading beauticians; *Sofiène*, 22 rue des Narcisses, Menzah V, T 766362, is a reliable address in the residential part of town. In Sidi Bou Saïd, *Enzo Martelli*, T 747973 and *Crystal*, T 741862, have a good name. For men, a short back and sides and a shave is available almost everywhere. *Am Ali* on the Blvd Bab Menara will do a good military cut.

Handicrafts: Tunisian craftsmanship can be excellent and it is possible (after a bit of bargaining) to get a very good deal. Leather goods and brass objects are plentiful and of very good quality. The best place to go, at least to find out the official prices and have an overall idea of crafts produced, is the *Office National de l'Artisanat (ONAT)* on Ave Mohammed V, just beyond the Tourist Office, off Place de l'Afrique has a showroom of local crafts and arts from around Tunisia. It is interesting to go there before leaving Tunis, as you will see the local diversities and specialities. It is also worth seeing the prices before entering the souqs. They also have a list of the official prices for carpets according to the quality. You will find many of these, among lots of less interesting goods, in the medina in rue Jemaa Zitouna. Be selective.

By the Great Mosque, the *Souq Del Attarine* specializes in perfumes and precious stones. Amber is generally well worked but watch out for plastic imitations (amber resists the heat of a match). **Jewellery** can be found in the *Souq des Orfèvres*, and *Souq el-Berka*. For **carpets**

Perfume

🦶 The art of distilling perfume essences has all but disappeared (Announ has a small distillation unit off Souq en-Nahhas) and many of the essences on sale today are imported. Unromantically, they come in metal cans (stamped and sealed). The advantage is that the salesmen in Souq el-Attarine can make up your favourite *eau de toilette* to the strength you require and at half the price. Maher in Souq el-Attarine (opposite the steps leading up to the 15th century ablutions building Midhat es-Soltane) does a fine imitation Kenzo for Men. More traditionally, various flower waters are on sale very cheaply (orange flower or geranium), and are excellent for perfuming fruit salads and Turkish coffee.

---

and blankets go to *Souq el Leffa*, but carpets are generally cheaper in Kairouan. If you get a carpet be sure you have the receipt and that there is a quality stamp on the back. For **leather**, go to the *Souq el-Sekkajine*, but be warned that the quality is sometimes mediocre.

Many of the market stalls which scattered the streets selling 'necessities' like toothpaste, fly-spray and ladies' stockings and most of the cheap eating stalls have been moved away to rue Moncef Bey, visited by buses Nos 2 and 100.

If you are not looking for souvenirs, the best place to go is Ave Charles de Gaulle in the new city where you will find supermarkets (*Monoprix*), chemists, and camera shops. There are many smart shops and boutiques in Tunis, especially in the area of Ave Habib Bourguiba, Ave Habib Thameur and Ave de France. (Don't miss the two Italian style galleries which are paved with geometric patterned mosaics though the crush of people prevents a good view.) Rue al Jazira to the E of the medina is more interesting and more useful, having small shops patronized by the locals, hardware, electrical goods, jewellers, food shops.

As a development from the souq, there is now a new shopping experience, new in Tunisia, the Lac Palace Shopping Mall. This is on the edge of the Marsa highway and is the focal point of the new suburb, Tunis El Buhaira. There is a large car park. Inside, in the air conditioned central square and two storeys of shops the elevators hum, metal birds 'fly' and the retailers wait for the consumers. Surely one does not come to Tunis for this.

● Sports

Diving: contact the Fédération des activités subaquatiques de Tunisie, Piscine olympique d'El Menzah, BP 486, 1082 Cité El Mahrajène, T 234041, they have a small office which can provide information on diving events – most notably, underwater photography competitions are held in Tabarka, where most diving activity takes place. Tunisian kids, equipped with goggles, spend many happy hours fishing for sea-urchins (poor man's oysters) on the rockier sections of coastline.

Gliding and Flying: the *Gliding Club* at Djebel Rassas S of Tunis was closed a few years ago after a particularly appalling accident. However, like the numerous birds of prey using the currents eddying round this strange mountain, hang-gliders continue to fly at weekends. There are instructors and equipment for those

Mosaic of a game bird on terrace of a Roman Villa in Carthage

interested in how to learn or to practise this sport, T 255762.

Golf: there is an 18 hole course at La Souqra (close to the airport), T 765919, F 765915, 4,432m, par 66.

Gymnastics and Martial Arts: Institute of Culture Physique et d'Arts Martiaux – opposite the girls' school at 14 rue de Russie leading left off Place de Barcelone, T 241801, open 0800-1200 and 1500-2100, closed Sun.

Riding: at Club Hippique de la Soukra, 15 km N of Tunis, T 203054 and Ksar Saïd, 10 km from Tunis. Race meetings every Sun at Ksar Saïd, T 223252.

Shooting: (pigeons and game birds) in Forest of Radès S of Tunis.

Swimming pools: at El Menza (Cité Olympique) and the piscine municipale in Belvédère Park, by Place Pasteur. You can also try the large 4-star hotels, *Hotel Africa* has a pool on the 3rd flr.

Tennis: in the Belvédère Park and Park des Sports, Ave Mohammed V. Tunis 'Open' in Mar.

Yachting: *Club of Goulette*, Port of Sidi Bou Said, Chief Mariner, T 741645, F 744217.

● **Tour companies & travel agents**
Abou Nawas Travel, 8 rue Ibn Jazzar, 1002 Tunis, T 781351, F 782113; *Ariana Voyages*, 80 Ave Habib Bourguiba, 2080 Ariana, T 71516; *Atlas Voyages*, 6 rue Saha Ibn Ab-bah, T 286299; *Carthage Tours*, 59 Ave Habib Bourguiba, T 347015, F 352740; *Cyrine Tours*, 3 rue Abou Dhabi, T 338063, F 243670; *Forum Travel*, 3 rue Houcine Bouzaine,

T 225193; *Key Tours*, 15 rue d'Angleterre, T 351122; *Loisitours*, 6 rue Tatouan, T 783653, F 788868; *La Maison du Voyage*, Ave Gamal Abdul Nasser, beside the Post Office; *Sedec* Tour, rue de Marseille; *Tourafrica*, Ave Habib Bourguiba, next to *Africa Hotel*; *Tunisian Travel Service*, 19 Ave Habib Bourguiba, T 348100 and 28 rue Hassan Ibn Noamene, 1002 Tunis, T 785855, F 780682; *Ulysse Tours*, 31 Ave de Paris, T 344727 and 20 rue 18 Janvier, T 255082; *Voyages 2000*, 2 Ave de France, T 248554.

● **Tourist offices**
The tourist information offices are: **Tunisian National Tourist Office**, 1 Ave Mohammed V (Place de l'Afrique), T 341077, F 350997, open 0730-1330 in summer, 0830-1200 and 1500-1800 in winter, closed Sun and public holidays; **ONTT**, branches at train station and airport, also at 51 Ave de la Liberté; **Regional Tourist Office for Tunis**, 29 rue Hatem Ettai (corner of rue de la Palestine), T 289403/288720, Tx 15347.

● **Useful addresses**
Ambulance: T 3412350, T 491286.

Car park: by *Hotel Abou Nawas*. This is a convenient and safe place to park having a barrier and a gate keeper. Convenient for the metro, a short taxi ride or a 10-min walk to Place de la République. Open every day, charges 0600-1300 TD0.35; 1300-2100 TD0.35; 2000-0600 TD2.

Doctor: T 341250, T 346767, T 780000.

Fire station and **Police**: T 197.

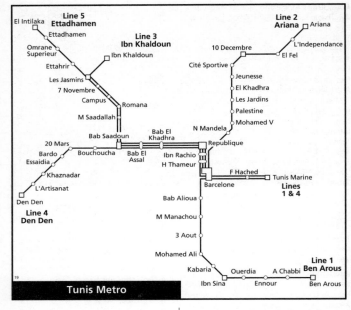

Tunis Metro

Line 5 Ettadhamen — El Intilaka, Ettadhamen, Omrane Superieur, Ettahrir, Les Jasmins, 7 Novembre, Campus

Line 3 Ibn Khaldoun — Ibn Khaldoun, Romana

Line 2 Ariana — Ariana, L'Independance, El Fel, 10 Decembre, Cité Sportive, Jeunesse, El Khadhra, Les Jardins, Palestine, Mohamed V, N Mandela

M Saadallah, Bab Saadoun, Bab El Khadhra, Republique, F Hached, Tunis Marine

Lines 1 & 4

20 Mars, Bardo, Essaidia, Bouchoucha, Bab El Assal, Ibn Rachio, H Thameur, Barcelone, Khaznadar, L'Artisanat, Den Den

Line 4 Den Den

Bab Alioua, M Manachou, 3 Aout, Mohamed Ali

Line 1 Ben Arous — Kabaria, Ibn Sina, Ouerdia, Ennour, A Chabbi, Ben Arous

● Transport

Local Bus: you will probably not need to use more than a few routes during your stay in Tunis. For more information go to the bus station in front of the train station on Place de Barcelone. Bus No 3 leaves from Ave Habib Bourguiba in front of Tunis Air, or from Ave de Paris in front of the *Hotel Majestic* and goes to the Bardo Museum and S bus station. Bus No 5 leaves from Place de l'Indépendance and goes to Place Pasteur by Belvédère Park. Bus No 35 leaves from Ave Habib Bourguiba for a 30 mins ride to the airport. **Car hire**: many firms have an agent at airport. **Avis**, Ave Habib Bourguiba, in the *Africa Hotel* lobby, Ave Habib Bourguiba, T 341249; **Ben Jemaa**, Excelsior Garage, 53 Ave de Paris, T 240060; **Budget**, 14 Ave de Carthage, T 256806; **Carthage Tours**, 59 Ave Habib Bourguiba, T 254605; **Chartago Rent**, 3 Ave Habib Bourguiba, T 349168; **Europacar**, 17 Ave Habib Bourguiba, T 340303; **Garage selection**, 65 Ave Hedi Chaker, T 284698; **Hertz**, 29 Ave Habib Bourguiba, T 248559; **Topcar**, 23 Ave Habib Bourguiba, T 344121; **National Automobile Club of Tunisia (NACT)**, 29 Ave Habib Bourguiba, T 349837; **SOS Car recovery**, 6 rue Ahmed Amine, T 891000. **Metro**: there is a brand new tramway system in Tunis which is rapidly expanding. At present there are five lines but many more are under construction. The tramway is the city's answer to severe congestion and has so far been successful. The central tram station is at the train station and another large station is on Place de la République. There is a ticket kiosk at each stop. Simply buy a ticket to the desired destination and board the next tram. Where more than one line is served by the same stop be sure to be in front of the correct ticket kiosk. The place names are clearly marked at each stop. **Taxis**: are quite cheap but may be difficult to find, particularly at rush hour. The maximum you should have to pay is about TD4-5 and that is for a long trip to La Marsa. All taxis have meters and use them, so make sure they have switched it on. The best place to find a taxi is in front of the main train station. Most taxis are painted yellow, but this is a recent decision and some older taxis are different colours. **Allo Taxi**, T 282211; **Telephone Taxi**, T 492422. Lovage station is at Place Moncef Bey.

Air To get to the airport either take a taxi or bus No 35 from Ave Habib Bourguiba, opp *Africa*

Hotel, 30 min. **Airline information** Aeroflot, 24 Ave Thameur, T 340845; Air Algérie, 28 Ave de Paris, T 341590; Air France, 1 rue d'Athènes, T 341577; GB Air, 17 Ave Habib Bourguiba, T 244261; Egypt Air, 49 Ave Habib Bourguiba, T 341182 in the *International Hotel*; KLM, 50 rue Lucy Faure, T 341309; Lufthansa, Ave Ouled Haffouz, close to the Belvédère Park, in the *Mechtel Hotel*; Royal Air Maroc, 45 Ave Habib Bourguiba T 249016, in the Le Colisée building, B stairs, 3rd flr; Tunis Air, 48 Ave Habib Bourguiba, T 259189, central office 133 Ave de la Liberté, T 288100. **Internal flights**: (Airport T 235000, 236000) by Tunisair to **Djerba** daily at 0800, 1200, 1430, 1530, 1900, 2200 (1 hr), costs US$50; **Sfax**, Wed, Thur 0700, Tues, Wed, Thur, Fri 1800, Mon and Sun 2000; **Tozeur**, Mon, Fri, Sat, Sun 2100; **Tabarka**, Fri, Sun 1310. Tunis Air subsidiary Tunisavia have introduced more flights using small 72 seater planes. In summer it is important to book well in advance as places are hard to come by. Typical flight prices – return:

Tunis-Sfax TD75.6 – daily; Tunis-Djerba TD90.6 daily; Tunis-Tozeur TD86 – daily except Tues and Wed.

International flights T 754000/755000, winter schedule (there are additional flights in summer): **Abu Dhabi**, Wed 2200; **Algiers**, at least 2 daily between 0840-1700; **Amman**, Wed 0825; **Amsterdam**, Tues, Sat 0825, Wed, Sun 1435; **Athens**, Tues, Thur 0855; **Barcelona**, Mon, Tues, Thur, Fri, Sun at 1330 and 1610; **Berlin**, Fri 0800; **Beyrouth**, Fri 1300; **Bordeaux**, Fri 1125; **Brussels**, Mon, Thur, Sat 0835; **Cairo**, Mon 1455, Wed 2200; **Casablanca**, Thur, Sat 0725, Tues, Fri, Sun 0830, Mon, Wed 1410, Thur 1555, Sat 1855; **Copenhagen**, Tues 0825; **Dusseldorf**, Fri 0845; **Frankfurt**, daily at 1345, Wed, Thur, Fri 0930; **Geneva**, daily at 0910 or 1550; **Istanbul**, Tues 0910, Thur 1515; **Jeddah**, Mon, Tues, Wed 1500; **Lille**, Fri 1345; **Lisbon**, Thur 1435; **London**, daily at 1200; **Lyon**, daily; **Madrid**, Mon, Fri 1530, Tues, Thur, Sun 1330; **Malta**, Thur 1230, Sun 1710; **Marseille**, daily; **Milan**, Mon 0915; **Munich**, Fri 0835; **Nice**, daily not Wed; **Paris**, daily 1400, 1805, Mon-Fri 0800 and 1105; **Rome**, daily 0830 and 1600; **Strasbourg**, Fri 1440; **Vienna**, Thur 0830, Sun 1445; **Zurich**, Thur, Sat 0910, Sun 1425.

Train TGM: the TGM (Tunis-La Goulette-La Marsa) is the train linking Tunis to the coastal resorts and suburbs. The station is at the end of Ave Habib Bourguiba, T 244696, beyond Place de l'Afrique. It is open 24 hrs a day with trains

TUNIS

LE BAC

LA GOULETTE

GOULETTE NEUVE

GOULETTE CASINO

KHEREDDINE

AEROPORT

LE KRAM

CARTHAGE SALAMMBO

CARTHAGE BYRSA

CARTHAGE DERMECH

CARTHAGE HANNIBAL

CARTHAGE PRÉSIDENCE

CARTHAGE AMILCAR

SIDI BOU SAÏD

SIDI DHRIF

LA CORNICHE

LA MARSA

TUNIS TGM LINE

every 10-15 mins during the day and every hour at night. The service goes to La Goulette, Carthage, Sidi Bou Said and La Marsa. The main train station is in the centre of the new city on Place de Barcelone. Information: SNCFT, Ave Farhat Hached, T 244440/252225. **National departures: Bizerte** 0550, 1130, 1600, 1830; **Bir Bou Rekba** and **Sousse** 0710 (on to El Djem, Sfax, Mahares and Gabès); 0900, 1840 (on to Monastir) 1205, 1535 (on to Monastir and Mahdia); 1305, 1410, 1730 (on to El Djem and Sfax); 2120 (on to El Djem, Sfax, Gabès, Gafsa and Metlaoui); Nabeul 1420, 1805 to Hammamet and Nabeul. To **Algeria**: only one train goes on to Algiers, all the others stop at the border. **Algiers** 1255; **Ghardimaou** (border) 0635, 1200, 1425, 1620, 1750. All trains go via Béja and Djendouba (except the 1425). Sample fare: Tunis to Sfax 2nd class TD8, bicycle TD6.5; to Sousse TD5, to Gabès TD12, to Metlaoui TD12, to Gafsa TD11.

Road Bus: there are two bus stations in Tunis. The N bus station is situated at Bab Saadoun. To get there take the bus No 3 from Ave Habib Bourguiba by *Hotel Africa Méridien*. Get off just after Bab Saadoun, the bus station is on the right. Buses from here go to the N coast. For information about buses to the N, T 562299/562532. Departures from here to Bizerte; Raf Raf and Ras el Djebel; Medjez el Bab and Béja, change here for Aïn Draham, Jenbouba and Tabarka; Mateur and Tabarka; Medjez el Bab, Teboursouq and Le Kef, change here for Thala. The S bus station is at Bab El Fellah and has buses to all other places including Algeria and Libya. To reach the station walk from the main train station, a distance of 800m. Take the rue de La Gare on the right of the station, at the end of the street the station is on the other side of the road. For information about buses to the S, T 495255/490440. Departures from here to Hammamet and Nabeul; to Kairouan via Enfida or El Fahs and on to Gafsa (change here for Tozeur and Nefta) or Kasserine; Sousse (change here for El Djem), Sfax and Gabès, change for Tataouine, Medenine, Ben Gardane, Zarzis and Matmata. **Buses to Algeria, Libya and Morocco: Algeria** (Annaba) daily at 0700; **Libya** (Tripoli) Mon, Wed, Fri and Sun at 1700 cost TD25 plus TD2/piece of luggage, takes 8-10 hrs; **Morocco** (Casablanca) Sat at 0630. **NB** During the summer it can be difficult to get a seat on a bus. You may have to put up a bit of a fight at the ticket office. The best thing is to book. This service is available for most lines, but it is best to check. **Louages**: are large taxis that take five people and go from one city to another. The city names shown do not necessarily indicate where the car is going, but only where it is licensed. The louage stations are sited next to bus stations, at the front of the N station and to the left of the S station. If going S during the summer you will find that most louages go in the evening or at night, as it is cooler.

Sea Ferry: T 255239 for information, see page 343, Compagnie Tunisienne de Navigation, 5 Ave Dag Hammarskjoeld, T 242999.

Brik

This is a very popular dish – either sweet or savoury – and requires *malsouqua* dough and a *malsouqua* tray as the first two steps.
Malsouqua dough is made from semolina (durum wheat) flour, water and salt. Leave it to stand for an hour then knead well, adding lukewarm water to make a really soft paste. A *malsouqua* tray is silver plate on copper and is warmed face-down over the fire.
To produce a sheet of *malsouqua* allow a little of the dough to run over the warm tray covering the surface. As the film of dough dries carefully remove the sheet and place it on a damp cloth. A little practice is required here. Repeat the process heating the tray each time, until all the paste is used and covering the sheets with a damp cloth so they do not become brittle. Prepare the filling such as Tuna fish with parsley and onion, minced lamb with cheese or chicken/pigeon with nuts.
Place a square sheet of *malsouqua* on a dish and place a spoonful of filling in the centre and over this break and egg. Fold the square into a triangle and nip the edges to keep the filling in place. Fry in hot oil until golden brown and serve with a slice of lemon. 250g of semolina flour make about 15 *malsouqua* sheets.

The area to the NE of Tunis encompasses the important historical sites, the most expensive suburbs and the nearest beaches. The northern suburbs of Tunis extend for over 20 km along the coast, a succession of small settlements described as 'pearls on a necklace'. La Goulette is the first port of Tunis, very popular and very lively at night in the many restaurants along the bay. Carthage is considered a 'smart' suburb and is famous for its Phoenician and Roman remains. Sidi Bou Saïd is the well known blue and white 'bird cage' village perched on the cliff top. La Marsa is quiet and has a beautiful beach while Gammarth is the area of modern hotels patronized by the Tunisians as well as international guests. Take the dual carriageway W from Place de l'Afrique.

LA GOULETTE

ACCESS from Tunis is very easy by the TGM or the road that runs alongside it on the causeway, a very interesting ride. There is a very practical, free ferry service between La Goulette and Radès which enables travellers going S to bypass Tunis. The service runs 24 hrs a day. The harbour has berths for 60 yachts, min-max draft, 3-6m.

La Goulette (The Gullet) is at the narrow entrance to the Lake of Tunis and is the main port of Tunisia. Ferries leave here for Europe. It is dominated by a fortress built by Charles V of Spain in 1535, when he assisted the Hafsids fight against Barbarossa. It functions as a harbour, an important naval base, a dormitory for Tunis and also as a highly industrialized area. Nevertheless in summer it is a very

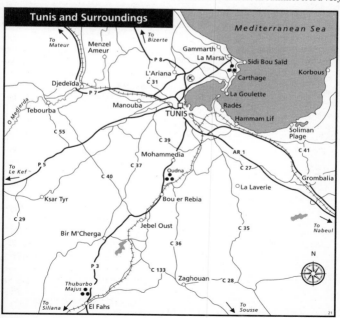

pleasant place to go for a meal of fresh fish or just to stroll. The main street, with restaurants and bars everywhere, comes to life in the evening. The fishermen in the small boats here in the Lac de Tùnis (El Bahira) are not fishing for fish but dredging for shell fish. These are sent to Korbous where they are suspended in sacks in the clean sea water there until the grime of their original surroundings has been washed from their systems. Each case sold from Korbous has a government controlled certificate.

Part of Lac de Tùnis has been filled in and the land reclaimed, with the help of a Dutch company, to form a new development site called La Lagune de Tunis or The New Medina. This is envisaged as a luxury town with shops, housing and an amusement park for 100,000 inhabitants.

From the **Fortress of Karraka** enjoy a splendid view over the harbour and the Gulf of Tùnis. The fortress was a prison and has a gruesome history. Entrance TD1, photography TD3.

Lunch is ready

👣 Along the roadside in the small settlements the time for lunch is signalled by the smoke of small charcoal grills. The owner wafts the fuel with a small straw plaited flag to increase the temperature. Adjacent to the grill are one or two chairs and a table set with bottles of soft drink. And what is for lunch? A recently removed sheepskin hangs on a pole to advertise the freshness of the meat. Nearby hangs the carcase, perhaps covered from the flies and the dust by a plastic bag or cloth. The customer chooses the pieces of meat and watches while they are grilled. How could a meal be better organized, the choice of meat and supervision of its cooking. Nearby, tethered to a tree or stump, are one or two sheep calmly grazing. Do they realize they are next on the menu?

La Goulette now has the equestrian statue of former President Habib Bourguiba which originally stood in Place d'Afrique in Tunis.

- **Places to eat** The best grilled fish restaurants are situated by the port. Recommended are ♦♦*Canal 11*, T 736251; *Le Chalet*, T 731145; *Le Café Vert*, T 736156. ♦*La Petite Etoile*, T 736205; *Les Boulevards*, T 735674; *L'Avenir*, T 730103; *Monte Carlo*, T 735338 and *Venus*, T 736717. We have given the telephone numbers but booking is not necessary. If one is full just go to the next.

- **Places of worship Catholic**: Station TGM, Sidi Dhrif, T 740854, services Sat at 1930 and Sun at 1000. Also 1 rue Scipion, T 734228, service in French Sat 1700, English Sun 0930.

- **Sports** Yachting Club de la Goulette, T 276017.

- **Tour companies & travel agents** *Asfar el Hana*, 64 Ave Habib Bourguiba, T 736761.

- **Useful numbers** Port de la Goulette, T 735300; Port de Radès, T 449300.

CARTHAGE

ACCESS From Tùnis drive along the causeway and through La Goulette or take the TGM from the end of Ave Habib Bourguiba. The stations are strategically situated for visiting the sites or, as an alternative, *calèches* are available at Carthage Hannibal station. Taxi from airport costs TD6.

Carthage is now one of the smart suburbs of Tùnis, well placed close to the sea. The remains of the old city of Carthage can be visited at various locations in the area, but there is little left of the grandeur. Nevertheless, the old Roman and Punic ruins are well worth seeing, to give an idea of past splendours.

History

According to Virgil, Carthage was founded in 814 BC by the **Princess Dido** (Didon), who came there as a refugee after her husband had been killed by her brother, Pygmalion. According to Greek legends, she fled from Tyre in the eastern Mediterranean to North Africa where she

Scipio – the Conqueror of Hannibal

🐌 Carthage was forever a thorn in the side of the Romans. So much so that Cato in the Roman Senate ceaselessly called for the defeat of Carthage, *'delenda est Carthago'*, even after the expulsion of the Carthaginians from Sicily in 241 BC. During a second war, 218-201 BC, Hannibal and his elephants invaded Italy and was undefeated though never able to take Rome itself.

Hannibal was finally defeated by the General Publius Scipio (218-183 BC), a high born Roman. Scipio's father died in battle in Spain fighting the Carthaginians after which Scipio offered himself as a military leader in Spain when others declined the task. His tactics were well thought out and in 209 BC he attacked New Carthage, the Carthaginian headquarters in Spain by sea and land at a time when the major Carthaginian armies were in central Spain and Italy. He went on to win two more major victories at Cadiz and Seville, thereby ending Carthaginian control in Spain.

The main Carthaginian forces were still at large, however, and Scipio returned to Italy, assembled an army and attacked in Sicily and then in North Africa itself. He won a victory at Utica (see page 175) in 204 BC and took Tunis in 202 BC. His most difficult battle was at Zama close to Carthage where he faced Hannibal himself but won a famous victory, ending the Second Punic War. He became known from that date as Scipio Africanus.

He later fell foul of politics in Rome and withdrew to live out his few remaining years farming in a country district. He stayed nonetheless a commanding individual of culture, an innovator of military tactics and a man who inspired great loyalty among his troops. He was also the only Roman to defeat Hannibal in open battle and he thereby ended the Carthaginian threat to the safety of the Roman Republic and its then growing Empire.

---

bought land from a local Berber chief. The story of her purchase is that Dido agreed to acquire land no more than could be covered by an ox hide. Cleverly, she cut the hide into narrow strips and so surrounded a much larger area than had originally been provided. It was enough to build a new city – **Kart Hadascht**, meaning New Capital.

Other largely apocryphal tales tell of Dido's courtship with Aeneas, the Trojan warrior, an affair celebrated in Purcell's 17th century opera *Dido and Aeneas*, based on Book Four of Virgil's classic the *Aeneid*. Dido reputedly died of a broken heart when Aeneas resumed his wanderings. In fact the two were not living at the same period – but why spoil a good yarn ?

Another suitor of Queen Dido was a local king, Iarbas, who wanted to marry her. Dido, determined, it is said, to remain faithful to the memory of her late husband, committed suicide on a funeral pyre to escape the attentions of Iarbas. Quite how this sense of loyalty squares with the story of Dido and Aeneas is difficult to see!

Certainly, the foundation of Carthage was an enormous success. It soon became a major power and trade centre, with as many as 500,000 residents, making it the third largest city in the Empire after Rome and Alexandria. It attempted to rival both the Greeks and the Romans by setting its sights, unsuccessfully, on Sicily. Everybody knows the extraordinary story of **Hannibal** (see box, page 120), who crossed the Alps with 40,000 men and 38 elephants to attack Rome. Unfortunately, the Romans eventually took revenge and Scipio's armies won a decisive battle in Zama in 202 BC. Carthage was subjected to a siege lasting

Hannibal: jumbos in the passes and carnage by Carthage

Hannibal, unfortunately recalled by many only as the man who crossed the Alps with a herd of elephants, deserves far greater acclaim.

He was one of the greatest army commanders of ancient times, recognized for his innovative military strategies and his charismatic leadership.

He was born in Carthage in 247 BC, the son of the military leader Hamilcar Barca. He spent much of his early life in regions of Spain controlled by Carthage, fighting wayward Spanish tribes and consolidating Carthaginian power. He made such an impression that at the age of 26 he was promoted to Commander-in-Chief of the Carthaginian army. His expansionist policies upset the Romans and led to the Second Punic War with Hannibal commanding the Carthaginian side. In a bold manoeuvre he advanced on Roman Italy, crossing the Pyrenées, the Rhône in France and the Alps. He started this incredible military exercise leaving Spain with some 40,000 troops, numerous horses and 38 elephants to use as battering rams. He lost men by desertion, guerrilla warfare by the Gauls and natural causes, but gained supporters on the way. His arrival in

the Po Basin, most probably via the Mt Cenis Pass, with 20,000 infantry, 6,000 cavalry and a handful of elephants showed conclusively Hannibal's considerable ability to organize and command. It was surely a glorious feat.

The first encounter between Hannibal's troops and Scipio's Roman forces sent N to meet them, was on the plains W of the Ticino River. Here Hannibal's numerically inadequate cavalry gained the upper hand. Their second meeting, known as the Battle of Trebia river, also went in Hannibal's favour. The Battle of

Elephant from mosaic at Oudna

3 years and was eventually seized and razed to the ground in 146 BC to the delight of Cato who had had this in mind for some time.

However this was not to be the end of Carthage as the Romans, under Caesar Augustus in 44 BC, returned to make it the capital of the Roman Province of Afrique, the cultural and intellectual centre. At this time Carthage was known as Rome's bread basket due to its highly fertile hinterland. It later collapsed as a significant power after the successive invasions of the Vandals, Byzantines and Arabs. After the Arab invasion, Carthage was mainly used as a source of building material for Islamic monuments and the

expanding city of Tunis (see History, page 28).

A quick history of Carthage:

814BC – founded by Princess Dido

260BC – beginning of the 3 Punic wars between Carthage and Rome

146BC – destroyed after a 3 year siege by the Romans

122BC – Gracchus attempted to refound Carthage

44BC – refounded as Colonia Julia by Caesar Augustus

14AD – increased in prosperity

439AD – seized by Vandals for one century

533AD – reconquest by Byzantines

698AD – fall of Carthage

Trasimene in the spring of 217 BC left thousands of Romans dead and Hannibal triumphant. Hannibal had one further impressive victory at Cannae where despite being far outnumbered, his troops encircled and trapped the Romans, and by attacking from the rear slaughtered about 50,000 enemy troops in one day. Hannibal's leadership and military tactics thus brought about the worst defeat ever suffered by the Roman army.

Hannibal did not take the opportunity to march on Rome but remained in Italy and, despite suffering from extended supply lines, a lack of naval support and allies who gave greater consideration to affairs of their own, continued to harass the Romans. His fighting strength gradually weakened and the Roman strategy of avoiding direct confrontation allowed him only minor victories.

Meanwhile the Carthaginians were forced out of Spain by Scipio, the Roman general who went on to invade Africa in 204 BC. Hannibal at this point abandoned his campaign in Italy and rushed home to protect his country. Despite the peace proposals agreed between Scipio and the Carthaginian army, Hannibal broke the armistice and concentrated the remaining forces on present day Sousse. Details differ on the campaign which followed that culminated in the Battle of Zama, but in essence Hannibal's troops were defeated, over 20,000 men died and Hannibal fled. A treaty was signed between Rome and Carthage in 201 BC, a disappointing end for Hannibal to his military career.

Carthage was allowed a deal of self government by the Romans, with Hannibal a leading figure. While Carthage recovered rapidly under his hands he was not universally popular and it is understood that his speedy removal to Ephesus was to avoid arrest. He outstayed his welcome in Ephesus, his advice to King Antiochus on how to conduct his war against Rome was not heeded and when Syria lost the war in 190 BC, part of the price was Hannibal's surrender. Accounts vary on what followed but eventually by 183 BC, the Romans were in a position to demand his surrender. To avoid arrest, at the age of 64, Hannibal committed suicide. Further details from Club Hannibal, Carthage Museum.

Know your Roman gods

It will certainly aid your visit to be able to identify the Roman gods mentioned frequently in association with the many Roman sites in Tunisia. The name of the Greek equivalent is given in brackets.

The Romans worshipped gods at various levels. There were everyday gods who protected hearth and home and those like the Triad (Jupiter, Juno and Minerva) on a much higher plain and more likely to be found in illustrations.

Amphitrite was one of the Nereids (see below) and the unwilling wife of Neptune. She ran off at the offer of marriage and was brought back by a dolphin dispatched by Neptune. The dolphin was rewarded by becoming a constellation while Amphitrite is portrayed spending the rest of her life riding round in a carriage pulled by sea-horses.

Apollo was a very important god particularly known for prophecy, medicine, law, courage and wisdom. On a lower plain he was associated with flocks and herds and archery. He and his twin sister Artemis were the children of Jupiter. Some of the women he wooed were not impressed. Daphne fled from his advances and was turned into a laurel tree, after which time Apollo wore a laurel wreath. Cassandra the daughter of the King of Troy also refused him and was punished by becoming the speaker of prophecies which no one believed. Coronis was unfaithful to him and was killed. In art he is represented as a young man with a bow or a lyre.

Ariadne was the beautiful daughter of Minos, the king of Crete. She fell in love with Theseus and gave him the sword with which he killed the Minator. She also gave him the ball of thread with which he found his way out of the labyrinth. There is some problem with the end of the story. Either he abandoned her and she hanged herself ... she was carried off to Naxos and left there to die ... she was carried to Naxos and married the wine god Bacchus (by whom she had six children) ... she died in childbirth on Cyprus.

Bacchus (Dionysus) was the god of fruitfulness and vegetation, especially known for wine and ecstasy. He was the only god with a mortal parent. He was the son of Jupiter and Semele, a daughter of the King of Thebes, who died (blasted with thunderbolts) when the full force of Jupiter's glory was revealed to her. Jupiter protected his son Bacchus by sewing him in his thigh until he reached maturity. Bacchus worship had great appeal for the women who 'abandoned their families, took to the hills, wearing fawn skins and crowns of ivy and shouting "Euoi", the ritual cry....'. Early pictures represent him as a bearded man but later he is portrayed as young and effeminate. Bacchic revels were a favourite subject on mosaics.

Ceres (Demeter) was the goddess of cereals and harvest and this extended to all the fruits of the earth. She was the daughter of Cronus and Rhea, sister of Jupiter. She was responsible for making the crops grow each year and the first loaf of bread from the new harvest was always sacrificed to her. She was intimately associated with the seasons. After the loss of her daughter Persephone to Hades she laid a curse on the earth which caused plants to wither and die and the land to become desolate. Although her daughter was rescued she had to return to Hades for 4 months each year so Demeter withdraws her gifts from the world during this time thus creating winter. Her daughter's return brings the spring. Her attributes were associated with her earth-mother role, an ear of corn, baskets of fruit and flowers and her favourite animal was a pig.

The **Cyclops** were thought to be Arges, Brontes and Steropes, the three sons of Uranus and Gaea, who made thunderbolts for Jupiter and the trident for Neptune. Hence when Apollo could not take revenge on Jupiter he slew the Cyclops who had forged the thunderbolt which killed his son Asclepius instead. Another interpretation is of a gang of one-eyed giant, savage shepherds who lived in caves and ate a number of Odysseus's crew before their leader was slain.

Diana (Artemis) the huntress was represented as the twin sister of Apollo and was the moon goddess. She originated as an Italian woodland goddess who was prayed to by women to assist conception and delivery. She was also the goddess of domestic animals. In Roman art she appears as a young huntress accompanied by a hound or deer.

Eros was the god of love, originally a primeval god, was later taken to be the son of Venus and (perhaps) Jupiter. He was the god not simply of passion but also of fertility. His chief associates were gods representing longing and desire. Quite a trio. He is represented as a beautiful winged youth, sometimes even a child. His golden arrows would inflame the passions of those impaled while his arrows of lead inspired hatred. He often set off two arrows at once, a recipe for disharmony. The plural form Erotes is used.

Hercules, although Jupiter's son, was a mortal. He was venerated for his labours and his power to avert evil. He had a very violent nature. He killed his wife and all his children and as penance was set the famous 12 Labours which he seemed to enjoy. After being poisoned by a jealous wife his body was burned on a funeral pyre but Jupiter caught up the immortal part (his soul) and took him to live with the gods. In art and literature he is represented as an enormously strong man, medium height, a huge eater and drinker, amorous and kindly but given to occasional violent outbursts.

Juno (Hera) was Jupiter's wife, the daughter of Time and of Rhea who was the daughter of Sky and Earth. She was the mother of Mars. She was the goddess of womanhood, of marriage and maternity. She was worshipped each year on 1 Mar as the goddess of women and marriage and at each new moon as the goddess of the moon. She was often portrayed as a matronly figure, of mature proportions, beautiful but rather severe, standing in a chariot drawn by sacred peacocks. She has a difficult private life, being jealous of the various women/goddesses with whom Jupiter associated and their offspring.

Jupiter (Zeus) was the chief god. He was the god of the sky, who could manifest himself as the bringer of light, the rain god worshipped at time of drought or the god of thunderbolts thus making all places struck by lightning sacred. The days of the full moon were sacred to him and he was also worshipped at the grape harvest. On a more moral tone he was concerned with the solemnization of oaths and treaties. His amorous adventures caused problems, especially with his wife.

Kore (Persephone) was the daughter of Zeus and his sister Demeter. She was abducted by Pluto and taken to the underworld from which she was rescued. As she had eaten food there (a pomegranate seed) she was forced to return to her husband for 4 months each year. These correspond to the winter or fallow time in the seasons.

Mars (Ares) was second only to Jupiter in importance. Initially he was a god of nature and fertility and protector of animals and crops. Later he became the god of war and protector of Rome.

Marsyas found the oboe that the goddess Athena had constructed and once he became a proficient player challenged Apollo to a musical contest, Marsyas on the oboe and Apollo on the lyre. The story has more than one ending. In one version the judge was King Midas (of the gold fingers) who foolishly declared Marsyas the better. At this Apollo turned Midas's ears into those of a mule. In another version the Muses are judges and declare Apollo the winner. Not content with his victory he tied Marsyas to a tree and had him flayed. Copies of the famous statue of the bound Marsyas, a symbol of autonomy, were taken to the colonies. A mosaic of the competition is in the Bardo Museum.

Mercury (Hermes) was the god of commerce and trade, of science and astronomy, of thieves, travellers and vagabonds, of eloquence and cleverness. As the messenger of the gods he was represented as a young man with wings on his shoes and his hat. As the representative of commerce he is clutching a purse.

Minerva (Athena) was Jupiter's daughter. She was the goddess of handicrafts and industrial life, the professions, art and sometimes war. The fifth day of the Ides of March was her festival.

The **Nine Muses** were the daughters of Zeus and Mnemosyne (Memory). They were known for their music, for their songs, which brought joy to all who heard. They were assumed to be maidens, or at least unmarried, but were also referred to as the mothers of important, usually poetic or musical, gods like Orpheus. When portrayed each had an attribute – a lyre, a mask, scroll. The nine were: Calliope – epic poetry; Clio – history; Erato – love poetry; Euterpe – lyric poetry; Melpomene – tragedy; Polyhymnia – songs of the gods; Terpsichore – dance;

Thalia – comedy; Urania – astronomy.

Neptune was really the god of fresh water and originally nothing to do with the sea. His festival took place in summer when fresh water was most scarce. Originally he was only a minor deity but as the Romans became seafarers he assumed a greater significance and was identified with the Greek god Poseidon.

The **Nereids** were daughters of the sea god Nereus and Doris (daughter of Oceanus) about 50-100 of them. They were imagined as attractive young girls inhabiting any water (salt or fresh), and harmless to mortals.

Orpheus was presented at birth with a lyre by the god Apollo and given instruction in music by the Muses. He could enchant men and beasts with his music and also move rocks and trees. When travelling to look for the Golden Fleece his music put the monsters to sleep and prevented the cliffs from falling. When his wife died he followed her to Hades and with his music persuaded hard hearted Pluto to let her return to earth. But he forgot his promise not to look back as they journeyed and he lost her for ever. In his grief he treated all women with contempt, and the story says they tore him to pieces in revenge. The Muses picked up the pieces and buried him at the foot of Mt Olympus and set his lyre in the sky in his memory.

Pan was the god of the goatherd and shepherd. He was quite human, though not handsome being rough in appearance, apart from his goat-like ears and horns and goat-like legs and hooves. He was an excellent musician and plaid the pipes beautifully. He was merry and friendly and often seen dancing in the woodland with the nymphs. He is always in pursuit of one or another of the nymphs but always rejected because he is so ugly. His name is the basis for the word *panic*.

Pegasus, the winged horse, sprang from the body of the slain Medusa. It was caught and tamed by Bellerophon by means of a golden bridle provided by the goddess Minerva. Pegasus was a faithful companion but when Bellerophon impiously attempted to ride up to heaven Jupiter sent a gad-fly which stung Pegasus so that he unseated his rider who fell to earth lame and blind. Pegasus was then placed as a constellation in the sky.

Perseus who was yet another son of Jupiter is noted as the god who cut off the head of the Gorgon Medusa and rescuer of Andromeda from a sea monster.

Pluto was the god of the underworld, the son of Cronus and Rhea, and the brother of Demeter. He took over control of Hades at the death of his father. (Didn't gods live forever?) He married Persephone (daughter of his brother and sister) who only stayed in Hades for 4 months of each year. He was depicted as stern, pitiless and unbending.

Saturn was a fire god and later an agricultural god who taught mortals how to till the land. His name comes from the Latin meaning to sow. He is represented with a sickle in his hand. His wife, Ops, was the goddess of plenty. A useful couple to have around. In his honour a yearly festival, Saturnalia, was held in December after the farming year was completed. This was a time of games and feasting when presents were exchanged including especially wax candles and dolls. This took place on 17 Dec and had a direct influence on Christmas celebrations. His name is given to Saturday.

Silenus was one of the Satyrs, the father of Bacchus.

Tellus was the goddess of fertility in particular of cereal crops.

Theseus a legendary hero, son of Aegeus the king of Athens, had numerous adventures, mainly killing cruel and wicked monsters. Being heir to the throne did not prevent him sorting out the fire-breathing bull of Marathon and offered himself as one of the 7 youths and 7 maidens sacrificed each year to the

Minator. He killed the Minator (see Ariadne above) and returned home. He unfortunately forgot to change the sails on his ship to white on the return voyage – a signal that he has succeeded. His father, seeing the black sails cast himself into the sea (the Aegean Sea) so Theseus became king. He had many other adventures. An uprising in Athens forced him to Scyros where he was killed. His bones eventually were placed in a temple in Athens.

Venus - Goddess of love and beauty - this mosaic is situated at Bulla Regia

Ulysses (Odysseus) is best known for his epic 10 year return journey from the Trojan war. His wisdom, courage and resourcefulness, all stretched to the limit with the horrific obstacles he encounters, eventually permit his return where, as a final task, he has to prove to his wife that he is her long lost husband.

Venus (Aphrodite) was originally a mere goddess of vegetable gardens but later became identified with Aphrodite the goddess of love and beauty. Venus was represented as the highest ideal of feminine beauty. She was honoured too for the belief that Romulus, the founder of Rome, was descended from her son Aeneas.

Vulcan was the god of fire, especially its destructive force-like volcanoes and was called upon to keep such fires from the people. He is portrayed as being a blacksmith. He was ugly and lame. He married Venus.

Places of interest

A short visit to Carthage only gives an overview. Tours provided by hotels are usually only half-day affairs hardly adequate to get from one end of Carthage to the other (3 km) and visit a few remains on some of the 12 main sites. Allow at least a full day if possible. All sites here open 0800-1900 summer, 0830-1730 winter, closed Sun. Entrance TD2, photography TD2 covers all sites and the museum, valid only for day of issue.

Local information
● **Accommodation**
A *Hotel Reine Didon*, rue Mendès France, on Byrsa Hill, T 733433, F 732599, close to the museum, 22 rm, expensive, very quiet, overlooking the sea, excellent restaurant.

● **Places to eat**
The best places to eat in this area are ◆◆*Baal* at Salammbo, T 731072 and *Le Phénicien, Phoenix de Carthage*, T 734555; ◆◆*Gerry* at Salammbo, T 730089 and *Neptune*, T 731456.

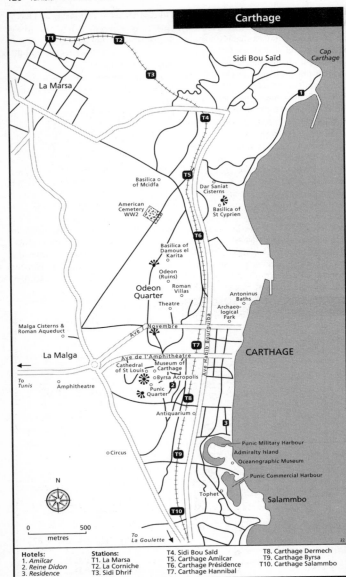

Carthage

Sidi Bou Saïd

Cap Carthage

La Marsa

Basilica of Mcidfa

Dar Saniat Cisterns

American Cemetery WW2

Basilica of St Cyprien

Basilica of Damous el Karita

Odeon (Ruins)

Odeon Quarter

Roman Villas

Antoninus Baths

Theatre

Archaeological Park

Malga Cisterns & Roman Aqueduct

Novembre

La Malga

Ave de l'Amphithéâtre

To Tunis

Amphitheatre

CARTHAGE

Cathedral of St Louis

Museum of Carthage

Byrsa Acropolis

Punic Quarter

Antiquarium

Punic Military Harbour

Admiralty Island

Oceanographic Museum

Punic Commercial Harbour

Circus

Salammbo

Tophet

N

0   500
metres

To La Goulette

Hotels:	Stations:		
1. Amilcar	T1. La Marsa	T4. Sidi Bou Saïd	T8. Carthage Dermech
2. Reine Didon	T2. La Corniche	T5. Carthage Amilcar	T9. Carthage Byrsa
3. Residence	T3. Sidi Dhrif	T6. Carthage Présidence	T10. Carthage Salammbo
		T7. Carthage Hannibal	

TOPHET, OCEANOGRAPHIC MUSEUM AND THE PUNIC PORTS

Get off at the TGM station at Carthage Salammbo and walk down towards the sea. First is the Tophet (crematorium) and then along the road, on the right, the Oceanographic Museum and the Punic Ports. It is then only a short walk up to the TGM station Carthage Byrsa.

At **Tophet** are the remains of the sanctuary of the Carthaginian divinities Tanit and Baal-Hammon, the oldest Punic religious site in Carthage. There is not much left to see. According to legend, for seven centuries, the noble Carthaginian families brought their children here to be ritually sacrificed and urns containing ashes and remains of many children have in fact been found. This site was discovered in 1921 and is considered to be the largest of all known sacrificial compounds. The ashes of the victims, sometimes small children but more often birds and young animals, were placed in a stone-lined trench.

Other offerings such as dishes and lucky charms were buried too. When the whole area was filled with covered trenches a layer of earth was placed across and the whole process began again.

The **Oceanographic Museum** is of most interest to those who are keen on fish and fishing.

Admiralty Island This small island in the harbour area was the subject of research by a British archaeological mission in the 1970s, which revealed a fascinating Roman docking system. The island was built up as a circular space, with a spine carrying an upper service gantry below which ships could be winched up into a covered dry dock (see plan, page). A bridge linked the island to the shore. This sophisticated dock was constructed to handle exports of wheat to Rome. Adjacent was the **Punic Harbour** joined to the sea by a dredged channel. This harbour was a large circular basin surrounded by large warehouses.

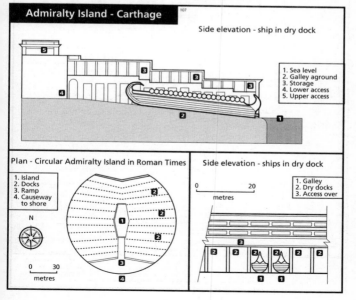

Admiralty Island - Carthage 107

Side elevation - ship in dry dock

1. Sea level
2. Galley aground
3. Storage
4. Lower access
5. Upper access

Plan - Circular Admiralty Island in Roman Times

1. Island
2. Docks
3. Ramp
4. Causeway to shore

N

0   30
metres

Side elevation - ships in dry dock

0   20
metres

1. Galley
2. Dry docks
3. Access over

The **Punic Ports** The main harbour used to be the very heart of Carthaginian prosperity. The N basin boasting safe anchorage for 220 vessels was the naval base. It was circular in shape and bordered by quays. The southern base, originally rectangular in shape, was for merchant ships. It is hard today to imag-

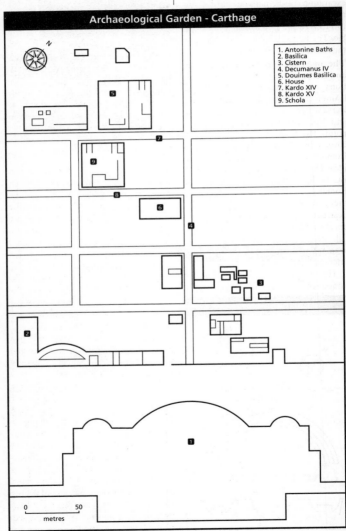

Archaeological Garden - Carthage

1. Antonine Baths
2. Basilica
3. Cistern
4. Decumanus IV
5. Douimes Basilica
6. House
7. Kardo XIV
8. Kardo XV
9. Schola

0   50
metres

ine the activity that must have been generated at these two ports.

The **Antiquarium** situated alongside Ave Habib Bourguiba has exhibits from excavations of the harbour and the surrounding area. There are numerous coins (over 9,000) and pieces of metal and marble. The best exhibit is the mosaic from the House of the Greek Charioteers.

The museum, amphitheatre, theatre and Roman Villas Alight at TGM station Carthage Hannibal. Walk up Ave de l'Amphithéatre to the summit of Mt Byrsa which was the Acropolis of Punic and Roman Carthage, an ideal view point. The Byrsa quarter recently discovered by French archaeologists, dates from the time of Hannibal and gives an idea of urban life in the early 2nd century BC. We have to be grateful that when the Romans returned to rebuild Carthage they covered over the ruins of the 146 BC destruction on Byrsa Hill with thick layers of rubble and earth – a Roman landfill programme. Hence the whole segment of history was preserved for later examination.

Here is the large cathedral named in honour of St Louis and seminary (now

Mosaic of a duck on a terrace of a Roman Villa

the museum) constructed by the French during the Protectorate which has been made into a cultural centre. On the southern slope are the remains of the Punic residential quarter (2nd century BC), built in a regular rectangular grid, houses, water tanks, drains, plastered walls, tiled floors. Down the other side of the hill the amphitheatre is on one side of the road and a collection of cisterns on the other. Returning towards the sea down Ave 7th Novembre on the left is the theatre behind which lie the Roman Villas. If you visit the Basilicas of Damou and St Cyprien next then backtrack to the Baths of Antoninus you will have visited all the major sites and be back at the TGM station.

The **Mago Quarter** dating from the 5th century BC is approached down Ave de la République. It was destroyed in 146 BC and rebuilt under Caesar Augustus. Following the excavations by the German Archaeological Institute the site was turned into a garden and it is possible to walk along the restored Roman road by the sea front. A small museum displays household items, found during excavations. Models and diagrams illustrate the development of the Punic settlement and the rebuilding a century

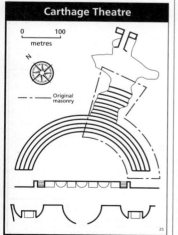

Carthage Theatre

```
0        100
  metres
```

N

- - - Original
masonry

25

Carthage - Ruins on Odeon Hill Site

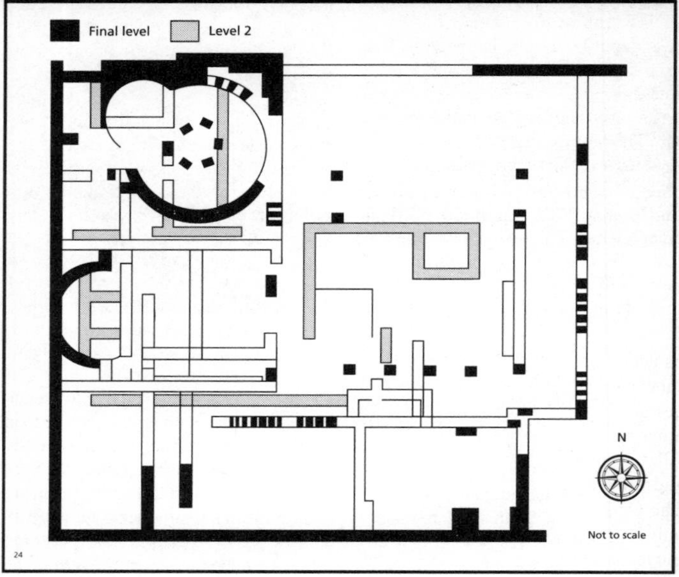

Final level | Level 2

N

Not to scale

after its destruction.

In the **amphitheatre**, built during Hadrian's reign and capable of seating 35,000 spectators, early Christians were thrown to the lions and gladiators as entertainment for the audience. Unfortunately there is very little to see since only limited excavation work has been carried out.

The **cisterns** were the main reservoirs for the Carthage water supply. Today they are in a bad state.

The Odeon Quarter is set to the W of the railway and Ave Habib Bourguiba. The **Roman theatre** which could hold 10,000 spectators is located in the Odeon area though almost all of what can be seen is a restoration. The original pieces exist only in fragmentary form (see diagram), but at least give an idea of what the entire seating area (*cavea*) of the monument was once like. The semicir-

cular *orchestra* with some of its original marble flooring can still be seen too. The building is not very interesting in itself as it is not very true to the original, but the International Carthage Festival held here every year receives great praise.

Also on Odeon Hill, N of the theatre, are a series of excavations of fine **Roman villas** (on the whole badly restored) and similar buildings reached via the entrance at the *nymphaion* with its water feature. The villas are of classical proportions, built around the peristyle or central pillared courtyard giving access to the main living rooms. This form can be seen clearly in the famous and now restored 5th-6th century **House of the Aviary**, named after the subject of a mosaic found at the site bearing a well executed polychrome of a fowl and fruit, now in the Bardo Museum. This house has an octagonal garden in the middle of

Horse used in chariot racing
around circus.
Mosaic from villa in Carthage

its courtyard. Many of the artefacts on show here in the house, including statues and a bust of Dionysus, are from other sites at Carthage. Other adjacent villas such as the **House of the Horse** and the Odeon itself are worth a visit. The Odeon was an indoor theatre but only its confused ruins remain – most of the material has long gone, used to construct new buildings.

The **Antonine Baths**, once the biggest baths in North Africa and the third largest in the Roman world, were truly enormous. They are in a splendid position between Ave Habib Bourguiba and the sea and are one of the best preserved sites in Carthage. Even though there are only a few pieces of building still standing they give, with a little imagination, a good idea of the grandeur that was.

Their construction began under Hadrian and Antonius officiated at the opening ceremony in the middle of the 2nd century. The finance for the project, donated by some rich inhabitant, gives an indication of the wealth at that time. The complex array of rooms in the baths is shown on the plan above. The layout is symmetrical around a central axis of the swimming pool, with the *frigidarium* and *calderium* running from the seashore frontage to the second façade facing W onto the archaeological gardens. The two wings each contained a *palaestra* or open pillared exercise yard, an indoor gymnasium, hot bath, *tepidarium* and *destrictarium* or warmed cleaning room. A *laconicum* or sweating room was included, while the main *frigidarium* was shared by both wings. Many of the minor rooms are hexagonal or octagonal in shape. Water for the baths came from the main city aqueduct. Being at sea level, the heating and service areas had to be built above ground, the boilers immediately below the heated rooms for efficiency and economy.

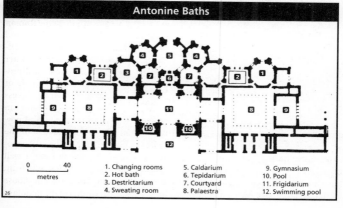

Antonine Baths

```
0        40
metres
```

1. Changing rooms
2. Hot bath
3. Destrictarium
4. Sweating room
5. Caldarium
6. Tepidarium
7. Courtyard
8. Palaestra
9. Gymnasium
10. Pool
11. Frigidarium
12. Swimming pool

26

Mosaic of long tailed bird on the terrace of a Roman Villa

To the S of the baths lie the present-day archaeological gardens, comprising two main NW-SE roads (Decumanus III to IV) of the original gridiron layout of roads and their crossroads (Cardo). Originally the road system was aligned along the summit of the acropolis of Byrsa (NW-SE) and defined all the blocks of property in the city. The residual area encompassed by the archaeological gardens is mainly in ruins but the former esplanade of the baths can be identified together with its porticos and annexes, of which the most singular is the **latrines**, laid out in two great 35m semicircles. There is a small **basilica** in this same corner featuring a main aisle and two side aisles, but the main church in the gardens is to the W – that of the late Byzantine Dermech Basilica (Douimès). Part of the Punic necropolis is the only sign of the older foundation in the gardens. The **Schola House** on Decumanus III has a peristyle and contained fine mosaics.

So many of the original stones of Carthage has been taken. Many originally here were used in the construction of Tunis. Others travelled much further and make up parts of a number of monuments including Pisa cathedral.

The **museum**, T 730036, situated by the cathedral at the top of Byrsa hills is a spacious showroom in which some fine exhibits are well presented. The approach road winds round the shoulder of the hill with vestiges of ruins protruding from the hillside. The road terminates in a car park in front of the cathedral. Entrance to the museum and the 2nd century Punic ruins is to the right, TD2 in addition to the antiquities fee paid at the kiosk to right between cathedral and entrance. It is worth making a short detour to wander among the partly restored walls. It is also worth a walk in the garden which faces the museum entrance. This stands on the site of an ancient basilica and here more examples of pillars and carved stonework can be examined. The walls of the garden are inlaid with small pieces found in the area.

Follow the path from the entrance kiosk and turn right to the toilets or left takes you to the museum door with some rather plain sarcophagi on display at either side. By contrast just inside on the

The North Africa American Cemetery

🐾 The US armed forces played their first and a significant role in WW2 in the western hemisphere on the battlefields of North Africa. The policy for a clear military victory in North Africa was determined at an Anglo-American summit meeting in Washington in Dec 1941. In Jul of 1942 the USA agreed to use its troops in Operation Torch for the liberation of the region, in which joint Allied forces, including a strong US contingent would drive from the Atlantic coast of Morocco and from the Mediterranean coast in Algeria to meet with British and Commonwealth troops moving in from the E. Operation Torch began on 8 November 1942 and, after a comparatively easy occupation of Morocco and Algeria, US troops invaded Tunisia in mid-Nov of 1942 in an unsuccessful attempt to take Tebourba and Djedelda on the way to Tunis.

Strong reinforcement of the Axis armies in the winter led to a fierce counter attack against the Allies in Jan 1943, pushing them from positions on the Kairouan and Hir Moussa passes. In Feb, however, the Allies once again attempted to close in against the Axis bridgehead around Tunis and faced an Axis defensive drive with severe fighting across a wide arc of territory from Le Kef, Sbeitla and Kasserine. Allied troops coming from the E were held at the Mareth Line, a defensive perimeter across the narrow plain in the Gafsa area originally built by the French. The decisive battle at this stage was probably at Kasserine where a powerful, mainly German force, failed to break through Allied lines to any damaging depth, though at the cost of heavy US casualties among the defending force. A second armoured attack on Allied positions in N Tunisia in the Sejenane and Ksar Mezouar area ran for over 2 weeks in late Feb and the first half of Mar. On 6 Mar Rommel failed to break the British lines at Mareth and lost significant numbers of tanks in his attempt. Throughout late Mar and Apr Allied forces advanced on most fronts, Gafsa falling to the American 1st Infantry Division on 17 Mar. The US 1st Armored Division cut the road from Tunis to Bizerte and thus hindered the Axis supply line leading to local combatants, including Tunis itself to the Allies in the N. The German army in the Cap Bon area was also cut off by Allied troops. Some 250,000 Axis prisoners were captured and on 12 May 1943 General Juergen Von Arnim surrendered his forces in Tunisia. The next day Field Marshal Hesse formally surrendered on behalf of the Axis command in North Africa.

US forces suffered heavy losses in the North African campaign with 10,290 men killed out of total Allied battle losses in Tunisia of 17,861 (British 6,471 and French 1,100).

2,841 US war dead are laid to rest in the US North African Cemetery at Carthage, including some who fell in Tunisia and others who perished whilst on duty with the US Persian Gulf Command. The cemetery occupies a 10 ha site which actually lies on the ruins of the ancient city of Carthage. The site has a Court of Honor, graveyard garden, chapel and visitor's building. The address is BP 346, Sidi Bou Said 20226, Tunisia, T 747767, F 747051, or enquiries in the USA to Department of State, Tunis, Washington DC 20521-6360. See page 324 for more information on WW2.

right are two carefully executed 4th century BC sarcophagi with recumbent statues on the lid. This is the room devoted to Punic stele and sarcophagi. The Paleo-Christian room is on the left as you enter. It contains some important terracotta tiles and two sculptured panels known as The Adoration of the Kings and The Annunciation. Opposite the entrance is the room devoted to modern scientific methods relating to excavations and archaeology. Upstairs to the left is an amazing display of oil lamps while the rest of the room is divided into the main periods of Carthaginian history. Items from Punic Carthage denoted with beige includes items from graves: Roman Carthage (blue) has ceramics, glassware and sculpture in marble; Christian and Byzantine Carthage (pink) has figurines, objects in ivory, terracotta tiles and glassware; Arab Carthage, mainly ceramics, is denoted in green. There is no leaflet to explain about the exhibits though most are named in Arabic, English and French. It is a worthwhile stop but is somewhat overshadowed by the magnificent collection in the Bardo museum.

The **circus** was on the extreme W of the city. Only the outline can be made out. It would have been used for chariot racing as depicted in the mosaic exhibited in the antiquarium, the four teams wearing distinguishing colours. The site became a cemetery.

After leaving Carthage and before reaching Sidi Bou Saïd take a left turn to the **American Military Cemetery**. There is a car park inside the entrance gates and a visitors' reception and restroom.

On a site covering over 10 ha are the graves of 2,841 American military men and women (240 unnamed) who died in the fighting which culminated in the liberation of Tunisia. Walk down the steps and along the tree shaded avenue to the immaculate lawn marked with rows of white crosses. The tablets of the missing consist of a wall 120m long on which names and particulars of 3,724 persons are inscribed. Three modern wall mosaics show the movements of the Allied Forces in North Africa and the Mediterranean during WW2. This is a fine example, if a sad one, of a cemetery in a foreign land, carefully designed to blend with the surroundings.

Open summer (16 Apr- 15 Sept) 0800-1800 Mon to Sat, Sun and holidays opens one hour later, in winter closes one hour earlier.

SIDI BOU SAÏD

Sidi Bou Saïd station is 10 mins' walk from the centre. The village is beautiful, a pleasant place to stay in contrast to Tunis. It is built on a cliff facing the Mediterranean, overlooking Carthage and Tunis to the SW and Korbous and Cap Bon to the E. All the white painted houses having blue painted windows and doors, the latter having traditional patterns picked out with black studded nails. The buildings go all the way down to the sea, ending by the small port. The narrow, winding streets follow the curves of the hill, and provide a most interesting walk. The architecture is superb and the houses have been very well preserved. There is an excellent view from the top of the hill where there is a small cemetery on the right. A steep climb, consider taking a taxi.

For refreshments try the picturesque but very expensive Moorish *Café des Nattes* in the cobbled square in the centre of the village. Another place to have a drink, particularly at sunset, is the *Café Sidi Chabaane*, situated at the end of the village. Coffee here TD1. The view from here over the sea is quite exceptional. Follow the walk down to the harbour and along the path which continues back up the hill at the end of the Cap. Being on every tourist's itinerary Sidi Bou Saïd can get very crowded, especially in summer, but most people tend to congregate in the main streets and it is possible to find some peace in the small back streets.

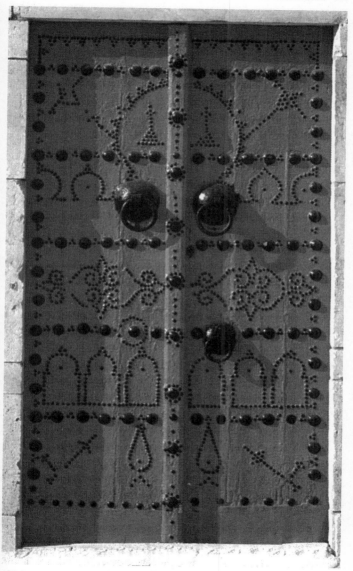

Door design of small and large nails

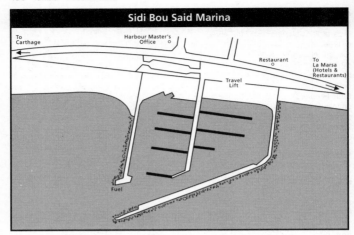

Sidi Bou Said Marina

A short distance to the N of Sidi Bou Saïd a presidential palace is being built to accommodate official guests.

Pilgrimages are made to the tomb of Abou Saïd each Aug culminating with the feast of la *kharja*.

The villa of Baron d'Erlanger, a musicologist is a very attractive setting for a **Museum of Traditional Music and Musical Instruments**. Called Ennejma Ezzahra Palace and is open summer 0900-1200 and 1600-1900, winter 0900-1200 and 1400-1700.

The elegant white painted (sometimes natural olive wood) bird cages with distinctive domes are made here by hand.

● **Accommodation B** *Hotel Amilcar*, at the foot of Sidi Bou Saïd cliff, T 470788, all 250 rms have a view over the Gulf looking towards the Cap Bon peninsula, private beach, pool; **C** *Hotel Residence*, 16 rue Hannibal, Salammbo, T 731072, 8 rm with heating and shower, no a/c, clean, attractive, restaurant, 10 mins from beach, excellent position for visiting Carthage; **C** *Sidi Bou Saïd*, on a hill slightly out of the village, T 740411, 34 rm, good standard, pool, unfortunately no sea view; **D** *Hotel Dar Zarrouk*, T 740215, F 336908, 100 yr old building built round an attractive central courtyard, beautiful mosaic walls, once housed the harem, 12 rm with high dome ceilings, bath, heating but no a/c as design and position do not require it, very very attractive, all rm with sea view, breakfast TD2 extra, other meals in restaurant adjacent to hotel; **E** *Hotel Boufares*, central, T 740091, 8 rm centred around a shaded patio in a typical house, very clean and cheap, cold in winter, excellent breakfast, no restaurant, it is vital to book in the summer season, ask manager to play his lute.

● **Places to eat** There is not much choice here. ◆◆*Restaurant le Pirate*, T 748266, by the harbour at the bottom of the cliff specializes in fish and sea-food, expensive but worth it as the food is excellent. ◆*Restaurant La Bagatelle*, at the bottom of the hill before the village, good setting, good, food, very popular; *Dar Zarrouk*, T 740591. ◆*Restaurant Chergui*, T 740987, on the main street, on the right of *Café des Nattes*, large terrace with a fantastic view, food is good value possibly more interesting in its layout and cheaper as less well known, built round a courtyard, one side is covered to give welcome shade, several tables with bench seats on either side covered with blankets and cushions, can seat 40, Turkish coffee TD0.6, orange juice TD0.6, cheese omelette TD3, chicken couscous TD4, mixed grill TD6. There are lots of stalls selling nuts and sticky sweets.

● **Banks & money changers** UBCI, in the new town at the bottom of the hill, on the road to La Goulette.

● **Entertainment Art Galleries**: there are a number of art galleries in this region N of Tunis. In particular **Galerie Cherif Fine Art**, 20 rue de la République and Galerie Ammar Farhat, 3 rue Sidi el Ghemrini. Also try the summer exhibitions at Driba – **Espace Art**, 4 rue Omen Ibn Abi Rabiad, La Marsa Plage; **Sêrail**, 9 Ave du 7 Novembre, La Marsa Ville; **Espace d'Art Mille Feuille**, La Marsa Ville. **Hammam**: recommended is Hammam Sidi Bou Saïd in the street opposite the Magasin Général in the lower part of the town, very modern, very clean, rec.

● **Hospitals & medical services Chemist**: all night chemist next to the bank.

● **Sports** The ancient fishing port has been developed as a marina, with a sailing club and a windsurfing school. There are 360 berths (min-max draft 2-4m) and all the necessary services are now in place including a 26 tonne travel lift.

LA MARSA

This town lies at the TGM terminus (or catch bus No 20) and is relaxed and quiet, full of luxurious villas. It has a beautiful beach lined by a promenade with palm trees, far away from the bustle of Tunis and therefore popular at weekends, especially in summer. This beach is particularly popular with wealthy Tunisians from the S who find the summer climate here a pleasant change from their own. There is little to do apart from sit on the beach, in a restaurant or in a café.

The 16th century Hafsid Al-Abdillia palace has been saved from ruin and is being reconstructed to house the new **Museum of Modern Art**. Legend says that Abu Abdullah Mohammed, the Hafsid ruler at that time, had a sickly daughter for whom fresh sea air was recommended. Not to be found wanting Abu Abdullah had three palaces constructed at La Marsa, of which only this, the third, remains. It follows the classic design with the main rooms arranged around an open central courtyard complete with fountain. The dominant feature, a high tower, offers superb views. It will be another 2 years before visitors will be able to view the 5,000 works of art and admire the carefully restored building.

● **Accommodation** is expensive along the coast, most of the hotels being 3 or 4-star. They have the advantage of being only 5 mins from the TGM station and having magnificent surroundings and views. **C** *Aqua Viva*, 110 rm, T 748567, F 342411; **C** *Cap Carthage*, 350 rm, T 740064, F 741980; **C** *Kahena*, 70 rm, T 748200, F 747911; **C** *Karim*, 220 rm, T 740700, F 741200; **C** *Molika*, 206 rm, T 740242, F 741646; **C** *Nova Park*, 70 rm, T 748764, F 748611; **D** *La Noria*, 460 beds, T 746348, F 743337.

● **Places to eat** ♦♦♦*Au Bon Vieux Temps*, T 774322; *Bistro Garden*, T 743577; *Les Mimosas*, T 746460. ♦Have a drink at the *Café Safsaf*, and try some of their pastries or Tunisian cooking.

● **Transport Local Car** rental: at *Hotel Cap Carthage*, T 741596 and at *Hotel Molika*, T 740118.

GAMMARTH

Here, there is a long line of expensive villas, luxury hotels and restaurants strung along the coast. However it is possible to reach the beach to the N beyond the hotels (most of them are right on the beach). The beach is good, but crowded in summer, when it can be noisy and the litter builds up. There is a French military cemetery in Gammarth.

● **Accommodation AL** *Abou Nawas*, Blvd Taieb Méhiri, T 741444, F 740400, 45 apartments, 127 rm with a/c, pool in summer, good beach, 6 restaurants/bars, excellent food, all sport activities are organized; **B** *Mégara*, on Blvd Taieb Méhiri, T 740366, F 740916, Moorish decor, 77 rm, large pool, lovely gardens; **C** *La Tour Blanche*, T 271697, is situated a little way up from the coast and therefore has a view, except *The Galaxy* – the trendiest nightclub in Tunis – is attached.

● **Places to eat** These are generally expensive. ♦♦♦*Le Grand Bleu*, T 746900; *Les Dunes d'Or*, Baie des Singes, T 743379; *Les Ombrelles*, T 742964; ♦♦*Le Pecheur*, T 741906, beyond *Les Dunes d'Or*; *L'Orient*, T 741906; ♦*Ellil*, T 743918; *La Vague*, T 747312.

The road continues NW to **Raoud** through the sand dunes and reaches Tunis via the P8. The coastal area is being developed as another tourist complex.

SOUTHEAST FROM TUNIS

On the other side of the canal of Tunis extend the southern suburbs. This region includes the 'middle income' cities of Radès, Ez Zahra, Hammam Lif and Borj Cedria.

These sprawling suburbs of Tunis hold little interest for the visitor, but **Radès** has one useful feature, the passenger and car ferry to La Goulette avoiding travelling through Tunis. It operates all day, carries 10 cars, takes 5 mins and costs nothing.

The small plantations of trees in the suburbs here are situated in areas of wasteland. This area is part of the national reforestation programme. Each autumn at the tree festival each person can plant a tree, provided free by the state. The first tree each year is planted by the President.

● **Accommodation Youth hostel**: Banlieu Sud, T 483631, 10 km from Tunis, 10 mins from Radès station, 56 beds, meals available, ring to book as it takes groups and can get full.

HAMMAM LIF

A coastal resort, once mainly for the bourgeois of Tunis, situated at the foot of Djebel Bou Kornine whose rocky outcrops slope steeply to the edge of the road. There is a therapeutic *hammam* here, (TD2.8 per session) not to be confused with the better establishment at Korbous. It is adjacent to *Hotel Majed*.

● **Accommodation E** *Hotel du Bon Repos*, rue Bel Hassen Chedli, T 291458, short walking distance from the main road on slope of Djebel Bou Kornine, fairly basic hotel, TD20 for rm pp, breakfast TD2, 18 rm some with separate bath and toilet, some have shared facilities, some rooms have fine view over bay to Sidi Bou Saïd, no restaurant; **F** *Hotel Majed*, 1 rue Salammbo which is the main road through the town, TD6.5 pp bed only, 10 rm shared facilities, very basic.

Further E, **Borj Cedria** has a quarry producing reddish marble of moderate quality stone. More importantly for the sun seeker it also has a good beach used by people from Tunis at weekends and in summer. Many of them come out by train. The German cemetery commemorating all who fell in the Tunisian campaign between Nov 1942 and May 1943 E towards Soliman turn right into a track leading through a large iron gateway into a parking area. A square archway has an austere reception room on the right and very clean toilets on the left. Continue along the flower-lined cobbled pathway up the hillside, just 2 mins walk, to the reach the monument. This is built of square grey/white stone blocks in terraces on 4 levels which overlook the Gulf of Tunis out towards Sidi Bou Saïd, a fine view. The terraces are built in the form of square bays with 3m high walls. The burial chambers are set into these bays. The higher terrace is built around a central square garden area with a few shrubs and small trees. It is all very depressing and only relieved by the view.

● **Accommodation C** *Dar*, T 290188, 144 beach bungalows; **C** *Salwa*, T 290764, 116 rm, pool.

Massicault with **Commonwealth WW2 cemetery** at Borj el Amri (1,576 graves), 28 km SW of Tunis beside the P5. Open 0730-1430 Sat-Thur. Bus No 23a from Tunis. *Hotel Magreb* and restaurant on S side of road.

● **Tour companies & travel agents** *Gulf Travel Agency*, 70 Ave de la République, Hammam Lif, T 292100, F 291954; *Romulus Voyages*, Km 12 Ezzahra, T 450544, F 450582; *Mondial Tours*, Place 9 Avril, Hammam Lif, T 293727.

SOUTH FROM TUNIS

The exit from Tunis is quick along the motorway but the suburbs of cheap housing, mixed small scale industry and uncontrolled development extend even this distance. On the P3, as an

Roman aqueduct near Bou Er Rebia

example, between Tunis and Fouchana there is an enormous car breaking yard, visible from the roadside, which extends over 1 km in length and about 100m deep. It has 47 entrances each dealing with different variations of vehicles. The Tunisian drivers seem to see this as a challenge to keep it working to capacity.

Beyond this point agricultural activity takes over and the journey is more pleasant. One delight of this route is the proximity to the aqueduct which once took water to Carthage. It appears first on the W and then on the E, the road cutting through a breach S at Mohammedia. Where parts of the supporting structure have crumbled away the actual aqueduct has fallen and here it is possible to view a cross section of the amazing structure. The channel carrying the water was oval, large enough for a man to walk along, lined with cement to prevent leakage and covered to prevent evaporation. Fascinating.

From here until Bou Er Rebia the aqueduct is visible to the E, particularly where the road dips down to cross the Oued Miliane 3 km from Mohammedia. To maintain the level the aqueduct re-

quires much higher supporting pillars. The accuracy of the engineering is awesome considering the equipment available. As you follow the aqueduct note that the pillars get wider where the structure gets higher and needs more support to soar above the land. As the contours rise again the structure is less spectacular and runs at about 1m above the ground here as it did when it cut through the centre of Mohammedia to the N.

At 23 km from Tunis is the left turn to **Oudna**. After a further 8 km take the C133 up and away from the valley with Djebel Oust to the W and Djebel Kefa to the E. **Moghrane**, in the centre of an extensive area of cereal cultivation, has an important agricultural college. **Bir M'Cherga**, with all the usual services, is another agricultural centre. The C133 continues to Zaghouan via an attractive avenue of huge eucalyptus trees (courtesy of the French).

UTHINA (OUDNA)

This site, nestling on the N facing foothills of the Djebel Mekrima, is famous for the quantity and quality of its mosaics. Only parts of the site have been excavated and it was from the upper class residential area to the N that these mosaics came. During the excavations a score of houses were uncovered. The largest, known as the Laberii, was a splendid dwelling with numerous rooms and even more numerous outbuildings. All the rooms and the atrium were paved with rich mosaics. You will have to go to the Bardo (see page 85) to see the lovely picture of Venus seated on a rock while three cupids play with her veil or the huge 'oceanic' picture with Neptune, Amphrite, sea-horse drawn chariots around three boats carrying three well-heeled females and a cluster of cupids. The large public baths was discovered, some huge cisterns and a theatre

Hot soups for cold desert nights (1)

Semolina Soup (Sdirr)
100g of coarse semolina
2 tablespoons of:
        finely chopped parsley
        chopped celery
1 tablespoon each of:
        tomato paste
        harissa
        pickled capers
        dried mint
1/2 tablespoon of:
        paprika
        caraway seeds
4 cloves of garlic
10ml of olive oil
1 fresh lemon (sliced)
salt to taste
small pieces of salt meat if required
1 1/2 litres water

Method
In a thick pan heat the oil, add salt meat, water, tomato paste and harissa, caraway, paprika and garlic. Simmer with plenty of water for 10-15 mins until meat is cooked. Add celery, capers, parsley, lemon and salt to taste. With the water simmering slowly add the semolina, stirring all the time. Simmer for 5 mins. Serve hot on heated plate.

and from other buildings inscriptions and a dozen important sculptures are displayed at the Bardo. There is much more to be discovered here on this exciting site.

ZAGHOUAN

Lying 60 km S of Tunis, Zaghouan, known to the Romans as *Ziqua*, has a regular bus service from Tunis and louages from Tunis and Hammamet. It is an interesting journey travelling inland and gaining in altitude. A complex system of cisterns and aqueducts once carried fresh water over 132 km, following the contours to Carthage. Parts of the aqueduct can still be seen on the road from Tunis. Zaghouan is dominated by the towering 1,300m high Djebel Zaghouan. The spring and the beginning of the aqueduct can be visited, about 2 km out of town. A few reservoirs can still be seen, but the real interest is the beauty of the site.

Zaghouan is built on to the hill slope. Climb up to the Triumphal Arch (2nd century AD), or rather to the little pavement café situated on the roadside opposite the arch and contemplate the panoramic view, E over the plain towards the sea or S towards Djebel Zaghouan. The Romans must have done just the same, from this very arch. The road continues up towards the Sidi Azouz mosque, and at lunchtime the open doorways allow the smoke and aroma of grilled meat to waft into the street. There is a square by the mosque, shaded by a large tree, and at the corner a fountain of running water in a neat, decorated ceramic tiled surround. There are in fact two mosques close together, one the square white 'wedding cake' variety, the other octagonal, balconies, gold and with green and a pointed green tiled cupola.

The narrow street continues upwards to the Temple des Nymphes some 2 km distant. A few stops are allowed on this slope – to admire the view. There is a small café at the top, with views towards the temple and across the plain. The temple is built into the hillside with steps leading up to a semi-circular wall. The 12 alcoves in the wall once held life size statues, unfortunately all have now gone. The pool in the centre has been restored and again holds water and the steps down have been renewed making access much safer. There is no entry charge. A number of smart villas have been erected on the wooded hillside between the town and the temple.

The Andalusians introduced the wild rose here in 1795 and from this has developed the rose essence production for which this region is justly famous. The rose essence is very popular in cakes and pastries. Zaghouan had just ended a project to increase the area of its already considerable rose gardens and the development of a wild rose nursery. The wild rose festival is held here each May.

● **Accommodation** *C Les Nymphes*, T 675094, Zaghouan 1100, PO Box 11, 1.5 km out of town towards Roman aqueduct, 80 beds, situated in quiet wooded surroundings along a track off the road up to the Temple. It is frequented (it is said) by government officials from Tunis who spend a quiet evening away from the stress of the town. **Youth hostel**: *Maison des Jeunes*, Zaghouan, 85 beds, meals available, T 675265.

● **Hospitals & medical services** A new regional hospital opened here Apr 1996.

● **Post & telecommunications Area code**: 02.

The C28 road E from Zaghouan leads to Hammamet. It leads down through the prairie-like cereal fields to the *oued* and the almond and olive groves. The road skirts a small lake with a hilly ridge as a backdrop and crosses the plain. It comes to the Berber villages of Hammam Jedidi and Sidi Jedidi, the latter to be avoided at all costs on a Tues when coaches deposit their passengers to view an 'authentic' market. The intensive cultivation continues to the motorway and the outskirts of Hammamet.

The C133 road S from Zaghouan which leads to Enfidia descends steeply to the plain. After 5 km take the right fork for an interesting ride. It ascends to the old village of **Zriba** (another 7 km) where you can sit among the ruins and watch the birds of prey circle overhead. This old Berber village clings to the mountainside overlooked by Djebel Zaghouan (1,295m). The village has a fortified granary or *kalaa*, a small mosque with an oblong crenelated tower and a *zaouia* to Sidi Abdelkader el Jilani complete with cupola. It is interesting to see the main streets paved with blocks of stone. Unfortunately the village is deserted. Zriba village, the French settlement, stands much lower down, on the C133, 10 km from Zaghouan.

The Berber village of **Djeradou** can also be reached from this road though easier access, avoiding a very rough road, is from the C35. The villagers work with esparto grass, making plaits which the men then make into a variety of bags and baskets, olive mats and panniers. From the ruined fort can be seen the square white mosque and the domed *zaouia*.

Jebel Oust, 30 km SW from Tunis is one of Tunisia's three main health spas. **Accommodation** *C Djebel el Oust*, T 679740, Complex Thermal, Djebel el Oust, bungalows, a/c in public rooms, views towards mountains; *C Les Thermes*, 98 beds, T 677127, F 677074; *D Cheylus*, 90 beds, T 677477, F 677074.

Bou Kornine National Park, 18 km SE from Tunis, near **Hammam Lif**, is home of the Bonelli's and short-toed eagle, a popular place for picnics. Reached by a minor road off the P1 in the centre of Hammam Lif.

THUBURBO MAJUS

This is 60 km S along the P3 from Tunis. Access by bus or louage from Tunis. Get off at El Fahs and walk (3 km) or get a taxi. If coming from Tunis, ask the driver to stop at Thuburbo Majus (before you get to El Fahs) from which it is a short walk to the site. It is better not to follow the signposts, but to cut across between the two hills, just behind the signpost. There is a car park at the entrance, a small café and a clean toilet. Open 0800-1200 and 1500-1900 in summer and 0930-1630 in winter, closed Mon, entrance TD2, photography TD1.

History

Thuburbo Majus was originally a Punic city, but when the Romans conquered Carthage they agreed to pay dues to Rome and so survived. In 27 BC the Emperor Augustus founded a colony of veterans in order to control the strategic situation of the city. Thuburbo Majus was placed in a strategic position, encircled by hills except to the W permitting a close watch on movement of people and trade between the plain and the coast along the route of the Oued el Kebir. The hinterland, a fertile land producing cereals in abundance, provided a further boost to the economy, added to that of toll/tax collection. The Punic heritage mixed well with the Roman presence and it was at this time that most of the major monuments were repaired or reconstructed, such as the Capitol and the Baths. The town declined as the Romans' authority slackened. With the Vandals in power the town reverted to a village.

Places of interest

Thuburbo Majus is a large site occupying the hill slopes overlooking a fertile agricultural plain and the Oued Kebir which provided the water. It was at an important crossing of trade routes which permitted collection of tolls. The production of cereals, olives and wine were important factors in the prosperity of the city.

This large city covered over 40 hectares. The **Forum** and the **Capitol** dominate the ruins. The forum is well preserved. It was built between 161-192 AD and restored with some changes in layout around 376 AD. It stands 49m square, surrounded by a portico on three sides. The fourth side leads, by means of a broad flight of stairs, to the Capitol

built in 168 AD. This is the best place to visit first as it enables one to view the whole site. Great efforts were made to raise the level of this building to give it the height it needed for its imposing position overlooking the town. Six fluted Corinthian columns each 8.5m high continue to dominate the site. Dedications were made to Emperor Marcus Aurelius and to Commodius. The temple is also dedicated to the triad of Jupiter, Juno and Minerva. The head and foot, all that remains of the statue of Jupiter, once an impossible 8m high, are in the Bardo Museum.

To the NE of the Forum are the remains of the **Curia** (town hall/meeting place of the council). The **Temple of Peace** adjacent to/part of Curia has a marble-paved courtyard with a peristyle leading on to a large hall paved with marble. It is thought a statue to Peace stood here.

The **Temple of Mercury** built in 211 AD has an unusual circular courtyard though the outer walls are straight. The eight column bases remain. He was the god of Merchants and overlooked the market area.

The **Agora**, the paved market place, stood opposite the Capitol and beyond the S corner of the Forum. There are two smaller annexes. This was used for retail of produce but also as a gathering place. The arcades on three sides were divided into 21 small shop spaces.

The **Winter Baths** covering 1,600 sq m were completely rebuilt between 395 and 408 AD. They were very luxurious. There were more than 20 rooms here decorated with elegant mosaics, square pools, round pools, fountains, latrines and urinals. The entrance from the small square was a four-column portico.

The **Summer Baths** were larger, covering 2,400 sq m. These were restored in 361 AD. Here there were cold, warm and hot rooms all with lavish decoration – much marble, many mosaics and fountains. These were fed from three large cisterns.

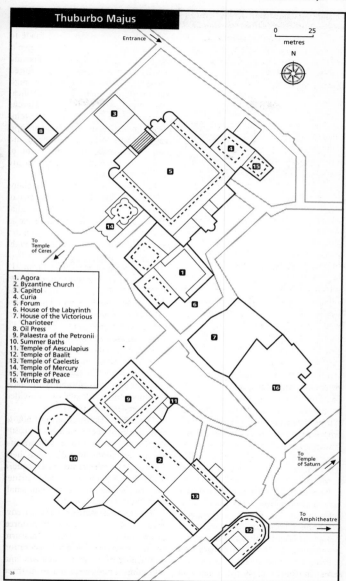

Thuburbo Majus

Entrance

0   25
metres

N

To Temple of Ceres

1. Agora
2. Byzantine Church
3. Capitol
4. Curia
5. Forum
6. House of the Labyrinth
7. House of the Victorious Charioteer
8. Oil Press
9. Palaestra of the Petronii
10. Summer Baths
11. Temple of Aesculapius
12. Temple of Baalit
13. Temple of Caelestis
14. Temple of Mercury
15. Temple of Peace
16. Winter Baths

To Temple of Saturn

To Amphitheatre

28

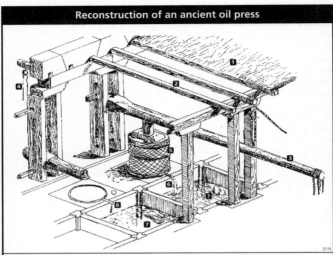

Reconstruction of an ancient oil press

1. Covering of straw or reed matting.
2. Beams supporting roof.
3. Tree trunk raised and lowered to press out the oil.
4. Pulley to lift tree trunk to desired height.
5. Sacking tied round straw mats with crushed olives between.
6. Channel for olive oil.
7. Container for oil with moveable partitions.

The **Palaestra of the Petronii** was built in 225 AD and named after the family who endowed the construction – Petronius Felix. This a rectangular area surrounded by a portico (supported by grey/black marble columns which still stand) was for games and gymnastic activities (wrestling, boxing) before bathing. The mosaic from here, depicting these activities, is in the Bardo Museum. In the S corner there are alphabetic signs carved into the pavement explained as a Roman game rather like Lexicon.

The large, very overgrown, area to the SE of Palaestra was a shrine to the god of healing, the **Temple of Aesculapius**.

Further E is the **Temple of Caelestis** (Tanit) who required the periodic sacrifice of young children (see Carthage).

On the other side of the track is the **Temple of Baalit**. She was a Punic goddess who slipped into the Roman mythology. The building has three straight sides while the short NE side is semicircular and has a door opening on to a small square, smaller than but similar to the square before the Winter baths.

The **Temple of Saturn** (not much left here) to W of site and at the highest point in town, later became a church. Again there is evidence of 'building up the land' before constructing the temple.

The ruins of the **Amphitheatre**, hollowed out of the hillside, can be found to the very edge of the site. Near by is one of the cisterns for water supply. This cistern to the S of the site is huge – large enough to have an inner gallery constructed on the inside rim.

The oil factories behind and to the W of the Capitol are a reminder of the activities which helped to make this town so prosperous.

In the residential area around the Forum were homes of wealthy Roman inhabitants. They are named after the mosaics found there – eg Neptune, Theseus. Another residential has been excavated in the SW area by the summer and winter baths. The **House of the**

Victorious Charioteer by the Winter Baths had rich mosaics and painted stucco. The **House of the Labyrinth** is by the market. From here was retrieved the well known 4th century mosaic which covered the floor of the *frigidarium* in the baths of this private house. The mosaic, in the form of a maze (labyrinth) has at the centre Theseus cutting off the head of the Minator. The ground surrounding the two figures is littered with bits of humans, the remains of the monster's previous victims. The mosaic is bordered with walls and gates, depicting the city. This mosaic is in the Bardo Museum.

The **Temple of Cérès**, to the W of the site, on sloping ground had a courtyard 30m x 30m, the centre decorated with mosaics and a portico with three gateways. Later this was turned into a church, using half of the courtyard. A number of tombs were found in the church, one containing jewels.

Local information
● Accommodation

There is no accommodation at or nr the site.

Thuburbo Majus makes a good day trip from Tunis, returning via Zaghouan. The nearest **youth hostel** is in Zaghouan convenient for travellers going E to Enfida and Sousse.

El Fahs, a busy agricultural centre, larger than Zaghouan, holds an important cattle market each Sat. Expensive harvesting equipment is for sale. There are several engineering establishments here, more advanced than the casual car/van repair merchants on the outskirts of every town.

SOUTHWEST FROM TUNIS

Tunis to Medjez el Bab
Take the minor road W to Toukabeur and after 16 km reach Chaouach at 490m, built round a fortress (Byzantine?). These two are typical Berber villages living on a very modest scale, olives, cattle and sheep, cereals. In the area are the ruins of Roman **Sua**, and earlier caves, called *haouanets* carved in the cliffs for burial places.

Couscous

The really good host/hostess makes his/her own couscous – of course, as follows.

Spread the coarse semolina in the base of a large shallow dish, gently add water and stir until the moisture is evenly spread. Over this sprinkle fine semolina flour and roll the mixture in the palm of the hand, adding more water or more fine semolina until the mixture turns into balls about the size of a chick pea. Use the first couscous sieve with the coarse mesh (*ghorbel qamh*) and shake and break up the mixture till it all goes through. Repeat the process with the medium mesh (*ghorbel kouksi*) again breaking up any larger pieces with the palm of the hand to help them through. Shaking the mixture in the small mesh sieve (*ghorbel tallaâ*) removes the too fine material and leaves the finished couscous.

Put water to simmer in the base of the couscous steamer and the slightly dampened couscous in the colander above and allow to steam. After 30 mins remove the colander and place the contents in a shallow bowl, sprinkle it with water and using a fork break up any lumps so each grain is separate. Return to colander and steam for a further 10 mins.

Couscous is served with countless savoury dishes and many of these can be cooked in the base of the steamer while the semolina is being cooked above it.

Cap Bon Peninsula

THIS REGION, which covers an area of 2,837 sq km and protrudes like a thumb into the Mediterranean, was an essential part of the Roman Empire for food supplies. Today it is rich in orchards, the source of fresh fruit and early vegetables for much of Europe, of olives, and of Tunisian wine from its 33,000 hectares of vineyards. Furthermore, with the growth of the all year holiday hotels built along the beautiful beaches, it is the Tunisia of the package tourist. Down the centre of this peninsula is a line of hills which culminate in the west at Djebel Sidi Abderrahman (421m) and in the east at Djebel Ben Oulid (637m) adding variety to the landscape and virtually separating the north coast from the southeasterly region.

The peninsula is well known for the almost uninterrupted ribbon of fine sandy beaches which extend for over 200 km. The coast to the north is more indented and has more rocks, but is equally less busy.

TUNIS TO HAMMAMET

Heading SE from Tunis there are two parallel roads, the A1 autoroute and the P1 trunk road, as far as Sousse. The booths on the new A1 section are being erected and soon a toll will be levied. This will still be a good route to take, avoiding the slow journeys through small towns and villages and providing a view over the rolling countryside towards the distant mountains. Nearer peaks include Djebel Bou Kornine (Two Horns) at 576m to the E, in the National Park and Djebel Ressas (Mountain of Lead) at 795m, about half way from Tunis to Hammamet. Do not relax your concentration as sheep still graze the verges and illegal U-turns are still practised. The P1 provides a slower journey with more people-based activity. The third route, by train, runs beside the P1 most of the way and having a higher position in the carriages, the view, especially over the vineyards near Grombalia is particularly good.

Cap Bon

Zembra

Zembretta

El Haouaria

Cap Bon

Sidi Daoud

Kerkouane

Mediterranean

Sea

Zaouiet El Mgaïez

Tazoghrane

C 27

Kelibia

Rass Dourdass

C 26

⛰ *Djebel Ben Oulid (637m)*

C 45

Skalba

Korbous

Sidi Aissa

Bir Meroua

Menzel Temime

⛰ *Djebel Bou Korbous (419m)*

⛰ *Djebel Si Abd Er Rahmane (602m)*

Gulf of Tunis

Sidi Rais

Barrage Chiba

Soliman Plage

⛰ *Djebel Sidi Abderrahman (421m)*

C 43

Cedria

Soliman

Menzel Bou Zelfa

C 27

⛰ *Djebel Rassas (576m)*

Beni Khalled

C 44

Korba

Grombalia

Belli

Tazerka

To Tunis

⛰ *Djebel Ben Kornine (795m)*

Es Somaa

⛰ *Djebel Makki (641m)*

Bou Argoub

C 27

Dar Chaabane

Beni Khiar

GP 1

Bordj el Hafaïed

⛰ *Djebel Reba el Aïn (328m)*

Nabeul

⛰ *Djebel Behelil (556m)*

Bir Bou Rekba

Aïn Tébournok

To Zaghouan

Sidi Jedidi

Hammamet

N

C 35

To Sousse

Gulf of Hammamet

0   10

km

Bou Ficha

HAMMAMET

ACCESS Frequent buses and trains come from Tunis and a train runs from Monastir airport. Buses and taxis stop near the medina. The station is a short walk away, or share a taxi.

Hammamet, known as **Pupput** to the Romans was a stopping point on the Roman road with linked Carthage to Hadrumete (Sousse). The city developed as a result of the expansion of agriculture and maritime trade and also thanks to the generous sponsorship of a wealthy patron, Salvius Julianus. Other 'visitors' included the Sicilians, the Turks, the Spanish.

Hammamet, 65 km SE from Tunis, is probably one of the best known resorts in Tunisia. In the 1950s this was a sleepy village adjoining a beautiful beach on fertile ground. There was a small population

Early tourists and gilded exiles

🦶 Like Capri and Taormina over the water in Italy and the red city of Marrakech, the Tunisian towns of Sidi Bou Saïd and Hammamet attracted artists and the internationally rich and famous in the first half of the 20th century. The myths of classical antiquity and variations on *Death in Venice* were a powerful draw. Some, like the writer André Gide, sought the primal scene, others like the painter Paul Klee left Tunisia with inspiration for life, and still others preferred the life of the lotus-eater.

By the end of the 19th century, the establishment of steamer lines had made travel sufficiently safe and easy for visitors to come and go between the ports of the Mediterranean and northern Europe. Italy, of course, was the primary destination, and travellers became tourists enraptured by the colour and animation and the rich cultural heritage.

Travel to 'the south' had been a natural complement to a classical education since the 18th century. It was the journey out of the library and as the French built roads and railways across North Africa they also took care to excavate the Roman cities, emphasizing the Latinity of the recently acquired territories. As modern quarters grew up alongside the old medinas wealthier travellers would stay a whole winter in their southern Arcadia, enjoying the mild climate or living out their exotic fantasies, or both.

The heyday of tourism for would-be writers and men of leisure was between the two world wars. Rodolphe, Baron d'Erlanger, scion of a French banking house which had done well lending money to Tunisia in the mid-nineteenth century, built himself a neo-Moorish palace at Sidi Bou Saïd in the twenties, and having constructed this latter-day Alhambra with all the conveniences of an English country house, he proceeded to organize scholars into producing a voluminous

and two hotels. The small population prospered on agriculture, fishing, crafts including weaving and embroidery and the production of essence from the orange flowers. Now it has a population of 100,000 and welcomes tourists in their thousands. The change has been very carefully executed, with attention to the preservation of the site, no hotel permitted higher than a palm tree! It stretches now over 2 km N inland and slightly uphill and to the E and W some 7 km along the coast. This is where the holidaymakers spend their vacation in the hotels by the beach, some never leaving the hotel complex.

The development of the town started in the 1920s, when Rumanian millionaire, **Georges Sebastian**, built a beautiful villa and invited many of his artistic friends such as Paul Klee, André Gide and Frank Lloyd Wright to visit. In 1959, Georges Sebastian's house was bought by the state and made into an International Cultural Centre (see below). During most of the year the house and gardens can be visited. The caretaker will show you round. The lounge is worth seeing with its long table and simple wrought iron chairs and the walls hung with 'modern art'. The novel 4-seater sunken bath is set in the shape of a cross (presumably mixed bathing – all very avant-garde) rather like four hip baths. The caretaker will operate the water system. (A similar system can be seen at Kerkouane.) The rather small guest bedroom can be viewed. Here Von Arnim, Rommel, Montgomery and Churchill were accommodated as the varying fortunes of WW2 permitted. Entrance TD1, photography TD1. Open

treatise on Arab music and also found time to execute some nicely splodgy oils of his adoptive village and its people.

Hammamet at the turn of the century consisted of a walled town, its ramparts overlooking the sea, with kilometres of beaches stretching away on either side and a hinterland of fragrant orchards. A wealthy Anglo-American couple, the Hensons, came in 1923 and chose Hammamet as a retreat. The handsome Jean Henson had arrived in France in 1917, in service with the US Navy. Caught up in the artistic atmosphere of the twenties' Paris, he remained after the war, friend of artists and immortalized by the photographer Man Ray. On Capri he met a divorced Englishwoman, Violett, and the two headed S for Hammamet, where they made their home. Instead of opting for the most refined Hispano-Moorish decorative techniques like Rodolphe d'Erlanger, the Hensons chose the domes and vaults of Tunisian vernacular architecture, the simplicity of the modular patio house of Mediterranean tradition. In 1925 Georges Sebastien, a mysterious Rumanian millionaire arrived and followed the Hensons' example, to be followed later by a Baltic aristocrat George Hoyningen-Huene and his protégé, the photographer, Horst.

Romantic residential tourism continues today. From the ramparts of the Hammamet kasbah it is possible to see lovingly preserved summer houses and a restored Sidi Bou Saïd home is much sought after by wealthy Tunisians. Happily for those without the Jet Set connections the Dar Ennejma Ezzahra, as the d'Erlanger palace is called, is now the Centre for Arab and Mediterranean Music (see page 386), open for public tours and the occasional concert. Dar Sebastien, also now state-owned, is more drama oriented and the mini theatre in the grounds is home to an annual summer festival of the performing arts (see page 149).

0830-1800 daily except Mon. An open-air theatre was built in the grounds and a very interesting **International festival** is held here annually in Jul/Aug with dance, theatre and music (ranging from jazz to classical).

The town has kept some of its charm, even though a commercial centre (find the banks and a supermarket here) was recently constructed. Equally the medina, surrounded by its walls and lying adjacent to the sea, has kept some of its oriental mystique. The beach continues to be an attraction, to the E, from the cemetery up towards the hotel region it is of fine white sand, some 30m wide with safe bathing. The development of the newly planted palm trees along the promenade will provide necessary shade. Escape from the tourist shops and walk around the small back streets. Walk on the beach and watch the fishermen mending their nets. There are several bench seats along the medina wall which give a more comfortable view of the same activity. Fishing no longer has the importance of earlier days and some of the boats on the beach are more attractive than they are seaworthy. Stepping off the main street, Ave de la République, for a glimpse of the real Hammamet will reveal a host of small workshops, small food shops, even live chickens for sale. Note the smart new villas set among the older run-down dwellings. Notice the door decorations of black nails which form stylized, traditional designs and the decorated door surrounds.

Places of interest

The **Medina**, fairly small, is the main landmark in Hammamet, built right on the beach. Originally constructed in 904, frequently damaged and restored, the walls protect the **Great Mosque**, the baths and the narrow, winding streets. Near the kasbah these contain numerous stalls intent on attracting the tourists and the fresh food stalls of the daily market. The rest of the medina is made up of private dwellings, the attractive doors set into the otherwise blank walls are an attraction in their own right. Some restored dwellings have window balconies.

The medina contains many reminders of the holy men who spent time in Hammamet. Among them are **Sidi Bou Hadid** (12th century) may have come from Morocco, perhaps Sakiet el Hamra. It is said that shortly before he died he instructed his family to put his corpse into a coffin and throw it into the sea. He wanted the waves and currents to decide on his final resting place. His tomb was to be built where his coffin was washed ashore. Legend has it that the sea gods built his tomb by the town walls, from where he can keep watch over the Gulf of Hammamet. For this reason he has become the particular saint of the fishermen who make offerings to him and in times of real danger call on his assistance. He is said to be buried in the medina in the place which bears his name.

Other holy men with tombs in Hammamet include **Sidi Mohammed Attiq** (late 14th century), a religious thinker who stayed awake at night to protect the town (while, it is said he read the Koran over 1,700 times) and **Sidi Abdallah** the mystic (early 15th century), who despite his wealth spent most of his time within the fort at Hammamet – thinking. His marabout still exists. Each has an area in the medina bearing his name. **Sidi Bou Ali** (early 14th century) has his tomb in the kasbah. This ascetic is revered today and his marabout in the courtyard is visited by those who hope to receive his blessing.

There is also evidence of Hammamet's other famous men: **Cheikh el Fnaich** came to Tunisia from Andalucía in 1691. He was a holy man, a scientist and a poet. He built a mosque in the medina where he taught the Koran and where he was murdered by robbers.

Hedi Ouali Ben Ahmed (the street named after him runs beside the railway to the N of town) was from an important local family. He died at just 25 fighting in the Tunisian army for the control of Bizerte.

Taieb Ben Mohammed Azzabi (for street named after him see map) was born in Hammamet and died just 26 fighting for the liberation of Tunisia.

Chaabane Ben Othman Merhbene was born in Hammamet in 1917. He lead the Destourian movement in the town until 1956 when he was promoted. He eventually became president of the Destourian confederation. In 1952 he was sentenced to 10 years in prison and 10 years in exile for his part in the struggle against the French for independence but independence was gained in 1956 and he was honoured by President Bouguiba.

The **Dar Hammamet** in the medina is a **Museum of Traditional Dress**. The three rooms have an interesting collection of traditional female clothing and wedding garments. One room is set out as a bedroom. There are additional costumes in the cabinets. Entry TD1.5 for adults, TD0.5 children under 10 years, open 0900-1700 every day of the year, T 281206. Enter from the square by the cemetery or follow the signs by the sea front. This is another place recommended for watching the sunset from the roof.

The **Great Mosque** is most easily reached through the gate from the market place from where the minaret can be seen. It is not outstanding but is obvious by its white square tower where the upper part, just below the crenelations, is covered with yellow tiles patterned in black. At ground level in the white wall there are several light brown wooden doors set in a stone surround. On each is

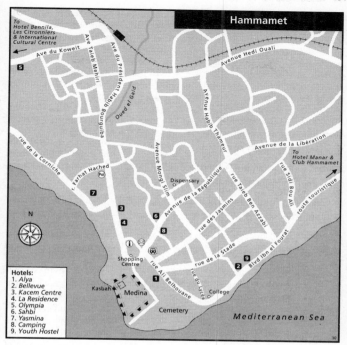

Hammamet

Hotels:
1. Alya
2. Bellevue
3. Kacem Centre
4. La Residence
5. Olympia
6. Sahbi
7. Yasmina
8. Camping
9. Youth Hostel

a clear message in four European languages to keep out.

The **Kasbah** was originally built in the 12th century and has now been heavily restored. The building you see today dates back to the middle of the 15th century (between 1463 and 1474) and was built while the Hafsids were in power. It is more impressive as a setting than as a place to visit. It stands in the western corner of the medina and has some splendid views to the NW over the beach with its holidaymakers among the colourful fishing boats pulled up on the sand and over the esplanade with its restaurants and boutiques, to the SW over the Mediterranean sea where here the walls actually rise out of the water, and to the S and SE it overlooks the white walls and roofs of the medina. More

distant aspects include the expanse of the Gulf of Hammamet and to the W Djebel Zaghouan (1,295m). These magnificent views from the walkway and the battlements are certainly worth the TD1 entrance fee (photography free). Situated in the N corner of the kasbah is a squat tower on which is a small café (there are many pleasanter places) while the inner courtyard is bare apart from a few trees which provide welcome shade in the summer. There are three cannons and several horse-drawn ploughs on display but no museum.

Located beside the sea, the fort gave rise to the foundation of the town of Hammamet. It was first constructed between the end of the 9th and the beginning of the 10th centuries (between 893 and 904) under the Aghlabite Dynasty.

As it stands today most of the work is from the middle of the 15th century while the Hafsids were in power.

The Sidi Djedidi site has some Roman mosaics, entrance TD1, open daily summer 0900-1300 and 1500-1900, winter 0830-1730.

Visit the archaeological site of Pupput which was a staging post on the road from Carthage to Hadrumete. There are some fine Roman mosaics here. Entrance TD1, open daily summer 0800-1300 and 1500-1900, winter 0830-1730.

The Centre International Culturel on Ave des Nations Unies, some 3 km W of the town is a rather pretentious name for an organization which promotes a few festivals in summer and theatrical productions in the open-air amphitheatre in its extensive grounds. The sea makes a magnificent backdrop. The stone tiered theatre (don't forget your cushion!) was built with money provided by the Gulbenkian Foundation. The International Festival takes place in Jul-Aug, presenting in Arabic and French folklore, theatricals, ballet, concerts, musicals

Take a stroll

The following walk is recommended on a calm day. Follow the medina wall past the market place with the cemetery on the left. Carry on round the next corner and half way along there is a breach in the wall. Continue to the beach (or call into the Dar Hammamet museum if you have not been yet) where the wall begins again by the sea. Hop down to the beach. Keep the medina wall to the right and the beach soon disappears to become a narrow rocky path which can be affected by sea spray. This terminates about half way along at a small quay with a gateway into the medina. Walk through the narrow alleys of the dwelling area of the medina back to the Great Mosque and the market place. The tall white modern memorial, sweeping skywards, commemorates the dead of WW2 and adjacent to it, on the wall forming the boundary between the market place and the cemetery is a high relief frieze depicting the horrors of war. This is some 36m long and 1½m high, of modern styling formed in flowing lines in a cement plaster (not carved). It is worthy of closer inspection. Weekly market Thur morning.

Local information
● **Accommodation**

As there are lots of expensive hotels along the coast to the N and to the S of the town, it is easy to find somewhere to stay. These same rooms, however, are much cheaper if booked as part of a package.

B *Dar Hayet*, 10 mins walk along the beach from Kasbah, T 283399, decor outstanding, comfort superb; **A** *Hotel Manar*, route Touristique, T 281333, F 280772, 200 rm, 6 floors, a/c, 2 pools, 5 tennis courts, golf, banks, shops, restaurants; **A** *Hotel Miramar*, rue de Nevers, T 280344, F 280586, 3 km W of Hammamet centre, gardens lead on to beach, all facilities expected, this is one of the original tourist hotels that has recently been extended, make sure to get a room in the newer part as those in the older part are showing their age (this part only **B** standard) and the a/c is noisy; **A** *Hotel Phénicia*, Ave Moncef Bey, T 226331, F 280337, somewhat isolated, 7 km W of Hammamet, in 14 ha of garden fronting on to the beach, 370 rm incl suites, all facilities plus indoor heated pool which connects to outside pool, also separate outside pool, luxurious reception lounge, this hotel is very highly rec.

B *Hotel Bel Azur*, T 280544, F 280275, Ave Assad Ibn el Fourat about 2½ km N of town centre, 620 beds, located on water's edge in

Tipped off

🐾 The all too numerous feral cats found scavenging around the hotel areas although appealing are best not handled. The Society for the Protection of Animals in Tunisia along with the London based Society for the Protection of Animals in North Africa are working to control the numbers. The cats are caught, neutered and marked by the removal of the tip of the left ear and released to continue an active, but thereafter, unproductive life.

Thalassotherapy

🦶 One of the most comprehensive ranges of treatment backed up with good organization is the Bio Azur centre in the grounds of *Hotel Bel Azur*, best known for its heated seawater treatments of rheumatism, arthritis, gout, backache, nicotine dependency, stress and for slimming and post-natal depression. Cost of any four treatments per day is TD75.

Individual treatments such as a total marine mud bath TD25, general massage TD25, local massage TD15 are only three of the total of 25 treatments on offer. A beauty salon forms an integral part of the centre providing facial treatments – from an antiwrinkle course TD220 to an evening makeup TD20. Contact *Centre de Thalassotherapy Bio Azur*, Hammamet, T 2788500.

Other centres are Abou Nawas Abou Jaâfar in Sousse opened 1993, Gammarth (planned) and Djerba (planned).

extensive (10 ha) landscaped grounds, very high standard, all sports facilities available; **B** *Hotel Club-Hammamet*, route Touristique, T 281882, F 281670, 337 rm on 2 floors, a/c, very good, beach, indoor pool complex, outdoor Olympic size pool, many activities, good food, large rooms facing the sea; **B** *Hotel Continental*, T 280220, F 280409, right on the beach, a/c, with bath, terrace, restaurant, bar, covered pool, TV, shop, boutiques, sauna, fitness room, tennis, watersports, shares with adjacent *Hotel Parc Plage*, all facilities; **B** *Hotel Fourati*, rue de Nevers, T 280388, F 280508, 3 km W of town centre, enter through gardens to reception, gardens lead down to beach, 772 beds, all facilities, 1 heated indoor pool, 2 outdoor pools; **B** *Hotel Kacem Centre*, Ave Habib Bourguiba, nr train station, T 279580, F 279588, 67 rm with 2 ring hob and fridge, crockery and utensils, 2 pools, roof top terrace with BBQ, a/c, 800m to private beach shared with *Yasmina*, restaurant, fitness centre; **B** *Hotel Le Hammamet*, rue de Nevers, T 280366, F 282105, 3 km W of town centre, of high standard but does not front the beach which is about 5-mins walk away, 674 rm, all services incl a/c and heating, 1 heated indoor pool, 1 outdoor pool; **B** *Hotel la Residence*, 72 Ave Habib Bourguiba, T 280406, F 280396, Moorish style, 184 rm with 2 ring hob, fridge, utensils and crockery, roof top pool heated in winter, full a/c, restaurant, 10 mins from beach, 4 km to golf.

C *Hotel Khella*, Ave de la République, T 283900, 10-mins walk from medina, home quiet, 71 rm with bath, a/c, heating, good, clean, modern hotel; **C** *Hotel Les Oranges/Hotel Les Oranges Beach*, rue de Nevers, T 280144, F 280157, 766 beds in total,

typical tourist hotel providing all facilities which are shared between the two establishments, indoor pool, outdoor pool; **C** *Hotel Olympia*, Ave Des Nations Unies, T 280622, F 283142, 36 rm with shower and heating, no restaurant but many in vicinity, a clean, tidy hotel.

Our special recommendation – **Samaris** family hotel and campsite to the W of town but convenient after coming off the motorway. Don't be put off by the approach for once inside there is a warm welcome from the owner. The hotel lobby and reception are decorated in traditional style with a pleasant lounge and easy chairs. To the right is the comfortable small restaurant while straight ahead is the terrace where meals can be served. The centrepiece is an ancient olive press, in perfect condition, found on the site. In the evenings there is traditional entertainment, folk music, dancing etc, at no extra charge. The 20 rm, situated round the courtyard, nr the main building, are simply furnished with twin beds, a/c, heating, shower and wc. There are three studios which sleep 4 persons and have cooking facilities at TD50/day. The thick stone walls make this a rarity – a quiet hotel. The adjacent camping ground in 2 ha enclosed site, electricity, toilets and showers, shares the pool. Fees TD3 pp; TD1.5/car and per tent; TD2.5/caravan. The beach is 5 mins by car.

D *Hotel Alya*, rue Ali Belhouane, T 280218, F 282365, central, very clean, half the rooms look over the medina, the others over a street, roof terrace, bar, 300m from beach; **D** *Hotel Bellevue*, Blvd Ibn el Fourat, T 281121, F 283156, beach, central, clean rooms, most with view; **D** *Hotel Sahbi*, in town centre, T 280807, central, 200m from beach, pleasant large rooms, some with views; **D** *Les Citronniers*, route des Hotels, by *Hotel Bennila*, T 281650, F 282601, modern, very close to beach, no views, barbecue, drinks, food on the beach.

E *Hotel Bennila*, route des Hotels, from the centre take the road to Sousse and turn left by the UIB bank, T 280356, clean, pleasant rooms, pool, quite cheap.

Camping: *Ideal Camping*, 34 Ave de la République, T 280302, adequate, restaurant, electric hook-ups, shaded area, book in summer, tent TD2.5, car TD2.5, person TD1.5/night.

Youth hostel: T 280440, 100 beds, meals, central location, beside *Hotel Bellevue*.

● **Places to eat**

♦♦♦*Chateau Neuf*, Centre Sunset City, T 282976; *La Cupola*, Ave du Koweit, T 281138; *Dar Sidi*, Centre Khayem, T 289985; *Fiesta*, Centre Commercial, T 280985; *Oasis*, Feten Centre, T 227881; *La Pergola*, Centre Commercial, T 280993.

♦♦*Restaurant Achour*, T 280140, central, rue Ali Belhouane, reputedly the best fish restaurant in Hammamet, terrace; *Aquarium*, Ave des Nations Unies, T 282449; *Restaurant Barberousse*, in the medina, wonderful terrace, pleasant decor, very touristy; *Jugurtha*, Ave des Nations Unies, T 280432; *La Medina*, in square nr kasbah, T 281728, popular, pleasant Tunisian style café, seating 60 people, get a table on the terrace if possible for a fine view over the medina, beach and esplanade, especially interesting on market day, use the entrance from the sea front, sample price seafood salad TD12, royal couscous TD7; *La Brise*, Ave de la République, close to medina, no alcohol, quantity rather than quality; *La Sirene*, Ave Assad Ibn el Fourat, right on beach opp sports stadium, 10-15 mins walk from town so very quiet.

♦*Pizzeria* T 80825, Shopping Centre, central; *Restaurant de la Poste*, central square, opp the medina, terrace has a great view over the medina and the golf course, good food, quite cheap; *La Rosa*, Ave du Koweit, T 282864; *Shehrazade*, Ave des Nationes Unies, T 280436; *Sidi Abdel Kader*, junction rue Ali Benhouane and rue du Stade, opp *Hotel Alya*, a clean pleasant restaurant seating 20, sample prices fillet steak TD6, spaghetti TD4, seafood salad TD2, several cheap cafés and restaurants overlook the esplanade and the beach.

Look out for the French style pâtisserie on the junction of Ave de la République and rue Ali

Belhouane, the window displays are nearly as attractive as the produce.

● **Banks & money changers**

Money can be changed in the big hotels or the banks in the centre of town. **BDS**, Ave du Koweit; **BT**, Ave Habib Bourguiba; **STB**, Ave du Koweit, has automatic cash dispenser (dinars) for Visa and Mastercard; **UIB**, Ave des Nations Unies, an exension of Ave du Koweit. There is a bank in the medina, in the square by the kasbah which is open Sun when all other banks are closed.

● **Entertainment**

Cinema: in shopping centre, performances at 1500 and 2100. Prices TD2 and TD1.5.

Hammam: the Turkish bath (Bain Maure) is to the right of the Great Mosque in the medina.

Nightclubs: mainly to the S of Hammamet, on the road to Sousse, in the direction of the route des Hotels. *Ranch Club*, Ave Moncef Bey; *La Tortue*, *Manhatten*, *Calypso*, Ave Moncef Bey, and *New Mexico* all in Hammamet Sud. *Bedouina*, T 280095, Ave des Nations Unies, an extension of Ave du Koweit; *Tropicana*, Route Touristique and *Sunset City*, Merazka.

Theatre: Centre Culturel, T 280656, Ave des Nations Unies.

● **Hospitals & medical services**

Chemist: open nights, two on Ave de la République, T 280876 or T 280257.

● **Places of worship**

Catholic: 13 rue du Lycée, off rue du Stade, adjacent to college, marked Eglise Catolic in ceramic tiles. The church, built in traditional Arab style, is only open for service Sat 1700 and Sun 1100 but the tree shaded garden and bench seats are available at all times. Contact the priest at Grombalia, T 255232 (winter) and Hammamet T 280865 (summer). Protestant services are also held here. Contact Pastor Dobson at Sousse medina, T (03)224073.

● **Post & telecommunications**

Area code: 02.

Post Office: Ave de la République, T 250598, Mon-Sat 0730-1230 and 1700-1900 in summer, winter 0800-1200 and 1500-1800. Sun always 0900-1100.

● **Shopping**

Most shops are content to sell trinkets and souvenirs, the high quality hotels have a better selection in their boutiques and serious shoppers are advised to go to Sousse. However, the following shops have been rec as having handicraft goods of reasonable quality. In the Medina try Bazaar Mahmoud, Boutique Abdessalem Boudhina, Boutique Negro, Dar Braham, Gharbi Bazaar, Maison Arabe and Sindabad Bazaar.

Bookshops: there is a good bookshop in the shopping centre, selling informative books and booklets in many European languages.

Market: Market day – Thur.

● **Sports**

All watersports are available, also horse (and camel!) riding, golf, tennis, and go-karting. Ask at any hotel. Yasmin Golf Course, T/F 226722, has 18 holes, 6,114m and par 72. Cytrus Golf Course, T 226500, F 226400, 2 18-hole courses of 6,175m at par 72, fees TD 28-30/day. Hot air ballooning. *Leisure Centre*, T 280656, Ave Habib Bourguiba.

● **Tour companies & travel agents**

Carthage Tours, rue Dag Hammarskjold, T 281926, F 281166; *Hammamet Travel Service*, rue Dag Hammarskjold, T 280193, F 281936; *Royal Travel Club*, rue de Nevers, T 281413, F 281488; *Tourafrica*, rue Dag Hammarskjold, T 280446, F 278225; *Tunisia Explorer*, Ave des Nations Unies, T 283275, F 282766; *Tunisian Travel Service*, Ave des Nations Unies, T 280040; *Visit Tunisia*, 48 Ave du Koweit, T 287427, F 283120; *Voyages Loisirs Tourisme*, Ave Habib Bourguiba, T 224600/900, F 223777.

● **Tourist offices**

The tourist information office is at 32 Ave Habib Bourguiba, by the new shopping complex in town centre, T 280423.

● **Useful addresses**

Police: Av Habib Bourguiba, T 280079.

Toilets: are situated at the gate from the market place towards the mosque, shared entrance but separate inside. Only for an emergency.

● **Transport**

Local Car hire: Avis, route de la Gare, T 280164; **Europacar**, Ave des Nations Unies, T 280146; **Hertz**, Ave des Hotels, opp *Hotel Miramar*, T 280187; **Intercar**, Ave des Nations Unies, T 280423; **Topcar**, Ave des Nations Unies, T 281247; **Tri Car**, Ave Habib Bourguiba, T 283580, F 283576. **Cycle hire**: TD2/hr or TD10/day from *Hotel Kacem* Centre. **Taxi**: can be hired from in front of the medina.

Noddy

The Noddy train is operated privately and consists of three rubber tyred coaches open at the sides but covered on top. Each coach has 6 bench seats, each seating 3 persons. Price for a 5 km ride is TD2 per person which is more expensive than a taxi shared between 2 people and much slower – but not so much fun....

Some attempt is made at destination colour coding, but check.

Train There is one train daily to Tunis at 0603 and two to Nabeul at 1546, 1926, otherwise the nearest trains are at Bir Bou Rebka reached by bus or louage. Information: T 280174. From **Bir Bou Rebka**: to Tunis at 0819, 1020, 1641, 1943 and 2100; to Sousse (Sfax and Gabès) 0700, 0816, 1304, 1500, 1609 and 1850. A Noddy Train provides a shuttle service from the hotels to the town centre on a leave when full basis. At slack times it waits by the medina for customers.

Now only one train each day operates from Tunis on the branch line to Hammamet. The main train station for both Hammamet and Nabeul is **Bir Bou Rebka** where a fine new station building is under construction. The continuation of the journey is by taxi or bus, the fare to Hammamet being TD4 and TD0.6 respectively. The second class train ticket to Tunis is TD4.6 plus the admission ticket of TD0.5 on the return journey. Take care at Bir Bou Rebka as the name is marked on the station building but not on the platform – and cannot therefore be seen by passengers on the train.

Road Bus: the bus station is front of the medina. Frequent departures for **Tunis**, **Sousse** and **Nabeul**. Hammamet to Nabeul to Hammamet from 0630-1915, every 30 mins; Hammamet to Kelibia at 0830, 1300, 1620 and 1720; Kelibia to Hammamet 0500, 0600, 0630 and 1445; Hammamet to El Haouaria 1720; El Haouaria to Hammamet 0525. All journeys to Korbus are via Soliman; to Monastir via Sousse at 0705; to Kairouan at 0620 with return from Kairouan at 1130; to Mahdia via Sousse at 0735, arriving Sousse at 1035; return from Mahdia at 1400 leaves Sousse at 1530; to Zaghouan (and El Fahs) at 0550, 1120, 1420 and 1720; to Tunis at 0530, 0650, 0715, 0930, 1045, 1246, 1300, 1500 with return buses at 0730, 0915, 0930, 1230, 1430, 1450, 1730, 1815, 1830.

Excursions from Hammamet

Sidi Jedidi, about 12 km W of Hammamet, is named after a holy man of Moroccan birth called Cheikh Mohammed Jedidi who lived in the region. He was favoured by Mohammed Ben Hassan, a Hafsid prince, who gave him 18,000 ha on which this hamlet stands. Many tour operators offer a visit to a typical country market at Sidi Jedidi. By their very interest they have changed the nature of the market and items for tourists are now being retailed.

A far more natural local market can be visited any Wed at **Bou Argoub**, on the GP1 17 km N of Hammamet. There are no trinkets or souvenirs for tourists here. There are (as yet) no tourists. Many of the dwellings in this region and on towards Grombalia are Italian style, with pitched roofs and clay tiles. A very different experience from the domed roofs. The railway station buildings at Fondouk Djedid, Grombalia and Bou Argoub are typical country town Italian, especially the latter with its 2 storeys surmounted by a sloping roof and its shuttered windows. Even the whitewashed walls and blue painted woodwork do not disguise its unusual style.

NABEUL

ACCESS The bus station on Ave Habib Thameur. Taxi rank by hospital on Ave Farhat Hached.

Nabeul, 65 km SE from Tunis, with a population of 50,000, is considered the capital of tourism in Tunisia, though it is difficult to know why. The centre of the town is only a collection of shops and services for tourists. Nabeul is the capital town of the Directorat of Cap Bon and the regional government buildings are here on Ave Taieb Mehiri as are the colleges.

New in Nabeul on Ave Habib Thameur, standing in the middle of the road near the hospital, is a monument to Cap Bon's orange production. It depicts a basket of oranges surmounting a tiled tower some 5m high.

The Romans knew this town as

Another holiday romance?
Mosaic from Neapolis – reclining Neptune makes his intentions
quite clear while Mars looks on.

Neapolis. The actual site is beside the *Hotel Aquarius*, almost on the beach, must not be missed. This Phoenician city was occupied by Roman troops during the 3rd Punic war in 148. Under Caesar Augustus it grew in importance, developing quickly, and by 258 had obtained the status of a Roman city. Here can be seen the 'House of Nymphs' from which the seven beautiful mosaics now exhibited in the town's museum were removed. It is also said to be the place where Artemonis, a superb horse, doted on by his Roman master, was buried.

Just beside it there is a 'factory' where fish entrails were processed to make the famous highly flavoured *garum* seasoning. This condiment was used in most Roman dishes.

Colonia Julila Neapolis, apparently developed by Julius Caesar on an earlier Punic site, lies 1 km to the E of town. The entrance to the site off the Route Touristique is a gate with a sign over 'This is closed'. Continue about 50m further E and take the track which leads to the sea. About 200m down the track on the left is a small gate, the entrance. Open daily 0900-1200, entry TD1, photos TD1. The site, which is privately owned, extends to about 8 ha and it is now you wish you had memorized the map from the entrance of the museum in Nabeul. The site is very overgrown and the excavations appear haphazard, the half revealed foundations of a villa, a few fallen columns or a poorly preserved mosaic among the uncut grass.

Places of interest

Museum, 44 Ave Habib Bourguiba, just next to the railway station and the famous Jarre, displays the best of the local remains from nearby Neapolis and a few from the excavations at Kerkouane and Kelibia. It is built round the traditional square courtyard with a gallery to the left exhibiting Punic pottery and statuettes and an extensive display of pottery and oil lamps through to the 3rd century AD.

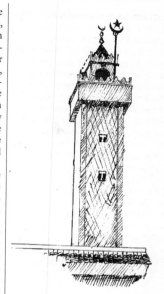

Mosque Salamba – The Minaret

Opposite the entrance is a fine display of mosaics. The best by far is a life-size mosaic showing the vanquished Pryum (?) kneeling before a seated Agamemnon with Mercury and Achilles (?) standing behind them and another showing Mars standing behind a reclining Neptune. Take special notice of the baked earth statues from the rural shrine of Thinissut. One represents the goddess-mother breast feeding her baby and others are lion-headed goddesses (fertility symbols). This museum, unfortunately, does not provide a descriptive leaflet, and while the pottery has labels in Arabic and French, for the mosaics it is necessary to use the services of a guide who will require a tip.

There is a map of the site of Neapolis on display at the entrance to the museum. Open winter 0930-1630, summer 0800-1200 and 1500-1900, entrance TD1 plus TD1 for photography, closed

Mon. The adjacent park provides benches and shade.

Mosque Salama is quite striking with a fine entrance off Ave Habib Bourguiba, opposite the post office. The front façade has a gallery of three arches, each side of which is supported by two pillars. The side and back walls are completely covered in decorative ceramic tiles. It is surmounted by a central dome of white patterned plasterwork. The square tower which is patterned with a geometric form in pale yellow is surmounted by a crescent.

Nabeul's speciality is **pottery**, its largest industry after tourism. The art of polychrome ceramics was introduced in the 15th century by the Andalusians. Try and visit a workshop to see how the various shapes are achieved. Originally the pottery was made in the town – now it is made on the outskirts. The main factories are Maison de l'artisanat on Ave Habib Bourguiba, well down towards the beach, T 285438, no showroom; Ceramics Kedidi on route de Tunis, T 287576, about 1½ km from town centre, extensive showroom, mainly tiles; Poterie Artistique Gastle, Zone Industrielle, route de Tunis, T 222247, abut 1½ km from town centre, employs about 100 people and will allow visitors to view the manufacturing process (no need for individuals to book, parties must contact M Hedi Hichaeri or M Farmi Naghrebi). Showroom at 190 Ave Habib Thameur, shop at 117 Ave Farhat Hached.

Behind the ONAT shop there are several lock-up workshops in the form of a square in which artisans ply their trade. Visitors are free to look around.

Nabeul is noted for mats woven from rushes and esparto grass, silver and silk embroidery, and the distillation of jasmine, wild orange flowers and roses. These fragrant essences called *zahr* are prized by the locals for their soothing qualities. (Be assured a few drops in the milk will make a fretful baby sleep soundly.) Other local crafts are **straw products**, **ironwork** and **sandstone** carved into intricate patterns.

Local information
● Accommodation

A *Hotel Kheops*, outskirts of Nabeul, T 286555, F 286024, good restaurant, Olympic size pool, indoor pool, 300 rm, a/c, bath, TV, phone, terrace, watersports, tennis, disco.

B *Hotel Les Pyramides*, E end of Ave Habib Bourguiba, T 285444, F 287461, large hotel with accommodation in 350 bungalows, beach, pool, organized activities.

C *Hotel les Jasmins*, Ave Habib Thameur, T 280222, F 285073, 188 beds, pool, restaurant, about 1 km in direction of Hammamet, an older hotel, comfortable, not central.

D *Hotel Fakir*, opp the Roman remains of Neapolis, T 285477, brand new, small, pleasant rooms, 200m from beach, very welcoming owner prefers individual travellers to groups;

D *Les Hafsids*, 4 rue Sidi Maaouia, T 285823, just off Ave Habib Thameur nr orange monument, 16 beds, toilet in rooms, shared bath, small Tunisian style hotel close to town centre.

E *Pension Mustapha*, Ave Habib el Karma on corner with Ave Ali Belhouane, T 222262, 5 rm with wash basin, shared toilet and bath, no restaurant, clean Tunisian style hotel close to the souqs.

F *Pension el Habib*, Ave Habib Thameur, T 287190 outskirts of Nabeul coming from Hammamet, beach, very clean, communal bath/toilets, all rooms with handbasin, roof terrace, main road is slightly noisy; **F** *Pension Les Roses*, rue Farhat Hached, T 285570, clean, well kept, central, communal bath/toilets.

Camping: *Hotel les Jasmins*, T 285343, on the road to Hammamet, 1 km out of town, hot/cold water, shop, restaurant, outdoor theatre in an extensive orange grove, 1 ha under shade, prices TD1.9 pp (under 18 TD1.3), tent TD1.3, caravan TD1.5, car TD1.1, electricity TD1.7, shower TD2.

Youth hostels: 2 km from town centre at the end of Ave Mongi Slim, by the beach, T 285547, 56 beds, closed all Feb. Also *Centre de Séjour et de Vacances 'La Gazelle'*, T 221366, 70 beds, meals available. Also *Maison des Jeunes*, Ave Taieb Mehiri, T 86689, 80 beds, clean, meals available, don't expect hot water.

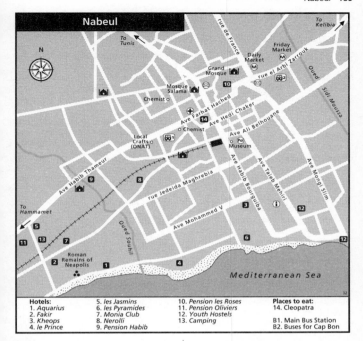

Nabeul

To Tunis

To Kelibia

rue de France

Friday Market

Daily Market

Grand Mosque

rue el Arbi Zarrouk

Mosque Salama

Chemist

Ave Farhat Hached

Ave Hedi Chaker

Ave Ali Belhouane

Local Crafts (ONAT)

Chemist

Pol Museum

Ave Habib Thameur

rue Jedeida Maghrebia

Ave Habib Bourguiba

Ave Taieb Mehiri

Ave Mong Slim

To Hammamet

Oued Souhil

Ave Mohammed V

Roman Remains of Neapolis

Mediterranean Sea

Oued Sidi Moussa

Hotels:	5. *les Jasmins*	10. Pension les Roses	Places to eat:
1. *Aquarius*	6. *les Pyramides*	11. Pension Oliviers	14. Cleopatra
2. *Fakir*	7. *Monia Club*	12. Youth Hostels	
3. *Kheops*	8. *Nerolli*	13. Camping	B1. Main Bus Station
4. *le Prince*	9. *Pension Habib*		B2. Buses for Cap Bon

● **Places to eat**

◆◆◆*Les Oliviers*, T 286613, Ave Hedi Chaker, decor and food delightful; *Monia*, Ave Habib Abdelwaheb, T 285713, fish, crustaceans, shell fish, French cuisine.

◆◆*Au Bon Kif*, Ave Habib Thameur, T 222783; *Le Corail*, Ave Habib Bourguiba, T 223342; *La Rodinella* (The Swallow), 116 Ave Habib Bourguiba on corner of Ave Farhat Hached, pleasant, central.

◆*Cleopatra*, Ave Habib Bourguiba, small, clean; *Er Rachida*, Ave Habib Thameur on corner of Ave Habib Bourguiba, excellent to sit and watch people going by, an attractive café decorated in traditional Tunisian style, up several steps above street level, tables on covered area overlooking street in town centre; *Karim* snack bar in central square; *Le Malouf*, Ave Habib Bourguiba, close to post office, small Tunisian style café; *La Rotonde*, T 285782, Ave Taieb Mehiri. Also restaurants down by the beach.

● **Banks & money changers**

Most banks are on Ave Habib Bourguiba and Ave Farhat Hached, in the town centre. **STB** has automatic cash dispenser – for 24-hr service.

● **Entertainment**

Festivals: **Nabeul International Fair**, Ave Habib Bourguiba (early Apr each year), details from T 285374, F 223242. **Nabeul Summer Festival** of folk arts and concerts, Ave Habib Bourguiba (Jul and Aug), details from T 286683.

Nightclub: *Monia Club*, T 285713, route de l'Hotel Neapolis.

Theatre: *Maison de la Culture*, T 286817, Ave Farhat Hached.

● **Hospitals & medical services**

Regional Hospital, Ave Mohammed Tahar Mâamouri, T 285633; *Clinique Les Violettes*, route d'Hammamet, T 286668, F 286240; *Clinique Ibn Rochd*, rue Mongi Slim, T 286668, F 286240.

● **Post & telecommunications**
Area code: 02.

Post Office: main office, Ave Habib Bourguiba, open Mon-Sat 0800-1800, also Ave Mongi Slim.

● **Shopping**
Crafts are the best buys in Sousse. Visit *ONAT* on Ave Thameur to see the local products and check the prices without having to buy them. The traditional green/yellow pottery is a good buy. The wrought iron, like the stone carvings, are very weighty items to fit in your suitcase!

Some rec outlets where craft goods of a decent standard may be found; go first to *SOCOPA* in Ave Mongi Slim to get an idea of the style and prices and then try: Ave Farhat Hached for *Authentique*, *Dar Braham*, *Poterie Gastle*; Ave Habib Thameur for *Poteries La Caravan* and *Poteries Kharraz*; Ave Habib Bourguiba for *Ceramique d'Art* for more unusual ceramics and pottery, the speciality being the glassware with gold fired into the glaze.

Nabeul Shopping Centre is opp the hospital on Ave Habib Thameur. There is no medina in Nabeul and the souqs in shopping areas along Ave Farhat Hached and through to Ave Habib el Karma take its place. The better quality shops and restaurants are found on Ave Habib Bourguiba between Ave Farhat Hached and Place du 7 Novembre where a full grown pine tree can be seen growing out of a decorative ceramic pot which forms the middle of the roundabout.

The local daily market (vegetables, fruit and fresh meat, chicken and fish) is off rue de France. It is full of local interest and not crowded with tourists like the Fri camel market.

● **Sports**
Adjacent to Nabeul the port of Béni Khair has moorings for 15 pleasure boats, with a depth of 1-3m. All facilities are available, incl security and comfort. *Club de Chasse du Cap Bon* with 1,400 members is situated in Nabeul. The whole of Cap Bon is designated as a Nature Reserve and hunting is carefully controlled to take place from Sept to Mar **in certain regions** as follows: end Sept-end Dec each Sun it is permitted to shoot partridge, quail and hare; mid Oct-mid Jan wild boar; end Oct-end Mar on Thur, Fri and Sat the thrush.

● **Tour companies & travel agents**
Delta Travel, 156 Ave Habib Bourguiba, T 271077, F 271177; *Eagle International Travel*, 58 Ave Habib Bourguiba, T 223355,

F 223263; *Leader Tours*, Nabeul Centre, T 271626, F 271166; *Salama Voyages*, 18 Ave Habib Bourguiba, T 285804, F 287043; *Sept Voyages*, 10 rue de l'Oranger, T 286998, F 286998; *Tunisian Travel Club*, 76 Ave Mongi Slim, T 287427, F 286977.

● **Tourist offices**
The **Regional Tourism Bureau** stands back from road on Ave Taieb Mehiri, T 286737. Towards the beach, from town centre. Bus and train times are normally posted outside the office. Closed in winter. The **Nabeul Tourist Office** is at Place 7 Novembre, T 223006.

● **Useful addresses**
Police: Ave Habib Bourguiba, T 285474; Garde National, Ave Taieb Mehri, T 286153.

● **Transport**
Local Car hire: Avis, *Hotel Kheops*, T 286555; Hertz, Ave Thameur, T 285327; **Europacar**, Ave Farhat Hached, T 287085; **Express Car**, Ave Habib Thameur, T 287014; **Matei**, Ave Habib Bourguiba, T 285967; **Méditerranée Car**, Nabeul Centre, T 224835, and Ave Farhat Hached, T 221073; **Next Car**, Ave Habib Bourguiba, T 285967; **Nova Rent**, Ave Habib Bourguiba, T 222072; **Rent a Car**, Ave Thameur, T 286679; **Royal Car**, rue Sidi Maaouia, T 287333.

Train There is one train a day to Tunis 0545 otherwise the nearest trains are at Bir Bou Rebka reached by bus or louage. Information T 285054.

Road Bus: the bus station is on Ave Thameur. Information on T 285261. Frequent buses to **Hammamet** starting at 0530, **Tunis** (every ¹/₂-hr), **Kelibia**, **Zaghouan** 8 each day, **Sousse** starting at 0645, **Mahdia** starting at 0730 and **Kairouan** (direct at 0600, 0800 and 1215). Buses frequent from Nabeul to Kelibia and El Haouaria with final departure from Kelibia at 1830. **Louages**: Ave Farhat Hached, T 286081. **Taxi**: Allo Taxi Express, T 222444.

DAR CHAABANE EL FEHRI

Dar Chaabane el Fehri, population 25,000 just 2 km N of Nabeul is noted for its exquisite statuary sculpted from the local stone. The particular way of dressing the stone can be seen in the older (and new) traditional style houses in the town in the surrounds of the doors and windows. The stone is a local limestone, soft enough to work into patterns either hollowed out or as a relief. In Dar Chaabane the mosque has an interesting, finely-sculpted doorway. Otherwise the town has little charm. On Fri a large market is held, but this is simply a tourist attraction. Busloads of tourists arrive and prices and quality respectively go up and down. Further S you can visit more authentic markets.

The beach, 20 mins walk, has fine sand but the promenade has no seats, no shade, no cafés. Neighbouring Hammamet is much more attractive.

BENI KHIAR

The Hilalians, nomadic tribe from Upper Egypt, established a settlement here in the 11th century. A century later the founder Kheridine established a *ksar*, carefully set back from the pirate infested coast. The nomads of this colony settled here and supported themselves by weaving, a handicraft for which they are still famous today. The mosque was built later, outside the main *ksar*, and is all that remains of this settlement.

Beni Khiar still specializes in the spinning and weaving of wool, using natural dyes yet now there are few local sheep. It produces the traditional stripped blankets, the *kachabia*, a hooded cape and the fine weave and black stitched needlework carpets in small workshops or individual homes. Some of the workshops were built half underground. The finished material is also used in the making of traditional clothing like the *burnous* as well as tents. These, like the reed mats, produced in the same small-scale fashion, are part of the Cap Bon tradition.

There are many *koutab* and *zaouia* indicating the importance of Beni Khiar as a long established centre of Koranic learning.

At 4 km from the town is a small attractive lake. It is long and narrow, but the water is clear and deep.

A natural gas field has been located in the area of **Es Somaa**, 8 km N of Nabeul and **Belli**, some 20 km W of Nabeul. A gas flare amidst the fields indicates production is underway.

A CIRCULAR TOUR OF CAP BON

If there is a choice tour this peninsula in a clockwise direction. This is by far the best way to do the journey, the NW coast being the most attractive. If time runs out you have seen the best and the road on the SE is faster for a quick return.

The countryside

There are over 180,000 ha of arable land on the Cap Bon peninsula. The annual rainfall varies between 360 mm and 670 mm. Irrigation water used to be raised from wells by camels or donkeys but to-day the few wells that remain are backed by 8 dams and many hill lakes which provide a storage capacity of over 200 million cu m. Cap Bon is eager to show its importance in a national capacity. Here production is given as a % of the country's total:

Strawberries from the Korba region 90%

Citrus fruits, oranges, clementines, mandarins and grapefruit from Menzel Bou Zelfa, Soliman and Beni Khalled 70%

Grapes for eating and wine from Grombalia, Bir Bou Rekba and Bou Argoub 80%

Olives, almonds and market garden produce (early potatoes, fennel, carrots and broad beans) are produced in vast quantities – making best use of its position between the capital and the tourist centres. Local markets as well as national markets play an important part. Cereals are also grown and there is some pasture for beef rearing.

Production:

citrus	180,000 tonnes
vegetables	156,000 tonnes
potatoes	85,000 tonnes
tomatoes	53,000 tonnes
grapes	45,000 tonnes
strawberries	2.2 tonnes
spices	2 tonnes

Prickly pears or barbary figs (*Opuntia Vulgaris*)

The hedge of prickly pear cactus, with large flat spined leaves, is explained as necessary to protect precious crops from marauding donkeys or untended flocks. This explanation is highly suspect. On the first count donkeys, sheep and goats are all too valuable to the owner to allow them out of sight. Consider how carefully flocks are herded away from crops, consider how often you have seen a donkey, away from its overloaded cart, that has not been hobbled. On the second count these hedges are not continuous and gaps to allow access are not closed. No the truth is, these are most probably boundary hedges or less commonly shelter belts to deflect wind from delicate plants.

The attractive flowers of yellow or cyclamen occur from May onwards, providing a bright splash of colour. If your visit occurs in July or August do not hesitate to try the delicacy, the fruit of the Barbary fig. Obtain them ready peeled from roadside sellers and certainly DO NOT pick them yourself as they are protected by a multitude of fine spines, almost invisible to the naked eye, which can only be removed, painfully, by an expert.

Consume these fruits in moderation as more than two or three can cause constipation.

Wine growing

The vine grows well in the favourable Tunisian climate, producing good table grapes and feedstock for wine making. Most table grapes were originally grown on a small scale by Moslems. The Tunisian local varieties include Razzegui, which is a white grape found for sale throughout the country during its harvest at the end of Aug. Many introduced varieties are now also grown and grapes are cultivated even in the southern palm oases.

The main vineyards are found, however, in the NE of the country where abundant water for irrigation and light soils are available, such as in the Cap Bon peninsula, Tunis, Grombalia, Korbous and Tebourba. These areas are mainly frost-free and do not suffer from desiccating winds like the wetter and higher N and NW of the country.

Wine became an important commodity after the settling of parts of the country by Italian and French immigrants. In the 1890s the attack of phylloxera on vines in mainland Europe gave encouragement for grape-growing in Tunisia though in the inter-war years phylloxera took its toll of Tunisian vineyards too. New grafted stocks have been introduced.

The area under vine cultivation fell from 150,000 ha in 1985 to 29,000 ha in 1995. Approximately half the grapes grown are for wine making. Wine production runs at between 200,000-400,000 hectolitres/year, two-thirds of which is consumed in Tunisia. The wine industry has great difficulty in marketing its wines in the developed countries as a result of adverse tariffs.

The main varieties of wine grapes are:

Alicante Bouschet (red), from France gives a high alcohol wine with a good colour. It is often used as a blending wine.

Alicante Grenache (red), from Spain with a high alcohol level and rich in tannins but with a tendency to deteriorate quickly.

Carignan (red), from Spain and makes a good wine for immediate consumption and is also used for blending.

Cinsault (red), from southern France is low in alcohol but has a rich fruity taste and full colour.

Monica (red), from Sardinia is a fine wine with good bouquet and is better for aging.

Mouvedre (red), from Spain, has a light colour and matures well.

Pedro Ximines (white), from Spain gives a slightly acidic wine but is a good wine without blending.

Sangiovese (red), from Tuscany provides a deeply coloured wine which benefits from being laid down for some years.

Ugni Blanc (white), is from Tuscany with a somewhat high acidity though palatable as a light and fruity wine. Often used for blending.

A variety of other stocks, of which the principal are Cabernet, Merlot, Morrastel, Pinot and Syrah are also in use.

Most wine in Tunisia is produced as full-bodied reds or light rosé. White Muscadet wines are also popular. Among the most palatable of wines in hotels and supermarkets are the Tebourba reds (try Magon Vieux) and the reds from Mornag (try Haut Mornag or Chateau Mornag). Muscat Sec de Kelibia from the Cap Bon peninsula is a good dry white wine. Of the many rosé wines few are unpalatable, though those from Mornag and Tebourba are probably the most rewarding.

Part of mosaic in Bardo Museum

GROMBALIA

Grombalia with 20,000 inhabitants is an important market area and a focus of routes. It was known to the Romans as *Colombaria* but of their habitation there is no trace. The oldest remains here are 16th century, the time of the evacuation of Andalucia by the Moors. The oldest mosque here, built by Mustapha Cardinas, dates from that time.

He also had constructed a public fountain and a public *hammam* as well as a beautiful dwelling for himself. The olive presses found here which date from that time indicate the quick growth in prosperity of the region. The feast of the wine is held in Sept to celebrate the town's central and important position in the wine and table grape production. Market day – Mon.

The main vineyards in the Cap Bon peninsula are centred around the town of Grombalia. During colonial times much of the wine was exported to France for blending and the vineyards covered a greater area than they do today. While the vine still plays an important part in the agricultural scene here there is less evidence of future development, few young vines being brought on for replacement or new vineyards. The vine produces a good crop for up to 50 years and then in reducing quantities for up to 100 years so although it may look old and gnarled in the winter it will burst forth in the spring. Unlike the terraced fields of France and Germany the vineyards here are planted on flat ground.

The countryside on the C41 between Grombalia and Soliman is flat agricultural land with cereals. These are less well cared for than the cereals around Zaghouan. The fields are small and there are bare patches and heavy weed infestation. The farmers here lack the necessary resources. The frequently seen collections of white painted brick sheds with half-cylinder roofs are for storage, and beef and veal rearing.

As Grombalia is the centre of the vine growing region there are many roadside stalls in the season and much activity when the grapes are ready for wine production. There is a large market for clothes and shoes each Mon in the street by the railway station. The goods are piled high on trestle tables, a lively affair. This town has the advantage of being able to go about its business without being hindered by visitors.

● **Transport Train** Trains from Grombalia to **Tunis** (via Hammam Lif) 0634, 0717, 0823, 1451, 1655, 2103; Grombalia to **Nabeul** 1512, 1851; Grombal ia to **Sousse** with onward travel to Mahdia, Sfax, Gabès and Gafsa 0745, 0945, 1245, 1450, 1616, 1922.

Excursions To **Aïn Tébournok** from Grombalia take the road from Grombalia towards the Tunis-Sousse motorway but continue straight across to Aïn Tébournok (Tebournoug), a further 7 km. Here is a most splendid *duor*, rising from the middle of which is an ancient fortress, built on a small, high plateau surrounded by mountains. A restoration company has been engaged to sort out the piles of stones of this once magnificent construction and to preserve and display the site. A cleared area at the foot of the building overlooks a paved alley and from here is clear evidence of a forum and adjacent roads which have massive foundations of dressed stone.

Once here it is worth continuing E to the Barrage Masri which shelters under Djebel el Behelil (556m) or on the return take the left turn to a smaller, and rather more attractive barrage (depending on the rainfall) which shelters under Djebel Makki (641m).

Beni Khalled   Orange growing is located around Beni Khalled and Menzel Bou Zelfa. These towns have no other intrinsic interest than the support they provide for the orange production (and that they both have a monument to oranges in the centre of the town).

Menzel Bou Zelfa with a population of around 15,000 is known as the 'Queen of Oranges', the Maltaise. It has a daily orange market in season where it is possible to buy a 25 kg crate of oranges for as little as TD1.5. The Orange Festival is held each Apr/May. It is one of the principal suppliers of citrus fruit. It is also one of the oldest cities in Cap Bon but the rich heritage has not been well preserved. The best piece to see is the mausoleum of Sidi Abdelkader and the adjacent mosque, in the town centre next to what remains of the medina. This mausoleum is the place of pilgrimage of the Kadria brotherhood. Market day – Thur.

Menzel Bou Zelfa, 44 km from Tunis on the C43, can be reached via Soliman and Grombalia, 41 km from Tunis, is on the main P1 from Tunis to Hammamet and the main railway line from Tunis.

Soliman, with its Andalusian style buildings and unique minaret is well worth a visit. The town is named after its patron, a rich Turkish farmer who came to this area around 1600 and began the construction of a new town. The subsequent influx of immigrants from Andalucia left their mark in the form of building style, irrigation methods and even culinary preferences. Note the typical square minaret of the mosque, covered with semicircular green tiles, all that remains. **Accommodation D** *Solimar*, T 290105, F 290155; **E** *Andalous*, T 290199. **Travel agents**: *Mek Tours*, 9 bis Ave de la République, T 290177, F 291600; *Soly Holiday*, 8 rue Hedi Chaker, T 291649, F 291753.

Soliman Plage across the flat marsh land towards the NW has a broad expanse of fine sand and two hotels. A Noddy train connects the beach and the town of Soliman during the summer, a journey of 4 km. It is a lovely beach, very popular in summer and at weekends. **Accommodation D** *Solymar*, 400 beds, T 290105, F 290155, right on beach of fine white sand, 200 rm with bath and toilet, restaurant, pool, disco/nightly entertainment;

E *El Andalous*, 288 beds, T 290199, F 290280, right on beach, 100m from *Hotel Solymar* and share entertainment, 127 rm with bath and toilet, closed in winter.

The main road from Soliman through the flat marshlands to the W connects with the P1 near Bordj Cedria. From Soliman to the E the road rises through prosperous agricultural land towards Sidi Aïssa with the Djebel Bou Korbous rising up on the W to cut out any prospects of the sea. The detour via Korbous is recommended even if you have no intention of stopping there. It is a very scenic route which circles the hill and on reaching the coast follows the cliff with the sea literally straight below. The view towards La Goulette and Sidi Bou Saïd is very impressive.

Sidi Raïs is 3 km from the C26 across flat marshland. It is interesting for its seaside holiday homes built on stilts over the water's edge on a beach of fine sand. This is where the Tunisian families from the surrounding areas come each weekend or for their longer holidays. There is a small jetty where a few local fishing boats tie up and from which they sell their daily catch of fresh fish. The coast N from Sidi Raïs through to Kerkouane is one of rugged, wild, unspoilt splendour.

KORBOUS

Korbous is a small thermal spa resort of seven springs, with prospects of expansion, overlooking the sea. Korbous was first discovered and used by the Romans who named it *Aquae Calidau Carpitanae*. At the end of the last century the king at that time, Ahmed Bey, had a pavilion here for enjoying the thermal springs. On the hilltop is a beautiful villa, previously used by Bourguiba as one of his summer resorts. The thermal institute and its baths which could be cleaner, can be visited and used. Strange atmosphere as many visitors have come for health reasons. The thermal spa, Kilani ben Aziza, is open 0800-1600, every day of

the year, T 284520. This area is also known for watersports, in particular underwater fishing.

● **Accommodation** Most of the hotels are expensive and used by the people undergoing treatment at the spa. **A** *Aïn Oktor*, T 284552, 4 km along the road to Soliman, 128 beds, overlooking the sea, no beach, thermal cures; **A** *Chiraz*, route de Korbous, T 293230, 16 beds; **A** *Les Sources*, T 284535, large terrace overlooking the sea, 103 beds, thermal cures, pool; **B** *Residence des Thermes*, T 284664, on main road in town centre, 5 mins walk from spa baths, clean, tidy rms with balcony on 2 floors, 18 twin bedded rm, all with bath and toilet, heating, meals if required are provided in newly built restaurant across the road.

● **Places to eat** *Chez Korbsi* and *Restaurant Dhrib* in town centre serve good cheap meals, and *La Brise* at Sidi Rais.

Aïn Atrous (Goat Spring), 1 km N of the village is a spring that gushes out of duct in the hillside at 50°C and runs along a stone gully for a few metres before tumbling down about 3m over a few rocks into the sea. The typical smell of rotten eggs (hydrogen sulphide) cannot be avoided and the wisps of steam rise from the heated water. Even in winter it is possible though not really pleasant to bathe in the sea here. There is a car park and a few small cafés and restaurants close by. It is a favourite spot for locals so Sat and Sun are very busy.

Aïn Oktor (Kidney Spring) is named after a cold spring 1 km on from Aïn Atrous – on edge of the sea on this rocky coastline. The hotel is completely isolated being out of the village. It nestles in a ravine as the road winds down to the water's edge. An unusual stop. The spring water emerges slowly, its name meaning the spring which emerges drop by drop, and contains a high proportion of chlorine and soda used in the treatment of kidney disorders and urinary problems.

Beyond Hammam el Hatrous the main road swings right but by keeping to the coast the resort of **Rass Dourdass** can reached after a further 3 km ride.

Seven Springs

At **Korbous** therapy has been available for over 30 years – the treatment being adapted to modern techniques. Here rehabilitation treatments are offered as well as relief from stress and overwork. Cures are sought here for rheumatism, paralysis and nervous disorders. These springs have slightly different but complementary powers. The waters contain sodium, chlorine and a little sulphur.

The region has seven springs all reputedly beneficial in some way for medical problems from arthritis to obesity. In addition to Aïn Atrous there is Aïn Thalassira, Aïn Fakroun (Tortoise Spring), Aïn Ichfa (Health Spring), Aïn Arraka (Hot Spring) and Aïn S'Bya (Virgin Spring) and the most important of all Aïn el Kebira (Great Spring) in which clients can indulge themselves in the spa rooms built by Ahmed Bey right on the shore line. Many of the visitors here are in good health and intend to remain so by following a programme of relaxation in the thermal waters in healthy and attractive surroundings. Typical prices are: Simple bath TD2.4; Massages TD8; Clay/mud bath TD7; Jacuzzi TD5.5; Water jets treatment TD3; Vapour treatment TD2.

This is a lovely approach through bare rugged hills, the lower level covered with scrub and aromatic *maquis* sloping down to the sea.

Bir Meroua is on the C26 reached directly from Soliman or recognized as the sharp left turn towards El Haouaria when approached from the coast.

After **Sidi Aïssa** the flatter fertile plain is used for vineyards and olives where vines won't grow. Vines, cereals and vegetables (lots of tomatoes) are cultivated by the now settled Bedouins whose villages are at intervals along the C26. The higher, less fertile areas, are covered with stunted pine. **Tazoghrane** is one such Berber village, built on a slight rise at the junction.

Continuing towards Sidi Daoud the road is further inland with only glimpses of the sea. In this locality canes are grown which are harvested and used to make fences and awnings to provide shade.

At **Zaouiet el Mgaïez** a street market is held in the main street each Wed, an honest description is crowded rather than colourful.

SIDI DAOUD

This small fishing village just off the coast road to Korbous has a large and obtrusive fish canning plant. It hosts a traditional Fishing Festival in late May/early Jun each year. This festival, known as the *Matanza*, is quite violent, as the shoals of large tuna fish at times weighing more than 200 kg, en route from the Atlantic Ocean via the Straits of Gibraltar are caught in carefully positioned nets, dragged towards the shore and then harpooned, filling the sea with blood. Pacifists might prefer the splendid view from the village towards the island of Zembra. Bus from Bab el Fellah in Tunis. Sidi Daoud has factories which deal with the tuna fish and then export it to other Mediterranean countries.

There are moorings here for pleasure boats with between 1.8m and 3m depth – with all the expected facilities, security and comfort. Near here is the tiny beach, Bir Jeddi, about 2 km down a wooded track from the village. The beach is fine sand, but has lots of pebbles too. There are some huts for hire and a cool freshwater spring near the remains of an old cemetery.

The road continues NE towards El Haouaria, Ghar el Kebir and Cap Bon.

EL HAOUARIA

ACCESS The louages and bus station are on Ave Habib Bourguiba in the town centre.

7 km NE from Sidi Daoud, is El Haouaria (*Pop* 10,000), a small village famous for its falconry festival and its position at the end of the Cap Bon peninsula. The village itself is of little interest, but the surrounding countryside and beaches are delightful.

Places of interest The **Falconry Festival** is held each May or Jun. This is when the country people bring their hawks to put them through their paces in front of other bird handlers. This is certainly a festival worth seeing if one can stand the cruelty. Live prey are used for these displays. The small birds are trapped during the spring migration and kept until the festival, any left over being released back into the wild. Obviously it takes a large number of birds for these displays. There is a very carnival atmosphere about the town during the festival. The falcon festival coincides with the start of the hunting season.

The monument in the town centre is a magnificent hawk with outstretched wings.

Other attractions are the beach, just 5 km from the village, fine white sand stretching SE to Hammam el Ghezaz and seas calm and clear enough for underwater fishing. 3 km from the village on the shore near the extremity of the Cap are the **Ghar el Kebir Caves**, entrance TD1, open winter 0830-1730, summer 0800-1200 and 1500-1900. It is thought that the rock quarried from here was used to build parts of Carthage. You are advised to let the official guide show you round as he knows more than the unofficial ones! There are said to be 97 caves in total. There is a car park and small café by the path that leads to the entrance (TD1). It is a short easy walk to the main caves which are interlinked and have small openings in the roof, originally for the exit of the quarried stone, so daylight can now enter. Bats enter too through these vents and roost during the day in the caves. They also roost in the natural caves in the hill nearby. Your guide will point out the 'camel' of stone in the big hall, a female we are told. The mountains along the coast and behind the villages offer interesting walks.

Towards the end of the Cap Bon peninsula there is a beautiful little beach, **Ras Ed Drak**, which is quite secluded and still relatively unknown. It is 4 km from the village along a road leading to the end of the peninsula. The view from the end of **Cap Bon** is superb. It is said that on a clear night the lights of Sicily, 140 km away, can be seen. The migrating birds make El Haouaria their first call when arriving in this part of the continent. They certainly have not heard about the falcons.

● **Accommodation** D *De l'Eperrier*, Ave Habib Bourguiba, T 297017, F 297258, 28 beds in 10 rm, with bath, very good restaurant; **D** *Le Pacha*, T 226077, F 280031; **D** *Le Ribat*, T 280403, F 282099; **D** *Sahbi*, T 226213, F 280134; **F** *Dar Toubib*, T 297163.

● **Places to eat** Restaurant in *De l'Eperrier* (English spoken) rec. Try ◆◆*Les Grottes*, T 297296, Grottes Romaines, *Idéal Restaurant*, Ave de la République, T 280302 and cheaper ◆*Fruits de la Mer*, T 297078, Ave Hedi Chaker, with fresh fish; *La Rosa*, Ave du Koweit, T 282864.

● **Banks & money changers** BNA and STB on Ave Habib Bourguiba nr the Post Office.

● **Post & telecommunications Post Office**: at the start of Ave Habib Bourguiba, by the louages and bus station.

● **Sports** Hunting, enquire at the Association de Chasseurs de Tunis for details of quail, woodcock, partridge and hare hunting. *Club de Fauconniers*, Aquilaria, on road to quarries, open 1000-1600 daily.

● **Transport Road Bus**: there is an irregular bus service, either via the N coast from Tunis (but this takes a while because the bus stops everywhere) or via Kelibia. **Louage**: taking a louage is much faster.

Zembra and Zembretta are small islands clearly visible from the end of Cap Bon with steep cliffs making access difficult. The sea for 1.5 nautical miles

Falcons for a festival

🦶 Haouaria, situated at one of the closest points between the African continent and Europe, lies right on the twice yearly migration path of thousands of birds, particularly large birds of prey. Falconry is an old tradition here and in 1967 the local tourist board set up a festival in June to attract some trade to this rather out of the way corner of the Cap Bon peninsula.

The people of Haouaria use two species of birds of prey for falconry, the sparrow hawk (épwevier in French or es-saf in Tunisian) and the peregrine falcon (faucon péléri or el-burni). Sparrow hawk are captured up on the mountain at the the time of the April migration and after two or three weeks are ready for hunting. Quail is the favourite prey. Generally after the festival most of the sparrow hawks are released. Takes of the rarer peregrine falcons are much more closely controlled. Only one or two nestling may be taken each year and the young birds are then reared in captivity. Permits are issued to bona fide falconers only.

The festival went into decline in the 1980s, to re-emerge as a 3-day event in 1995. The falconers parade with their birds through the town centre and then there are displays on the hillside. The devotees of falconry (el-bayzara in Arabic) now have a gleaming new centre up on the hill towards the Roman quarries complete with aviaries and meeting rooms which can be visited.

For birdwatchers the best time to visit El Haouaria is the last two weeks in April when the migration of a huge variety of birds is at its height or in the late autumn though this is less spectacular. Take up an observation position on Djebel Sidi Aboid.

beyond low tide is designated as a *nature reserve* with no fishing, professional or sports allowed. Grey puffins nest here. Once these islands had a hotel and a scuba diving centre. Now they are occupied by the military and no access is permitted.

Zembra a small rocky island about 8 nautical miles NW from the coast by Sidi Daoud. It rises up straight out of the sea to its summit of 435m. Evidence shows that it was colonized from the time of the Phoenicians and by the Romans who called it *Aégimures*. Here is found a special type of rabbit. Zembretta which is smaller has a lighthouse.

KERKOUANE

About halfway between El Haouaria and Kelibia a small signposted road goes down towards the sea and the site. This remarkable example of the only purely Punic town, still well preserved, is thought to have been built in 6th century BC and abandoned following the fall of Carthage to the Romans but some remains have been found dating from the

3rd century. It was never inhabited after that time, which accounts for its good state. After it was razed to the ground in 146 BC by the Roman general Regulus the sand gradually covered it and it was forgotten until the middle of this century. Proceed towards the sea and the site through well maintained flower borders. The walls have been restored to about 1m in height. The roads continue right down to the rocky water's edge, no sandy beach here. Standing at the top of the slope the street layout and house foundations are clearly visible, with all the houses following the same pattern of rooms round a central courtyard. All the houses had baths, saying something about the sophistication of Punic civilization. The main economic activity seems to have been the manufacture of an expensive purple dye known as Tyrian purple and very popular for ceremonial robes. It was made from decomposed shell fish. Perhaps this explains the baths! They could not have been nearer the sea for their raw material.

On the site you will be shown the bread oven, the temple and a mosaic of the goddess. Open summer 0900-1900, winter 0900-1630, except Mon. Entrance TD1, photography TD1, T 294033.

There is a large car park close by the entrance gate. There are toilets on the left and a small museum on the right with exhibits which are exclusively Punic in origin. They include sarcophagi, jewellery, ceramics, terracotta statuettes and ritual objects.

Beyond Kerkouane the land is flatter, less interesting, less commanding views, a marshy coastline with salt water lakes. The C27 is a wider, faster road, generally well surfaced except around Kerkouane where the road edge has deteriorated and falls away at the edge at times with a tyre splitting drop of 5 cm.

Hammam el Ghezaz (Rezèze) (*Pop* 8,000), has the best beaches in Tunisia, a peaceful expanse of fine, white sand stretching for 5-6 km. The dunes behind the beach are covered in conifers.

KELIBIA

Kelibia has a population of 34,000. It is a fairly small, pleasantly authentic, modern fishing village dominated by an impressive Byzantine fortress. The village offers the visitor peace and quiet, particularly welcome if coming from Nabeul. The best beaches are situated 4 km NE of Kelibia at the corner of Cap Bon though in every small bay there are sandy stretches.

Kelibia is home to an important fishing fleet with a commercial fish market on the quayside. The main catch is 'blue' fish. The quiet port was modernized to become the main fishing port of Cap Bon and is at times haven for the whole Cap Bon fleet which comprises 360 coastal fishing boats, 46 trawlers and seven boats for game fish. Despite the modern facilities fishing with lamps at night in the traditional way still continues from this harbour.

There is also a thriving shipbuilding and ship repair section here. Kelibia also provides a ferry link to Europe. Great investment has taken place here, particularly by the Italians (quick hydrofoil links) and Kelibia is set to be another large tourist base. The port must be visited to view the recent alterations to take hydrofoils and the new pleasure yacht harbour. It is a popular evening promenade and the departing fishing fleet, for night fishing by lamp, adds to the spectacle.

Agriculture is the mainstay of this region, and the white wine Muscat de Kelibia is greatly prized. The vineyards here and tradition of winemaking have been established for centuries. Other cash crops include ground nuts and tomatoes. While Kelibia may be well known for its fishing fleet how many people know that the best lettuces in Tunisia are grown here? It is also an important furniture making centre and many workshops are to be seen on the road S from town. The equipment used by the craftsmen is rather basic and the furniture rather utilitarian by European standards.

Other crafts include the making of ornate garments decorated with embroidery, in particular wedding dresses.

Places of interest Kelibia fortress, built on top of a 150m high rocky promontory during the 6th/7th century, has been changed and rebuilt many times. The crenelated walls, almost complete, are made of huge blocks of stone and are reinforced with square towers at the corners. The fortress surrounds the remains of an much more ancient fort and some deep wells. Inside the fortress there are several vaulted rooms, one of which, with three naves, was probably a chapel. Turn right off main road N of the village for a magnificent view. Entrance TD2, free for students, open summer 0800-1900, winter 0830-1700. Excavations in the vicinity of the fort are of Roman **Clupea**. Alternate years in Jul an international amateur film festival is held here. Watch the fishermen at night using power lamps to catch sardines, anchovies and mackerel.

● **Accommodation** C *Palmarina*, T 274062, F 274055; **D** *Ennassim*, meaning 'the breeze' by the sea, T 296245, rooms around a small courtyard; **E** *Florida*, by the sea, T 296248, small hotel next door to *Ennassim*, 25 beds, most rooms with sea view, shaded terrace; **F** *Amis*, T 285777; **F** *El Mansoura Holiday Village*, 232 beds, T 295992, F 296156; **F** *Mammounia Holiday Village*, 208 beds, T 296088, F 286858. **Youth hostel**: T 296105, 80 beds, on the road to Mansoura, by the sea.

● **Places to eat** The restaurants in both the hotels are good, as is *Café Sidi el Bahri* by the port where it is pleasant to have a drink in the afternoon and watch the fishing boats return. Try the fish, it should be fresh! ◆◆*El Mansoura*, T 296321, and *Cluppea*, T 296296, both on the beach, in very good setting, fish dishes rec; ◆*Le Relais*, T 296173, route de la Plage. Kelibia is noted for its dry wine. Try in particular the Muscat sec de Kelibia.

● **Sports** Some watersports are available but the resort is not really set up for this. Harbour has berths for 20 yachts, min-max draft 2-5m,

Table grapes

Despite the small area suitable for this crop Tunisia produces some delicious eating grapes. Of the 29,000 ha under cultivation half is for table grapes. In season the sellers at the roadside tantalize the taste buds by swinging huge bunches of fruit at passing cars.

Taking into account the earlier ripening in the S look out for:

Cardinal, variety of the above, end of June in S and from beginning of July in N. Skin completely red. Very popular as can withstand more heat than most vines.

Perlette, a very compact bunch with small and medium size grapes, second half of July,

Muscat de Kelibia/Muscat de Raf-Raf, depending on where you are, ripens second half of August. Golden/green – can also be used for winemaking.

Razzegui, this is the most common eating variety in Tunisia. Some of the grapes are really huge. Green tinted with pink. Ready at end of August.

The deep purple, *Bezzoul el Khadem*, attractive grey bloom, ready in September.

The rosy pink/green *Ahmeur*, originating in Algeria, ready end of September.

Sultainine, this one can be relied upon to be seedless, makes a change, mainly small grapes in long tapering bunches. End of July to beginning of August.

Mosaic from Sousse Museum

with all the expected facilities, security and comfort.

● **Tour companies & travel agents** *Kerkouan Voyages*, Place Sidi Abdessalem, T 295370/410, F 296836.

● **Transport Road** Buses leave every hour in the morning to El Haouaria and there are frequent departures to Nabeul. Bus from Tunis leaves from Bab Aliona. **Sea** An interesting hydrofoil link with Trapani in Sicily is advertised during the summer, taking 4 hrs and carrying up to 180 passengers. For information T 296276. Details of these ferry crossings are given in **Information for travellers**, page 352.

Mansourah is a wealthy suburb to the N of Kelibia, with several fine sandy beaches. The construction of private dwellings along the coast road between Kelibia and Nabeul has increased. The structures advance when funds are available so the impression is of being at times in a building site.

Menzel Temime with a population of 30,000 is a very busy town, its prosperity depending on the local agricultural region. Peanuts/groundnuts appear in this market and are grown in the area to the N of the town up towards El Haouaria. For those who want to see the first stage of the salted peanuts this is the place to look. The plants actually push the seed pods down into the ground – hence the name. The area is well known too for its cultivation of pimentoes. This is one of the beef rearing areas though by European standards the herds are very small and the animals much less robust.

It is an ancient town, founded by the 4th century BC. Some ruins occur in the agricultural land in the area. There are some ancient caves, perhaps 1st century BC, badly signposted, dug in the rocks overlooking the beach. The various invaders/settlers have left their mark, Roman cisterns, fortresses, mosques and mausoleums.

The strings of pimentoes drying in the sun are like garlands on the front of the houses. A cheerful sight. Market day – Tues, cattle and sheep market, agricultural produce, oranges, pimentoes and peanuts in season.

Accommodation D *Temime*, 88 beds, T 298262/266, F 298291. **Youth hostel**: 40 beds, T 298116.

The road from Menzel Temime to Korba is in good condition. The verges are lined with eucalyptus trees. The land on both sides of the road is extensively cultivated, the soil is rich and taking advantage of the beef rearing is organically enriched, and water is provided from well heads at intervals along the way. The stage of mechanization ranges from camel and horse-powered ploughs to sophisticated, Tunisian assembled, heavy machinery. Approaching Korba the salt lakes and marshes on the E become more extensive. The land on the W side produces large quantities of tomatoes and pimentoes which are processed/concentrated in local factories. Chicken and egg production units are common here. Nearly every Tunisian meal offers egg or chicken in some form. The roadside stalls selling vegetables, eggs and chickens are both useful and colourful.

Korba is a small town on the coast road just 20 km N of Nabeul. It stands on the Oued Bou Eddine which is used by *Club Mediterrané*. A rough road leads inland up to a barrage on the *oued*.

Pimentoes, tomatoes and strawberries are produced here, hence the nick-name 'red city'. Very little of the ancient city of *Julia Curubis* remains though the remains of the aqueduct are worth a visit. It is thought to have been the seat of an archbishop associated with the presence of St Cyprien here in 275AD. From the Islamic period there are remains of the mausoleum of Sidi Maouia and a mini *ribat* to protect the settlement from attacks by pirates. One week each year in Aug there is a national festival of amateur theatre. Market day – Sun. **Accommodation** *Club Mediterranée*, T 226400. **Youth hostel**, 100 beds, meals provided, family run, T 289296.

Northern Tunisia

THE NORTH of Tunisia has so far escaped the mass tourism of elsewhere in the country, but this may not be for long as there are many impressive Roman sites to visit and the landscape is exceedingly attractive. In summer the temperature is high but more bearable than in the south, with the mountains and thickly wooded areas behind the coast being most welcoming. The coast between Bizerte and the Algerian border offers steep cliffs, small bays and many secluded beaches, well off the main routes. Most of the country's king prawns, lobsters and crayfish are caught off this northern coast. The Bizerte region's varied natural environment includes forests, lakes, a rocky coastline and sandy beaches. In particular the East facing beaches are particularly fine – extending as far as Raf Raf and Ghar el Melh.

The fertile region of the Medjerda valley is noted for its vineyards. Originally, in colonial times, these covered a greater area, but since exports of wine to France for blending have declined so has the area given over to this crop. The towns of Bizerte, Tabarka and Le Kef have much to interest the traveller and the Roman remains in Dougga are not to be missed.

Small villages permit sights of pink pinafored school girls, boys in blue smocks and seasonal farm produce on sale on road side – melons, grapes, live chickens. There are three important dams in the region – Joumine, Sejnane and Ghezala where commercial projects are underway to breed red mullet, grey mullet, pike, perch and carp.

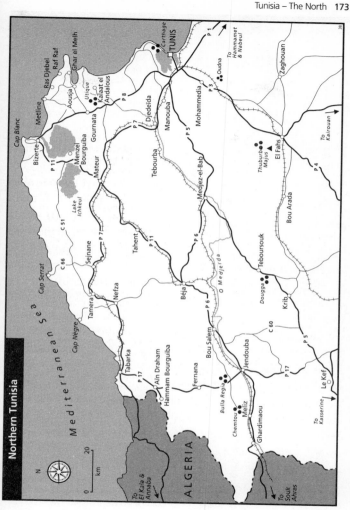

Northern Tunisia

BIZERTE

ACCESS Bizerte is 64 km from Tunis, bus Nos 44 and 62, 1 hr by taxi, a pleasant, slightly hilly, journey through fairly fertile farmland with large areas of olive and citrus. Leave Tunis on the P8 heading NNW for Bizerte. The road crosses the wide flood plain of the Oued Medjerda, the only permanently flowing river in the country and the river responsible for the alluvial deposits which silted up the bay and reduced important trading ports to insignificance.

History

(*Pop* 400,000; *Alt* 5m) Bizerte is the biggest town on the N coast and the fourth largest town in Tunisia. Its history goes back to Punic times when the natural harbour attracted the Phoenician sailors. The town was destroyed with the fall of Carthage, but later rebuilt by Caesar, and known as **Hippo Diarrythus**. Conquered by the Arabs in 661, Bizerte expanded during the Hafsid Dynasty. The arrival of the Moors from Spain in the 17th century, as in other cities in Tunisia, gave it a new lease of life and guaranteed its fortune. The opening of the Suez Canal in 1869, and the arrival, in 1882, of the French who appreciated its strategically important position and turned the town into a naval arsenal, were other important factors in Bizerte's development.

Since Independence the industrial sector has expanded. There is an oil refinery and a large ironworks. Bizerte lies N of the swing bridge over the 8 km long canal which joins the inland Lake of Bizerte (111 sq km and noted for its oysters and mussels) to the open sea. Here some commercial fishing takes place – mullet, bream and sole. The road from the bridge leads into the regular grid pattern of streets, a legacy of the French, beyond which lies the well preserved medina and the old port. The town is currently undergoing an expansion of the tourist infrastructure. Bizerte is a Free Trade Zone and it is hoped this will contribute to the development of convention and business tourism within the city.

Places of interest

The old harbour is charming with its blue and white houses overlooking the fishing boats and in the evening it has a different but equally pleasant atmosphere. From there you can penetrate into the **kasbah**, the old fortified town. The labyrinth of little streets with painted walls is fascinating to walk through and, leaving the old town, you can wander into the newer medina, peeping into doorways where craftsmen can be seen at work using techniques that are centuries old. Behind the town the old 'Spanish' fort actually built by the Turks gives atmosphere and historic interest. It has been sufficiently repaired to be used, once in a while, for open air theatre. The new city is of little interest except for the bustling life and cafés. **Local markets** are held. The main market is behind the old harbour and there is another on Ave Taieb Mehiri, before the town hall. Bizerte has an **Oceanographic Museum** which is not as impressive as it sounds. There are some good **beaches** on either side of the town, but the most popular one is at Remel, over the bridge

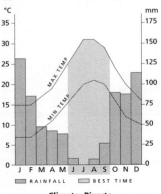

Climate: Bizerte

Utica

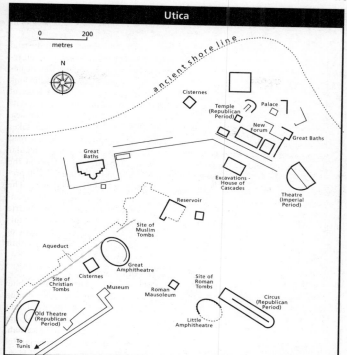

to the S. North of town the Corniche with hotels and restaurants leads to Cap Blanc, an old fort and scrubland used for picnics.

Festival of Sidi el Béchir, 1st Thur in Sept; Festival of Bizerte Jul/Aug; International Festival of Mediterranean music alternate years; Khémais Ternane Conference – every third year.

Excursions

Utica is an old Roman city of which little remains. The museum on the site contains some small items of interest. Worth a visit if transport is available but a long walk on a hot day for little reward. It is $2\frac{1}{2}$ km E from the new town of **Utique**, on the main road. The site is clearly signposted. The museum is on the left, shade

for parking and picnics, and the site itself is another 500m down the road. Open winter 0830-1730, summer 0800-1900, closed Mon and public holidays. Entrance TD2 and TD1 photography charge.

Like many ancient cities in Tunisia, Utica founded in 1101 BC was first a Punic city, later taken over by the Romans. It was, at one stage, the first capital of the Roman province of Africa and, as such, rich in public monuments. The city was not as it is today, surrounded by expanses of agricultural land, but by the sea, exporting agricultural produce from its rich hinterland. The Oued Medjerda has filled in with alluvium the bay on which it stood leaving it 15 km from the

Tunisian mosaics

The Romans made a fine art of 'decorating a surface with designs made up of closely set, usually variously coloured, small pieces of material such as stone, pottery, glass, tile or shell', mosaics.

These first mosaics were constructed of natural materials, pebbles and small stones set in clay, and usually the colours were black or white. The inclusion of other coloured stones, glass, and even broken pottery and shells was introduced at a later date. The production of small, natural clay and polychrome tiles known as tesserae developed even later as designs for mosaics became more complicated and regular shaped pieces were required.

Although Africa was one of Rome's first overseas provinces the actual process of Romanization was very slow and there were certainly no major developments before the late 2nd century AD. Although development was late in total the mosaics of North Africa are more numerous and much better preserved than those remaining anywhere else in the empire due to a combination of climatic conditions and lesser population pressure. The area we know as Tunisia is richer in mosaics than any other country and provides an enormous number of examples, from urban houses, mainly from the 4th century.

The earliest mosaics in North Africa were very simple and it is assumed that early examples of more elaborate designs were produced by imported labour or constructed in Italy and carried to their final positions.

The wealthy Romans decorated both their private and public buildings with mosaics. These were a luxury item, expensive to produce. They were primarily decorative, though their size and sophistication would certainly advertise the wealth of the patron. Generally the finer specimens were in the better, more visited parts of the house and ornamental/geometric rather than pictorial designs

shore. Bearing that in mind it's easier to see that its strategic location was responsible for its important position, second only to Carthage. With the fall of Carthage in 146 BC Utica became the capital of the province and the settlement prospered as a garrison for Roman troops and the residence of many rich and powerful Roman citizens. The reinstatement of Carthage returned Utica to 'second place'. Utica's collapse, like that of other Roman cities, came with the invasions by the Vandals and the Byzantines. The final fall was the Arab conquest.

The Roman site is not extensive and has only been partially excavated. There is evidence of the replacement of smaller buildings by something much larger and grander (due to the more important role as capital perhaps) and in some cases a duplication (two theatres). One of the theatres is centrally placed, the other cut into the hillside.

The residential area contains houses, built in the classical style, such as The Hunt, The Treasure, The Cascade etc, generally known after their mosaic decorations. The **House of the Cascades** is a large dwelling centred round a patio on to which opened the imposing *triclinium* as well as smaller chambers, many with basins and fountains. The adjacent **House of the Hunt** had a large garden surrounded by a patio and numerous rooms, one of which contained

were found in less important areas.

There are clear indications that the central part of the mosaics were constructed by 'master' craftsmen while the geometric designs and borders were done by workers who were less well trained, and often produced a lower standard of work. Subject matter of the mosaics is frequently repeated and similar examples can be found on many different sites. Examples of the pattern being drawn in the underlying clay have been found but are not common. The workmen must have followed some pattern especially where the work was more complicated. The recurrence of identical motifs across a wide area shows that designs were probably chosen from a common stock and not drawn for each building.

The common themes to look out for are:- hunting scenes and scenes showing rural life; seasons and seasonal activities; scenes from literature; scenes from mythology. The all important central medallion was set in a circle, square, oval or polygon and the whole mosaic was surrounded with a border usually exhibiting a geometric design. Most common were the gillouche (three strand rope) and Greek key borders.

the famous mosaic. The **House of the Capitals** had capitals representing human figures. The **House of the Treasure** produced a hoard of coins. Some mosaics remain, preserved under wooden covers which the guide will lift for you. The scenes are mainly fishing. The huge Utica mosaic with Neptune and Aphrodite in a sea-horse drawn chariot, Nereids on sea tigers and all overlooked by Oceanus can be seen in the Ulysses Room at the Bardo Museum. Look out for the use of yellow Chemtou marble as well as the white and green marble from Greece. At the foot of the hill are the great baths, great in size, covering over 26,000 sq m. The cisterns and conduits to service this were fed from an aqueduct and water tower which came in at the highest point where the remains of the water tower, sometimes referred to as the citadel, can be found.

The **Museum** is very small, divided into two rooms. The Punic room has some gold brooches and earrings of 4th-3rd centuries BC, oil lamps from 7th-1st centuries BC, vases from Greece and Italy indicating trade and small sarcophagi for the bones and ashes of children who, according to legend, were sacrificed here. The Roman room has statues, an inscription from 1st-2nd centuries AD, a mosaic of a hunting scene and an interesting diagram of the excavations of the House of Cascades. There is no accommodation at Utica.

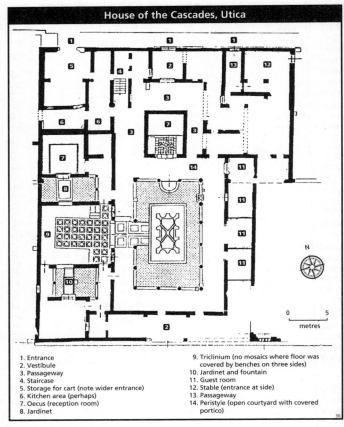

House of the Cascades, Utica

1. Entrance
2. Vestibule
3. Passageway
4. Staircase
5. Storage for cart (note wider entrance)
6. Kitchen area (perhaps)
7. Oecus (reception room)
8. Jardinet
9. Triclinium (no mosaics where floor was covered by benches on three sides)
10. Jardinet and fountain
11. Guest room
12. Stable (entrance at side)
13. Passageway
14. Peristyle (open courtyard with covered portico)

Kalaat el Andalous village stands on what was a headland before the sea retreated, an agricultural area, mainly vines. Houses are part of Medjerda development project sponsored by World Bank. Market day – Wed. Beside main mosque are post office, bank, petrol and Haj Ali café. The views S and E to **Sidi Bou Saïd** and **Cap Bon** are well worth the walk.

Also worth a visit is **Cap Blanc**, a rocky headland just 10 km N of Bizerte. This is the most N tip of Africa and is very beautiful.

Local information
● Accommodation

Most of the large hotels are situated on the Corniche which is about 3 km out of the town.

C *Apart'hotel Résidence Aïn Mereim*, T 437615/438859, F 439712, 296 beds; **C** *Corniche*, route de la Corniche, T 431844, F 431830, 4 km out of town, low season prices acceptable, beach, 87 rm with sea view, fly screens, no a/c, pool, many organized activities, large nightclub, fully booked in summer;

C *Holiday Village – El Kébir*, T 431892-4, F 439534, has 782 beds; **C** *Nador*, T 431848, F 433817, next to *Corniche* and very similar, 105 rm, beach, pool, no disco, tennis, fully booked in summer.

D *Petit Mousse*, route de la Corniche, T 432185, very pleasant, 12 rm, good atmosphere, beach across the road, excellent restaurant, eat outside in summer.

F *Hotel Africain*, next to and similar to *Zitouna*, on edge of medina, T 434412; **F** *Continental*, rue d'Istambul, T 431436, probably one of the best deals if you want a cold shower and a clean, cheap bed, but don't expect much else; **F** *Zitouna*, Place Slaheddine Bouchoucha, T 431447, edge of the medina, very noisy external rooms, no showers.

Try also the unclassified hotels: *Jalta*, T 431169, F 434277; *Sidi Salem*, T 432126; *El Kebir*, T 431892.

Camping: camping is permitted at Remel Plage hostel.

Youth hostels: 1 km N of city centre up Blvd Hassan en Nouri, beyond the medina on route de la Corniche, kitchen, meals provided, 100 beds, T 431608. Also *Remel Plage*, 3 km from city centre, any bus going S of the canal will stop at the turn off, 50 beds, closed Feb, T 440804.

● **Places to eat**
♦♦*Belle Plage*, Corniche, T 431817; *De Bonheur*, rue Thaalbi, T 431047; *L'Eden* on Corniche, T 439023 for seafood; *Le Petit Mousse*, in *Hotel Petit Mousse*, excellent food and fresh fish, not cheap but worth the price.

♦*La Mamma*, T 433695, rue Ibn Khaldoun, sells pizzas and pancakes; *Restaurant de la Liberté*, next door to *Hotel Continental*, good, cheap food.

● **Banks & money changers**
The banks operate a rota so one always stays open later. **BNT**, rue 1er Juin; **STB**, rue Farhat Hached, there is also another branch behind the ONAT, by the old harbour; **CFCT**, Ave Habib Bourguiba which takes Eurocheque and Visa.

● **Hospital & medical services**
Chemist: all night, *Sparfi*, 28 rue Ali Belhaoane, T 439545.

Hospital: on rue du 3 Août, T 431422.

● **Places of worship**
Catholic: 120 Ave Habib Bourguiba, T 432386, service Sun at 1030.

● **Post & telecommunications**
Area code: 02.

Post Office: main office, 6 Ave d'Algérie, takes parcels as well. Around the back of main building is the telecommunications office, also on rue el Medina and Place Pasteur.

● **Shopping**
Visit the *National Handicrafts Centre* (*ONAT*) just by the old harbour on Quai Khémais Ternane, T 431091. They have a good selection of regional art. Bizerte specializes in ironwork, woodwork, pottery, carpets and embroidery.

● **Sports**
Club Nautique, T 432262, on the right of the main beach in town, hires out surfboards and does various other watersports. Sub-aqua fishing is very popular. Otherwise try one of the hotels on the Corniche. The *Corniche* hotel organizes water skiing and rents surfboards. Horse riding is offered at some of the hotels. Some of the big hotels and small enterprises hire out bicycles, which is a cheap way of getting to the beach. Municipal swimming pool (heated) on Blvd Hassan en Nouri. Marina for 100 boats. Harbour Master's Office, T 431688.

● **Tour companies & travel agents**
International Voyages, 35 Ave Habib Bourguiba, T 432885 and 439666, F 433547; *Tourafrica*, Ave Habib Bourguiba, T 432315; *Transtour*, 7 rue d'Alger, T 432174; *Tunisia Line*, corner of rue Ibn Khaldoun and Belgique, T 431944, F 432700; *Via Bizerte*, rue 1er Mai, T 432901.

● **Tourist offices**
National Tourist Office (ONTT), 1 rue d'Istambul, T 432703/432897. The office is hard to find. It is situated by the canal, about 100m before the bridge, towards the sea. Will provide a map of Tunisia, a map of Bizerte and information about places to stay in the region.

● **Useful addresses**
Police: T 431200/1, rue du 20 Mars 1956

● **Transport**
Local Bicycles & Motorbike hire: Ben Othman, Ave Habib Bourguiba; Ben Kilani, Ave Habib Bourguiba, T 431622 and Ben Aleya, rue Sassi Bahri. **Car hire**: ABC, 33 Ave Habib Bourguiba, T 434624, F 436350; Avis, 7 rue d'Alger, T 433076; Budget, 7 rue d'Alger, T 432174; Europcar, 52 Ave d'Algérie, T 439018, also at 19 rue Med Rejiba, Place des

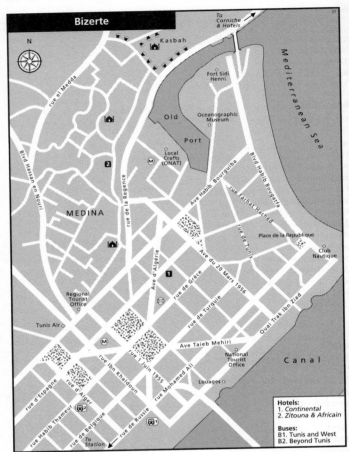

Bizerte

Labels on map:
- To Corniche & Hotels
- Kasbah
- Fort Sidi Henni
- Old Port
- Oceanographic Museum
- Mediterranean Sea
- Local Crafts (ONAT)
- rue el Medda
- Blvd Hassan en Nouri
- rue de Regence
- MEDINA
- Ave Habib Bourguiba
- Blvd Habib Bougatfa
- rue Farhat Hached
- rue de Tunis
- Place de la République
- Club Nautique
- rue d'Algérie
- Ave du 20 Mars 1956
- rue de Grèce
- Regional Tourist Office
- Tunis Air
- rue de Turquie
- Quai Trak Ibn Ziad
- Ave Taieb Mehiri
- National Tourist Office
- Canal
- rue Ibn Khaldoun
- rue 1 Juin 1955
- rue Mohamed Ali
- Louages
- rue d'Espagne
- rue d'Alger
- rue Habib Thameur
- rue de Belgique
- To Station
- rue de Russie

Hotels:
1. *Continental*
2. *Zitouna & Africain*

Buses:
B1. Tunis and West
B2. Beyond Tunis

Martyrs, T 431455; **Hertz**, Place des Martyrs, T 433679; **Inter Rent**, 19 rue Mohammed Rejiba, T 431455. **Mattei**, rue d'Alger, T 431508; **Next Car**, 80 Blvd Hassan en Nouri, T 433668. **Shipping Co. Navitour**, 29 Ave d'Algérie, T 431440.

Air The nearest airport is Tunis. Information from Tunis Air, 76 Ave Habib Bourguiba, T 432201.

Train The station is approx 15 mins walk SW along canal out of town. Information on T 431070. To Tunis 0540, 0810, 1350, 1835.

Road Bus: the main bus station is by the bridge over the canal. Information from *Société Régionale de Transport*, Quai Tarak Ibn Ziad T 431371/736. A short walk N up Ave d'Algérie to the town centre. Information from Société Nationale de Transport on T 431222/431317 Bus station for places W, as far as Tabarka, i on rue d'Alger. Frequent buses to **Tunis** an **Ras Djebel**; change at Ras Djebel for **Raf Ra** and **Ghar el Melh**; **Aïn Draham** (via Tabarka leaves early morning. **Louages**: leave by the canal under the bridge to all destinations, but some are harder to obtain if the demand is low. Louages terminate on the Quai Trak Ibn Ziad under the bridge or at the N end of Ave d'Algérie. Sometimes available at the station.

Sea Navitour, 29 Ave d'Algérie, T 431440. Port – Harbour Master's Office, T 431688.

RAS DJEBEL

This is a large modern settlement on the coast E of Bizerte on the road to the beaches of Raf Raf. The town has a café, a patisserie called FSRD and *Hotel Okba* but not much else of interest. By contrast the surrounding area is very beautiful. The beach at Ras Djebel is very crowded in the summer and as most people prefer to camp near the town, anywhere further W is better. To the N, Cap Zebib offers magnificent views and the road from Bizerte to Ras Djebel is very scenic with a panoramic view over the coast by Bizerte. On the beach is a tiny marina with fishing boats. Drive with care as the road stops dead 1m from cliff edge ... those in the know turn left.

RAF RAF

ACCESS The buses from Bizerte, Ras Djebel and Tunis stop just by the beach. Bus No 1B from Tunis.

The town of Raf Raf at the top of the hill which houses the well-to-do of Tunis in attractive villas is not particularly special. Take the steep (10%) road to Raf Raf plage which is very beautiful. The white sand backed by dunes and the settlement extending virtually to the beach makes it a unique setting. Unfortunately there is little accommodation. It makes a pleasant day excursion from either Tunis or Bizerte. Consequently in the summer, on Fri market and especially at weekends, Raf Raf gets very crowded with trippers and the approach roads become jammed with cars. Raf Raf produces the best table grapes in Tunisia, on sale, in season, all along the road. They are known as the *Raf Raf muscat*.

The Ile Pilau just off the coast, looks just like a fortress and makes an interesting photographic subject.

Local information
● **Accommodation**

It is possible to stay in straw huts on the beaches which can be rented overnight for about TD10, but you will have to bring everything you need.

C *Hotel Dalia*, T 447668, small, only 22 rm, about half have sea view, very clean, close to beach, open all year, expensive due to location.

● **Places to eat**

The restaurant in the *Hotel Dalia* is good, clean and cheap. You can eat outside and watch the sea and the visitors. There are a few other restaurants along the beach, try *Restaurant Andalous*, but they tend to be overpriced.

Locals are occupied making traditional bird cages to sell to tourists.

● **Transport**

Road Bus: departures for Bizerte and Ras Djebel. Three daily to Tunis. **Louages**: also available, but in summer towards the end of the day it can be quite crowded as everybody is leaving. Hitching may take time as most cars are already full.

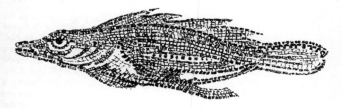

Fish mosaic

GHAR EL MELH

ACCESS Ghar el Melh via Aousdja on buses Nos 5 and 3A from Tunis and Bizerte. There are no buses E to Sidi Ali el-Mekki.

This is a clean, S facing fishing village by a shallow salt lagoon with a notorious past of piracy and smuggling. when it was known as Port Farina. The lake extends over 3,000 ha, with a depth of around 1m. The main fish caught here are mullet, bream, perch, sole and eel. Very busy in season, quality restaurants. The road continues past the village and on 6 km to the splendid beach of **Ras Sidi Ali el Mekki** with a small café/shop and straw cubicles for camping, rented at TD5/day. At the end of the peninsula, built partially into the cliff is the *marabout* of Sidi Ali el Mekki, a place of pilgrimage. This is an attractive and secluded spot.

Sounine, further N, has a rocky beach, expensive villas, show huts for rent on beach, café Budan on corner, also *Café l'Escale* for snacks. In spring every electricity pylon has a storks' nest. In autumn the fields are full of tall white squills.

Metline is a small town built into the hillside. Take the road round it to the W for a splendid view. **El Alia**, built on the crossroads, is a splendid example of the settlements built by returnees from Andalucía. Here thistles are grown for the felting of *chechias* (see page 94). The road SW from here towards Menzel Bourguiba has been upgraded and is very busy. Once across the P8 it skirts the lake shore. Good views as no buildings beside lake.

MENZEL BOURGUIBA

A large provincial town on the W side of Lake Bizerte with nothing particular to attract visitors. The pollution it produces is most unpleasant. Menzel Bourguiba does make a good base from which to visit Lake Ichkeul.

● **Accommodation** E *Younès*, 32 beds, T 461606.

● **Tour companies & travel agents** *Via Bizerte*, rue du 18 Janvier, T 460756.

This animal sanctuary of 12,600 ha, 1m-3m deep, is 25 km away and is arguably the most interesting of Tunisia's six National Parks. Access off P11 S of Menzel Bourguiba just after the railway crossing. Water birds and waders are among the thousands of over-wintering migrants (over-wintering Grey-lag geese can number 15,000) found here and 75 species of mammal such as water buffalo, wild boar, porcupine, otter and jackal and around 500 species of reptile live in this protected marsh/lake/mountain habitat. Expeditions to watch the 180 species of bird (best Mar, Apr and Nov) are offered by some tour agents. Visitors may be lucky enough to identify the long legged wading bird on this mosaic. The Tourist Office in Bizerte arranges visits to the area which was designated by UNESCO in 1977 as a biosphere reserve. (The only other such site acknowledged by UNESCO is the Everglades in Florida.) As well as the lake the surrounding wetlands and Djebel Ichkeul are included.

There is a small Ecological museum high above a car park overlooking the lake. Minor road beyond the museum is closed to traffic but walkers are welcome on the circular route round Djebel Ichkeul. The numerous tracks across the dry lake floor are not recommended.

Long legged wading bird - Sfax Museum

Warning The minor road marked S of the lake on Michelin 172 to the C51 does not exist.

Water flows from Lake Ichkeul into Lake of Bizerte via Oued Tindja which is only 5 km long.

FROM BIZERTE TO TABARKA

The coast between Bizerte and Tabarka is quite wild, the sea hidden by thick forests noted as refuge for the last lion (1925) and the last panther (1932) in Tunisia. The coastline is worth trying to reach, especially if you like deserted beaches, although access is difficult. By car from Bizerte to Tabarka take the road W towards Menzel Bourguiba and turn right 5 km after Bizerte on the C51, in the direction of **Sejnane**. This road, running in a valley for much of the way, is very beautiful. At Sejnane the route rejoins the main road to **Nefza** and **Tabarka**.

SEJNANE

This is a pretty mountain village rich in metal ores and producing unusually decorated pottery, animals and statuettes, in Berber style. Packed with donkeys, Peugeot trucks and women in colourful tribal dress on market day, Thur. It is a good base from which to visit Sejnane dam. Although this is on the 'tourist itinerary' it should not be missed. From here too it is easy to visit the attractive and very secluded N beaches, though you will need to have your own transport or be very lucky with lifts. Don't set off for any of these out of the way coastal spots without plenty of provisions. There is a small unclassified hotel at Sejnane, *Sidi Mechrig*.

On the C51, 11 km from Sejnane turn right at the cross roads (signposted) to **Cap Serrat**. This is a headland with a lighthouse and a good, often deserted, beach. It may be possible to buy food at the kiosk on the beach – but don't rely on it.

At Tamera, 10 km before Nefza on the Bizerte road, turn right and follow the winding track signed 'plage' for about 10 km. At the end there is a small fishing village, **Sidi Mechrig**, overlooked by a Roman fortress, and, of course, a beautiful beach. People set up camp here for the summer. There is a hotel. Leaving Tamera, branching from the Sidi Mechrig track, there is a rough scenic ride to the coast at **Cap Negro**, an area once known for its coral fishing.

The closest beach to Tabarka is **Zouara** beach, only 20 km before the town. Turn right off the Bizerte road before Aïn Sebna (a sign indicates the way) and follow a fairly easy track for 5 km. This is a beautiful beach with fine sand, but again there is no infrastructure whatsoever.

TABARKA

ACCESS The louage station is on the main street Ave Habib Bourguiba. From the long distance bus station on rue du Peuple turn left down the hill to the central square. The local bus station is about 50m up the hill from the main square. The airport lies 9km E of town at Ras Rajel.

A minor seaside resort, 175 km W from Tunis, situated where the forested slopes of the Khroumirie range meet the sea. It is a magnificent setting and although this small resort is being enlarged the new hotel complex, good quality and well designed, is situated to the E of town and does not intrude. By the seafront, in town, Porto Corallo has been sympathetically developed with a new hotel, marina and restaurant. The wrecks in the bay add a gruesome interest.

The origins of the town can be traced back to Haron (5th century BC) who is said to have established a trading post here. The Phoenician town was called *Thabraca* meaning 'place in the shade'. As a 3rd century Roman town it was noted for its trade in 'big cats', export of wood for building, lead and iron from its mines and the yellow marble (see Chemtou page 190).

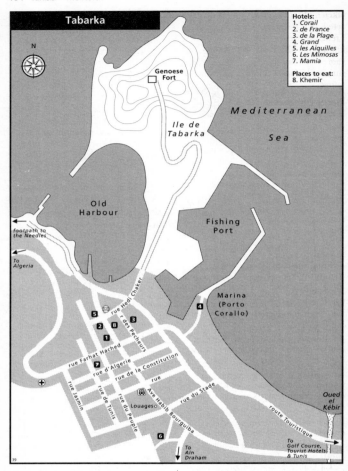

Thabraca played an important role in developments associated with luxurious buildings – painters, decorators, sculptors and ceramic artists made it the town of 'arts'. Mosaic artists founded a school here whose prestige won wide renown abroad for 3 centuries. The walls of the staircase in the Bardo Museum which leads from the ground floor to the galleries above are covered with tomb mosaics from Tabarka dating from the 4th and 6th centuries.

The town prospered with the spread of Christianity in the 5th century and especially during the reign of the Fatmides in the 10th century. In the 16th century it regained its status as a strategic harbour for merchant shipping. More than once the Genoese took possession of it, only to lose it again. It was taken by Tunisia in the 18th century and acted as a fortress in WW2 under the French Protectorate. Today it is better known for the deep depressions off-shore and to the E where lobsters, shrimps, prawns and crayfish can be found.

Places of interest

Tabarka is the centre for diving on the N coast and the diving centre in the Yachting club on the seafront is open all year. The club also organizes other watersport activities including underwater photography. In autumn, hunting, especially of wild boars, is an expanding tourist industry. **Archaeological museum** open 0830-1730 winter, 0900-1300 and 1500-1900 summer, closed Mon, entrance TD1. This museum which contains a basilica and Roman mosaics is currently closed for restoration.

From the town walk along the coast past the old fort built by the Genoese to the **Aiguilles** (needles), some 20m high, carved out of the rock by sea and wind. The view from the top of the old fort is impressive and worth the effort of walking up. An 18 hole golf course has recently been opened along Route Touristique. The course overlooking the sea is in 100 ha of pine and oak forest. Coral jewellery is on sale and there is a **coral festival** in Jul with street fairs and markets when the town is certainly more lively. Market Fri. There is a **WW2 cemetery** with 500 graves 15 km E of town on the P7, open 0730-1430, Sat-Thur.

La Galite is a small archipelago of seven islands (Gallo, Plastro, Ganton and Galite are the largest) in the Mediterranean about 60 km from Tabarka. A few fishermen, wine producers and their families live here. There are remains of Roman tombs and Punic relics. Contact the Tourist Office in Tabarka from a visit here. It is a restricted area for fishing and a classified **nature reserve** with a colony of Mediterranean monk seals.

Local information
● Accommodation

The new A/B grade hotels along Route Touristique have increased the number of beds available but in summer booking is essential.

A *Abou Nawas Montazah*, T 643532/508, F 643276, 306 rm with balcony, phone, heating, no a/c, no fly screens, Olympic size pool, beach site, tennis, windsurfing, scuba diving tuition, exercise room and sauna, minimal carpeting so noise echoes through hotel at every step. Look out for **A** *Grande Hotel* currently under construction in the Porto Corallo complex in the marina; **A** *Iberotel Mehari*, T 670001/3, F 643943, 200 rm, much quieter than Montazah, good restaurant, pool, beach site, tennis.

B *Les Mimosas*, on the left as you enter the town, T 643018/28, F 643276, on top of a hill overlooking the bay, pool, 60 rm with sea view. Similar hotels are **B** *Morjane*, on the road behind the sand dunes, T 644453, F 643888, 160 rm, the first hotel built on the beach, very convenient; **B** *Paradise Golf*, T 643002/440, F 643918; **B** *Royal Golf Marhaba*, T 644002, F 643838.

C *Hotel Corail*, 76 Ave Habib Bourguiba, 50 beds, cheap, but only rec if funds are low or everything else is full; **C** *Hotel de la Plage*, rue des Pecheurs, T 644039, 14 beds; **C** *Hotel Novelty*, Ave Habib Bourguiba, T 644176/8, F 643008, brand new, 26 rm, central, very clean.

D *De France*, Ave Habib Bourguiba, T 644577, 38 beds, restaurant, old fashioned charm, probably the best of the cheap hotels but has certainly known better days.

● Places to eat

◆◆*Hotel de France*, Ave Habib Bourguiba, good food at very decent prices. *Le Pirate*, Porto Corallo, T 644061; *Les Arcades*, Porto Corallo, T 644069.

◆*Hotel Corail*; *Les Agriculteurs*, T 644585, good, cheap, very filling food; *Novelty 66*, Ave Habib Bourguiba, T 644367.

● Banks & money changers

BNT and UIB on Ave Habib Bourguiba; BNA on rue de Peuple.

● Hospital & medical services

Hospital: on rue de Calle, T 644023.

● Post & telecommunications

Area code: 08.

Post Office: Ave Hedi Chaker, T 644417, Mon-Fri 0830-1230 and 1500-1800, Sat 0830-1330.

● **Shopping**
Market day: Fri.

Handicrafts: incl olive wood carvings, basket work, carpets, Berber pottery and Tabarka briar pipes.

● **Sports**
Diving: **Deep sea diving**: *Scuba Diving Club*, Port de Tabarka, T 644478, the first sub-aqua sports centre in Tunisia, open all year, best season Apr-Oct. Dive sites only 15 mins by boat. **Underwater diving**: at *Mehari Diving Centre*, 'Le Crab', T 643136; *Aquamarin*, T 643508; *Loisirs de Tabarka*, T 643002. The Yachting Club at Porte de Pêche Tabarka is rec by the Tunisian National Tourist Office as the best place to learn snorkelling and scuba diving. Snorkels can be rented from Magasin Sinbad d'Equipment Marin, at the port. Only those with club membership may participate in diving – in other words you have to join – but the club premises are of a very high standard and the changing facilities are excellent. Rescue equipment is available.

Golf: 18-hole course, 6,400m, par 72, fees TD30-35/day. *El Morjane*, T 644028, F 644026.

Horse riding: can be arranged at the hotels.

Hunting: *Hunting Club*, route d'Aïn Draham, T 644417.

Sailing: the marina has 50 moorings with planned extension to 280 berths.

Tennis: at the hotels.

● **Tourist offices**
32 Ave Habib Bourguiba, T 670111, open 0900-1200 and 1600-1900, after the main square on the right. Only basic information.

● **Tour companies & travel agents**
Tabarka Voyages, Ave Ennasr (route d'Aïn Draham), T 643740, F 643726; *Tunisie Voyages* in *Hotel Mehari*, T 643136/325, F 643868; *Ulysse Tour*, Blvd de 7 Novembre, T 643582, F 643622; *Vaga Tours*, Cité des Arts, T 644416, F 654803.

● **Useful addresses**
Police station: on rue du Peuple, T 644021; **Maritime police**, Port de Tabarka. **Border police**: Melloula, T 632889/860. **Police-Babouche-Algerian border**: T 655150.

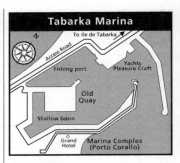

● **Transport**
Local Car hire: Hertz, Port Corallo, T 644570. Interlo, Blvd de 7 Novembre, T 643595; **7 Novembre** at Airport, T 640005, F 640133.

Air T 655150, internal flights to Tunis Fri 1600, Sun 1830 take 40 mins. From Tunis Fri 1450, Sun 1730.

Road The long distance **bus** station is in rue du Peuple (1st street on the right going uphill from the central square). Information from Société National de Transport, rue de Peuple, on T 444048. Departures **Tunis** (via Mateur) 0400, 0500, 0730, 0900, 1545; **Tunis** (via Béja) 0600, 1000, 1300. The local bus station is 50m uphill from the central square. Frequent departures to **Aïn Draham** and **Jendouba**. Two buses a day to **Bizerte**. Information from Société Régionale de Transport Général de Jendouba, Ave Habib Bourguiba, on T 644097. **Louages**: the station is at the beginning of Ave Habib Bourguiba. Departures for **Jendouba**, **Aïn Draham**, **Le Kef** and sometimes **Tunis**. **Tuf tuf**: from tourist hotels to marina/old harbour along tourist road. Leaves on the hour from old harbour.

Sea Port – Harbour Master's Office, T 644599, F 643595.

TABARKA TO AIN DRAHAM AND LE KEF

The road from Tabarka S to Aïn Draham is a typical mountain road and very scenic, with a wonderful view towards the coast. At Babouch there is a turning W to Hammam Bourguiba, 17 km, a thermal spa greatly prized by the Romans. Ruins here of vaulted arches, high rendered brick w-alls and columns with ornamental capitals. There are two springs the

Cork

The Cork Oak, *Quercus suber*, is a native evergreen of the Mediterranean coastal region. It flourishes on the N facing slopes of the coastal hills, the Northern Tell, up to an altitude of 1,200m and is highly prized for its economic value. It can be instantly recognized by its orange-brown smooth trunk from which the 'bark' has been gently stripped away, from the ground up to the main branches.

It takes 20 years for a Cork Oak to mature and after that time the dead outer layers of 'bark' can be harvested every 8-9 years. As these trees which rarely grow more than 15m high can live for 300-400 years it is a good long term investment.

The outer layer of the bark is dead and is separated from the inner, living bark by a layer of cells known as *phelloderm*. From this new cork is produced when the outer layer is stripped away. The first cutting away of the cork is known by the fanciful term 'demasclage', used also to describe castration of animals. This first stripping is referred to as male, thereafter all strippings are female.

The cylinders of cork are carefully removed in the summer and taken to processing plants. There is one in Tabarka and another in Aïn Draham. After boiling to dissolve the tannic acid present in all oaks and to soften the material, the rough outer layers are removed and the sheets left to mature.

Cork is perhaps best known as a stopper in wine bottles, a practice introduced in the 17th century and thereby revolutionizing the storage of wines. Cork has many other uses. Its lightness, buoyancy and resistance to burning means that it is excellent material for insulation. It is also used for floor tiles, notice boards, fishing floats, and formerly for cricket balls. Furthermore there is evidence that Hellenic women work high heeled shoes of cork and that Egyptians, seeking comfort to the end, used this most versatile of materials to line their coffins.

lower emerging at 38.5°C and the higher at 50°C with different chemical properties said to relieve respiratory conditions. **E** *Hotel Hammam Bourguiba*, T (086) 32517, F (086) 32497 open all year, has 40 rm and 20 bungalows and is used by Tunisians taking treatment. This road also leads to the Algerian border but the crossing in this area has about 10 km between control posts, a walk not to be undertaken lightly. Border post control at Babouch, T 647150.

AIN DRAHAM

Aïn Draham, which means 'silver spring or stream', lies 175 km W of Tunis and 26 km S of Tabarka. It is known as a spa town. It is a very picturesque village, many of the older houses having particularly red tiled roofs. It is surrounded by thick cork-oak forests way up at 1,000m in the mountains. It is an ideal place in summer away from the unpleasant heat, but can be quite chilly in winter when snow is common. Aïn Draham is also the heart of the wild boar hunting region and it can be difficult to find places in hotels during the season from Oct to Mar. It is a quaint little town with one steep, central street (one way), and is important as a market town for the region. Housing has spread to other side of valley.

Places of interest

The Association du Patrimoine Populaire et Historique Aïn Draham is found in a small office where products of the regional arts are displayed. It is interesting and the people are very welcoming.

Just N of Aïn Draham, to the W of the road, is Col de Ruines. This small detour has splendid views as does the terrace of *Hotel Nour el Aïn*.

Benir M'Tir is a spectacular detour off the main road S of Aïn Draham. It is

Hunting dogs (from a mosaic found at El Djem)
chase wild boar into a net for capture.

one of Tunisia's largest reservoirs on a tributary of the Oued Medjerda.

Local information
● **Accommodation**

B *Hammam Bourguiba*, in Hammam Bourguiba, T 647217.

C *Hotel Nour el Aïn*, T 655000, F 655185, 60 rm, open all year, covered heated pool, health club, international menu, busiest in hunting season. Look out for the new hotel, *La Forêt*, almost complete.

D *Beau Séjour*, Ave Habib Bourguiba, T 647005, 30 rm, an old hunting lodge, restaurant, central, book in summer; **D** *Les Chênes*, T 647211, 32 rm, out of town, 7 km towards Jendouba, looking very worn, good, food, rather secluded, set in the middle of the forest, organizes wild boar hunting; **D** *Rehana*, T 647391, at the S end of the village on the road to Jendouba, 75 rm, comfortable hotel with a very memorable view overlooking the valley, within walking distance of the village, book in summer.

Youth hostel: is at the top of the hill, kitchen, 150 beds, T 647087.

● **Places to eat**

◆◆*Grand Maghreb* is good but expensive.

◆*Café de la Republique*, on Av 7 Novembre is rec.

● **Banks & money changers**
Are all on Ave Habib Bourguiba. **BNT**, **STB** are opp Association du Patrimoine, and **BNA** is beyond the Tourist Office.

● **Hospitals & medical services**
Hospital: is on route de l'Hôpital, T 647047.

● **Post & telecommunications**
Area code: 08.

Post Office: Ave Habib Bourguiba, T 647118, further up the road after the Association du Patrimoine.

● **Sports**
Wild boar hunting Oct-Feb and woodcock shooting are advertised for this region in winter, see *Hotel Les Chênes*. Huge new

sports complex 6 km S of town.

● **Tourist offices**

Syndicat D'Initiative, Ave Habib Bourguiba, towards the top, T 647115.

● **Useful addresses**

Police: Ave Habib Bourguiba, T 647150.

● **Transport**

Road Bus: the bus station is at the bottom of Ave Habib Bourguiba, on the right, by the cemetery. Frequent buses to **Tunis**, **Jendouba** and **Tabarka**. **Louages**: the station is situated at the top of Ave Habib Bourguiba, on the square. Main routes are to <F85MJendouba and Tabarka.

BULLA REGIA

ACCESS Bulla Regia lies 3 km E of the Aïn Draham-Jendouba road. Take a bus from Jendouba and ask to get off at Bulla Regia. The intersection is 6 km N of Jendouba and is signed only to Bou Salem. You will have to walk or hitch the remaining 3 km. There is no accommodation at the site. Open summer 0800-1900 and 0830-1730 winter, closed Mon, entrance TD1, photography fee TD1. Visit the museum first (café and toilets) where you may be able to buy a guide book.

History

In 2 BC, Bulla Regia was the capital of one of the three small Roman kingdoms in Numidia, but prosperity came under the rule of Hadrian, when the town was annexed to the Empire. The economic development of the town was based on the strategic position for trade and the fertility of the surrounding plain which produced grain in abundance.

Places of interest

The ruins are laid out on terraces on the steep slopes of Djebel Rebia (647m) overlooking a large plain, which is particularly hot in summer and cold in winter and there is no doubt that it was to escape the unpleasant extremes of this climate that the houses were built partly underground, as they are at Matmata (see page 309). These **underground villas** are the main attraction here. Despite earthquake damage to the surface features, due to the unusual architecture, many of the villas are well preserved. The general style was to have the eating and sleeping rooms centred around a large underground courtyard. Judging from the luxurious decoration, most of them belonged to rich inhabitants. Notice the ceilings are arched. The vaulted roof in the House of Hunting is supported by hollow tubes of terracotta. Most of the better mosaics have been taken to the Bardo Museum (see Tunis page 85), but in the **House of Fishing** and the **House of Amphitrite** some magnificent mosaics are still in place. Above ground structures which are still visible include the **Theatre** complete with stage, the **Memmian Baths** near the entrance, the **Forum**, the **Temple of Apollo**, and a Christian Basilica. There is a festival here each Sept. The **Forum** is a rectangular area with religious and public buildings on all four sides. To the W is the Capitol of which little remains, to the N stands the Temple of Apollo, more ancient than the Forum on to which it

Triton from Triumph of Venus

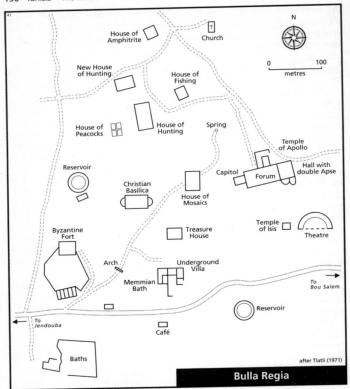

House of
Amphitrite

Church

N

0   100
metres

New House
of Hunting

House of
Fishing

House of
Peacocks

House of
Hunting

Spring

Temple
of Apollo

Reservoir

Christian
Basilica

House of
Mosaics

Capitol

Forum

Hall with
double Apse

Byzantine
Fort

Treasure
House

Temple
of Isis

Theatre

Arch

Memmian
Bath

Underground
Villa

To
Bou Salem

To
Jendouba

Reservoir

Café

Baths

after Tlatli (1971)

Bulla Regia

opens by means of a small courtyard. A quite remarkable group of statues found here are on display in the Bardo Museum, in particular that of Apollo which gave its name to the temple. A Hall with double apse and paved geometric mosaics in very poor condition stands to the E.

The Memmian Baths, some of the walls of the *frigidarium* still standing, are by the entrance to the site. Beneath are basement rooms with groin vaults.

In 1942, a hoard of 70 7th century Byzantine pieces of gold was discovered in an underground villa N of the Memmian Baths, now renamed the Treasure House, indicating occupancy up to that late period. Here an examination of the mosaic pattern shows the arrangement of the dining room.

Return from Bulla Regia W across the P17 towards **Chemtou**. Look out for the abrupt change of surface after the village. The rough track continues W then turns S to the ruins of **Simithu** or **Shimitus** which was a Numidian town and then a Roman colony founded under Augustus 27 BC-14 AD and famed for its yellow marble (giallo antico) quarried until Byzantine times. This city was situated at the junction of two important routes, those coming W from Carthage through Bulla Regia and the other coming S from Tabarka (*Thabraca*). It covered a large area, about 80 ha, both on the hilltop by the quarries where there are huge masonry blocks belonging to a ruined Roman temple (perhaps dedicated to Saturn), and below where there are large baths (ruins) and the complicated water system that supplied and connected them to the aqueduct. Here too was a theatre, parts of which have been excavated, a forum, a basilica and a building thought to be a *schola*.

The remaining arches of a huge bridge, built in Trajan's reign, stand beside the Oued Medjerda. The system set up for a water-driven cornmill either by or on the bridge (locks, sluices and water channels) can be discerned. In May 1993 a treasure hoard was found here. A ceramic pot containing 1,123 solid gold coins was discovered. They covered a period of over half a century and weighed just over 7 kg. This site is certainly worth a visit!

The current Tunisian/German project has plans for a museum on the site.

The blocks of marble from the nearby quarry were each marked with name of the reigning Emperor, the proconsul for Africa and the quarry manager. The stone was an important export, and a road 60 km long and 5.1m wide was constructed to the port at Tabarka.

The track across the river bed leading S to the P6 requires a 4WD vehicle.

The track directly W from Chemtou leads to **Thuburnica**, a visit for the really dedicated.

JENDOUBA

Jendouba, 44 km S of Tabarka and 154 km W of Tunis, is an important crossroads and administrative centre. This town provides easy access to Bulla Regia and the Algerian border. There are branches of all the main banks here.

● **Accommodation** D *Similthu*, on the right, by the roundabout when arriving from Bulla Regia, T 631695, F 631743, new hotel, 26 rm, restaurant, on the main road, not very appealing; E *Atlas*, rue du 1er Juin 1955, T 630566, behind the police station, probably the only decent hotel in town. **Youth hostel**: 60 beds, meals, T 631292.

● **Transport Train** The train station is off the main square, by the police station. Departures **Tunis** 0554, 1033, 1240, 1515, 1653; **Algeria** (Annaba/Algiers) 1539. **Road Bus**: the bus station is to W of town, past the railway lines. Information on T 630411. Frequent local buses to **Tunis**, **Le Kef**, **Tabarka** and **Aïn Draham**, also buses to the border at Ghardimaou. They do not cross the border so you will have to cross on foot. **Louages**: for **Ghardimaou** they leave from the station on Blvd Sakiet Sidi Sousse. For Tunis they leave from rue 1 Juin 1955.

Excursions

Ghardimaou, 34 km W of Jendouba, is on the way out towards Algeria. It is not worth a visit on its own account. There is the **E** *Hotel Thubernic* if you wish to stay on the way to **El Feidja**, one of Tunisia's six National Parks, in the hills near the Algerian frontier, set up to protect the Barbary deer. The nearest town is Aïn Soltane. Take the P6 out of Jendouba and turn N just before the frontier post. Border at Ghardimaou T 645004.

Before proceeding S to Le Kef, visitors are recommended to find time to make a journey NE to **Béja**, either by road or railway. For the first 22 km to Bou Salem, both are alongside the Oued Medjerda, the only river in Tunisia which flows all year round. The road, which never seems to be free of roadworks, crosses the two main tributaries, the Oued Mellègue and Oued Tessa which can be spectacular in flood and very disappointing at other times, while the railway line from Jendouba to Béja runs along the far side of the main valley. Bou Salem is a large successful market town dealing with the agricultural produce, mainly cereals but some grapes and some livestock, of this fertile valley. It is possible to see in this journey the area that the Romans used as their 'bread basket'. From Bou Salem the road climbs up the wooded slopes to

Béja providing panoramic views back towards the route travelled, while the railway crosses and recrosses the main river before turning N to Béja.

BEJA

ACCESS The bus and train stations are at the bottom of the main street with frequent connections to/from Tunis and Jendouba.

(*Pop* 35,000; *Alt* 234m) This town has had an eventful history, marked by various unfriendly visitors over the centuries razing it to the ground! Today, fortunately for the residents, there is less excitement but it is worth a wander round the medina and up the keep in the kasbah for a fine view of the town and the fortified walls. Try to count all the 20 square towers. Béja has an attractive location, surrounded by excellent agricultural land with hills to the NW. It is possible to see from the expanses of cereals which this town was the largest grain market of the Roman Africa. Today it is still very busy as it commands the junction of six important roads.

Places of interest

Trajan's Bridge, once part of the Roman E-W road network lies on the minor road C76 about 13 km SW of Béja. The road leaves Béja beside the station and crosses the railway before crossing the Oued Béja. This Roman bridge, which seemingly has nothing to do with Trajan at all, is still in splendid condition. Its 70m span is a monument to the workmanship from the time of Tiberius. Barrage Kasseb another, very large barrage on the Oued Medjerda lies 16 km W.

There are **WW2 cemeteries** in the area. One is just outside the N limits of the town with 396 graves and another with 99 graves about 800m N of Thibar village which lies on the C75 between Béja and Teboursouq, adjacent to the agricultural college. Both open 0730-1430 Sat-Thur. At **Thibar** see the ruins of the Castle of the Seven Sleepers.

Local information
● **Accommodation**

There are two small hotels.

D *Hotel Vaga*, T 450818, with 36 beds.

F *Hotel Phoenix*, T 450188, with 30 beds.

Youth hostel: T 450621, opp the bus station, 80 beds, meals available.

● **Tour companies & travel agents**

Vaga Tours, Ave 18 Janvier, T 451805.

LE KEF

Le Kef (The Rock) 58 km S of Jendouba is perched 750m up on a rocky hill. It is a very beautiful little town with a long history, mainly military in nature due to its important strategic position. It became a Roman colony in the 2nd century because of its situation. When the French entered Tunisia, they captured Le Kef in 1881 and made it an important military centre. During WW2 it became the provisional capital of the still free Tunisia. Today the town is an important economic and cultural regional centre. It is an interesting place to visit and remains authentic and relatively untouched by tourism. Also, due to its long history, it is rich in monuments.

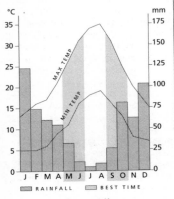

Climate: Béja

RAINFALL   BEST TIME

Mosque of Sidi Bou Makhlouf

Places of interest

If you want to visit the town, it is a good idea to stop off at the **Association de Sauvegarde de la Medina**, on Place de l'Indépendence. They have a charming little office and are very helpful. The best way to visit the medina is to walk around with no fixed itinerary. Some parts are as beautiful as Sidi Bou Saïd, with the advantage that here there are no crowds.

The **Regional Museum of Popular Arts and Traditions** is on the square at the top of the town. An interesting museum set in the old and very beautiful Zaouia Sidi Ali Ben Aissa. There are four rooms, the most interesting presents elements of the everyday nomadic life, including a large tent of the type seen only occasionally today in the southern regions. Open winter 0930-1630 and summer 0900-1300 and 1500-1900, closed Mon, entrance TD1.

The **kasbah** is an old Turkish fort built in 1601 using much 'recycled' more ancient materials. It has an impressive view. Entrance TD1. In summer the **Bou Makhlouf festival** takes place in the courtyard.

The **Mosque of Sidi Bou Makhlouf**, a reminder of the Andalasian presence so widespread in the area, is just behind the kasbah. This is a very beautiful mosque with interesting domes and an octagonal minaret. The inside is highly decorated with ceramics and stucco. Also worth a visit is **Dar el Kous** behind Ave Habib Bourguiba. This is a 4th century Christian basilica dedicated to St Peter. Ras el Aïn was/is the spring which supported the town in Roman times. Evidence of channels and a cistern remain.

A minor road, the C72, climbs N to the side of the 1,500 ha lake held back by the Nebeur Dam. The lake is an impressive 18 km long. A better view is obtained from the dam on the Oued Mellègue by turning off the road to Jendouba after the steep winding road passes Nebeur.

Local information
● **Accommodation**

D *Hotel Sicca Veneria*, Place de l'Indépendence, T 221561, ugly, 34 rm, central, relatively cheap, restaurant.

E *Hotel Chez Venus*, Ave Habib Bourguiba, T 224695, 20 rm with bath, good value, helpful owner, organizes wild boar hunting.

F *La Medina*, 18 rue Farhat Hached, T 220214, simple, new, fairly clean and welcoming; **F** *La Source*, Place de la Source, T 221397, 9 rm, central, set around a patio next to the Muezzin's loudspeaker, not very clean, slightly shabby.

● **Places to eat**
◆◆*Restaurant Chez Venus*, Ave Habib Bourguiba, very pleasant atmosphere, probably the best food in town, a bit more expensive than the others.

◆*Restaurant l'Auberge*, Ave Habib Bourguiba, good, cheap Tunisian food; *Restaurant Ed Dyr*, Ave Hedi Chaker, good value.

● **Banks & money changers**
STB, Place de l'Indépendence; BT, Ave Hedi Chaker.

● **Post & telecommunications**
Post Office: Ave Hedi Chaker.

● **Sports**
Wild boar hunting.

● **Tour companies & travel agents**
Nord Ouest Voyages, rue Essour, T 221839.

● **Transport**
Road Bus: the bus station is a 20-min walk downhill from Place de l'Indépendence. Information on T 20105. Frequent buses to Tunis and Jendouba, connections also to Sfax; Kairouan; Nabeul; Gafsa; Sousse; and Bizerte. Louages: the louages station is by the bus station.

Know your Romans – Who was Emperor Diocletian?

Gaius Aurelius Valerius Diocletianus (245-313 AD) was Emperor of Rome 284-305. Co-emperor Numerian at that time in charge of eastern areas died in 284 and Emperor Carinus in charge of western areas was assassinated in 285 leaving Diocletian in full control. He was revered as an able soldier and an energetic ruler. Initially he split the empire into two, then four administrative divisions, instituted domestic reforms, fiscal reforms and reorganized the army. He is particularly remembered for his persecution of the Christians (303-305) having them thrown to wild animals, stretched on racks and burned during public demonstrations. He abdicated in 305 and retired to Yugoslavia.

Excursions

Hammam Mellègue, a thermal spa 4 km SW of Le Kef, turn right off P5. **Kalaat Es Senam** and **Table de Jugurtha**, turn right off P17 29 km S from Le Kef, before the railway and after 14 km bear left and S. Table de Jugurtha is 1,271m and for the energetic there are views over to Algeria!

LE KEF TO KASSERINE

Just 42 km W of Le Kef is Sakiet Sidi Youssef and the Algerian border. It was on 8 February 1958 that the French Air Force dropped bombs here to destroy what they considered to be Algerian rebels. The raids left a large number of Tunisian and Algerian soldiers and civilians dead and caused the destruction of the town.

HAIDRA

Haïdra, known as *Ammaedara* to the Romans, is well off the main tourist track – in fact few visitors reach here – all the more reason for your journey.

The main site lies to the SE of the town and the old Roman road runs parallel to the P4 from which many ruins can be seen. The main function of Haïdra was always to protect the borders of the Roman Empire.

Coming from the E one first encounters the Triumphal Arch of Septimus Severus which spanned the Roman road to Carthage. It has the dedication date of 195 AD inscribed in the frieze. Its present state of preservation is due to being incorporated in a small Byzantine fort.

Further S and E are the remains of a Byzantine church with three naves. Excavations show that this covers a more ancient church. In both the apse faced E. This church is dedicated to the martyrs who perished under the persecution of Diocletian. A small chapel there is dedicated to these unfortunates.

About 300m to the S, just before the

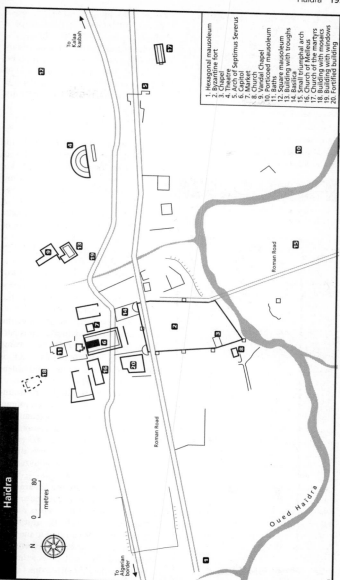

Haïdra

N

0   80
metres

1. Hexagonal mausoleum
2. Byzantine fort
3. Chapel
4. Theatre
5. Arch of Septimus Severus
6. Capitol
7. Market
8. Church
9. Vandal Chapel
10. Porticoed mausoleum
11. Baths
12. Square mausoleum
13. Building with troughs
14. Basilica
15. Small triumphal arch
16. Church of Melleus
17. Church of the martyrs
18. Building with mosaics
19. Building with windows
20. Fortified building

To
Ksar lac
kasbah

To
Algerian border

Roman Road

Roman Road

Oued Haïdra

43

oued, is the beautiful Porticoed Mausoleum. It is well preserved, still having a second storey. The upper floor is in the style of a small temple and the façade of four columns supporting a pediment gives it its name. Any statues which stood between the columns have long since been removed.

At 200m N of the road and in line with the Church of the Martyrs is the Square Mausoleum decorated with Corinthian pillars and stylized garlands. The Theatre also stands to the N of the road. This

is a great disappointment as the restorations of 299 AD have not prevented it from being now just a pile of stones on hard to distinguish foundations.

The Building with Troughs has stone basins topped by arcades, the purpose of which may have been storage of grain. The adjacent Vandal Chapel with three naves, refers to these invaders from the 5th century who left funerary inscriptions.

Travelling E by the present road is the old customs post then what was a very large temple, thought to have been the Capitol. Between these two buildings the discernible square with many jumbles of stones was the market.

The Church of Bishop Melleus was a most distinguished building with two massive columns supporting an arch at the perimeter of the courtyard. Inside there were three naves, a semi-circular apse on either side of which was a sacristy. It is said the remains of St Cyprien were here in the 6th century.

To the S of the main road, just by the ruined bridge over the *oued*, stood a Hexagonal mausoleum. A building of greater distinction is the Byzantine Fort built at the time of Justinian (527-565 AD). It has claims to be the largest Byzantine fort in Africa. This building had a ground area of 200m by 110m and the walls reached up to 10m. The evidence of the nine square towers is clear. Halfway down the E wall was a circular tower. The main N-S route actually passed through this fortress and at the S led to a bridge over the Oued Haïdra. A small chapel with three naves was incorporated into part of the W wall against one of the towers. There was a side aisle on the S side and a high tower, as high as the wall. Parts of the ribbed vaulting are still preserved. Renovations to the N elevation of this fortress were undertaken by the Turkish beys.

Just outside the walls of this fortress to the SW is another small church.

Church of Bishop Melleus

```
0        6
metres
```

semicircular apse

sacristity

sanctuary

steps down

West Chancel

Altar (perhaps held remains of St Cyprien)

East Chancel

Altar

Porch

Remains of two massive columns

Courtyard

42

LE KEF TO TEBOURSOUQ AND TUNIS

The P5 from Le Kef NW towards Tunis, passes through an interesting mixture of small present day Tunisian towns and ancient remains of Roman and Byzantine origin. This is a rich agricultural area of pasture, cereals and wooded hills.

Just N of the small town of Krib, on the left at Km 119 – are the ruins of the triumphal arch and several other remains of the Roman settlement of **Musti**.

The site is entered through a green gate and the visit will not take more than 15 mins. The best of the ruins is the Byzantine citadel, the walls of which are clearly defined. This is constructed of pieces removed from the older buildings. Parts of the Christian basilica with three naves, to the W, are less obvious. There are temples to Apollo, Cérès and Pluto and to the SE of the site is the *zaouia* of Sidi Abd Rebba. There is a triumphal arch at each end of the town, the better preserved is along the road towards Teboursouq 300m E of the main group of ruins. The date of original construction is not known. Just 10 km further along what remains of a Byzantine fort stands on a hill to N of road. This is the site of the ancient settlement of **Agbia**. There is no sign, just take the track across a field. Immediately beyond, on the left is a turn to **Dougga**. This is a very rough route and a long walk – best approach is from Teboursouq.

On towards Tunis the older part of **Teboursouq**, on a hillside, overlooks the P5 while the modern part of town lies

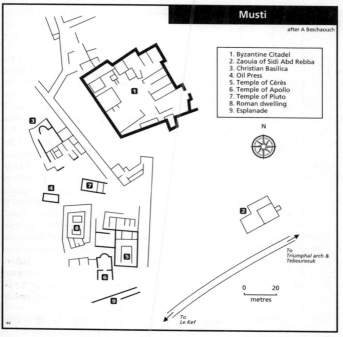

Musti

after A Beschaouch

1. Byzantine Citadel
2. Zaouia of Sidi Abd Rebba
3. Christian Basilica
4. Oil Press
5. Temple of Cérès
6. Temple of Apollo
7. Temple of Pluto
8. Roman dwelling
9. Esplanade

N

To Triumphal arch & Teboursouk

0   20
metres

To Le Kef

along the main road. **Aïn Tounga** immediately to the E of the road contains an imposing Byzantine fortress and remains of Roman Thignica, while **Testour**, the ancient town of **Tichila**, still reflects its Andalusian origins, home of the Moors driven from Spain in the 15th century. The large mosque here is remarkable for its minaret which is in the Andalusian style at the base and in Tunisian style at the top. WW2 cemetery to N of road at Km 61 post.

DOUGGA

ACCESS Take a bus or louages to the new settlement of Dougga (set up to house the folk who were dwelling on the site) and walk up a track behind the village. The ruins are 3 km further on along a track. The easiest way is to go from Teboursouq and take a taxi or louages.

History

The Roman ruins known as **Thugga** are 100 km W of Tunis, 7 km S from the town of Teboursouq and very clearly signed. They are spread out across the plateau and on to the steep side of the *djebel* which overlooks the Oued Khaled. It was originally a Punic town allied to Rome against Carthage. As a consequence, after the downfall of Carthage, the town was granted a certain degree of independence. Romanization only started towards 150 AD, after 2 centuries of coexistence. By the time Carthage had been rebuilt by the Romans, Dougga had become the economic and administrative centre of a very rich agricultural area and controlling the route to the coast, thus enjoying great prosperity. Having become a Roman colony by the end of the 2nd century, the town reached the height of its wealth under the rule of Septimus Severus. It was a very important city in this area with the imposing name of Colonia Licinia Septima Aurelia Alexandriana Thuggenses. Its downfall in the 4th century was caused by the heavy dues paid to the Romans and religious quar-

Fisherman - mosaic at Dougga

rels. When the Vandals invaded, most of the population had moved to Teboursouq. Today the ruins of Dougga spreading over 25 ha still give a very good idea of the everyday life in the ancient city.

Places of interest

Dougga is the largest of the Roman sites in Tunisia and is considered the most dramatic. This is the one site not to be missed. The ruins are on the slope of a small hill and the view and situation are beautiful. It is possible to do a superficial visit in an hour or so, but it is really worthwhile spending a great deal more time. On arrival, one of the 'guides' hanging round the entrance will no doubt want to show you around. Most of these guides are not official and do not hold a card issued by the Tourist Office. If you are in a hurry, it can be a good idea to take one, but be careful to agree on the price beforehand. Café and reasonable toilets at entrance.

The Monuments are open 0830-1730 winter and 0700-1900 summer, closed Mon, entrance fee TD1, photography TD1. The shorter **recommended route** is outlined here first. It takes in all the major buildings which are marked on the accompanying map. The monuments are described in the order they are encountered. A longer route, taking in more, but even then not all, of the important monuments is described straight after. If possible do find time to do both. Begin by the museum.

1. Museum

2. The much restored **Theatre** originally built in 168/9 AD, is a typical example of a Roman theatre. It is quite modest in size, but could nevertheless seat 3,500 people on its 19 semicircular tiers, in three stages, cut into the hill slope. This ensured the stability of the structure and simplified construction. The seating was closed off at the top by a portico, since destroyed and it is suggested that a temporary screen or blind was erected over the seating to protect the spectators from the sun. Some of the columns have been re-erected on the stage but now that the back wall of the stage has disappeared a person seated in the *cavea* obtains a splendid panoramic view of the plain below.

3. **Temple of Augustan Piety** was a small raised sanctuary with an even

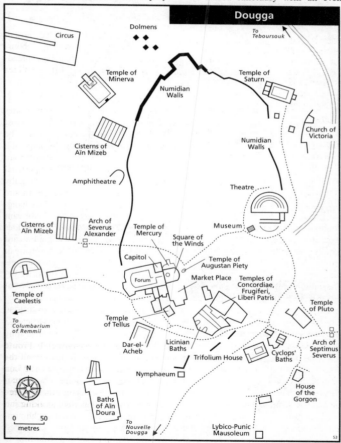

Dougga

- Circus
- Dolmens
- To Teboursouk
- Temple of Minerva
- Numidian Walls
- Temple of Saturn
- Church of Victoria
- Cisterns of Aïn Mizeb
- Amphitheatre
- Numidian Walls
- Theatre
- Cisterns of Aïn Mizeb
- Arch of Severus Alexander
- Temple of Mercury
- Square of the Winds
- Museum
- Capitol
- Forum
- Temple of Augustan Piety
- Market Place
- Temples of Concordiae, Frugiferi, Liberi Patris
- Temple of Pluto
- Temple of Caelestis
- To Columbarium of Remmii
- Temple of Tellus
- Dar-el-Acheb
- Licinian Baths
- Trifolium House
- Cyclops' Baths
- Arch of Septimus Severus
- Nymphaeum
- House of the Gorgon
- N
- Baths of Aïn Doura
- To Nouvelle Dougga
- Lybico-Punic Mausoleum
- 0   50 metres
- 53

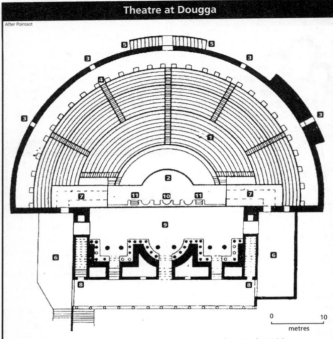

Theatre at Dougga

After Poinssot

1. Cavea (19 semicircular tiers of seating)
2. Orchestra
3. Doorway/entrance
4. Staircase (interior)
5. Staircase (exterior)
6. Large room (permitting entrance under orchestra to cavea)
7. Tribunalium (positions for V.I.Ps)
8. Stairs up
9. Proscaenium (stage)
10. Pulpitum (about 1m high with rectangular and semi-circular niches)
11. Stairs from orchestra to stage

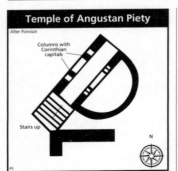

Temple of Angustan Piety

After Poinssot

Columns with Corinthian capitals

Stairs up

N

smaller vestibule entered from the W by a small stair. The engraving on the architrave supported by columns with Corinthian capitols indicated its name and use.

4. **The Square of the Winds** is named after a compass-based inscription naming 12 winds cut into the paving. This square has in fact a semicircular wall at its E end behind which stands the Temple of Fortune and Temple of Augustan Piety.

5. **Temple of Mercury** This section contains the Temple of Mercury con-

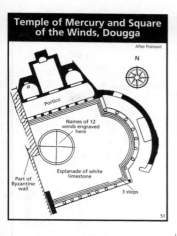

**Temple of Mercury and Square
of the Winds, Dougga**

After Poinssot

N

Portico

Names of 12
winds engraved
here

Esplanade of white
limestone

Part of
Byzantine
wall

3 steps

51

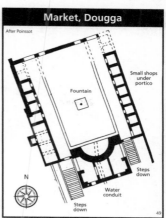

Market, Dougga

After Poinssot

Small shops
under
portico

Fountain

N

Steps
down

Water
conduit

Steps
down

49

structed between 180 and 192 AD and
composed of three chapels, the rectangular central one being larger, the lateral
chapels, much smaller are almost hemispherical in plan. All three are dedicated
to the same god, Mercury. This temple
dedicated to the god of, among other
things, trade faces towards the market
(see also Thuburbo Majus where a similar arrangement exists), donated by the
same patron.

6. **Market** is bordered on its two longer
sides by a series of small shops which were
built under the portico – now disappeared.
Each shop was exactly the same size, 2.8m
x 2.7m. In the centre stood a fountain. The
S end held a large alcove which probably
held a statue of Mercury. To the right and
the left of this alcove a doorway leads out
to separate stairways which descended to
rooms below.

7. You cannot miss the **Capitol** with its
impressive set of steps and six huge
fluted monolithic columns over 8m high
on the edge of the portico. It is considered by some to be the most beautiful
Roman monument in the whole of North
Africa. It was built between 166 and 169
AD and dedicated to the deities Jupiter,
Juno and Minerva. This is a remarkable

monument, drawing the eye of the visitor. The decorative Corinthian capitols
on these huge columns support an ar-
chitraved frieze which bears the dedication to the Triad for the salvation of the
emperors Marcus Aurelius and Lucius
Vérus and a pediment in the decoration
of which can be seen an eagle making off
with a human figure. Behind the portico
is a *cella* 13m x 14m, entered by a central
doorway and divided into three parts,
each with a niche in the end wall. The
central, largest niche once held a white
marble statue of Jupiter and the smaller
side niches statues of the other two deities. Beneath the podium constructed to
lift this capitol to its elevated position is
a crypt, in three compartments and used
at one time as a fort and at another
perhaps as a church.

An ancient model of the square of the
Capitol is on display in the Dougga
Room at the Bardo Museum. Another
ancient model at the Bardo is of the
Theatre.

8. The open piazza in front of the Capitol (24m x 38m) at the base of the staircase leads W to an open space which is
the **Forum**, also dating from the end of
the 2nd century. It was the centre of

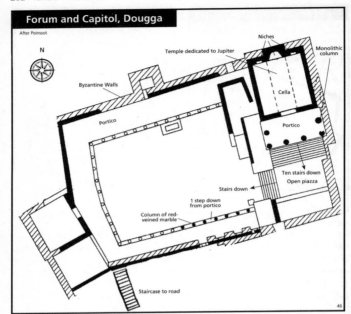

Forum and Capitol, Dougga

After Poinssot

N

Niches

Temple dedicated to Jupiter

Monolithic column

Byzantine Walls

Cella

Portico

Portico

Ten stairs down

Stairs down

Open piazza

1 step down from portico

Column of red-veined marble

Staircase to road

46

public life and administration. Few of the original 35 columns (red veined marble from Chemtou with white capitals) and bases remains. The floor beneath the porticos which once surrounded three sides of the building was mosaic tiles.

9. **Vestiges of the Byzantine Fort** can be seen to the N (a rectangular tower) and S (a rectangular support) of the Forum. The fort covering some 2,800 sq metres in fact enclosed both the Forum and the Capitol and the gateways to N and S are marked on the diagram. Much of the stone used to construct this fort was taken from older buildings on this site.

10. **Temple of Caelestis** (Juno?) also constructed during the reign of Severus Alexander (222-235 BC). The rectangular sanctuary which is entirely enclosed by columns is approached up a flight of 11 steps. It is set in a large, closed semi-circular courtyard which has a portico on the curved side. Definite Greco-Roman influences can be seen here. A number of columns still remain. The broad esplanade in front of the sanctuary has doorways to the E and W.

11. **Dar-el-Acheb** The four rectangular basins enclosed in the larger rectangular building were accessed from a door to the N reached up two steps. Perhaps these basins were for the storage of oil or perhaps for ritual washing.

12. **Temple of Tellus** the goddess of crop fertility. This is a small temple, a square central area and three chapels on the NW wall, the central one being largest and rectangular, the lateral chapels being almost circular.

13. **Roman dwellings to left hand side**, known after the mosaic removed from there and now in the Bardo Museum portraying the welcome *omnia tibi*

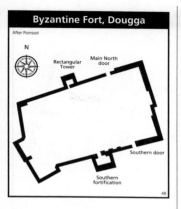

Byzantine Fort, Dougga

After Poinssot

N

Rectangular Tower

Main North door

Southern door

Southern fortification

48

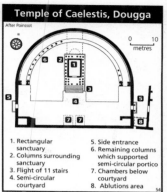

Temple of Caelestis, Dougga

After Poinssot

0   10
metres

6 2 1

5 3 5

4

7 7

8

1. Rectangular sanctuary
2. Columns surrounding sanctuary
3. Flight of 11 stairs
4. Semi-circular courtyard
5. Side entrance
6. Remaining columns which supported semi-circular portico
7. Chambers below courtyard
8. Ablutions area

54

felicia. Despite the removal of the mosaic the house is interesting for the arrangement of water collection and distribution. In this vicinity there are a number of dwellings, all in ruins and difficult to distinguish.

14. **Roman dwellings to right hand side** The House of Dionysus and Ulysses is in very good condition and a great deal can be learned about these dwellings, their layout, plumbing, by wandering from room to room. This particularly splendid private house with most sumptuous decorations, produced the well known scene from Homer's Odyssey of Ulysses bound to the mast by his friends to prevent him being bewitched by the Sirens and the most remarkable mosaic of the child Dionysus admonishing the pirates who had taken him hostage and turning them into dolphins. These and others from this house are in the Bardo Museum.

15. **Licinian Baths**, 3rd century, a very large and complicated building, dominating that part of the site. The fireplace which heated the water, the hot room with the pipes visible in the walls, the cold room and the *palaestre* or 'exercise room' remain.

16. The **Temples of Concordiae,**

Frugiferi and Liberi Patris were constructed between 128-138 AD. Liberi Patris is the largest and has a large square central area flanked by porticos while at the NW side are 5 rooms, the largest in the centre while in the opposite direction was a small theatre, seats still present.

17. Ancient walls – **Numidian** – part of the same fortifications running N of the Theatre, running N from the Byzantine fort and found in smaller sections among the Roman houses to the right hand side of the road, House of Dionysus and Ulysses etc.

18. **Trifolium House**, the brothel, dates from the 3rd century and is the best conserved and largest house yet discovered on the site. It is built at two levels with the entrance at street level and the rooms one floor below.

The staircase at the N side of the house leads down to a peristyle, a rectangular central garden, a small semicircular pool at one end, surrounded by a portico with a mosaic floor. The private quarters to the SW have the vaulted, trefoil shaped room from which it takes its name.

19. **Cyclops' Baths**, to the NE of and associated with Trefolium House stand

Public Baths – Roman style

🐟 Although the larger private houses had their own bathing facilities most Roman citizens made use of the public baths – for which a charge was made. The men and women were strictly segregated, using separate facilities or using the baths at different times of the day. Associated with the public baths was the *palaestre* or exercise room, small shops and sometimes even a library. Visitors to the public hammam in Tunis will find this account very familiar.

The first room in the bathing part was for the removal of outdoor garments – there were niches in the wall for storing the clothes. The body was smoothed with oil, generally olive oil, and then the would-be bather went into the exercise room to get his circulation moving and to raise his body temperature. From there he went to the hot room and steam room where attendants removed the oil and perspiration with a strigil. The journey then was next to the warm room and then to the cold room which was normally large enough to contain a swimming pool. Fresh oil was smoothed on the body at the end of the operation.

Obviously this smooth operation only worked because of the ingenious and complicated engineering of the building, the organization of water supply and the numerous servants and attendants stoking fires.

the Baths of the Cyclops, named after the magnificent mosaic taken from the floor of the cold room here and now on display at the Bardo Museum (see page 85). The baths are not in a very good state, except for the communal latrine. The extremely realistic mosaic, dated as 4th century, shows the three giants, the Cyclops, working at the forge in the cavern belonging to Vulcan who was the god of Hell (see **Gods**, page 121). It is unusual to find figures of such gigantic proportions (well they were giants) or with such dark skins depicted on Roman mosaics.

20. **House of the Gorgon** is named after the mosaic of the head of the Gorgon held in the hand of Perseus.

21. **Lybico-Punic Mausoleum**, perhaps Tunisia's most famous pre-Roman ruin. This is certainly the oldest monument in the area dating from the 3rd-2nd century BC – the mausoleum dedicated to the Numidian Prince Ateban, son of Iepmatath, son of Pallu (said the inscription in both Libyan and Punic which also gives the name of the architect as Abarish. It is thought Ateban was a contemporary of Massinissa. It stands in an olive grove on the brow of the hill and is an impressive 21m in height. It was virtually destroyed by the British Consul in Tunis in the 1840s, who took the stones bearing the bilingual inscriptions back in to the British Museum. The reconstructed, 3-storey tower rises from a plinth of five steps and culminates in a pyramid. The central section is reminiscent of a Greek temple. Note bas reliefs of four-horse chariots with drivers. Take a minute to place this in context – it was an ancient monument when the Romans were building Dougga!

22. **Arch of Septimus Severus** (205 AD) The Triumphal Arch of Emperor Septimus Severus (193-211 AD) was erected in his honour after Thugga was made a *municipium* at his command, giving the community at Thugga partial rights of Roman citizenship. It stood at the eastern entrance to the site astride a road of some 5m in width made of large limestone pieces set in a herring bone pattern. This was the main road to Carthage.

23. **Temple of Pluto** who was the god/protector of Thugga. There is no certainty that this was the dedication of this temple. The large rectangular court-

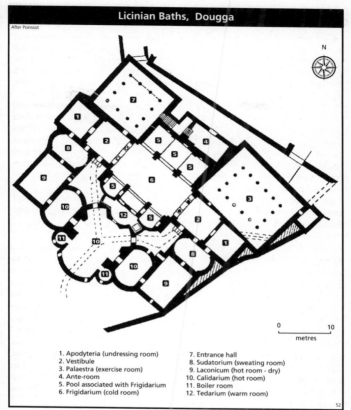

Licinian Baths, Dougga

After Poinssot

N

0   10
metres

1. Apodyteria (undressing room)
2. Vestibule
3. Palaestra (exercise room)
4. Ante-room
5. Pool associated with Frigidarium
6. Frigidarium (cold room)
7. Entrance hall
8. Sudatorium (sweating room)
9. Laconicum (hot room - dry)
10. Calidarium (hot room)
11. Boiler room
12. Tedarium (warm room)

yard was reached up steps from a smaller portico. The small sanctuary was raised, again more steps, only pieces of which remain.

24. It seems **The House of the Seasons** and the **House of the Duck** (again named after pieces of mosaic) were interconnecting or perhaps just one dwelling. The plan is not easy to discern and there are other houses where the arrangement is clearer.

From here this shorter route takes the visitor back to the museum from where the longer route can be accessed, going round the theatre to the top of the *cavea* and continuing N alongside the Numidian wall at the edge of the plateau. Take time to admire the views.

25. **Neptune Sanctuary** A small rectangular sanctuary down off the plateau built near the now non-existent road that lead to the Temple of Saturn. Entrance via a door in the E wall and a small niche in the W wall opposite.

26. **Temple of Saturn** (195 AD) This was built in a dominant position, overlooking the valley. Apparently it was built over the site of an earlier Baal-

Hammon-Saturn sanctuary. It is aligned almost E-W. The outer vestibule (some of the original Corinthian columns still stand) leads into the rectangular central courtyard which originally had a gallery to S,W and N. At the W end are three equal sized chapels. The central chapel once contained a marble statue of Saturn and that to the left a statue of a man dressed in a toga, the benefactor. Changes in the construction have made the entrance arrangements a little complicated.

27.   Down seven steps to the **Crypt** in which have been found many sarcophagi.

28.   In a small Christian cemetery stands the **Church of Victoria** (4th-5th century AD). Many stones were taken from the Theatre and the Temple of Saturn are used in its construction. There are three aisles separated by two rows of columns. The central aisle is wider and longer ending in an altar. Two sets of stairs lead down to the crypt.

From the church return to the top of the plateau and follow the line of the Numidian walls.

29.   There is one small section, only 130m in length, of very ancient walls with parts of two towers on the outer side.

30.   **Dolmens** These are large stones set up as funerary monuments.

31.   **Circus** This is a very large rectangular area aligned E-W on the edge of the plateau. It is dated at 214 AD with additions some 10 years later. Down the centre is the *spina*, a raised area 190m long which ends in semicircles. Did the spectators sit on the rocks to watch the charioteers race round this central spine?

32.   The **Temple of Minerva** constructed 138-161 AD remains really only in outline. Enter by a central door into a large rectangular courtyard with a line of columns at each side. The sanctuary (outer and inner) at the NW was reached up stairs.

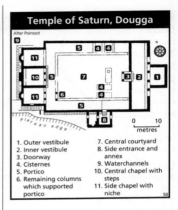

Temple of Saturn, Dougga

After Poinssot

1. Outer vestibule
2. Inner vestibule
3. Doorway
4. Cisternes
5. Portico
6. Remaining columns which supported portico
7. Central courtyard
8. Side entrance and annex
9. Waterchannels
10. Central chapel with steps
11. Side chapel with niche

0   10 metres

50

33.   The **Cisterns of Aïn Mizeb** were a vital part of the town's survival. They are made up of seven long reservoirs (each 35m by 5m) set 1m apart which stored water from the spring to the W. The method of construction and the lining to prevent leakage can still be examined where these cisterns are exposed. Having separate compartments prevented total loss if one part was damaged and permitted cleaning and repairs without cutting off the supply.

34.   Considering the size of the **amphitheatre** in El Djem did Thugga have nothing similar? Is this the remains?

35.   The **Cisterns of Aïn el Hammam** are similar to those further N. There are five parallel reservoirs (each 34m by 3m) and one short one across the end all fed from a spring a distance to the SW.

36.   **Arch of Severus Alexander**, an indistinguished emperor, 222-235 AD. The arch (4m wide) spanned a road, paved in herring-bone style which eventually lead to Carthage.

Walk past the **Temple of Caelestis** and climb gently up the hill.

37.   **A private chapel to Juno** The remains of the aqueduct from Aïn el Hammam is crossed shortly before reaching the next building.

38. **Columbarium of Remmii** A large funerary monument containing the tombs of the Remmii family.

39. **Baths of Aïn Doura and cistern** Here are the ruins of a public baths. To the N is the cistern fed from the Cistern el Aïn and the W the semicircular latrines.

40. **Nymphaeum** The ruins of this fountain are passed on the return to the main site. The water for here also came from Aïn el Hammam.

Local information

● **Accommodation**

It is best to stay overnight in **Teboursouq**, although there is only one hotel there.

D *Hotel Thugga*, on the main road to Tunis, T 465713, 66 beds, has obviously seen better days, rather poor quality. Used by tour groups for a lunch stop.

Youth hostel: in Teboursouq, T 465095, 40 beds.

● **Transport**

Road Bus: there is an hourly bus to **Le Kef** and **Tunis** and many links to **Béja** and **Jendouba**. Information on T 465016.

The town of **Testour** on the S side of the Oued Medjerda stands halfway between Teboursouq and Mejez-el-Bab. It stands on the old Roman site of Tichilla and small pieces of this are found incorporated into the more modern fabric of the town. The modern town dates from the flight of the Moors from Andalucía. It retains its Spanish character. There are many mosques. The Great or Fri mosque is 17th century and built in the Spanish Renaissance style, the ribbed tiled roof being dominant in the town and the minaret has a sun dial (quite unusual) perhaps to aid the timing of the call to prayer. This stands at one end of the main street and at the other end is the dome of the *zaouia* of Sidi Nasser el Buirouachi built in 1733. A visit to his *zaouia* is made by women hoping to improve their fertility. Here too is the grave of the famous rabbi – Fredj Chaoua. Another Jewish figure is remembered here for his Tunisian wife/mistress who murdered him or for love of whom he killed himself. The story is unclear but the house he built for the singer Habiba is now the town's Maison de Culture! Life is strange.

The town is best noted for its tile making introduced from Spain for which it has been famous these last 300 years. Examples of the beautiful tile work from the *zaouia* are included in box on **Tiles**, above.

An annual Festival of Mahlouf is held at the end of Jun. *Mahlouf* is Hispano-Arabic classical music brought from Andalucía by the escaping Moors. Accommodation and good places to eat are not to be found here. Market day – Fri.

MEDJEZ-EL-BAB

This is a market town and an important crossing point of the Oued Medjerda. A new bypass and bridge have been constructed. Take the minor road back to Tunis, the C50. From here the Berber village of Chaouach is accessible along a narrow, climbing, winding road. Drive up the ridge to the village which is in the shadow of a Byzantine castle. The ridge has an abundance of ancient Berber monuments and the remains of the Roman settlement of Sua. The British First and Eighth armies played an important part here in WW2 (see The Desert War, page 324). It has two **WW2 cemeteries**. One is 3 km SW of town on the P5 with 2,900 graves and a memorial to soldiers who died in Tunisia and Algeria and have no known grave. The other has 240 graves and is 17 km W of town on the P6 beside the church in the old town of Oued Zarga. Both open 0730-1430 Sat-Thur.

● **Accommodation E** *Hotel Membressa*, small, 14 rm, communal shower, T 460121.

Tiles from Tunisia

Zellij or multi-coloured ceramic tiles were traditionally used to decorate the walls of the Tunisian city home. The fashion probably came from Andalucía in the 17th century – or possibly with the 'integration' of Tunis into that most loosely articulated of empires, the Ottoman Empire, as of the late 16th century. The great Sidi Mehrez mosque in the northern part of Tunis medina had red, green and blue Iznik-type wall tiles until its restoration in the late 1970s.

In folk memory, the holy man named Sidi Kassem el-Ziliji (the tilemaker) is generally cited as having brought tilemaking to Tunis. Little is known about him except that he was a skilled tile maker, a pious man and that he was highly esteemed by the Hafsid sultans. In 1496, he was buried at his home on the western edge of the medina. Under the dome, behind the cenotaph, a later inscription gives his full name: Abu Fadhl Kacem Ahmed as-Sadafi al-Fasi. He may therefore have been a native of Fez, taken on a Moroccan name and not come from Andalucía as thought. His *zaouia* today houses a small museum of Tunisian ceramics, with a fine collection of both urban and rural pottery, see page 104. The building, situated on the Place du Leader, is instantly recognizable with its pyramid-shaped green-tiled roof, recalling the palaces of Morocco and Andalucía.

From the late 16th century, Tunis' potters and tilemakers set up their kilns and workshops close to Bab Souika on the eastern side of the medina, in an area which even today is still known as *Kallaline* (the plural form of *kallal*, potter). Three influences were at work in Kallaline pottery – Andalusian, Ottoman and Italian, and the result was a uniquely Tunisian style. The *cuerda seca* or dry cord technique was used to imitate the geometric designs of Hispano-Moorish ceramic mosaic: fine lines of manganese and oil were used to define a pattern on the tile and isolate areas to be filled in later with coloured ceramic. *Cuerda seca* tiles are rather rare. The technique must have required considerable skill and was therefore expensive. In the 18th century homes which have survived with their decoration intact – notably Dar Lasram (see page 97), the preference is to cover large surfaces with small (12cm x 12cm) tiles in two or three colours.

Exuberant floral motifs, stylized cypresses, minarets and domes, and occasionally animals too, feature in large panels executed in harmonious shades of green, blue and yellow on a white ground. Tile manufacture at Iznik in Turkey was at its apogee in the 16th century and the stylized yet fluid lines of the tulips and carnations of the Perso-Turkish decorative vocabulary came to feature in Kallaline tiles. Some of the best examples can be seen at the 17th century palace Dar Othman (see page 98). The craftsmen of Kallaline were, however, never able to imitate the celebrated Iznik red.

In the 18th century, Kallaline products were in high demand. The increasing prosperity of Tunisia under two strong Husseinid rulers, Ali II (1759-82) and Hammouda Pasha saw the development of a pronounced taste for richly decorated interiors which was to the great benefit of the ceramic tile industry. Great

Kallaline, 18th century tile work
- part of long floral border

Modern tile work - Nabeul

expanses of interior walls were covered with tiles in luminous shades of green and blue, egg yolk yellow contrasted with black and white, the whole set between the grey white of marble flooring and bands of elaborately carved white stucco.

In the early 19th century, Tunisois or *beldi* taste moved on towards the more naturalistic leaves and flowers of Italianate tiles. Large quantities of *zellij* were imported from Italy, and to satisfy market demand, Hammouda Pasha (1782-1814) created new workshops at Gammarth on the coast N of Tunis, employing foreign artisans.

To deal with the Italian competition, the artisans of Kallaline made use of Italianate motifs, adapting them to local taste. Times were changing, however, and large Italian and Spanish 18cm x 18cm tiles came to be used before giving way to modern industrial tiles with a fine biscuit, more suitable for the modern apartment. As the way of life changed, the demand for traditional pots declined as well. Kallaline was unable to compete, and by the 1960s, the workshops and kilns had completely disappeared.

Tile making continues to prosper in Testour (see page 278), and the Tunisian ceramic industry is still very much alive in the holiday town of Nabeul. As tourism developed, some smart entrepreneur realized that large quantities of blue and white plates and dishes were what the visitor wanted to buy in a Mediterranean resort. Observing the quantities of pots sold to tourists, Jean Genet expressed the fear that in a few decades time there would be nothing left of Tunisia. Today, the traditional subtle greens, yellows and aubergine have practically disappeared – except for a few of the larger *khabia* type jars. The higher quality traditional pots, often with metal decoration, are imported from Morocco. However, there is some rather pleasant contemporary Nabeul stoneware, and German expertise has established La Rose des Sables, a company manufacturing fine porcelain for the upmarket dinner table.

Where to see (and buy) tiles and pots

After a visit to the potters of Kallaine, Georges Duhamel wrote "I looked for potters, I found poets". The traditional ateliers and kilns of the medina of Tunis have long since vanished, and there is not much poetry about a visit to Nabeul, although this is definitely the place with the most ceramic showrooms – something for all tastes. In Tunis, **El Hanout** (in the medina, 50m up on the left on the rue de la Zitouna) has the best selection of contemporary Tunisian pottery, ranging from the neo-Habitat to the natural browns and reds of Sejnane pottery from the N. Further up the same street, **El Hanout Arabe** has a more interesting range of rural pottery. Owner Kate Daoud is a mine of information on the subject. For fans of old ceramic panels, the **Café Mnouchi** (at the intersection of souq es-Sekkajine and souq el-Kebabjiya) has a fine collection, many with figurative designs. Older collectors' pieces may sometimes be found at the antique dealers on the rue des Glacières (street to the right of the British Embassy) and in any of the antique shops in the La Marsa/Le Kram zone. Look out for work by the Chemla brothers. Perhaps the most reliable antique junk emporium is **Le Serail**, just opposite the bus station in Marsa Ville. On occasion they also have some interesting contemporary pieces.

Some of the finest tiled interiors are in the medina of Tunis, notably at **Dar Lasram** (rue du Tribunal), **Dar Husseïn** (place de Château) and **Dar Ben Abdallah**, which houses museum displays of traditional life in the medina. Fine tile detailing can also be seen on many buildings in parts of the city dating from Protectorate (1881-1956).

Glazed Pottery Tiles

Fig 2a Glazed pottery tiles from Sidi Nasser el Buirouachi *zaouia* in Testour. The top band is a distinctive crenolated geometrical freize and beneath is a floral band. The black band between two white stripes is extremely bold, separating the two designs.

Fig 2b These tiles, also from the Sidi Nasser el Buirouachi *zaouia*, display a composition which is symmetical about a central axis. The plant figures involve both foliage and flowers. The strongly marked serrated edge of the leaves stands out against a blue background.

Fig 2a

Fig 2b

Central Tunisia

CENTRAL TUNISIA contains a diversity of interesting sights. It includes the Sahel, the major feature, a zone of thousands upon thousands of regularly spaced olive trees, Tunisia's most important product; the busy coastal resort area accessed from Monastir airport; the holy city of Kairouan; Sbeitla and El Djem, the best preserved and most important Roman remains in the county; the busy city of Sfax and the peaceful Islands of Kerkennah. These are separated by long distances and the route we have devised takes in all these places and returns you, eventually, to the coast at Sousse.

The Sahel, or shoreland, is the low-lying E coastal plain of Tunisia extending from the Gulf of Hammamet to the Gulf of Gabès, and inland some 50 km, reaching a maximum altitude of around 275m. The region has a long history, going back to the Carthaginians and the Romans, with the amphitheatre in **El Djem** (Thysdrus) being one of the most important remains in North Africa. The cultivation of olive trees, introduced by the Romans, continues today with **olive oil** making an important contribution to the region's prosperity (see below). The Sahel region was greatly influenced, both culturally and architecturally, by the Arab invasions and the founding of **Kairouan** which became the fourth holy city of Islam. The medinas in most of the coastal towns have been preserved as well as monuments dating back to the 7th and 8th centuries. The Sahel, because of its good beaches and pleasant climate which is tempered in summer by cool sea breezes, has become an important tourist area centred on Sousse and Monastir. Nevertheless, there are many areas where few tourists visit, such as the charming town of Mahdia and the quiet Kerkennah Islands.

The olive – a symbol of peace and harmony

In the 2nd and 3rd centuries AD, while under Roman rule, the cultivation of the olive tree (*oleo europeae sylvestris*) spread through North Africa – from Morocco to Libya. Oil 'factories' and stone olive presses are common finds on the Roman sites (see Sbeitla museum, page 251). Today crossing this region by air the chequer-board pattern of olive cultivation is very distinctive. On the ground the endless hectares of olives are even more impressive.

The most important olive producers are in the Mediterranean Basin, Spain,

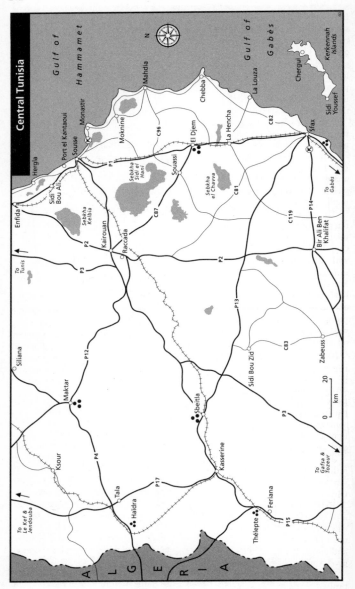

Central Tunisia

Gulf of Hammamet

Gulf of Gabès

Kerkennah Islands

N

Hergla
Enfida
Sidi Bou Ali
Port el Kantaoui
Sousse
Monastir
Moknine
Mahdia
Chebba
La Louza
Chergui
Sidi Youssef
Sfax

To Tunis

P1
P2
P3

Sebkha Kelbia
Kairouan
Raccada

Sebkha Sidi el Hani

C96
C87

El Djem
Souassi
La Hencha

Sebkha el Chavva

C81
C82

C119

Bir Ali Ben Khalifat

To Gabès

P14

Siliana
Maktar
Ksour

P12
P4

Sbeitla
Sidi Bou Zid

P13

Zabeuss
C83

P2

P3

20
0
km

Tala
Haïdra
Kasserine
Feriana
Thélepte

P17
P15

To Gafsa & Tozeur

To Le Kef & Jendouba

A L G E R I A

Italy, Greece and **Tunisia**. The olive is a sub-tropical, broad-leaved, evergreen tree, both fire and drought resistant. It grows 3-12m high and many trees are said to be between 50-100 years old. The leathery, lance shaped leaves, growing in pairs are dark green above and silvery underneath. From the tiny white flowers the green olives develop.

The olive branch, synonymous with peace, was Noah's first indication of the receding flood.

In modern olive cultivation on the plains the trees are planted 10m x 10m apart, leaving room for machinery and yields reach 50 kg per tree. Traditional methods produce 15-20 kg per tree.

The method of harvesting and production has not essentially changed. Removal of the fruits must be done with care. Tunisians are forbidden to hit trees with sticks to remove the olives. Reminders are given on television at the harvest season. It damages the tree and bruises the olives which lets in the air and allows oxidisation which reduces the quality. The harvested berries are washed in tepid water then crushed. The oil is separated from the water by centrifuge, filtered, kept at a regulated temperature in airtight steel vats, then bottled. The older method incorporates rotating stone grinders, the resulting paste being fashioned into rings on esparto grass mats which are then squeezed by an animal turning the screw tighter and tighter. The resulting oils, dark and thick, are then purified.

The oil varies in quality and colour, rather like wine. Some oil is a clear yellow, some is thick and golden like honey. Olive oil is classified as:

Extra virgin oil – oil with no flaws – is produced from olives which are picked ripe and processed immediately. Acidity must not be above 1%. It adds flavour and aromatic fragrance to dishes. Like good wine it is rich and delicious.

Virgin olive oil – from olives not bruised, damaged or subjected to adverse temperatures or too much air. Can only be blended with other virgin oils. Acidity maximum 1.5%.

Pure olive oil – lacks the quality of the above, being more acidic and cheaper. Read the labels on the bottle with care.

Olive oil is good for you. It is one of the easiest oils to digest. It is healthy, containing no cholesterol. It is safe for frying, heating up to 210°C without igniting. It is also very handy for anointing passing royalty.

SOUSSE

ACCESS Buses come here from all the major cities to one of the two bus stations, either on Bab el Djedid or by Place Farhat Hached, the main square. The train station is very convenient, right in the middle of the town on Blvd Hassouna Ayachi. Taxis and louages arrive by Bab el Djedid on Ave Mohammed Ali. The nearest airport is Skanes/Monastir.

(*Pop* 300,000; *Alt* 6m) Sousse is the third largest city in Tunisia after Tunis and Sfax. It is highly industrialized, being well known for its production of denim jeans, but the town centre is still very pleasant. It is a city of many facets making it an interesting place to visit. Situ-

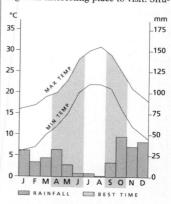

Climate: Sousse

The Ribat

ated by the sea on the Gulf of Hammamet, with the harbour right by the main square, it has long beaches and an elegant promenade. The walled medina, looking down towards the sea, contains narrow, winding streets.

History

Founded in the 9th century BC by the Phoenicians, Sousse is one of the oldest ports in the Mediterranean. In the 4th century BC, Carthage became the leading city, and Sousse entered into its sphere of influence. During the second Punic-Roman war, Hannibal used Sousse as his base, but was beaten in 202 BC. During the third Punic-Roman war, Sousse changed its allegiance to the Romans thereby avoiding destruction and gaining the status of free town. Unfortunately, with the victory of Caesar over the armies of Pompeii in **Thapsus** (46 BC), Sousse was again in the position of having chosen the wrong side and Caesar imposed heavy taxation on the town. Nevertheless under the rule of **Trajan** (98-117 AD) the city became an important commercial centre.

Sousse managed to survive the many invasions that followed until the Arab invasion in the 7th century when it was destroyed. In the 9th century, with the coming of the **Aghlabite Dynasty** to Kairouan, it again prospered, as that inland city's port, but it was conquered again in the 12th century by the Normans and in the 16th century by Spain. During WW2 it was again seriously damaged.

Places of interest

The old **Medina** is still surrounded by the original walls, built in 859 and restored in 1205. The way to enter the medina is either via Bab el Djedid, or through the Place des Martyrs beside the central square which leads to the Great Mosque. The breach in the walls was the result of bombardments during 1943.

The **Great Mosque** is by a large esplanade leading towards the ribat. Built in the 9th century by the Aghlabite Emir Abou Abbas Mohammed, it was prob-

The Ribat

ably a conversion of a kasbah built a few years earlier. Further renovations and restorations have taken place. On two corners, large, round towers dominate the marble floored courtyard and make it look like the fortress it may originally have been. Overall the monument is very simple, the courtyard being decorated solely by inscriptions around its sides. Only the courtyard can be visited. Open 0800-1300, closed Fri. Entrance tickets TD1 can be bought opposite the mosque and at the local ONTT.

The **Ribat** is a type of fortified monastery. It formed part of a chain of forts built by the Aghlabites along the coast which functioned as religious centres and a means of protection for the Muslim population against potential invaders. They communicated by smoke signals or flames, since they were all in sight of one another. The ribat at Sousse was built in 820, using some materials from older sites, as can be seen at the entrance where antique columns are placed on either side of the door. It is

38m square with towers at all four corners, the main one being the lookout tower. The interior is very plain. On the 1st floor a large prayer room takes up all the S side. Go to the top of the watch tower, up the narrow stairway, where the view over the city and the sea is fantastic. Open 0800-1900 in summer, 0930-1200 and 1400-1800 in winter, closed Mon. Entrance TD1, photo fee TD1.

The Zaouia Zakkak is a beautiful building dominated by a small Turkish octagonal minaret. You cannot visit the inside,

Not on the menu today - stuffed gazelle from a mosaic in Sousse Museum

but from the outside it is splendid.

The **museum** is set in the **kasbah**, at the SW end of the medina. The kasbah was built in the 11th century and extended in the 16th, around an old signal tower (the Khalef) dating back to 859. The museum's main exhibits are collections from the Trophet of Hadrumete, steles, sacrificial urns and Punic jars. It also contains many mosaics which are well presented and well preserved. Though less numerous and interesting than the Bardo's collection in Tunis, Sousse has its share of masterpieces. The majority of the mosaics are from the 3rd and 4th centuries, the central theme being the sea. Particularly worth seeing is the 3rd century *'Bacchus' Triumph'* in room 8. This mosaic, found in Sousse, illustrates the victory of a young god over the forces of evil. Another mosaic nearby portrays Zeus and Ganymède. See also the *'Lion and the Dog catching a Hare'* in room 14 dating from the end of the 2nd century. Entrance is via Blvd Maréchal Tito. Open 0800-1200 and 1600-1900 in summer, 0930-1200 and 1400-1800 in winter. Closed Mon, entrance fee TD2, photo fee TD1, T 233695.

The **Souqs** are mainly situated around the N end of the rue d'Angleterre. The souq or bazaar economy of North Africa has distinctive characteristics. In Tunis a series of large souqs continues successfully to exist while bazaar economies elsewhere are faltering. In Tunis as a whole, Islamic ideas and traditional trading habits have remained strong in Egyptian cities.

The bazaar originally functioned as an integral part of the economic and political systems within the Middle Eastern and North African regions. Traditional activities in financing trade and social organizations were reinforced by the bazaar's successful role in running international commodity trade. The bazaar merchants' long-term raising of credits for funding property, agricultural and manufacturing activities was strengthened by this same trend.

There is a view among orientalists that there is an Islamic city of specific social structure and physical shape, of which Tunis and Kairouan are frequently quoted examples. The crafts, trades and goods are located by their

Mosaic of two fishermen at the Sousse Museum

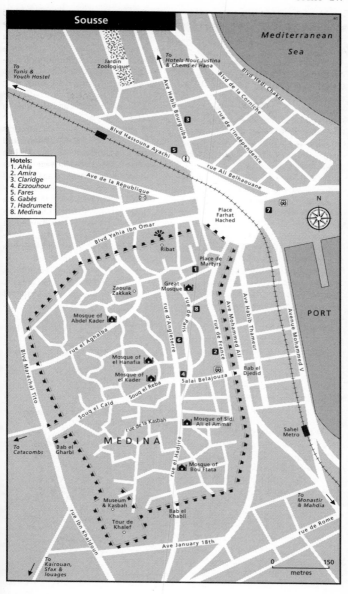

Sousse

Hotels:
1. *Ahla*
2. *Amira*
3. *Claridge*
4. *Ezzouhour*
5. *Fares*
6. *Gabès*
7. *Hadrumete*
8. *Medina*

Mediterranean Sea

To Tunis & Youth Hostel

Jardin Zoologique

Blvd Hassouna Ayachi

Ave de la République

Ave Habib Bourguiba

To Hotels Nour Justina & Chems el Hana

Blvd de la Corniche

Blvd Hedi Chaker

rue de l'Independence

rue Ali Belhaouane

Blvd Yahia Ibn Omar

Ribat

Zaouia Zakkak

Mosque of Abdel Kader

rue el Aghalba

Blvd Marechal Tito

To Catacombs

Place Farhat Hached

Place de Martyrs

Great Mosque

rue d'Angleterre

rue de Paris

Mosque of el Hanafia

Mosque of el Kader

Souq el Reba

Souq el Caid

rue de la Kasbah

MEDINA

Bab el Gharbi

rue Ibn Khaldoun

To Kairouan, Sfax & louages

Museum & Kasbah

Tour de Khalef

Bab el Khabli

rue el Hadjira

Mosque of Bou Ftata

Mosque of Sidi Ali el Ammar

Salai Belajouza

Ave de France

rue de France

Ave Mohammed Ali

Ave Habib Thameur

Bab el Djedid

Avenue Mohammed V

PORT

Sahel Metro

To Monastir & Mahdia

rue de Rome

Ave January 18th

N

0   150
metres

'clean' or 'unclean' status in an Islamic sense, and whether these goods can be sold close to the mosque or medersa. Valuable objects are on sale near to the main thoroughfares with lesser trades needing more and less costly land pushed to the edge of the bazaar. There is a concentration of similar crafts in specific locations within the bazaar so that all shoe-sellers for example are in the same street. These ground rules do not apply in all Tunisian bazaars but in many cases they are relevant in different combinations.

The allocation of land within the bazaar as outlined by the orientalists fits the operation of economic principles of land rents. Thus, there is a hierarchy of crafts, modified at times by social custom and Islamic practice, which gives highest priority to book making, gold and silver jewellery over carpet selling and thence through a graded scale of commodities through metal work, ceramics, sale of agricultural goods and ultimately low grade crafts such as tanning and dyeing.

On the W is Souq el Reba, where material and perfume are sold. Again on the right is the Kalaout el Koubba, a building whose original function is unknown but which was probably built in the 19th century. Continue up the Souq el Reba and go out by Bab el Gharbi and turn left along the walls to come to the kasbah and the museum. After visiting the museum re-enter the medina by following the walls to the Bab el Khabli. Following the rue el Hadjira will bring you back to the rue d'Angleterre. Shopping in the tourist shops on rue d'Angleterre can be expensive. Either drive a hard bargain or buy your souvenirs elsewhere. **Markets** are held each Sun, slightly out of town on the Sfax road.

The **Catacombs** are to the W of Sousse, consisting of more than 250 galleries containing up to 15,000 tombs over a distance of 5 km. They were built and used between the 2nd and 4th centuries and are rather a disappointment. Currently closed for repairs which may take some years. Ever hopeful, the Tourist Agency gives entrance TD1, and opening hours 0800-1200 and 1500-1900 in summer and 0900-1200 and 1400-1800 in winter so perhaps the repairs are nearly complete.

The **Jardin Zoologique**, to the W of Ave Habib Bourguiba, has several shaded walkways between the aviaries with birds which range from budgerigars to ostriches. It provides a shaded resting area for entrance TD0.25 and there is a café and a toilet by the gate.

The **beach** of fine sand which is cleaned every morning starts in front of the Corniche, but it is much nicer, and less crowded further N. Surfboards can be rented all along the beach. The seafront promenade Blvd Hedi Chaker has recently been resurfaced with modern block paving and diagonal patterns. It makes a pleasant walk of about 1 km.

Local information

Price guide

Hotels:			
AL	over US$75	D	US$20-40
A	US$75	E	US$10-20
B	US$60-75	F	under US$10
C	US$40-60		

Places to eat:			
♦♦♦	expensive	♦♦	average
♦	cheap		

● **Accommodation**

There are more than 80 hotels in Sousse, with over 31,500 beds, 20% capacity of all Tunisia. Aim is 50,000 beds in 2001. Most are fully booked in summer.

AL *Orient Palace*, 558 beds, T 24288, F 243345; **A** *Abou Nawas Boujaafar*, 474 beds, T 226030, F 226595; **A** *Hotel Chems el Hana*, T 226900, F 226076, elegant, 243 rm with bath, a/c, phone, TV, terrace, 2 restaurants, 2 pools, fitness centre, tennis, golf, Turkish baths, floodlit watersports, situated in palmery by the sea and quite nr the medina, conference rm for 150, wheelchair access.

B *Nour Justina*, on Corniche, T 226382, 422 beds, seafront, food and service is reputedly

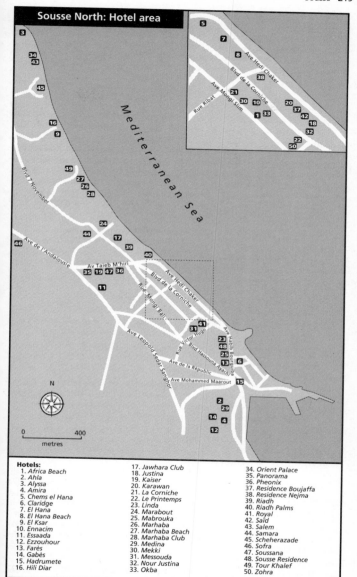

Sousse North: Hotel area

Mediterranean Sea

Ave Hedi Chaker
Blvd de la Corniche
Ave Mongi Slim
Rue Ribat

Blvd 7 November
Ave de l'Andalousie
Av Taieb M'hiri
Blvd de la Corniche
Ave Hedi Chaker
Rue Mongi Bali
Rue Victor Hugo
Blvd Hassouna Yachi
Ave Habib Bourguiba
Ave Leopold Sedar Senghor
Ave de la Républic
Ave Mohammed Maarout

N

0   400
metres

Hotels:

1. Africa Beach
2. Ahla
3. Alyssa
4. Amira
5. Chems el Hana
6. Claridge
7. El Hana
8. El Hana Beach
9. El Ksar
10. Ennacim
11. Essaada
12. Ezzouhour
13. Farès
14. Gabès
15. Hadrumete
16. Hili Diar
17. Jawhara Club
18. Justina
19. Kaiser
20. Karawan
21. La Corniche
22. Le Printemps
23. Linda
24. Marabout
25. Mabrouka
26. Marhaba
27. Marhaba Beach
28. Marhaba Club
29. Medina
30. Mekki
31. Messouda
32. Nour Justina
33. Okba
34. Orient Palace
35. Panorama
36. Pheonix
37. Residence Boujaffa
38. Residence Nejma
39. Riadh
40. Riadh Palms
41. Royal
42. Said
43. Salem
44. Samara
45. Scheherazade
46. Sofra
47. Soussana
48. Sousse Residence
49. Tour Khalef
50. Zohra

not quite up to scratch.

C *Hotel Farès*, Blvd Hassouna Ayachi, just off Place Farhat Hached, T 227800, 180 beds, central, private beach 200m away, a/c, high rm with view; **C** *Le Claridge*, Ave Habib Bourguiba, T 224759, 60 beds, centre of new town, very noisy, very clean; **C** *Le Printemps*, Blvd de la Corniche, T 229335, F 224055, 69 rm for 2/4 persons, with hob, fridge and utensils, bar, tea room, hairdresser, commercial centre, restaurant, 5 mins walk from town centre.

D *Hotel Ahla*, Place de la Grande Mosquée, T 220570, 100 rm, clean, pleasant, very quiet; **D** *Hotel Hadrumete*, Place Assed Ibn el Fourat, T 226292, by port, 35 rm with bath, clean, good restaurant, pool, enclosed terrace café, 2 mins to sea – better value for money than *Azur*; **D** *Sousse Azur*, 5 rue Amilcar, off Ave Habib Bourguiba, T 226960, F 228145, 20 rm, restaurant, coffee lounge, 10 mins from town centre.

E *Hotel de Paris*, 15 rue des Rempart, by the walls close to Place Farhat Hached, T 220564, very clean, some rm on the roof, close to the medina and the new town; **E** *Hotel Medina*, behind the Great Mosque on rue de Paris, T 221722, very clean, some rooms with bath, roof terrace, restaurant/bar, no phone bookings, so arrive early in summer; **E** *The Hotel Amira*, 52 rue de France, nr Bab Djedid in the medina, T 226325, clean, half rm have bath, some with view, panoramic roof terrace.

F *Hotel de Gabès*, 12 rue de Paris, T 226977, best of the cheap hotels, very clean, some rm on roof, good views from terrace, only 14 rm so book in summer; **F** *Hotel Ezzouhour*, 48 rue de Paris, T 228729, in the medina, very simple, some rms with bath, otherwise communal shower, very cheap, pleasant manager; **F** *Hotel Perles*, 71 rue de Paris, T 224609, in the medina, very small, could be cleaner, communal shower, cheapest hotel in Sousse.

Youth hostel: T 227548, 3 km out along Tunis road, at Plage Boujaafar, 2 km from station, kitchen, meals available, 90 beds.

● **Places to eat**
Good choice available on route de la Corniche and Ave Habib Bourguiba. Most restaurants cater for tourists, menus in many languages. Some cafés in the medina advertise only in Arabic.

◆◆◆*Le Bonheur*, T 225742, Place Farhat Hached, good grilled meat and fish, large terrace on the street; *Restaurant Cherif*, by the harbour, specializes in fish and seafood; *Restaurant des Remparts*, T 226326, rue de l'Eglise, by medina walls close to Place Farhat Hached, more expensive because it serves alcohol; *Restaurant Mahlouf*, T 226508, Place Farhat Hached, excellent food, particularly the fish, large terrace.

◆◆*L'Escargot*, Blvd de la Corniche, T 224779, space for 65, French cooking; *La Fiesta*, Blvd Mongi Slim, better than average; *Restaurant le Golfe*, Ave Habib Bourguiba in Boujaafar complex, clean, good choice.

◆*Restaurant Ben Henda*, rue de Paris, in the medina, simple but tasty food; *Restaurant Hassoumi*, rue de Rabat, just off the Corniche, very cheap, good Tunisian food, clean; *Restaurant Populaire*, rue de France, typical medina restaurant; *Restaurant Tunisien*, rue Ali Belhaouane, nice setting, some dishes a bit more expensive, very good fish.

● **Banks & money changers**
BDS and STB on Ave Habib Bourguiba; UIB, Ave Habib Thameur; BT, rue Ali Belhaouane; BNT, rue de l'Indépendence. Money can also be changed in any of the large hotels. STB has an automatic cash dispenser (dinars).

● **Entertainment**
Casino: El Hana Palace Hotel, T 243000.

Concerts: *Sousse International Festival* in Jul/Aug, open Air Theatre.

Nightclubs: *Balaoum*, Kalaa Kebira, T 227599; *El Borj*, Sidi Bou Ala, T 268523; *Le Douar*, Sidi Bou Ali, T 247155.

● **Hospitals & medical services**
Chemist: open nights, 38 Ave de la République, T 224795; 45 route de la Corniche; Ave H Thameur. Chemists display names of those open late.

Hospital: *University Hospital*, Ave Farhat Hached, rue Ibn el Jazzar, T 221411; *University Hospital Centre (CHU)*, Sahloul, Hammam-Sousse, T 241411; *Les Olivers Clinic*, Blvd 7 Novembre, T 242711; *Dialysis Centre*, Blvd 7 Novembre, Route Touristique, T 242711.

Thalassotherapie: *Abou Nawas Boujaafar* offers a range of treatments for total well-being incl indoor heated sea-water pool, two saunas, Turkish baths, gym, solarium and relaxation room.

● **Places of worship**
Catholic: *Eglise St Felix*, 1 rue de Constantine, T 224596/220554, service in French, Sat 1815

and Sun 0930.

Evangelical Church: 16 rue de Malte, T 224073.

Synagogue: in rue Amilcar.

● **Post & telecommunications**

Area code: 03.

Post Office: Ave de la République, just off Place Farhat Hached, T 224750.

● **Shopping**

Fixed price articles, good selection at Socopa in *Hotel Abou Nawas Boujaafar* and the larger Soula Centre off Place Farhat Hached. *Monoprix*, Place Farhat Hached; *Magasin Général*, rue Khaled Ibn Walid; Blvd de la Corniche, Complex Nejma; Port el Kantaoui.

Market day: Sun, Rank de Sfax. Animal market on Sat, Sahloul, Hammam Sousse.

● **Sports**

Harbour: the harbour has berths for 10 yachts, min-max draft 3-9m.

● **Tour companies & travel agents**

Atlas Voyages, Blvd du 7 Novembre, T 240270, F 240116; *Carthage Tour*, Ave Habib Bourguiba, T 227954, F 225301; *Chams Tours*, 8 rue Ali Belhaoune, T 225357, F 227328; *King's Travel*, 10 rue du Caire, T 228750, F 228307; *Meditours Tunisie*, 95 Blvd Abdelhamid el Cadhi, T 227466/7, F 223265; *Tourafrica*, rue Khaled Ibn Walid, T 224277; *Tunis Air*, Ave Habib Bourguiba, T 227955; *Tunisian Travel Service*, route des Oranges, T 241599, F 243499; *Tunisie Voyages*, Blvd du 7 Novembre, T 242134, F 242664.

● **Tourist offices**

The tourist information offices are at Regional ONTT, 1 Ave Habib Bourguiba, by Place Farhat Hached, T 225157, open 0730-1930 most days. The local office is opp, T 220431.

● **Useful addresses**

Customs Authority: Place de l'Indépendance, T 227700.

National Guard: Ave Leopold Sedar Sanghor, T 225588.

National Security: rue de l'Indépendance, T 225566.

Parcel Post: rue Ali Bey, T 225492.

Police: rue Pasteur, T 225566.

Society for the Protection of Animals: rue Taieb Driss, route de Monastir, T 233347.

Toilets: Train station, Tourist Office, medina in rue el Achalba.

● **Transport**

Local Car hire: Avis, route de la Corniche, T 225901; **Ben Jemma Rent a Car**, rue 2 Mars, La Corniche, T 224002; **Budget**, 63 Ave Habib Bourguiba, T 224041; **Europcar**, route de la Corniche, T 226252; **Hertz**, Ave Habib Bourguiba, T 225428; **Inter Rent**, route de la Corniche, T 227562; **Touaregs**, 13 route Khezama, T 243975; **Tunisia National Rent-a-car**, route de la Corniche, T 226333; **Young-car**, route de la Corniche, T 226416.

Air Tunis Air, Ave Habib Bourguiba, T 227955, for details of flights from Skanes/Monastir airport, T 260300.

Train 'Sahel Metro' is one line which goes all the way to **Mahdia** along the coast stopping at all the resorts, small towns and Monastir international airport (TD0.6 single). Hourly from 0600-2000. The trip **Sousse-Mahdia** takes just under 1½ hrs (TD3.75 return). The station is at the S end of Ave Mohammed V, 100m down from the Bab Djedid towards the harbour, T 225321.

   For Tunis: The station is on Blvd Hassouna Ayachi, up the road from Place Farhat Hached. Information on T 221955. Departures to **Tunis** 0348, 0530, 0650, 0757, 1310, 1418, 1527, 1830, 2012; **Gabès** 0918, 2324; **El Djem/Sfax**, 0918, 1509, 1618, 1935, 2324; **Gafsa/Metlaoui** 2324. For **Hammamet** and **Nabeul** get off at **Sidi Bou Rekba** and continue journey by bus or louage. Trains leave Sousse for Sidi Bou Rekba at 0348, 0530, 0650, 0757, 1310, 1418, 1527, 1830, 2012. 'Noddy' road trains between Sousse and Port el Kantaoui leaves Place Boujaafar in Sousse on the hour 0900-1800 in winter 0900-2300 in summer, returning at half past the hour. There is a blue train and a yellow train, tickets cannot be transferred. Adults TD3 return, children under 8 years TD2. Noddy Train, T 240353.

Road Bus: there are 2 bus stations. The first is on Place Sidi Yahya by the Bab Djedid, the second by Place Farhat Hached, on the Place du Port. Information on T 224202. Departures from Bab el Djedid to **Kairouan** (1½ hrs, TD2.39); **Hammamet** (2 hrs, TD2.99); **Nabeul** (2¾ hrs, TD3.45); **Gabès** (5 hrs, TD9.27) and **Sfax** (2½ hrs, TD4.96); **Djerba** (via Zarzis), **Kebili** (7¼ hrs, TD12.96); **Douz** (7¼ hrs, TD13.9); **Medenine**; **Matmata** (7 hrs, TD10.74); **Tataouine** (9 hrs, TD13.11; **Port el Kantaoui** (30 mins, TD0.45). Departures from Place du Port to **Tunis** and Bizerte. **Louages**: the louage station has moved from Bab el

Djedid, on rue Mohammed Ali to Souq el Ahad, nr camel market on route de Sfax. Take a taxi as it's a 30-min walk. **Taxi**: yellow taxis have meters.

Sea Compagnie Tunisienne de Navigation (CTN), rue Abdallah Ibn Zoubeir, T 224861, F 224844.

EXCURSIONS NORTH FROM SOUSSE

PORT EL KANTAOUI

10 km N of Sousse, Port el Kantaoui was developed as a tourist town. It has been created with a certain amount of good taste with many restaurants and cafés and lots of 4-star hotels. In addition, it boasts a 340 berth marina, yacht basin and golf courses. The overall impression is, fortunately, not too overpowering. Offering every imaginable facility, Port el Kantaoui is geared, unashamedly, towards mass charter tourism.

• **Accommodation AL** *Diar el Andalous* T 246200, F 246348, luxurious, 300 rm, beach, a/c, indoor and outdoor pools, tennis, disco, free watersports; **AL** *Marhaba Palace* T 243633/240200, just like a palace, 250 splendid rm, indoor and outdoor pools, tennis, garden; **C** *Hotel Salem*, Ave Habib Bourguiba, 261 rm, no a/c, pool, disco, no credit cards. **NB** Don't look for cheap hotels in this area.

• **Places to eat** Are all expensive. All hotel restaurants provide good (pricey) meals as do ◆◆◆*Le Beach Club*, T 241799, *La Durade*, T 244893 is very good, but very pricey; *Le Yacht Club*, T 241799 and *Le Club House*, T 241756. ◆*Neptune VI*, floating restaurant, T 241799, giant prawns special; also *Les Emirs*, T 240865; *L'Escale*, T 241791 and *Le Méditerranée*, T 240788. For cheap meals go into Sousse.

• **Sports Diving**: Port el Kantoui International Diving Centre, Port de Plaisance, T 241799, is recognized by the watersport federation and is open all the year. Prices at Diving centre: First dive TD20; Exploration TD22; Night dive TD25; 6 dives DT110; Open water training TD250. **Fitness club**: Beach club nr swimming pool at N end of harbour, T 241799, TD4/session, offers many sporting and health activities. **Golf**: International 'Open' each Apr. El Kantaoui T 231755/6, has a 27 hole tournament golf course, par 108, 9,576m where green fees are TD30-TD40/round and lessons are available. Palm Links Golf Course and Monastir Golf Course, shaded by olive trees, are both 18 hole, par 72, 6,140m. **Sailing and fishing**: Yachts and catamarans can be hired from the yacht basin or you can take a trip in an ancient sailing boat. Aquascope trips are available to view underwater life. The harbour has berths for 340 yachts, min-max draft 2-4m. See piece on Yachting, page 356, for further details. Organized at quayside are: Sailing trip, daily weather permitting at 1000 and 1430, 3 hrs, TD20 – with an hour for swimming and fishing. Catamaran trip, daily 1000, 1200, 1400 and 1600, 2 hrs, TD15. Fishing day trip 1000-1800, TD80, winter half day for TD40, eat what you catch or take it home. Aquascope, 3 vessels operating daily 0700-1800, an hour for TD12-15, goes down to 25m – but as sea bed is featureless and the water murky not worth it. **Scuba diving**: with tuition and equipment.

• **Tourist offices** The tourist information office is on the left as you enter through archway into the marina, manager Mohammed Lakhdar very helpful, T 241799.

Beyond Port el Kantaoui is **Sidi Bou Ali**

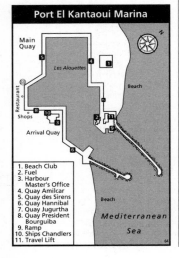

Port El Kantaoui Marina

Main Quay

Les Alouettes

Beach

Restaurant

Shops

Arrival Quay

Beach

Mediterranean Sea

1. Beach Club
2. Fuel
3. Harbour Master's Office
4. Quay Amilcar
5. Quay Des Sirens
6. Quay Hannibal
7. Quay Jugurtha
8. Quay President Bourguiba
9. Ramp
10. Ships Chandlers
11. Travel Lift

where the folklore centre should be visited. Beyond again is **Hergla**, formerly Horraca Coeila, a cliff village dominated by the mausoleum in honour of Sidi Bou Mendil. Sidi Bou Mendil (more commonly known as the saint with the handkerchief) was said to be able to transform any piece of cloth into a magic flying carpet which took him to the Holy Land of Arabia. In Hergla esparto grass is still woven into *scourtins*, round mats used in the olive oil presses to filter the oil.

● Useful addresses **Area code**: 03. **Harbour Master's Office**: T 240500, F 240506.

ENFIDA (ENFIDAVILLE)

43 km N of Sousse, Enfida is an agricultural and administrative centre not caught up in the tourist circuit. It is situated where the P2 to Kairouan leaves the main P1 route from Tunis to Sousse. The train station is 10 mins walk E of town centre. Buses run from Sousse hourly on the half hour. Everything on the main road – bus station, police, museum, market. No hotels, no restaurants, no taxis. Tourist information by talking to museum curator.

Places of interest The **Museum** in the old French church on the main street contains a mixture of old tombstones and mosaics. It is interesting as it demonstrates the diversity of Tunisia's cultural and religious past. Entrance 600 mills, photography TD1, open 0930-1630, closed Mon. Each Sun a highly colourful **market**, where all the farmers and bedouins from the surrounding areas meet, is held at the S end of town on the road to Sousse and Kairouan. Many things, including material and clothes, are much cheaper here than in Tunis. Covered vegetable/fruit market open daily.

A WW2 cemetery lies to the W of town containing graves of 1,551 soldiers from Britain and the Commonwealth who died in 1943 during the Eighth Army's advance across N Africa. There is a French WW2 cemetery at Ouled Abdallah about 4 km N of Enfida.

Roman remains at Gheguernia, called Henchir Fraga, about 7 km N of town; also at Aïn M'Deker 16 km NW on C113. Spa at Aïn Garci 16 km W.

TAKROUNA

A small Berber village perched 195m high on an outcrop, Takrouna has an amazing view. It is reached by leaving Enfida on the C133 to Zaghouan and taking the signposted 2nd turning on the left after 5 km. The village is noted for its honey as well as the traditional work with plaited esparto grass in particular producing mats to spread over the bench of the bridal chamber. This settlement, like Zriba, has a *zaouia* to Sidi Abdelkader el Jilani, a smart square building with dark tiled dome and blue door. The mosque has a square white minaret and a tall white lantern tiled in green. This settlement too is almost deserted. Climb up and explore the remaining Berber grain stores.

Returning to Sousse there is the choice of the P1 which cuts through the salt march and salt lakes or the better alternative the new motorway, from which the views are quite splendid, but do keep your eye on the other drivers who are also looking at the view.

Kaala Kebira which stands between these two main routes on the northern outskirts of Sousse has lost some of its agricultural charm but the Olive Festival in Dec is well worth a visit.

SOUTH FROM SOUSSE

SKANES

Between the coast road and the sea, in some places actually adjacent to the airport, stand the hotels of Skanès. This tiny settlement is still no more than a small centre with many, many tourist hotels dealing almost exclusively with the package tourist, though not averse to finding a room for the individual traveller. It has

View of Ribat

the advantage of easy access to the airport, and to the Sahel Metro which goes to Sousse. There is a lovely long sandy beach, ideal for children and relaxation.

● **Accommodation** The cutting into the gorse-covered sandy cliffs continues as more and more hotels are created. Here is a selection: **A** *Dkhila Jockey Club*, T 461833; **A** *Kuriat Palace*, T 460855; **A** *Regency*, T 460033; **A** *Robinson Club*, T 427515; **A** *Sidi Mansour*, T 460023; **A** *Skanès El Hana*, T 462256; **A** *Skanès Palace*, T 461350; **B** *Sunrise*, T 427144; **C** *Chems*, T 433350; **C** *Les Palmiers*, T 61151.

MONASTIR

ACCESS The 'Sahel Metro' runs from the airport, 9 km away, to town. The bus, train and louage stations are on Ave de la République just 5 mins walk to the town centre.

Lying on the coast about 25 km S of Sousse on a headland at the S point of the Gulf of Hammamet, Monastir is an attractive fishing port with an elegant promenade along the bay. The journey from Sousse improves as the industrial area of Sousse is left behind. The huge factory on the outskirts makes couscous! The salt pans at Sahline Sebkha are extensive, an unusual sight for visitors from northern Europe but common in these warm Mediterranean areas. The dried salt is collected, purified and exported. At least the raw material is free.

Sponge fishing is carried on here as well as the catching of most indigenous fish and shellfish.

Monastir was originally called **Ruspina**, a corruption of the Punic name Rous Penna, and it served as Julius Caesar's operations base for his African campaign. Part of the triple ramparts from this time still survive. During the 11th century, when nearby Mahdia was the Fatmid capital and Kairouan was out of favour, Monastir was the holy city to which pilgrims came.

History

Habib Bourguiba was born here in 1903, and this has largely contributed to the development of the town. It is now part of a large tourist complex which continues N to Skanes and Sousse. Monastir's history goes back to Phoenician times, later becoming a major military base for Caesar. During the 7th century, with the construction of the ribat, it became part

View of Ribat

of the coastal defence system. Then, after the fall of Kairouan in the 11th century, Monastir became the religious capital. The Turks made it into a stronghold and it was not until 3 August 1903, when Bourguiba put in an appearance, that Monastir made it back onto the map.

Places of interest

The **Ribat** was built in 796 by Harthouma Ibn el Ayoune, as part of the coastal look-out system. One of the oldest and largest of the military structures built by the Arabs in N Africa, it was later refortified and surrounded by an additional wall during the 9th and 11th centuries, which gives the whole edifice an interesting mixture of contrasting styles and shapes but the initial plan remains – a courtyard surrounded by accommodation (primitive) for the defenders and a prayer hall now beautifully set out as the **Ali Bourguiba Islamic Museum**. It is very interesting actually to see the inside of one of these forts but do be careful as there are no safety barriers and some of the steps and walks by the walls are unprotected. It is used by film makers whenever they want to photograph an 'authentic' fort so

may be closed to the public. The 13 episodes of the serial *Jesus of Nazareth* were filmed here and many other well-known films such as *Raiders of the Lost Ark*.

The entrance is at the foot of one of the polygonal towers, where a corridor flanked by rooms originally for the guards, and now used as a ticket office, leads into the central courtyard. The view over the sea from the top of the Nador (lookout tower) is recommended, especially at sunset. The Museum is clean and neat, well laid out, with good details about the exhibits: gravestones, a Kufic stele, glass, pages of Koran (as seen

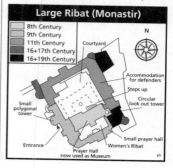

Large Ribat (Monastir)

- 8th Century
- 9th Century
- 11th Century
- 16+17th Century
- 16+19th Century

N

Courtyard

Accommodation for defenders

Steps up

Small polygonal tower

Circular look out tower

Small prayer hall

Women's Ribat

Entrance

Prayer Hall now used as Museum

65

also in Kairouan Museum), small pieces of pottery found here at the Ribat, small pipes, pots and oil lamps, leather covers, exquisite ancient fabrics, pottery, a display of coins and a unique wooden Arab astrolabe (for measuring altitude), made in Cordoba and dating back to the 10th century.

There are, in the courtyard, more engraved steles and tombstones dating back from the 11th and 12th centuries. Open 0800-1900 in summer, 0900-1200 and 1400-1800 in winter. Closed Mon, entrance TD2, photography TD1, no flash or tripods, T 461276. Allow at least an hour to potter about here and get the feel of the place.

There is a nearby, smaller, Ribat of Sidi Dhouib. Also ruins of a similar construction are to be found at the entrance to *Hotel Esplanade*. Plans are to preserve these ruins as they now stand. Another

Fishing off Monastir

The continental shelf here has a very gradual fall and in places is almost flat. Trawling is possible. At depths of around 50m the sponges for which this area is famous are found. Alongside these are found echinoderms (sea urchins). Fish caught include mullet, hake, bream, dogfish, octopus, and squid.

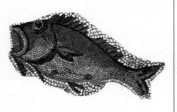

From a mosaic found at a Bizerte, now in the Bardo Museum

ruined fort stands at the end of Cap Monastir.

The style of the **Great Mosque** is simple, in contrast with that of the ribat. Built in the 9th century, it was later extended in the 11th century. Notice that some of the pillars have capitals of an earlier date.

The **Habib Bourguiba Mausoleum** at the N end of the cemetery is an imposing affair, a huge square building with a huge golden cupola flanked by two splendid matching minarets. It is approached via a vast paved concourse which cuts through the Sidi el Mazari cemetery (what happened to the graves that were beneath?) at the S end of which are two new ornate tombs. As one approaches the ornate iron gates (with decorative script on each gate) a man with a key will appear and let you get even nearer – for a tip. Don't rush in as actually the building looks better through the gates. This is where ex-President Habib Bourguiba is buried. It was built in 1963 at the same time as the **Habib Bourguiba Mosque**. The mosque is on rue de l'Indépendence in the old town and was built following the richly decorated traditional style of architecture using more green tiles than can be imagined. The mosque which cannot be visited by non-Muslims is built in traditional style, a very sophisticated building with some remarkable decoration. The entrance to the prayer hall is through 19 intricately carved teak doors made by the craftsmen of Kairouan. Once inside, the huge vaulted prayer hall is supported by 86 pink marble columns. There is a large dome before the *mihrab* which is inlaid with golden mosaics and decorated with small onyx columns.

Knowledgeable travellers will notice that this **medina** is NOT like other medinas with donkey-wide streets and obscure courtyards behind generally closed doors. This is in fact an enclosed Mediterranean style (French/Italian) suburb of the 18th century with more recent additions. Note the iron work balconies and tilework, neither usual in a normal medina. Although it has been restored and is very clean and tidy it is nevertheless an interesting area of Monastir with small retail outlets but none of the associated small scale manufacturing. There is a small tower on the corner of the medina opposite the post office which seems to have no function now.

There is a weekly Sat **market** in Souq Essabt on Place Guedir El Foul and the rue Salem B'Chir near the bus station.

A **Museum of Traditional Costume**

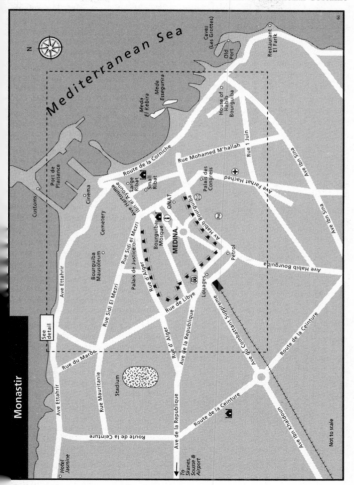

on rue de l'Indépendance near the Tourist Office. Open Mon-Sat 0900-1200 and 1400-1730, closed Sun, entrance TD1. **Museum of National Movement** in rue Trabelsia in the medina is recommended.

The **birth place of Habib Bourguiba** is in Place 3 Aug, on the route de la Corniche overlooking the old fishing port. It has a blue door and tile work round door and windows. A faded plaque to the right hand side of the door indicates its importance.

There are some interesting **caves** cut into the sandstone rock which protects the S side of the old fishing harbour as a breakwater. These were used as stores and some still have doors. The shore of the harbour here is covered with many rusty anchors.

The islands off-shore are **Meda el Kebira** and **Meda Esseguira**. There is a causeway to walk out on foot to the outer island and a track to drive out to the inner island.

In the cemetery near the Habib Bourguiba Mausoleum is the **Koubba of Sidi el Mazari** built in 1149 AD, a holy man. This can be visited, please note the request to be correctly dressed.

Day trips can be arranged to the **Kuriat islands** which lie about 15 km E. For more information, see office at end of port. These islands are used by the Cap Monastir diving centre.

Walk to the **Cape – Isle Gdamsi**. Follow the track at the end of port area which leads out to the point and to the small (inaccessible on foot) Pigeon island beyond. It is a pleasant walk (30

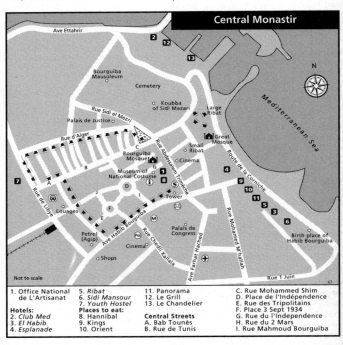

Central Monastir

1. Office National de L'Artisanat	5. *Ribat*	11. Panorama	C. Rue Mohammed Shim
	6. *Sidi Mansour*	12. Le Grill	D. Place de l'Indépendance
Hotels:	7. *Youth Hostel*	13. Le Chandelier	E. Rue des Tripolitains
2. *Club Med*	**Places to eat:**		F. Place 3 Sept 1934
3. *El Habib*	8. Hannibal	**Central Streets**	G. Rue du l'Independence
4. *Esplanade*	9. Kings	A. Bab Tounès	H. Rue du 2 Mars
	10. Orient	B. Rue de Tunis	I. Rue Mahmoud Bourguiba

mins) round the koubba and, surprisingly, three good quality tennis courts. There are good views, close down to the tiny natural harbour with the El Kahlia caves are cut into the promontory, where the fishermen pull up their boats and wash their nets and beyond over Monastir or N to Skanès. At the very end of the promontory are the remains of a fort which is being excavated and renovated. The path goes round the edge of this fort and in places there is very limited foot room over a steep drop. Do take care.

Local information
● Accommodation
The number of places to stay in Monastir is quite limited. The hotels are expensive but not of high quality. Out of season many are closed or are undergoing redecoration. You are advised to go to Skanès or Mahdia for 4-star comfort or Sousse for a wider choice.

A *Club Med*, T 431155, has some excellently located accommodation on the port.

B *El Habib*, T 4629941; **B** *Hotel Ribat*, all on route de la Corniche; **B** *Sidi Mansour*, T 462944.

C *Esplanade*, T 461146/7, F 460050, central location with access through garden to Corniche, 7 km from airport, 5 km from international golf course, 130 rm with bath, telephone, and balcony overlooking pool and within view and sound of the sea, bar, restaurant. Visitor's comment – the restaurant is very gloomy, hard to read the menu, service is off-hand and the food good in itself but poorly presented on cold plates on not too clean table cloths.

E *Hotel Jasmin*, route de la Falaise T 462511, very pleasant, 23 beds in 16 rm, cheap, welcoming, with a beach across road and a very good restaurant frequented by locals.

Youth hostel: on rue de Maroc, town centre, T 461216, 60 beds, TD4 pp, only dormitories, no double or family room.

● Places to eat
♦♦*de Tunisie*, Ave Ali Belhouane, behind *Hotel Hadrumete*, Dutch owned, Tunisian and Indian food; *El Medina*, Place de l'Independence, corner of Ave de l'Independence, opp medina wall, small, clean, pavement tables, friendly staff, menu in English, open 0900-1800; *Restaurant*

Hannibal in medina behind Office National de l'Artisanant, T 461097; *King's* restaurant on route de la Corniche, good service, adequate; also on route de la Corniche are *Orient* and *Panorama*. On the marina *Restaurant Chandelier* is worth a visit; *Le Grill*, T 460923; *Le Grill* on marina, T 460923.

♦*La Pizzeria*, T 460923, Port de Plaisance, on marina. Also on marina are *Le Central, La Marina, La Rosa*. It really depends on how much noise you can stand with your food. Good snack bar at airport.

● Banks & money changers
STB, Ave Habib Bourguiba, T 261383; **UIB**, Ave Habib Bourguiba, T 261400; **BNT**, Place de l'Indépendance, T 261057; **BNT**, Place de l'Indépendance, T 261495. Money can also be changed in large hotels.

● Entertainment
Cinemas: there is a number of cinemas in the town, incl one in the marina.

Hammam: in the medina, rue de Tunis.

● Hospitals & medical services
Chemist: *Charhine* on Ave Habib Bourguiba and *Karoui* on Ave de la République.

Hospital: *Hôpital Fattouma Bourguiba*, Ave Fattouma Bourguiba, T 461141.

● Places of worship
Catholic: *Chez les Soeurs*, Zone du Stade, T 431931, services Sat 1800 and Sun 0900.

● Post & telecommunications
Area code: 03.

Post Office: Ave Habib Bourguiba, by the Palais des Congrès (conference centre), T 260176, also at railway station and airport.

● Shopping
Office National de l'Artisanat, open 0900-1900 daily, except Sun 1100-1700, has a good selection of items to choose from, or from which to learn about prices. On outer edge of Medina facing E towards *Hotel Esplanade*. *Magasin Général*, Place de l'Independence, in town centre. *Monoprix*, rue de Tunis, opp medina wall.

● Sports
Golf: *Palm Links* golf course, T 466910/2, F 466913, 10 km out of town, on road beyond Skanes towards Sousse, 6,140m, 18 holes, par 72, green fees TD30-40.

Fishing: excursions from Monastir – weekly mini-cruises to the Kuriat islands. Trip on El

Kahlia for amateur anglers, provision of rods, lines and trolls. For details contact T 461156.

Horse riding: available, ask at any large hotel for details. Horse racing each Sun.

Watersports: incl scuba diving and sailing, at the Cap Monastir. Underwater diving school, T 461156. Monastir Yacht club has 386 berths. Marina T 462305/462509. Cap Marina Monastir – Port de Plaisance Latitude 3546'11"N, longitude 1050'50"E, T 460951/3/5, F 462066, nearest airport 8 km, adjacent marinas are Sousse 10 M, Port El Kantaoui 14 M, Mahdia 31 M, 400 moorings, max boat length 45m, depth at entrance channel 6m, harbour 4-5m, outer jetty 7m, mooring rates for a 11m boat is TD 7 per day in high season, or TD 704 per year, facilities include fresh water, electricity on pontoons, toilets, showers, fuel, oil, refuse disposal, telephone and television to boats exceeding 12m.

● **Tour companies & travel agents**
ATAC Tour in *Hotel Rivage*, T 230955; *Atlas Voyages* in *Hotel Chems*, T 233350; *B'Chire Voyages*, Ave Habib Bourguiba, T 261066; *Carthage Tours*, in *Hotel Habib* on Corniche, T 461847; *Skanes Travel Service* in *Hotel Sahara Beach*, rue de 2 Mars 1934, T 261088; *Tourafrica*, Ave Habib Bourguiba, T 461381.

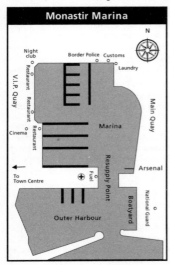

Monastir Marina

● **Tourist offices**
The tourist information office is at ONTT, Quartier Chraga, in front of the Habib Bourguiba Mosque, T 461960. Also in front of the airport, T 461205.

● **Useful addresses**
Customs: at port, T 462305.

Fire: on rue de Libye, T 197.

Garage: there are 3 garages on Ave Habib Bourguiba.

Petrol: at Agif, Mobil or Ruspina, all on Ave Habib Bourguiba.

Police: on rue Chedli Kallala, T 461432.

● **Transport**
Local Car hire: Avis, airport, T 463031; Europcar, airport, T 461314; **Hertz**, Ave Habib Bourguiba, T 461404, and at airport, T 461314; **Inter rent**, airport, T 461314; **Nova Rent**, Av Habib Bourguiba, T 467826.

Air *Tunis Air* at airport, T 460300 and in Monastir close to *Hotel Ribat*, T 462550, *Nouvelair*, airport, T 460300. Flight information Skanes/Monastir airport on T 461314. Departures to Djerba Tues, Thur, Sat 1600; *Tozeur* Tues 1710. **Scheduled international flights**: Amsterdam Tues 0850; Brussels Tues 0915, Sat 0745; Casablanca Mon 0815; Frankfurt Tues 0930; Istanbul Mon 0835; Luxembourg Tues 0850, Sat 0921; Lyon Fri 1510; Marseilles Thur 1025; Paris Sat, Sun 1530; Rome Mon 1600; Vienna Sat 1520. There are numerous charter flights too.

Train Opposite the bus station. Information on T 460755. **Tunis** (via Sousse) 0610, 1238, 1758 (TD5). 'Sahel Metro' goes to the airport and to **Sousse** and **Mahdia** along the coast every hour from 0600-2000.

Road Bus: the bus station is at the S end of Ave de la République. Information on T 461059. Departures to **Tunis** 0445; **Sfax** 0500, 0600, 1100. There are also frequent buses to **Sousse** (TD6). **Louages:** leave from in front of the bus station. **Taxi**: some taxi drivers take advantage of tourists – check there is a meter or agree a price.

Sea Cruises: to Kuriat Island in Gulf of Hammamet T 461156.

15 km S of Monastir is **Uzitta** (also identified as Henchir Makhreba) which was closely associated with Caesar's campaign in Africa. Its ruins are on a slightly elevated position, overlooking the plain.

During excavations a residential district was uncovered with a number of villas. Many were very luxurious with private baths and mosaic tiled floors.

From Monastir to Mahdia

This route can be done on the Sahel Metro train, which has stations at Khnis, Ksar Hellal and Teboulba in addition to those on the published timetable (see page 349).

This part of Tunisia is one of the most crowded, after the capital itself. There are many small settlements, some running one into another and the serenity of the rural area, glimpsed at intervals, olive groves and small gardens, has become harder to find. The corniche to the S of the old fishing port at Monastir soon loses its attraction and the area becomes one of small industry. Turn right, away from the coast, towards the main road and head S.

The village of **Khnis** stands right on the coast with a small fishing fleet and relaxing views. It is S of this area that we have the first signs of agriculture, olive groves right up to the coast.

While the minor road continues along the coast to Saiada the road to **Ksar Hellal** swings inland, leaving behind the views and becoming increasingly congested. Ksar Hellal has a busy main road, a continuing line of shops, small workshops and medium grade housing. This runs on to become **Moknine** (noted for its jewelled Berber costumes as well as its pottery) where the road returns us to the coast, with salt flats to the W and the sea to the E. Moknine is connected to Sousse and Mahdia by train, by the 'Sahel Metro'. Some of this area is used for market garden produce, peppers, melons are common but the main crop is tomatoes (used as a garnish on nearly every meal) for the larger towns. The area of land covered by plastic green houses increases year by year. There are olives under-cultivated with cereals. Produce of the area also includes potatoes.

Teboulba, a surprisingly large centre, has grown up on agriculture. This is a very good area for farming, hence the density of population. Fruit trees have more or less replaced the olives here, along with potatoes and tomatoes under plastic cover. The use of prickly pear as hedges adds interest, especially when this cactus blooms.

The small port of **Bekalta** lies S of the ruins of **Rass Dimasse** which stand on the headland.

MAHDIA

ACCESS Bus station by the market and the harbour. The train station and louage station are nearby.

Mahdia, Tunisia's second largest fishing port, 60 km S of Sousse, and 50 km from the airport, is a charming little town which has to some extent escaped the tourist mania of the rest of the coast. Situated on the headland of Cap d'Afrique the town is surrounded by sea on three sides. An ancient Punic port, Mahdia followed Carthage and Kairouan as the capital of Tunisia in the 10th century. It is impressive for its position, its old city, its busy fishing port and its massive cemetery at the far end of town.

The traditional olive cultivation around the town and especially N of Mahdia has been taken over by extensive market gardening – plastic covered, tunnel shaped, head high greenhouses – growing tomatoes, pepper, melons, fennel etc.

Shi'ite Islam and the North African connection

Islam, one of three great revealed religions emanating from the Middle East, remained solidly united only for the brief period, 632-661 AD, under the rule of the early Caliphs. The succession was contested, however, in the reign of Ali (656-661) and led to a divide in Islam, in which Ali's son Hussein was killed in 680 at Karbala in Iraq after a series of unsuccessful battles against the Ommayyad Caliphs who had gained control of the empire. The dynastic schism led to religious divisions on ideology and ritual, the followers of Ali and Hussein, Shi'ites, believing that the Imam was not dead but merely hidden from sight (in occultation) and who would return to lead a crusade for the purging of Islam and the re-establishment of the proper succession usurped in the 7th century AD. The Shi'ites also understood that communication with God could be done in individual ways, and importantly, through God's interpreters on earth – the eminent authorities of the Islamic teaching schools at Karbala, Najaf, Qom and Messhed (ayatollahs and hojjatolislams). The formal teachings of the Islamic jurists and the religious consensus of the Sunni Muslims was rejected by the Shi'ites.

One reason for the survival of Shi'ism in the face of an all-powerful Sunni tradition and military supremacy was that the Persians adopted Shi'ism and incorporated it into their cultural and political resistance to the Arabs and gave the religion a geographical base in what is present day Iran.

Muslim cemeteries

🐾 One of the lasting monuments in Islam is the *maqbara* or graveyard. All are different, ranging from undefined rocky areas near villages, where unnamed head and foot stones are barely distinguishable from the deserts surrounding them, to the elaborate necropoli of Cairo where a veritable city of the dead is established. In all cemeteries bodies are interred with head towards the *qibla* – Mecca.

In Tunisia graveyards often contain a series of simple whitewashed mud brick tombs of holy men or *marabouts*, around which his disciples and their descendants are laid in. At Mahdia, there is a large and complex example of a long-used cemetery beyond the town, where stylized marble mausoleums, tombs and graves are densely packed in. Similarly ornate and walled cemeteries occur in cities elsewhere, there is a fine one at Monastir with the mausoleum of the late President Habib Bourguiba adjacent to it. In Tunis itself the Silsila cemetery is of ancient foundation – probably dating from the 7th century and located in the shadow of the Ez-Zitouna mosque, known as the Great Mosque. Muslim graveyards in Tunisia have no flowers unless they grow wild and by chance. Instead of buying flowers to ornament family graves on their routine weekly visit, relatives will often give a simple dish to the poor to provide a meal for the children.

Important or noble families have private cemeteries called *tourbet*. Most frequently, *tourbet* are part of a complex of religious buildings – schools or mosques – with separate rooms or a distinct domed area. In Tunis the most well-known are the Tourbet al-Bey, mausoleum of the Husseinid sultans of the 18th-20th centuries located in the central section and the Tourbet Aziza Othmana of the medina (see page 102).

Death and funerals are times for noisy outbreaks of wailing and crying. In traditional families, the approach of a person's death is signified by wailing, increased on actual death by the addition of the mourning neighbours and relatives. Occasionally in villages the body is laid in a large room where funeral dances are performed by wailing women, singing the praises of the deceased. Corpses are washed and wrapped in a simple shroud for interment. Mourners follow the cortege to the cemetery often in large crowds since every person who walks 40 paces in the procession has one sin remitted. At the graveside a *shedda* or declaration of Islamic faith is recited. Urban funerals are more ornate than those in the country districts and the passing of public figures is often accompanied by some pomp.

Things might have been different and Tunisia could have been a principal Shi'ite centre of the world. A group of Ismaelis, Shi'ites who broke away from the main Shi'ite group in 765, believing that the death of Ismael, the seventh Imam, in 770 AD brought the line to an end and began the Imam's occultation, moved to Tunisia and set up a capital at Mahdia in 912 AD (page 28). They were wandering preachers teaching a creed of humanity and equality, which was attractive to the North African Berber communities. In 893 AD one teacher, Abu Abdallah, converted the powerful Katama Berbers to his side and this eventually led to the move to North Africa of the Ismaeli leadership under Abed Allah and the foundation of Fatimid state (so-called because of the succession in the caliphate from Fatima, the prophet's daughter).

Tunisia served as a base for the Fatimids for the period 909-973 after which time their ambitions to convert the Islamic world back to Shi'ism led them successfully to attack Egypt, found Cairo in 969 and give up their hold on Mahdia. Tunisia was thus a mere stepping stone for the Fatimids. Shi'ite Islam all but died out in North Africa under the impact of Arab invasions by the Beni Hilal and Beni Sulaim beginning in 1050 AD.

The Fatimids of Mahdia

Al-Mahdi (Abed Allah)	909-934
Al-Qa'im	934-946
Al-Mansour	946-952
Al-Mo'iz	952-975

History

The history of Mahdia is closely linked with the Shi'ite branch of Islam. The Shi'ites believe that the Caliph must descend from Ali and Fatima (the prophet's daughter) and that the Sunnis are usurpers and heretics. After a 7-year war with the Aghlabites, **Obaid Allah**, known as **El Mehdi** (the Saviour), the founder of the Fatimid Dynasty (followers of Fatima)

finally secured victory and sought to establish his own capital. Mahdia was founded in 912 on an easily defended site and El Mehdi settled down in the still unfinished town in 921 in order to reinforce his power and protect himself. However his cruelty and his enemies' hatred made peace short-lived. In 944 the city was kept under siege for 8 months by the army of Abou Yazid. The siege was unsuccessful. The new dynasty moved to a city closer to Kairouan, Sabra el-Mansouriyya. The inhabitants of the abandoned capital concentrated on the sea for their welfare with the profits from fishing, commerce and piracy bringing a period of prosperity.

However reprisals followed, with first an unsuccessful Christian expedition to dislodge the pirates in 1088, then the occupation by Roger of Sicily in 1148. Later various other attempts were made to rid the town of the pirates, by a joint French-Genoan force in 1390 and in 1550 by Charles V of Spain. The Spanish were finally successful in 1554. As a result, the inhabitants were forced to revert to more traditional ways of life, such as olive cultivation and the production and weaving of silk. Today Mahdia is one of the largest fishing ports in Tunisia. The industry specializes in 'blue fish' such as mackerel and sardines, shining bright lamps at night to attract the fish.

Places of interest

The best way to start a visit to this town is to walk right round the edge of the promontory beginning on the N side, on the Blvd Cap Afrique up to the light-house and back down on the S side. Once that circuit has been completed and a call paid to the *Café Sidi Salem* to relax and admire the view, the centre of the town can be explored. The views from Cap Afrique are really well worth a visit and as most of the other inhabitants of the area are dead (this is a huge cemetery) the place is quiet.

The **medina** is beautiful even though there are not many specific things to see.

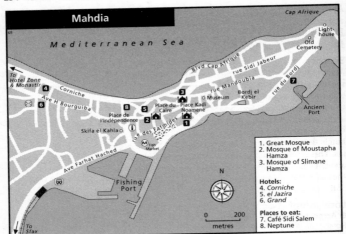

Mahdia

1. Great Mosque
2. Mosque of Moustapha Hamza
3. Mosque of Slimane Hamza

Hotels:
4. Corniche
5. el Jazira
6. Grand

Places to eat:
7. Café Sidi Salem
8. Neptune

Stroll around on the marble paved streets and peep into the doorway of one of the numerous weaving workshops producing high quality silk and cotton material for wedding dresses. At night, walk towards the main square in the medina, Place du Caire, and have a drink in the café under the arcades. This is the local social centre and has a lot of atmosphere.

Good spot to watch the sunrise is S shore near Grande Mosque, just you, the sun and all the fishermen.

Skifa el Kahla (Obscure Gateway), is the main gate into the town. The tip of the Cap and the medina used to be behind a large wall and only 'safe' people were permitted to enter. At the time of El Mehdi only troops and a few, privileged people lived within the walls in order to minimise the risk of rebellion. The people lived outside, but within the walls were their shops and workshops. This meant that starting a rebellion during the day could jeopardize the life of their families outside, while to do so during the night would lead to the loss of their livelihood. The present gate was built in 1554, after El Mehdi's time, following the departure of the Spanish.

The **Great Mosque** is on Place Kadi Noamene, at the top of the main street. The mosque was totally rebuilt in 1963 following the original 10th century Fatmid plans. The work was done with great skill and faithfulness to the original which was the first Fatimi mosque ever built. Unfortunately the mosque can only be entered by Muslims.

The **Bordj el Kebir** was built around the same period as the Skifa el Kahla. The Bordj is an impressive fortress built on the highest point of the headland overlooking the sea. The view from the top is good, but a visit to the Bordj is of limited interest. Open 0930-1630 winter and 0900-1200 and 1400-1800 summer, closed Mon, entrance TD1.

Salakta Museum which is situated on the site of Sullectum on the edge of the Punic cemetery. Inside is a splendid mosaic showing a lion, the emblem of a rich shipowner of the city at that time. Open daily (not Mon) 0930-1630 winter and 0900-1200 and 1400-1800 summer.

Special events:

Mar – National festival of the professional theatre

Apr – National festival of folk music and arts

Jun – Fishing festival

Jul – 'Nights of Mahdia' festival

Beaches

Mahdia has very beautiful beaches. By the village the shore is rocky, but the water is very clear. Further N along the Corniche, towards the hotels, the beaches are excellent. A 'Zone Touristique' has been built N of Mahdia where, as well as hotels there are new, very expensive villas. This is some distance from the town, about 5 km N up a new road right beside the coast. It is served by the local bus No 36B and *calèche*.

Local information
● **Accommodation**

Hotels with **A** grade in the tourist area incl: *Abou Nawas*, Bordj, Paradise el Mansour, 214 rm, T 696694, F 694968; *Paradise el Fatima*, 290 rm, T 696733, F 696731. The approach road is still being constructed, take care.

B *Club Cap Mahdia*, along route Touristique, T 681725, F 680405, 250 rm, beautiful, newly built, beach, quality service, pool, nightclub, tennis, horse-riding and all watersports, closed Nov and Dec, value for money; **B** *El Mehdi*, route de la Corniche, T 681300, F 680309, on beach of fine sand, 260 a/c rm with bath, telephone and balcony, some family rm, restaurants with local and international dishes, bar, Moorish café, TV rm, indoor and outdoor pools, disco.

D *Corniche*, Ave 7 Novembre, T 694201, F 694190, 16 rm with bath, small, cheap, clean, good restaurant, 2 km from town, not on beach side; **D** *Sables d'Or*, 3 km N out of town, along the Corniche, T 681137, F 681431, by the sea, beach, 68 rm are individual bungalows, sea view, most watersports.

E *Hotel Rand*, 20 Ave Taieb M'Hiri, T 680525, 22 rm with bath, breakfast incl, no restaurant, central, clean, pleasant staff and owner, hairdresser.

F *Hotel el Jazira*, rue Ibn el Fourat, close to Skifa el Kahla, T 681629, only hotel in the medina, very simple, clean, communal bath/toilet rather antiquated, uninviting, some rooms with sea view.

Youth hostel: in Mahdia, T 681559, 60 beds, meals available, family rooms, very clean, good view from roof, signposted from train station, about 5 mins walk. Another at Chebba, T 683815, 37 km from Mahdia, 60 beds, convenient for those taking the coast road C82 S to Sfax.

Camping: El Asfour, close to *Sables d'Or*, large, well organized site.

● **Places to eat**

◆◆*Neptune*, Ave 7 Novembre, start of *Corniche*, T 681927, clean, tidy, fish dishes sold by weight before cooking, seats 40; *Restaurant le Lido*, Ave Farhat Hached, by harbour, very good fish, T 681867.

◆*L' Espadon*, nr Hotel Corniche, T 681476, small, pleasant decor, close to beach, cheap, seats 26; *Restaurant el Moez*, between main gate and market, very cheap, good food, typical local restaurant, no alcohol; *Café Sidi Salem*, see map, hardly matters about the food, the views are excellent. All along the side of the harbour there are small cafés, fish appearing frequently on the menu.

● **Banks & money changers**

BNT on Place de l'Indépendence; BT and STB on Ave Habib Bourguiba.

● **Post & telecommunications**

Post Office: in the new part of town on Ave Habib Bourguiba.

● **Shopping**

Interesting carpet shop on rue du Bordj, opp *Café Sidi Salem*.

Market: on E side of port sells fish daily and other fresh produce and general goods on Fri.

● **Sports**

Harbour: 20 yacht berths, min-max draft 3-6m.

Health & Fitness Club: *Hotel Abou Nawas* in hotel zone.

● **Tour companies & travel agents**

Abou Nawas Travel, Ave Tahar Sfar, La Corniche, T 696222, F 696224; *Cap Voyages*, 196 Ave Habib Bourguiba, T 680355, F 680629; *Fatimides Voyages*, 191 Ave Habib Bourguiba, T 680763, F 694590.

● **Tourist offices**

The tourist information office is inside the medina's main gate, Skifa el Kahla, on the right in rue el Moez, T 681098, friendly but uninformative.

● **Useful addresses**

Taxis: T 695900.

Police: Ave Habib Bourguiba, nr supermarket.

Port: Harbour Master's Office, T 681595.

● **Transport**

Local Car rental: Avis, T 696342; Hertz, T 695255; Jet Car Loisirs, T 681796; Self Drive, T/F 696863. All on Ave Habib Bourguiba. **Taxis**: Abou Nawas, T 695900.

Train 'Sahel metro' train every hour 0500-1800 to **Monastir**, **Skanes/Monastir airport** and **Sousse**. Train station, T 680177, is down the street from the bus station, by the harbour. **Tunis** (via Sousse) 1135, 1645. Takes 4 hrs (TD1.5).

Road Bus: the bus station, T 680372, is by the harbour on Place 1st May. Frequent buses to **Sousse** and **Monastir**. Less frequent buses to **Tunis**, **Sfax**, **Gabès** and **Kairouan**. **Louages**: by the harbour, beyond the bus station, destinations **El Djem**, **Kairouan**, **Monastir**, **Sfax** and **Sousse**.

Mahdia to El Djem South of Mahdia are a few small coastal settlements, Er Zgana and Rejiche being the main ones. Ksour Essaf, 7 km inland and 10 km from Mahdia is larger, depending on the surrounding agricultural produce for its prosperity. The bypass to the N through the market gardens and olives leads on to El Djem (see page 262).

KAIROUAN

ACCESS The bus station is SE of Bab ech Chouhada, 15 mins walk from the centre. Louages from Tunis arrive at Bab ech Chouhada. All others arrive outside the Post Office.

(*Pop* 100,000; *Alt* 60m) The recommended route goes inland now to Kairouan, situated 65 km SW from Sousse along the P12 in the middle of a large plain and visible for miles around. The spiritual and religious capital of Tunisia, the city was the first base for the conquering Arab, and Muslim armies from the E. Still surrounded by the original walls, the town has a particular charm. The early morning or evening light over its ochre buildings is especially beautiful. Kairouan is also the capital of traditional **carpet manufacture** and the market town for Tunisia's main fruit growing area. It has a healthy climate thanks to its altitude. It stands at the junction of roads to Tunis, Sousse and Gafsa.

Tunisian handmade carpets

There is a good variety of high quality

Example of a Tunisian Mergoum carpet pattern

Tunisian handmade carpets. They are not graded as 'oriental carpets', though some are every bit as valuable and decorative as most Persian and Turkish products. A carpet or traditional hand-made rug makes a fine memento of a visit to Tunisia. A better choice can be made with a little knowledge and by taking your time in making your selection. Above all, if you do buy, make sure that you pick a rug that you like and can live with. Acquiring carpets as an investment is only for the experts.

In Tunisia as in other North African countries there are two main types of handmade carpet – the flat woven **kilims** and knotted carpets usually of wool on a cotton base. Whereas Tunisian carpets and rugs have a good reputation internationally, the *kilims* are more valued inside Tunisia. The classical carpets come from the workshop and home-based vertical looms of Kairouan in a variety of weaves. The patterns are geometrical, usually based on a central medallion in the form of single and double diamond shapes, with the linework reflected in similarly geometrical serpentine borders. Most of the original patterns were developed from prayer rugs, perhaps with roots in the Anatolian carpet, and some of the oldest of Tunisian carpets can still be found in mosques such as in the Zaouia Sidi Sahab in Kairouan (see page 243). Colours are at their best in blues, though Kairouan carpets can also come in very pleasant pastel and deep reds. Their weave is of hand knots of the *ghordes* type, with long tufts looped around the warp. *Merghum*, the other popular weave, is different, having short tufts emerging on the underside of the warps with regional variations as tapestries in Gabès, Matmata, Kebili and Gafsa and as *kelims* in Djerba and Sbeitla.

The finest carpets in Tunisia are made in silk or a mixture of silk and wool and come with knot densities of 250,000-500,000 knots/sq m at prices of over US$1,500 per sq m. For those without a desire for silk, there are excellent and cheap natural colour hand-woven carpets such as the *alloucha*, made of undyed lambswool.

Each carpet will need to be bargained for with patience and humour. The following points might help during this process. (1) Before entering the bargaining process make sure that you know what you are looking for – rug, tapestry or carpet – and what size of carpet your rooms can accommodate (and you can comfortably carry with you out of Tunisia). (2) If possible take an independent Tunisian friend with you to the shop who understands carpets and rugs. He will help to overcome language and bargaining hurdles. Remember, however, that tourist guides will lead you to carpet shops which give them commission on your purchase. (3) Take your time by shopping around and calling more than once at a shop before purchase. There is no need to be rushed whatever the inducement. (4) In Tunisia carpets ought to carry a lead government seal indicating their date of manufacture, material, area and quality. In official handicraft shops such as the very good one in Tunis, Office d'Artisanat in Ave Mohammed V, T 346899/348588, fixed prices are generally the rule, though this might not make them cheaper than the *souq* for the avid bargainer. (5) Remember that you must pay for your purchase in Tunisian dinars – exchanging currency through a shopkeeper can be very expensive – and that posting a carpet home from Tunisia is technically possible but best avoided – a 15% discount is normal for a cash and carry transaction. Cash-on-delivery terms for a carpet dispatched to the nearest EU port of London Heathrow Airport is 30% down payment and the balance on receipt. Remember that VAT and customs duties may be levied at the point of entry/receipt to the customer's home country.

History

The city was founded in 671 by Aqbar ibn Naffi as an outpost for the conquest of the Maghreb. He chose the site for its strategic value, being both far enough away from the coast where Byzantine fleets still threatened, and from the Berbers in the mountains who were strongly opposed to the new invaders. The town was attacked by the Berbers who won two significant victories, the more important in 688. The hostilities did not last long, however, with the Berbers soon converting to Islam. During the 9th century and the rule of the Aghlabids, the town found prosperity, and independence from Baghdad.

With the arrival of the Fatimids in N Africa in 909 a break occurred within Kairouan, an established centre for Sunnism, and the new Shi'ite leadership. As a result, El Medhi founded Madhia and moved his capital there. After the rebellion of Abou Yazid, in 953, the new Fatimid Caliph El-Mansor moved the capital back to a new city, Sabra el-Mansouriyya, just 2 km away from Kairouan. This meant the older settlement was bypassed commercially, most trade being done in the new city.

The curse of the Fatimids The real decline came with the invasion from Egypt in 1157, when Kairouan changed its allegiance from the Fatimids in Cairo to the Abbasids in Baghdad.

Tunisia and Libya were deeply affected in ethnic origin, religion and culture by two invasions of Arab groups from the E – the Beni Hilal and the Beni Sulaim.

The Beni Hilal confederation consisted of the three tribes, the Atbeg, the Riah and the Zoghba which originated in the central area of Arabia before moving to Egypt. A parallel tribal group, the Beni Sulaim, had similar origins and structure. It was made up of tribal elements – the Beni Hebib, the Beni 'Auf (Ku'ub), the Beni Debbab and Beni Zegb. They both came with reputations as brigands and trouble-makers, attributes confirmed in Egypt by their constant uprisings against the authority of the ruling elite. When in 1047 the Zirid successors to the Fatimid rulers in Tunisia changed their allegiance from the Shi'ite branch of Islam to Sunni and recognized the Abbasid Caliphs, the Fatimids retaliated by ridding themselves of the Beni Hilal and the Beni Sulaim to whom they bequeathed their former ter-

---

How the site for Kairouan was chosen – another fable

Long, long ago in 671 AD a companion of the Prophet Mohammed and a mighty warrior, governor of Ifriqiya by the name of Aqba ibn Naffi was travelling in the area. He drew up his horse and halted his troops at the very edge of 'a dangerous rubble filled valley strewn over with weedlike growth and infested with all manner of wild beasts' as the ancient guide books describe it. His troops required some reassurance to cross this dangerous area. This he provided by invoking the miraculous discovery of a golden goblet, unearthed from the sands beneath their feet. This he proved to be a special goblet that had been lost in Mecca. Aqba ibn Naffi's horse chose to stumble at this point (perhaps overwhelmed at the resourcefulness of his master) and water immediately sprang from the ground – a source which was proved to be directly linked to the well of Zem-Zem in Mecca which had first been discovered by Abraham. To make a final point he spoke to the wildlife in the valley in 'fiery speech' and the might of his words drove the scorpions from their hideouts and the wild beasts from their dens – leaving the area clear for the founding of a campsite (a *qayrawan*) and the basis for a magnificent city.

The invasion of the Arab tribes C10 and C12 AD

Legend:
- Islamic Conquest
- Direction taken by Beni Hilal & Beni Sulaim

Map labels: 1156 AD, Kairoua, Kairouan, Kairouan fell in 1157 AD, Mediterranean Sea, Beni Hilal 1156AD, Tripoli, Benghazi (Berka), Beni Sulaim C12, Cairo (Fustat), Beni Hilal 1152 AD, Red Sea, Medina, N, 69

ritories in North Africa. The Beni Hilal began their journey W in 1050-51 AD and first settled in Cyrenaica before moving, first, into Tripolitania where the Zoghba took control, then second, into Tunisia in the 11th century. They defeated the Zirid governors of Tunisia at Gabès in 1052 and by 1057 Kairouan fell to the nomadic invaders. The Beni Hilal fought the ruling Muslim rulers in North Africa, fought amongst themselves and were a thoroughly disrupting force in the area until they and the Beni Sulaim were contained by the Almohads of Morocco.

The Beni Hilal and Beni Sulaim are thought not to have been soldiers of Islam bent on a crusading conquest but rather bedouin and marauders looking for loot and land. Little was done on behalf of the Fatimids in the religious domain. Indeed, most scholars believe that the Islam of the tribes was learned from the already Islamised local populations. They remained as nomads and herders entirely unabsorbed into the city and its civilization, often making bedouins of other Berber and Arab populations.

There are always two sides to every story in North Africa. The saga of the invasion is celebrated in poetry, notably the *Saga of the Beni Hilal*, which tells of love, conquests and tales of derring do. On the other hand, Arab historians remember the two tribes of nomadic invaders as rapacious and "no better than a cloud of locusts". The civilization of the towns was largely destroyed or alienated so that the surviving cities in Libya and Tunisia were foreign depots in a sea of nomadic backwardness. Cultivation was largely abandoned and irrigation systems fell into disrepair.

The curse of the Fatimids on North Africa in the form of the Beni Hilal and Beni Sulaim was a total success, not that it did the Fatimids much good either!

It was not until the Hafsids were in control of Kairouan in the 13th century that the city redeveloped. Finally, under the Husseinid Dynasty in the 18th century, the city regained some of its past glory. Today Kairouan is a very important **religious centre**, the primary holy city in the Maghreb region, preceded in status only by Mecca, Medina and Jerusalem.

Islamic Medicine in Kairouan

Isaac Ben Saloman, known as Isaac Judaeus in the West, was a notable medical man of Kairouan. He came to that city from Egypt in 905 AD and established a great reputation as a writer on the treatment of human illness and as philosopher and scientist. He was a contemporary of the premier Islamic scientist Razi (Rhazes). By an ironic but important twist of history, Isaac Ben Saloman built on foundations of medicine provided originally by the Greeks. To these he added the then current Arab scientific

Miniature from an Arabic manuscript of the 14th century showing use of an instrument for measuring the amount of bloodletting from a patient by Al-Jazari. From L MacKinney, *Medical Illustrations in Medieval Manuscripts*, London, Wellcome Historical Medical Library, 1965, p 234.

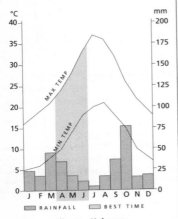

Climate: Kairouan

knowledge and together these were channelled into Europe as a result of translations of his work by writers such as Constantine the African in approximately 1080 AD. His works were basic to European mediaeval medical knowledge and were still in use as late as the 16th century. His topics of research seem to be rather specialist and even modern such as *The Anatomy of Melancholy*! He did not lack a psychological view – he advised that doctors should "Comfort the sufferer by the promise of healing, even when you are not confident" and "Ask your reward while the sickness is at its height, for being cured he will forget to pay."

One of his students, Ibn al-Jazzar, who lived and worked in the 10th century, wrote the famous books *Provision for the Traveller*, which was a directory of cures for diseases, and *Care of Children*.

Places of interest

If time is short there are numerous guided tours of the town which take in the main sights. These leave from the Tourist Office.

Kairouan is a most confusing town. Street names are frequently changed, some have two names and the locals you ask will recognize neither. Accept this as a challenge which adds to the charm of the place.

Buy your ticket first at the tourist office. It costs TD4 for seven sites. Mosquée Okba – the Great Mosque; Mausolée Abi Zomaâ – Zaouia Sidi Sahab or Barber's Mosque; Bassins Aghlabites – Aghlabid Pools; Mausolée Sidi Abid – Zaouia of Sidi Abid el Ghariani; Musée Rakkada – National Museum of Islamic Art; Mausolée Sidi Abada – Zaouia of Sidi Amor Abbada; Barrouta – Bir Barouta.

Photo fee TD2 at each site. Official guide TD7 for all the sites, for a group about TD10.

The **medina** is still surrounded by its original walls and is an interesting place to walk around, particularly in the early

A
journey of
1000 miles
begins with
your first
footprint...

With apologies to
Lao Tzu c.604 - 531 BC

Footprint Handbooks

Win two Iberia flights to Latin America

Welcome to Footprint Handbooks - the most exciting new development in travel guides since the original South American Handbook from Trade & Travel.

We want to hear your ideas for further improvements as well as a few details about yourself so that we can better serve your needs as a traveller.

We are offering you the chance to win two Iberia flights to Latin America. Iberia is the leading airline for Latin America, currently flying to 34 destinations. Every reader who sends in their completed questionnaire will be entered in the Footprint Prize Draw. 10 runners up will win an exclusive Footprint T-shirt!

Complete in a ball-point pen and return this tear-off questionnaire as soon as possible.

1 Title of this Handbook_____

2 Age Under 21 ☐   21 - 30 ☐   31 - 40 ☐
        41 - 50 ☐   over 50 ☐

3 Occupation _____

4 Which region do you intend visiting next?
   North America ☐ India/S. Asia ☐ Africa ☐
   Latin America ☐ S.E. Asia   ☐ Europe ☐
   Australia   ☐

5 Which country(ies) do you intend
   visiting next?
   _____

6 There is a complete list of Footprint
   Handbooks at the back of this book.
   Which other countries would you like
   to see us cover?
   _____

Please enter your name and permanent address:

Name_____

Address_____

_____

_____

E-mail_____

Offer ends 30 November 1997. Prize Draw
winners will be notified by 30 January 1998.
Flights are subject to availability.

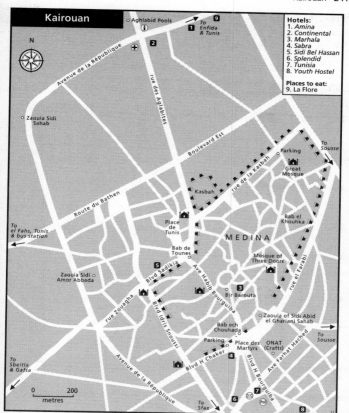

Kairouan

Hotels:
1. Amina
2. Continental
3. Marhala
4. Sabra
5. Sidi Bel Hassan
6. Splendid
7. Tunisia
8. Youth Hostel

Places to eat:
9. La Flore

morning when shops are opening and the sun is coming up. The medina is centred around the main street, Ave Habib Bourguiba. Walking up here from Bab ech Chouhada, on the right after the Bir Barouta, is a small covered souq. Further up, again on the right following the signs for the *Hotel Marhala*, is a small busy market. The medina gets very lively in the morning towards the Bab de Tounes, at the N end of Ave Habib Bourguiba.

The **Great Mosque**, built by Aqbar ibn Naffi, dates from the founding of the city in 671, and was built to be the centre of the new town using many pillars and capitals that were originally Roman and Byzantine. As such it is the oldest western mosque. It was severely damaged by the Berbers in 688, was virtually rebuilt in the 9th century and later enlarged, but nevertheless has kept its original style. The main dome is of ribbed brick in a herring-bone design. The shape of the mosque is not quite rectangular, but actually trapezoid in shape, the shorter sides measuring 70m and 74m and the longer sides 124m and

125m. The courtyard also trapezoid, the shorter sides being 52.45m and 50.25m, the longer sides both being 67m. Here there are pillared cloisters with wooden ceilings, often ignored by the casual visi-

tor. Both the E and W porticos have two aisles supported by three lines of arches. The N portico backing on to the minaret has four small rooms in one corner. The courtyard is very large, half-paved in

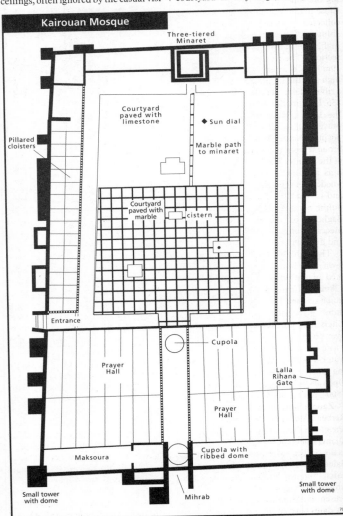

Kairouan Mosque

Three-tiered Minaret

Courtyard paved with limestone

◆ Sun dial

Marble path to minaret

Pillared cloisters

Courtyard paved with marble

cistern

Entrance

Cupola

Prayer Hall

Lalla Rihana Gate

Prayer Hall

Cupola with ribbed dome

Maksoura

Small tower with dome

Mihrab

Small tower with dome

white marble, the remainder paved with limestone blocks in which there is a differentiated path, not quite central, which leads to the minaret. Towards one corner is an interesting sundial indicating the times of the five daily prayers. Close to the sundial the rain water was collected in a cistern for use in ritual ablutions. The square minaret is 31.5m high, built in three successively smaller sections. The first is 10.7m square and 19m high, the next 7.7m square and 5m high and the smallest 5.5m square with a ribbed dome. It is thought to date from 836. Enquire if it is possible to climb up the 128 steps for a superb view. The prayer hall is filled with numerous imposing granite and marble columns brought from older sites in other parts of the country. Unfortunately non-Muslims are unable to view the internal wooden ceilings, the lavishly decorated and carved doors, woodcarving on the pulpit nor the 9th century tiles from Baghdad in the niche which faces Mecca. Open daily 0800-1800 except Fri and during prayers.

The **Aghlabid Pools** to the N of the town were built by Abou Ibrahim Ahmed in the 9th century. One is large, 128m in diameter, while the other is much smaller. They were part of a much more elaborate water system. The Cherichera aqueduct carried water from over 36 km away and the smaller pool was used to settle the silt carried in the water. The clear water was stored in the big pool, diameter 128m, depth 5m. Open 0830-1730 winter, 0800-1200 and 1500-1900 summer.

Zaouia Sidi Sahab (also known as the Barber's Mosque) is the burial place of one of the Prophet's companions, Abou Djama El Balaoui. The Zaouia is known as the Barber's Mosque because Abou El Balaoui carried about with him three hairs from the Prophet's beard, from which he would never be parted! The present building with its elegant minaret dates back to the 17th century. It is

Minaret of Great Mosque

beautifully decorated with Andalusian style ceramics. To get to the mausoleum, you first enter into a small room and continue along an open air corridor, richly decorated in multi-coloured ceramics. The next small room with a finely worked plaster ceiling opens on to the delightful main courtyard (square in shape and bordered on three sides by colonnades), with the mausoleum which houses the tomb. Access is reserved to Muslims. Notice the painted wooden ceilings under the arcade surrounding the courtyard. On Fri when circumcision ceremonies take place and during the Mouled (the Prophet's birthday), there are numerous pilgrims.

Mosque of the Three Doors (Thlethe Bibane), on the E side of Bir Barouta near the far end of rue de la Mosque de Trois Portes, built in 866 by a holy man from Córdoba, is one of the oldest mosques in Kairouan which takes its name from the three large doors leading inside. It has a beautiful façade all decorated with calligraphy and discretely carved reliefs. There are interesting inscriptions above the doorway.

To reach the **Zaouia of Sidi Abid el**

Ghariani, in the medina, take the 2nd road on the right after the main gate. This burial place of Sidi Abid, a 13th century saint, was constructed in the 14th century. Of particular interest is the room with the mausoleum. The ceiling is extremely finely worked wood, with fine plasterwork all around. The building in itself is very beautiful, based around three courtyards. The archways here are supported by Byzantine columns. Today it houses the office of the Association de Sauveguard de la Medina (an organization dedicated to helping to

---

The unforgiving Imam

Orthodox Sunni Islam evolved as a diversity of schools of thought depending on the great jurist whose opinions, none diverging far from the norm, were accepted as law - Abu Hanifa, Malik ben Anas, Ash-Shafi'i, Ahmad Ben Hanbal and Da'ud Al-Zahiri. In North Africa those following the view of Malik ben Anas (the Malikiyya group) became the most prominent and have remained so to the present day.

The Malikiyya favoured local practice as a principal guide in legal interpretations of Islam, with the opinions of the great religious teachers and application of human reason within the current Islamic community being more important for Muslims in deciding their courses of action than the rather tortuous analogies drawn from the *Hadith*, the written traditions of the Prophet Mohammed's life and times.

The widespread observance of the Malikiyya doctrine arose from the activities of a great Muslim teacher and thinker, the Imam Sahnun of Kairouan, who was a dedicated disciple of this school of Islamic jurisprudence in the 8th and 9th centuries (approximately 777-855 AD). Sahnun became known for his longevity, his adherence to the Malikiyya doctrine and his unforgiving persecution of Islamic scholars with opposing beliefs to his own. His success was that, with the exception of a handful of Ibadi Muslims in Djerba and a tiny minority of Hanafis, all of North Africa and much of Andalucía was converted Malikiyya Islam. Despite the Shi'ite Fatimid intrusion in the 10th century, the Malikiyya remained dominant throughout the region ever since.

Universal orthodoxy had a price, however, and Islamic philosophy was tightly confined to acceptable topics. Fortunately, Arab artistic and scientific innovation in Kairouan and Tunisia continued with Jews and Christians also playing key roles (see below).

> "Praise be to Allah, lord of the creation,
> The compassionate, the merciful,
> King of the last judgement!
> You alone we worship, and you alone we pray for help.
> Guide us to the straight path,
> The path of those whom you have favoured,
> Not of those who have incurred your wrath,
> Nor of those who have gone astray."
> *The Exordium*

Excerpt from the Blue Koran of the Great Mosque in Kairouan, 11th Century AD

preserve the medina) and the regional office of the National Art and Archaeology Institute. Open during office hours.

Bir Barouta, in the centre of the medina, is an old well which functions by the movement of a camel going round in circles. Not an essential visit!!

Zaouia of Sidi Amor Abbada was built by a 19th century blacksmith who designed huge objects, deemed to be useless, such as huge anchors to held Tunisia on to the land, huge swords, giant guns etc many of which are on display in his tomb with seven domes.

National Museum of Islamic Art and Culture, 11 km SW of Kairouan at Raccada on the P2, open daily 0900-1600, Fri 0900-1300, closed Mon. Entrance TD1.5. This was one of ex-president Habib Bourguiba's palaces so the setting is beautiful and the building elegant.

Raccada (meaning the Sleeper) was the second royal town of the Aghlabid rulers and as such has archaeological importance in its own right.

There is no written guide to the museum though general books are on sale. The displays, in a surface area said to cover over 20 ha, are neatly set out and with clear explanations. In the entrance hall is a wooden model of the great mosque of Kairouan on a scale of 1:50. It is quite superb. The interior of the minaret and central nave are exposed and allow the observer a better grasp of the layout of this magnificent building. On the other side is a copy of the mosque's *mihrab* where the sculpted plaster work of floral and geometrical designs has been faithfully reproduced. There are 28 panels of stucco arranged 7 by 4.

Exhibits include old, leather bound books from the Great Mosque in Kairouan dating from the late 10th century and leaves of old Korans with the most beautiful script while the walls are hung with old views of the ribats in Monastir, Sousse etc. There are cases of bronze coins from various eras and some 19th

century jewellery. One display has glass bottles from Mansuiyya. There is a very useful chronological table of the different dynasties that ruled in this region since the Arab conquest of 648 AD. It is useful to set in time, as well as space, the historical items in this museum and museums elsewhere in Tunisia.

Visits could also include demonstrations of how *Makrouth* the famous sweet (a very sticky pastry filled with date or fig paste and when cooked steeped in a thick syrup) unique to Kairouan is made, as well as carpet weaving, and copper beating.

There is a new dam at El Haouareb on the Oued Merg Ellil some 10 km W of Kairouan. This, in addition to providing extra, and always welcome, water for irrigation now protects Kairouan from the serious flooding previously caused by the irregular rainfall.

Local information
● Accommodation

Don't worry about the address, all the hotels are all clearly signposted in English. This is not, however, the main problem. While Kairouan is an important city and tourists come in their thousands to see the magnificent sights at present the accommodation available is not up to standard. A great deal more effort is required to produce the cleanliness, comfort and service as provided by the hotels on the coast.

B *Hotel Continental*, route de Tunis, to N of town by the Aghlabid pools and the Tourist office, T 220607, 175 rm, a/c, large pool, garden, restaurant, visitors could be forgiven for turning round and leaving, thinking they had arrived at the wrong place, with the current state of the hotel probably the best thing to do.

C *Hotel Amina*, route de Tunis, GP2, 300 Kairouan, T 226555, F 225411, 3 mins from city centre, 62 rm and 5 suites all with bath and balconies, telephone, a/c, 2 restaurants, coffee shop, bar, large pool, garden, nr Tourist office and Aghlabid pools, disco each evening, good lunch for TD7 served from 1230, hence popular with coach parties, at present this is the best hotel in town, but then there is no competition.

D *Le Splendid*, T 220522, rue du 9 Avril, 28 rm with bath, a/c, clean, basic, bar and busy restaurant, slightly over-priced; **D** *Tunisia*, T 221855, Ave Farhat Hached, 44 rm with bath, breakfast, no restaurant, comfortable, very clean, no a/c but fans on ceiling.

F *Hotel Marhala*, T 220736, F 229527, 35 Souq El Bey in the medina nr Bir Barouta, 30 rm with bath, very pleasant, real Tunisia, well run, small, view from top rm, roof terrace, no lift; **F** *Hotel Sabra*, T 220260, rue Ali Belhaouane, by place des Martyrs, clean, pleasant, friendly staff, roof terrace, 30 rm, rm at back are quieter, *hammam* next door, rec.

Youth hostel: Ave de Fés, T 220309, in the new town, kitchen, 70 beds, reports say noisy and not clean.

● **Places to eat**
♦♦*Le Flora*, route de Tunis; *Raschid*, Ouled Farhane; *Hotel Amina*, see above.

♦*Restaurant des Sportifs*, Place de la Victoire, couscous speciality; *Restaurant El Karawan*, rue Souqeina Ben El-Houssein, behind *Tunisia Hotel*, typical Tunisian cooking, family run; *Restaurant Fairouz*, signposted off Ave Habib Bourguiba in the medina, good food, cheap; *Restaurant Sabra*, Ave Farhat Hached, an excellent, cheap place to eat typical Tunisian food; *Roi du Couscous*, Place du 7 Novembre, Tunisian food at cheap prices, closes in late afternoon, best for lunch or early dinner. *Restaurant La Tabouna*, of Place des Martyrs, another, just about adequate cheap eating place, plenty of chips.

● **Banks & money changers**
BDS, UIB and BT on Place de l'Indépendence. STB has automatic cash dispenser for Visa and Mastercard.

● **Entertainment**
Hammam: Sabra, next to the hotel of the same name, close to the tourist office by Bab Ech-Chouhada. Immaculately clean. Men only, closes around 1600.

● **Hospitals & medical services**
Hospital: by the Aghlabid pools, T 220036.

● **Post & telecommunications**
Area code: 07.

Post Office: Place du 7 Novembre, rue Farhat Hached.

● **Shopping**
Bargains: Kairouan is one of the major centres for **carpets** in the country. Visit first the display of old and new carpets at the ONAT on Ave Ali Zouaoui, to get an idea of real prices even though carpets can be cheaper elsewhere. Be careful when walking around, the 'Musées de Tapis' (carpet museums) are really shops which have their own carpets on display. For an experience of purchasing carpets try *Société Tapis Sabra*, rue Sidi Abid, T 223068 or *Centre Kairouanais du Tapis*, 35 Souq des Tamis, T 226223. A typical rounded doorway in a plain wall leads into what was a private dwelling. There are 10 magnificently decorated rooms with a wealth of patterned tiles. The domed ceilings are about 7m high and the sunlight filters through to light up the hundreds of carpets, spread on floors, hung on walls and piled in rolls at every turn. In one room there is a loom and a woman or women will appear to demonstrate how a carpet is woven. Seating is provided in the largest room where any carpet you would like to see is rolled out for inspection. Even if you decide not to buy a carpet go up on to the roof terrace for the view.

● **Tourist offices**
The tourist information office is opp *Hotel Continental*, nr Aghlabid pools. There are 2 offices, turn left for information and right to buy tickets for the monuments. Welcoming competent staff will organize you a tour or an official guide if requested. Open 0800-1730 daily except Sun 0800-1200 T 220452/221797.

● **Useful addresses**
Police: T 220577.

● **Transport**
Local Car hire: Budget, Ave de la République T 220528; Hertz, Ave Ibn el Jazzar, T 224529.

Road Bus: the station is on the road to Sousse. For information T 220125. Departures to Tunis; Kebili/Douz; Gafsa; Tozeur; Djerba Zarzis; Medenine and Nefta. **Louages**: departures for **Tunis** are from Bab ech Chouhada. All other destinations leave from the Post Office. To **El Djem** possible by louage, requires changes and patience.

AROUND KAIROUAN

The road N for Kairouan towards Tunis (P2) is in a very poor condition. Road works at intervals, in an attempt to smooth the way, make this a slow and dangerous journey.

Kelbia Lake is halfway between Kairouan and Sousse. It lies to the SW of the P2, the main road from Nabeul to Kai

Mosaic of a wild duck from
a villa at Carthage

rouan just after the intersection with the MC48 road to Sousse. The best way to view the lake is to walk around the shore, but clear paths and viewing points are rare as the water level of the lake changes during the year. There is no other way to the lake but through fields or olive groves. However, at 25 km from Kairouan a small loop to the E takes one nearer to the water. In summer it is dry. It is an important **Wildlife Reserve**, with a wide variety of birds. During the summer you may spot squacco herons, purple gallinules or the fantailed warbler. In the winter, migrating birds such as flamingo pass through.

KSAR LEMSA

Take the slightly more northern route NW from Kairouan towards Siliana. The C99 is much more interesting climbing up the eastern side of the pass between Djebel Ousselat and Djebel Bou Dabouss. Take the bypass round Djelloula for a better road. Bear right once over the pass and cross the wide Oued Maarouf to reach the ruins of Ksar Lemsa.

Like all Roman cities Ksar Lemsa was situated in a position of strategic importance. It overlooked the valleys of the Oued el Kebir and the smaller, nearer Oued Maarouf. It controlled movement from the plains of the W to the coast and was itself protected by its position on a low plateau backed by the Djebel Bargou.

This fortress (hence the modern name *ksar*) is dated from the 6th century BC, the reign of Justinian though re-use of older building stones complicate the issue. The battlements of the almost square fortress (29m by 31m) remain. Entrance was through a gate on the N side. Inside the fortress was a large, deep water cistern fed by a conduit from outside – a supply in times of siege. Around the fortress are many ruins, few excavated and even fewer published.

MAKTAR

Maktar, population 7,500, lies 900m above sea level and 114 km W of Kairouan along the scenic P12. The new city was built by the French a century ago but the Roman city of Mactaris which dates from around AD 200 was built on the site of an earlier Numidian defensive position. The Oued Saboun protects one side. The ruins are entered by the museum through the Roman gate. Open winter 0830-1730, summer 0800-1200 and 1500-1900, entrance TD1, photography TD1. The remains of the **amphitheatre** lie to the left and further left, across the Roman road are the remains of a **temple** dedicated to the Carthaginian god Hathor Miskar. The central section of the site contains the former forum and the remains of Trajan's Arch, looking less triumphal than in its heyday of 115 AD. Beyond are the foundations of the **5th century Basilica of Hildeguns** and after another 100m are the **Baths** which are considered the best preserved thermal baths in Africa. Much of the splendour is in its mosaics.

To the W lies the **Schola Juvenum**, claimed as one of the prettiest ruins in Tunisia, once an educational establishment for young people and in the area around this is a temple dedicated to Bacchus, an open space that was the Forum, a cemetery and yet more baths.

Maktar town lies to the N of the site and at an altitude of over 900m is refreshingly cool. The town is built on the hillside and the buses stop at the lower end of the town while the louages stop higher up the main street.

● **Accommodation C** *Mactaris*, T 876014, 20 rms, reasonable standard.

17 km E of Maktar, towards Kairouan on the P12, on a small loop road is the Berber village **La Kesra** standing at 1,078m. This is a magnificent defensive position, has its own spring and outstanding views. The ancient Numidian city of Chusira stood here, the Romans constructed the main streets and the walls of the old buildings echo these ancient civilizations. Traditional crafts, particularly cloth weaving, are carried on here.

Just 1 km from Kbor-Klit is Ksar

Toual Zammel. This small agricultural town has origins from pre-Roman times. The Ksar is actually a 2-storey mausoleum and other remains include part of a street, a temple, a Christian church (?) and two necropoli. The Roman name was *Vicus Maracitanus*.

SBEITLA

ACCESS The bus station is in the centre of the new town and the louages are next to it. Many buses come here from Kasserine, Gafsa, Tunis and Kairouan. The train station is on rue Habib Thameur to S of town.

The 75 km journey S from Maktar to Sbeitla is along winding minor roads through the Dorsal region. Within 2 km

Mactaris

To Kairouan
To Maktar and Sbeitla
Museum

N

0   100
metres

Amphitheatre

1. Roman Road
2. Temple of Hathor Miskar
3. New Forum
4. Byzantine Tower
5. Basilica of Hildeguns
6. Great Eastern Baths
7. Temple of Bacchus
8. Old Forum
9. North Baths
10. Schola Juvenum
11. Baths
12. Monument
13. West Baths
14. Numidan Tombs
15. North Gate

Temple **2**

Forum

3

Trajan Arch

4

Basilica

5

Temple **7**

Forum **8**

Great Baths

6

9

13

14   **12**   **11**   **10**

74

f leaving Maktar, there is a magnificent
iew N to the mountains and as the P4
limbs through the Djebel Skarna
1,076m), the Tunisia seen by the visitor
ere is in sharp contrast to the level
lains of the Sahel. As the road descends,
he ruins of the ancient settlement of
ufes at Sbiba lie to the left. 40 km
eyond is Sbeitla.

The new city is of no special interest,
ut the old Roman ruins of **Sufetula** are
eally worth a visit, being considered one
f the best preserved sites in Tunisia.
Enter opposite the museum into the
Byzantine quarter where there are three
orts/dwellings constructed of materials
aken from older buildings and with for-
ifications necessary at those unsettled
imes were divided into rooms and there
vas a well to provide water during a
iege. The nearby **Byzantine church** is
edicated to Saints Gervais, Protais and
Tryphon; **baths** badly damaged and par-
ially rebuilt with a mosaic of fish and
rustaceans and an oil press (originally
here were two presses and a windmill).
The **Arch of Diocletian** forms part of
he old walls to the S of the site.

In the central area is a large **cistern**
vhich supplied water to the city, the
ainwater being perhaps supplemented
y an underground canal. Close by are
he remains of a large public **baths**, with
ot and cold rooms and a geometric mo-
aic decorating the room dedicated to
xercise. The **fountain** is one of three
ublic fountains dating from the 4th
entury.

Turn right here to the **theatre**, a
hadow of its glorious past. The tiers are
n ruins but the orchestra pit is clearly
isible as are the colonnades round the
tage. Worth the detour if only for the
nagnificent view over the Oued Sbeitla.
The **Church of St Servus** was built in
he courtyard of a Roman temple, now
nly four columns of stone mark the
orners of the building. Turn left along
he street originally with shops on either
ide to the magnificent **capitol** entered

through the **Arch of Antonius Pius**.
This gateway was built in the style of a
triumphal arch and formed part of the
ancient walls though not quite so thick.
It has a large centre arch flanked by two
smaller ones. It can be dated between 138
and 161 AD thanks to an inscription
which refers to the Emperor Antonius
Pius and his two adopted sons, Marcus
Aurelius and Licius Verus. The three
massive **temples** which stand side by
side opposite this gate, across the vast,
almost square, **Forum** are assumed to be
dedicated (from right to left) to Juno,
Jupiter and Minerva. The central temple
was more opulent in decoration. The
columns of the temple of Minerva are
especially delicate. The side temples can
be approached by wide steps but the
main, central temple is fronted by a tribune without steps. One can imagine the
processions moving up the two sets of
stairs to meet before the main temple.
Vaulted cellars stand below these temples. The Forum, paved with huge stone
slabs, is surrounded by a wall which

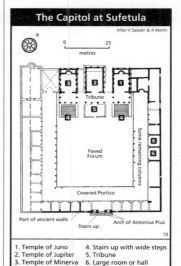

The Capitol at Sufetula

After H Saladin & A Merlin

0 — 25
metres

Tribune

Paved Forum

Some remaining columns

Covered Portico

Part of ancient walls

Stairs up

Arch of Antonius Pius

73

1. Temple of Juno
2. Temple of Jupiter
3. Temple of Minerva
4. Stairs up with wide steps
5. Tribune
6. Large room or hall

shows evidence of several restorations. Against this wall stand large rooms or halls. In most cases these rooms were fronted by a covered portico supported by colonnades. The use to which these rooms were put has never been clear. The central square has been enlarged at one time. Close to the Forum is another church constructed on the site of an older building. This is in poor condition but visible are the central aisle and the two smaller side aisles separated by a double colonnade.

The group of buildings to the NE, known as the episcopal group, comprises two churches, a baptistery, a chapel and

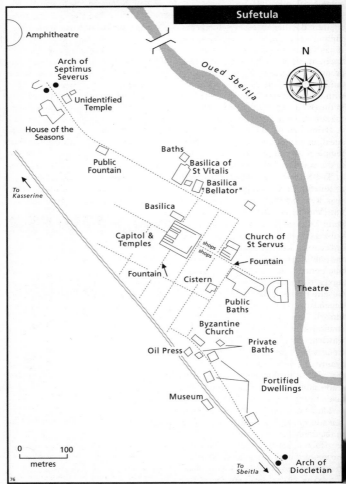

Sufetula

- Amphitheatre
- Arch of Septimus Severus
- Unidentified Temple
- House of the Seasons
- Ou ed Sbeitla
- N
- Public Fountain
- Baths
- Basilica of St Vitalis
- Basilica "Bellator"
- Basilica
- To Kasserine
- Capitol & Temples
- shops
- shops
- Church of St Servus
- Fountain
- Fountain
- Cistern
- Public Baths
- Theatre
- Byzantine Church
- Private Baths
- Oil Press
- Fortified Dwellings
- Museum
- 0   100
- metres
- To Sbeitla
- Arch of Diocletian

76

small baths. The **Basilica Bellator**, excavated in 1907 is named after a fragment of inscription found there. It measures 34m by 15m, has a central nave and two side aisles and a double apse. The mosaic floor in the choir still remains. The baptistery was converted into a chapel dedicated to Bishop Juncundus (5th century) who is believed to have been martyred by the vandals. The adjacent **Basilica Vitalis** is a later building and is larger measuring 50m by 25m. It has 5 naves and double apses and like the Basilica Bellator has evidence of long occupation. Its mosaic pavements are quite special. A marble table decorated with biblical themes found here is now in the Bardo Museum. The museum on the site has only a photograph.

If time permits explore the NW of the site through the houses and unidentified temple to the amphitheatre and across to the much restored bridge.

The Roman town, originally known as Sufetula, was probably built in the year 3 BC, but little is known about it until the period under the rule of Emperor Vespasian (69-79 AD). The town was very prosperous during the 2nd and 3rd centuries, judging by the remains of the public buildings. During the Byzantine period, the town was briefly made capital of the province then, in 646, the Governor Gregory declared himself independent from Constantinople called himself Emperor and moved his administration from Carthage to Sufetula, which he considered to be a better centre from which to defend the country against the Arabs. This proved not to be the case when Gregory was killed defending Sufetula in 647 and the town was taken by the Arabs.

The best time to visit this impressive ruined town is early in the morning or in the evening when the soft sunlight is particularly beautiful on the stones of the temples and one is less likely to have to share the experience with a bus-load of tourists. Open 0830-1730 winter and

Christian theme on a mosaic
(Sbeitla Museum)

0600-2000 in summer. Closed Mon, entrance TD1, photo fee TD1. Most of the site is accessible in a wheelchair.

Opposite the ruins (adjacent to the Coca-cola stall and coach park) is a museum containing artefacts and photographs of Sbeitla divided into five sections covering prehistory, Roman sculptures, ceramics, Christian/Byzantine and Muslim periods. A visit to the museum first may make the site visit more valuable. Open daily 0600-2000. Entrance included in fee for ruins. There are toilets beside the museum.

Sbeitla museum Room 1 contains local material from Sufetula accompanied by maps and plans. The Libyan period is represented by megalithic tombs from Djebel Selloum and Thala

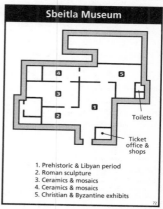

Sbeitla Museum

Toilets

Ticket office & shops

1. Prehistoric & Libyan period
2. Roman sculpture
3. Ceramics & mosaics
4. Ceramics & mosaics
5. Christian & Byzantine exhibits

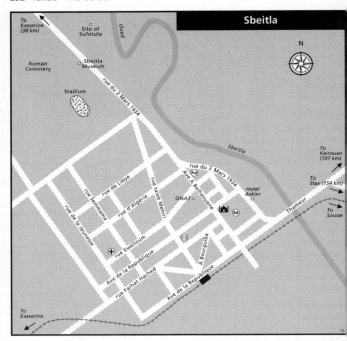

Sbeitla

and by an inscription from the region of Djediliane-Rouhia to the N of Sbeitla. The early Roman period is represented here by a series of votive and funerary steles.

Room 2 has marble statues and busts including a statue found at Sufetula, Bacchus, god of wine, accompanied by a panther from whose open mouth once came a fountain of water. From Kasserine came the statue of a feminine figure, perhaps Diana the huntress. Look too for the female bust from Haïdra and a smaller statue from Sbiba.

In Rooms 3 and 4 there are two important mosaics, from Sufetula and Sbiba. The rest of the space is given over to the economic life of the region at that time which was firmly based on olive oil. There are presses, containers for carrying the oil, lamps, plates and dishes. The marble head of Mercury from Sufetul is on display here and a special piece o very ancient leather from Sbiba.

Room 5 is devoted to Christian an Byzantine exhibits. From the 2nd cen tury the Christian religion was expand ing its influence. Here in Tunisia ther were many churches, as many as 6 a Sufetula and Haïdra. The display a tempts to give an idea of the richness o the period with photographs and arte facts. There are sarcophagi, bronze, glas and descriptions.

While the modern town of Sbeitla i not very attractive it does have all th necessary facilities a traveller could re quire and looks its best on a Wed whe there is the weekly market. There is bank, a telephone booth, a post offic and sufficient shops.

● **Accommodation** is available at **B** *Hotel Sufetula*, just before the ruins on the way to Kasserine, T 465074, pleasant, clean, good pool (available to non-residents), the only good hotel in Sbeitla and charges accordingly, you may find yourself rubbing shoulders here with the tour group you tried to avoid at the site; **D** *Hotel Bakini*, rue 2 Mars 1934, T 465244, has 80 beds.

North from Sbeitla to Sbiba

This city of Sbibes (Sbiba) stood on the route between Le Kef and Sbeitla overlooking the Oued el Hattab and protected by the Djebel Oust to the W and Djebel Mrihila to the S. It is said that the strategic position and the fertility of the soil were the two factors which allowed this city to survive until the early Middle Ages. There are records of strong Christian influence (two basilicas), ramparts erected by the Byzantines, parts of which still stand, but perhaps the best remnants of this interesting city are to be found in the mosaics and statues on display at the museum in Sbeitla.

Excursion to Kasserine

Kasserine lies 38 km SW of Sbeitla. Behind it to the W stands Djebel Chambi (1,544m) the highest peak in Tunisia providing an interesting dimension to the spectacular sunsets. The ruins (very few) of the Roman town of Chambi are here to the left of the road. **Chambi National Park** protects the last of the mountain gazelles. Take the P17 N from Kasserine and before the Oued Hatab turn left/W on the P13. 5 km after crossing the railway look for a track to the left which skirts Djebel Chambi and returns to the P17. Kasserine depends on esparto grass for its livelihood (see above), and little else grows here. The town is dominated by the huge cellulose processing factory. Kasserine stands by a very important junction and controls an important pass. Even the Romans noticed that and in more recent times the American troops tried to hold the area from the German advance. The Oued Eddarb, tributary of the Oued el Hattab is crossed between the junction

and the town proper. There are plenty of banks, small and medium size shops, a chemist and a hospital. It is large enough to have two of the regulation issue square faced clock monuments, confusing when getting directions, but the central monument is a hand clutching a few stalks of cereal (perhaps it is esparto grass!). Bus and louages stop in middle of town. The main ruins are a good walk or a short taxi ride to the W.

● **Accommodation** **C** *Hotel Cillium*, T 474406, 5 km from town centre, just before the ruins en route from Kasserine, interesting circular design, 72 beds, all rm have bath, 770m above sea level, splendid views, pleasant, clean hotel, pool, a/c, it is the only good hotel in Kasserine and charges accordingly. very popular for lunches (TD7), can organize wild boar hunting in the vicinity; **F** *Hotel Ibis*, by Mobil service station; **F** *Hotel Salam*, on N side of town nr Shell petrol station. **Youth hostels**: in **Kasserine**, 67 km from Sbeitla, 3 km from Kasserine centre, T 07 470053, 92 beds, meals available; **Siliana**, 35 km N of Maktar, T 08870871, 70 beds.

CILLIUM

This is the most important Roman site in the region, set up at a strategic location controlling routes both N-S and E-W. Once the local nomads were subdued it was settled by the Romans. The site is on a plateau overlooking the Oued Derb, a tributary of the much larger Oued el Hatab. As the present town of Kasserine was built on the far side of the *oued* much of the site has been preserved though the necropolis was unnecessarily destroyed when *Hotel Cillium* was built. So what is there to see? Among the ruins stand the Mausoleum of Petroni, the remains of the 3-storey Mausoleum of the Flavii (better condition) near the main road, the Triumphal Arch (3rd century AD) with a dedication from which the town gets its name, the dam on the Oued Derb and a number of small Byzantine forts. The mosaics, some in the Bardo, were found in the houses which stood about 100m W of the Triumphal Arch. Best known is the panel with Venus, surrounded by Tritons, Nereids on sea-monsters and Erotes on dolphins.

For those searching for finer details – the water for the baths was supplied from the *oued* and here is a small channel which leads from there to the baths – but at present the water in the *oued* is some 50m below the channel entrance – no baths today.

Just 5 km S of Cillium, near the tiny settlement of Henchir el-Guellali is the remains of a reservoir, to provide water for Cillium and irrigation water for the nearby fields.

There is no direct bus to Gafsa from Sbeitla. Taking louages to **Gafsa** requires changes at Kasserine, Fériana and Mejel Ben Abbès each leg costing about TD1.5. If you get stuck in Fériana try **E** *Hotel Mabrouk* near bus and louage stop.

Haïdra can be accessed from here, or from Maktar. It is off the main routes and not very easy to get to from anywhere. For details of this Roman site (see page 194).

KAIROUAN TO GABES

This is a busy route going directly S. It passes the National Museum of Islamic Art at Raccada in a beautiful palace. Don't miss this. Further S where the P2 crosses Oued Zeroud and the railway line and where the C86 cuts off to the SW is the Zaafrane Centre. Here is a large café set back off the road, clean, welcoming and with all facilities. The eucalyptus trees bordering the route have been reduced by road widening and careless pruning but are sufficient in size and quantity to remind one of this attractive French legacy.

This is a rich agricultural area, dairy cattle which can survive in these northern parts and olives under-planted with cereals so that no waste is permitted. This really is the plain of the olives which stretch as far as the eye can see both to the E and W.

Bouhajla is a small settlement set up at a crossroads. Here you will find the National Guard, yet another square-faced clock on a central pillar, chemist, bread shop, louage and bus stop. There is a café by the bus stop and a slightly better café to the N of village on E side by the new mosque and petrol station.

Djebel Khechem closes in on the W and Djebel Kordj on the E. At the road junction P13 and P2 are two fairly basic cafés. This area in spring has the delight of the prickly pear hedges in flower, bright pink and yellow clusters, and the nut trees in bloom too, much more delicate shades of pink and white. Nut trees are generally at the fields' boundaries and there produce an eerie irregular network of pale blossom.

Salt lake Mecheguig, to the W, in right conditions a very large expanse of water,

Esparto grass – paper in the desert

Esparto grass, also called *Alfa* or *Halfa*, is a needlegrass (*Stipa tenacissima*) indigenous to northern Africa and southern Spain. It is very common on the infertile, dry, sandy soils of interior Tunisia and Algeria where nothing else will thrive. The plants grow in clumps maybe 2m across with the cylindrical stems reaching 1m in height. The young grass can be used as animal fodder but later becomes too tough even for camels to chew.

This grass has been used over the centuries to make ropes, mats, storage utensils, baskets and sandals. Today it is harvested for the manufacture of paper by a process developed in the UK in 1856. Esparto has a very high cellulose content. The fibres are strong and flexible, and standard in size and shape and make a better paper than either wood pulp or rags. The resulting paper is of high quality being uniform in texture, opaque and very smooth.

can support rich bird life, especially water birds like flamingos. These have the advantage of being visible easily from the road.

North of Bir Ali Ben Khalifat is a government resettlement project with small individual houses rather than a small village. Ben Khalifat has a hotel and café, very popular at lunch times. Good choice of food, pizza, cakes, tea, coffee, juices, also a restaurant, clean toilets, welcoming staff. Hotel has 8 pleasant rooms.

SFAX, THE KERKENNAH ISLANDS AND EL DJEM

SFAX

ACCESS The main bus station is at the E side of Ave Habib Bourguiba, in front of the train station. There is another bus station at the other end of Ave Habib Bourguiba at Ibn Chabat, beyond the market for services to Gabès and all destinations S. The train from Tunis takes 2 hrs. Louages stop on Place de la République. The airport, El Maou, 6 km to the SW, T 241700, handles international package tours and internal flights.

Those wishing, perhaps understandably, to avoid Sfax can use the clearly

signed road which skirts it to the W. It is a dual carriageway with the main storm drain in between. There are numerous, slow junctions with lights. In places it is three lanes wide and the turn to Sfax generally has a filter. Don't get into the wrong lane.

(*Pop* 400,000; *Alt* 21m) Sfax is the second largest city in Tunisia and is an important agricultural, industrial and commercial centre. The older part of the city has, however, retained a lot of its charm. Sfax is a thriving city with two distinct parts: the new town, built to a geometric pattern, and the medina, still surrounded by its original walls. It is a delight for tired visitors for the site is absolutely flat.

History

Nothing remains of the ancient town of Taparura, but its commercial tradition is still well in place. In the 7th century the town was already a trade centre, exporting olive oil to Italy. By the 10th century, Sfax declared itself an independent state, only to be conquered by Roger of Sicily in 1148. It later put up a valiant resistance to the Venetians in 1785 and surrendered to the French in 1881 only after fierce attacks. Bombardment during WW2 destroyed a large part of the town. Today, its main activity is centred around phosphate exports, but olive oil continues to be a major industry.

Places of interest

The **Archaeological Museum**, is in Place Hedi Chaker (in the new town), T 229744, off Ave Habib Bourguiba. This small museum of seven rooms displays Islamic, early Christian and Roman exhibits, mostly mosaics, manuscripts and pottery. There is a 3rd century Roman painted funeral artefact. Open 0900-1200 and 1500-1830 in summer, 1400-1730 in winter, closed Sun, entrance TD3.

The **medina** is one of the best preserved and most authentic in Tunisia. Unlike the souqs of Tunis and Sousse, it is primarily aimed at the locals, who do

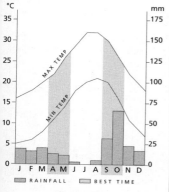

Climate: Sfax

most of their shopping there. Many artisans and craftsmen still work here and earn a living in a traditional way. This all makes the medina very interesting for visitors, particularly as its walls are still intact and the difference in atmosphere between the old and new cities is clear.

Dar Jellouli, T 221186, houses the **Regional Museum of Popular Arts and Traditions** at 5 rue Sidi Ali Nour, off rue de la Driba. Set in a beautiful 17th century palace, the museum is extremely interesting and enables one to have a very good idea of life in Tunisia in the last century. On the ground floor the rooms are organized around a small courtyard. Each contains well-explained lifesize pictures of traditional Tunisian living. In one room is a kitchen complete with implements, in another living rooms with all the furniture and so on. On the 1st floor is a display of the traditional clothes and jewellery of each social class. A visit is definitely worthwhile and the setting is superb. Open 0930-1630, except Mon and public holidays, entrance TD2.

The **Great Mosque** was built in the late 9th century, and altered in 988 and 1035. From the outside the minaret, made of three superimposed towers in the same style as the Great Mosque of Kairouan, can be seen. In shape it is almost rectangular, with an addition to the SE face and a piece missing from the western corner. It measures 52m from NW to SE and 41m in the other direction. The paved courtyard is surrounded by high porticos with horse-shoe arches on pillars, many from more ancient sites. The L-shaped prayer room has 9 aisles and 6 bays leading to the courtyard (16m by 14m) and 12 bays leading to the minaret which stands centrally in the NW wall. The courtyard was originally twice the size. Half has been taken to extend the prayer room. There are two cupolas, one central on the S face of the courtyard and the other at the end of the same aisle, at the far end of the prayer room, adja-

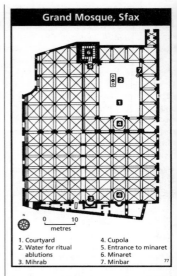

Grand Mosque, Sfax

1. Courtyard
2. Water for ritual ablutions
3. Mihrab
4. Cupola
5. Entrance to minaret
6. Minaret
7. Minbar

cent to the *quibla*. The *mihrab* indicated in the wall beneath this cupola no longer exists. The five groups of three columns to the right of the current mihrab are an unusual feature, necessary to support some particularly thick arches and a structural wall.

The bronze-faced main doors to the prayer room are worked in a geometric design of squares. Unfortunately, the interior is closed to non-Muslims.

An interesting itinerary is to enter the medina by the main gate, **Bab Diwan**, and go up the road on the left, leading to the **Great Mosque**. Passing by, only glimpses of its interior, reputed to be very beautiful, can be seen since it is closed to visitors. Continue down rue des Teinturiers and enter the **souq**. Within the souqs, one can find everything from clothes and meat to saddles for donkeys. At the end of this street are the city walls and the rue des Forgerons (blacksmiths). Opposite is the **Bab Djebli**, a gate looking over a recently built market, where food is generally sold. This can be

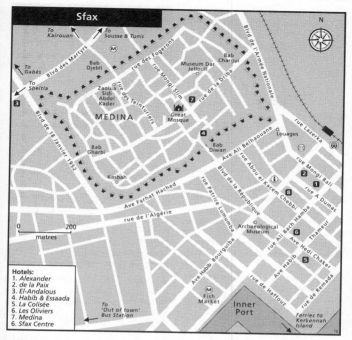

Sfax

To Kairouan
To Sousse & Tunis
Bab Chargui
Blvd de l'Armée Nationale
To Gabès
Blvd des Martyrs
Bab Djebli
rue des Fogerons
Museum Dar Jellouli
Zaouia Sidi Abdel Kader
rue des Teinturiers
rue Mong Slim
rue de la Driba
To Sbeitla
Blvd de 18 Janvier 1952
MEDINA
Great Mosque
rue Lazerka
Bab Gharbi
Bab Diwan
Louages
Ave Ali Belhaouane
Ave Abou el Kacem Chebbi
rue Mongi Bali
Kasbah
Blvd de la République
Ave A Dumas
Ave Farhat Hached
Blvd de Patrice Lumumba
rue de l'Algérie
Archaeological Museum
rue Ali Bach Hamba
Ave Thameur
Ave Hedi Chaker
Ave Habib Bourguiba
Ave Habib
rue de Haffouz
rue de Remada
Fish Market
Inner Port
To 'Out of town' Bus Station
Ferries to Kerkennah Island

0   200
metres

Hotels:
1. Alexander
2. de la Paix
3. El-Andalous
4. Habib & Essaada
5. La Colisée
6. Les Oliviers
7. Medina
6. Sfax Centre

worth a visit. In the rue des Forgerons, artisans work in little workshops doubtless in the same way as they have for centuries. Go right up rue Mongi Slim. Again, this is the heart of the souqs. Some buildings have superb façades. Follow rue de la Driba and on the left is the **Dar Jellouli Museum**. Without doubt, the best way to see the medina is to spend a few hours walking around, particularly as this is really one of the few authentic medinas left. Also of note is Place de la Kasbah, to the W of Bab Diwan. The **kasbah** itself is of no great interest, but there is a beautiful private building on the square. In the streets leading into the medina from here notice the iron grilles on the first floors of most houses. Also notable is a beautiful 17th century private house on Place Barberousse.

Local information
● Accommodation
A *Hotel Sfax Centre*, Ave Habib Bourguiba, T 225700, F 225521, 115 rm, 8 suites, brand new, very little character, all mod cons.

B *Syphax Novotel*, route Souqra, T 243333, F 245226, 127 rm, rec to all travel agents.

C *Hotel el-Andalous*, Blvd des Martyrs, T 299100, F 299425, 90 a/c rm, bar, 2 restaurants, on busy street but quiet inside and in rear rooms, free underground parking; **C** *Hotel Les Oliviers*, Ave Habib Thameur, new town centre, T 225188, charming, 50 rm, old style, good condition, pool.

D *Hotel Alexander*, rue Alexandre Dumas, T 221911, in new town, extremely well kept, 30 rm, clean, very good restaurant; **D** *Hotel Amine*, 40 rm, T 245601, has been rec; **D** *La Colisée*, rue Taieb M'Hiri, T 277800, F 299350, 40 rm with bath, a/c, heating, restaurant.

F *Hotel de la Paix*, rue Alexandre Dumas, T 221436, in new town, 30 rm, pay showers, very clean; **F** *Hotel El Habib*, rue Borj Ennar, T 221373, in medina, 22 rm, clean, communal showers; **F** *Hotel Essaada*, rue Borj Ennar, T 220892, opp *El Habib*, 43 beds, small, clean, communal showers; **F** *Hotel Medina*, 53 rue Mongi Slim, T 220354, 32 beds, in medina (not surprisingly!), small, clean, pay shower.

Youth hostel: on the road to the airport, T 243207, 126 beds, train station 1 km.

● **Places to eat**
♦♦♦*Le Corail*, T 227301, Ave Habib Maazoun, very comfortable restaurant, excellent seafood, expensive, fixed menu is value for money; restaurant in *Hotel Alexander*.

♦♦*Chez Nous*, rue Patrice Lumumba, good choice at a good price; *Le Baghdad*, T 223085, Ave Farhat Hached, very good restaurant, nice decor, but a bit expensive.

♦*La Renaissance*, 77 Ave Hedi Chaker, T 220439, choice of fish and meat dishes, clean; *Le Printemps*, 57 Ave Habib Bourguiba, T 226973, wide choice; *Restaurant Tunisien*, just inside Bab Diwan on the right, cheap, good food.

For a **drink** go to Place de l'Indépendence and the surrounding streets, or to the medina. Try *Café Diwan*, on the left after the main gates following the walls.

● **Banks & money changers**
STB and UIB, Ave Hedi Chaker; BIAT, rue Salem Harzallah; BT, Ave Habib Bourguiba; BNT, rue Taieb Mehiri; UBCI and BS, rue Abou el Kacem Chebbi; BC, Place de l'Indépendence. STB has automatic cash dispenser for Visa and Mastercard users.

● **Hospitals & medical services**
Chemist: all night, *Rekik, Polyclinique Ettaoufik*, T 241105, 25 rue Alexandre Dumas; *Kilani*, Ave Habib Bourguiba, T 220740.

Hospital: *Hôpital Hedi Chaker*, route d'El Aïn, T 244422.

● **Places of worship**
Catholic: 4 rue Dag Hammarskjold, T 210253, Sat at 1830 and Sun at 0930.

● **Post & telecommunications**
Area code: 04.

Post Office: large building at E end of Ave Habib Bourguiba, T 224722.

● **Shopping**
Markets: Central Market on Ave Habib Bourguiba; Fish market Bab Jedid to SW of town;

also route de Gabès/Ave Farhat Hached. Monoprix, 12 rue Abou el Kacem, open daily 0800-1900.

● **Sports**
Fitness centre: Samorail, route Sidi Monsour, nr beach.

● **Tour companies & travel agents**
Bahri Travel Agency, 32 bis Ave Habib Bourguiba, T 228654; *General Voyage*, Ave Hedi Chaker, T 221067; *Mediterranean Travel Agency*, 10 Quatier Commercial, T 224679; *Siwar Voyages*, 26 bis rue Habib Thameur, T 226400; *Tourafrica*, Ave Hedi Chaker, T 229089; *Tunisia Line Service*, 16 rue Habib Maazoun, T 296983; *Univers Tours*, Ave Habib Bourguiba, T 222029.

● **Tourist offices**
The tourist information office is at Place de l'Indépendence, in a little kiosk, T 224606.

● **Useful addresses**
Customs: rue Mongi Bali, T 229184.

Garde National: rue Victor Hugo, T 227688.

Police: rue Victor Hugo T 229710.

● **Transport**
Local Car hire: Avis, rue Tahar Sfar, T 224605; Budget Immeuble Taparura, T 222253; Europacar, 40 rue Tahar Sfar, T 226680; Hertz, 47 Ave Habib Bourguiba, T 228626; Locar, rue Habib Maazoun, T 223738; Mabruk Car, 46 rue Mohammed Ali, T 297064; Rent a Car, rue Habib Maazoun, T 227738; Solvos, rue Remada, T 229882.

Air *Tunis Air*, 4 Ave de l'Armée, opp the Post Office, T 228028, F 299573; *Air France*, rue Taieb Mehiri, T 224847; *Tunisavia*, rue Habib Maazoun, T 222736. The airport, T 241700, is about 6 km SW on the road to Gafsa. Flights to **Tunis**, T 240879/241740, Tues-Thur 0700, Tues-Fri 1920; **Djerba** Thur 1800; **Paris** Thur 1030, Sat 1435.

Train Information on T 221999. Departures for **Tunis** (via Sousse) 0555, 1225, 1325, 1825, 0145; **Gabès** 1128, 0210; **Metlaoui** (via Gafsa) 0143. 2nd class return Sousse TD7 plus 650 mills fee each way. Takes 2 hrs.

Road Bus: services for **Gabès, Djerba, Zarzis, Tataouine, Ben Ghardane** and **Tunis** leave from the bus station on Ave Habib Bourguiba, by the train station. Information on T 22355. All other destinations are served from the bus station at the other end of Ave Habib Bourguiba. **Louages**: leave from Place de la République.

Very fishy

Today in Tunisia the sign of the fish is still a sign of a blessing. Look around now and see delicate pendants of gold and silver fishes in jeweller's windows, fish above shops, dangling fish rather than dangling dice in the taxi, fish-shaped amulets on babies'clothes, fish-shaped biscuits at a feast, fish motifs on mosaics and fish on every menu. After all, the fish was the symbol of early Tunisian Christians. In Sfax the bride and groom still step seven times over a large fish elaborately decorated with ribbons which is afterwards part of the wedding feast. Listen for the blessing *Al hoot aleekum* meaning the blessing of the fish be on you. For a country with 1,600 km of fishy coastline – why not?

Sea Ferry: to the Kerkennah islands in summer (Jul-Aug), departures every 2 hrs 0600-2000. Winter 4 boats/day 0700-1900. Foot passengers TD0.5, motorbikes and cars TD4 and the crossing lasts just over 1 hr. For further information contact Sonatrak, Ave Hedi Khefacha, T 222216.

Sfax to Gabès The outskirts of Sfax on the P1 are very unpleasant, with a huge and dirty phosphate works covering the land between the road and the coast. The Roman ruins of **Thaenae** near present day Thyna are clearly indicated at 10 km out of Sfax. There is a sign at the S end of Thyna pointing to the land between the coast and the road. Follow the track through a small agricultural area to the coast beside the lighthouse.

Thaenae was at the coastal end of the line marking the limit between Numidian and Roman territories. It has suffered from thoughtless pillage and the necropoli on the town's periphery were 'turned over' for profit. Even the mosaic, Orpheus, set aside for protection, was destroyed in WW2. Later excavations produced evidence of a huge square enclosure having a side over 2 km long with semicircular towers. A Baths

was discovered nearer the coast, and it was suggested that the bathing facilities originally of individual ownership had been changed into public use. Mosaics and painted frescoes are recorded.

The Baths of the Months excavated in 1961 had walls several metres high, roofing with groin and barrel vaults. There were some noteworthy mosaics but to cheer the workers a treasure hoard of gold coins was discovered dating back to the 3rd century AD. The better objects were taken to the Bardo and to Sfax Museum where they are on display.

MAHARES

Maharès, 24 km to the S of Sfax, is a linear settlement. The main street (Ave Habib Bourguiba) is a dual carriageway. There are numerous petrol stations (Mobile, Shell, Esso), repairs of cars, tyre repairs, metal-workers, mini-supermarket, chemists, and lovely fresh bread. The new mosque is set back at the S end of town while the older mosque is right on the road.

There is a skeleton of small whale, reconstructed and on display in the sculpture gardens near to the harbour by the fishing boats. There are metal 'fun' sculptures, entertaining and decorative, in the gardens too. Market day is Mon and the carpets for sale in large quantities are laid out along the harbour wall – very colourful.

● **Accommodation** D *Hotel Marzouk*, Ave Habib Bourguiba, T 290261, F 290866, 20 rms, restaurant, nice pool, clean, good restaurant for evening meals, café, snacks all day, pleasant management; D *Hotel Tamaris*, Ave Habib Bourguiba, to S of *Hotel Marzouk*, 60 beds, is very popular with Safari Tour groups; E *Younga*, T 290334, 20 beds.

● **Places to eat** Restaurants *Pizzeria*, *La Sirene* and *Las Rene*.

Sekhira is 42 km N of Gabès. Linear settlement, some new housing on the coast side with lovely views. This is a major junction with a flyover, hence good cafés both sides of road dealing with tour coaches, petrol, car repairs, bakers. The agriculture here consists of beans and moderate grazing land. Perhaps there is more money to be made out of selling food and drink to passing lorry drivers.

THE KERKENNAH ISLANDS

ACCESS Daily crossings from Sfax, six in summer, four in winter. Crossings take just over 1 hr. For information contact Sonatrak, Ave Hedi Khefacha, Sfax, T 222216. Most hotels in Sfax have timetables available. In Kerkennah the ferry lands at Sidi Youssef, on the island of Gharbi, about 20 km from the hotel zone. The islands are linked by a Roman causeway. A minibus service is provided and will meet the incoming ferries, though this costs more than the service bus. A bus will go directly to the hotels, so be sure to take the right one! All buses go to Remla. For El Attaya, there are a few buses a day, but they tend to stop early, so check the times. Buses for the ferries leave about an hour before ferry departure time. Times can be checked at the bus station in Remla, beside *Hotel el Jazira*. All other hotels should have this information. Otherwise, rent a bike, particularly as the islands are flat!

There are seven islands in the group with a total area of 15,000 ha made up of 6,000 ha of agriculture, 4,000 ha of palm trees and the rest uncultivated salt flats. The two large inhabited islands, Gharbi to the W and Chergui to the E, lie 20 km from the mainland. They are very beautiful, with wonderful, almost deserted, gently sloping sandy beaches, ideal for small children. The islands are almost flat (maximum altitude 13m) and covered in palm trees and with many lagoons. Historically they have been a place of exile, from Hannibal to Bourguiba. At the moment tourism is just developing with most of the hotels concentrated around the *zone des hôtels* in Sidi Frej, with a few in Remla.

The rest of the island is almost untouched, making it quite easy to 'get away from it all'. A good way to get around is to rent a bicycle from *Hotel Farhat*. Some of the beaches are difficult to get to without transport as the buses only go through the main villages. The inhabitants have the reputation of being the most hospitable in Tunisia. The people live largely off fishing and now tourism. The fishing is indeed an interesting

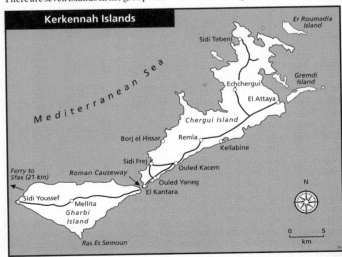

Kerkennah Islands

Mediterranean Sea

Er Roumadia Island

Sidi Tebeni

Echchergui

Gremdi Island

El Attaya

Chergui Island

Borj el Hissar — Remla

Kellabine

Sidi Frej

Ouled Kacem

Ferry to Sfax (21 km) — *Roman Causeway*

Ouled Yaneg

El Kantara

Sidi Youssef — Mellita

Gharbi Island

Ras Es Semoun

N

0   5
km

event to watch as very unusual techniques are used. The traditional technique, known as '*sautade*', resembles a hunt rather than fishing. The fishermen place baskets, made out of reeds and split palm leaves, on the seabed and stand in the shallow waters surrounding the island, hitting the sea with palm tree fronds. The fish (mullet in this case) hide in the baskets and are consequently trapped. This is truly an interesting sight and can be viewed at very close range since many fishermen, for a small fee, will take a passenger with them. It is also possible to rent a *felouka* (traditional fishing boat) with a captain and go either for a day trip round part of the island and probably a quiet lunch out at sea, or for a week and a total tour of the island. Information for these trips at either El Attaya, a small fishing village in the N of the island, or at one of the two larger hotels, the *Grand Hotel* and the *Hotel Farhat*, in Sidi Frej. Sponge fishing is also important. The sponges are kept in ceramic jars called *carour*.

Otherwise activity is restricted to lying on the beach and taking life easy! In Remla it is possible to visit a carpet factory, without the anxiety of sales pressure as here they don't sell, but ship them to the mainland for retail.

Places of interest

Visit the museum in **Résidence du Salud du President Bourguiba** beyond El Attaya on the NE of Chergui. It commemorates Bourguiba's escape by boat into Libya in 1945 and contains the shack he hid in and some photographs. From Remla ½-day island tour TD13 or 'sea picnic' for TD20. The *Festival of the Siren* takes place in Aug.

Local information
● **Accommodation**
Many hotels are closed in winter and those that remain open are often poorly heated.

C *Grand Hotel*, Sidi Frej, T 281266, F 281485, large hotel, 114 rm on 2 floors, half with sea view, a/c dining room, pool, tennis, organized watersports, cycle hire, nightclub, beach restaurant, open all year; **C** *Hotel Farhat*, Sidi Frej, T 281240, F 281237, next to *Grand Hotel*, 308 beds, well decorated, pleasant, pool, tennis, beach virtually non-existent.

E *Hotel Cercina*, Sidi Frej, T 281228, F 281262, very good, beach, 70 beds, half rm have bath, most rooms are bungalows, some have sea view, restaurant has typical Kerkennian fish specialities.

F *Hotel el Jazira*, Remla, T 281058, well kept, small, 24 rm, communal bath/toilet, bar, good restaurant open all year but cold in winter.

Try also the unclassified *Aziz*, 88 beds, T 259405, F 259404; and *Kastil*, 32 beds, T 281212.

Youth hostel: Remla, just behind the stadium, T 281148, 80 beds, meals available, family rm.

Camping: in El Attaya.

● **Places to eat**
◆◆*Restaurant La Sirène* by the bank in Remla, very good fish and seafood, alcohol available, shaded terrace.

◆*Le Régal*, El Attaya, N of Remla, by the harbour, very good simple, cheap food, welcoming owner. Try the special Kerkennah sauce of tomato and garlic which is excellent on shellfish.

● **Bank & money changers**
UIB is in centre of Remla, beside *Hotel el Jazira*.

● **Hospital & medical services**
Chemist: *Behiri* in centre of Remla, T 281074.
Hospital: Remla, T 281119.

● **Post & telecommunications**
Area code: 04.

Post Office: T 281000, Centre of Remla. There are a few other branches, the closest to the hotel zone being in Ouled Kacem.

● **Shopping**
Best buys are olive oil and saffron.

● **Sports**
All watersports incl windsurfing and octopus fishing, horse and camel riding and tennis.

Harbour: El Attaya has berths for 10 yachts, min-max draft 3-4m.

● **Useful addresses**
Police: in Remla and El Attaya, T 281053. Maritime police, Mellita, T 223615.

● **Transport**
Sea Ferry: office on Ave Hedi Khefacha, T 223615, frequent ferries summer 0600-2000 about every 2 hrs and winter 0700-1700

4 return journeys. Car TD3.5, passengers TD0.5, motorbike TD1.

SFAX TO EL DJEM

This road, a journey of 64 km, goes through an area devoted almost exclusively to agriculture. The small settlements providing ample petrol stations, local cafés and the occasional baker and small shop. **El Hencha** is an exception, a larger linear settlement with a small industrial zone, bricks, cement as well as the usual metalwork and car repair outfits. There are more cafés, one or two of better quality and small stores. The prosperity is signalled by the construction of a new mosque. The station is 2 km to the W. Any slight elevation along the route gives a good view to the W over the distinctive Sahel – huge expanse, thousands and thousands of olive trees and to the E the salt flats which go on to the coast.

EL DJEM (EL JEM)

ACCESS The train station on main Tunis-Sousse-Sfax line is 10 mins E of the amphitheatre and the bus station is by the museum, 500m from the amphitheatre. In summer the buses are full and it is difficult to find a place. The louages terminate in a street by the station.

This is a small town of around 10,000 people in the middle of a plain full of olive trees that would be of little interest if it were not for its imposing Roman amphitheatre, one of the most surprising sights in Tunisia. The sheer bulk is breathtaking. Here this largest of all Roman monuments in Africa attracts several hundreds of thousands of visitors each year to admire its grandeur. It really is a superb monument, and the sheer size of the ochre stone walls rising above the ordinary dwellings is an experience not to be missed.

The entrance to the town from the E

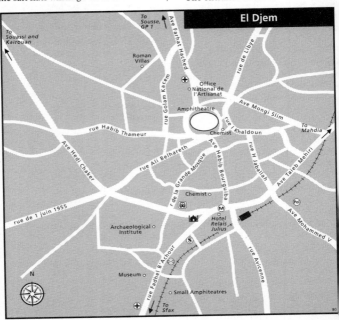

El Djem

Carnage under the sun – Thumbs up for the great amphitheatre of El Djem

A good guide to the level of the 'Romanity' of a city was the presence of an amphitheatre. These great buildings for public entertainment existed right across the Roman Empire. The amphitheatre of Thysdrus in the sleepy modern town of El Djem was, after the Colosseum in Rome and the amphitheatre in Capua, the largest in the Empire.

It is difficult to see where the Roman practice of public slaughter came from. The Greeks were certainly too refined for such practices. Yet the populace of the Empire developed a taste for the *munera*, the bloody spectacles provided as bounty by the magistrates or as a tribute to the deceased. Pliny in his *Natural History* tells the tale of the origin of the amphitheatre. In 53 BC, in Italy, a candidate for the tribune's office, in search of votes, devised a new electioneering technique. Two semi-circular wooden theatres were set up back to back, mounted on a swivel. Thus two plays could be put on at the same time. But the gimmick was revealed in the afternoon, when the two theatres were swung round on their pivots to form a circle where a *munus* or gladiatorial show was held.

Under Augustus the *munus* became an important (and sinister) way for rulers to interact with those they ruled. The primitive wooden structures gave way to magnificent stone buildings and the word *amphitheatrum* was coined to describe these settings for various brutish 'sports' depicted in gory graphic detail in the mosaic floors of the ancient Thysdritan home. In addition to the *hoplomachia* or gladiatorial fights there were re-enactments of various myths (Pasiphae and the bull, amongst others) and in the later Empire, the followers of Christianity, then viewed as a dangerous sect with secret ceremonies, were a particular target. Blood spilling on to the ground and disguising of Christian martyrs as initiates of Caelestis would transform torture into sacrifice. *Damnatio ad bestias* (being condemned to the beasts), however, was reserved for common criminals and certain prisoners of war. The huge resources devoted to the shipping of rare beasts to Rome for slaughter is testimony to the importance of the amphitheatre shows and also evidence of the wealth of the Empire and the extent to which this wealth could be squandered.

The inhabitants of the province of Africa, to go by the evidence of the mosaics, preferred *venationes* or the exhibition and 'hunting' of big cats and other wild beasts. (See the tiger attacking two wild asses in the El Djem museum.) For a long time it was thought that mock sea battles were a feature of Thysdritan entertainment but unfortunately archaeology has laid this particular myth firmly to rest.

Today's visitor to Thysdrus can clamber up into the highest parts of the seating and look down into the arena just as the Roman spectator would have done. Mercifully the slaughter of people and beasts is no longer considered great entertainment and little disturbs the quiet of the great building apart from the clicking of camera shutters and cooing of pigeons nesting in the crumbling stonework.

Entertainment in the amphitheatre from a mosaic from Korba

is graced by three columns, part of the great heritage and on the other side of the road is a workshop which produces mosaics. Does nothing change?

History

The ancient town of **Thysdrus** was probably founded by the Punics, but it was only under the Romans, in particular the rule of Hadrian (117-138), that the town prospered. Hadrian encouraged the continued cultivation of olive trees and the town became an important centre for the manufacture and export of olive oil. By the 3rd century the town reached its peak, as the ruins of luxurious villas testify. The population was over 30,000. In addition to the owners of the villas there was a large rural population. But, due to political rivalries within the Empire, El Djem's fortunes gradually decreased, and were finally brought to an end during the Arab invasion, when the olive groves were set on fire, definitively ending El Djem's commercial prosperity.

Places of interest

Thysdrus covered an area of between 150 ha and 200 ha, the size of the remaining monuments gives a clear indication of the size of the original city. The huge **Amphitheatre**, 148m long by 122m wide, has a perimeter of over 425m. The long axis of the arena is 65m and the shorter axis 39m. The tiers rose to more than 35m providing seating for a capacity of 45,000 spectators. It was the third largest amphitheatre in the Roman Empire and the most famous and best preserved in Africa. Lack of inscriptions prevents accurate dating but construction, which is attributed to Emperor Gordien I who owned land and property in the area, began in the 2nd century between 230 and 238 AD and when one considers that the nearest quarries were over 30 km away the task must have been enormous. It was never completed due to lack of funds and political instability. The stone was too soft for fine sculpture – hence the simplicity of the decoration. The theatre was used for some of the spectacular shows so dear to the heart of Emperor Gordien – wild beasts fighting to the death, martyrs or prisoners being thrown to the wild animals, good family viewing. Some of the scenes were recorded in the mosaics found here.

It was used throughout the centuries as a fortress or stronghold. The legend of the underground tunnels leading from El Djem to the sea refer back to Kahena, a Berber princess who rebelled against Islam and used the amphitheatre as a fortress. She is said to have waved wriggling fish at the troops surrounding her stronghold, taunting them with her freedom of movement. In 1695, Mohammed Bey ordered a hole to be made in the amphitheatre's walls to prevent its use during any further uprisings by the local population who protested about his heavy taxation. The breach in the walls was further enlarged in 1850 during another revolt about taxes. The theatre was thereafter used as a convenient supply of building stones by the inhabitants of the town. Nevertheless much of the original building remains and is very well preserved; it is a truly impressive sight. Open daily from dawn till dusk.

Mosaic: five medallions containing fish and the figure five, the symbol of brotherhood and mutual help (El Djem Museum)

Entrance TD2. Photography permit TD1 includes visit to museum.

There are two smaller amphitheatres more or less superimposed. These are just a short distance to the S of the main amphitheatre and can be found on the other side of the road to Sfax. The older one from the 1st century, a very primitive fort, was simply cut into the rock and the second one, which was to last until the building of the large amphitheatre was erected against the hillside on top of the remains of the first. Behind the museum, about 250m to the W of the small amphitheatre, there is a group of villas bounded by a Roman necropolis to the S and a well preserved, paved, street to the E. The houses are of the classic Roman style with a garden surrounded by a peristyle with richly decorated rooms. Mosaics dating from the 3rd century when their production at El Djem was at its prime included medallions with *Xenia* motifs representing animals, fish, fruit, flowers; Dionysaic themes (one dwelling being known as the House of the Dionysaic Procession) and a lovely illustration of the Minerva judging the musical contest between Apollo and Marsyas (see box, page 87).

Some 30 **Roman villas** have been excavated here, all of which indicate a considerable wealth. The dwellings, built round an inner courtyard and surrounded by a colonnaded gallery, were paved with colourful mosaics depicting mythological themes.

Mosaics from the earlier excavations of these villas, described as 'the most beautiful' are now displayed in the Bardo National Museum in Tunis (see page 85), in Sousse and in the local museum in el Djem. In the more recently discovered villas the mosaics have been left in situ. The baths, covering a surface area of over 2,000 sq m revealed some fine mosaics too.

There are more pleasures to come, but not yet. Aerial photographs indicate the existence of another huge amphitheatre measuring 165m by 33m and a circus measuring 550m by 95m and estimated to hold 30,000 spectators.

The **Archaeological Museum**, clearly signed, is 500m from the amphitheatre on the road to Sfax, set in a replica of a Roman villa. It is very interesting, with magnificent mosaics. In the main room is the famous mosaic *'Orpheus and the animals'* while, particularly notable in the end room, are two mosaics, *'Lions devouring a wild boar'* and next to it *'Tiger attacking two wild asses'*. These were found in a villa which once stood beside the museum. Open 0700-1900 in summer and 0730-1730 in winter, entrance included with ticket to amphitheatre. Clean toilets here and at the site.

The **International Music Festival** takes place each year 15 Jul-7 Aug in the Amphitheatre. The first took place in 1986 and this important cultural event of symphony concerts, in its magnificent setting, is attracting a greater and greater following. During the interval, when hundreds of candles are lit, the atmosphere of ancient history and present splendour is impossible to describe.

Mosaics at El Djem

The proprietors of the museum in El Djem are very proud of their mosaic collection and wish to draw to the public's

Urania, the muse of astronomy with her astral disc

attention three exhibits of special merit which reflect the richness of the mosaics of Thysdrus and the material and cultural wealth of the 'upper middle class' of that Roman town.

The first is from a large drawing room of a very luxurious villa which measures some 33.5 sq m. There is a wide border of geometric and vegetable patterns. Set in a rich background of garlands and floral motifs are nine medallions, set three by three, each depicting one of the Nine Muses (see box, page 121). Each figure is a delight and such young and graceful figures would have been an attractive decoration for any public room. In the first row is Thalia (muse of comedy) with her mask and *pedum* (cross-shaped stick). The second row has Melpomene (muse of tragedy) and Terpsichore (muse of dance) with her lyre and plectrum. Our attention is also drawn to Urania (muse of astronomy) in the third row represented with an astral disc and astrologist's rod.

The second mosaic of merit comes from another large villa of which only one wing has so far been excavated. This is smaller (only 12 sq m). The centre is a hexagon, bordered by half hexagons and half circles. The central medallion is the bust of an old bearded man. The six circles contain the Sun (Apollo), the Moon (Artemis) and the four seasons, Spring in green, Summer in red, bare breasted and vine draped Autumn and darkly cloaked Winter.

There is a strange assortment of smaller characters included here well worth searching out – grasshopper, frog, rat, lizard. On the artistic level the plant imagery with its attention to detail makes this a very special item.

The third ornamental pavement came from the same house as the second, another Dionysian scene. The border is acanthus tufts where tiny creatures lurk. Look for the grasshoppers, frogs, rats, snails and lizards as in previous mosaic. The entire pavement is trellised with vines which emerge from the four corners and in which tiny birds, animals and cupids reside. Great play is made of the ladder-carrying cupid. Don't miss him. The central medallion is unusual three small children, urged on by a naked woman, are tying up a bald, bearded and pot-bellied man with floral garlands. He is Silenus, Bacchus's father who despite his love of drink and his unflattering figure, is not to be underestimated. Details from Sousse Tourist Office (no office in El Djem).

Local information
● **Accommodation**

C *Hotel Club el Ksar*, 5 km from El Djem on route de Sousse, 35 rm, bar, restaurant, 3 pools nearing completion.

E *Relais Julius*, off the main square by train station and nr bus stop, T 03 690044, simple clean, cheap, 15 double rm with bath round the courtyard, restaurant, ask for a room with a view of the amphitheatre.

● **Places to eat**

The cafés in front of the amphitheatre are expensive, prices reduce with distance from site. Café Bacchus (no alcohol despite name) opp site, distinctive blue and white décor, shaded terrace, good coffee, mint tea, basic toilet. A meal at ◆◆*Relais Julius* is better value for money.

Mosaic of a young woman, symbol of Spring.

● **Shopping**
Supermarket: on Ave Habib Bourguiba. Market day Mon, opp train station.

● **Transport**
Train Departures for **Tunis** (via Sousse) 0701, 1323, 1425, 1915, 0252; **Sfax** 1014, 1604, 1712, 2033, 0018; **Gabès** (via Sfax) 1014, 0018; **Gafsa** and **Metlaoui**, 1014.

Road Bus: the bus station is by the museum. Frequent buses run to **Sfax**, **Sousse**, **Gabès** and **Tunis**. **Louages**: by the train station, 5 mins E of the amphitheatre.

Not on the menu today - Thrush from a mosaic in a dining room at El Djem

The Djerid

THE CHOTT EL DJERID gives its name to this low-lying region of salt lakes stretching from the Algerian border to the sea. Most of the oases lie on its perimeter. The Chott covers approximately 5,000 sq km, twice the size of Luxembourg and is mainly dry lake covered with a crust of salt. It is an impressive sight, especially from the P16 which links Tozeur and Kebili where mirages are frequent. The area has more on offer, however, than just the Chott. The oases, situated on the very edge of the desert to the west and east, are magnificent. Nefta and Douz, the doorways to the Sahara, are easily accessible and have a distinctive charm. The whole area abounds with fascinating landscapes and oasis villages and time should be spent here in order to explore thoroughly. In summer the temperatures reach 45°C and moving around becomes a slower and less comfortable process. The best periods to visit are spring and Nov when temperatures are more agreeable, the dates are being harvested and many festivals are held.

GAFSA

ACCESS The train station is 3 km E of town in the new suburb of Gafsa Gare. Buses and louages terminate in the main square, in front of *Hotel Gafsa*.

(*Pop* 60,000; *Alt* 313m) Gafsa (Roman Capsa) is the capital of the region, the largest and most important oasis town in the Djerid. It stands at the junction of the P3, P14 and P15, the crossroads between the deep S and the N. This pink-walled town is built in a mixture of styles from both N and S. The large boulevards and modern buildings are reminiscent of the N, while the narrow streets close to the Piscines Romaines have a definite echo of the S.

Gafsa made the headlines in 1980 when a commando troop of 300 exiled Tunisian came from Libya and captured the city. I took the army 3 days to dislodge them. Th reasons behind the seizure of the town remain something of a mystery.

The industrial basis of the town is phosphates and sections near the railway to the SE are to be avoided for that reason. Gafsa sees many tourists but pays attention to them only as a source of income and offers no real welcome. As a gateway to the S Gafsa is best passed through quickly.

Places of interest

The **Piscines Romaines** (Roman baths) are at the end of Ave Habib Bourguiba and consist of two deep rectangular pools which overflow into a *hammam*. Open 0800-1200 and 1500-1900 in summer, 1930-1630 in winter, closed Mon, fee TD1. In the summer, youths jump from their side or from the top of a palm tree into the pools. Fun to watch but they will expect a tip! The surrounding square has recently been carefully redeveloped and has a small café. The tourist information office and the museum are also here.

On the same street is the **kasbah**. From a distance the kasbah looks like a splendid pink fortress. It was built by the Hafsids and work is in progress here to repair/reconstruct and make it into a government building. It ought to be made into a 5 star hotel. Gafsa has plenty of government buildings and not one decent hotel.

The **Museum** of Gafsa, is situated by the pools and next door to the Tourist Office. It has a neat display. In addition to the expected local artefacts there are two absolutely superb mosaics of sporting activities. The better one shows the course of an athletics tournament from start to the award of prizes. Open 0930-1630, closed Mon.

The **oasis** starts just behind it, containing over 100,000 palm trees and numerous citrus trees. Follow the extension of rue Ali Belhaouane into the oasis. This is a pleasant ride/walk with numerous side turnings. The direct road through the oasis emerges at the P3 about 7 km W of town. The main products are oranges and lemons which are better quality than the dates.

Local information
● Accommodation

C *Hotel Jugurtha*, 4 km W of town, in the oasis of Sidi Ahmed Zarroug which is now a built up suburb of Gafsa, T 221467, impressive site, 78 rm, pool, tennis, unfortunate approach via used car/bus dump, still closed for refurbishment, may be upgraded when completed; **C** *Hotel Maamoun*, Ave Taieb Mehiri, T 222740, central, modern, relatively nondescript building, 46 a/c rm, pool, restaurant used by tour companies, indifferent service but all modcons.

D *Hotel Gafsa*, on the main square in town centre, rue Ahmed Snoussi, backing on to louage station, T 224000, F 224747, modern, soulless, a/c.

E *Khalfallah*, rue Mohammed Khadouma, by police station, T 221468, clean, on a noisy road, rather expensive for what is provided; **E** *La Lune*, Ave Taieb Mehiri, T 222212, S out of town on left beyond *Maamoun*; **E** *Hotel Moussa*, Ave de la Liberté, T 223333, clean and cheerful, a little out of town which makes it quieter.

F *Ennour*, Ave du 13 Février 1952, T 220620, very cheap, outside showers; **F** *Hotel de la République*, Ave Ali Belhouane, T 221807, quite new, clean, 20 rm, probably the best of the cheap hotels, named only in Arabic. Other hotels worth trying are **F** *Ali Pasha*, 4 rue Ali Belhaouane, T 220231, which is more than adequate; **F** *El Bechir*, 40 rue Ali Belhaouane, T 223239, reported as cosy; **F** *Tunis*, Ave 2 Mars,

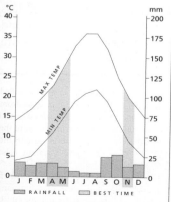

°C / mm chart with MAX TEMP and MIN TEMP curves, months J F M A M J J A S O N D along the bottom.

RAINFALL · BEST TIME

Climate: Gafsa

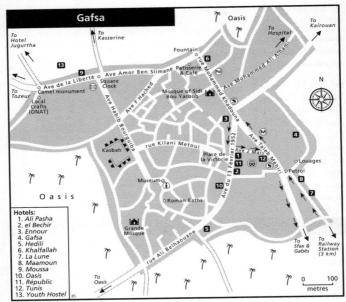

Gafsa

Hotels:
1. *Ali Pasha*
2. *el Bechir*
3. *Ennour*
4. *Gafsa*
5. *Hedili*
6. *Khalfallah*
7. *La Lune*
8. *Maamoun*
9. *Moussa*
10. *Oasis*
11. *Républic*
12. *Tunis*
13. *Youth Hostel*

T 221660, very nr to bus station, perhaps a bit too near; also *Hedili* and *Oasis*.

Youth hostel: 2 km from station, T 220268, kitchen, meals provided, 56 beds, N side of Ave de la Liberté, beyond *Hotel Moussa*.

● **Places to eat**

◆◆*Restaurant Semiramis*, rue Ahmed Senoussi, T 221009, by *Hotel Gafsa*, one of the best places in town for French and Tunisian cooking, a bit expensive.

◆*Restaurant de Carthage* on the main square, good, cheap, typical Tunisian food.

● **Banks & money changers**

BDS is on the main square, under *Hotel Gafsa*; STB nearby.

● **Places of worship**

Catholic: Chez les Soeurs, Quartier Doualy, T 223785, ring for details of services.

● **Post & telecommunications**

Post Office: Ave Habib Bourguiba N of the kasbah.

● **Shopping**

Excellent fruit shops on S side of Ave 2 Mars, fruit

is beautifully arranged, and still better to eat.

Handicrafts: the craft centre is clearly signposted at the N end of Ave Habib Bourguiba. This is a school set up by the ONAT to train people in the art of carpet making. Make a visit to the workshops. The best buys are the striped and geometrically patterned woollen blankets and woollen rugs and shawls.

● **Tourist offices**

The tourist information office is by Piscines Romaines at the end of Ave Habib Bourguiba, T 221644, has limited written information, but very willing to talk, open 0900-1700.

● **Transport**

Train The station is rather inconveniently situated 3 km outside the town in the suburb of Gafsa Gare, along the road to Gabès. One train daily at 2056 goes on to **Tunis** (via Sfax and Sousse) and one to Metlaoui at 0526.

Road Bus: the bus station is by the main square. Information on T 221587. Frequent departures to **Tozeur** and **Nefta**, also buses to **Kairouan**, **Sfax**, **Sousse**, **Gabès** and **Sbeitla**. **Tunis** 0730, 1030, 1230 (TD4). **Louages**: on the main square in front of *Hotel Gafsa*.

EXCURSIONS FROM GAFSA

The routes have been described out of Gafsa, not because it is a good place to stay but because it is at the centre of five important roads.

GAFSA TO SFAX

The road S out of Gafsa crosses the Oued Sidi Aïch and turns NE. The road to Tunis continues in this direction while that to Sfax takes a right turn. Just at this junction is the '*Wild life*' park, very popular in the evening and at weekends. Visitors at other times may find the gates firmly locked. Here gazelle and ostriches roam in enclosures. There is a small café.

The road runs adjacent to the railway for much of the journey. Around Zannouch is a richer area, here there are lots of cereals and some roadside grazing. This is a government settlement area with expanses of plastic greenhouses and wells at intervals for the irrigation. This availability of water encourages plasticulture which is not perhaps the most economic return for such an expensive commodity.

The view is of small settlements as far as the eye can see, not as villages but as individual hamlets. On the less favoured areas the esparto grass appears (see box, page 254).

Senned Gare has grown up round the railway station. Try the station café. The small *oued* which runs through the vil-

---

Mirages – illusions in the desert

👣 A mirage is a type of optical illusion caused by the refraction (bending) of rays of light as they pass through air layers of varying temperatures and densities. The most common mirage occurs in the desert where what appears to be a distant pool of water, perhaps surrounded by palm trees turns out, to the disappointment of the thirsty traveller, to be only another area of dry sand.

The rays of light that come directly to the eye show the palm trees in their correct position. The rays of light that travel through the warmer, less dense air travel faster as they meet less resistance and change their direction. They bend nearer to the ground but are assumed to have come directly to the eye so the brain records the trees and the blue sky as reflections in a pool of water.

The rays are real, just misinterpreted, thus a mirage can be photographed but that does not, alas, make the shimmering 'water' available to quench the thirst.

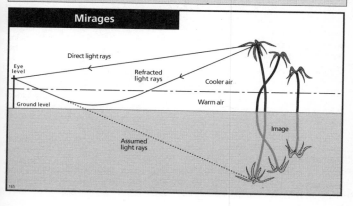

Mirages

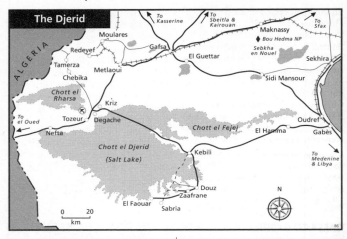

The Djerid

lage is dammed for small-scale irrigation. Djebel Majoura, 874m, stands to the N. Old Senned is a Berber village about 10 km S of here along the track to the W of the station. It nestles into the N. slope of Djebel Biada (1,163m) into which are cut many caves. Some of the houses make use of caves and are semi-troglodyte in nature. At about 3 km E of Senned Gare where change of governorate is indicated look out for railway lines which are raised well above the level of the road. These could cost a tyre or two.

At slightly greater altitudes, where the soil is thinner and less fertile there is no cultivation. This is an amazing contrast to the abundant green of the cereals. Then down to another fertile basin and the regular arrangement of olive groves. New olive orchards have been planted, as yet these are too young to produce a harvest. The almond trees have been left at the boundaries and by the road bringing a bright touch of colour in the early spring. There are a few small settlements on the road – don't run short of petrol – few buses and few louages.

Maknassy, 80 km from Gafsa, is the first settlement of size. The main street, Ave Habib Bourguiba, is dual carriageway and the main square is Place des Martyrs complete with blue square-faced clock, chemist, post office and petrol. There is a bus station with an unpleasant café and at the E end a training school for those employed in tourism. The C83, of good quality road, goes N from here to Sidi Bouzid, and a track suitable only for walkers or mountain bikes goes S round Djebel Bou Hedma to Bou Hedma National Park though this is better accessed from Gafsa via the C124 (see page 268).

Bou Hedma National Park is an area of pre-desert steppe, where Dorcas gazelles, Addax antelopes and ostriches have been reintroduced. Permission must be gained before entry from the Ministry of Agriculture. Really determined visitors to this National Park will have this arranged in Tunis and have suitable transport available.

The road climbs out of the basin on to the edge of Djebel Bou Hedma and down to the next basin of olive cultivation and almonds. The road is straight and level, the pointed summit of Djebel

En Nedjilet a feature on the right. At Mezzouna, 93 km to Sfax, the C89 to the S cuts down to Gabès and N to Sidi Bouzid. There is a railway station and all facilities – but not an exciting place to stay. Note the road indicated from Maknassy to Bir Ali Ben Khelifa avoiding Mazzouna and going through el Ghriss is not recommended. From here it is 31 km to Bir Ali Ben Khalifat then a straight run E through typical Sahelian scenery to Sfax a further 42 km.

● **Accommodation** **C** *Bir Ali Ben Khalifat* hotel and café, very popular at lunch times, good choice of food, pizza, cakes, tea, coffee, juices, also a restaurant, clean toilets, welcoming staff, hotel has 8 pleasant rm, not quiet as this is right on the busy road.

GAFSA TO GABES

This journey along the P15 is 146 km. First recommended stop is the oasis of **Lalla** clearly signposted to E of road just 5 km out of Gafsa. Turn left after crossing the railway track. It is very pleasant here after the bustle of Gafsa, a thriving oasis community and very popular at weekends when the small cafés are busy. Much quieter and more typical is **Lares**. At 18 km from Gafsa turn off S on a good surfaced road. After 4 km is Lares, no tourists here, a delightful mixture of palm, olives, figs, almond trees, and prickly pear hedges. This is a splendid example of an oasis garden. The road through the oasis rejoins the main road after 5-6 km. The C124 goes off E at **El Guettar**, taking advantage of lower land between the Djebel Orbata and the Djebel Ank and is a road of variable quality which gives access to Djebel Bou Hedma National Park – 63 km. 37 km out of Gafsa there is a turning S to Kebili across the Chott el Fedjadj. It is wise to check this road is open after the winter rains, some parts are very low-lying. For details of Sfax see page 255.

El Guettar is a small settlement of about 15,000 inhabitants on the foothills of the Djebel Orbata, 1,165m. It owes its existence, and evidence shows there has been a settlement here some thousands of years, to the unusual (for Tunisia) system of water supply to the oasis. The water source was within rock layers in the foothills and was lead by gravity to the fields of the oasis. At one time 28 *khattara* were recorded providing between 5-6 litres of water per second and this supply was shared between the fields on a 6 hourly basis. Unfortunately these do not function today though in places remnants of the shafts to the underground channel can be distinguished (see box, page 357).

GAFSA TO KASSERINE

Given the choice do this route from N to S, Kasserine to Gafsa, this way the *djebel* in the far S acts as a backdrop and gives a distance and a perspective to the view.

In Gafsa, at the junction with the square-faced clock, take the road N to Kasserine. At Barroucka, on the left, set well back off the road, is a huge ornate mosque. The road runs alongside the Oued el Kebir, with open plain used as grazing land on the E and Djebel Bou Ramli to the SW, reaching a height of 1,128m. The spring flowers are a delight. A number of small settlement, on the road such as Ennadour are encountered.

Colour discrimination – among camels

It takes a little imagination but the connoisseur can distinguish five different colours of camel. The most beautiful and the most expensive is the white and it is said to be the fastest though that may just be to excuse the higher price; the yellow beast is a very popular second; the red animal is solid, dependable and a good baggage animal; the blue is really black but called blue to avoid the evil eye and as such is not high in the popularity stakes, while a camel which is a mixture of white, red and yellow is just another beast of burden.

Water technology of yesteryear

Tunisia, like other North African countries, benefited in the past from the introduction of the *khattara* or *foggara* (or *mkeil* as they are known locally in S Tunisia), which is an underground water channel that taps the water table in alluvial fans of hill areas. The technology was brought probably from as far away as E Iran or W Afghanistan in the mediaeval period, though Roman systems with well-engineered and large diameter channels also exist in Libya. Water can be transported to fields and villages over considerable distances. The *mkeil* in S Tunisia was formed by a narrow diameter inclined channel with 20-30m deep vertical shafts spaced at 15-20m intervals for the removal of detritus during building or maintenance and for ventilation afterwards (see illustration). In the villages in El Guettar, located on Highway 15 between Gabes and Gafsa, the remnants of the *mkeil* can still be seen but sadly not in current use.

The *mkeil* illustrates the virtues of traditional Islamic technology. It has a generally long life cycle. Once it has been completed, it will keep flowing, given adequate maintenance. It will run continuously day and night and, except in a few cases, throughout the four seasons. The *mkeil* needs no power other than that provided by gravity. The *mkeil* is a friendly influence on the water table.

Despite these major advantages, the *mkeil* and its traces, as with so many other kinds of traditional technologies, are now at great risk of complete extinction.

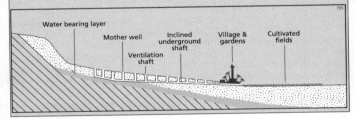

Few offer any facilities for the traveller. At 32 km from Gafsa cross the Oued el Kebir which is very very wide. It is hard to imagine such a valley full of rushing water. The route is an interesting mixture of almond trees, cereals and grazing, sheep rather than goats. The only settlement of any size is Maajen Bel Abbès, which has developed due to its position by the railway station.

The road and rail now run parallel all the way N to Fériana (72 km from Gafsa). Alterations to the centre of this long narrow settlement may make some improvement but it is little to recommend it. All services are available, plenty of petrol and small shops selling basic supplies.

● **Accommodation** F *Hotel Mabrouk*, T 485202 in town centre, directly opp bus station and adjacent to louages.

There are Roman ruins on the W side of the road just S of Thélepte, the ruins and the village have the same name. There is not much to see except ruined walls of dressed stone. Access by walking across to have a look! Thélepte itself has a splendid air of decay. Some of the original bungalows remain, typically French style. The new houses are not up to the same standard. From Fériana to Kasserine there are very few settlements, an expanse of cereal, fruit trees and olive plantations. (For details on Kasserine see page 253.)

GAFSA TO TOZEUR

From the centre of Gafsa at the square-faced clock take road W to Tozeur. A junction to the N hopefully indicates *Hotel Jugartha*. At 7 km from town the road from the oasis joins on the left. The route is pleasant, lined with stands of young eucalyptus trees. After crossing the Oued el Melah (Salty River), the major *oued* of the region, the railway accompanies the road on the right and the *djebel* on the right too gradually closes in until Metlaoui is reached. Once a separate town, but now incorporated into Metlaoui, is Phillippe Thomas named after the discoverer of the phosphate deposits which are mined here. At the approach of Metlaoui, by the railway station, there is a restaurant and a number of small cafés used by tour buses and safari trucks. Metlaoui has a pleasant, busy, tree-lined main street and a smart mosque with a striking bright green dome marks the centre. There is a good provision of necessities, chemists, food stores, many petrol stations, a hospital on the main road, and the National Museum of Mines. The bus station and louages are in the town centre. At the square-face clock is the junction N to Moulares and the station from which the Red Lizard train departs daily at 1100 except Mon. Here too you will find the STB bank, a chemist, the police and *Restaurant Ellafir*. **Accommodation E** *Hotel Ennechim Touristic* is situated to W on road to Moulares. **Transport Train** The station is to the E of the town. One train daily to **Tunis** (via Gafsa and Sfax) at 1915; **Redeyef** at 1555; **Moulares** at 1505.

Once through the town the junction W to the **Seldja Gorges** is clearly signed by the Mobil petrol station. At this junction is *Café Seldja*, busy if the tourist coaches arrive, but clean and good service. The exit road is lined with large eucalyptus trees.

SELDJA GORGES

These amazing gorges with 200m high sandstone cliffs are best seen from the train to Redeyef which departs daily from Metlaoui. This is a tourist train, the Red Lizard, and was once used to transport the Bey. It comes complete with the original furniture and fittings which have seen better days. It does the journey in about 2 hrs and leaves daily at 1100, except Mon, TD10. A fascinating trip, but some days full of tourists, which is only to be expected. Alternatively, take an ordinary train which is advertised to leave at 1500 to Moulares and 1555 to Redeyef. This is much cheaper but less appealing. Both trains return to Metlaoui at 1830. To travel the 5 km W to the Gorges by car, take the track on the S end of Metlaoui going towards Tozeur. At the end of the track there are two tunnels. Walk through into the Gorges. It is best to do this in the morning before the temperature gets too high.

Continuing S to Tozeur, the P3 is a good surface road and a straight road, watch out for the police! This region is still used by the nomads, their black tents and their grazing dromedaries looking incongruous beside the high-tech vehicles constructing a new bridge of the Oued el Melah which is crossed again here.

TOZEUR

ACCESS The airport is 4 km out of town. The bus station on Ave Farhat Hached is used by buses from Tunis, Nefta, Gafsa and Kebili. The louage station is opposite.

The town is famous for its oasis and more particularly its 2 million or so palm trees fed by 200 springs. The oasis is a splendid place to walk, or take a swim in one of the tepid springs. Ras el Aïn is well known, a spring emerging at 30°C at the foot of the cliff, from where the water is diverted for irrigation. The atmosphere is fresh, the vegetation is surprisingly dense and the area is large enough to be able to absorb the crowds. The old town is very beautiful and still untouched. Nevertheless, Tozeur is the well established political and commercial centre of the Djerid and with its new international airport is starting to develop an significant tourist industry. Tourism is still a relative newcomer, but many hotels are being built.

Places of interest

The old town is fascinating. Go down Ave Habib Bourguiba, turn left before the market into Ave Ibn Chabbat. Down this street on the right, follow rue de Kairouan (signposted to the museum) which passes under an arch. This is the oldest part of the town with many archways and intriguing side streets. Some of the houses date back to the 14th century. They are wonderfully decorated with inscriptions from the Koran or with floral and geometric patterns, most of them built out of earthen bricks in an elaborate decorative style particular to this region. Notice that few houses have windows on to the street. They are organized in the traditional style with the rooms set round a central courtyard. The doors are also interesting, decorated with nails and bearing three door knockers. The one on the left is for women, on the right for men and the lowest for children. Each knocker emits a different sound, eg deeper for men, enabling residents to recognize who is at the door.

The small **Museum of Popular Arts and Traditions** in rue de Kairouan is very interesting and clearly displayed, set in the old Mosque (Sidi Aissa). Everyday objects are on view giving a good insight into the daily life of people in Tozeur. The rooms contain such diverse objects as traditional clothes for celebrations, jewellery, oil lamps, cooking implements and weapons. Also on display are manuscripts written by Ibn Chabbat in the 14th century, setting out the complex water distribution system in the oasis. In the courtyard you can see one of the doors with the three knockers. This is a worthwhile visit, due to the simple charm of the museum and its setting. Open 0900-1200 and 1500-1800 in summer, closes 1700 in winter. Closed Mon. Entrance TD1 includes services of a charming guide.

The Oasis is the very reason for the existence of the town. It is beautifully fresh in summer, due to the large number of irrigation canals fed by more than 200 springs. Get there by following the signposts to the 'Jardin du Paradis' or

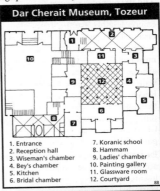

Dar Cheriat Museum, Tozeur

1. Entrance
2. Reception hall
3. Wiseman's chamber
4. Bey's chamber
5. Kitchen
6. Bridal chamber
7. Koranic school
8. Hammam
9. Ladies' chamber
10. Painting gallery
11. Glassware room
12. Courtyard

Who's there?

Doors in the Museum of Popular Arts and Traditions in Tozeur have on display two doors. These are very informative. The door from the rich man's house is made of apricot wood, a lovely colour. On it there are three knockers. The largest with the deepest note is used by a man wishing to gain admittance, the medium knocker has a lighter tone and is used by the women while the lower, small knocker with the lightest tone is used by the children. The door to the house of the poorer man is made of slices of palm tree trunk. On it there are two knockers, a higher one for the women and a lower one for the children. When the man of the house wants to be in – he gives the door a kick and shouts for his wife ...

take the road leading to the Belvédère, on the left after the Tourist Office. If the peace of the oasis is to be appreciated the well advertised tour by *calèche* is to be avoided. Problems with water supply and neglect have resulted in the loss of some of the palm trees. While the people of Tozeur turn to tourism for their income they would do well not to ignore the oasis which attracts the visitors.

The Belvédère is a large cliff by the side of the oasis where many of the springs emerge. Bathing in the hot springs has been recommended. The road to the Belvédère (3 km) goes through one of the most picturesque parts of the oasis. It is a long, but nevertheless very pleasant, walk starting on the left along Ave Abul Kacem Chebbi, beyond the Tourist Office, and following the river. From the top of the Belvédère the view over the Chott and the oasis is most impressive, particularly in the late afternoon.

Le Jardin du Paradis and **Zoo du Désert** are through the oasis (about 3 km), following the well signposted road which starts just before the *Hotel Continental*. It is a superb garden, with amazing trees and plants, particularly impressive in the spring time, and pleasantly fresh in the summer. Try the special, very refreshing drink, reputedly unique to the Jardin, with natural pistachio, banana, violet, rose or pomegranate flavourings. Next to the Jardin is the Desert Zoo with examples of many desert animals and reptiles including snakes and scorpions. A sorry place with many of the animals trapped in minute cages. Not recommended. Open daily from 0700 until dusk. Entrance TD1.

The **Dar Cheraït Museum**, past the Tourist Office, is not easy to find as all the signs are only in Arabic. The best indications are the groups of parked tour coaches just beyond on the left or the tourist-trap shops on the opposite side of the road. This brand new building is located in an imitation bourgeois Tunis house. It is a private endowment, the founder and patron Abderrazak Cherai wished to preserve parts of the past heritage so that they should not be forgotten. He called it a window into the Tunisian civilization. The collection is, as usual, the reconstruction of traditional life in the previous century with rooms set up as kitchens, living rooms and even *hammams*. There are also many exhibits devoted to the life of the Beys and some of their weapons (more works of art than instruments of death), ceremonial clothes, jewellery, furniture including the Bey's bed. An interesting museum, perhaps a little too flashy, but nevertheless an impressive collection of many authentic works of art from recent Tunisian history. Open 0800-2400. Entrance TD3. Photography fee TD1.5, video recorder TD10.

The house was based on the style of a nobleman's establishment with rooms round a spacious central courtyard complete with star-shaped fountain and an L-shaped hallway that opens on to a grand staircase. Grand houses had a number of vestibules, the greater the importance the greater, the number. Suppliers and tradesmen never progressed beyond the first, distant relatives would reach the second but only very close friends and members of the family would reach the last which opened out on to the patio. The patio here is surrounded by four galleries the number originally reserved for royal palaces, lesser mortals having to make do with three or even only two.

Take time to study the architectural decoration. The tiles in the museum are new but designed on old traditional patterns (diagrams of parsley flower, lion's paw or sparrow's wing?). The intricately carved plaster work, as delicate as lace, is reported to require 15 separate tools to complete the designs. This work, perhaps not surprisingly, being called in Arabic *naqch hadida* or iron sculpture.

Details of displays in Dar Cherai Museum:

1. The figures in the entrance hall are positioned as a welcoming party. When the head of the household or important visitors arrived drums and tambourines would be played as greeting and a drink served from the brass trays. Note the ornately carved door.

2. The long reception hall contains interesting tile work and pottery, some of these are copies of tiles dating back to the 18th century come from Testour, an important production centre. There are 4 tiles from Tourbet el Bey, Tunis dating from 1737 (see page 102).

3. The 'wise man' who inhabited this chamber would have been a religious dignitary or a man of law. He has gathered around himself items relating to his occupation – old ink pots, pen holders and parchment and pieces of importance

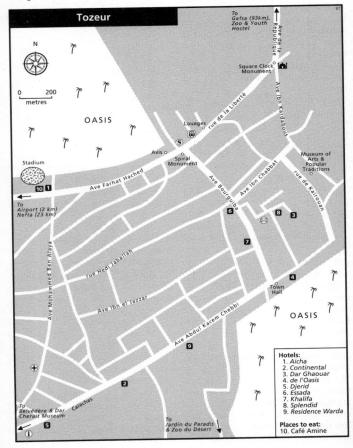

Tozeur

To Gafsa (93km), Zoo & Youth Hostel

Ave de la Republique

Square Clock Monument

Ave Ibn Kardabou

N

0   200
metres

OASIS

rue de la Liberté

Louages

Avis

Spiral Monument

Museum of Arts & Popular Traditions

rue de Kairouan

Stadium

10 1

Ave Farhat Hached

Ave Bourguiba

Ave Ibn Chabbat

6   8 3

7

Ave Mohammed Ben Ataya

rue Hedi Jaballah

Ave Ibn el Jazzar

4

Town Hall

OASIS

Ave Abdul Kacem Chebbi

9

To Airport (2 km) Nefta (23 km)

Hotels:
1. Aicha
2. Continental
3. Dar Ghaouar
4. de l'Oasis
5. Djerid
6. Essada
7. Khalifa
8. Splendid
9. Residence Warda

Places to eat:
10. Café Amine

To Belvédère & Dar Cherait Museum

Calèches

2

5

To Jardin du Paradis & Zoo du Désert

such as old Korans. The varied headgear is interesting. Look out for the door knocker in the shape of a lion's head.

4. The bey receives dignitaries in his chamber, an elegant room, with exquisite tapestry embroidered with silver threads. To the left is a mixed collection with Moncef Bey's watch, an opium pipe and a pearl inlaid water pipe. To the right are weapons, elegant silver handled sabres and rifles inlaid with mother-of-pearl.

5. The old-fashioned kitchen, dating back some 25 years, is still found today in many traditional houses. Cooking by wood or charcoal is still common. The red-copper utensils, each with a special role, were made in Kairouan.

6. The bridal chamber has some magnificent displays of expensive jewellery and jewellery boxes of mother-of-pearl and tortoise shell, part of the trousseau. Examine the furniture – octagonal pedestal tables with inlaid mother-of-pearl used to make geometric and floral designs. On these stand a rose water sprinkler and an incense holder.

7. The small Koranic school contains many associated items. It has the pupils' slates complete with a lesson to learn, a prayer mat belonging to the instructor and an ancient tool of punishment used for beating on the soles of the feet – a *falka*.

8. The *hammam* follows the normal design, a steam room, a cool room and a room in which to relax. All the utensils are displayed.

9. Here ladies are being exceedingly industrious, making lace and working embroidery. On the left are examples of their handiwork. The stages in the production of a *chechia* from the knitting of the woollen cap to the final shaping and felting are presented here though this was not a woman's task.

11. The red glass collection comes from a variety of sources. Red glass is expensive to produce as gold powder is amongst its ingredients. Look out for the unusual red Venetian glass chamber pot. Perhaps more use than a blue glass pistol.

In addition to the museum, the Dar Cheriat has a garden, no charge, with palm trees and amazing lighting, exchange, 2 restaurants (one with a floor show), good food and a Moorish café! Try their hot chocolate.

Local information
● **Accommodation**

There are a number of new hotels in the Zone Touristique to the W of the town. They incl: **AL** *Abou Nawas*, T 452700, F 452686; **B** *Basma*, T 452488, F 452799; **B** *Palmyre*, T 451588; **C** *Hotel Oasis*; **C** *Phedre*, T 452698, F 451599; **C** *Ras el Aïn*, T 452003, F 452189.

B *El Hafsi*, on route Touristique, past the Tourist Office, T 452966, F 451577, very pleasant, modern, restaurant, pool, 62 rm, being extended.

C *Hotel Continental*, Ave Abdul Kacem Chebbi, T 450411, conveniently situated adjacent to oasis, 150 rm, slightly rundown, pool, less expensive than l'Oasis; **C** *Hotel de l'Oasis*, on Ave Habib Bourguiba, T 450522, 125 a/c rm, modern, tasteful, pool, garden.

D *Hotel Dar Ghaour*, rue de Kairouan, T 452782, F 452666, beside *Hotel Splendid*, opened 1993; **D** *Hotel El Djerid*, Ave Abdul Kacem Chebbi, T 450488, F 451160, has definitely known better days, pool, 50 rm, clean, slightly over-priced.

E *Hotel Aicha*, rue Farhat Hached, T 450988, F 452873, some rm with bath and a/c; **E** *Hotel Splendid*, opp the Post Office, T 450053, faded charm, requires some attention, clean, most rm with bath, pool, restaurant.

F *Hotel Essada*, Ave Habib Bourguiba, opp the market, T 450097, very simple, noisy, communal bath/toilets, TD1 for a hot shower; **F** *Pension Warda*, off Ave Abdul Kacem Chebbi, just before road to oasis, T 450597, very cheap, simple, very clean rm, very welcoming, dry your laundry on the roof.

Youth hostel: Ave de la République, close to the station, T 450235/450213, 47 beds.

Camping: at Degache, 10 km N of Tozeur on the C106. *Bedouin Camping*, down the track opp the piscine municipale, clean facilities, food available, shady sites. TD5 for 2 people, 1 car and 1 tent – rates pro rata. *Camping les Beaux Rêves* – turn left at Tourist office into the palmery.

● **Places to eat**
Are all on or around Ave Habib Bourguiba.

♦♦*Restaurant Le Petit Prince*, Ave Habib Bourguiba, set in pleasant surroundings, very good, more expensive than the others. *Dar Cherait Restaurant*, in museum complex.

♦*Restaurant de la République*, Ave Habib Bourguiba, similar to *Paradis*, particularly good couscous; *Restaurant du Paradis*, by the *Hotel Essaada*, off Ave Habib Bourguiba, very good, cheap, a few pleasant tables outside, rec; *Restaurant du Soleil*, Ave Abdul Kacem Chebbi, good atmosphere; *Restaurant El Faouiz*, Ave Habib Bourguiba, very good, simple Tunisian food, cheap.

● **Banks & money changers**
STB and BDS on Ave Habib Bourguiba, BNT and BIAT on Ave Farhat Hached. STB has automatic cash dispenser (dinars) for Visa and Mastercard holders.

Entertainment
Hammam: 1 min from *Hotel Essada*.

● **Hospitals & medical services**
Chemists: on Ave Abdul Kacem Chebbi, T 450491; Ave Farhat Hached, T 450370; Ave Habib Bourguiba, T 450153.

Hospital: *Hôpital Régional de Tozeur*, Cité de l'Hôpital, T 450400.

● **Post & telecommunications**
Post Office: on the main square off Ave Habib Bourguiba.

● **Shopping**
Bargains: there are many shops in Tozeur, but it is important to sort out the cheap imitations from the real bargains. Carpets and blankets are a very good buy, but be careful. In season the fresh dates are excellent.

● **Sports**
Hot air ballooning: *Aeroasis Club* offers a trip in a floating balloon every day of the year, weather permitting. Trips last about 2½ hrs and are a very peaceful way to see the Sahara. The club has 3 balloons and can cater for 15-18 people at a time. Time your trip to coincide with the sunrise, early morning or sunset (remembering to incl something warm to wear). Too little or too much wind and extreme heat prevent the programme going ahead, for safety reasons. Expect to pay about TD85 and be as flexible as possible in your arrangements, T 452361.

Sand yachting: on the Chott el Djerid is organized by *Hotel El Jedrid*. The best season is from Nov to May after which it is too hot.

● **Tour companies & travel agents**
Most of these are to be found on Ave Farhat Hached going out towards the airport. From the junction with Ave Habib Bourguiba, they are in order on the right: *Tozeur Voyages*, T 452439, F 451440; *Cartours*, T 450547, F 451077; *Tunis Air* on the right beyond the stadium; then on the left *Meheri Voyages*, T 450387, F 451211; *Passion Voyages*; *Etoile du Sud*, T 451055; *Carthage Tours*, T 541300; *Europ Tours*. In addition there is *Abdelmoula Voyages*, route de Degache, T 451130 and *Voyages Chaabane*, Ave Abdul Kacem Chebbi, T 451011.

● **Tourist offices**
The tourist information office is **ONTT**, Ave Abdul Kacem Chebbi, close to *Hotel Djerid*, T 450503. Organizes camel trips from Tozeur. There is an official price list for all excursions. *Pension Warda* and *Hotel de l'Oasis* offer 4WD tours to Nefta, Tamerza and Seldja Gorge.

● **Useful addresses**
Police: T 450126, 1 km down route de Gafsa.

● **Transport**
Car hire: Avis and Car Tours, 3 Ave Farhat Hached, T 453547; **Europacar**, Ave Abdul Kacem Chebbi, T 450119; **Hertz**, Ave Farhat Hached, T/F 450214.

Air *Tunis Air*, Ave Farhat Hached, T 452127; at the airport, T 450388. The airport is 4 km along the road to Nefta, T 450345. Flights to **Tunis**, Mon, Tues, Thur, Sat and Sun 0615; **Djerba** (TD30), Thur and Sat 0710; **Monastir**, Tues 0710; **Brussels**, Tues 0710; **Lyon**, Thur 0840; **Paris**, Mon 0930 and Fri 1625; **Zurich**, Sat 0710. There are seasonal changes, always check.

Road Bus: frequent buses to **Tunis**, **Nefta**, **Gafsa** and **Kebili**. A few buses a day to **Gabès**, **Kairouan** and the N. Information on T 451557. **Louages**: opp the bus station. Louages have destinations marked only in Arabic, ask for your destination. Be early at the stop and be sharp as Tunisians with less luggage slip quickly into the seats. Six a day to Kebili, none direct to Chebika, go via Redeyef (or hitchhike).

The Talisman

The 'evil eye' is a powerful force in the local societies of North Africa. It is believed that certain people have the power to damage their victims, sometimes inadvertently. Women are thought to be among the most malignant of possessors of the evil eye – a factor associated with the 'impurities' of the menstrual cycle. Even a camera can be considered as an alien agent carrying an evil eye – so only take photographs of country people where they are comfortable with the idea and be exceptionally careful in showing a camera at weddings and above all funerals. Envy too is a component of the evil eye and most conversations where any praise of a person or object is concerned will include an *mashallah* or "what god wills" as protection against the evil spirits that surround human kind. Likely victims of the evil eye are the young, the female and the weak. Vulnerability to it is seen to be worst in marriage, pregnancy and childbirth, so that women in particular must shelter themselves from the evil eye. Uttering the name of Allah is a good defence against the evil eye. Alternatively amulets are used, this practice originating from the wearing of quotations from the Koran written on to strips of cloth which were bound into a leather case which was then strapped to the arm. The amulet developed as a form in its own right, made of beads, pearls, horn or stone brought back from a pilgrimage. Amulets also have the power to heal as well as to protect against the occult.

The Romans too were keen to fend off the effects of the evil eye and incorporated in the mosaics at the threshold of their dwellings 'good' components to fight off the 'evil'. The mosaic from Moknine and now in the museum at Sousse shows the 'good' fish and snake keeping an 'evil' eye in bounds.

For Tunisians particular talismans are the hand of Fatima, the five fingers known as the *khamsa*, and the fish symbol, which is regarded as very effective as a protection for women and new-born infants. Both symbols can be bought as pottery, textile or precious metal.

In contemporary North Africa, medicine, superstition and ornament combine to give a wonderful array of amulets and decorations worn for both everyday and specific use.

EXCURSIONS FROM TOZEUR

TOZEUR AND THE ALGERIAN BORDER OASIS

For those with their own transport this is a splendid day's outing. There are three wonderful oases not to be missed. **NB** It is much better to do this circuit in the anticlockwise direction as described here, to get the best of the views and to drive through the potash first.

Drive N to **Metlaoui** and turn left at the junction with the square-faced clock. The area to the N of town is like a moon-scape with a road through. No one here has heard of protecting the environment. There is no attempt to keep the place tidy, just piles of dark gritty material, huge lorries, and dust. Note, this is a very dangerous area through which to drive, the lorry drivers must be on piece-work and few give consideration to other road travellers. There is also much heavy industrial plant being moved. The road runs adjacent to the conveyor belt for a while, interesting but not scenic. The road winds up slowly to the top of the *djebel*. The Michelin map has a green line on this road to indicate a scenic route – don't you believe it – and the road surface is as dreadful as the surroundings.

At the top, after 16 km of grime, everything changes. Turn left to Moulares going directly W through green grazing land with Djebel Bou Ramli to the N, Djebel Mrata (948m) and Algeria directly ahead. **Moulares** means 'mother of the bride' and a more badly chosen name is hard to find. Moulares is a collection of government buildings, small shops and petrol stations. It is dedicated to phosphates and the railway line goes through the middle of the town carrying wagons of phosphates. There has been some attempt to brighten the environment with a few palm trees but to little effect.

From Moulares to Redeyef is 18 km. There is a bypass round **Redeyef** which

is recommended. It means missing the bus station and the regulation issue square-faced clock but little else.

The journey from Redeyef to Tamerza is along a very attractive piece of road, considering all that has been before. In spring it is a delight. The road surface is quite rough but there is very little traffic. This road crosses many *oueds* and the engineering is erratic. At times the dip down to the *oued* bed is very steep, not something to meet at speed. At Aïn el Ouchika you can get your papers checked here for Algeria, under more normal circumstances. 5 km further on is Midès.

Midès, Mades in classical times, 8 km from Tamerza, is on a good surfaced road as it goes on to Algeria. Take the signed road to the canyons where there are three small cafés. This means being greeted by three small boys each hoping to entice you to their small area of seats, to take you to the canyon, to take you round the old town, to take you to the oasis. The oasis itself, lies to the W, an expanse of palm trees under-planted with pomegranates and vegetables. There are caves cut into the hillside here as in a number of Berber hill villages. The village clings to the mountainside and is surrounded by canyons on three sides, looking as though it is suspended in mid-air. Driving through at sunset is unforgettable.

There is no other road out of Midès so return to the junction and turn right to Tamerza. The road dips down to the Oued el Horchane at an amazingly steep angle – watch the car.

Tamerza named as Ad Turres in classical times and also part of the Limes Tripolitanus fortifications is another beautiful village built along the top of the mountain. The old village has been abandoned after heavy flood damage, apart from the neatly painted white *marabout*, but is worth a visit for the view. In the old village walk down the deserted main street from the highest point, the *kalaa*, to the lowest point around the

The Marabout

The North African landscape is dotted with small white painted buildings scattered about the hillsides, hilltops and cemeteries. These are the burial places of the holy men or marabouts (*marabit* in Arabic). The marabout was a religious teacher who gained credibility by gathering disciples around him and getting acknowledgement as a man of piety and good works. Marabouts were in many cases migrant preachers travelling to and from Mecca or were organisers of sufi schools. Place names of marabout sites are mainly after the names of the holy man interred there usually prefixed by the word 'sidi'. Some sites are very modest, comprising a small raised tomb surrounded by a low wall, all whitewashed. Other marabouts have a higher tomb several metres square topped by a dome (*koubba*). In some instances, marabout tombs are large house-like structures acting as mausoleums and shrines. Most tombs in rural areas can carry stakes bearing flags in green cloth as symbols of the piety of their donors and as a token of continuing protection from the marabout.

In Libya annual processions are made to the marabout shrines for good luck, fertility and protection against the evil spirits. This is particularly the case where the area around is occupied by a tribe claiming descent from the holy man in question.

In the old Tunis medina there are no less than 38 marabout sites. Look particularly for the tomb of Sidi Bou Abdullah in Souq el Sekkajine.

mosque and *marabout*. The extensive oasis with abundant water, produces excellent dates as well as vegetables. The new village in a neat square pattern is of no real interest, but a walk along the river bank, the Oued Sendess, responsible for the damaging floods, is interesting.

Local festivals Each year the *Festival of the Cascades* is held here, from 25-27 Mar. This event of music and action is becoming internationally famous.

● **Accommodation** The area's only hotels are here, **B** *Tamerza Palace*, T/F 453722, just 70 km from the airport at Tozeur, 65 spacious rm, a/c, heating, bath, bar, good restaurant, panoramic views over old village, shaped pool, Moorish café, conference room, tennis, deals with tours for lunchtimes, and safari tours overnight, a lovely place to stay, tasteful architecture so hotel blends with scenery and deserves to be visited for this alone; **D** *L'Hotel des Cascades*, T 445365, 150 beds, outdoor restaurant, pool, beautiful location, excellent views at sunset, rec, more central position, set down to the E to the palmery – follow the signs to the cascades about 100m from the main road, 50 individual bungalows are made out of palm fronds, screened windows indicate the presence of mosquitoes. A cheaper and more pleasant alternative is to rent a tent from the locals at the entrance to the village (TD5 pp) and spend the night in the oasis by the river. This is not an official camping area.

● **Places to eat** ◆◆*Tamerza Palace* for a good choice; ◆down by *Hotel des Cascades*, are a couple of cheap restaurants.

From Tamerza to Chebika the very poor condition of road makes it unsuitable for coaches and requires care. There are splendid views from this elevated position across to the Chott. No service buses up here and no louages in evidence so very little traffic encountered. Between Tamerza and Chebika the waters of the Oued el Horchane actually runs across the road. Stop here and walk back up the stream to the gorge to the waterfall. This avoids the tourist trap but does include some climbing. Above is the source of the river and further, to the left there is a good view across the oasis and the plain.

Chebika, Ad Speculum in classical times and part of the Limes Tripolitanus fortifications, is a small oasis of palms and vegetables in a narrow gorge. It is very beautiful with an amazing landscape. The old, abandoned village appears to be hanging to the rocks while its residents have moved out to the new village. New Chebika is a small village, just a shop and a post office, the mosque does not even have a minaret. There is parking at the top near the waterfall for coaches and cars, a real tourist trap but approaching this way one does not have to clamber up. At the junction where the P16 meets the P3 is restaurant/grill *Oasis*, terrace has good views, food better than average, popular with tour operators.

Hot soups for cold desert nights (2)

M'Hammas (Bean Soup)

250g of bean flour
200g spinach (washed and finely chopped)
100g chickpeas (soaked for at least 12 hrs)
2 large carrots (peeled and cubed)
4 tablespoons of tomato paste diluted in water
2 tablespoons of: finely chopped parsley
                         olive oil
1 tablespoon of chopped celery
small pieces of salt meat if required
salt to taste
2 litres of water

Method

In a thick pan heat the oil, and add all the ingredients except the bean flour and simmer for 15-20 mins. Thicken with the flour stirring to prevent lumps. Serve hot on heated plate.

The road from Tozeur to Nefta is straight with a good surface. Alongside the road 'fields' of new palm trees have been planted. In all these line the road, with some breaks, for more than half the distance. With a little rain and not too much wind this will be a very scenic ride in 10 years time.

NEFTA

ACCESS The bus station is on the N side of the main street, Ave Habib Bourguiba. The louages stop opposite.

Nefta is a small oasis town 23 km W of Tozeur at the edge of the Sahara. The real desert is encountered just along the P3 towards the Algerian border only 36 km away. The oasis in Nefta has about 400,000 palm trees which produce some of the best dates in Tunisia and has the advantage of being visited by fewer tourists than Tozeur. The Corbeille, a wide, deep basin which originally had springs flowing from its sides, must be seen as well as the old town.

Nefta is known as the home of Sufism, an Islamic sect formed by ascetics who were concerned with trying to achieve communion with God by means of spiritual development rather than the study of the Koran. The participants are called *faqirs* or dervishes and only a few ever reach the end of the path, ie unity with God, at which stage they can be called a Sufi. Sufism was rejected by orthodox Islam but became quite popular due to the open-minded view it promoted, and the incorporation of local rites and traditions.

One of the visible peculiarities of Sufism in Tunisia is the importance of saints and their shrines. This partly accounts for the large number of *marabouts* and mosques in the S and in Nefta in particular which has over 125. In many cases, as with the *marabout* of Sidi Bou Ali, they became places of worship. According to legend, Sidi Bou Ali was the creator of Nefta and of Sufism. There are over 120 *marabouts* in Nefta! Every year, 3 days after the *Id el Kebir* (end of Ramadan) a large celebration takes place, attracting people from all over Tunisia. Many activities including music and dance take place in the courtyard of Sidi Bou Ali's *marabout* and in Nefta's main street. It is nevertheless basically a religious festival.

The Romans were here, though no traces remain, and called the settlement Aggasel Nepte.

Places of interest

The **Corbeille** is a large depression situated to the N of Ave Habib Bourguiba and from the ridge surrounding it there is an excellent view over the **oasis** below and towards the Chott el Djerid in the distance to the E. The best view is from the *Café de la Corbeille* which is reached by taking the road N from the Tourist Office or by foot through the old town N of the Place de la République. Walk down into the oasis. Notice the numerous *marabouts* which are particularly beautiful at sunset. Children will want to act as guides but this is not necessary. The Tourist Office provides guides who are both competent and friendly.

The **old part of town** on the W side with its maze of narrow arcades is easily accessible from the Corbeille. It is recorded as having 24 mosques. The old town continues on the other side of the Ave Habib Bourguiba and this is well worth strolling around, particularly as not that many tourists make the effort.

The **Zaouia of Sidi Brahim** (his tomb) is at the head of the Corbeille adjacent to *Café de la Corbeille*. **Sidi Salem's Mosque**, also known as the Great Mosque, is on the ridge above the Corbeille.

The Route Touristique is signed more in hope than in actuality. There are one or two hotels here, overlooking the scrap yard and the rubbish blowing in the wind. Something needs to be done about this area – avoid it. At present the Sahara Palace is closed for refurbishment and the celebrated *Café de la Corbeille* looks unlikely ever to open again.

Local information
● Accommodation

A *Sahara Palace*, just behind the Corbeille, T 457046, 100 a/c rm and 9 suites, large, luxurious, Olympic size pool, disco, well situated overlooking the oasis, closed for refurbishment.

The newest hotels are to the E of the town, on the road towards Algeria. They incl:

C *Caravanserail*, T 457416, F 457344; **C** *Horizon*, T 457088, F 457700; **C** *La Rose*, T 457366, F 457385; **C** *Neptus*, T 457378, F 457447.

D *Hotel Marhala*, T 457027, brand new hotel, pool, restaurant, tasteful decorations.

E *Hotel Les Nomades*, at the entrance to town on the left, T 457052, typical rm with beds on the flr, all rm have bath, original, very welcoming staff, pool, currently being renovated.

F *Hotel El Habib*, well situated in the centre of the old town, signposted, T 457497, clean and very basic, some rm with bath, rooftop restaurant.

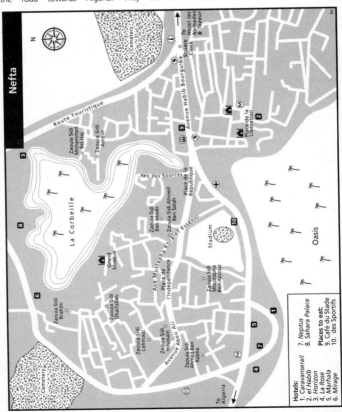

Nefta

Hotels:
1. Caravanserail
2. el Habib
3. Horizon
4. La Rose
5. Marhala
6. Mirage
7. Neptus
8. Sahara Palace

Places to eat:
9. Café du Stade
10. des Sportifs

● **Places to eat**
◆*Restaurant du Sud*, Ave Habib Bourguiba, good, cheap Tunisian food; *Restaurant la Source*, by the Tourist Office on Ave Habib Bourguiba, Tunisian specialities; *Café du Stade*, for local flavour.

● **Banks & money changers**
BDS and UIB on Ave Habib Bourguiba.

● **Hospitals & medical services**
Hospital: Hôpital Local de Nefta, rue des Martyrs, T 457193.

Chemist: on Ave Habib Bourguiba, T 457159.

● **Post & telecommunications**
Post Office: Ave Habib Bourguiba, 150m beyond the Tourist Office.

● **Shopping**
Best buys: Desert Sand Roses, found a few metres under the desert surface, are unusual and attractive objects. They are formed due to evaporation from the mineral barites and are created in beautiful patterns. They make an excellent buy, particularly as they are not well known in Europe. The only problem might be transport as they come in all sizes, the biggest being really big. The market is about 10 km beyond Nefta on the road to Algeria. It is necessary to bargain as prices generally start three or four times higher than the actual value. The market is by the Chott and is very beautiful in the late afternoon or early morning light. You are also less likely to meet a bus load of tourists whose arrival would have the inevitable effect of increasing prices.

● **Tourist offices**
The main tourist information office is on Ave Habib Bourguiba, on the right as you enter the

---

Asses, donkeys and mules

There is a certain amount of confusion when naming the normally overladen and generally undernourished beasts of burden found in the countries of North Africa. While there can be no confusion as to what is a **horse**, *Equus caballus*, or even an **ass**, *Equus asinus*, despite the fact that it is most commonly called a **donkey**, a **mule** requires some definition.

The term **mule** can refer to any hybrid but as a beast of burden it is the offspring of a male donkey (jack) and a female horse (mare), while the offspring of a male horse (stallion) and a female donkey (jenny) is correctly termed a **hinny**.

A mule is a horse in the middle with a donkey at either end. It has longer ears, and a thinner mane and tail than its mother and carries the typical 'cross' markings on the shoulders and back. The hinny is less popular, being nearer the size of a donkey and has the shorter ears and thicker mane and tail of its father.

A mule is stronger than a horse, has a much longer working life under the right circumstances, can withstand extremes of temperature without long-term ill effects, is less vulnerable to sickness and can survive on a very limited diet. Mules are noted for being surefooted and for being fast and accurate kickers. Mules are generally considered to be infertile though instances of offspring are recorded.

The Algerian wild ass originally roamed the Atlas Ranges. The Romans carefully preserved them on mosaics but are held responsible for their demise. The Nubian wild ass, of a distinctive reddish hue, roamed the semi-desert areas between the River Nile and the Red Sea shores. It survived into the 20th century.

The Egyptians used asses. Illustrations from 2500BC show us that even then these domesticated beasts were carrying loads and passengers out of all proportion to their size. They also had mules which are thought to have first been bred around 1750BC. Models of this hybrid were found in the pyramids and a mule drawing a chariot is depicted on a vase found in Thebes.

The Romans placed heavy reliance on the mule, for riding, to draw carts and farm implements and to carry equipment. To assist copulation they devised a wooden cage with a ramp to enable the shorter jackass reach the taller mare.

town, T 457184. It organizes *calèches* and camel rides round the oasis. They also organize excursions into the desert and the dunes. Guides are available. Open daily 0800-1800.

● **Useful addresses**

Police: T 457134, on Ave Habib Bourguiba.

Repairs & fuel: *El Kaoui* and *Chkoba* both on Ave Habib Bourguiba.

● **Transport**

Road Bus: departures to **Tunis** (takes 8 hrs); Sfax; Kairouan; Gafsa; Hazoua and the Algerian border. Buses do not cross the border but taxis do, otherwise you are faced with a 5 km stretch of no-man's land to get to the Algerian border post. From the other side, it is an 80 km stretch to the first town, El Oued, but louages are available. **Louages**: depart frequently to **Tozeur** (takes 20 mins). There is a service to **Hazoua** and the Algerian border.

Excursion Algeria is only 35 km W of Nefta and El Oued another 64 km. An interesting excursion for those with a visa, in more settled times, but not to be considered at present.

Asking the way – who nose

👣 It is considered rude to point so when asked a direction an Arab may well indicate by facing the desired way and tipping up his nose as a pointer. The more the nose is tilted the further the distance to be travelled to the requested destination. This habit is more prevalent in the countryside but not uncommon in the towns. The young lady in the Tourist Information in Tunis indicates the direction in this rather ambiguous manner which makes the finding of a hotel or bus station more of a challenge than necessary. Of course if one is unaware of this custom even the general direction will not be understood.

TOZEUR TO KEBILI AND DOUZ

This is a worthwhile route to follow. It goes via the small oases of Degache and Kriz right through the centre of the massive salt lake, Chott El Djerid. It is a most impressive sight, a single black line of road cutting through the white salt deposits. Mirages and interesting optical illusions are frequent. The Chott begins about 20 km from Tozeur where the road dips down. The W side of the Chott is not so tidy. The amount of debris left by drivers, abandoned vehicles, split tyres and old petrol/oil cans, certainly detracts from the scenery. A number of small palm thatched huts are set up at the side of the road at about the centre point, all with the same facilities, selling sand roses (some dyed garish hues), cups of tea and coffee and providing a primitive toilet a few steps across the salt flat. These are frequented by coach tours.

Where the chott is at its lowest salt is extracted. At each side of a road a channel, about 1m wide, has been dug in the white sand. In winter and spring this is full of water which will evaporate and leave a deposit of salt. Occasionally work with mechanical diggers is in progress lifting this salt.

Souk Lahad 75 km from Tozeur is a small settlement with all services, banks, chemist, two or three cafés of which *Café Salam* by the bus stop and the municipal garden is rec.

These small villages along this route provide opportunities to see small gardens fed by water which drains into this low-lying area. For a salt sea there is a surprising amount of vegetation at the rim. New palm groves have been introduced to the S of the road, the trees are almost mature, between are olives and cereals. In less fertile places the scrub provides grazing land. Just after the Chott el Djerid, at Zaouia, 20 km before Kebili, is **C** *L'Hotel les Dunes*, T 99211, F 99153, 89 rm, built 1991, exchange and boutique, excellent, very well decorated, pool, entertainment includes *mecheoui* under tents with traditional dancing and music! Turn off opposite the petrol station. **Menchia** has cafés for a rest en route. **Telmine** is another compact oasis reached before **Kebili**.

KEBILI

ACCESS The bus station is in the main street (the road to Douz) with buses to Douz, Gabès and Tozeur. The louages station is central.

This is a small regional town of military importance just W of the main road at the E end of the Chott el Djerid. One of the few interesting sights is the hot baths 4 km out of town towards Douz. There are two pools, one for the men and – another further up the stream for women. An early morning bathe is very refreshing.

The old village of Kebili is not to be missed, it is certainly as interesting as

the new one and much more peaceful. Follow the signs more or less opposite the spring-fed pool on the road to Douz and take the track which winds through the oasis. The oasis gardens under the palm trees are well cared for and have a prosperous air. The crops are good quality. The irrigation system is in good order. Yet the houses in the village are deserted and decaying. In places roofs have fallen in and walls collapsed. Only 20-30 years ago it was a busy centre but the people moved into more modern accommodation. The village has no inhabitants but is not deserted. The men come to tend the gardens and pray at the mosque. The blue painted koubba in the village is in good repair. Take this opportunity to walk through the village, examine the houses and obtain an idea of what such a village must have been like.

Local information
● **Accommodation**
C *Fort des Autruches*, signposted off the road

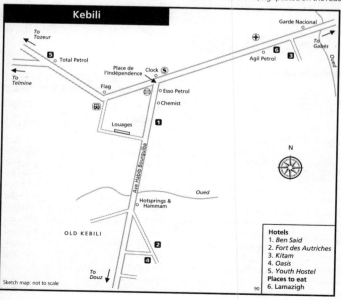

Kebili

To Tozeur

5 Total Petrol

To Telmine

Place de l'Indépendance · Clock Ⓢ

Flag

Garde Nacional

6 · 3

To Gabès

Agil Petrol

Ⓢ Esso Petrol

○ Chemist

Louages

1

Oued

N

Hotsprings & Hammam

OLD KEBILI

2

4

To Douz

Sketch map: not to scale

90

Hotels
1. *Ben Said*
2. *Fort des Autriches*
3. *Kitam*
4. *Oasis*
5. *Youth Hostel*
Places to eat
6. *Lamazigh*

to Douz, T 90233, 96 rm in an old fort, recently renovated, pool, bar on a terrace overlooking the oasis and the Chott, clean, has very large heated pool, views over oasis, can organize rides and tours, a good place as stopover, but in summer it is advisable to book, name for this hotel derived from when ostrich feathers were in fashion and an abortive attempt was made here to breed the birds that produced them; **C** *Hotel Oasis*, Zone Touristique, T 491222, F 491295, 1 km from town centre, has 256 beds in 124 rm, all with bath, good view, telephone with direct line. Reception has change facilities, takes major credit cards, will book you on 4WD excursions, camel treks, car hire, restaurant has 300 places, local and European cuisine, mainly buffet meals, large pool with two different levels joined by a waterfall, conference centre for 300, disco, mini souq, *hammam*, sauna, provision for handicapped visitors.

D *Hotel Kitam*, nr town entrance from Gabès, 32 rm, a/c, telephone, good restaurant, exchange, open all year, 2 pools – small one for children, disco.

F *Ben Said*, Ave Habib Bourguiba, T 491573, on left of road to Douz, nr centre of town and louage stop, clean rm, shared bathroom, highly rec.

Youth hostel: T 490635, 60 beds, bathrooms awful, meals available, catch bus in town centre towards Tozeur to Total petrol station.

● **Shopping**
Museum of Kebili nr spring-fed pool on way to Douz is really a shop selling *kilims* where someone will work a loom as a demonstration but the quality of the produce is not high.

Bazma 4 km S of Kebili on the E side of the road. This has at its centre an old *ksar*, and an old minaret, among the palm trees, both abandoned.

M'Said is 10 km S of Kebili, and a further 5 km from the road to the W. This has the advantage of being on slightly elevated land and completely encircled by a cool and inviting palm oasis. The squat minaret with a small cupola on the top, is in the centre of the new settlement, the old settlement of mud bricks being completely abandoned. There seems to be more birds here and this is certainly a more pleasant place to visit than Bazma.

Djemma 16 km from Kebili, shows a bright face to the passing traveller, the road edges are painted, trees have been planted at intervals along the way and the settlement is just big enough to offer all services. Set back from the road the newly settled areas still have a raw appearance. It is noted for the water in the public fountain which, unlike most water in the area, is not brackish.

El Golaa is really a suburb of Douz, standing to the N. The town centre is marked by a square-faced clock (another!) on brick pillars. The oasis covers a large area and a wide road, running parallel to the C206, takes one along a pleasant ride into Douz, a recommended alternative to the main road.

DOUZ

This really is the gate to the desert, where the oasis meets the sand dunes! Unfortunately the new hotels have not been positioned with consideration for anyone else's view. The village is compactly built with narrow streets in order to protect against the summer heat and keep the sand at bay. The fight against the sand is incessant and women sweep the sand away from the doorstep, only to repeat

The tribes of Nefzaoua

The region is called the **Nefzaoua** region and in it there are five tribes. These are the *Marazik* of the Douz area numbering around 29,000; the *Adara* of the Zafrane region numbering around 5,000; the 7,000 *Sabria* in the region of the same name; the *Grips* of the Faouar region numbering 3,000; and a final 3,000 *Aoulad Yaghoub*. While to the visitor they may seem all alike there are obvious distinctions, clear to themselves and each tribe can be recognized by the clothes, the bags, the tents and domestic objects and, on the women, their head and face coverings.

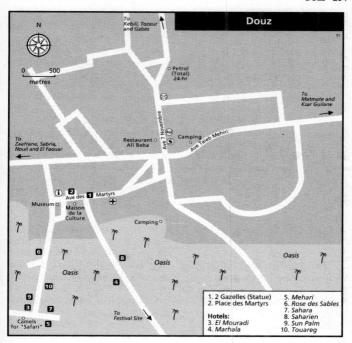

1. 2 Gazelles (Statue)	5. Mehari
2. Place des Martyrs	6. Rose des Sables
	7. Sahara
Hotels:	8. Saharien
3. El Mouradi	9. Sun Palm
4. Marhala	10. Touareg

the process a few hours later. Douz is also the meeting point between the nomads and sedentary population. The citizens of Douz call themselves the M'Razigues. An increasing number of nomads are settling down. By the large hotels lies a small, modern village inhabited mainly by settled nomads. The desert is all around Douz and after a few km out of town the road is hemmed in by dunes. Douz makes a good centre from which to study the oases.

The interesting statues at the road junctions – directions from these are by far the best way of finding one's way about the town – are by a sculptor from Kairouan, Negib Abana. His man on a camel dominates the northern entrance to the town and his two lifelike gazelles are on the road towards the oasis and the Ofra sand dune.

Places of interest

The **Ofra Sand Dune**, one of the largest easily accessible sand dunes. Take the road towards the hotels and park by one of them or, alternatively, hire a camel by the Tourist Office. The official prices are posted in the Tourist Office. Particularly attractive at sunset. Small museum on way to dunes.

Aïd el Idha or the **Feast of the Sheep** is celebrated in Douz 2 months and 10 days after the end of Ramadan. Just before this event it's possible to see more sheep than usual being brought into the villages, men haggling with shepherds about the price of one individual animal, and the occasional lone sheep, tied up in gardens, by houses, on waste ground by apartments, waiting for its inevitable end. The feast is a reminder of the brave gesture made by Abraham to God, the

The Sloughi

These animals originated in the Oued Souf in the S of Algeria but this particular breed of hunting dog has been bred here in Douz from generation to generation. There are only three families with permission to breed these special animals, Mamoun, Gharslah and Ghrirett and it would be unwise to purchase from anyone else. Litters can be as large as 12 puppies but the average is 4 making these creatures quite expensive to produce. They are reared – it is said – on a diet of milks, dates and bread and from this they develop strong, intelligent and speedy animals, able to run as fast as a hare. The active life, as a hunter, after training, is about 9 years. Regular exports of dogs are made, from the registered breeders, to Europe, to Libya and Saudi Arabia and even to the USA where they are in great demand. Prices depend, as on all such animals, on age and pedigree.

sacrifice of his only son. The sheep is slaughtered and the meat is eaten by the family and shared with the poor. A special dish is cooked at this time, for the feast, prepared from the sheep's intestines which can be seen hanging on strings to dry lime washing on a line.

Douz International Festival also known as **Festival du Sahara** is held at the end of the period of celebrations all over the Djerid. It includes special exhibitions of the traditional ways of life. The 'entertainers' include numerous folklore troupes and theatrical groups. Being faithful to the oral tradition the Festival receives a number of popular poets, story tellers, wandering minstrels and artists from all walks of life. At the festival itself the eye-catching displays include the horse races and demonstrations by acrobatic riders, camel races and mock combat on camels, and the ever popular Sloughis, only bred in the Douz region, who pit their speed against hares. In addition there are dancers and jugglers, singers and musicians. One of the highlights is the 'wedding celebration' in all its finery. This is a 3-day festival with a wonderful atmosphere and something for everyone. Merchants are attracted to the area in ever greater numbers and set up their stalls along the route and on the main roads in the villages. There are some fierce contests for position and at times a problem to find a way through

the throng. The time of the festival is a time when the people of Douz invite their friends and families – thus swelling the crowds and the village to bursting point. The Festival takes place every year around the end of Dec. There is also a *Folklore Festival* in Mar. Check exact dates with the Tourist Office. At this popular period be sure to have booked a hotel room.

Museum of the Sahara, only open 'in the season' has displays of local crafts, costume and domestic items.

There is a **market** each Thur attended by many nomads. There is also an animal market which sometimes has camels. Get there early if you want to buy one! Buyers and sellers collect in the designated area off Ave des Martyrs, beside the oasis.

Douz is an important point of departure for many **desert trips**. One of the most interesting is a week's camping trip through the desert to Ksar Guilane by camel. For the less adventurous, trips in 4WD vehicles are a good way of seeing the desert. Remember that in summer the desert gets much too hot for these trips. If interested, contact Agence Abdel Moulah Voyage in Douz, 150m from the Tourist Office, T 495484, F 495366. Camel Trekking is organized by *Douz Voyages*, T 495179 and by *Abdelmoula Voyages*, T 495484, F 495336. Douz to Ksar Guilane (8 days) or Douz to Sabria

(3 days). Price of TD21 per day includes camels and drivers, cooks, blankets, sleeping bags, breakfast, lunch and dinner.

Excursions

South from Douz The road S runs through the small palm gardens, neatly laid out, carefully irrigated, protected from the elements and the blowing sand by palm frond fences. But soon the salt encrusted land appears and small salt lakes. This is not 'the desert' just semi desert but nevertheless very spectacular. Some small lakes provide opportunities for seeing small birds, pied wagtails and sandpipers.

It is interesting to note the way in which the sand dunes have been stabilized to prevent them encroaching on the road. It all looks very attractive. The lines of palm fronds stick out of the top of the dunes, the sand gleams almost white due to the high salt content, the road is a thin black line and the sky an amazing blue. A lovely picture. Young eucalyptus trees line the road as part of this stabilization process.

Zaafrane is accessible by bus, louage or hitchhiking from Douz. Zaafrane really is a village in the desert. The old village has been abandoned and is slowly being covered by the sand. The surrounding landscape of endless dunes and sand with the occasional palm tree is very impressive. New Zaafrane is a linear settlement with the palm gardens to the N. It has a police station, a water tower, a school (the girls wear pink overalls here), two bakeries, a butcher and Taxiphone. The Tourist office is open only in 'the season', unspecified, and is situated by the café and the dromedaries. There are many dromedaries here, already harnessed to take the tourists a very short ride to see the sand. The settlement has increased in size very rapidly as the nomads have been settled. The new village has modest housing. Each property has a square house with a window on each side of the central door

and three half cylinders making up the roof, and store built round a courtyard. All to the same plan, but modified by the individuals. **E** *Hotel Zaafrane*, T 491720, small, cheap hotel, clean and very simple, café. Excursions by camel are available TD25/day, following a circuit around the water holes and eating biscuits cooked in the sand. A superb walk from Zaafrane back to Douz (3-4 hrs) via the sand sea. Navigate using Douz Post Office tower which is visible from the top of the dunes. Real desert environment including animal tracks in the sand. If a storm comes head N to the oasis and back to the road. Carry plenty of liquid and a compass. Sabria between Zaafrane and El Faouar has little to see except more dunes and an old cemetery with two *marabouts*.

Zaafrane to Sabria and El Faouar The land S of Zaafrane is very flat, the bed of a dried lake. Sabria is marked as 3 km S off the C206 but the palm trees are within 1 km. The roads which bends sharply through the palms to the village soon deteriorates into a track. Although the settlement has spread the palm trees have been retained beside the houses, giving a less stark appearance to the settlement. Here the newly settled status is indicated by the retention of the bright tribal dress of the women. It is a most attractive village, chickens in the streets, goats by the houses, women by the well. The houses here follow the same pattern as those in Zaafrane. This is certainly an interesting place to visit.

Approaching El Faouar the flat dried lake bed gives way to small dunes which have been stabilized with palm fronds and planted with mimosa and acacia. Moving sand seems to be a major occupation here. The ever encroaching sand is removed from the roads by means of powered vehicles, in El Faouar a bulldozer is used; men with shovels and donkey carts move sand from the surrounding land, where to and why is

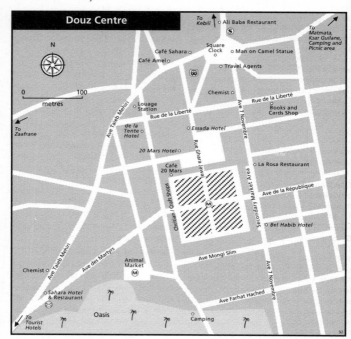

Douz Centre

To Kebili
Ali Baba Restaurant
To Matmata, Ksar Guilane, Camping and Picnic area
Café Sahara
Square Clock
Man on Camel Statue
Café Amel
Travel Agents
N
Chemist
Rue de la Liberté
Books and Cards Shop
0   100
metres
Louage Station
Rue de la Liberté
Ave 7 Novembre
To Zaafrane
de la Tente Hotel
Essada Hotel
20 Mars Hotel
Café 20 Mars
La Rosa Restaurant
Ave de la République
Secondary Market Area
Christian / Craft Shops
Bel Habib Hotel
Ave des Martyrs
Animal Market
Ave Mongi Slim
Chemist
Ave 7 Novembre
Sahara Hotel & Restaurant
Ave Farhat Hached
To Tourist Hotels
Oasis
Camping

not explained; the women sweep the sand from their homes as a repeated regular chore.

El Faouar is also accessible by bus, louage or hitchhiking. This is the last village on the road. Try and see the **market** on Thur when any nomads and locals assemble. It is at its most interesting when dates are in season. Go early in the morning as many goods have disappeared by 1000. El Faouar is surprisingly large and busy. Here we have the police station, a clinic, a large school, in a large palm oasis. The *Café de Tunis* stands at the entrance to the town on the S of the road, the chairs and tables are set up across the street. The central square, from which the buses and louages leave, is marked by the mosque and a square-faced clock. Here stands *Restaurant Salam*. The first bus of the day (good

quality but exceedingly crowded) leaves just about 1000 from El Faouar. **D** *Hotel El Faour*, T 491576, F 224747, international telephones, satellite TV, 106 rm with 300 beds, a/c and heating, comfortable shady lounge area, bar, sand skiing, folklore during dinner under tents, is virtually built in the desert, with pool, restaurant. The hotel organizes 4WD and camel trips (2-3 hrs) in the desert and you can learn dune skiing! The palmery closes round the village to the W. Here beyond the football field the surfaced road ends. Beyond there is a direct route for 4WD vehicles from El Faouar to Kebili (54 km) via Blidet and Touiba.

Local information
● **Accommodation**
There are a number of new hotels now in the Zone Touristique nr the oasis and by the famous

Ofra Dune. These incl: **B** *Iberotel Mehari*, T 495088, F 495589, 127 rm, pool, opened 1989, built to look like a ribat, so plain exterior but inside a fresh and peaceful environment, luxury, all rooms telephone, a/c, heating, 2 pools, one is a thermal pool, sulphurous water to a temperature of 25°C all year round, nightclub, boutiques, conference facilities; **B** *Oasis El Mouradi*, T 470303, F 470905, lovely atmosphere, this is a lovely hotel, used by safari tours but treats people like individuals, 342 beds in 180 rm with a/c, outdoor pool and indoor covered pool with a solarium, *hammam*, sauna, and a fitness centre, conference facilities, well appointed restaurant with a good choice of food.

C *Le Sahara Douz*, T 495246, F 495566, 300 beds, opened in 1990, all with balcony, covered heated pool; **C** *Sun Palm*, (was *Caravanserai*), T 495123, 172 beds, opened 1992; **C** *Touareg*, T 470057, F 470313, 315 beds.

D *Hotel Saharien*, on route Touristique, T 495337, F 495339, accommodation in over 100 bungalows most with bath, very clean, pool, deals almost exclusively with tour groups for lunches and one night stays, limited conference facilities for 200 persons, delightful setting, really is in among the palms, rooms spacious, a/c and heating, hot water, the advertised gourmet refined meals are in reality a no-choice dinner and nothing to choose from for breakfast, call in for a coffee but don't stay here.

E *Hotel Rose du Sable*, route Touristique, T 495484, not quite as nice a position as *Saharien* but cheaper, recently renovated and enlarged, 200 beds in 90 rm, all with bath and a/c and heating, pool, restaurant.

F *Hotel Bel Habib*, in Place des Souq, T 495309, newly opened, clean, very cheap, welcoming owners, communal bath/toilet, large breakfast, interesting views from terrace over fruit and vegetable market. Owner will organize lifts – eg Ksar Guilane in 4WD for TD5; **F** *Hotel de la Tente* next to louage station, dormitories, bath with hot water, sleep on the roof in a bedouin tent for 2TD, manager very kind, rec; **F** *Hotel Splendid* in town has been rec; *Hotel 20 Mars*, in town, unclassified, TD7/night, T 470269.

● **Places to eat**
◆◆◆*Hotel El Mouradi*, very good buffet evening meal in splendid surroundings for TD15.

◆◆*Restaurant Ali Baba*, by the police station to N of town, serves excellent couscous; *Restaurant Petite Price* between the two tourist offices on Place des Martyrs; *Restaurant la Rosa* in the town centre.

◆*El Khods*, 100m from Tourist Office, good simple food, cheap.

● **Post & telecommunications**
Post Office: in the centre of the town.

● **Sports**
Karting: on the dunes for ages 10-90.

● **Tourist offices**
The tourist information office **ONTT**, Place des Martyrs, route de Zaafrane, T 495350, is in the same building as the local tourist office. They are separated by a café. Local office, T 470351, where Mr Amor Boukris has very little information to hand out but everything you want to know in his head. He is most helpful. Open 0830-1400 and 1500-1800 every day. They organize excursions into the desert on camels.

● **Transport**
Road Bus: from the station at the roundabout by the cemetery there are frequent buses to **Kebili**; **Tunis** 0600 (via Kairouan) and 2030 (via Gabès and Sfax); **Gabès** 0700, 1000, 1430; **Tozeur** 0630; **El Faour** (via Zaafrane) 0645, 0800, 0900. The local buses are absolutely jammed – a problem to get on and even worse to get off. **Louages**: are based opp the bus station in the centre of town. Louages to Kebili TD1.5, to Gabès TD6.

Southern Tunisia

THIS IS where the north fringe of the Sahara begins. The architecture and landscape change noticeably as one goes south. There are few sites of historical acclaim but a great many interesting places to visit such as the unusual troglodyte dwellings in Matmata and the beautiful *ksour* of Medenine. The Sahara is the main attraction for visitors who want to see white desert sand dunes and palm tree filled oases, so the number of tourist centres is increasing with alarming speed but the distances are such that it is possible to avoid the crowds.

The coastal area must not be overlooked. In addition to the tourist beaches of Djerba the sea itself contributes to the region's economy. The king prawns found in the region of Gabès are a valuable export, with octopus, squid and cuttlefish important too. There are 12 varieties of tuna fished throughout the year along with the popular red mullet.

The province of Gabès relies on truffles to boost its employment and exports. This strange white fungus which develops underground is in great demand in Europe and the Middle East.

The traditional view of Tunisia as a divided country arose from the French colonial opinion that there was a rich, fertile and well-watered NE around Tunis which was 'utile' (useful) and the rest of Tunisia which was not useful. There is still a lot of truth in this view, which has been reinforced by events since independence. For example, population has increasingly flocked to the NE where one third of the population now live. Investment in modern agriculture and industry has also followed the same pattern. Tourism and petroleum based manufacturing have slightly redressed the balance, though almost all of the

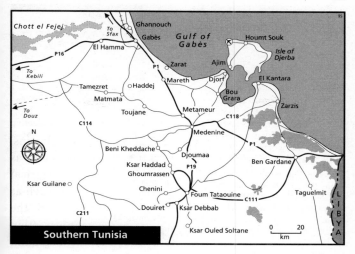

Southern Tunisia

kind of employment has tended to be on the coast, so that the central and S inland areas have been left at best with low-paid primary mining for phosphates or low productivity agriculture.

This is all now in process of change thanks partially to petroleum exploration and much more to tourism and new agricultural ventures. Petroleum exploration is mainly offshore but workers are drawn in from the S with a tolerance for long hot days at work and no qualms about long periods spent away from home. In the last 5 years there has been a strong expansion of tourism in the S. Provision in the S of new and first quality hotels such as the *Tamerza Palace*, the *Dar Cheriat* in Tozeur has made an entirely new extended tourist circuit in the desert for European visitors most of whom would never have found their way to this region. 4WD tourism is getting (perhaps unfortunately) to be big business and a major source of income for the local people. The one-day visitor routines by air have ended and a full one-week itinerary is now the norm in the south-

ern region. Features such as the Red Lizard train at Redeyef in the Djerid have brought a new form of industry to what was a tired backwater.

Less dramatically visible than the convoys of 4WDs, has been a revolution in farming in the S. In addition to the age-old export of dates, the climatic advantages of the S is now being used to grow crops demanded out of season in the prosperous industrialized states of the EU. Recent ventures have seen specialist melon and soft fruit growing for the tables of restaurants in France and there is scope for much more intensive development using new technology and recently found underground water resources. The signature in 1995 of an arrangement with the EU for free trade will further open up this market provided of course the high rewards of tourism do not draw labour away from the land.

Certainly, the S of Tunisia, including the Djerid, can no longer be dismissed as economically irrelevant to the fate of the country as a whole.

Bypassing Gabès

Coming S from Kairouan or Sfax there is a pleasant bypass to the W of Gabès. The turn from the N of Gabès goes towards Oudref to Kebili and the W. About 16 km before Gabès there is a sign right, the turning is alongside the military zone, guard posts with armed guards – definitely not the place to take photographs. You will know you are on the right road if you almost immediately cross the railway. There is a right turn to Oudref (a bit confusing when you know you want to be going S) and then a left turn on to the 208. On the road S ignore the industrial pollution from the cement works to the W of Gabès and note the ruined Ksar up on the hillside to the E of the road instead. In this area too a number of black tents are to be seen. The nomads are not fully settled and these tents are erected adjacent to the grazing herds.

The 208 crosses the main Gabès to Kebili road, take your choice, or go on SE, to meet up with P1 again.

GABES

ACCESS The bus station is on the main street, Ave Farhat Hached, at the W end, after the roundabout, towards the oasis. Walk E to the town centre. Trains from Tunis and the coastal resorts, Gafsa and Metlaoui arrive at the station on Ave 1 Juin, in the centre of town. The louages station is also on Ave Farhat Hached.

(*Pop* 94,000; *Alt* 4m; *Best seasons* spring and autumn) Gabès, 138 km S of Sfax, with its characteristic ochre buildings, is the first town along the route which gives a feel of 'the South'. It extends along the Oued Gabès which feeds the oasis and provides the harbour. The main attraction is the very large oasis which comes right down to the sea.

Gabès is a relatively new city, much of it having been rebuilt after WW2 and the serious flood in 1962. Despite the long beaches and fine sand, the coast is not very appealing. A major industrialization programme in the area over the last 15 years means the sea is probably pol-

Libyan traffic

Libya is currently under UN sanctions arising from the Lockerbie bombing in 1988 and the shooting down of a French airliner over the Sahara in 1989. The sanctions began on 15 April 1992 and were subsequently renewed in 1993, 1994 and 1995, despite last ditch attempts by the Libyan authorities to stave them off. The sanctions include the banning of all civil aviation connections with Libya.

Thus at the present time the only routes into and out of Libya are by sea or land. A principal land route is via Tunisia with travellers going overland in Libya but taking international flights from Djerba or other Tunisian airports. In consequence, there is a strong flow of traffic to and from the Tunisian-Libyan land border at Ras Ajdir. This is in addition to the high level of commercial goods that has always been moved between the two countries at that border crossing.

Visitors to southern Tunisia can spot a Libyan vehicle by the colouring of the number plates. Libyan trucks and taxis carry a yellow number plate, government vehicles red and private cars green. For those who can read Arabic, Libyan private plated vehicles also have their town of origin marked. The number of Libyan cars travelling to Tunisia is limited by shortages of foreign exchange and occasional arbitrary official constraints on movements of Libyan nationals by their government. Libyan drivers are not always versed in international traffic conventions and the conduct of vehicles is often erratic and not within the norms of Tunisian drivers. So, when you see Libyan number plates on vehicles, take double care! Fortunately the density of Libyan vehicles diminishes with distance N.

luted, but it is nevertheless worth a stop to enjoy the coolness of the oasis. Gabès is also an excellent centre for visits to the surrounding villages of Chenini (do not confuse this with village of same name near Tataouine), and Matmata and a good stop over on the way to Kebili, Medenine and Djerba.

History

Thought to be of Phoenician origins, by 161 BC Gabès was part of Carthage, and a trading link with the S. It later came under Roman influence when it was known as Tacapae and was destroyed during the Arab invasion. The rebirth of the town is linked to the arrival of Sidi Boulbaba, the Prophet's companion, in the 7th century. He is now revered as the town's patron saint. Gabès later became a *fondouk*, or halt on the way S. During WW2 the Afrika korps settled in Gabès, using it as a strategic point on their supply lines to Libya, see information on Mareth (page 470). The town was finally liberated in Mar 1943 by British and French troops, but only after extensive damage had been done. Today, apart from traditional industries such as fishing and agriculture based on fruit from the oasis and the 300,000 palm trees, Gabès has become highly industrialized with a massive cement and brick factory, an oil refinery, harbour and projects for petrochemical industries. Oil and gas wells have been drilled offshore in the Gulf of Gabès. Fortunately, though, the industries are dispersed over the surrounding suburbs, making them less conspicuous.

Places of interest

Today no ancient monuments remain in Gabès. Nonetheless, there are traces of the Roman dam across the Oued Gabès, several pillars and capitals that have been incorporated in the mosque of Sidi Idris and in the mausoleum of Sidi Boulbaba. Some other fragments of lesser value have been used in buildings in the older quarters. In the quarter of Jara, which was already fully urbanized at the end of the 11th century BC, are concentrated the mosques of Sidi Idris, Sidi al-Hajj 'Umar and Sidi ben Isa. The building of these mosques has been attributed to a small Arab dynasty called Banu Jami.

The most important building in the quarter of Jara is the **mosque of Sidi Idris**. The old columns bear horse-shoe arches which span the aisles in two directions supporting vaulted ceilings which cover the entire room. There are seven aisles perpendicular to the wall of the *qibla* and five aisles parallel. The room which preceeds the narthex gallery has columns in pairs. There are galleries on the two long sides of the courtyard.

The **mosque of Sidi al-Hajj 'Umar** is smaller and has suffered some alterations over time. The columns, from which arches diverge in two directions, support the six vaulted ceilings which cover the paved terraces.

The **mosque of Sidi ben Isa** is of asymmetrical plan. It seems a later extension on one side has made it unbalanced. There are 4 aisles down the length and 3 aisles across. Here, again, outrepassé arches support the vaulted roof. The central square, opposite the *mihrab*, is covered by a cupola made of tubes of terracotta, and constructed in the traditional ways of the country.

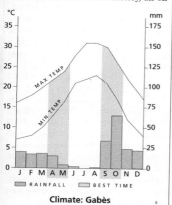

Climate: Gabès

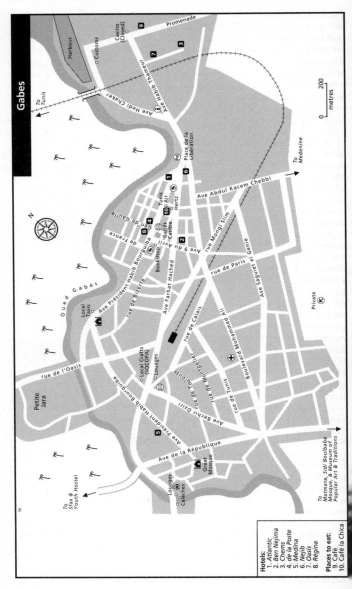

Gabes

To Tunis

Harbour

Customs

Casino (Closed)

Promenade

Oued Gabès

N

0 200 metres

To Medenine

Place de la Libération

Ave Habib Thameur

Ave Hedi Chaker

Ave Abdul Kacem Chebbi

Ave President Habib Bourguiba

Ave 9 du Avril

de France

de Gaulle

Tunis Air

Hertz

Gabès Centre

Bookshop

rue de Bizerte

Local Taxis

Ave Farhat Hached

rue de Paris

rue Mongi Slim

Ave Saguiet el Genie

Boulevard Mohammed Ali

Private

rue de Calais

rue de Toulouse

Local Crafts (SOCOPA)

Louages

rue de Montréal

rue de Tunis

rue Bechir Dziri

Ave President Habib Bourguiba

Ave de la République

Great Mosque

Petite Jara

rue de l'Oasis

To Sfax & Youth Hostel

Louages

Calèches

To Matmata, Sidi Boulbaba Mosque, & Museum of Popular Art & Traditions

Hotels:
1. Atlantic
2. Ben Nejima
3. Chems
4. de la Poste
5. Medina
6. Nejib
7. Oasis
8. Régina

Places to eat:
9. Café
10. Café la Chica

The **Great Mosque** at the junction of Ave de la République and Ave Bechir Dzir was built in 1938 and in itself is of little interest, but the surrounding area has a souq and many shops selling handicrafts made of plaited palm fronds – everything from hats to baskets and mats. Shops also sell jewellery, food and spices, giving the whole market a colourful touch and interesting aroma. Both spices and plaited items are very good buys.

The **Oasis** is very large, covering 10 sq km, and has more than 300,000 palm trees which shelter hundreds of olive and fruit trees in addition to numerous vegetable gardens. To get to the more attractive parts of the oasis you can go by car towards the village of Chenini by taking the main road towards Sfax, turning left in the direction of Kebili, then left again, signposted Chenini. Alternatively go on foot by the other end of the oasis, by the bus station, crossing the little bridge. Following the road it is 7 km to Chenini, but it is not necessary to go that far since there are pleasant walks along the small, shaded paths between the palm trees, especially in summer. A more picturesque way to see the oasis is to take a *calèche* from the end of Ave Farhat Hached. The price from a travel agent is lower. It takes 1¼ hrs to make the whole tour. The price, TD12, for up to 4 people, is set by the Tourist Office which is close to the louage and bus station. These are a tourist trap, strictly for the undiscerning as is the zoo (entrance TD0.5) complete with crocodiles and scorpions. Neither is recommended. At the end of the oasis, towards the source of the river, are located the **Sidi Ali el Bahoul Mausoleum** and a very small, but refreshing, waterfall. The region attracts a very high proportion of tourists but the oasis is large, and it is easy to get away from the crowds.

Mosque Sidi Boulbaba, one of the most important religious monuments in the area, is on the road towards Matmata, down the continuation of Ave de la République. This is the burial Place of Sidi Boulbaba, who was the Prophet's barber after he came from Kairouan. The building is very elegant, with beautiful arcades. Only the inner courtyard is open to visitors. On Fri afternoon the smell of incense is spread around the mausoleum. The portico is crowded by people drinking tea kept hot by small charcoal fires.

The **Museum of Popular Arts and Traditions** is next to the Sidi Boulbaba mosque, set in an old *medersa* which has a simple but appealing architectural style. It was built during the reign of Mohammed Bey. The rooms around the courtyard used to be occupied by the students of the *medersa*. Nowadays, those rooms constitute the main part of the museum which has a collection of everyday objects demonstrating the traditional way of life in Gabès. The material is well displayed but unfortunately there is a disappointing lack of information. An official guide on site will explain them to you – in Arabic. The items exhibited fall into four categories: domestic craftsmanship, marriage, agriculture in the oasis and feeding.

Museum of Popular Arts & Traditions (Gabès)

Displays of:

1. Wool and associated crafts
2. Veils
3. Cushions, blankets, kilims and embroidery
4. Embroidered blouses and embroidered motifs
5. Wedding dresses and finery
6. Agriculture in the Oasis

Fingers of light – or the dates of Tunisia

In Tunisian cities, the feathery foliage of the date palm waves majestically over squares and avenues. In the southern oases of Tunisia, it is the tree of life, its fruit, leaves and wood the basis of the local economy. The Swedish naturalist Carl Linnaeus rendered homage to the beauty and generosity of the palm tree when he classified it in the order of Principes, the order of princes. The Latin name of the date palm, *Phoenix dactylifera*, may be translated as "the Phoenician tree with fruit resembling fingers" and Tunisia's top variety of date, the famed *deglet nour*, are also referred to as *doigts de lumière* for their translucent appearance.

The date palm is a close relation of the grasses. Its trunk is in fact a stem with no branches. It has no bark, being simply covered by the base of the old fallen leaves. A cross section of a palm trunk reveals a multitude of rigid tubes containing sap bearing vessels, rather than the annual growth rings of a true tree.

In the wild state, the young palm tree tends to resemble a hedgehog due to the uncontrolled development of buds at the base of the initial trunk. If severed with skill, these buds can be planted elsewhere. There are both male and female trees. Broadly speaking, a male tree can pollinate some 50 female trees but to ensure maximum fruit production, the farmer will place a sprig of male flowers next to the female flowers.

In Mar or Apr, the tiny green date is round like a marble. Its future is uncertain for if the sand winds are too fierce, it may be blown from the tree before its time. During the summer, the date reaches full size; becoming smooth and yellow, rich in vitamins but bitter to taste. In the heat of the summer and autumn, the fruit slowly matures on the tree, softening and turning an amber colour, deep brown or black, depending on the variety. The date sugars change as well and little by little, the date dries out and becomes a preserved fruit while still on the tree.

For the oasis dwellers, the date is so precious that they have a name for each stage of its growth. The date palm may produce up to 100 kilos of dates annually for a whole century. However, in order to do this, it needs manure and a lot of water, anything up to 300 litres a day!

Each country has its top varieties of date. As well as Deglet Nour, Tunisia produces the Kuwat, a rather dry dessert date, Kentra which is very sweet, the Menakher variety, the date of the beys, the robust Allig and Ftimi, and the Kentichi, a dry date which is stored in pottery jars and does not harden.

The date is no longer a providential food for oasis dwellers. The date palm orchard, now limited to the top producing varieties, has become more fragile. The market economy now regulates the palm grove with all that this implies in terms of processing and packaging. Whereas in the traditional palm grove, apricots, pomegranates, figs and oranges were grown in the shade of the palms, newly planted groves are laid out to permit greater mechanization. Whereas once there were tiny allotments between the irrigation channels, the modern palm grove is devoted to dates alone.

Domestic crafts are typically a female activity and can be split in two branches: weaving and embroidering. Entering the building turn left into the first room. Here different kinds of wool are displayed, together with the spinning, combing and dyeing tools, jars with different vegetable dyes (tannin, henna, etc), a vertical loom and examples of typical headwear called *hambel*, *bett aniya* and *ferrashiya*. In the following showcase are different veils: on the right the white veil typical of Gabès, in the centre the veil decorated for wedding ceremonies at Gabès, on the left the Matmata veil. Other glass cases contain cushions, blankets, kilims and a selection of embroidery. In the following rooms admire the embroidered blouses, mostly white, with decorations on the sleeves. The embroidery is either with crochet needles on tulle. Embroidery motifs are displayed.

Marriage The next room is exactly opposite the main entrance and was the prayer room of the *medersa*. Here the trousseau, traditionally given to the bride by the groom, and the dowry are shown. The trousseau contains fine fabrics, embroidered blouses, trousers, silk cloth, ankle bracelets, earrings, necklaces, tie-pins, threads, mirror, comb, spices and incense. The dowry is composed of fine fabrics, veils, blouses, henna, chains, old silver jewels. In the middle of the rooms three different bridal dresses are displayed; the first to be worn during the ceremony, the second when she was introduced to relatives, the third for the last day of the wedding feast (the seventh day). Over the blouses, in tulle or crochet material, the bride used to wear silver jewels.

Agriculture in the oasis is the last developed part of the museum. Different tools, straw jars to transport foodstuffs, irrigation and cultivation patterns are displayed.

Feeding is divided into food conservation – (jars containing spices), boxes with vegetables and cereals, photographs of 10 different types of dates); food transformation – oil-press, mortar, millstones, jars and pots; food storage – containers, such as leather bottles and straw jars; food preparation – pots and plates.

Leaving the museum turn right into the small garden where, among the fruit trees, you can find Roman and Punic capitals. At the end of the garden it is possible to see the old minaret of the *medersa*. Open daily 0800-1300 and 1600-1900 in summer, 0930-1630 in winter. Closed Mon, entrance TD1.10 plus TD1 photograph fee, flash prohibited, T 281111.

In Gabès there are two ports, the pleasure marina with the harbour in town and the industrial port 6 km away.

Local information
● **Accommodation**

B *Hotel Chems*, end of Ave Habib Thameur first on the right after the railway line, 5-mins walk from the centre, just beyond *Hotel de l'Oasis*, T 270547, F 274485, 1 min to beach, over 200 a/c rm with telephone, most parts tastefully decorated, each with a small terrace, some with sea view, adults' pool, childrens' pool, 500 seat restaurant, open air theatre, covered parking room, sauna, boat hire, live music; **B** *Hotel de l'Oasis*, at the end of Ave Habib Thameur, T 270381, F 273834, first on the right after the railway line, just 5 mins walk from town centre and 1 min from beach, 112 a/c rm with bath, private terrace, telephone, sea view, also 9 luxury apartments, safe car parking, conference facilities for 20-200 persons, good size pool with ample and varied sitting areas by pool and in garden, best and most expensive hotel in town, organizes excursions to S.

D *Chelah Club* (Village de Vacation), in Chenini in the oasis, 20 mins from the beach and 300m from the zoo, T 270442, T/F 227446, clearly signposted, accommodation in 50 small bungalows (damp in winter and spring), ask for hot water as heating runs independently in each bungalow, indoor restaurant only fair, during summer outdoor restaurant under an arbour of vines, pool could be cleaner and not adequate for real swimmers, no credit cards, no money change, from Gabès yellow taxi to Chenini is TD1.2 but TD0.3 if you share; **D** *Hotel Anis*, about 3 km from town on road to Medenine, T 278744, very new; **D** *Hotel Nejib*, corner of Ave Habib Bourguiba and Ave Farhat Hached, T 271686, 56 rm, all modcons, a/c, noisy due to main streets on both sides, slightly over-priced but very comfortable and convenient, showing signs of age; **D** *Régina*, 135 Ave Habib Bourguiba, T 272095, only 14 rm with bath, arranged around central courtyard, clean, restaurant, in summer dinner is served on the patio, best of the cheap hotels.

E *Hotel Atlantic*, 4 Ave Habib Bourguiba, T 220034, old hotel retains some charm but needs decorating, clean, all 64 rm have bath, restaurant, good value, rec; **E** *Hotel Khenini*, Ave Habib Bourguiba, T 270320, 34 rm with bath, breakfast only TD1.5; *Hotel Medina*, nr Great Mosque, T 274271, 40 rm.

F *Ben Nejima*, 68 rue Ali Djemel, nr train station, T 271591, clean, quite pleasant and very simple, hot communal showers, rooms at front rather noisy, good restaurant; **F** *Hotel de la Poste*, 116 Ave Habib Bourguiba, T 270718, very cheap but not really very clean, communal bath and toilets.

Youth hostel: is known as *Sanit el Bey* or *Centre de stage et de vacance*, Rue de l'Oasis, T 270271, F 275035, in quarter called 'Petite Jara' N of the souq, small rooms, 80 beds, 60 beds, clean, TD4/night, breakfast TD1, dinner TD3.

Camping: on main road, follow sign opp Agil petrol station. Cheap and adequate, also at Youth Hostel, TD2 pp, TD1/tent, per car and per van. Palm trees here provide some shade.

● **Places to eat**
♦♦*Restaurant Chez Amori*, 82 Ave Habib Bourguiba, has good, simple Tunisian food, choose the fish before it is cooked, very friendly; *Restaurant l'Oasis*, 15-17 Ave Farhat Hached, T 270098, a very popular restaurant especially for locals at lunch time, evenings are quieter, more expensive than the others; restaurant in *Hotel Chems*, serves international and some Tunisian food, buffet TD11, menu TD7.5; try also restaurant *El Mazar*, Ave Farhat Hached, T 272065; restaurant in *Hotel Ben Nejima* has good, well presented food.

♦*Le Pacha*, Ave Farhat Hached, good, filling food, served by welcoming people; *Restaurant à La Bonne Table*, Ave Habib Bourguiba, good, cheap food; ♦*La Ruche*, on the road to Sfax, T 270369; *El Khalij*, Ave Farhat Hached,

T 221412; *Chez Amori*, 82 Ave Habib Bourguiba, is not quite as good as it used to be, choose the fish before it is cooked.

There are also several very small, very cheap restaurants beside the daily vegetable market off Ave Farhat Hached which serve Tunisian food.

● **Banks & money changers**
BCT, rue Mohammed Ali, T 271203; **BIAT**, Ave Farhat Hached, T 270459; **BNA**, Ave Habib Bourguiba, T 272323; **BS**, 131 Ave Habib Bourguiba, T 271499; **BT**, Ave Habib Bourguiba, T 270093; **UIB**, Ave Habib Bourguiba, T 274881, open 0800-1200 and 1400-1700. On Sat and Sun there is always one bank open at 0930. **STB** has an automatic cash dispenser (dinars) for Visa and Mastercard holders.

● **Entertainment**
Hammam: there are 4 to try, in the souq, on Ave Mohammed Ali, by the *calèche* station and close to the Sidi Idris mosque. Open morning and evening for men, afternoon for women, entrance TD1.

● **Hospitals & medical services**
Chemist: all night, two in Ave Habib Bourguiba.
Hospital: *Hôpital Universitaire*, Cité M'Torech, T 282700; *Clinic Bon Sécour*, 10 rue Mongi Slim, T 277700; *Dialysis Centre*, 112 rue Mongi Slim, T 273200, F 275822.

● **Places of worship**
Catholic: 25 rue d'Alger, T 270326, service Sa at 1830.

● **Post & telecommunications**
Area code: 05.
Post Office: T 270544, Ave Habib Bourguiba opp *Hotel Régina*, change available

● **Shopping**
Bargains: SOCOPA (part of ONAT) on Blvd Farhat Hached in front of post office has range of quality goods. Open 0900-1300 and 1600-1900 in summer; 0830-1230 and 1500 1830 in winter, closed Sun afternoon. Gabès is well known for its straw work which can b bought in the souq or the markets. Also rec the Berber jewellery. Gabès is the last tow where you can buy a European newspape although it will probably be several days ol The daily **vegetable market** gives a goo insight into Tunisian life.

Books: bookshop marked on map, very good selection and very helpful.

Crafts: The ONAT school/workshop on A

Farhat Hached, T 270775, is worth a visit to see all the local handicrafts on display, closed afternoons on Fri and Sat. This is where the various craft techniques are taught. The course lasts 2-3 years for jewellery making, the majority of the young artisans opening their own shops on completing the course. There are courses, too, on palm frond weaving and carpet making and the demonstrations show how these skills are taught.

Food: In the area of the Sidi Boulbaba mosque and the museum, on the corner on the right there is a baker who sells lovely fresh bread and mouthwatering Tunisian sweets. The baker by the tourist information office sells excellent bread with seeds on.

General: the *Gabès Centre* on Ave Habib Bourguiba is only a collection of small and noisy boutiques, not for any serious shopping.

● **Sports**

Harbour: 20 yacht berths min-max draft 2-4.5m, T 270367.

Sponge fishing: also fishing for tuna fish, king shrimps, octopus.

● **Tour companies & travel agents**

Etoile du Sud, Ave Farhat Hached (same office as Express Rent), T 650244, F 651076; *Voyage Najar Chabane*, Ave Farhat Hached, T 272158, F 277555; *Europtours*, 12 Ave Farhat Hached, T 274720; *Sahara Tours*, Ave Farhat Hached, T 270930; *Gabès Voyage*, Ave Farhat Hached, T 270797; *Carthage Tours*, Ave Habib Bourguiba, T 270840.

● **Tourist offices**

The tourist information office is at Place de la Libération, T 220254, open 0830-1300 and 1500-1745, closed Fri, Sat and Sun afternoon.

● **Transport**

Local Car hire: Hire here as there are no facilities in Medenine or Foum Tataouine. **Avis**, rue du 9 Avril, T 270210; **Budget**, 57 Ave Farhat Hached, T 270930; **Europcar**, 12 Ave Farhat Hached, T 274720; **Economic Rent-a-Car**, 159 Ave Farhat Hached, T 257515; **Express**, 154 Ave Farhat Hached, T 274222, F 276211; **Hertz**, 30 rue Ibn el Jazzar, T 270525. **Cycle hire**: enquire at the Youth hostel or at *Hotel de la Poste*.

Air (nearest airport is Sfax 137 km N or Houmt-Souq on Djerba 106 km E) **Tunis Air**, Ave Habib Bourguiba, T 270697; **Tunis Avia**, route de Sfax, T 272501.

Train The train station is off rue Farhat Hached.

Information on T 270744. Departures as follows: **Tunis** (via Sfax and Sousse) 1535, 2310.

Road The bus station is at the end of Ave Farhat Hached, by the entrance to the oasis. Information on T 270008. In Gabès there are 3 bus companies, all in the same place. **Sotregames** (timetable only in Arabic) Tunis via Sfax and Sousse at 0600, 0945, 1230, 1235, 2115, 2200, 2215, 2250 and 2350. Medenine 0600, 0730, 0800, 1000, 1700, 1730. Matmata 1015, 1100, 1200, 1400. Djerba 0930, 1345, 1530; **Entri** Tunis 0600, 0945, 1230, 1235; Sousse 0815, 0915; Djerba 0930, 1345, 1530; Zarzis 1345; El Hamma 1400; Sfax 1500; Foum Tataouine 1615; Ben Gardane 1735. **STE** Foum Tataouine via Medenine 1000; Zarzis via Medenine 1100, 1330; Djerba via Djorf 0945; Ras Ajdir and Libyan border via Medenine and Ben Gardane 1145, 1530. Departures to: **Matmata** (takes 1 hr, TD2); **Ben Gardane**; **Chenini** from the corner of rue de la République and rue Haj Jilani Lahbib; **Djerba**; **Gafsa**; **Kebili**; **Sfax**; **Sousse**; **Tunis**. **Louages**: the louage station is close to the bus station. Sample fares Tunis TD14, takes 6 hrs; Djerba TD5; Sousse TD10; Medenine TD3.5; Tripoli (Libya) TD25. It is possible to get a round trip visiting all the villages and the area surrounding Gabès. Tour operators offer a variety of options, including travel by 4WD vehicle with a group of 5-10 people (see Travel agents).

GABES TO KEBILI

At 4 km N out of Gabès the P16 W to Kebili is clearly signed. This first part is through the pleasant oasis region. At Maqsef where the P208 'Gabès bypass' crosses the route is a government subsidized agricultural estate with surprisingly large grain silos, large areas under plastic, olives and a few date palms. About 5 km before El Hamma on the N side is an area used by coaches and safari tours, **Station Chincou Tourisme**, a good place for a coffee. This is decorated with huge desert roses and is impossible to miss. It is here that the gas pipeline crosses the route and where a number of tracks lead out N across the sebkha.

El Hamma de l'Arad, 32 km W of Gabès, is situated between the salt lake to the N and the foothills of Djebel Tebaga to the S. The Romans called it

Aquae Tacapitane. The hot water in the springs which feed the hot baths is very sulphurous. The road in through the triumphal arch just beyond the *oued*, by the hospital and the grain stores leads past a few villas to the date palm oasis. The road into the oasis turns off N and the dual carriageway, complete with smart double globe lights, goes right through the town. Here you will find plenty of shops (try *Ulysses* for size), tyre and car repairs, 2 pâtisseries, chemist, petrol, calor gas, cafés, 3 banks near the square clock and even the opportunity for photo development. The louages gather near the Shell petrol station while the post office is opposite the road to Matmata.

In El Hamma there are several thermal springs and three *hammams*. Unlike many *hammams* which use the same facilities and divide out the time, here the bathing areas and entrances for men and women are quite separate so no timetable is needed. The *hammams* here differ in condition of the buildings, some less pleasant than others. Hot showers are available in all.

From Place 7 Novembre go towards the banks and turn right. On the left is **Hammam Aïn el Borj**, entrance TD0.12, 4 pools for women and 4 for men. This is probably the most friendly and most colourful *hammam*. At the women's entrance, soaps, panties and bras, combs, shampoo, henna and *suak* (to clean the teeth) are sold.

The *hammam* on the road to Gabès is not clearly signed, though there is a white label with a red arrow and the name of the bath house in Arabic script. Turn right before the hospital into a nameless and dusty road. At the very end there is the **Hammam Esghaier**, entrance TD0.20. This is the cleanest and the most expensive *hammam* in town and also the least crowded, probably because it is a 15-min walk from the centre. The building is well kept, with blue columns and a light blue ceiling. Both the women's and the men's areas are provided with lockers,

one big and one small pool, and a hall with benches for resting before leaving. Unfortunately the toilets are unpleasant. The outdoor thermal pool is a suitable length for swimmers. Parking available. Situated near the souq in a popular area, is **Hammam Abd el Kader**, entrance TD0.12. This is the most crowded *hammam*. There are 2 big pools for women and 1 for men, high ceilings but unpleasant atmosphere and unhygienic toilets.

There have been reports of children being too attentive to tourists and causing problems when their demands for money, biros and even clothing were not met. This is most unusual in the S but perhaps the increase of tourists is the cause.

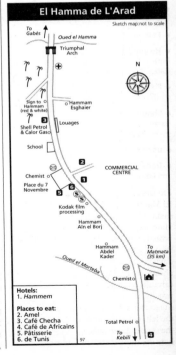

El Hamma de L'Arad

Sketch map:not to scale

To Gabès

Oued el Hamma

Triumphal Arch

N

Sign to Hammam (red & white)

Hammam Esghaier

Shell Petrol & Calor Gas

Louages

School

Chemist

COMMERCIAL CENTRE

Place du 7 Novembre

Kodak film processing

Hammam Aïn el Borj

Hammam Abdel Kader

To Matmata (35 km)

Oued el Morteba

Chemist

Hotels:
1. *Hammem*

Places to eat:
2. Amel
3. Café Checha
4. Café de Africains
5. Pâtisserie
6. de Tunis

Total Petrol

To Kebili

97

● **Accommodation** F *Hotel Hammam*, 80 Ave Habib Bourguiba in front of Banque de Tunisie, 8 rm small and mostly dark, extremely cheap (TD3 without breakfast), is the only hotel in town, management can speak only Arabic and is not very pleasant towards tourists.

● **Places to eat** ♦♦*Restaurant de Tunis*, Ave Habib Bourguiba/Place 7 Novembre nr Bank de Tunisie, couscous with lamb is better than elsewhere, the *gateaux maison* (home made sweets) are actually bought in the nearby pâtisserie, try the *Kairouan gateaux*, the typical biscuit made in Kairouan with dates, semolina and sesame seeds. ♦*Restaurant Amel*, in the commercial centre, has food on display, good chicken kebab, very cheap, no tables. Try also restaurants *Checha* or *Africanes* (at the W end of town). Coffee shops and restaurants are found on both sides of the main street.

● **Banks & money changers** BT and BNA in Ave Habib Bourguiba nr *Restaurant de Tunis*.

● **Entertainment Hammam**: see details below.

● **Festival** of the *hammam* each Mar.

● **Hospital & medical services Chemist**: on Place 7 Novembre. **Hospital**: on the road to Gabès in a very new building, T 234127.

● **Post & telecommunications** Post Office on the right in Place 7 Novembre.

● **Shopping** Commercial centre behind *Hotel Hammam*. The souq has a good selection of spices. **Market day**: Mon.

● **Useful information Police**: T 234141.

● **Transport Road Bus**: to Gabès and Kebili and **Louage** in Ave Habib Bourguiba.

Excursion

El Hamma to Matmata Nouvelle Matmata Nouvelle can be reached from El Hamma via a track (34 km) clearly signposted in the town centre. A normal car will do it in good weather conditions with daylight. At Km 6 crossroad, go straight ahead. In El Magcem, at Km 12, drive carefully as there is a school and children usually try to get a lift. At Km 15, El Magcem ends, there are some houses on the left and a crossroad with a fountain in the centre. Take the road on the left. From here the route is straightforward.

Sembat is just a continuation of El Hamma with the same central reservation with double globed lights. The cheap housing with half cylinder roofs is very obvious here. There is a huge brick works – everywhere around is bright red. In contrast, immediately after the *oued* is the oasis, with good quality soil and adequate water providing good crops, particularly pomegranates. From here to Kebili it is a very long straight road, the Djebel on the S with serrated summits and scrub land, hardly good enough for grazing, as far as the eye can see. Watch out for the white posts with red writing. The sign says 'danger of death' but only in Arabic script. **Don't check. Don't enter.** There are very few small settlements but in this region they are easy to spot by the essential tall water towers.

Keep a watch at 57 km from Kebili for a restaurant on the N side of road, and reward yourself with a coffee. The 'feature' marked on the Michelin map at **Saidane** was a fort, then a hotel and now a police post so no photographs please.

Finally the road turns S and cuts up through the Djebel Tabaga to take you to Kebili (see page 289).

GABES TO MATMATA

ACCESS Ensure the buses from Gabès or the daily bus from Tunis drop you in the original Matmata (which is 15 km down the road), not Matmata Nouvelle. A minibus runs between Matmata Nouvelle and Matmata costing 800 mills. It leaves when it is full.

MATMATA

Matmata is an amazing **troglodyte** village set in the mountains. The scenery round about is like a lunar landscape, with the houses being dug into the ground (see box, page 308). The only visible signs above ground are the TV aerials! There are also many very beautiful *marabouts* scattered over the mountainside. The village is inhabited by 3,500

Downstairs only – the Troglodyte tendency

👣 Underground living has its advantages. Where soft rock permits easy digging out of the initial dwelling and allows later extensions when necessary, the owner of an underground house is better off than one with a building on the surface. In addition, the rock insulates the troglodyte dwelling keeping it even in the hot lands of S Tunisia or the Jabal Nafusa in Libya at a constant 17°C, cool in summer and cozy in winter – no trouble with noisy neighbours either!

The layout of the troglodyte house in North Africa is similar throughout the area, with a large circular depression or *housh* in the rock with its ramp, stairs or tunnel to the surface. Occasionally hillside houses are built laterally into the rock and have stone walls and doorways directly into the *housh*. The *housh* is often in the Matmata area of Tunisia as high as 7m with a diameter of 10-15m and open to the sky. It acts as a central courtyard, with cooking, animal stabling and storage facilities, off which up to seven or eight small rooms, some 2-storey, are cut into the surrounding earth or rock to serve as bedrooms, stores and stables. Large dwellings for an extended family can have several inter-connected courtyards. An example of this is the troglodyte hotel in Matmata (see page 310).

Troglodyte houses are usually impeccably clean and well-appointed with white-washed walls, rock-cut shelves and tiny excavated cupboards. In the Berber troglodyte houses of Techine, close to Matmata, houses are decorated with elaborate clay built furniture, including dressing tables in their bedrooms. Some dwellings have been suitably modernized by the provision of electricity and water supplies.

Although the troglodyte house is associated with the Berber villages of Tunisia (see map, page 64 , Tribal Origins in Tunisia) and Libya and reached its peak of development in the Monts des Ksour around Matmata, in some areas such as Gharyan in Libya (see page 524), troglodyte dwellings were used by Jewish families until as late at 1948.

In 1996 at Boumalne in Morocco a new hotel, Kasbah Tizzarouine, was set up including troglodyte rooms in traditional form. The underground house is thus alive and well !

people, but about half of them leave to work in the N or in Europe at some point in their lives, often setting up as bakers. Some who return, having earned sufficient money, build themselves a 'real' house in Matmata Nouvelle, 15 km down the road to Gabès. A section of the population still live in the underground dwellings, but their number is slowly decreasing. If you want to see the inside of one of the underground houses it isn't really necessary to take a guide, but doing so is one way of obtaining entry. The fee should be negotiated but is generally very reasonable, in the region of TD1-2.

The Berbers, known as the Matmata, have been living in these houses for over 700 years. They originally constructed their homes underground in the soft rock to protect themselves from possible attacks and from the harsh climate. Habits are only now starting to change due to the exodus of the young people who set off to the large cities in the hope of finding work and an easier life.

There is little scope for agriculture in Matmata due to the harsh climate and the lack of water, which explains the tendency to migrate. However there is still some work to be found in the village particularly in the ever-expanding tourist sector, and many locals make their money from the tourists who flock here during the day. Indeed it is worth staying

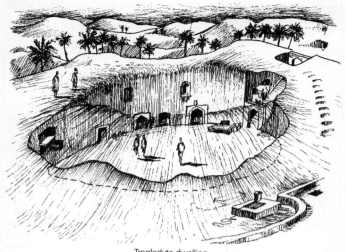

Troglodyte dwelling

overnight in Matmata in order to appreciate the village once the crowds have left and drive out to Zeraoua and Tamezret to see the sunset. Doing so, especially in one of the underground hotels, is quite an experience.

Places of interest

Underground dwellings On arriving in Matmata it is unclear where to go since nothing is visible, but walking around will reveal one of the 700 underground houses. Many of these can be visited in return for a small payment at the end of the tour. Take the opportunity to see the unusual living conditions. Even if you are not planning to spend a night in Matmata, go and visit a hotel, access being free, and see the labyrinth of tunnels leading from one courtyard to another. For further detail, see page 308.

Overlooking the village is a small fort which, unfortunately, cannot be visited since it is in a military zone. The **museum** is in a typical troglodyte house, on the left coming in from Gabès. It is well signed but the opening hours are erratic.

The tour of Matmata is possible by camel. Camels and guides are to the SE of town on the way to Toujane. Don't pay all the fee till you get down or it may cost you more.

Excursions

Matmata Nouvelle, 15 km away, is often ignored but a visit here will help explain the reasons why the villagers moved and give also some insight into the process of settlement of the nomads. By car there is a variety of places to visit. Going SE towards Médenine, take the track which goes via Toujane. This is shorter, but not necessarily quicker, and a very picturesque route (see Toujane, see page 313). If you are travelling to Douz or Kebili or feeling adventurous, take the track to Tamezret. (See Tamezret below.)

Local information

● **Accommodation**

All the water in Matmata has a distinct yellow hue. Accept it as part of the excursion. **C** *Hotel les Troglodytes*, name soon to be changed to *Ksar el Amazigh* because it is not actually underground, T 230062, F 230173, 1 km

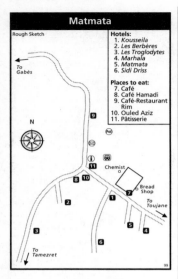

Matmata

Rough Sketch

Hotels:
1. Kousseila
2. Les Berbères
3. Les Troglodytes
4. Marhala
5. Matmata
6. Sidi Driss

Places to eat:
7. Café
8. Café Hamadi
9. Café-Restaurant Rim
10. Ouled Aziz
11. Pâtisserie

To Gabès

N

Pol

Chemist

Bread Shop

To Toujane

To Tamezret

down road to Tamezret on left, pool, clean but unusual shape prevents any real swimming, 50 a/c rm, opened 1993, during the late evening and night water is not very hot, no credit cards, private parking, best and most expensive hotel in the village, lunar landscape, rec; **Hotel Kousseïla**, arriving from Gabès turn right and the hotel is on the left after 100m, T 230303, F 230265, 34 rm, 100 beds, a/c, no pool, no credit cards, very clean, opened 1995.

D **Hotel Matmata**, F 230177, quite small, above ground (so no troglodyte charm), all 32 rm have bath, a/c, comfortable, clean, small pool, restaurant, management offers large discounts to groups of over 10, be warned.

E **Hotel Marhala**, T 230015, slightly out of the village, up the road towards the fort, the best of the 3 underground hotels, very clean, very basic (bed, door without lock, light bulb!), communal bath/toilet, quiet, good traditional restaurant, book in summer, composed of 5 holes around which the rooms are located, neither humid/cold in winter, nor hot in summer, cheap, friendly management, do not miss a night here! Owned by Tunisian Touring Club.

F **Hotel Berbers**, T 230024, F 230097, most recent and smallest underground hotel, communal bath/toilet, restaurant, book in season,

a curious experience, 13 rm, 120 beds (some rooms have 9 beds), the holes in which the hotel is built are less deep than usual and are therefore less impressive, watch your head! F **Hotel Sidi Driss**, T 230005, largest and most touristy, endless corridors and courtyards, communal bath/toilet, bar, restaurant, not very clean, not all the management is fluent in English or French (Arabic only).

● **Places to eat**
For a decent meal it is best to eat in the hotels, open to all visitors, although there are a few restaurants in the market place.

◆◆**Hotel les Troglodytes**, try the warming barley soup (winter only) and as a dessert the nehchi Tataouine, a pancake filled with almonds, sesame seeds and peanuts, lunch TD7.5.

◆**Café Restaurant Ouled Aziz, Chez Abdul**, at the entrance to Matmata in front of post office and tourist office, has good traditional Tunisian food and is quite cheap, here try something different: chicken or lamb tajine and pepperoni filled with rice and vegetables, complete meal (salad, main course, dessert or fruit) is TD5, the manager is an official guide and can give you some (free) information on the area, rec; **Café Hamadi**, nr Chez Abdul, has good cakes but the best sweets can be bought in a small shop nr the pâtisserie; **Café Restaurant Rim**, arriving from Gabès at the beginning of Matmata on the left, T 230023, opened 1996; **Café de la Victoire** has only coffee, tea and soft drinks.

● **Banks & money changers**
Banks are situated in Matmata Nouvelle, 15 km along the road to Gabès.

● **Hospitals & medical services**
Chemist: on the main road in front of bus station.

● **Post & telecommunications**
Post Office: in the centre of town, changes money.

● **Shopping**
Market day: Tues.

● **Tourist offices**
The tourist information office is next to the Post Office.

● **Useful addresses**
Police: on road to Medenine, T 270390.

● Transport

Road Bus: the bus station is located nr the mosque and just in front of the track to El Hamma (buses to Gabès every hour, TD1.1, no buses to Medenine). **Tunis** 2030; **Sousse** 2215; **Gabès** 0530, 0730, 0900, 1100, 1230, 1330, 1400, 1600, 1730, 2000; **Tamezret** 1400. **Louages**: on main road in town centre but very few cars. Matmata to Matmata Nouvelle is TD0.8.

EXCURSIONS FROM MATMATA

EL HADDEJ

This village is located on the road to Gabès. After 6 km N from Matmata turn right where the tourist shop and the **Relais Touristique des Troglodytes** are situated. *Relais* is a restaurant with a circular courtyard and, around it, 10 small dining rooms, T 230129, prices from TD4 to TD6. Better to book as in low season

they do not cook every day, suitable for groups. After the *Relais* the paved road ends. The track is narrow, full of curves and has many ups and downs. The landscape is beautiful and the best time to arrive here is in late afternoon to see the sunset. Access is difficult without your own transport. Takes 1 hr to walk. El Haddej is made up of several cave dwellings hidden in the ground which resembles a lunar landscape riddled with giant holes. It is similar to Matmata but less involved with tourism so it is possible to see what Matmata must have been like before the tourist influx. Nonetheless, guides are easy to find. There are three main things to see: the oil-press, the marriage cave and the typical troglodyte house. Bargain and arrange the tour price in advance.

Going around in El Haddej may seem

Surrounding area of Matmata

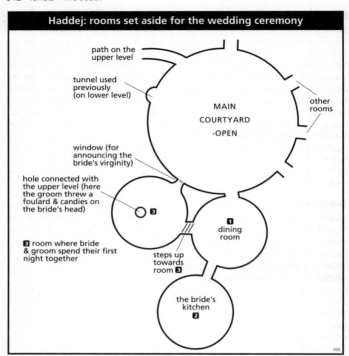

Haddej: rooms set aside for the wedding ceremony

path on the upper level

tunnel used previously (on lower level)

MAIN COURTYARD -OPEN

other rooms

window (for announcing the bride's virginity)

hole connected with the upper level (here the groom threw a foulard & candies on the bride's head)

3 room where bride & groom spend their first night together

3

1 dining room

steps up towards room **3**

the bride's kitchen **2**

100

familiar as the American film producer Steven Spielberg used this landscape to great effect in his famous films *Star Wars* and *Raiders of the Lost Ark*.

The **oil-press** is made of a huge stone trough and an enormous mill wheel once turned by a camel.

The **marriage cave** is a troglodyte dwelling only for wedding ceremonies. Around the courtyard are several rooms. One of them was the bridal kitchen, where the food for the guests of the marriage ceremony was prepared. Another was the wedding room, where the bride and the groom consummated their marriage. In this room there was a hole in the ceiling connected to the upper surface. Through this hole the groom threw a foulard and some candies. The bride waited here, sitting below the hole in the wedding room and if the foulard and the candies touched her, it was considered good luck. In the wedding room there was a window from where the groom shot his rifle signifying the bride was a virgin. The rifle fire meant that the wedding feast could start and that dinner could be served to the guests waiting in the courtyard. Watch your head when you enter the rooms.

The **troglodyte house** In Haddej almost all troglodyte houses are inhabited. Tourists are allowed to enter a house only with a guide. Part of the money the guide receives will be given to the family visited. Do not be surprised: since 1995 electricity is available in Haddej and radio is quite widespread in the village.

BENI AISSA

From the centre of Matmata drive W towards Tamezret. Measure the journey. After 1 km turn right towards El Hamma. After another 500m you pass on the left a troglodyte dwelling. After a few hundred metres the road condition becomes very poor and there is, unfortunately, a lot of litter here. At 6 km, at the crossroad, turn left and on both sides are troglodyte houses almost hidden (of course) and still inhabited, although their owners might be with their sheep and goats. At Km 7 on the right there are two *marabouts*. The track ends here.

TAMEZRET

This beautiful Berber village lies 13 km W of Matmata. The road here from Matmata is black top and amazingly good but very narrow. The scenery is quite extraordinary, a mixture of the moon and the Grand Canyon if the telephone and electricity supply lines are ignored. Troglodyte houses can be seen at Km 3 and Km 4½ on the left, and, if you look down, at Km 6½ on the right. At the crossroad (left to Zaraoua and Douz) go straight towards Tamezret. After a few metres on the right there is a *marabout*. The road is now through some lovely scenery, magnificent views but drive carefully as it is dangerous. The village is built on the side of a mountain. The houses built of dried earth blend in perfectly with the scenery. Stroll around the narrow, winding streets and walk up to the top of the village from where there is a marvellous view across the desert, particularly at sunset.

TAOUJOUT

From Tamezret drive to Taoujout (3½ km), which is worth a visit, perhaps even more than Tamezret because it is still unspoilt by tourism. It is a Berber hill-top village. For a normal car there is no way to go further from Taoujout. With a 4WD or a motorcycle it might be possible to drive from Taoujout to Beni Aïssa.

OLD ZERAOUA

Only 16 km NW of Matmata, and just 6 km off the road at Tamezret is Old Zeraoua, an abandoned Berber village. The inhabitants have moved to new Zeraoua. Feel free to wander through the streets and look into the houses which have survived better than those at, for example, Tamerza as they are stone constructions. Many have vaulted roofs and it is possible to climb the outside stone stairs for a view over the region.

TECHINE

To the S of Matmata is Techine, another troglodyte settlement. It is noted for the 'fixed' furniture in the dwellings, made of clay or clay covered wood which is painted white. They look to be delicate pieces, but replacement is not a problem.

TOUJANE

No buses go along this road but it is possible to get a lift. It is a very worthwhile trip either by car or by mountain bike. The track is not very easy (be sure to have a good spare tyre) but a normal car could do it. From the centre of Matmata take the paved road E towards Toujane. After 1 km on the right see the military fort and on the left admire the panoramic view over the plain below. On a clear day it is possible to the Djerba! Photographs are not allowed here, as this is all military area. Enjoy the trees, the birds of prey, and the ground squirrels. At Km 5 on the right a *marabout* and, at Km 7 on the right again, some troglodyte houses. At Km 8 are crossroads (right to Techine and Beni Kheddache) go straight ahead in the eucalyptus woods. The track here is in very good condition. At Km 10 more crossroads (right to Zriba, Techine and Beni Kheddache), go straight on here and also at the next crossroads (left to Beni Zelten and Mzata). Keep an eye on the track as its condition gets worse and worse, and look down on the right at the small lakes (during spring) or at the *oued* (during winter and autumn). The landscape is gorgeous. At Km 14 on the right a troglodyte house. At Km 20 you will be on the edge of the mountain. Park on the left (there is a parking space) and admire the shadows and light over the flat mountains. At Km 24 crossroad (right to Cheguine) turn left and start the descent to Toujane which will suddenly appear, apparently clinging to the mountain side. It is a beautiful village on an exceptional site. Wander around and look at the carpets and the *kilims*, small smooth woven carpets with traditional designs originally used as prayer mats and in tents. They are all made locally and are cheaper here than in the main towns. Purchases can be made at Chez Laroussi on the road.

At the end of the village, after Chez Laroussi, on the left is the *Relais Mohammed Esnani*, kilims, *semen* (cooked butter used on couscous), honey and tea herbs are sold here, drinks, coffee and tea are available too, unpleasant toilet.

AIN TOUNINE

Aïn Tounine is a small village N of Toujane. It can be reached from the centre of Toujane a distance of about 6 km.

Toujane to Beni Kheddache (33 km) After the café in Toujane take the C104 towards Medenine. After 7 km is Dkhelet Toujane. This is not an interesting place but has *Café du 7 Novembre* on the left and a post office on the right. After 5 km a track goes N to Mareth (66 km), the main road (unsurfaced) goes on to Medenine (25 km) so turn right to El Hallouf and Beni Kheddache (see page 318). The track is good at the beginning but soon deteriorates. There are some herders' huts, magnificent views and plenty of holes in the road. It is an interesting ride, quite an adventure.

Jouant a la Kherbga or playing draughts Tunisian style

This popular game requires no board or manufactured counters. Everything required is readily available. A small pile of earth, sand or roadside dust is scraped together with the foot and patted flat with the hand. Seven rows of seven holes are impressed into the surface and the playing area is ready. Pieces used in the game are small pebbles, date stones or dried dates, all to hand.

The aim of the game is to eliminate systematically the pieces of the other player in a style similar to our draughts. Although this is a 'game for two' everyone around takes part with well-meaning advice or noisy criticism about the mode of play.

The game can be set up so that the players and spectators can also watch the activities in the village street while the shepherds set up their games in a position from which they can watch over their flocks.

MATMATA TO DOUZ VIA THE DESERT TRACK

This journey can be done in a car which does not have 4WD (but don't tell the hire agency your plans!!!). It is an exciting experience and 60 km shorter than the route via El Hamma-Kebili, although not necessarily faster. Don't forget to take water and do not travel after rain as the vehicle will sink. (See Travel and Survival in the desert, page 43.) Take the black top road to Tamezret and follow the track W. Turn left at the junction after the pipeline, and about 2½ km further is the small *Café Djelili* where the food is excellent. Another 10 km will bring you to the *Café Sahara Centre* offering food, accommodation and selling 'Arab' headgear to tourists. Here you can sleep out in the open under an incredible star-studded sky. The road from here on is more or less a straight 43 km to Douz.

Camels – ships of the desert

There are two kinds of camel, *Camelus Dromedarius*, the Arabian camel with one hump and *Camelus Bactrianus*, the Bactrian which has two. Arabian camels, found in North Africa, though only as domestic animals, are about 3m long and about 2m high at the shoulder. They range in colour from white to black.

They are not the most attractive of creatures, looking particularly ragged and scruffy at the spring moult. Large bare leathery areas on legs and chest look like some serious skin complaint but are normal and act as cushions when the animal kneels down.

Interesting physical characteristics which allow these animals to survive in the desert include hairs inside the ear opening as well as the ability to close the nostrils between breaths, both preventing sand penetration; thick eyebrows to shade the eyes from the sun's glare; a pad of skin between the two large toes on each foot forming a broad, tough 'slipper' which spreads the animal's weight over a larger area and prevents sinking in the loose sand; the ability to store a reserve of fat in the hump and to go for days without water. Each eye has three eyelids, the upper and lower lids have very long eyelashes to protect the eyes from sand whipped up by desert winds, while a third, thinner lid blinks away dust from the eyeball. The skin inside a camel's mouth is so tough that cactus thorns do not penetrate, hence a camel can eat anything, 'even its owner's tent'.

Camels can go for many days without food as the hump can store up to 35 kilos of fat as emergency rations. They can go without water for even longer, depending on the weather and the kind of food available. As camels do not sweat but instead function at a higher body temperature without brain damage, their demands of fluid are less. At a water hole they drink only enough to balance their body moisture content.

Less pleasant characteristics include a most unpredictable nature, especially in the mating season, which includes nasty habits like using its long sharp teeth to bite people and other camels, viciously kicking with the back legs, spitting and being generally awkward. When a camel stands up it moves in a series of violent jerks as it straightens first its hind legs then its front legs. When a camel walks, it moves both the legs at one side at the same time, giving a very rolling motion which can give the rider travel sickness.

Camels are unwilling beasts of burden, grunting and groaning as they are loaded and generally complaining at being made to lie down or stand up. Once underway though, they move without further protest.

These large, strong beasts are used to pull ploughs, turn water wheels and carry

large loads for long distances across difficult terrain. They can carry up to 400 kg but usually the load is nearer 200 kg. Despite moving at a mere 6 or 7 km an hour, camels can travel 100 km in a day. They also provide their owners with hair for cloth, rich milk and cheese, dried dung fuel and eventually meat, bones for utensils and hides for shoes, bags and tenting and live for up to 20 years.

The Arabian dromedary, bred for riding and racing, is of a slighter build but can cover 160 km in a day and reach speeds of up to 15 km per hour.

MEDENINE AND SOUTH TO FOUM TATAOUINE

MEDENINE

ACCESS The bus station is on rue du 18 Janvier and the louages stop in a small street opposite.

This is an important crossroads town. However it holds little interest for the visitor, having been extensively modernized with few traces of its past remaining. Medenine is at the centre of the **ksour** area. A *ksar* (plural *ksour*) is a fortified village built in a characteristic style with curved, whitewashed houses and the typical *ghorfas* (granaries). Originally the villages were not fortified, but with

the Arab invasion and other dangers the Berbers were obliged to build defences. The *ksour* were generally built on the top of a hill, in an easily defensible position, out of dried earth which blends in with the colour of the landscape. Medenine is a good place for the start of excursions towards Metameur and the surrounding area where some *ksour* have been better preserved than in Medenine. This region is a frontier between two cultures, the nomads and the settled people. Once the area was totally controlled by nomads but today the tents have been replaced by small concrete houses and the camel by a Peugeot truck.

Increasing tourism has made some

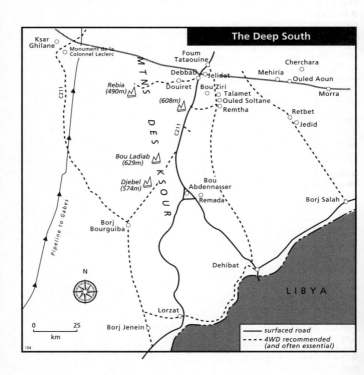

The Deep South

surfaced road
--- 4WD recommended
(and often essential)

Roadside sales

☞ The produce of the local countryside can often be deduced by the items on sale by the roadside. Containers of unrefined olive oil, cans of olives, live geese and turkeys and chickens held by their legs, nuts, grapes, oranges even fresh fish. It is certainly an interesting and effective method of retail. Fossils, amethysts and huge desert roses are on display and often held in the hand of determined and foolhardy youths who stand in the road, so take care. Look out too for the can and the plastic funnel advertising fuel for sale. The small motor bikes have a very small tank and need frequent replenishment. On the main road S of Gabès, onwards towards the Libyan border, bundles of green notes are waved at the face of the driver – Libyan dinars – the best exchange rate is here but perhaps the best opportunity is for a fresh sheep skin, still warm.

souvenir sellers more aggressive.

Market days are Sat afternoon and Sun.

Local information
● **Accommodation**

C *Hotel Ibis*, Place du 7 Novembre in the centre of town, 200m from the *ksour*, T 643878/9, F 640550, 44 rm, all a/c, some rooms with terrace, conference room, clean, a bit noisy as sport teams usually stay here, opened 1994.

F *Hotel Essaada*, Ave Habib Bourguiba, T 640300, 28 rm, 6 rm with shower but none with toilet; *Hotel El Vazira*, off Ave 7 Novembre, nr the *ksar*, clean and cheap; **F** *Hotel Hana*, T 640690, in Ave Habib Bourguiba, quite noisy, but well placed, central.

Youth hostel: rue des Palmiers, on the road to Djorf, T 640338, 60 beds.

● **Places to eat**
♦♦*Restaurant in Hotel Ibis*.

♦*Restaurant Echana*, Ave Habib Bourguiba, T 640690, good food and cheap, parking available; *Restaurant de la Liberté*, in front of *Hotel Ibis*, good and cheap; *Restaurant l'Olivier*, road to Gabès (Km 14, Koutine), T 630017; *Pizzeria Plaza*, Ave Habib Bourguiba; *Restaurant Carthage*, rue du 18 Janvier; restaurant in *Hotel Hana*, Ave Habib Bourguiba.

● **Banks & money changers**
BS, Ave Habib Bourguiba, T 640087; **STB**, rue 2 Mai, T 640053; **BNT**, Ave Habib Bourguiba, T 640088; **Banque Centrale**, at the crossroads to Foum Tataouine; **Amen Bank**, behind *Hotel Ibis* in Place du Festival.

● **Post & telecommunications**
Post Office: Ave Habib Bourguiba, on the

crossroads towards Foum Tataouine, where the Gouvernatorat and public gardens are to be found.

● **Tour companies & travel agents**
52 rue de 18 Janvier, T 640817.

● **Useful addresses**
Police: T 640033.

● **Transport**
Road Bus: information on T 640427. Buses to Tunis; Djerba, Tataouine, Zarzis, Ben Gardane, Gabès, Gafsa and Sfax.

AROUND MEDENINE

Metameur can be reached by louage (about TD2.5), hitchhiking or a bus to the junction. Take the road to Gabès, turning left after 6 km to the village which is 1 km further up the road. Metameur is a beautiful village with *ghorfas*, which are still in relatively good condition, on the small hill.

● **Accommodation E** *Hotel El Ghorfa*, T 640294, 35 rm, shared toilets and showers, a charming little hotel built in the ghorfas, a wonderful place if you want to get away from everything for a few days. Visitor's comment: choose half board as the food is good and you will not find a restaurant unless you drive to Medenine. The manager, Mr Hachim Drifi, is very talkative and knowledgeable on the neighbourhood and local culture. Try to arrive early or make a reservation, as he lives a distance from the hotel and might leave before you arrive. Bring sleeping bag as sheets and blankets are not provided. Good place to meet people either driving to Libya or to the desert. Dinner is the best way to chat, as all guests sit at the same long table and the manager will introduce everybody.

Gightis on the coast 27 km N of Medenine on the road to Djorf has remains of Romano-African style buildings, Capitol, Forum, Temples, Baths and is an interesting excursion. Gightis **museum** open 0830-1730 in winter and 0900-1300 and 1500-1900 in summer, closed Fri, entrance TD1.

Djoumaa is situated 36 km SW of Medenine on the C113 to Beni Kheddache. There are buses here from Medenine at 0815 and 1000, returning at 1000 and 1400. It is worth a trip to this most attractive hill top village with splendid views. The *ksar* has only recently been abandoned.

Beni Kheddache, beyond Djoumaa, 65 km from Ksar Guilane and 14 km from Ksar Hallouf, can be reached by the same buses from Medenine at 0815 and 1000. The village is of little interest in itself except on Thur which is market day, but from here you can take the desert track S to Ksar Haddad and on to Foum Tataouine.

● **Accommodation** F *Hotel Zamour*, on a track a few kilometres after the postal office and the hospital (better ask), T 647196, F 647197, 13 rm, 40 beds, very basic (bring your own sleeping bag and be prepared to sleep on a mattress on the floor), built in a cave structure, therefore no windows, communal toilets and showers, clean, very quiet as you are surrounded by the mountains, excellent restaurant. Open 1995.

● **Places to eat** Restaurant in *Hotel Zamour* (booking rec).

● **Hospitals & medical services Hospital**: 647010.

● **Post & telecommunications Post Office**: in the centre of town, close to the hospital and behind louage.

● **Useful addresses Police**: T 647025.

● **Transport Road Bus**: buses to Medenine at 0700, 1400. Buses from Medenine at 1000, 1600. **Louage**.

MEDENINE TO BEN GARDANE

This 77 km of road is very busy as goods go into Libya this way. Getting a lift is easy. There are 3-4 buses daily.

● **Accommodation** Stay in Ben Gardane at E *Hotel de l'Algerie*, rue 20 Mars, T 665279; F *Baghdad*, rue de Zarzis, T 666123, next to bus station, clean, shared toilet facilities; F *Hotel El Ounz*, rue de Medenine, T 665920, 20 rm, most with bath, fairly clean, good views over town from terrace on upper storey.

● **Places to eat** *Restaurant de l'Espoir*, in front of *Hotel Baghdad*, rue de Zarzis, a very good unofficial exchange rate for Libyan dinars is available here, you are now just 33 km away from the Libyan border.

MEDENINE TO FOUM TATAOUINE

With your own transport the most interesting route is via Beni Kheddache and S via Ghoumrassen. The track is not difficult and the landscape is fantastic. This is the area inhabited by the Haouia. Without transport, the quickest and easiest way is to do the 49 km by bus. For the more determined there is a bus from Medenine to Beni Kheddache and a bus from Ghoumrassen to Foum Tataouine and it is possible to hitch a ride between the two villages.

If you decide to drive straight from Medenine S to Foum Tataouine be prepared to be stopped several times by the police. In fact, on the road there are at least seven police checkpoints. Policemen will check your passport and, being a tourist, you simply have to smile and to be polite. Bear in mind that this road leads to Foum Tataouine but also to the desert and to the Libyan and Algerian borders. At 16 km before Foum Tataouine is a *ksar* on the right. The landscape is not so flat and the mountains appear ahead.

FOUM TATAOUINE

ACCESS Buses from Medenine, Zarzis Houmt Souk, Ghoumrassen and Tunis arrive at the bus station on Ave 1 June 195 The louages station is on the same street

The major town in the *ksour* area, Tataouine is a good place to start a circuit round the *ksour*. It is not a very interesting town, but more charming than Medenine. Especially lively and interesting is the market on Mon and Thur.

Places of interest

A very colourful **market** is held Mon and Thur on Ave Farhat Hached. There is a possibility of finding a bargain in the carpets, jewellery, straw goods, and particularly the materials from the bedouin women.

Local information
● **Accommodation**
The choice is very limited.

B *Hotel Dakyanus*, 6 km from Foum Tataouine on the road to Chenini turn right at the crossroad towards Ghoumrassen, the hotel is a earth colour building on the left recently built by Oued El Ferch, which supplies a source of drinkable water to Foum Tataouine itself, T 862932, F 862932, 100 beds, pool suitable for swimmers but if you plan to stay in this hotel for a while check to see if there is water in the pool; **B** *Sangho*, T 860124, F 862177, 62 rm, 9 km S at the Douiret/Remada intersection turn right towards Ghoumrassen el Bled, clearly signed, spotlessly clean, tastefully decorated, pool, tennis, restaurant, opened Jul 1993.

E *La Gazelle*, Ave Hedi Chaker, T 860009, F 862860, a/c, all 23 rm have bath, could be better looked after and cleaner, decent restaurant, 62 rm, definitely over-priced and not very welcoming, but unfortunately one of the few suitable hotels in town.

F *Hotel Medina*, Ave Habib Mestaoui, T 860999, 20 rm with sink, hot showers, restaurant, breakfast TD1.5; *Hotel Ennour*, Ave Habib

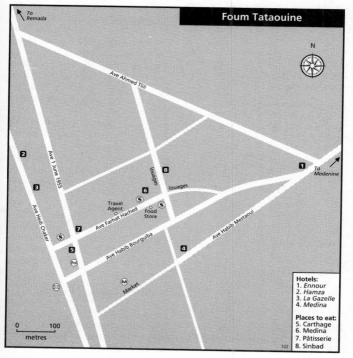

Foum Tataouine

To Remada

To Medenine

Ave Ahmed Tlili

Ave 1 June 1955

Ave Hedi Chaker

louages

louages

Travel Agent

Ave Farhat Hached

Food Store

Ave Habib Bourguiba

Ave Habib Mestaoui

Pol

Market

| Hotels: |
| 1. *Ennour* |
| 2. *Hamza* |
| 3. *La Gazelle* |
| 4. *Medina* |

| Places to eat: |
| 5. Carthage |
| 6. Medina |
| 7. Pâtisserie |
| 8. Sinbad |

0   100
metres

Ghorfas

Throughout the S of Tunisia grain was stored in small stone cells known as *ghorfas*. They were each about 2m high and 6-10m in length. More units were added as required both at either side and above sometime reaching up to 8 units in height. Eventually the whole formed a courtyard, the blank outside walls deterring raiders.

A skill you might just require – how to make a ghorfa.

1. Build two walls of rock and mud about 2m apart and 1½m high.

2. Place vertically between the walls two straw grain baskets packed with earth. These must fit exactly between the walls to support them. Place a third straw grain basket of earth horizontally on top of the first two.

3. Over this place a previously manufactured plaited reed/straw mat to make an arch.

4. An arched roof of rocks held by a fine clay and gypsum mortar can then be gradually constructed, using the matting and grain baskets as support.

5. Construct a rear wall if necessary. Remove the supporting baskets and plaster the internal walls with lime and mud. Decorate if required with figures and handprints or fish to ward off the evil eye.

6. Construct a front wall with a wooden access door of palm.

Typical Ghorfas

Bourguiba, T 860131, by the main road to Remeda, not very clean and quite noisy; **F** *Hotel Residence Hamza*, Ave Hedi Chaker, T 863506, 9 rm, communal toilet and shower every 3 rooms, very cheap and clean, ask for hot water because the heating has to be switched on, nice management but the lady who works in the morning speaks only Arabic, in the afternoon somebody can speak French, rec.

● **Places to eat**

◆ *Restaurant Carthage*, rue 20 Mars, T 863167, good and cheap, try the grilled meat, the owner speaks only Arabic but his young son can get by in French, rec; *Restaurant El Medina*, nr louage, T 861978, very cheap. *Restaurant Sindbad*, 13 Ave 1 June 1955, nr bus station and louage, varied menu; *Maray Ben Jabeur* m in front of louage in 66 Ave Farhat Hached, T 860093.

● **Banks & money changers**

BS close to Post Office, in the centre of town; **Amen Bank**, on the corner between Rue

Farhat Hached and Ave 1 June 1955.

● **Hospitals & medical services**
Hospital: on the road to Medenine, T 860114.

Private clinic: nr *Hotel Hamza* and *Hotel La Gazelle*, T 860710.

● **Post & telecommunications**
Post office: in the centre of town, close to *Café de Paris*.

● **Tour companies & travel agents**
Rue 20 Mars, T 860937; rue Farhat Hached, T 860103, F 862438. They do not organize excursions in the desert.

● **Useful addresses**
Police: rue 20 Mars nr *Restaurant Carthage*, T 860871, ask here how to apply for permission to drive from Remada onward in the desert (the *Gouvernatorat* is the authority that releases such permits).

● **Transport**
Road Bus: buses to **Medenine** at 0630, 1000, 1300; to Gabès at 0630 and 1000. **Louage**: on the corner between Ave Farhat Hached and Ave 1 June 1955. Fare to Medenine is TD2, to Gabès TD5.

AROUND FOUM TATAOUINE

Ksar Ouled Soltane is one of the best preserved *ksour* in Tunisia and has virtually no tourists. The circular outer wall of the *ksar* is still virtually intact. The *ksar* is built on a slight rise allowing good views across towards Libya. The people stored their grain in *ghorfas*, and in this village two superb courtyard *ghorfas* survive, the older dating from the 15th or 16th century. Take the road directly S of Foum Tataouine, to the left of the main road to Remada, in the direction of Maztouria where on the right are three *ksour*, and overall some splendid views.

On the way to Ksar Ouled Soltane there are some small villages in which it is possible to buy bread and drinks. In Tamelest there is on the right a small shop (bread, vegetables and drinks) and, after the mosque on the left another (bread and yoghurt). There is a café in the square in Ksar Ouled Soltane but neither a hotel nor a restaurant as the inhabitants oppose the massive coming of tourists. People are, nonetheless, very nice and knowledgeable about the history of their *ksar*.

From Ksar Ouled Soltane the road goes into the desert towards Algeria and Libya. The road, recently partly paved, used to be exclusively military. Going further after Ksar Ouled Soltane, there is Mghit and after 1 km the track starts. It is not in good condition and this explains why there are no tourists behind this point. Getting a lift here is quite difficult but you might be lucky with a truck delivering supplies.

Ksar Ouled Soltane to Azzahra (Krachaoua) and back to Foum Tataouine Azzahra, 10 km from Ksar Ouled Soltane used to be called Ksar Retbet or El Krachaoua. It is an impressive village on the top of a hill. The village itself is a *ksar* built around a square in the middle of which two eucalyptus give shade. From the main square pass through the arch which joins a second square, which rather looks like a courtyard and where the 3 and 4 floor *ksour* are still inhabited. Be as quiet as possible as the inhabitants of Azzahra voted against a touristic campaign which meant the opening of restaurants, cafés and hotels.

From Azzahra to Foum Tataouine is a 21 km drive on a paved road. Leaving Azzahra after 500m on the right there is a *marabout*. At Km 3 on the right the tiny village of Bir Yekzer, at km 5 Khatma, at Km 6 on the left Maaned, at Km 10 on the left Ksour Jlidad (worth a visit). After 500m crossroad (Beni Mhiva on the right), turn left to admire the *ksar* there. After 300m, there is another crossroad, turn right for a panoramic view. Drive carefully as the road is up and down and there are many curves. Just keep to the surfaced road and Foum Tataouine will appear.

Ksar Ouled Debbab is about 10 km along the P19 on the road S to Remada. Arriving in the new village at the foot of the hill, walk left towards the mosque.

You will find a path on the left. If you have your own transport it is possible to drive up to the hill. This beautiful hilltop *ksar*, now abandoned and falling into ruin, blends into the surrounding landscape. Steps and arches can still be identified. It looks like a lonely place, but actually many boys and men spend their lazy days on the top of the dwellings. Their presence is almost concealed and they might reveal it by banging on something in a rhythmic way.

Douiret The road for Douiret, 9 km through land cultivated after the winter rains but barren in the summer, is W from the centre of Ksar Ouled Debbab. Drive with care as the road has many bends and drivers are looking at the view. The old, almost abandoned village is perched on the hillside 2 km further along the track. Only five families remain here. It is very impressive, quite eerie, the place has a mystical touch. The white mosque attracts attention while the earth coloured houses tone in with the hillside. There is a small *marabout* on the left on the way into the village. Watch out for dogs. Notice the inscriptionless tomb stones. Douiret has the privilege of having so far escaped the tourists. However, a restaurant and shop are almost ready to open. There is a youth hostel with 4 large rm and 4 tents.

Douiret to Chenini A possible route on to Chenini is via a scenic track N through the mountains. Take the usual precautions regarding water and spare tyres. It can be done in a Peugeot 205 or Citroen AX. Cross the new village of Douiret and take the track on to the W. It is best to check with one of the villagers to make sure the route is not closed by floods. The other road to Chenini is S of Tataouine, turn right after 2 km on the C207 to Ghoumrassen el Bled and 3 km further on keep straight ahead when the main route swings right. Total distance 10 km. There is no need to stop in the new town, rather follow the road round the hill to the only restaurant which serves excellent couscous.

Good news for walkers. Chenini is only 5½ km from Douiret over the top past the highest houses. It takes 1½ hrs to walk. Seek a guide at least for the first half of the walk as the only people en route will be girls herding goats. Leave Douiret early and wear strong shoes since the path is, in some parts, rocky. Don't miss this walk! You will arrive in Chenini Nouvelle, where it is possible to visit the old mosque on the top of the hill. Near the mosque on the right there are a *marabout* once inhabited by a woman and graves covered by stones and grass. If you do not have your own transport don't leave it too late to look for a lift back.

CHENINI

(Do not confuse with village of same name near Gabès, page 299). This is an amazing Berber village built on either side of a rock crest. The houses which are built into the rock have a small courtyard, where animals are kept. There are some *ghorfas* at the top of the village, but only a few are still in use. Chenini men are traditionally known as newspaper sellers. Visit the underground mosque with its particularly intriguing long tomb stones. Chenini has become part of the tourist route but, despite the crowds climbing up and down the village, it is worth seeing for the extraordinary setting. The streets here are just ledges, scarcely wide enough for two people to pass! The restaurant *Relais de Chenini* at the bottom of the hill has good, reasonably-priced food. At lunch (TD3.5) service can be slow since many groups call in here. With a packed lunch and a drink you will have more time for seeing the sights.

GUERMESSA

About 4 km along the road to Tataouine, after the new town of Chenini, take a dirt track on the left. Follow the telephone poles. After 2-3 km the track forks, keep left still following the poles. At the end of

Tunisia and Libya in WW2

The physical marks of the destruction wrought by WW2 are still very apparent in Tunisia and Libya – if mainly now in the large cemeteries of war dead.

Italy, the colonial power in Libya at the outbreak of WW2, invaded British-held Egypt in the closing weeks of 1940 mistakenly believing that the campaign there would be brief and successful. In reality, the war raged, with many changes of fortune for the combatants, until May 1943. The prize of winning Egypt from the British was the destruction of British lines of communication to the Middle East, India and the Far East together with access for the Italian and German commands to the rich oil fields of Iran and the Arabian peninsula. Great Britain and the Commonwealth countries, for their part, desperately needed to hold their grip on Egypt, their lines of communication such as the Suez Canal and the natural resources of the region. Scarcely surprising, therefore, that the battle for control of North Africa should be so protracted and bitter.

The local populations were for the most part unwilling spectators of the desert war though their suffering was considerable. In Libya, the Senusi movement backed the British against the colonial Italy and Libyan troops did ultimately have a hand in the re-conquest of their country. In Francophone North Africa there was uncertainty and confusion in the ranks of the French colonial authorities and their colonial peoples as a result of the Pétain régime's accommodation with the Nazis.

Although the Italian armies made some progress in Egypt in 1940, they were soon expelled. Faced with what appeared to be an Italian collapse, German troops and armour were moved into Tripolitania in Feb 1941. The combined German and Italian army pushed back the British to the Egyptian frontier by April. The Axis army was led by General Rommel with skill and audacity, supported by a strong air force. Rommel's eastwards advance was slowed by the protracted resistance of the garrisons, first Australian, then British and Polish, at Tobruk. Meanwhile the main armies fought pitche battles around the Libyan-Egyptian frontier until Rommel withdrew temporarily in Dec 1941. Once back in Libyan territory, Rommel reorganized and, taking advantage of improved lines of communication, prepared a counter attack which pushed the British back as far as Gazala, near Derna, in

this road you will come to the village of Guermessa. The new village is of no interest but behind, along a dirt track to the W, is the old village. It is similar to Chenini, but without the tourists. From the top (½ hr climb) the panorama of the surrounding area is breathtaking.

GHOUMRASSEN EL BLED

Ghoumrassen is only 8 km further on to the W from Guermessa. The most interesting part is towards the centre of the town. Behind the town, to the N, you can see the old abandoned village clinging to the cliff topped by a small mosque, as if watching over the inhabitants. If you

have the energy, it is worthwhile going up to the mosque. From here you will see the old *ghorfas* and the rest of the old town and a large new house owned by a rich business man. This is a good example of how the inhabited area changes as circumstances alter.

To walk to the top to the old mosque on top of the hill ask in centre of town where the path starts. It is not very clear. It is a stiff climb but rather dangerous. The mosque is small and its plan is quite irregular. On Thur evening many people walk up to the old mosque.

Market day is Fri.

● **Places to eat** The natives of Ghoumrassen

Jan and Feb 1942 as, after a pause, into Tobruk and deep into Egypt in Jun though this advance was finally held at El-Alamein after a fierce battle. Rommel made a final attempt at Alam Halfa, E of El-Alamein, to push aside British and Commonwealth forces and break through to the Nile Valley in Aug 1942 but failed in the face of a strong Allied defensive effort and his own growing losses of men and equipment.

The balance in the desert war changed in mid-1942. The Allies gradually won superiority in the air and gained freedom of movement at sea. The Germans and Italians increasingly lacked adequate armour, reinforcements and strategy as Rommel's personal health also deteriorated. On the Allied side General Montgomery took over leadership and began a build-up of the Eighth Army sufficient to overwhelm the well-trained and experienced Afrika Korps. Montgomery opened his attack at El-Alamein on 23 October 1942 and, after 11 days of hard fighting the Axis army was beaten back and retreated by rapid stages to the W to make a last stand in Tunisia.

The German attempt to hold on in North Africa was made difficult by sea and airborne landings by Allied, including American, troops in Morocco and Algeria in Nov 1942. These two countries were liberated with comparative ease when French Vichy units, formerly collaborating with the Germans, were brought round to supporting the invasion. German and Italian reinforcements were rushed to Tunis and a battle began to stop the advance of Allied units from the W as they fought their way in from Algeria and from the S through Libya. German attacks in the Battle of Kasserine in the hills N of Gafsa during Jan and Feb 1943 almost succeeded in halting the Allied progress. Rommel's final assault against Montgomery's advancing Eighth Army arriving from Libya failed in early Mar. Axis troops retreated northwards behind the Mareth Line on the Gulf of Gabès (see page 327) before being outflanked and being forced to withdraw by Montgomery's troops. A concluding series of battles in northern Tunisia saw the Allies push through the Medjerda Valley to Tunis and Bizerte in May 1943, effectively ending Axis resistance in North Africa.

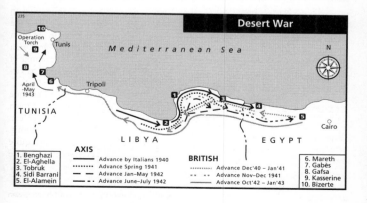

Desert War

AXIS	
——	Advance by Italians 1940
·········	Advance Spring 1941
— —	Advance Jan–May 1942
— ·· —	Advance June–July 1942

BRITISH	
››››››	Advance Dec'40 – Jan'41
— ·· —	Advance Nov–Dec 1941
⌁⌁⌁⌁	Advance Oct'42 – Jan'43

1. Benghazi
2. El-Aghella
3. Tobruk
4. Sidi Barrani
5. El-Alamein
6. Mareth
7. Gabès
8. Gafsa
9. Kasserine
10. Bizerte

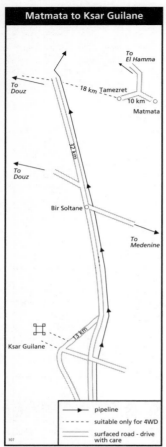

Matmata to Ksar Guilane

To
El Hamma

To
Douz

18 km Tamezret

10 km
Matmata

32 km

To
Douz

Bir Soltane

To
Medenine

13 km

Ksar Guilane

➤➤ pipeline
- - - - suitable only for 4WD
═══ surfaced road - drive
with care

107

are reported to be famous throughout Tunisia for their skill in the preparation of fritters. It is a matter of opinion. There are, despite this, unfortunately no good restaurants in Ghoumrassen. Nonetheless, the *pâtisserie* in Ave Habib Bourguiba and, in the same road, the baker can provide some basic food. Avoid the restaurant in the small road close to the police station as it is neither good nor cheap.

● **Bank & money changers** BS, Ave Habib Bourguiba, T 869147. **STB**, Ave Habib Bourguiba, T 869115.

● **Post & telecommunications Post Office**: Ave Habib Bourguiba.

● **Useful addresses Police**: Rue Ibn Arfa (in front of post office), T 869175.

KSAR HADDAD

A quiet little village 5 km N along the road after Ghoumrassen el Bled. The only *ghorfas* left have been beautifully conserved and transformed into a hotel. The **E** *Hotel Ksar Haddad*, T 869605, is very cheap, 26 simple rm, with bath/toilets which could be cleaner, restaurant serving good, traditional meals at reasonable prices, even if the comforts are limited and the management not very cordial, a night in the hotel is an experience not to be missed, some rooms have 3 floors and up to 7 beds.

In the main square by the hotel, *Café Etoile* has recently opened, it is very touristic and expensive, particularly good is the Turkish coffee.

KSAR GUILANE

A very beautiful village, it is only accessible from Chenini with a 4WD vehicle, though it is preferable to take a guide. From Douz a normal car will do. This is a magnificent oasis in the middle of the desert and no opportunity to visit it should be allowed to slip by. It is quite out of this world! Unfortunately some tour agencies have 'found' this area and it is not now so peaceful.

Ksar Guilane can also be reached from Matmata. Drive to Tamezret (10 km) on the paved road, then take the track (18 km, not in good condition, full of stones) to the pipeline. After 59 km with the pipeline on your right there is a crossroad, turn right and, after further 13 km, you will arrive in Ksar Guilane.

There are 3 campsites equipped with big tents, 150 beds each. Prices range from TD6 to TD9 depending on position of the camp itself, breakfast not included, all have unpleasant toilets. Bring your own sleeping bag. Try to arrive in Ksar Guilane as soon as possible because

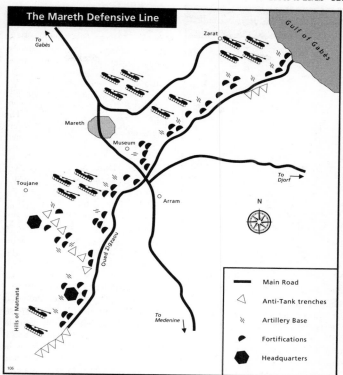

The Mareth Defensive Line

To Gabès

Zarat

Gulf of Gabès

Mareth

Museum

Toujane

Arram

To Djorf

N

Oued Zigzaou

Hills of Matmata

To Medenine

	Main Road
◁	Anti-Tank trenches
∖∖	Artillery Base
◖	Fortifications
⬡	Headquarters

106

campsites are often fully booked by tour agencies and you might have to sleep somewhere else.

REMADA

This is a military town 78 km S of Tataouine. This can be the starting point for travelling to the military posts of Borj Bourguiba (41 km), Lorzot (75 km), Dehiba (50 km) and Bir Zar further S on the Libyan border. Travelling after Remada, either in the desert or to the Algerian or Libyan borders, requires special permission. The competent authority is the Gouvernatorat in Foum Tataouine. Tents and sleeping bags are required, as there are no hotels in the area.

GABES TO ZARZIS

Just 4 km from Gabès, on the right in Teboulbou is *Restaurant Lanternes*. In the village of Kettana on the Oued El Ferch, on the right under the shadow of the palm trees, a permanent market of small shops sell any kind of local handicraft. It is open overnight too! The main market day is Wed.

Mareth is 37 km from Gabès and 39 km from Medenine. It survives on its historical record. There is little else.

Excursions The Military Museum of the Mareth line is located out of Mareth on the road to Medenine. Open from 0900 to 1645. Closed on Mon. Entrance TD1, permission to take photographs

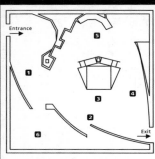

Plan: the Military Museum of the Mareth Line

Entrance →

← Exit

1. State of the war in North Africa, November 1942 - February 1943.
2. Main Allied and Axis forces in Tunisia, March 1943.
3. Model of the battle of Mareth, March-April 1943.
4. Military operations in Tunisia, April - March 1943.
5. Weaponry exhibition.
6. Audio-visual theatre.

TD2. Free entrance for students, children (less than 8 years old) and disabled.

Military history The Mareth Defensive line was located in the Mareth-Toujane region. This line was built between 1936 and 1940 by the French forces in response to a possible Italian offensive on Tunisia from Libya, which was at that time an Italian colony. The Mareth line was also called the *desert Maginot line*. It played an important role in the development of operations in the Tunisian Campaign of Nov 1942 to May 1943. This line stretched 45 km from the sea to the Matmata mountains and lay alongside the Oued Zigzaou. The line fortifications comprised 40 infantry emplacements, 8 large artillery bunkers, 15 command posts and 28 support points.

After the occupation of French territories by the Germans in 1940 and the Franco-German and Franco-Italian armistice treaties, a German-Italian commission proceeded to demilitarize the Mareth line. The German-Italian troops commanded by Field Marshall Rommel withdrew from Tunisia via Tripolitania as a consequence of their defeat against the British 8th Army led by General Montgomery (4 October 1942, battle of El Alamein). In order to enable Rommel's forces to hold up the British advance, the Mareth line was rearmed and reinforced by the Axis High Command. This rearming took place between Nov 1942 and Mar 1943. As a result, the Mareth line became an insurmountable obstacle, especially during the flood season.

The battle of Mareth took place in March 1943. It coincided with the pressure exerted on the Axis forces – led by General Von Arnim – in central and northern Tunisia, and with the start of maritime and aerial supremacy in the Mediterranean Sea of the Allied Forces – led by General Anderson. The battle began on 16 March 1943 when the British attacked the Mareth line on two fronts, the first along the coastal area between Mareth and the shore, the second across the Dahar plateau. On the 20 and 21 Mar the British attempted to cross the Oued Zigzaou, but met the fierce resistance of the Axis forces led by General Messe. The battle ended on 28 March 1943 following the British success through the El Hamma-Tebaga gap. The Axis forces were forced to abandon their defensive positions on the Mareth line and withdrew towards the N.

● **Places to eat** On the main road there are several cafés.

● **Banks & money changers BNA**, on the right arriving from Gabès; **STB**, on the left.

● **Tour companies & travel agents** *Mareth Voyage*, on the left coming from Gabès.

MARETH TO MEDENINE

At Km 24 there is the village of **Koutine**. Here food and drinks can be bought in the several cafés located on the main road. Try *Restaurant 7 Novembre* which is just at the beginning of Koutine on the left or *Restaurant l'Olivier*, T 630017.

ZARZIS AND THE ISLAND OF DJERBA

ZARZIS

ACCESS Buses arrive some 100m from central square, by the Esso garage, and the louage station is next to the nearby Shell garage.

The town has long been associated with Djerba as a tourist resort, and is not without certain similarities. The architecture is quite similar and the landscape, with large olive groves and long, white beaches is indeed very reminiscent of Djerba. The town, originally the market town for the area, is highly developed for tourism and generally well organized. The main point of interest in the town, apart from the market on Mon and Fri is the Sponge Festival (from 15 Jul to 15 Aug) which is celebrated with traditional dances and music, fishing boat competitions and, of course, sponge fishing. Zarzis is the road access to Djerba, across the causeway which was originally built by the Carthaginians and later rebuilt by the Romans. The road as it stands today was rebuilt in 1953. The only other access to Djerba is by the Djorf ferry.

Local information

● Accommodation

C *Zarzis Hotel*, T 680160, F 680292, 600 beds; *Club Sangho*, T 680124, F 680715, 722 beds; *Club Oamarit*, T 680770, F 680685, 844 beds; all in the touristic area.

D *Hotel Zephyr*, T 681027, F 681026, 652 beds; **D** *Hotel Zita*, T 680246, F 680359, 600 rm, a/c, adequate restaurant, coffee shop, an old building.

F *Hotel Amira*, T 680188, 22 beds; *Hotel Anis*, T 681409, 36 beds; *Hotel Haroun Rachid*, T 681332, 20 beds; *Hotel Medina*, T 681861, 40 beds; *Hotel du Port*, T 680777, 24 beds; *Hotel Soltana*, 20 beds; *Hotel de la Station*, T 680667, 51 beds; *Hotel du Sud*, 20 beds.

F *Hotel l'Olivier*, close to the bus station, T 680637, 20 beds, simple, clean, probably the best of the cheap hotels.

Youth hostel: rue de l'Algérie, 40 beds, T 681599.

Camping: Sonia site rec.

● Places to eat

♦♦♦*Restaurant Abou Nawas*, route des hotels, T 680583.

♦♦*Restaurant El Borj*, route des hotels, T 680928; *Restaurant El Bibane*, Ave Farhat Hached nr Place de la Jeunesse, T 681344, very good fish (choose the fish you like before they cook it), good, cheap and clean, rec; *Restaurant l'Oasis*, on the road to *Club Sangho*, T 680124; *Restaurant Les Palmiers*, town centre, T 680114; *Restaurant Le Pacha*, route des hotels, T 680497; *Restaurant Nozha*, route de Sonia Plage Municipale, T 681593; *Restaurant République*, town centre.

♦*Restaurant l'Olivier*, Ave Farhat Hached after *Restaurant El Bibane* on the same side of the road, T 680721, try lamb steak or chicken, cheap and not touristic.

● Banks & money changers

STB, town centre, T 680082; BNT, rue de Pales-

Zarsis

Sketch map: not to scale

To El Kantara & Djerba

Route Touristique

Ave Mohammed V

Hotels:
1. Amira
2. Club Oamarit
3. Club Sangho
4. Oliver
5. Zarsis
6. Zephir
7. Zita

Places to eat:
8. El Bibane

Place de la Jeunesse

Place 7 Novembre

Ave Farhat Hached

Ave du 20 Mars

Poli

To Medenine

Ave Habib Bourguiba

To Ben Gardane

Port

105

tine, T 680020; **BT**, rue de Palestine and rue d'Algérie, T 680024; **BDS**, town centre; **CFCT**, Ave Mohammed V, T 680818; **BS**, town centre, T 680318. There are also bureaux de change along route Touristique, 100m beyond the Tourist office. One takes VISA and Eurocheques.

● **Hospital & medical services**
Hospital: Ave du 20 Mars, in town centre, T 680302.

Chemist: all night, Ave Farhat Hached, T 681124.

Clinic: on the road to Djerba, T 682240.

● **Post & telecommunications**
Area code: 05.
Post Office: is in Ave Habib Bourguiba, T 680125. There is another Post Office/ telephone centre in the hotel zone, about 1 km N of the Tourist Office.

● **Sports**
Zarzis is a typical resort town with provision for watersports such as swimming, windsurfing and water skiing at all the large hotels along the beach. **Harbour** has 60 yacht berths, min-max draft 2-4.5m. Sponge fishing is advertised. Tennis can be practised at *Club Sangho*, T 680124.

● **Tour companies & travel agents**
Agency Globus, T/F 668288; *Majus Voyages*, T 680666; *Syndabad Tours*, Zarzis, Ave Mohammed V, T 681896; *Tunisirama* at *Club Sangho*, T 680124; *Zarzis Loisirs* at *Hotel Zita*, T 680246; *Zarzis Travel Service*, route de Djerba, T 681072; *Zarzis Voyage*, route de Ben Gardane, T 680654.

● **Tourist offices**
The tourist information office is at route des Hotels, route du Port, close to the *Hotel Zarzis*, T 680445.

● **Useful addresses**
Police: Ave du 20 Mars, T 680063 and Ave Farhat Hached, T 680745.

Port: route de Porte, T 681827.

● **Transport**
Car hire: Africar, T 680152; **Avis**, T 681706; **Europcar**, T 680562 and **Hertz**, T 680284, all on route des Hotels; **Express**, in *Club Oamarit*, T 680770; **Mattei**, next to *Club Sangho*, T 680124; *Zarzis Loisirs*, *Hotel Zita*, T 680246. **Louage**: Ave Farhat Hached, T 680078; **Taxi**: Ave Mohammed V, T 680063.

Road Bus: Tunis 2100; **Sousse** 1300 (via

Hot soups for cold desert nights (3)

Chickpea Soup
600g of chick peas
1 tablespoons of: cumin
                      harissa
1 teaspoon of caraway seeds
3 cloves of garlic (crushed in mortar)
10 ml of olive oil
1 lemon
salt to taste

Method
Soak the chick peas overnight then simmer gently until tender. Add harissa, cumin, garlic and salt. Serve hot on stale bread sprinkled with oil and lemon juice.

Medenine); there are about 4 buses a day to **Medenine** and **Ben Gardane**, TD1.7, more frequent departures towards Djerba, TD2.1. Information on T 680661.

Zarzis to Ben Gardane If you have your own transport drive on the C109, which follows the coast, skirts the salt lakes and reaches Ben Gardane 46 km away. Otherwise take the bus (the bus station is near the port). The ticket costs TD1.7 and the trip should take 1 hr, but it might take more as stops are on request. As you arrive in Ben Gardane, the market, held on Sat, is on the right. The bus station is 100m from the louage. Going to the Libyan border with the louage costs TD10.

ISLAND OF DJERBA

Djerba, with an area of 614 sq km, is a virtually flat island. Altitude reaches only 55m in the centre and it measures 29 km E-W and 28 km N-S. The island is surrounded by 130 km of white beaches, while the centre is covered with olive groves and palm trees. Djerba has a long history of independence and the architectural style, unique to the island, testifies to this. The number of settlements is small as, in general, the houses are spread around the countryside and Houmt Souk in the N is the only significant town. Unfortunately Djerba is well established in the tourist circuit and can be very crowded in summer. Nevertheless, the tourists tend to congregate in Houmt Souk or stay in their hotels. The centre of the island is relatively quiet, is less well adapted to tourism and has only the basic facilities.

History

Djerbian history began with Ulysses in the Odyssey. Homer wrote that Ulysses landed in Djerba and had great difficulty in leaving again, not least because of the attractions of the lotus flower he found on the island. The island then became in turn Phoenician, Carthaginian and Roman. Known at the time as 'Menix' it went through a period of turbulence, as did most of Tunisia, due to the decadence of the Roman Empire and successive invasions. Djerba was finally conquered by the Arabs in 667, but was later involved in the rivalries between the Kharejite sect and the orthodox Muslims.

By the 15th century Djerba had become a den of pirates and various efforts were made to dislodge them, the most fateful being in 1560 when an attempt was made to fight off the pirate Dragut (see page 381). This failed and Dragut built a tower with the skulls of the slain Christians. The tower was fortunately demolished in 1848! Since then, Djerbian history has been marked by French colonization. The Djerbians were actually quite happy to see the French come, fearing attacks from rebellious inland tribes.

Today Djerba's main resources are agriculture, fishing, handicrafts and, most

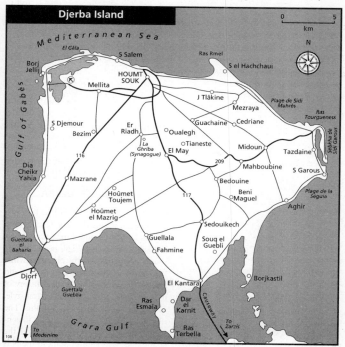

importantly, tourism. Agriculture is difficult on the island due to the lack of water. There are many palm trees but they produce poor quality dates, due to the high salt content of the water. Olive trees are more successful and olive oil is an important industry. Over 80 varieties of fish inhabit the sea around Djerba including shark, skate, and swordfish, but fishing is an occupation that is slowly declining, due to the continued use of traditional fishing methods and the preference for employment in hotels, usually for a bigger salary. Crafts are still important, particularly catering for the large tourist market.

The people

Those living on Djerba have always been quite isolated from the mainland. The effect has been the development of a unique style of life and architecture. The population is now mostly Berber in origin but, until recently, there was also a significant Jewish population on the island, one of the oldest communities in the world, dating back to 566 BC and the fall of Jerusalem to Nebuchadnezzar. Now there are only about 1,000 Jewish people left here, a large number having emigrated to Israel. The Arab population, numbering over 100,000, belong to the Ibadite sect which derives from the rigorous and austere Kharejite sect, established shortly after the Arab invasion. It is said the Djerbians followed this branch of Islam so as to keep some independence from the mainstream Islam preached by the Arab invaders.

Today, the population is faced with the new problems of tourism and the influence of western culture. Having lived for so long in isolation, they were perhaps less well equipped than other places for the large influx of tourists. The industry is having an adverse effect on the island's population and way of life since many of the traditional occupations such as agriculture and fishing are being abandoned for easier and better paid jobs in the tourist industry. Other residents have been forced to change jobs or leave due to the ever increasing cost of living, making Djerba an island with a very high emigration rate. In Tunisia and the Mediterranean region the word Djerba is synonymous with trader and grocer.

Architecture

Djerba is well known for its particular style of architecture. Houses, or *menzels* are found randomly scattered around the countryside, with no real village centres. The houses were organized in this way against the danger of attack and depending on the location of wells. Houmt Souk (the quarter of the souqs) was until recently the only town and, in effect, the market place for Djerba. The striking white-painted, often single-storey houses are organized around central courtyards, with no external windows. They resemble small forts since each has at least one tower. Each house has a cistern to collect the precious rain water. There are also many small, fortified mosques (as many as 200) which add to the attraction of the scenery. Driving or cycling round the centre of the island is a discovery and a delight.

HOUMT SOUK

ACCESS By road is either from Zarzis across the 6 km causeway, or via the ferry from Djorf to Ajim. Coming from Gabès, the ferry saves a lot of time but in summer be prepared to queue. The crossing only takes 15 mins. The ferry runs every 30 mins until 2000 when it is hourly through the night. Free for foot passengers and motorbikes, TD1 for cars by day and TD1.5 at night. All buses arrive at the bus station in the centre of Houmt Souk. Djerba has its own international airport to the W of Houmt Souk receiving scheduled flights from Frankfurt, Lyon, Geneva, Zürich, Brussels and Paris, as well as regular internal flights from Tunis (one way TD46) or Tozeur.

This is the only real town (40,000 inhabitants) on the island and therefore its capital. It has a certain charm when not taken over by tourists. Notice some of the houses are old *fondouks* where nomads rested for the night. Some have been transformed into hotels just as some houses in the small squares have been converted into cafés and restaurants. The town has nevertheless preserved a careful balance and has not been totally destroyed by tourism.

Places of interest

The **souq** is in the centre of the town. The

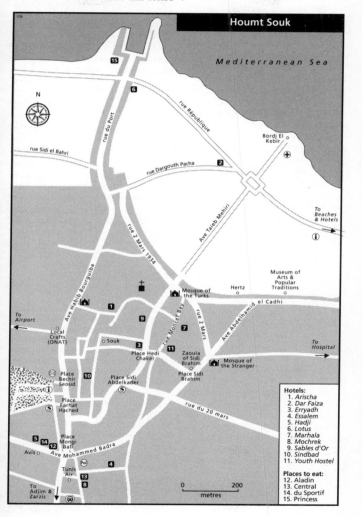

Houmt Souk

Mediterranean Sea

N

rue du Port
rue République
rue Sidi el Bahri
rue Dargouth Pacha
Bordj El Kebir
Ave Taïeb Mehiri
To Beaches & Hotels
rue 2 Mars 1934
Ave Habib Bourguiba
To Airport
Local Crafts (ONAT)
Souk
Mosque of the Turks
Hertz
Museum of Arts & Popular Traditions
rue Moncef Bey
rue 2 Mars
Ave Abdelhamid el Cadhi
To Hospital
Place Hedi Chaker
Zaouia of Sidi Brahim
Mosque of the Stranger
Place Sidi Abdelkader
Place Sidi Brahim
Place Bechir Seoud
Place Farhat Hached
rue du 20 mars
Place Mongi Bali
Ave Mohammed Badra
Avis
Tunis Air
To Adjim & Zarzis

0   200
metres

Hotels:
1. *Arischa*
2. *Dar Faiza*
3. *Erryadh*
4. *Essalem*
5. *Hadji*
6. *Lotus*
7. *Marhala*
8. *Mochrek*
9. *Sables d'Or*
10. *Sindbad*
11. *Youth Hostel*

Places to eat:
12. *Aladin*
13. *Central*
14. *du Sportif*
15. *Princess*

main souq, not to be missed, is covered and has many small shops selling mainly silver, brass, leather goods, shoes, material and clothes. Prices tend to be high, shop around for the best price. Don't forget to bargain! Djerba is noted for its straw mats, blankets, jewellery (most still made by the Jews) and pottery, particularly from Guellala. The typical Djerbian pottery has a special white colour obtained by the addition of sea water. The market is held around the souq every Mon and Thur. The pottery and straw mats are sold on the main square, by Ave Habib Bourguiba. Get there early.

Walking around the town will not take very long as it is quite small. Little streets lead on to charming squares with cafés. Notice the large doorways indicating an old *fondouk*.

The **Zaouia of Sidi Brahim**, built in 1674, is particularly interesting with its multiple arches. Across the road is the **Mosque of the Stranger**

The **Bordj el Kebir** (the Great Tower) by the harbour is a 15th century Arab fort which was later reinforced by the pirate Dragut. Inside it is possible to see the ruins of an earlier fort built in the 13th century, though the site goes back further to Roman occupation. Open 0800-1200 and 1500-1900 summer, 0830-1730 winter, closed Fri. Entrance TD3. From the top of the fort is a wonderful view over the sea and harbour. There is the **market** by the harbour held every Mon and Thur. The fish auction is particularly interesting.

The **Museum of Popular Arts and Tradition** on Ave Abdelhamid el Cadhi is set in an old *zaouia* dedicated to Sidi Zitouni who used to come here and heal the mentally ill. The collection is very interesting and well labelled. The first room displays the traditional Djerbian costumes and jewellery and explains the history of the island. Another room shows a pottery workshop, the instruments used and the fabrication process. The last room is particularly special, as it was once a place of pilgrimage. This room is known as *quoubet el khyal* (the Ghost's Dome). Open 0800-1200 and 1500-1900 in summer, 0930-1630 in winter, closed Fri, entrance TD2.

Beaches

Close to Houmt Souk the beaches are not very pleasant. The nearest to be recommended is 6 km E along the road towards the hotels. Turn left along a track just before the *Hotel Ulysses*. There are other good beaches further along the coast, but the litter problem is increasing.

Local information
● **Accommodation**
There are over 50 hotels on the island.

A *Hotel Ulysses*, T 657422, 300 rm all a/c, on beach, pool, restaurant, nightclub, sports activities, 10 km from Houmt Souk.

B *Aquarius Club*, T 657790, 600 beds and **Meridiana**, 400 beds, both beach hotels at Taguermes 28 km from Houmt Souk; **B** *Djerba Orient*, T 657440, opp *Hotel Ulysses*, 56 beds, 10 km from Houmt Souk, not on beach.

C *Hotel el Machrek*, Ave Habib Bourguiba, close to the police station, T 653155, F 650717, 40 a/c rm, some with terrace, parking, very clean, very new, rec.

D *Dar Faiza*, rue Ulysses, T 650083, pool, tennis, restaurant; **D** *Hotel Sables d'Or*, rue Mohammed Ferjani, T 650423, charming old house transformed into a small hotel, some rooms rather dark.

E *Hotel Le Hadji*, off the main square, T 650630, old, not very clean hotel, all 45 rm with bath, 17 have a/c; **E** *Hotel Erryadh*, off Place Hedi Chaker in rue Mohammed Ferjani, T 650756, an old *fondouk*, Berber style room with bath arranged around a central courtyard, very clean, lots of charm, important to book in season; **E** *Hotel Lotus*, 18 rue Republique, on beach, T 650026, F 651765, 17 rm with bath, shaded courtyard for outside eating; **E** *Hotel Marhala*, beyond Place Hedi Chaker on rue Moncef Bey, T 650146, F 653317, small, beautifully decorated, clean and cheap, rooms around attractive central courtyard, communal bath/toilets, rec.

F *Hotel Arischa*, on the street on the right opp ONAT, at the bottom on the left, T 650384, converted *fondouk* with a central patio, clean; **F** *Hotel Sindbad*, Place Mongi Bali, T 650047, in town centre, opp the Post Office, old *fon*

Fishing in Djerba

Djerba's coastline is composed of rocky shallows, sandy ledges and clay banks. It is occasionally cut by *oueds* which meander through vast fields of eelgrass. There are approximately 86 fish species living off the shores of Djerba. Generally speaking, bass and mackerel can be found off the northern coast (Borj Jellij, Houmt Souq, Ras Rmel and Ras Tourgueness), made up of limestone tables and sandbanks constantly beaten by waves and by the eastern Barrani wind. Mullet, carangidae and flat fish off the S coast (Ajim, Guellala, El Kantara and Aghir), deep and sandy, where the Ghibli wind blows. The E and W coasts are both rocky and dotted with lagoons. Off the E coast are perch, bass and dace. Off the W coast are weevers and dogfish. Fishing methods widespread in the island of Djerba are hook fishing, *la palangrotte* (hook fishing from the shore), rod fishing, troll fishing (nocturnal and winter only), long line fishing, fishing *à la lenza* in shallow waters, net fishing and fishing *à la sautade*.

douk with simple, clean rooms, communal bath/toilet, one of the cheapest in Houmt Souk; **F** *Hotel Essalem* nr market, rec as cheap, clean and friendly.

Youth hostels: 11 rue Moncef Bey, T 650619, 120 beds, very basic, pay a bit more and go to a hotel.

● **Places to eat**
♦♦♦*Restaurant La Princesse d'Haroun*, T 650488, by the harbour, specializes in fish, cosy atmosphere and decor.

♦♦♦*Blue Moon*, Place Chaker, T 650559, tables in the inner courtyard and inside.

Cheaper restaurants are: ♦♦*Le Mediter-ranéen*, 5 rue Moncef Bey, seafood and Tunisian food; *Restaurant du Sud*, Place Hedi Chaker, a bit touristy but the food is good; *Hassime Baaziz*, central, what it lacks in comfort and presentation is certainly made up for by the fish dishes and kebabs, only serves fresh food available in season.

♦*Restaurant Aladin*, Ave Badra, small and

cheap; *Restaurant Berbère*, Place Farhat Hached, small, typical, good couscous; *Restaurant Central*, Ave Habib Bourguiba, good, cheap food; *Restaurant du Sportif*, Ave Habib Bourguiba, very good, cheap Tunisian food.

Delicatessen: *M'Hirsi*, rue Abdelhamid Belkadhi, T 651206, best but most expensive; *Boukhris Marina*, also in rue Adbelhamid Belkadhi, good, sells pancakes too.

● **Banks & money changers**
STB, Place Farhat Hached, T 650140; BNT, Place Ben Daamech, T 650025; BT, rue du 20 Mars, T 650004; BTS, Ave Habib Bourguiba, T 650729; CFCT, Place Farhat Hached, T 650320. There are also many bureau de change offices around the town which accept credit cards and are open more flexible hours. Even better, STB now has an automatic cash dispenser for Visa and Mastercard holders.

● **Hospitals & medical services**
Hospital: main hospital on Ave Habib Bourguiba, T 650018. Private hospital 'El Yasmin' on Ave Mohammed Badra.

● **Places of worship**
Catholic: 2 rue de l'Eglise, Houmt Souk, T 650215, service Sun and holy days at 1000.

● **Post & telecommunications**
Area code: 05.

International exchange: on the side of the Post Office.

Post Office: Ave Habib Bourguiba, after the main square.

● **Shopping**
Handicrafts: the main ONAT craft shop is on Ave Habib Bourguiba, where the workshops and training centre are open for viewing.

● **Sports**
Aerobics & Martial Arts: can be practised in the gymnasium in Place Archa, which used to be a church.

Golf: by the sea shore, 18 holes, T 659055, F 659051.

Harbour: 10 yacht berths, min-max draft 1-3m. All water sports. Tennis. Fishing (see box, page 259). Scuba diving and undersea fishing (with permit) are allowed, though there are no facilities.

● **Tour companies & travel agents**
All can organize 2-4 day tours of the desert and into the towns and villages of Southern Tunisia. *Carthage Tours*, centre of town, T 650308; *Djerba Voyage*, Ave Habib Bourguiba, T 650071; *Malik Voyagec*, rue Habib Thameur, T 650235; *Sahara Tours*, Ave Taleb Mehiri, T 652646, F 652822; *Tourafricac*, 146 Ave Habib Bourguiba, T 650104, F 653240; *Voyages Najor Chabane*, Ave Habib Bourguiba, T 652633, F 652632.

● **Tourist offices**
The local information office is on Ave Habib Bourguiba, just before the Post Office, T 650157. Main office at the start of route Touristique, slightly out of town, T 650016, Tx 651956. Closed on Sat afternoon, Fri, Sun and public holidays.

● **Transport**
Local Bus: Djerba has a good public bus service to most parts of the island. There is a bus link with most major Tunisian towns. The bus station, through which all buses pass, is in the centre of Houmt Souk. Information on T 650076. Buses No 10 and 11 go hourly round the island, along the coast past the major hotels; No 12 goes to Ajim and the Djorf ferry; No 13 to Beni Maquel; No 14 to Guellala and No 16 to Sedouikech. **Car hire**: although cars can be rented they are expensive and there is a minimum 24 hour rental. However it is a good idea if you intend to go down to the S. Be careful in Houmt Souk when you park, as the Police have clamps (same problem as in Tunis: the difficulty is not the fine but finding the person with the keys to come and remove the clamp!). **Avis**, Ave Mohammed Badra, T 650151; **Budget**, rue du 20 Mars 1934, T 650185; **Europacar**, Ave Abdelhamid el Cadhi, T 650357; **Hertz**, Ave Abdelhamid el Cadhi, T/F 650039, highly rec; **Topcar**, rue du 20 Mars 1934, T 650536. **Cycle hire**: the island is small and flat making bicycles, which can be rented at most large hotels and in Houmt Souk, an attractive means of transport. In the tourist area to the E of Houmt Souk try Holiday Bikes Tunisie, close to *Hotel Medinan*. At *Hotel Arischa* half day hire (0900-1300 or 1400-1900) is TD6, all day is TD10. **Moped**: from Location Cycles, Ave Abdelhamid el Cadhi, in front of Shell petrol station, T 650303, TD15-20/day. **Taxis**: are a good way of getting around but can be hard to find, particularly at night, on market day or away from main routes. Taxi to airport costs TD5. Taxis from airport to Tripoli, Libya take 4-5 hrs. The route to Libya is from Djerba to El Kantara, Zarzis, Ben Gardane, Ras Ajdir and over the border, cost is TD100.

Air T 650233 or 650408, **Tunis Air**, Ave Habib

Bourguiba, T 650586; **Air France**, Ave Abdelhamid el Cadhi, T 650461. The airport is 8 km from Houmt Souk, served by a bus from town, but be sure to check the times beforehand. Flight information on T 650233. In the summer there are many more flights in addition to those listed below. **Scheduled international flights**: Brussels, Sat 0850; **Frankfurt**, Tues 0715; **Lyon**, Thur 1020; **Geneva/Zurich**, Sat 0910; **Luxembourg**, Sat 0745; **Marseilles**, Thur 0840; **Rome**, Mon 0845; **Vienna**, Tues 0900; **Paris**, Mon 0750, Thur, Sun 0900, Sat 1550, Sun 1245; **Sfax**, Thur 0900; **Monastir**, Tues, Thur, Sat 0730; **Tozeur**, Mon, 0745 and 1740, Thur and Sat 1645; there are 6 daily flight to Tunis between 0600 and 1715, (1 hr), cost US$50.

Road Bus: the bus station is in the centre of Houmt Souk. Information T 652239. Departures to: **Sfax**; **Gabès**; **Medenine**; **Tataouine** (2½ hrs); **Zarzis** and **Tunis**. **Louages**: by the bus station.

Sea Ferries: Ajim to Djorf run by CTN.

EXCURSIONS

Taxi tour of the island takes 2 hrs.

Midoun is the island's second largest town. A large black community, descendants of slaves brought from Sudan, exists here. It has a particularly good weekly market each Thur afternoon and Fri. To see an interesting olive press over 300 years old take the road towards Houmt Souk and turn right at the crossroads, rue Salah Ben Youssef. It is about 400m on the left by the well and hidden by an olive tree. A mule or camel was used to turn the stone roller to crush the olives which were then transferred to a sieve where a large palm tree trunk squeezed out the oil into a jar underneath. All around are chambers once used for stocking olives.

● **Accommodation** The only hotel is el-Jawhara, completely renewed but it is better to stay at a hotel on the beach.

● **Places to eat** ◆◆*Restaurant el-Guestile*, T 657724, rue Marsa Ettefah, typically Tunisian, eat on the terrace, on the verandah or the upper floor in one of the small dining rooms. ◆*Restaurant el-Constantine*, Ave Badra, less smart, food good, no tourists here!

● **Banks & money changers** STB, T 657723; CFCT, T 657493, both in town centre.

Ajim is the island's main harbour and

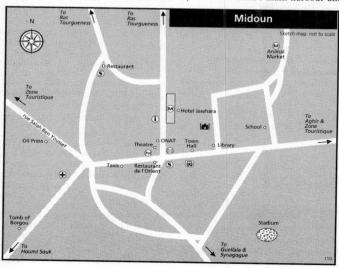
Midoun

The Jews of Tunisia: ancient community, modern diaspora

The Jews were the first non-Hamitic people to settle in the Maghreb, and their presence goes back 26 centuries to the time of King Solomon and his friend and son-in-law, King Hiram of Tyre. The two kings worked together in establishing trading posts in the western Mediterranean. Recent (1991) archaeological discoveries at Carthage confirm this. After the Arab conquest in the early 8th century, the Jews remained important in the region: across the Maghreb there were Jewish communities (the hypothesis that the majority of these communities were Judaized Berbers is supported by most writers), and the historian El Idrissi was struck by the importance of Judaism on Djerba. (Hara Sghira was founded in 586 BC on Djerba after the destruction of the first temple in Jerusalem (see page 339.) In the 16th century, Testour became a leading centre of the *megorashim*, the Jews expelled from Andalusia.

In the 17th and 18th centuries, with Tunisia a regency of the Ottoman Empire, the Jews came to play an important role in the developing trade with Europe. In the 18th century, numerous Jews of Iberian origin, established in Livorna, took up residence in Tunis, forming the core of the Grana community, as opposed to the Twansa or Tunis Jewish community. As of 1741, each community had its own synagogues and institutions. An 1846 agreement with Tuscanny allowed the Grana Jews to settle in Tunisia while retaining their original nationality. Under the protection of the Tuscan consul, the community grew rapidly.

As elsewhere in the Mediterranean, the Jews were quick to understand the importance of modern education. In 1878, the United Israelite Alliance opened a school with a modern French curriculum. The coming of the French Protectorate in 1881 opened new possibilities for an increasingly educated, energetic group. As they prospered they left their insalubrious quarters in the medina for new areas like Lafayette – where the community's wealth is reflected in the great

---

the departure point for ferries to Djorf on the mainland. Foot passengers free, car only TD0.6. It was once an important sponge fishing harbour. This activity is now virtually abandoned, due to the difficulties and dangers of the job. Today, Ajim is an important fishing port.

● **Places to eat** The village itself is of minimal interest, but there are a few cafés and restaurants with large terraces and long rows of street stalls. Arriving from Houmt Souk or Borj Jellij, in Ave Habib Bourguiba, on the left is ◆◆ *Restaurant Ouled-M'barak*, the fish here is excellent and is served with fried rice or chips, choose your fish and bargain, the meal is as cheap as you can get it! Towards the port, on the right, ◆◆*Café du Port Fafi*, and on the left ◆◆*Fast Food Fethi*, serving spaghetti, fish and chicken. All cheap.

Cedriane, further E off the road to Midoun from Houmt Souk is an oasis where the huge menzels (now abandoned and in disrepair) can be seen. The oasis has ample water and produces pomegranates as well as citrus.

El May has a typical Djerbian mosque with thick walls and a low, rounded minaret, resembling a fort. On Fri afternoon and Sat morning, a small local market takes place here. There is a livestock market too. *Restaurant Aladin*, rue Salah ben Youssef in front of the market place is small, good and cheap, take a small cup of strong tea at the end of the meal to wake you up, they are not used to tourists here.

Er Riadh was originally known as **Hara Sghira** or Little Ghetto. It was here that most Jews moved after the introduction of Islam to the area. They were treated with tolerance and produced jewellery,

Art Déco synagogue on Ave de la Liberté.

With a tradition of publishing religious works, the Jews were active in the press. Popular literature in Judaeo-Arabic was published along with newspapers like La Justice. Unlike Algeria's Jews, who received French nationality en masse, Tunisia's Jews remained subjects of the bey in their great majority – which by no means stopped them from joining the Communist Party and the Nationalist Movement. By 1950, the community was at its peak with 120,000 members, of whom 25,000 had foreign nationality.

After independence in 1956, Tunisia's Jews voted to elect the Constituent Assembly on equal footing with their Muslim fellow citizens. Again in contrast with Algeria, most felt secure enough to remain in their newly independent country, even if the new government aimed to remove any trace of separatism. Hence, in 1957, the Rabbinical Courts were dissolved, followed by the Community Council in 1958. More serious, however, was the transformation of the main Jewish cemetery into a public park, today's Jardin Habib Thameur. Anti-Semitic incidents took place during the 1961 Bizerte crisis and the 1967 Six Day War which saw Jewish property ransacked. With the cooperative movement under super-minister Ben Salah, the climate for private enterprise continued to deteriorate.

A spiritual people, deeply attached to their traditions, the Tunisian Jews were almost too well prepared to receive the ideology of the 'Promised Land'. Some 50,000 opted for Israel, in the years after independence, some 35,000 for France. Today, the community numbers a few thousand, with a handful of families still important in business. Nevertheless, the sacred books are still carried in procession during the annual pilgrimage to the El Ghriba Synagogue on Djerba, the oldest synagogue in the world.

of great reputation. In the village a sign-posted road on the left leads to the **El Griba Synagogue**. The original synagogue is said to have been built at the time of the first Jewish settlement in 586 BC, after the time of the destruction of King Solomon's temple in Jerusalem. The story goes that the place for the first synagogue was marked by a sacred stone falling from heaven and by the arrival of a strange woman to supervise the construction.

Griba means miracle and there is an annual procession which takes place on the 33rd day after the Passover – called Lag be Omer to commemorate these miracles. The congregation, swollen by many pilgrims, take the holy books through the streets on a covered platform. The present building was constructed in the 1920s and has become a spiritual centre for the study of the Torah. It is an interesting stop in an Islamic country. Inside the synagogue heads will have to be covered (head covers provided).

The Griba synagogue is a smart building, freshly whitewashed each year. The huge studded wooden doors open into the first (main) room. This is large, rectangular and the large blocks of marble which make up the floor are covered with rush matting. The walls are tiled in blue, pale blue columns, blue and gold arches with blue and gold tiles above. The coloured glass in the windows (blue, gold and green) is reflected by the sun on to the dark and heavy wooden furniture. Here old men recite from the holy books oblivious to their surroundings.

Some of the older men wear baggy trousers which fasten at a black band below the knee. The black signifies mourning for the destruction of Solomon's temple. The second room holds what is said to be one of the oldest Torahs in the world. Open 0700-1800 except Sat. A small contribution is appreciated.

Guellala, called **Haribus** in classical times, is renowned for its **pottery**, particularly the typical Djerbian white coloured ware. The clay for the pottery comes from galleries cut into the small hill nearby, on the road to Sedouikech. After lying in seawater the clay goes white. Guellala has over 500 artisans making pottery, now mostly selling to the tourists. Indeed it has shops from one end of the village to the other. Fabrication de Poiterie in the main street will provide details on how the pottery is made.

Melita, near the airport on the W side of the island had a white block shaped mosque with a very low minaret. Most of the older houses in the village have a domed roof. There are 2 cafés here. The one on the right sells typical biscuits. Drinks are cheaper here than in Houmt Souk. In a small street on the left is a Tunisian take-away.

Sedouikech, on the main road from Houmt Souk to the ferry was once well known for its pottery. Today all that remains of this craft are long underground stores. Other crafts still plied include grass plaiting for baskets of various styles.

Mahboubine is 30 mins by bus from Houmt Souk. It has an interesting mosque, a picturesque and peaceful village square and provides an opportunity to become acquainted with the real people of Djerba. Don't spoil it by taking photographs. The taxi driver said "At Mahboubine there is nothing" – nothing more enjoyable than this visit. Certainly

don't expect to find a hotel or a restaurant. There is only the café in the main square, alongside the mosque and the bus stop.

The West coast is still untouched by tourism and is ideal for walks, or a trip along the coast. Unfortunately the coast is mainly rocky, but there are a few beaches. To get there, take the road to the airport and continue straight on towards Borj Jellij, until the road goes right. Here you should take the track to the left and follow it S, all the way to Ajim. A few km along the track, on the right, there are a few beautiful houses and a mosque by the sea. Allow ½ day to Borj Jellij and all day to Ajim. Borj Jellij is a very wild and small port with a few simple fishermen's houses and a small lighthouse. The fishermen spend from 3-15 days here in the huts and then return to their village and their family elsewhere on the island. There is no organized transport here, no facilities and certainly nowhere to buy food. Make sure the taxi driver knows exactly where to meet you.

The Northeast coast Here you will find the tourists and all the large hotels. There are lovely beaches kept clean near the hotels, but not elsewhere, with white sand but they get very crowded in summer. Surfboards can be rented and various other watersports are organized in all the major hotels. If you want some peace, go to the W coast!

The East coast There is an excellent walk, takes 3 hrs, from Aghir to Borj Kastil which is a fort falling into ruin. There are interesting views, especially S across the mainland and the causeway. A very primitive overnight stop, if necessary, is available at the fisherman's cottage at the end of the walk. The only drawback is the litter on the beach.

Information for travellers

BEFORE TRAVELLING

ENTRY REQUIREMENTS

● **Visas**

Passports Check all passport and visa requirements with your nearest Tunisian Embassy. For stays of over 6 months (US citizens 4 months) a residence visa is required. Tourist visas are not needed by nationals of EU, USA, Canada or Japan. Cost of a visa into Tunisia for USA passport holder is US$20. At passport control you will be asked your hotel name. If you are undecided, give the name of any hotel in the town you plan to visit to avoid unnecessary questions.

For a private car you will need a driving licence, registration document (log book), and a Green Card valid for Tunisia. Stays of over 3 months are expensive as extension of vehicle permits is costly.

● **Tourist Information**

Tourist offices in Tunisia are open Mon-Thur 0830-1745, Fri-Sat 0830-1330, Sun and public hols 0900-1200. They are open longer in summer.

● **Tunisian Hotel Associates**

Is at 304 Old Brompton Rd, London, SW5 9JF, T 0171 3734412.

WHEN TO GO

● **Best time to visit**

The best season to visit is spring when the N is still green after the winter rains, the S is not yet too hot and the summer tourists have not arrived. The second best time is autumn when it is cooler, but tends to be very dusty. Summer can be extremely hot. Even in Tunis the summer temperatures can reach a maximum of 40°C while the S is even hotter. Despite this, it is the most popular time of the year for visitors. Winters are cold, very cold at some altitudes, and it can be damp in the N.

● **Climate**

There are considerable differences between the N and the S. Spring is a good period but it sometimes rains in the N. The summer is very hot, particularly inland and in the desert areas. On the coast the heat is made bearable by a light sea breeze. Autumn is the best period to visit the S and the oases. It is still warm, but can get very cold at night. Swimming in the sea is possible until Oct. In Nov it rains over most of the country, but never for very long. Winter is the ideal period for excursions in the Sahara, even though the nights are very cold the days are warm and the sky is blue.

● **Clothing**

Requirements depend on the time of year and the place. In summer it is necessary to be protected from the sun and to dress with consideration for the heat, bearing in mind that temperatures can fall very sharply at night in the desert. From Nov to Mar a warm coat is recommended and from Oct to May an umbrella or raincoat may be needed in the N.

HEALTH

● **Staying healthy**

No vaccinations are necessary but a tetanus

injection could make you feel more secure. The tap water in Tunis and most tourist centres is fit to drink but bottled water is easily available and may be better in the long run. Protection from the sun is essential. Most proprietary drugs are available over the counter from chemist shops in the main streets of even the smallest towns. Chemists can generally give advice on small problems. See regional sections for hospitals and chemists. Rabies is not to be lightly dismissed. While commonly associated with dogs, too many trusting tourists have been bitten by stray cats and had to undergo a series of very unpleasant injections.

The Society for the Protection of Animals in N Africa, 15 Buckingham Gate, London SW1E is working with the Society for the Protection of Animals (SPA) of Tunisia to control the number of feral cats which are found scavenging especially near hotels (see box, page 152).

● **Further health information**
Read the section on Health, see page 453.

MONEY

● **Cost of living**
It is much cheaper to live in Tunisia than Europe with a hotel costing as little as TD10-25 a night and food TD7-10 a day. Transport is cheap, too, making it therefore quite possible to live well on TD120 a week. Sample prices: bottle of water TD0.45; litre of milk TD0.45; bread TD0.30; cup of tea/coffee TD1/TD0.80; glass of beer TD1.80; haircut TD3-4.

● **Credit cards**
Cards of various types are accepted by most banks. STB and BT accept Visa and most of their branches accept Mastercard. American Express is accepted in certain travel agencies and bureaux de change and in some branches of the BIAT. Obtaining money with a credit card is generally very easy and the wait very short, just the length of a phone call. Credit cards can be used in all major hotels, restaurants and tourist shops. For all money changes a passport is necessary. STB have automatic cash dispensers (dinars of course) for Visa and Mastercard at Tunis Airport and at their main banks in Hammamet, Nabeul, Sousse, Sfax, Kairouan, Gabès, Tozeur and Djerba.

Most hotels of 2 stars and over and most good restaurants accept Visa, Diners Club, American Express and Mastercard. Some shops in the souq will accept credit cards. AmEx office in Tunis is at Carthage Tours, 59 Ave Habib Bourguiba.

Credit cards are required for deposit when hiring cars.

● **Currency**
The monetary unit is the dinar TD1 = 1,000 millimes. Exchange rates are fixed daily by the Central Bank. For rates for Jul 1995 see table, page 10. The exchange rate is fixed, with no black market price, and no need to shop around. Notes in circulation 5, 10, and 20 dinars. Coins in circulation 5, 10, 20, 50, and 100 millimes ½ and 1 dinar. Often prices over a dinar are still given in millimes which can be confusing. A taxi meter from the airport to central Tunis may say 3000 which is TD3. Be careful.

Tunisian dinars can only be obtained in Tunisia. You can take in as much foreign currency as you like. If you are carrying over £300 in foreign currency, complete a currency declaration so you can take it out again. No dinars can be taken out of the country. At the end of your stay you may change back up to 30% of the total value of foreign currency converted during the trip up to a maximum of TD100 dinars – so don't change more than you need at any one time and save all paperwork associated with financial transactions.

Money can be changed at all border crossings. Eurocheques and TCs in European currencies and US dollars are accepted at all banks and post offices.

Tunisian dinars are not accepted beyond customs control at the airport.

● **Taxes**
There are no direct taxes levied on visitors. Indirect taxes are included in prices.

GETTING THERE

● **General note**
There are no problems getting into Tunisia. Tourists are encouraged and visitors are made very welcome. Package holidays and tours are probably the cheapest way of seeing the country in some comfort. Individual travellers will find this the easiest country to move around within N Africa.

● **Air**
From Europe There are six international airports in Tunisia: Tunis, Djerba, Monastir, Sfax, Tabarka and Tozeur. In summer there are numerous charter flights from Europe, mostly to Djerba and Monastir. These can be very cheap but generally have restrictions regarding length of stay and legally must include accommoda

tion. In summer, book well in advance. For information on charter flights, contact the Tunisia National Tourist Office, 77a Wigmore St, London, W1H 9LJ, enquiries, T 0171 2245561.

British Airways services to Tunis are operated by the independent carrier GB Airways who offer regular direct scheduled services from London Gatwick to Tunis. For further information and reservations T 0345 222111.

Tunisair and Air France (via Paris or Marseille) also have scheduled flights to Tunis from London. All major European airlines fly to Tunis.

From the USA There are no direct flights. The best and cheapest way is to fly to London and get a charter or cheap scheduled flight from a bucket shop.

From North Africa Tunisair, Royal Air Maroc, Air Algérie and Egyptair fly into Tunis. Prices are generally reasonable and there are many scheduled flights. In summer finding places can be difficult.

Airfares Economy fares on scheduled flights, generally quite cheap, are more expensive in summer. Cheaper tickets can be purchased at bucket shops.

Best deals are with charter flights and tour operators who fly into airports further S, contact the Tunisian Tourist Office (see above). Air fares from adjacent N African countries are generally cheaper. Return fares – Casablanca to Tunis TD325 (3 hrs), Algiers to Tunis TD197 (1 hr). Airport tax of TD2 is payable in Tunisia, but this is generally included in the ticket price.

● **Train**

There is a daily train from Algeria at 1900 entering Tunisia via Ghardimaou, return journey leaves Tunis at 1255. One way 2nd class fare TD20 for a 24 hrs journey.

● **Road**

There are regular buses from Algeria and a daily bus to Annaba from Tunis at 0700 returning at 1700 and to Casablanca each Sat at 0630 returning at 2100. The main crossing in the S is at Hazoua beyond Nefta on the P3. Road crossings into Libya are at Ras Ajdir on the coast and at Ghadames. The bus for Libya leaves Tunis on Mon, Wed, Fri and Sun at 0700. Where the bus service fails there is generally a taxi service to the border.

● **Sea**

Important telephone numbers: Port de la Goulette, T 735300; Port de Tunis, T 255239; Port de Radès, T 449300.

Cruises that call in to Tunisia: Costa Cruises, call into Tunis and Gabès, 45/49 Mortimer St, London, W1N 8JL, T 0171 3232200, F 0171 3234566; **P&O Cruises**, the Victoria, Oriana and Canberra call in at Sidi Bou Saïd. P&O Cruises, 77 New Oxford St, London WC1A 1PP, T 0171 8002222, F 0171 8001280.

Ferries: La Goulette, the main port at Tunis is the all year entry point for car and passenger ferries. If you want to bring in a car during the summer book at least 3 months in advance.

Agents for **Tirrenia** in UK are **Serena Holidays**, 40/42 Kenway Rd, London SW5 0RA, T 0171 3736548, F 0171 2449829, they charge a £2.50 handling fee per ticket.

Agents for **CTN** (Compagnie Tunisienne de la Navigation) in UK are **Southern Ferries**, 179 Piccadilly, London W1U 9DB, T 0171 4914968, F 0171 4913502; in France are **SNCM**, 61 Blvd des Dames, Marseilles, 13002, T 91563010, F 91563100; in Italy are **Tirrenia**, Stazione Maritima-Moloangiono, Naples, T 817201111 or **Tirrenia**, Ponte Colombo Stazione Maritima, Genoa, T 258041, F 2698255; in Holland **Tunis Travel**, Overtoom 4000, 1054 Amsterdam, T 6164596, F 5134137; in Belgium **SNCM**, 53 rue de la Montagne, Brussels, T 5133818, F 5134137.

Agents for **SNCM** are **Southern Ferries** in London and **SNCM** in Marseilles (see above) and **SNCM**, 47 Ave Farhat Hached, Tunis T 338222, F 330636.

Agents for **USTICA** lines are **Voyage 2000**, 2 Ave de France, Tunis, T 348717, F 353263; **Sudovest**, Via Torre Arsa, 91100 Trapani, T (0923) 27101, F 547302.

Agents for **Linee Lauro** are **Carthage Tour**, Ave Habib Bourguiba, Tunis, T 347015, F 352740; **Place Municipio**, 88 Naples, T 5513352, F 5524329.

Ferries from: **Marseilles**, France (takes 24 hrs) operated from Joliette Ferry Terminal by CTN weekly in winter on Wed at 1600 or 1700, Jun every Wed at 1700 and Sat at 1200, and 3/4 a week Jul-Sep at varying times. In Jul there are two return sailings by CTN between Marseilles and Tunis. A single journey costs £109 (seat only) and £187 (cabin), return £197-£336. Children half price. A dog or bicycle £14 single and £28 return. A small car costs £215 single and £343 return. A motor cycle £91 and £147. There are equivalent sailings from Tunis to Marseilles and Sfax (33 hrs), Bizerte (24 hrs) and Sousse (28 hrs).

SNCM/Ferryterranee sail once a week on a Fri or Sat and retun Sun. In Jul and Aug there are 2/3 sailings per week. Prices are very similar to those for CTN quoted above but offer reduced return fares for students and have special offers for 2 people in a car.

Trapani, Sicily (takes 8 hrs) – Tirrenia Navagazione – one a week all year, each Mon (Tues in Ramadan), depart Trapani at 0900, arrive Tunis 1600. Depart Tunis at 2000 and arrive Trapani next day at 0800. Fares single – high season, first class cabin £82, deck £42, group 1 car £70, bicycle £7.50, motorcycle £24. Low season first class cabin £69, deck £35, group one car £60, bicycle £6, motorcycle £19.

Linee Lauro sail to Tunis, 4 times a month, Jun-Sep inclusive. Cheapest single fare TD84.

USTICA lines from Kelibia via Pantelleria, Jun-Sep, Sun, Wed and Fri, foot passengers only. TD50 plus TD3 for each piece of luggage.

Cagliari (takes 21 hrs) – Tirrenia Navagazione via Trapani. Departs Sun 1900. Fares single – high season first class cabin £94, deck £50, group 1 car £72. Low season first class cabin £79, deck £42, group 1 car £62.

Genoa/Naples – Tirrenia Navagazione via Cagliari and Trapani.

Genoa (from Ponte Colombo) CTN – once a week on Sat at 1300 or 1650 in winter, 2 a week in Jun and Sep and 3/4 a week Jul and Aug, takes 24 hrs. A single journey costs £77.40 (seat only) and £124.50 (cabin), return £136 – £242, children half price, a dog or bicycle £14 single and £24 return. A small car costs £145 single and £247 return.

Naples from Moloangiono by CTN, 3 sailings per month Jun-Sep inclusive all leaving in the afternoon. Equivalent return sailing from Tunis are all at weekends.

A single journey costs £56 (seat only) and £93 (cabin), return £90 – £175, children half price, a dog or bicycle £11 single and £21.40 return, a small car costs £91 single and £162 return.

Linee Lauro, to Tunis, 4 sailings a month Jun-Sep inclusive, takes 670 passengers and 170 vehicles, cheapest single fare TD65.

Malta operated by CTN, once a week via Catania (Sicily) taking 12 hr.

Valetta (Malta) commencing summer 1996 – Contact Eagle International Travel, 58 Ave Habib Bourguiba, Nabeul, T 271885.

Kelibia in summer only – (4 hrs) jetfoil from Trapani, Sicily – takes 90 foot passengers only. Aliscafi SNAV, £70 single, services cancelled in rough weather, 3 services a week, book, con-tact **Eagle International Travel**, 58 Ave Habib Bourguiba, Nabeul, T 271885.

● **Customs**

Customs at the airport are slow as most bags (particularly those belonging to Tunisians) are searched. Be patient. Leaving Tunisia the customs officials are rarely in evidence.

Duty free allowances You may take into Tunisia 2 cameras of different types, 20 films, cassette player, 2 tapes, video camera (which will go down on your passport), portable type-writer, portable radio, binoculars, child's push-chair, sports equipment, 1 litre of spirits, 2 litres of wine, 400 cigarettes or 100 cigars or 500gm tobacco, $1/4$ litre of perfume, 1 litre of toilet water and gifts to value of £30.

Duty free goods to take out of Tunisia such as perfume, cigarettes, wine, spirits and gifts are available in varying quantity and quality in airport departure louages, note Tunisian money is not accepted beyond passport control.

Import/export bans Weapons may not be taken in or out of Tunisia. Permits can be obtained for hunting weapons on organized visits. Possession of underwater weapons is a serious offence. The Tunisians are, understandably, strongly opposed to people exporting genuine pieces of their archaeological heritage.

Registration Other than the usual embarkation card filled in on arrival at a port or airport, no other formalities are necessary. Hotels register their guests. Informal visitors will need to register themselves with the nearest police station.

ON ARRIVAL

● **Conduct**

Clothing It is as well to remember that this is a Muslim country and you should dress casually but decently. There are strict rules for acceptable clothing for visiting a mosque. See the chapter on travelling in a Muslim country, (page 19).

Hammams Modest behaviour is expected in the *hammam* so cover yourself somehow.

● **Electricity**

The current is 220V on 2 pin plugs. Take an international adaptor plug. In the far S you may encounter 110V.

● **Hours of business**

Vary in summer, winter and Ramadan. These

are minimum times: **Shops** between 0800-1230 and 1430-1800, Sat 0800-1300 but they open earlier in summer with one session 0730-1300. Shops in tourist areas are always open!!

Banks 0800-1100 and 1400-1700 Mon-Thur, 0800-1100 and 1300-1500 Fri. Closed afternoons in summer. Ramadan 0800-1230. In Tunis, some banks are open outside these hours, and in most tourist resorts, money can be changed in large hotels at the aiports and in bureau de change establishments.

Government and Public Services 15 Jul-15 Sep 0730-1330. 16 Sep-14 Jul 0830-1330 and 1500-1745. Fri-Sat 0830-1330. During Ramadan opening hours are different and everything is generally closed in the afternoon.

● **Official time**

Tunisia is on Central European Time which is one hour ahead of GMT.

● **Photography**

Taking photographs is no problem in Tunisia, but be aware that some people object to being photographed and taking pictures of women is best avoided without their permission. However children love to be photographed – again and again! Avoid photographing military installations or risk losing your film, your camera or even gaining some hospitality in a police station. Film is readily available throughout the country, check the sell-by date. Bring your own specialist and video films.

● **Safety**

There is no threat to personal security in Tunisia. Normal vigilance is recommended against petty crime and basic common sense used with respect to personal property, especially money and passports.

● **Shopping**

A good range of crafts is available in Tunisia. You have the choice of buying them in tourist shops, the souqs or in the Office National de l'Artisanat Tunisien (ONAT). It is a good idea to go to the ONAT first where the official prices are listed. Even though the prices are higher here than in the streets, the quality is guaranteed. The best place for shopping is undoubtedly the souq in the medinas. The prices are generally lower and bargaining is part of the fun. No prices are fixed and, as a general rule, the real price is 50% less than the price first given (but could be 90% less).

Carpets are made throughout Tunisia but best bought in Kairouan where the quality is superior and the prices cheaper. All carpets should have a sealed quality certificate. There are three main types – the *Alloucha*, made with natural long wool; the *Zerbia* again with long wool but coloured (the colours used are generally artificial and not all natural as claimed) and the *Mergoum* made of short wool or silk. Don't forget to bargain. For advice on types and official prices go to ONAT.

Copper and brass goods vary in quality and price. The most common items are beaten copper plates, in different sizes. Some are still handmade, but most are mass produced.

Hammams open for women in afternoons, men either before or after. Modesty essential, nudity not acceptable. TD1, massage TD5.

Jewellery is either Berber or Arab in origin and sometimes a mixture of both. When buying gold or silver, be sure it has the official stamp on it: a horse head for 18 carat gold and a scorpion for 9 carat. A grape cluster is used for silver of 900 mills/gram. Anything without the stamps should be treated with care. Prices vary with the degree of craftsmanship and some items can be very expensive. A traditional design is the Hand of Fatima (the daughter of the Prophet). See page 50.

Leather goods are of very good quality but not always cheap. Be sure to check the sewing as it is often of poor quality and the item may soon fall to pieces.

Perfumes many different types are available in various quantities, but the 'staying' qualities cannot be guaranteed.

Pottery is produced in large quantities, but good quality ware is found in both Nabeul and Guellala on the island of Djerba.

Straw goods are actually woven palm leaf fronds, mostly from Gabès and Djerba. They are cheap and range from simple baskets to touristy camels.

● **Tipping**

Service is included on bills in restaurants and hotels. If you intend to stay for a while at a café, or return to a hotel it pays to leave something. Tips of 5-10% are the norm in restaurants.

● **Weights and measures**

The metric system is used throughout. See conversion table on page 14.

● **Worship**

Anglican services in St Georges' Church, Place Bab Carthage, Tunis each Sun at 1000, also each Sun in Sousse, at 0930, 16, rue de Malte. **French Protestant service** in Eglise Réformée, rue Charles de Gaulle, Tunis, each Sun at 1000. **French Catholic mass** in Jeanne d'Arc Chapel, Tunis and daily in the Cathédral Saint-Vincent-de-Paul 0815 and 1830, Sat 1800, Sun 0900 and 1100.

WHERE TO STAY

● Hotels

Hotels and hostels in Tunisia are all controlled by the Tourist Board, and divided into five categories. The top is 4-star luxury, the lowest one star. Each year the Tourist Board checks the hotels and renews their ranking, but it is often hard to understand their criteria as it is perfectly possible to find an unclassified (NC) hotel far cleaner and more pleasant than a 3-star one. The ranking also fails to take into account the level of service. The best way of judging a hotel is not to rely on the ranking, but to **ask to see a room**. The differences can be enormous. It must also be said that some hotels are really

Hotel classifications

AL US$75+. International class luxury hotel. **All** facilities for business and leisure travellers are of the highest international standard.

A US$75. International hotel with air conditioned rooms with WC, bath/shower, TV, phone, mini-bar, daily clean linen. Choice of restaurants, coffee shop, shops, bank, travel agent, swimming pool, some sport and business facilities.

B US$60-75. As **A** but without the luxury, reduced number of restaurants, smaller rooms, limited range of shops and sport.

C US$40-60. Best rooms have air conditioning, own bath/shower and WC. Usually comfortable, bank, shop, pool.

D US$20-40. Best rooms may have own WC and bath/shower. Depending on management will have room service and choice of cuisine in restaurant.

E US$10-20. Simple provision. Perhaps fan cooler. May not have restaurant. Shared WC and showers with hot water (when available).

F under US$10. Very basic, shared toilet facilities, variable in cleanliness, noise, often in dubious locations.

dirty with decrepit furniture. In this guide, we have tried to cover a range of hotels, all of them clean (well, fairly clean), but with a difference in comfort levels. It is also impossible to give a totally accurate description of a hotel as managements can change. Equally, you will be very surprised to find excellent, very clean small hotels in the medinas, with very friendly management. Quite a few hotels, which are generally still clean, have a distinctly 'past-it' look and urgently need refurbishment. All prices are posted in the reception and can be consulted. All official prices are per person and not per room. In all classified hotels, and even some unclassified ones, breakfast is included in the price. It may be a good idea to request half board, as the difference in price is often very small. If travelling out of season check heating (some hotels have none) and number of blankets. In many hotel restaurants it is usual to pay for the wine/water consumed at the end of the meal.

● Youth hostels

Tunisian hostels are part of the International Federation and accept YHA cards. In all there are 35 hostels. Hostels are located at Aïn Draham, Béja, Bizerte (2), Chebba, Gabès, Gafsa, Djerba, Hammamet, Jendouba, Kairouan, Kasserine, Kebili, Kelibia, Korba, Mahdia, Matmata, Médenine, Menzel Temime, Monastir, Nabeul (3), Nasrallah, Remla, Siliana, Sfax, Sousse, Teboursouq, Tozeur, Tunis (3), Zaghouan and Zarzis. Minimum age for unaccompanied children is 15, no maximum but priority is given to younger members. Open 0700-2300. Some close in middle of day. Price/night TD3-4. Hire of bed linen and sleeping bags possible at all hostels for 500 mills/night. Use of kitchen 300 mills. Breakfast 700 mills, lunch and dinner TD3.

● Camping

Organized sites with full facilities are relatively few and far between but clearly signed when provided. Always ask permission of the landowner and/or local police before attempting 'casual' camping. None is allowed on tourist beaches. Camping is permitted at the Youth Hostels at Nabeul and Remel (Bizerte). The major camp sites are at Hammam Plage, Nabeul, Hammamet and Zarzis.

FOOD AND DRINK

● Food

In Tunisia food is very good, quite varied and

generally cheap. The small restaurants which do not serve alcohol are cheaper. Restaurants with alcohol are more expensive, even though the quality of the food and service is not necessarily better. Most local products are fresh and good quality. Food is cooked with spices but is never too hot. Along the coast and on the islands, fish is the main dish, and this is always fresh. Fish prices are often by weight, and you can have a nasty surprise if you haven't had it weighed before eating it. In most main towns you will find a large number of French restaurants which can generally be relied on for quality and price. Prices are not always indicated on the menu. Be sure to check before you order.

Specialities – Starters

Chorba – flavoured soup with lots of pepper.
Brik – deep-fried pastry containing egg and tuna, minced beef, lamb or vegetables, usually spinach, very popular.
Salade Michouia – cubed, mixed cooked vegetables with tuna and egg, can be very spicy, served cold.
Salade Tunisienne – Salade Nicoise with tomatoes, onions, tuna and egg.

Main Dishes

Keftaji – seasoned meat balls served with onions, courgettes and peppers.
Chakchouka – ratatouille with chick peas, tomatoes, peppers, garlic and onions, containing pieces of veal and served with a poached egg.
Couscous – steamed coarse semolina or millet served with vegetables and meat or fish. Typical dish eaten throughout the Maghreb.
Mechoui – grilled meat (usually lamb), very spicy, with peppers and capers.
Tajine – solid cheese quiche, with meat and vegetables, cooked in the oven.
Coucha – roast lamb with potatoes and peppers cooked in the oven, excellent.
Merguez – small spicy mutton or beef sausages, generally grilled, the red colour gives an indication of the amount of chilli used in their preparation, and is a guide to how fiery they will be.
Kamounia – a slowly cooked meat stew,

strongly flavoured with cumin, a delight to find this on the menu.
Lablabi – a hearty soup of chick peas, served at any time of the day.
Marcassin – wild boar meat, the only pork you are likely to find in this Muslim country, is very strong flavoured and is served with a sweet, tasty sauce.
Mermiz – stewed mutton with beans.
Soboku – steamed mutton with tomato sauce.

Fish: the best are the *Rouget* (red mullet), *Mulet* (mullet), *Merou* (grouper), *Lou de Mer* (perch) and sole; seafood is also very good.

Tunisian desserts

Delight your friends after your visit to Tunisia with these delicious desserts.

Stuffed dates

Split the date across the top and remove the stone. Fill the space with ground almond paste or pistachio nut paste. Dip each stuffed date in a thick sugar syrup and roll in granulated sugar. Allow these to dry (overnight) before serving.

Samsa

For these you require sheets of *malsouqua* cut in half.

For the filling:
500g finely crushed almonds (hazelnuts will do)
1 tablespoon dried grated orange peel
250g of granulated sugar
lemon juice/rose water

Form small triangles round a spoonful of filling and fry in very hot oil until golden brown. Soak in thick sugar syrup and sprinkle with roasted sesame seeds.

Date maqroudha

For the base mix a thick semolina dough using medium grain flour, baking soda, warm water and a pinch of salt. While it rises make the purée filling using pitted dates, ground cinnamon, olive oil and fresh grated orange rind. Roll and cut the dough into stips 7-8 cm wide and 1-2 cm thick, place the purée filling down the centre of each strip from end to end, fold the sides across the middle and press flat. Remove ragged edges and cut into *maqroudha* diamond shapes. Bake for 25 mins in a hot oven and when cool soak for 2-3 mins in a thick sugar syrup.

Desserts

Like all Mediterranean countries, Tunisia has many varieties, all very sweet!

Baklava – puff pastry with lots of honey and nuts.

Maqroudha – semolina cake with crushed dates, baked in oil and dipped in honey.

Halva – very sweet cake made from sesame seeds.

Loukoum – Turkish delight.

Bjaouia – almonds, pistachio nuts and puffed rice in a cake mixture.

Masfouf – a dessert made from fine semolina flour served with dates, raisins, pistachio nuts and pine nuts, a meal in itself.

Fruit

Dates – the season for fresh dates is Oct. There are over 100 types but the best, the deglet nur, come from the desert oases, particularly Tozeur and Nefta.

Pastèque – watermelon, particularly refreshing in summer.

Grenade – pomegranates, served with sugar and sprinkled with jasmine flavoured water.

● **Drink**

The national drink is tea, generally mint tea. Try not to refuse if you are offered some as this may be seen as insulting! Tea is also served black with lots of sugar, or green tea TD1/cup. Coffee is also widely drunk TD1/cup. Two types are served, expresso and cappuccino. (In local bars coffee and tea is only TD0.5.) The most common and cheapest beer is Celtia (a Tunisian make) but Tunisian made Tuborg and Stella, as well as imported beers, can be found.

Wine The Tunisians have been making wine for over 2,000 years. Wines sold under certificate are under the strict control of the state. The **red wines** are more acidic than western palates are used to and vary in quality. It is difficult to recommend any particular wine but for experience try one from the medium-priced *Magon Rouge* to the cheaper *Vieux Thibar*. The **rosé** is by far the best bet. It can be drunk with anything and is rarely awful. Recommended are *Haut Mornag* and *Sidi Rais* and the more expensive *Château Mornag*. The **white wines** are generally dry – try *Sidi Rais*. Also considered worth a try are *Blanc de Blanc* and *Muscat sec de Kelibia*. Tunisian *vins gris* (untranslateable!) include *Gris de Tunisie* and *Gris de Bizerte*.

Other alcohol Tunisia also produces three types of very strong alcohol. **Boukha** is made from distilled figs, **Laghmi** is palm tree sap

drunk immediately after it is collected and **Thibarine** is palm sap left to ferment for a while. Most imported alcohols are available generally in hotels and rarely in bars, but they are very expensive. Take your own alcohol to 'dry' restaurants.

Soft drinks are widely available. Bottled water is very good and is offered, but not free, with all meals. The larger 1.5 litre bottle costs about 1/2 TD. The smaller, resealable plastic bottles are just right for taking on short journeys.

Cafés are an interesting experience. They are generally packed with men (no women) and intensely smokey and noisy! A good way to make contact with the locals is to try a Shisha. They are water pipes, but the tobacco is slightly different from cigarette tobacco, and flavoured with honey or sometimes apples. Stronger than cigarettes (but not the local Crystal cigarettes) it is nevertheless a good way to start up a conversation as somebody will invariably ask you if you like it.

GETTING AROUND

● **Air**

Flights: Tun Inter (reservations via Tunis Air) run regular internal flights between Tunis, Tabarka, Monastir, Djerba and Tozeur. They are generally arranged so that travellers from other towns can spend the day in Tunis. Flights are not expensive but places are scarce. Tunisavia are flying smaller 72 seater planes on internal flights and have small planes for hire. Air-Liberté, part of Tunis Air, now flies under the name of Nouvelair.

● **Train**

This is a good way of travelling in the main areas. The trains travel quite slowly so there is ample opportunity to see the scenery. From Tunis the lines go N to Bizerte (1 hr 50 mins) and Tabarka, W to Jendouba (3 hrs) and Algeria and S as the 'Sahel Metro' to Hammamet (1 1/2 hrs), Sousse (2 1/4 hrs), Sfax (4 1/2 hrs) and Gabès (7 hrs) through all the coastal resorts. The TGM runs frequently from Tunis to Carthage and La Marsa stopping in all the suburbs. The only line inland goes to Metlaoui (11 hrs), via Gafsa (10 hrs). The service is quite efficient, nearly all trains leaving on time. First class trains with modern rolling stock, adjustable seats and refreshments are good but lack the atmosphere, interest and cheapness of the 2nd class. On a return ticket, 25% reduction cards can be obtained, valid 8 days. Timetables

Timetable of Sahel Metro

Southbound (Sousse → Mahdia)

Sousse Bab Djedid	0605	0655	0745	0825	0900	1000	1125	1220	1315	1400	1500	1615	1720	1825	1910	2015
Sousse Sud	0613	0703	0753	0833	0908	1008	1133	1228	1323	1408	1508	1623	1728	1833	1918	2021
Sahline Sebkha	0622	0712	0802	0842	0917	1017	1142	1237	1332	1417	1517	1632	1737	1842	1927	
The Hotels	0625	0715	0805	0845	0920	1020	1145	1240	1335	1420	1520	1623	1740	1845	1930	
Airport	0627	0717	0817	0901	0932	1036	1147	1242	1337	1422	1522	1637	1742	1847	1932	
Monastir	0641	0727	0817	0901	0932	1036	1157	1252	1351	1432	1536	1651	1752	1901	1946	
Moknine	0710		0930	0932		1105		1248	1420		1605	1720	1815	1844	1930	2015
Bekalta	0721		0938			1113			1428		1613	1731	1852	1930	2023	
Mahdia Tourist Zone	0728		0945						1435			1802	1859	1938	2015	
Mahdia	0740		0957			1132			1447		1632	1750	1823	1911	1957	2042

Northbound (Mahdia → Sousse)

Mahdia	0500	0550	0625	0700	0750	1020		1315		1515		1710	1830				
Mahdia Tourist Zone					0712	1032						1722					
Bekalta	0520	0610	0647	0720	0810	1040		1335		1537		1730	1853				
Moknine	0528	0618	0657	0728	0818	1048		1315	1343	1545		1738	1901				
Monastir	0600	0650	0734	0740	0806	0850	1000	1130	1215	1310	1343	1415	1520	1617	1715	1810	1933
Airport	0610	0700		0750	0816	0900	1010	1130	1215	1320		1425	1530	1627	1725	1820	1943
The Hotels	0612	0702		0752	0818	0902	1012	1132	1227	1322		1427	1532	1629	1727	1822	1945
Sahline Sebkha	0615	0705		0755	0821	0905	1015	1135	1230	1325		1430	1535	1632	1730	1825	1948
Sousse Sud	0625	0715		0805	0834	0915	1025	1145	1240	1335		1440	1545	1642	1740	1835	1958
Sousse Bab Djedid	0552	0632		0722	0812	0841	0922	1032	1152	1247	1342	1447	1552	1649	1747	1842	2005

trains run every day except Sundays and holidays

connects with trains on Tunis–Gabes line

Let the train take the strain

The main line trains from Tunis to Gabès and Metlaoui are hauled by diesel-electric locomotives of General Electric of USA or Alstrom of France and consist of Comfort class, 1st class and 2nd class coaches. The 2nd class is adequate but the seats are not very comfortable and the coaches become crowded and for the long distances involved it is recommended that 1st class tickets are purchased. This way you can see the sights in comfort. A word of warning. The smaller stations on this line are only named on the actual station building and not on the platform. To be quite sure you know when your reach your destination sit near the front of the train – and keep asking. The public address system is not often used except at the major stations and where the announcements come first in Arabic and then in French.

There is no buffet car but an attendant normally pushes a refreshment trolley through the carriages serving snacks (half a baguette with salad) and a soft drink for TD1. He will want the bottle back.

The Sahel Metro which covers the region between Sousse and Mahdia is a overhead electric train stopping at all stations and is a convenient way to visit the coastal towns and villages.

available from any station and most tourist offices in Tunisia and abroad. In addition to the return ticket an extra 'admission' fee is charged to enter the return train, about 350 mills, most unusual.

● **Road**

Bicycles and motorbikes: are a good way to see the country, depending on the terrain. Mountain bikes are recommended. Summer heat may make progress difficult, autumn or spring being a better choice. Bring essential spare parts, though if a problem occurs help is easily available as all towns and villages have mechanics. Spare parts for motorcycles may prove harder to find. Cyclists are advised to wear bright colours. **Bus**: is the cheapest means of transport, and therefore the most popular. There is a well developed bus system, both long distance and local. However, to use these successfully requires a lot of patience and the asking of many questions. The destinations on local buses are only in Arabic. Long distance buses have the destination in French written on a placard at the front by the driver. You need to be sharp to see it and then get on the bus. If in doubt get folk nearby to look out for you – even if they are not getting your bus. It is an easy way for them to be helpful. Virtually all towns and villages are on a bus route. Local buses can be a very interesting experience, as everything from fruit to chickens is transported. The inter-city lines are generally fast and comfortable. On most lines there are slightly more expensive a/c buses available, vital in summer,

check the different companies for facilities available. Times available from bus stations and tourist offices. Advance booking is possible on most inter-city lines, very useful during summer. Arrive in advance, as buses are more likely to depart early than late. **Car hire**: is probably one of the best ways of seeing the country, but prices are quite high as cars are expensive here. Expect to pay TD370-500/week with unlimited mileage. There are a many agencies, everything from the large internationals (which tend to be the most expensive) to smaller local companies. The standard cars are generally Peugeot 205 and Citroen AX. Shop around as prices can differ and when comparing prices check the 17% VAT is included. It can also be cheaper to buy a package including flight and car in London or Paris. International driving licences are normally required but a current European licence is usually sufficient. Be warned that insurance is unlikely to include the tyres, the wheels or the windows and replacement can be extortionate. Read the small print on the contract and check on the excess charge. Consider bringing your own car. Balance the hire charges against the ferry charge and greater flexibility.

Examples of car hire charges 1996 one week unlimited travel from Tri Car in Hammamet or Holiday Autos UK.

Group A – Citröen AX, TD450/£289

Group B – Peugeot 205 or Renault Super 5, TD490/£329

Group C – Renault 19, TD550/£359

Group D – Peugeot 309 or Citröen ZX, TD630/£391

Group E – Citröen ZX with a/c, TD1,080/£449, Peugeot 405 with a/c, TD1,400/£459.

Car breakdown You may be rescued by a patrolling Garde Nationale. Failing that, hitch to the nearest village for a mechanic or to ring the hire firm. Travellers intending to drive in the S are advised to read the section on travelling in the desert (see page 43).

Driving in Tunisia is on the right. The roads are generally good but the number of cars on the road far exceeds the number of competent drivers. Be particularly careful when driving through villages, as children and animals have little road sense. Be very careful, too, of Peugeot pickups, which are more than likely to turn suddenly or stop without indicating. In town, the real danger is the pedestrians. Obey the speed limits, a strict 50 km in towns and 90 km on the main roads and 110 km on the autoroute from Tunis to M'saken (beyond Sousse). There are numerous police controls, particularly by speed limit signs. Infringement of traffic regulations can cost up to TD500. If you are stopped, smile. It will make things easier. Safety belts are compulsory. Petrol is very cheap and there is no shortage of petrol stations. Avoid no parking zones in cities as illegally parked cars are clamped (TD7) or towed away which is tedious rather than expensive. Roads signs are French/International with Arabic translations.

Hitchhiking is easy, particularly going along the coast. Inland can be more difficult but is generally not a problem. Normally the ride is not free except in an emergency. Shared taxis are found on many routes and private cars and pickups will act in the same capacity, expecting payment as a matter of course. Foreign travellers may get a free ride. Remember drivers have a choice and may not choose heavily laden, unkempt passengers, especially not for a free ride. While the editors appreciate that hitchhiking may be the only way to reach a given destination, travellers do so always at their own risk.

Louages are large long distance taxis, generally estate cars, taking up to 5 or 6 people. They operate between certain fixed points, are a very popular mode of transport and often the fastest. They leave as soon as they are full and have a station in virtually every town. They are excellent transport for a group or large family even though all children count full fare. Be sure to settle the price before leaving. For long trips don't sit at the very back as that is the least comfortable position. You are unlikely to find a non-smoking vehicle. They are generally a little more expensive than the train. The town indicated in the window of the louage does not indicate where it is going, but only where it is licensed! Be warned that some of the cars are old and slow, but some are brand new and travel fast (often too fast). In summer, it can be a good idea to travel in the evening, or at night, when it is considerably cooler.

Taxis The ubiquitous yellow taxis are seen in most towns, they are numerous (over 300 in Sousse alone) and cheap, though not as cheap as the bus. Watch the meter has been set at the start of the journey. If the driver says it does not work you can always get another taxi. Any problem take the driver's number and say you are going to the tourist department – this will do the trick. If you hire a taxi for yourself,

Tolls for the Tunis-Msaken Autoroute

Tolls are charged for vehicles using the autoroute at Mornag, Hergla and Sousse and at the exits for Boufica (Km 65), Enfidha (Km 90) and Hergla (Km 101). Toll rates in 1997 were set at:

Toll site (TD)	Motorcycles, cars light vans, caravans	Minibuses large vans, light trucks	Heavy trucks large buses
Mornag	1.00	1.60	2.30
Boufica	0.30	0.50	0.70
Enfidha	0.80	1.30	1.80
Hergla exit	0.30	0.50	1.70
Sousse exit	0.40	0.60	0.90

Travellers can buy magnetic pre-payment cards from *Tunisie autoroutes*.

charges run at 200 mills plus 120 mills/km with an extra charge for luggage (sometimes for each piece of luggage). Higher fares after 2100. Taxi is the best mode of travel for people with mobility problems. The local bus is difficult enough for the able-bodied, long distance buses have high steps and trains have high and narrow steps.

● Boat

Ferry services ply to Djerba and the Kerkennah Islands. The journey takes 1 hr. There are 6 daily crossings in summer and 4 in winter.

● Walking

Walking is not usual but with a good map, adequate supplies and stout footwear it is possible. French series 1:50,000 maps, now out of date, are available in some parts of Tunisia, via France. Dogs can be a problem. Take a stout stick or an umbrella which can double as a sun shade!

COMMUNICATIONS

● Language

Arabic is the first language but virtually everyone has some French. In the tourist areas shop keepers and hotel staff speak 3 or 4 European languages, (see page 447).

● Postal services

Stamps are available from post offices, some shops, some kiosks and most hotels. Post offices open Mon-Thur 0800-1200 and 1400-1700, Fri-Sat 0800-1230. Summer opening 0730-1200 except Sun. During Ramadan Mon-Thur 0800-1400, Fri-Sat 0800-1200. Postcard reaches the UK in one week, USA 2 weeks. Postcard to Europe costs 350 mills, to USA 400 mills. Letters 450/500 mills. Parcels about TD25 for 10 kg.

● Telephone services

The telephone system is quite efficient and

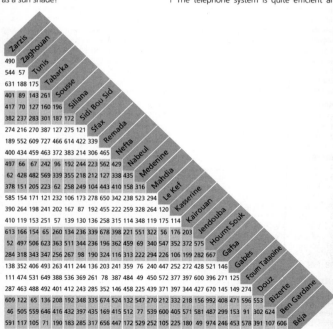

	Zarzis	Zaghouan	Tunis	Tabarka	Sousse	Siliana	Sidi Bou Sid	Sfax	Remada	Nefta	Nabeul	Medenine	Mahdia	Le Kef	Kasserine	Kairouan	Jendouba	Houmt Souk	Gafsa	Gabes	Foum Tataoine	Douz	Bizerte	Ben Gardane
Zaghouan	490																							
Tunis	544	57																						
Tabarka	631	188	175																					
Sousse	401	89	143	261																				
Siliana	417	70	127	160	196																			
Sidi Bou Sid	382	237	283	301	187	172																		
Sfax	274	216	270	387	127	275	121																	
Remada	189	552	609	727	466	614	422	339																
Nefta	400	434	459	463	372	383	214	306	465															
Nabeul	497	66	67	242	96	192	244	223	562	429														
Medenine	62	428	482	569	339	355	218	212	127	338	435													
Mahdia	378	151	205	223	62	258	249	104	443	410	158	316												
Le Kef	585	154	171	121	232	106	173	278	650	342	238	523	294											
Kasserine	390	264	198	241	202	167	87	192	455	222	259	328	264	120										
Kairouan	410	119	153	251	57	139	130	136	258	315	114	348	119	175	114									
Jendouba	613	166	154	65	260	134	236	339	678	398	221	551	322	56	176	203								
Houmt Souk	52	497	506	623	363	511	344	236	196	362	459	69	340	547	352	372	575							
Gafsa	284	318	343	347	256	267	98	190	324	116	313	222	294	226	106	199	282	667						
Gabes	138	352	406	493	263	411	244	136	203	241	359	76	240	447	252	272	428	521	146					
Foum Tataoine	111	474	531	649	388	536	369	261	78	387	484	49	450	572	377	397	600	396	271	125				
Douz	287	463	488	492	401	412	243	285	352	146	458	225	439	371	397	344	427	670	145	149	274			
Bizerte	609	122	65	136	208	192	348	335	674	524	132	547	270	212	332	218	156	992	408	471	596	553		
Ben Gardane	46	505	549	646	416	432	397	435	169	415	512	77	539	600	405	571	581	487	299	153	91	302	624	
Béja	591	117	105	71	190	183	285	317	656	447	172	529	252	105	225	180	49	974	246	453	578	391	107	606

Tunisia - Road distances in km

should present no problems. Look out for small kiosks/shops with signs **Taxi phone** – black lettering on a yellow background – which are **not** for calling taxis but for internal and international telephone connections. There are 5 or 6 in each town and at least one in each village. They are **much** cheaper than using the telephone in the hotel where the minimum charge is for 3 mins at TD5-10. Better still a Taxi phone usually has someone on duty who can give dialling codes and provide change.

Typical charges per minute from a Taxi phone are: France TD1.12; Ireland, Norway, Germany, Switzerland and UK TD1.28; Canada and USA TD2.4; Australia and Hong Kong TD4. These are normal coin operated telephones used exactly as in Europe, taking TD0.5 and TD1 for local use. International prices are on display.

Useful telephone numbers: all in Tunis, for introduction, permission to visit national parks etc:

Ministry of Foreign Affairs, T 1870.
Ministry of Religious Affairs, T 1863.
Ministry of Planning and Regional Development, T 1851.
Ministry of Agriculture, T 1873.
Ministry of Transport, T 1876.
Ministry of Culture, T 1866.

International code 216.

Local codes

01	Carthage, La Marsa, Tunis
02	Bizerte, Hammamet, Zaghouan and Nabeul
03	Monastir, Mahdia and Sousse
04	Sfax and Kerkennah
05	Gabès, Djerba, Medenine, Tataouine, Kebili and Zarzis
06	Tozeur, Gafsa and Sidi Bouzid
07	Kairouan and Kasserine
08	Tabarka, Le Kef, Aïn Draham, Jendouba, Siliana and Béja.
09	All car phones.
191	Speaking clock (French)
197	Police (anywhere)
198	Fire

ENTERTAINMENT

● **Media**

There are three daily newspapers in French, Le Temps, La Presse and L'Action. All international papers can be found in the main towns – usually the next day. Radio and TV is mostly in Arabic except for Antenne 2 (French) and RAI1 (Italian). There are no English programmes. BBC World Service can be picked up easily. For frequencies, see page 17.

Cinema in French and Arabic, costs TD1.5.

● **Sports**

Tunisia offers a variety of sports including:

Cycling is becoming increasingly popular and the standard of cycles for hire has improved. Quiet places like Kerkennah and Djerba can easily be explored in this way but main roads and Tunisian traffic is to be avoided. Serious cyclists may consider bringing in their own machine. Repairs are no problem.

Hunting and shooting of various game birds and wild boar. It is necessary to be part of an organized party for firearm permits during official hunting seasons. Expeditions for wild boar hunting (*sanglier*) can be organized by *Cilium Hotel* in Kasserine; *Sicca Veneria* in Le Kef; *Hotel Morjane* in Tabarka and *Les Chênes* in Aïn Draham. Contact Club de Chasse in Radès, T (01) 297011 for details.

Falconry: enthusiasts will find El Haouaria on Cap Bon the place to be in May and Jun. Contact Club to Fauconniers.

Fishing: is possible on inland waters of Cap Bon – a permit must be obtained from the Ministry of Agriculture in Nabeul on Ave Mongi Bali. There is no river fishing but lots of sea fishing with no permit required. The Kerkennah Islands are particularly suitable. Abou Nawas Marine arranges sea fishing for shark, tuna and swordfish, and provides all equipment, contact Tunis T 780450, F 780827 or Tunisie Sailing, Tunis T 761522, F 761866.

Rules on undersea fishing Any person wishing to undertake undersea fishing must file a request to the Director of Fisheries. The formula is the following: "I, the undersigned, family name, first name, date and place of birth, profession, address of residence, declare that I intend to take part in undersea fishing during this present year on the coastline of Tunisia. I certify that I am aware of the current regulations concerning this activity and I agree to exercise this activity in accordance with their provisions. Date and signature". This request should be accompanied by a medical certificate stating aptitude for undersea diving, by personal insurance and insurance for bodily injury to third parties.

Football: the national sport and Sun afternoon is the time to watch. See box, page 259 for an insight into this sport.

A Golfer's paradise in Tunisia Golf is an established sport in Tunisia albeit principally for foreign residents and visitors. There are eight first class golf courses across the country at Tabarka, Carthage, El Kantaoui and Djerba and two at both Hammamet and Monastir. All have coastal locations and all all set in fine countryside. Given Tunisia's excellent climate, with only a slight rainfall in the average winter/spring and southern Mediterranean temperatures, these are genuine all-year courses, with sunshine at its best in the southern resorts of Hammamet, Monastir and Djerba. For moderate temperatures go in the period Sept to Jun.

There are excellent and easy arrangements for a golfing break in Tunisia either by booking directly with the club or taking golf and accommodation as a package. Panorama Golf, for example (UK) T 01273 746877, F 01273 205338, offer golf resort holidays at Hammamet and Port El Kantaoui. Most courses offer facilities for experienced players and for beginners on a long weekend or weekly plus basis.

When pre-booking golf course starting times and discount rates can be negotiated. It is important that golfers take with them their *Handicap Certificates* since clubs in Tunisia demand sight of them before play is permitted. Tariffs for an 18-hole round run at approximately TD33 in high season and TD30 in low season, depending on the course and TD190 (high)-TD170 (low season) for a (6-day) week.

Tabarka course is set in more than 100 ha of pine and oak forest between the sea and the coastal hills. The course was designed by the Ronald Fream Group of the USA and comprises an 18 par golf course of 6,306m in length for 6,030m standard men's competitions and 5,190m for ladies' competitions. There is a 9-hole golf school course of 1,400m. The course is adjacent to the new Tabarka Montazah Tourist complex with good hotels and shopping facilities. The course is managed by Golf Montazah Tabarka, Route Touristique, El Morjane, 8110 Tabarka, T 644028-38, F 644026.

Tunisian Golf Courses

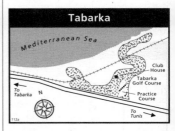

Carthage (La Soukra) Course is situated close to the Tunis international airport at La Soukra on the well wooded plain just above the salt lake, Sebkhat El Ariana. The course is 18-hole at par 66 with an overall length of 4,432m but a variety of course length selections offered down to 3,682m. There is a

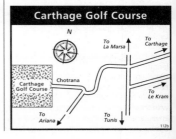

practice course and club house. The club runs amateur competitions throughout the year. Carthage golf course is only 10 km from Tunis centre and so there is easy access to first class hotel, shopping and entertainments. The ruins of ancient Carthage lie on the shore close by to the E. Contact Golf de Carthage, Chotrana 2, 2036 La Soukra, T 765919, F 765915.

El Kantaoui Golf Course is another Ronald Fream course, which was opened in 1979. It is the main feature of the town and is set in 100 ha of slightly undulating olive groves which drop right down to the sea front at El Kantaoui on the edge of the Sahel Plain. The course has 27 holes ranged in three 9-hole constellations with a further 9 holes planned. The men's championship course of 27 holes is 9,576m in length. There are practice and driving range areas attached to the club, whose club house is modern and well equipped. There is a club competition every Wed. The course is within easy reach of some of Tunisia's best hotels and the nightlife in nearby Sousse to the S. Contact Golf El Kantaoui, Station Touristique d'El Kantaoui, 4089 Kantaoui, Hammam Sousse, T 241500, F 241755.

Port El Kantaoui

Djerba Golf Club is set by the sea shore as an 18-hole links championship complex, designed by Martin Hawtree of the UK. It works in combination with an adjacent 9-hole intermediate course. The main course is 6,310m in length, 73 par (nine 4-par, six 3-par and five 5-par), beginning in a 9-hole loop through palms close to the sea, in which the 500m par-5 7th hole runs through dunes. A second loop, with three par-5 holes passes through a desert environment of palms and rocky outcrops. Djerba club house has a restaurant, bar and

golf shop. The club is in Zone Touristique 4116 Midoun, Djerba, T 659055, F 659051.

Golf Citrus at Hammamet on the NW of the town is large at 160 ha in flat country covered in olive and citrus groves and with six small lakes. Built in the early 1990s, it comprises two Fream designed 18-hole courses, *The Forest*, with 18 holes (par 72) at a length of 6,175m, which is regarded as fairly difficult, and *The Oliviers* of 6,178m (par 72), classified as moderately testing. A 9-hole *Executive* course runs over 1,220m with 8x3 par and 1x4 par to give in conjunction with the two other courses a total of 45 holes. There is a practice area, driving range and a club house featuring a pro-shop, restaurant and bar. The handicap requirement is 36. The course has a group of hotel shareholders – *Abou Nawas*, *Aziza*, *Manar*, *Méditerranée*, *Phénida* and *Sindbad*, though golfers can arrange accommodation at other hotels in Hammamet. Management at Citrus Golf, BP 132, 8050 Hammamet, T 226500, F 226400.

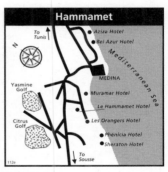

Hammamet

Yasmine Golf Course is located just to the N of the Citrus course. It was designed by Ronald Fream on a lightly wooded 80 ha site with two lakes in its southern section. It has a full 18-hole course and 9 training holes tucked into the centre of the complex together with a practice tee. The course has five separate teeing areas provided to give a good variety of challenge. For the 18-hole championship course par is 72 on a 6,115m length. Of noted difficulty are the 540m 10th hole with its adjacent lake and bunkers and the long angled 490m 15th, both with par 5. A good quality club house and a training school complete the facilities, all of which are within easy reach of the Hammamet resort. Contact Golf Yasmine Course, BP 61, Hammamet 8050, T 227665, F 226722.

Palm Links Monastir are located on the dunes between Sousse and Monastir. The course is less well-known than its neighbours to the N and S. It is nonetheless worth a visit at its coastal location in the dunes half an hour's drive S of Port El Kantaoui. Of 6,140m length the course has 18 holes with a par of 72. There is a golf school on a 9-hole course and a 360° driving range and practice area are available. The *Hotel Marhaba Palace* in El Kantaoui has a free daily shuttle to the links, T 466910/2, F 466913.

Monastir Golf Course is set in a magnificent site among scattered olive groves on the coast outside Monastir in slightly broken country which gives a great variety of topography between the various holes. The course itself is designed by Ronald Fream and is rated highly for its test of skills, 18 holes and par 72. The course is 6,140m in length with a choice of five tees per hole. There is a 3-hole training course, practice area and driving range. The course is a popular venue for golf holidays with a number of beginners and advanced courses running for 3-6 days. The golf course itself is convenient for hotels at Port El Kantaoui, Sousse and Monastir. Contact Golf de Monastir, Route de Ouardanine, BP 168 – 5000 Monastir, T 461095, F 461145.

Hang gliding: activities are based at Jebel Ressas, SE of Tunis. Contact the Federal Gliding Club in Tunis, T 906712, and see that section for details.

Horse Riding: there are plenty of horses for hire in the tourist areas. Better to hire from your hotel or a stable with a good reputation. Both Club Hippique in Ksar Saïd and Club Hippique La Souqra in the vicinity of Tunis are rec (see Tunis section). Horse racing takes place at Ksar Saïd, 10 km NW of Tunis, and at Monastir.

Hot air ballooning: at Aeroasis Club in Tozeur who offer floating trips in a balloon every day of the week, weather permitting. See that section for details.

The **Tunisia Rallye** is held annually in Apr in the S of the country. At the 1996 event there were 120 vehicles and 130 motorcycles participating.

Sand yachting/land yachting: on the dunes and on Chott el Djerid organized in Tozeur. Best season Nov-May. See that section for details.

Tennis: at most large tourist complexes. The quality of provision varies. Some complexes have a large number of courts. Cap Carthage in Tunis has 30, Club Mediterranée on Djerba has 20, while El Hambra, Les Maisons de Mer in Port el Kantaoui have 12 each. The Tourist Office publishes a booklet specifically for tennis enthusiasts.

Watersports: including sailing, skiing, wind-surfing, snorkelling, scuba diving, fishing and underwater fishing. Contact Centre Nautique International de Tunisie, 22 rue de Medine, Tunis, T 282209.

There are 30 ports and anchorages varying from 5 to 380 berths. The main pleasure ports are Port el Kantaoui, Monastir, Sidi Bou Saïd and Tabarka.

Yachting – entry regulations and information Except in cases of *force majeure* which must be proved, any pleasure craft arriving by sea from a foreign point of departure may only berth in a harbour where there is customs station and a police station – see chart page 357.

Upon arrival at the port all persons on board must show their passports and complete individual registration cards. Moreover, with regard to personal safety of the persons on board, the

Yacht Anchorages

Not to scale

Mediterranean Sea

Tabarka
Bizerte
Ghar el Melh
Sidi Bou Saïd
Sidi Daoud
TUNIS
La Goulette
Kelibia
Beni Khiar
Hergla
El Kantaoui
Sousse
Monastir
Teboulba
Bekalta
Mahdia
Salakta
Chebba
La Louata
Sfax
Ennajet
El Attaya
Mahrès
Sidi Youssef
Sekhira
Kerkennah Islands
Gabès
Houmt Souk
Ajim
Isle of Djerba
Zarat
Zaris
Bou Grara
N

Yacht anchorages – Tunisia

Anchorage		Pleasure craft berths	min draw (metres)	max draw (metres)	Facilities available
1.	Tabarka	60	2	4	hPBVWEFRLXsc
2.	Bizerte	25	2	8	HPBVWEFRLXsc
3.	Ghar el Melh	5	1.5	3	H BVWEfRLXs
4.	Sidi Bou Saïd	380	2	4	HPBVWEFRLXSC
5.	La Goulette	60	3	6	HPBVWEFRLXsc
6.	Sidi Daoud	10	1.8	3	HPBVWEF LXs
7.	Kelibia	20	2	5	HPBVWEFRLXsc
8.	Beni Khiar	15	1	3	HPBVWEFRLXsc
9.	Hergla	10	1	2	H BVWEFRLX
10.	El Kantaoui	300	2	4	HPBVWEFRLXSC
11.	Sousse	10	3	9	HPBVWEfRLXsc
12.	Monastir	400	3	6	HPBVWEFRLXsc
13.	Teboulba	20	2	4	HPBVWEFR Xs
14.	Bekalta	5	5	2.5	H BVWEF Xs
15.	Mahdia	20	3	6	HPBVWEFRLXSC
16.	Salakta	5	2	3	H BVWEFRLXSc
17.	Chebba	10	1.5	3	HPBVWEFRLXs
18.	La Louata	5	2	4	PBVWEF LXs
19.	Sfax	20	3	4.5	HPBVWEFRLXSC
20.	Sidi Youssef	6	2	3.5	HPBVWEF Xs
21.	El Attaya	10	3	4	VWEFR s
22.	Ennajet	10	1.5	2	PBVWEF LXs
23.	Mahrès	10	1	2	HPBVWEF LXs
24.	Sekhira	5	1.5	2	PBVWEF LXs
25.	Gabès	20	2	4.5	HPBVWEFRLXsc
26.	Zarat	5	1.5	2.5	BVWEf X
27.	Ajim	5	1.5	2.5	HPB WEF Xs
28.	Houmt Souk	10	1	3	HPBVWEF Xsc
29.	Bou Grara	10	1	2.5	HP WEF Xs
30.	Zarzis	60	2	4.5	HPBVWEFR Xsc

Facilities available:

H Harbour master		**P** Customs/Police		**B** Buoys	
V VHF		**W** Fresh water		**E** Electricity	
F Fuel		**R** Repairs		**L** Lifting gear	
X Watchman		**S** Shops		**C** Car hire	

upper case indicates on site
lower case indicates close by

harbour police may request that a list of equipment be completed and deposited at the harbour police office, on each occasion that a pleasure craft puts to sea.

On entering any Tunisian port, any foreign vessel should be flying, in such a manner that they are easily visible, its national flag and the flag of Tunisia on the rear mast and at the brow. Immediately upon entry the owner/user of the vessel must present himself at the customs office with all necessary registration and identity papers. The other occupants must remain on board until entry formalities are complete and a certificate of free circulation has been granted. This certificate allows use of Tunisian territorial waters without further formalities until departure for another country at which time the certificate will be surrendered.

Cats and dogs must have a certificate of health and anti-rabies vaccination dated within the last 6 months.

Fishing is authorized by the regional offices of the Commissariat General à la Pêche located at all coastal ports.

Documents and charts which are highly recommended: French Hydrographic Service maps no 7014, 5017, 4314, 4315, 4316, 4244 and 4245.

Forecasts may be obtained from the marine weather centres at La Goulette, Sfax, Mahdia and Bizerte and from the harbour master's office at Sidi Bou Saïd, El Kantaoui and Monastir where marine weather reports, wind strength warnings, special weather reports (gale warnings) and daily marine weather forecasts are available. In addition all Tunisian national radio stations broadcast daily weather reports.

Meteorology During winter the Tunisian coast is in the depression track between the Azores and Siberian anticyclones. In summer the Azores high stretches E bringing good weather with steady breezes to an otherwise sheltered coast. In particular: the NE coast as far as Bizerte commonly experiences winds from the NW to W and occasionally from NE to E. On all coasts the winds become very variable nearer to land. In summer the prevailing wind alternates from W to N with sea breezes blowing E to NE.

On the E coast winds from the E prevail during the summer and are almost always moderate (forces 2 to 4). The occasional winds from the SE can reach force 5 and cause heavy seas. Sirocco winds from the S may affect all sectors of the Tunisia coast. They are usually short-lived but can be strong and unpredictable.

The SE coastline is affected by major tides, with a difference between high and low water of approximately 1.8m at Gabès and 1.4m at Sfax.

● **Clubs**

Automobile Club of Tunisia: 29 Ave Habib Bourguiba, Tunis, T 243921/241176.

Bridge: **Sousse Bridge Club**, T 03226291/2; **Tunis Bridge Club**, *Hotel Abou Nawas*, International tournament in Jun, Mme Ghodbane, T 250255/393443; **Tunis Bridge Club**, Tunis Tennis Club, 20 rue Alain Savary.

Chess: there are 130 chess clubs in Tunisia with more than 3,000 members. There are three levels, national (10 clubs), honorary (30 clubs) and division (90 clubs). **Tunisian Chess Federation**, Cité des Jeunes, Ave Mohammed V, BP234, Tunis, T 682154.

Innerwheel Club: *Hotel Abou Nawas*, Tunis, T 234606.

Lion's Club: there are 15 Lion's clubs comprising 400 member and 3 Leo clubs. Area President, 8 rue Echmoun, 2016 Carthage.

Rotary Club: 68 Ave Farhat Hached, 1000 Tunis.

Scrabble: Tunisian Scrabble Federation, Radès. Major competition each Jan at *Hotel Omrane*, Ave Farhat Hached, Tunis.

Travellers' Club, Ave du 7 novembre, 2013 Ben Arous.

HOLIDAYS AND FESTIVALS

1 Jan:	New Year's Day
18 Jan:	Anniversary of the Revolution
20 Mar:	Independence Day
21 Mar:	Youth Day
9 Apr:	Martyrs' Day
1 May:	Labour Day
1 Jun:	Victory Day
25 Jul:	Republic Day
13 Aug:	Women's Day
3 Sep:	Anniversary of PSD
15 Oct:	Evacuation of Bizerte
7 Nov:	New Era Day

● **Local festivals**

Many towns have festivals, some more interesting than others and some invented for the tourists. Interesting ones are mentioned in the text. Major ones include:

Apr *Ksar Festival* in Tataouine – Berber folklore and tradition; Nefta; Nabeul Fair, display of agricultural products; *Orange Festival* in Menzel Bou Zelfa (close to Hammamet), orange picking and folklore.

May *Sparrow Hawk Festival* in El Haouaria, hunting scenes and hawk displays; *Tunis fair* – alternate years.

Jun *Ulysses Festival* in Djerba, folklore of the island and simulation of Ulysses' arrival; *Dougga Festival* at Roman theatre; *Malouf Festival* in Testour – Andalusian folklore with Spanish performers.

Jul Carthage – events at Roman theatre; Monastir and Sousse both have *International Festivals* of music, dance and theatre.

Aug Sousse *Baba Aoussou Festival*; Hammamet *International Festival* of music, dance and theatre; Carthage – cinema of the developing countries; *El Djem Festival* of folklore and theatre in Roman Colosseum; *Béja* – wheat festival.

Sep *Wine Festival* at Grombalia – between Tunis and Nabeul; *Cavalry Festival* in Kairouan – Traditional Arab horse display.

Oct Carthage film festival alternate years.

Nov Tozeur *Sahara Festival* – oasis tradition and folklore.

Dec Douz *Sahara Festival*: Sahara folklore, camel races, cavalry and music – the best of the oasis festivals.

● **Religious feast/fast days**

These change every year as they follow the lunar calendar. Approximate dates for 1997:

   12 Jan: Beginning of Ramadan

Tunisian holidays explained

March 20 Independence Day: celebrates Tunisia's independence from France in 1956. It had been a French protectorate since the Treaty of Bardo in 1881.

March 21 Youth Day: this was formerly celebrated in June but changed to the day after Independence Day to associate the importance of young people with the 'new' Tunisia.

April 9 Martyrs' Day: commemorates the events of 1938 when mass demonstrations in Tunis for the formation of a Tunisian parliament ended in violence and the death of 22 Tunisians.

July 25 Republic Day: on this day in 1957 Habibi Bourguiba deposed the Bey, proclaimed the Republic of Tunisia and himself President.

August 13 Women's Day: to acknowledge the fundamental role of women in Tunisia. There is a female minister in charge of women's affairs.

Nov 7 New Era Day: in 1987 Zine El-Abidine Ben Ali was sworn in as the new president of Tunisia.

(see page 23)

8 Feb:	Aïd Esseghir celebrated by parties, music in the streets
17-18 Apr:	Aïd el Kebir
7 May:	Ras el Am Hejri (New Year 1417)
16 Jul:	Mouled of the Prophet

● **Market days**

In every town there is a market, some of limited interest, particularly in the main tourist areas. However the genuine markets are both interesting and colourful.

Mon Tataouine, Houmet Essouq, Kairouan, Aïn Draham, Mareth, Maktar, Kelibia, Mahres.

Tues Ghardimaou, Kasserine, Béja, Bizerte, Haffouz, Krib.

Wed Sbeitla, Nefta, Moknine, Sers and Jendouba.

Thur Gafsa, Teboursouq, Le Kef, Djerba, Bou Salem and Douz.

Fri Mahdia, Zaghouan, Tabarka, Mateur, Sfax, Nabeul, Zarzis.

Sat El Fahs, Ben Gardane, El Alia, Thibar.

Sun Sousse, Hammam Lif, El Djem, Enfida, Fernana.

Libya

THIS part of the *Handbook* is concerned principally with West Libya, but Libya is a gateway to a large area of the North-Central Sahara both through Fezzan in the west and Al-Khalij in the east. Libya's desert heartlands are also a key part of the west-east trans-Saharan routeways and descriptions of the two southern provinces are included in this *Footprint Handbook*.

Libya, the fourth largest state in Africa lies between latitudes 33°N and approximately 20°N and longitudes 20°E and 25°E. It lies in a transitional climatic zone between the Mediterranean and the Sahara Desert, having only a narrow cultivated strip in the north and more than 90% of its territory in the arid zone. The two northern coastlands of Tripolitania and Cyrenaica have been associated throughout history with Mediterranean civilizations, notably the North African provinces of Rome and Byzantium. The Muslim invasion attached Libya to the Muslim and Arab worlds of the East, diversifying and complicating its affiliation to Mediterranean society and southern Europe. Libya came under the Ottomans and semi-independent local Turkish rulers or *bashaws* until the initial occupation of the country by Italy in 1911. Libya gained its Independence in 1951 as a monarchy under King Idris Senussi I. In 1969 a revolution saw the creation of a 'Jamahiriyah', or country of the masses, by Colonel Ghadhafi. Libya became increasingly an oil-based economy but after 1976 its economic and political relationships with other countries deteriorated, culminating in the severance of its worldwide air connections in 1992.

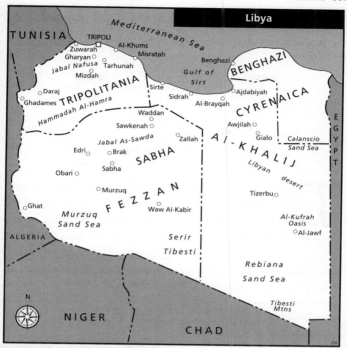

Libya

HORIZONS

BASICS

OFFICIAL NAME al-Jamahiriyah al-Arabiyah al-Libiyah ash-Shabiyah al-Ishtirakiyah (Socialist People's Libyan Arab Jamahiriyah)

NATIONAL FLAG Green.

OFFICIAL LANGUAGE Arabic.

OFFICIAL RELIGION Islam.

INDICATORS *Population* 5,407,000 (1995); *Urban* 86%; *Religion* Sunni Muslim 97%; *Birth rate* 45 per 1,000 *Death rate* 8.2 per 1,000, *Life expectancy* 62 men, 67 women; *GNP per capita* US$6,510.

THE LAND

GEOGRAPHY

The state of Libya has an area of 1,759,540 sq km, three times the surface area of France. It has a 1,750 km seaboard with the Mediterranean stretching from Zuwarah in the W to Al-Bardia in the E. Most people live and work along the N coast. Elsewhere the country fades immediately inland into semi, then full desert S into the deep Sahara. The desert regions are lightly populated and support major routes often over 1,000 km in length where N to S transport tracks pass from oasis to oasis, ultimately linking with Chad, Sudan and Niger in Central Africa. For all its extent, therefore, Libya is a country where the ambitious traveller can see much of

Libya and its North African neighbours

For travellers crossing North Africa either from W-E or E-W, Libya is an important transit zone, so that its relations with its neighbours are critical to open frontiers and a smooth passage through border formalities.

The situation is always volatile so that nothing can be taken for granted – check with the embassies in Tunis or Cairo close to the date of departure that there are no snags affecting links. From time to time Libya expels portions of its foreign work force, bringing misery to thousands of folk caught up in the problem and congestion to border crossings. The last exodus was of Palestinians in 1995, though Tunisian and Egyptian workers have been affected at various times.

Other than these difficulties, Libya is co-existing reasonably well with its North African neighbours. The Maghreb states to the W of Libya still have the remains of the regional arrangements of the UMA (Maghreb Arab Union) which includes Libya, to give a structure to joint trade and travel facilities.

Meanwhile, the political quiescence in Libyan foreign policy has reduced frictions. Libya is no longer an ideological or military threat to its neighbours. Indeed, Egypt and Tunisia share with Colonel Ghadhafi a dislike of Islamists and have a harder basis for cooperation than formerly. Libya is also dependent for air transit traffic on its near neighbours and needs its neighbours to argue the Libyan case at the international level for a lifting of UN sanctions.

All is not, however, sweetness and light since Libya harbours resentments for its neighbours' collaboration in the UN embargo and has other policy differences with them which can break out into political problems at any stage.

what exists simply by following the few key lines of communication.

Libya and North Africa

Libya is a cultural and geographic bridge firstly between Egypt and the Arabian lands to the E, the *mashreq* and the territory of the extreme Arab W, the *maghreb*. Secondly, Libya acts as a link between the Mediterranean/Europe and Saharan Africa. The Arabic spoken in Libya is generally different from the Berberized and French-influenced Arabic of the Maghreb with its quite separate accent and dialect from the Arabic of the Nile valley. The coming of oil wealth profoundly affected the attitudes of small groups of an often bedouin population, barely 1 million in all, with their Libyan attitudes, way of life, and political structure. Apparently less culturally stable and profound, it is immediately different to the great Nilotic civilizations to the E, and to the more Mediterranean and French influenced societies to the W.

Libya and Europe

Although Libya was colonized by the Italians for a brief period (1911-1943) as its 'Fourth Shore' and was politically allied to Europe under the Senussi monarchy until 1969, since that time the country has become detached from European values. In contrast to the Maghreb, Libya will seem to be alien to the traveller from the W. Management and administrative systems are generally slow except in the new, small but flourishing private sector. The role of the state is much greater and impinges much further on people's private lives than in West Europe.

Borders

Libya is bounded to the W by Tunisia and Algeria. In the extreme SW, the border is not fully agreed and travellers are advised to keep to the main roads. In the E, the Libyan frontier with Egypt is for the most part agreed. Libya shares a border with Sudan in the SE. The entire southern border was subject to dispute with Chad.

The Uzu strip was bitterly fought over until 1990 when it was settled by reference to the International Court of Justice.

Regions

Traditionally Libya was divided into three provinces – Tripolitania, Cyrenaica and Fezzan. Indeed, until recently, Libya was a united kingdom of these three provinces and Libyans still identify with these historic divisions. Recent political changes brought four new administrative districts including Tripoli, Benghazi, Sabha and Al-Khalij or 'Gulf'. Tribal territories are still observed in the popular culture of some districts.

Relief

A set of geographical districts naturally defined by relief features is recognized locally, the principal natural zones being the densely settled regions of the Jefara Plain, the Jabal Nafusa, Sirte, the Benghazi Plain, the Jabal Al-Akhdar, Fezzan and Al-Kufrah. In the centre and S very large scale features dominate. In the W the Hammadah Al-Hamra is a vast stony plain with no settlements and few lines of communication. Adjacent to the E of the Hammadah is the Jabal As-Sawda, the black mountains, a desolate and topographically broken area. In the S, Fezzan, is the great sand sea of Murzuq through which travel is feasible only via the few great *wadi* systems which traverse it. In the E, the settled zone of the Jabal Al-Akhdar is followed to the S by the Dahar, an extensive area of enormous sand seas, of which Calanscio is possibly the greatest. It is dangerous to travel off the few highways which link the small oases. Water holes are few and population numbers very thin. In the deepest SE lie the Tibesti Mountains, the land of the Tibu tribes, where security is unreliable and the traveller is advised to enter only when accompanied by an official courier.

Rivers

Libya has only one permanently flowing river, the Wadi Ki'am, in the W province between Al-Khums and Zliten. This is a tiny stream of no more than 2 km running from a spring source to a reservoir impounded in a lagoon adjacent to the seashore. Elsewhere the *wadis* run in spate after heavy rains but are dry for the rest of the year. *Wadis* in flood can fill at a dangerous speed. Among the major *wadis* of Libya are the Mejennin which runs through the W suburbs of Tripoli city. It is now mainly controlled through dams and diversion works in its upper reaches. The Wadi Soffejin drains much of S Tripolitania to the Gulf of Sirte, partly feeding the enormous natural salt marshes at Tauorga, located to the S of Misratah. In Cyrenaica the Wadi Derna is a rich area, its stream running for much of the year and providing irrigation water for a fertile oasis adjacent to the port. The generally waterless Wadi Al-Kuf runs through the hills of the Jabal Al-Akhdar in a steep, scenic gorge.

CLIMATE

The Libyan climate is very varied. The Mediterranean coast has warm winters with an unreliable rainfall, though on average over 200 mm. Extended periods of poor rainfall are experienced even in this coastal zone. Summers are hot and often humid. Relative humidity in Jul can reach an uncomfortable 80+% for days on end especially in Tripolitania. The mountains of the Jabal Al-Akhdar attract considerably more reliable rainfall in winter and early spring, while in summer the heights are cooler than the surrounding plains. Further S the climate becomes increasingly Saharan. Low temperatures and occasional random rainfall are experienced in winter with a large daily temperature range from 15-20°C during the day to sub-zero at night. Cold nights also occur in early and late summer. Summers are hot and very dry in the S with highs of over 50°C but one can also feel cold in the night when a sweater is welcome. Al-Aziziyah, inland on the Je-fara Plain behind Tripoli, has one of the world's highest recorded temperatures, 55°C.

The *ghibli* wind blows hot air from the Sahara across N Libya and carries a large amount of dust which severely reduces visibility. Relative humidity drops immediately at the onset of the *ghibli* to less than 15% and air temperatures rise rapidly. The wind is most noticeable in W Libya and is often associated with the spring solstice.

FLORA AND FAUNA

Outside the coastal plains, the Jabal Nafusah and the Jabal Al-Akhdar, the natural vegetation is dominated by tamarind, palm and fig trees. The acacia arabica, alfalfa grass, salt bush and a range of grasses grow thinly except after rain in the semi-desert. Other plants include the asfodel and wild pistachio. The dromedary was the principal animal of the region but is declining rapidly in importance. There is still a residual belief that the region was formerly, perhaps in Roman times, very rich and climatically more favoured than at present. Wall and cave paintings and graffiti of leopards, elephants, wolves and other animals of the Savanna suggest that this was so. There are antelope, gazelle and porcupine. Falcons, eagles, and other birds of prey are present in small numbers. During the period of bird migrations, many small migrant birds get blown into the Sahara and even the occasional exotic species strays into the oases. There are snakes, few dangerous, and scorpions which are to be carefully avoided. See also the introduction to North Africa, page 41.

AGRICULTURE

Agriculture remains an important occupation of the Libyans despite the protracted existence and economic dominance of the oil industry. In good years, as in 1995/6, rainfall turns the countryside green and the semi-desert

blooms with a profusion of flowers, the Jefara Plain being particularly attractive at such times. Poor rainfall means thin crops from rainfed farming and a reliance on underground water resources lifted by diesel and electric pumps. A series of dry years causes the water table to fall dramatically and leads to the excessive use of pumps. Around Tripoli, salt water from the sea has been drawn into deep aquifers more than 20 km inland from the coast. Water for both agriculture and human use has become increasingly salty over the years.

The Jabal Al-Akhdar of Cyrenaica has a generally reliable rainfall of more than 300 mm per year but has only limited underground water resources. Here agriculture is rainfed and is mainly concerned with grain production. In the S areas of the country farming activity is limited to small oases where underground water occurs naturally in seepages for traditional farming or can be pumped in modern development projects. The traditional farms have successfully resisted extinction as the economy has been modernized, though many modern reclamation schemes, as at Al-Kufrah, have been abandoned as costs have risen and environmental limitations taken their toll.

In much of the broad zone of N Libya, including the semi-arid steppes and the inland *wadi* catchments, various forms

of pastoral nomadism were important in the past. Tribal territories spread S from the coast to enable seasonal migrations of the nomads. In the central Jefara of Tripolitania, the fringes of the Gulf of Sirte and much of the S slopes of the Jabal Al-Akhdar, forms of full nomadism were practised. Other parts of the N were under types of semi-nomadism (family herding movement) or seasonal transhumance (movements of flocks by shepherds). The coming of the oil era, the imposition of firm boundaries between North African states and other processes of modernization brought much of the nomadic activity to a halt. Some semi-nomadic shepherding of large flocks of sheep and goats still goes on in traditional pasture areas but on a minor scale, involving only small numbers of people.

Agricultural land use in Libya is concentrated on the coastal strip. Only 1% of the country is cultivated with a further 7.6% as pasture, rough grazing or forest. The only natural woodland, mainly evergreen scrub, occurs on the Jabal Al-Akhdar, though this has been much reduced by clearances for agriculture. Total forested land is claimed at 0.4% of the land surface area.

The **land tenure** situation in Libya has evolved rapidly through the last 100 years. Communal, tribal land ownership was generally practised in Libya except in the settled oases. The Italian colonial period saw a great expansion of state-controlled lands which eventually devolved to the government of the independent state of Libya in 1951-61. Government intervention in all forms of ownership, ostensibly to socialize fixed assets in the country after the introduction of the Green Book decrees of 1973/75, led to more de facto nationalization of land. Small farmers are again being encouraged to remain in private ownership. In certain circumstances, individuals are also allowed to own more than one house. Some communal properties, mainly in the semi-arid steppes, are held by tribal groups. A gradual reassertion of private rights in land and other property began with the human rights decrees of 1977 and were reinforced by the privatization programmes implemented from 1989.

Economic potential

Libyan economic potential is greatly limited by the constraints of a harsh environment. No more than a fragment of the land receives rainfall adequate to support agriculture; underground water reserves are slight and declining. Even the costly movement of water from the S to the N by the Great Manmade River (GMR) projects inaugurated in late 1991 do little to mitigate the problem of water shortage. Other natural resources are scant. Oil, gas and some small chemical deposits occur. There is some potential for the development of the SW where yellow cake (low

Pan-Arabism

Feelings of pan-Arabism are very strong in Libya. The movement has established very strong roots in the country since the mid-1950s. It was Ghadhafi's adoption of pan-Arabist and Nasserist slogans which consolidated his grip on the country through the support of the people to these slogans. The Libyan people have always identified themselves with Arab issues such as the Algerian struggle for independence and the Palestine cause. These strong convictions of the Libyan people to pan-Arabism and the attitude to Islam as being the religion of the people has created a barrier that stood against the spread of fanaticism or the adoption of political Islam on levels similar to those in other Arab countries. However, it is a misconception to interpret the trend of the return to practising religion in Libya as a resurgence of Islam on the fanatical lines of its neighbours.

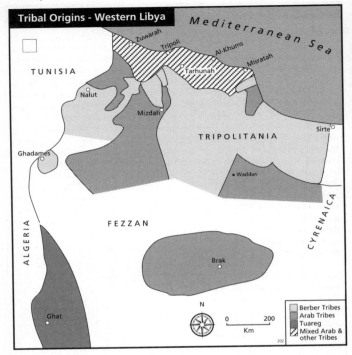

Tribal Origins - Western Libya

- Berber Tribes
- Arab Tribes
- Tuareg
- Mixed Arab & other Tribes

CULTURE

PEOPLE

grade uranium) is found. Overall, however, the country is poorly endowed and its physical resources inevitably must restrict its future development.

The **population** of Libya was estimated at 5,407,000 in 1995, 3.5% above the preceding year. There is great racial diversity. The original Berber population of W Libya gradually mixed with incoming Arab tribes after the 8th century BC, though some small groups of more or less pure Berbers from the Jabal Nafusa area of Tripolitania still exist. The peoples of E Libya are proud to be mainly Arab. Intermixture through marriage with

slaves and other peoples of negro origin such as the Tibu from the Tibesti mountains of S Libya gives a further dimension to the racial variety. The coastal cities originally contained populations of Jewish, foreign Arab, Maltese, Greek and many others.

Tribal traditions are strong. Outside Tripoli the country was economically and socially structured on *qabila* (tribal) lines with *lahmah* (clans) and extended family sub-clans. Each tribe had a defined territory and a specific history of alliances and friction with adjacent groups. During Italian colonial rule, the legal and economic basis of society was changed, partly through systematic removal of Arabs from the land but also by the economic upheaval that came with

The tribes of Libya

Libya remains a tribal society despite an attempt to undermine the system by the Italian colonial authorities, and strong forces for modernization since Independence especially since 1969. Perhaps the growth of an apparently all-powerful state control over the lives of ordinary people gave the tribal system the fillip it needed to survive. Caught up in a political regime many neither understood nor cared for, they turned to their traditional roots, the family, the extended family and the tribe. The genesis of the tribal system and its genealogies are all-important in giving strength to the tribes of the present day.

The tribes of Tripolitania are often of mixed Arab and Berber descent but might identify exclusively with one aspect of their ethnic origin. Geographically the tribes of different racial origin are in small areas so that there are few large confederations made up of a single ethnic source. In N Cyrenaica the tribes are exclusively Arab from the Obeidat of the Ulad Ali in the E to the Al-Magarba of Ajdabiyah and Sirt. All the tribes claim an individual or family as a common origin and it is not unusual for the pure Arab and Berber tribes to be able to establish long family trees. There are formerly saintly clans grouped around a *marabout* as a common ancestor. Some tribes claim their origins in a member of the family of the Prophet Mohammed. Other tribes have family trees which are suspect but which, nevertheless, serve to unite and bond the tribe. The still-practised custom of marriage between cousins brings a sense of closeness to those families involved.

Each tribe is made up of at least four different levels of organization, the nuclear family, the extended family, the large family group or sub-tribe and the tribe. The family and extended families are represented by the eldest male. The sub-tribe and tribe have a chosen or acknowledged head. Formerly the head or shaikh would act for his group in dealings with tribes or clans of a similar kind and with the outside world. This latter formality is less visible in modern society for, since 1969, the government has not given recognition to the tribal units. An element of social support and economic backing comes from the tribe together with a feeling of a shared territory. A person's identity originates powerfully in his tribal and family name, which declares ethnic origin, historical status and possibly current political strength.

colonial occupation and warfare. Nonetheless, tribal affiliation has social importance in marriage, kinship and status, especially outside the major urban centres.

Some 95% of people are found in the narrow N coastal strip, with 86% of all Libyans crowded into urban areas. Many of those registered as rural in fact commute to work in nearby towns. Tripoli attracts long-distance daily commuters and there are few areas of the NW not dominated economically by the capital despite recent attempts to decentralize. There is an average of three persons

per sq km, though in the coastal strip the densities are much higher.

It is estimated that about 46% of the Libyan population is less than 15 years old, 26% between 15 and 29 and a mere 4.1% above 60 years of age, a profoundly youthful population even by Third World standards. The balance between males and females is reported as 52% male and 48% female.

RELIGION

Libya is almost uniformly Sunni Muslim. Practice of Islam is normal for most people though, with some notable ex-

Libya and Islam

🐾 The Libyans see themselves as Arabs whose religion is Islam. They are Sunni (Orthodox Muslim) by persuasion and follow the Maliki rite with a small minority of Berbers who embraced Islam according to the Ibadite rite. The religion has never been a source of friction in the country and an absence of different interpretations of Islam has created a simple but strong bond between the people and religion. Although the first Shi'ite (Non-Orthodox) North African state was born in neighbouring Tunisia, with the establishment of the Fatimid State in the town of Mahdia, nothing can be encountered in Libya that is related to the Shi'ite practices of Iran, Lebanon or Iraq.

However, political Islam represented by Islamic movements advocating political points of view entered the country in the early 1950s following the purge by Nasser of the Moslem Brotherhood in Egypt. Some of the members of the movement fled to Libya and began to preach their thoughts to the Libyan youth. Later came Hizb al-Tahreer which called for the re-establishment of the Caliphate as well as Wahhabism, a puritanical form of Islam from Arabia. Out of the three Islamic movements only Wahhabism is rejected by the Libyan people because of its narrow interpretation of Islam and its belittling of the Libyan's Islamic practices. Wahhabism, through the support of Saudi Arabia has nonetheless introduced a new challenge to the Libyans who have a deep rooted belief in their Maliki rite. Using the political vacuum created by the rift between the people and the regime, the followers of Wahhabism succeeded in recruiting some Libyan youth to their movement. Hizb al-Tahreer and the Moslem Brothers have not gained a strong enough foothold in Libya to be capable of causing a threat to the regime, and their followers are not advocates of fanaticism or violence.

Fundamentalist Islam on the scale encountered in neighbouring Egypt and Algeria has not evolved in Libya to become a noticeable phenomena, and this is due, in part, to the nature of the Libyan belief in Islam, the resentment against religious-related violence, and a belief in a separation between politics and religion.

ceptions, Islam is kept as a way of life rather than a political force, in contrast to Algeria. Within Sunni Islam there is variation in attachment to different schools of jurists. Most Libyans are of the Malekite school, though Berber minority groups of Kharejite thought are also found.

LITERACY

Rates are much improved in Libya from a very poor base level at Independence. By 1990, 75% of males and 50% of females were literate. The educational system has been the subject of constant interference by the authorities, and standards, especially in higher education, have fallen in re-

cent years. Even so there are 72,000 persons each year in higher education with university levels, except in medicine and some other limited areas, approximating in most cases to those of European secondary schools.

INCOME

As an oil economy Libya generates an apparently high income per head at US$6,510. This figure can be misleading in the sense that the government controls and spends the greatest portion of national income which benefits the population at large. There is poor distribution of income, the isolated rural regions of the country being much worse off in real terms than the coastal cities.

Between individuals, however, there is less visible difference in income than in other Arab states. Libyan participation in the workforce is low at 25% of the total population with only 10% of women taking part in paid employment. By far the majority of Libyans work for the government or its agencies, leaving foreign labourers to work in industry and perform other menial tasks.

HISTORY SINCE INDEPENDENCE

British and French military administrations withdrew in 1951 when the state became independent as a United Kingdom of Cyrenaica, Tripolitania and Fezzan under the first Senussi monarch. The king kept close links with the British and Americans, permitting the retention of British land forces and American and British airforce facilities. Libya was economically poor at this period, having one of the lowest standards of living in the world. Foreign aid supported the state until an increasing volume of oil company expenditures in Libya on goods and services for exploration activity gradually improved the economy. Severe strains affected the Libyan nation as Arab nationalist and anti-western ideology generated by Gamal Abdel Nasser in Egypt spread to Libya.

Oil was struck in commercial quantities in 1959 and oil exports began in 1961. Libya rapidly became financially independent and initiated sensible reforms in housing, health and education. Employment opportunities improved and a development programme for agriculture, industry and infrastructure was set in motion. Young Libyan technocrats were given scope to implement their policies and the country made rapid steps forward from a low economic base level. The king took little part in the management of the country. Politically the nation was concentrated in a United Kingdom of Libya in 1963, with a parliament of limited powers centred in Tripoli. The Palestine question and the spread of Nasserite ideas made Libya politically unstable.

A coup d'état by a group of young army officers took place on September 1, 1969. The leader of the coup was Mu'amar Ghadhafi who was a disciple of Gamal Abdel Nasser, overtly anti-western and deeply convinced of the need to obtain full rights for the Palestinians. He banned alcohol and the use of foreign languages for official purposes. He closed down the remaining foreign military bases on Libyan soil. He abolished most private sector activities in the economy and promised a new Arab socialist society under the banner of the Socialist People's Libyan Jamahiriyah. He elaborated a set of philosophies encapsulated in his Green Book which set out his ideas on the nature of an Arab socialist state. He adopted the position of *qa'ed* (guide) and announced that democracy was untenable. Instead he set up people's committees in all administrative districts and work places as best representing the interests of the masses. Perhaps his greatest success was in threatening the assets of the foreign oil companies in Libya and in helping to force up oil prices in the early 1970s.

The Libyan role in favour of Arab unity and against western interests was pursued through the creation of a vast and expensive military establishment, political activities abroad designed to frustrate western interests and a solid pro-Palestinian stance. While oil revenues remained very high, Libya's international position gained some notoriety in Lebanon, Uganda and Chad. Military successes were denied the Libyan authorities and, as oil wealth declined first in the mid-1970s and then in the 1980s, Libyan foreign policy ceased to be significant in international affairs.

At home a series of economic plans promised rapid and integrated regional development of the country, but erratic implementation of projects, shortages of money and personnel and distraction abroad diluted the effort. Despite having a small indigenous population, Libya has never quite developed beyond oil as a productive and well-organized state with high personal incomes. In 1989 the socialist system of centralized national and economic management was abandoned piecemeal.

Political power is concentrated in the hands of Colonel Ghadhafi and, to a lesser extent, his close associates. An annual People's Congress permits some ventilation of other ideas and an apparent control system on spending of state revenues. In fact there have been few political changes to compare with the liberalization and privatization of the economy in recent years.

Despite official statements and propaganda images of Libya abroad, most Libyans are gentle and friendly, not least with foreign visitors who are clearly tourists and/or travellers. Travellers should, however, note that the security situation is slightly tense at the time of writing following harassment of foreigners in some southern locations.

MODERN LIBYA

GOVERNMENT

The ideal of government was expressed in the Third Universal Theory, expounded by Colonel Ghadhafi in the early 1970s and enshrined in the **Green Book**, the first sections of which were published in 1976. Ghadhafi attempted to bring together strands of his own beliefs – Islam, freedom from foreign intervention, equality of people and the welfare of the greater Arab nation – within a unified philosophy. He was never taken entirely seriously in this ambition outside the country. Events were also to prove that Libya itself was resis-

UN sanctions against Libya

The Libyan government has been in conflict with the United States of America, the United Kingdom and France over the matter of terrorism. The USA and UK are concerned particularly in the question of the downing of a Pan-Am flight at Lockerbie.

UN sanctions, imposed against Libya for its alleged involvement in the Lockerbie bombing in 1988 and the shooting down of a French airliner over the Sahara in 1989, began on 15 April 1992 and were renewed in 1993 and 1994. They were in accordance with Security Council Resolution 748, the UN having called in vain for the extradition of the two accused the previous January in Resolution 731.

The UN sanctions against Libya are as follows:
(1) the freezing of Libyan assets in the USA,
(2) the banning of all civil aviation connections with Libya,
(3) an arms embargo,
(4) UN sanctions were strengthened on December 1, 1993 with the imposition of controls on the transfer to Libya of oil related goods, aerospace equipment and training, in accordance with Security Council Resolution 883,
(5) constraints were placed on the international movement of Libyan financial assets, including special arrangements for the treatment of Libyan oil revenues.

Three permanent members of the Security Council are dedicated to the maintenance of UN sanctions until Colonel Ghadhafi hands over for trial two of his nationals indicted for involvement in the Lockerbie bombing and provides further evidence of its involvement in the shooting down of the UTA aircraft over Niger.

tant to his ideas. Despite the single minded expenditure of large sums on imposing socialism at home, including the devolution of bureaucratic powers to the four major regions – Tripoli, Sabha, Al-Khalij and Benghazi – and the removal of all private privileges of ownership of goods, property and even a fully private life, by 1987 the dream had to be abandoned. The structures he established persisted, however. A Basic People's Congress meets to manage the affairs of state, with Colonel Ghadhafi taking the position of 'guide' to the revolution. The congress acts officially through a series of appointed secretariats, which are now, for all practical purposes, ministries in the traditional mode. The revolutionary fervour, which characterized Libya in the 1970s and 1980s, has dimmed considerably and lives on only in the apparatus for security and military matters. Since he has these agents of political control in his hands, Colonel Ghadhafi effectively has the final say in decision-making in the country. There is no official opposition party and opponents of the régime have generally fled abroad.

The secretariats which look after day-to-day administration are spread out throughout the country as part of a deliberate policy of regionalizing management. Key ministries are in Sirte, though some scattered government offices also exist.

In foreign policy, Libya acted to harass the western powers at whose doors Colonel Ghadhafi laid many of the ills of Libya and the Arab nation. While he could play off the West against the USSR and had access to considerable oil revenues, he successfully worked against the USA and EU states in propaganda and support for their opponents. The demise of the USSR as a world power in 1991, a massive fall-off in oil revenues in the mid-1980s and the rise of the conservative states as leading elements within the Arab world left him vulnerable to foreign pressures to accept international legal norms for state activities. This was signalled in Libyan problems in 1992 with US and British demands over the Lockerbie incident.

ECONOMY

Libya is an oil-based economy. Oil was first exported commercially in 1961 and thereafter output rose rapidly so that at the end of the 1960s Libya was the fifth largest Opec producer of crude oil with more than 3 million barrels per day. This expansion was based geographically on the oilfields in the vast embayment of the Gulf of Sirte where small but prolific oilfields were found in the sedimentary rocks. While some oil was discovered by the major international oil companies such as Esso, Mobil and BP, there were also many small independent oil companies involved, for which Libya was the only source of traded crude oil. By the end of the 1960s a development of oilfields, pipelines and oil terminals had taken place in what had been a barren desert area lying between Tripoli and Benghazi. Following the revolution of 1969, economic policies were aligned towards making the country self sufficient.

Traditional agriculture

This was mainly self sufficient with small surpluses going to the many local occasional markets. The coastlands were comparatively rich agriculturally, favoured by adequate rainfall and available underground water for irrigation. Small fragmented farms were the rule on the coast, though many families had access to communal tribal lands for shifting cultivation and grazing animals to the S of the coastal oases.

Superimposed on this pattern of Arab farming and semi-nomadic herding is an Italian colonial structure established in the 1920s and 1930s but replicated since Independence by the Libyans themselves. The ex-colonial landscape is still a powerful feature of the country, espe-

Colonel Mu'amar Ghadhafi

Colonel Ghadhafi was born in the Gasr Bu Hadi area of Sirt on the coast of the Gulf of Sirte (Sidra) in 1942. His parents were from the Ghadhadfa tribe, a mixed Arab-Berber group, which practised semi-nomadic herding of animals with some shifting grain cultivation in the arid steppelands surrounding the traditional tribal territories. He went to secondary school in Misratah before joining the army as an officer cadet. He graduated from the military academy and was eventually posted to Sabha in the Fezzan area. He briefly attended the University of Libya in Benghazi and undertook a short stay in the United Kingdom on a training course.

He rose to fame in Sep 1969 as the head of a group of revolutionary officers who overthrew the monarchy and set up an Arab republic ruled by a Revolutionary Command Council. The political programme introduced by Ghadhafi was simple and based mainly on the ideas of the Egyptian nationalist leader Gamal Abdel Nasser. Colonel Ghadhafi was anti-western, anti-Israel and in favour of a centrally controlled social and economic system within Libya. British and American military bases in Libya were closed down after the revolution. All public signs had to be written in Arabic and all foreigners, including any remaining Italian residents, were no longer made welcome.

Initially Colonel Ghadhafi was received by the Libyan people with acclaim. His simple creed of Arab nationalism fitted the mood of the day. In the early 1970s Libya became immensely rich in oil revenues as, aided by Libyan actions against the oil companies, the price of oil rose dramatically on the international market. At the same time, Colonel Ghadhafi issued his philosophy to guide the revolution, the so-called **Green Book**, preaching a form of Arab socialism. He also saw for himself a role as messianic leader of all the Arabs and a focus around which the Arab world could be united. At home, he entered into bold programmes for economic development, with expansion of agriculture, provision of state welfare schemes and investments in industry and infrastructure. Power was, at least in theory, devolved down to regional municipal assemblies which reported annually to a General People's Congress.

By the end of the 1970s Colonel Ghadhafi faced increasing difficulties. Abroad, Libya's attempts at Arab unity had failed. Libya had been unable to affect events in the Arab-Israel dispute despite a great deal of fiery rhetoric. Colonel Ghadhafi had also made an unsuccessful attempt to intervene in a war in Uganda to support the unpopular leader Idi Amin. Meanwhile Ghadhafi's political credentials were eroded by the rise of revolutionary Islamic movements in Iran and the Arab world. The collapse of oil prices after 1980 weakened the Libyan economy at a time when Colonel Ghadhafi became deeply embroiled in a territorial dispute with Chad over the Uzu strip, a band of desert lying between the two countries. Despite huge outlays in men and material, the war against Chad was lost and was taken to the International Court for arbitration. Suspicions that there was Libyan involvement in international terrorism came to a head in 1988 when responsibility for the destruction by a bomb of a Pan Am aircraft from UK to the USA at Lockerbie in Scotland was attributed to two Libyan officials. Libya eventually fell under a UN air transport embargo and was isolated from the international community as a pariah state.

In Libya, Colonel Ghadhafi lost some popularity as a result of these adverse changes but remained as the political guide of the country, defended by loyal echelons of the armed forces and without real rivals.

cially in Tripolitania. Enormous areas of geometrically planted olive, almond and eucalypt plantations extend across the Jefara and parts of the Jabal Al-Nafusa, often in association with small colonial farmhouses. Although the Italian farmers have now gone, their legacy in the landscape, perpetuated 'by the local farmers who bought them out and by the government, remains and adds significantly to current output of olive oil and almonds.

The greatest single changes by Libyan farmers, though on a model mainly reminiscent of the Italians, is the introduction of citrus fruit orchards and the intensification of output through irrigation in what had originally been dryland or lightly irrigated Italian estates. The most important single field crop is fodder. Libyans prize their mutton enormously and sheep are kept by most farmers. There has also been an expansion of beef and dairy herding, which also requires abundant fodder production, mainly types of lucerne. On the Jabal Al-Nafusa, there is little irrigation and dryland crops are olives, figs and apricots. Grain of excellent quality is grown on the Jefara plain on lands owned by the Jabal tribes.

In E Libya, the Jabal Al-Akdar are used for dryland cereals, some fruit and a large area of fodder. In the S, Fezzan and Al-Khalij, oases survive using irrigation for intensive vegetable and fruit production. Libya's best dates come from the SW, the *deglet nur* being the most prized.

Modern farming

Contemporary agriculture other than the private sector activities already noted has until recently been mainly state managed. Underground water resources in the deep SE at Al-Kufrah, Tizerbu and Serir were developed for agriculture and new agricultural production units created in the SW at Sabha, Murzuq and other sites. Expensive imported technol-

ogy was employed in these schemes and imported labour from Sudan, Egypt and elsewhere since Libyans were generally not prepared to move to these inhospitable regions. Despite the investment of very large resources, the majority of agricultural schemes in the S were abandoned or run down when Libya's oil revenues declined during the mid-1980s.

Libya's biggest and most spectacular development, the Great Manmade River (GMR), will carry water in a large diameter pipeline from wellfields in Al-Kufrah, Serir and Tizerbu to the coast and thence to Benghazi in the E and Sirte in the W. A second pipeline, it is projected, will transport water from the Murzuq Basin in the SW to the Jefara Plain adjacent to Tripoli. The movement of water to the N is at the cost of the closure of most major irrigation schemes in the S. Although the government has promised that the new water will be used in the coastlands for agriculture in addition to supplying industrial and urban areas, high costs of the water delivered there make its use in irrigation questionable. The need for new water illustrates the other great problem for farming in Libya – the falling water tables and intrusion of sea water into aquifers in coastal areas.

Oasis economies

In the oases of the deep S and the small towns at a modest distance from the coast, there is little industry. Here life revolves around earnings from agriculture and remittance income from employment on the coast. Construction of private villas and other housing is the most pronounced area of economic activity in the countryside, though farming is still a way of life for many Libyans outside the major coastal towns and involvement in transportation also absorbs a great deal of energy in these areas.

Petroleum

Oil provides the government with its principal foreign exchange income, US$7,810mn in 1993, the main source of

Economic indicators US$ billion

	1989	1991	1993	1994
Oil revenues	7.500	9.600	7.650	7.800
Exports	7.750		7.700	7.826
Imports	5.497		8.260	4.386
National income	19.500	21.100	32.000	32.900
Current account balance	+2.253560		-560	+3.440
Inflation (%)	15		15	30
Foreign debt			3.500	2.592

Source: Economist Intelligence Unit

general revenues in the annual budget (90%) and the most important single commodity for export (99%). The two areas of production are around the W borderlands and the Gulf of Sirte, the latter with export terminals at Sidrah, Ras Lanuf, Al-Brayqah and Zuwetina. The main oilfields are linked by pipelines to coastal terminals. Serir oilfield and its associated installations in the extreme SE are tied in to a terminal at Marsa Hariga near Tobruk (Tubruq), while a small line runs on a NS axis in the W to Zaviyah oil refinery. An offshore field, Bouri, is sited on the Libyan continental shelf close to Tunisian waters in the NW. It was won from Tunisia in a judgment of the International Court of Justice in 1982. Libyan oil reserves are only moderate, rated at around 29,000 million barrels, which would last some 52 years at present rates of extraction. Libya produces approximately 1.5 million barrels per year and exports some three-quarters of its output, mainly to West Europe. The National Libyan Oil Co owns refineries in Italy and Germany. Domestic refineries are found at Zaviyah, Al-Brayqah and Ras Lanuf.

Economic plans

The comparatively short life expectancy of Libya as a major oil exporter has given emphasis to the need to develop alternative sources of exports for the future. A set of economic development plans has been adopted by the government, the latest being a programme for 1980-2000, with aims to bolster self-sufficiency, cre-

ate new jobs and lay the foundations for a future non-oil economy. Some successes were won, including an improvement in the country's transport infrastructure. Excellent road systems serve all parts of the country. New hospitals, hotels and schools have been set up so that even the most isolated settlements can offer good housing, health and educational facilities. Grandiose plans for a rail system to replace the old Italian lines closed in the 1960s have been delayed. A North African link through Libya from Morocco and Algeria to Egypt is under consideration, while a mineral and general purpose line from Brak (Brach) to carry iron ore to the Misratah steel plant is under consideration. Air transport in Libya serves most major settlements but its growth has been impeded by USA sanctions against Libya which have limited the availability of new aircraft to Libyan Arab Airways, the national carrier.

Industry

Economic development outside transport and other infrastructure has been expensive and limited. Only petrochemicals, with large scale complexes set up at Ras Lanuf and Bu Kammash with a smaller operation planned at Sirte, have shown rapid growth, but they depend on the oil sector for raw materials, are highly polluting and employ few Libyans. The Misratah iron and steel mills began operations in 1989 and brought great prosperity to this old market town. How commercially viable the plants are remains to be seen. Elsewhere in industry the state agencies set up a variety of new concerns in food processing, soap making, aluminium and construction goods materials. As from the late 1980s, Libyan entrepreneurs were encouraged to begin work in industry on their own account, a move which saw the opening of many small scale workshops, stores and corner shop businesses.

Economic trends

The poor performance of the oil sector since the mid-1980s has dominated trends since that time. The late 1980s was a poor time for Libya and things have picked up only as better management of limited oil revenues and improved internal economic liberalisation has had an effect. The growth of private enterprise has been the main area of economic growth in the immediate past. Indicative of Libya's difficulties, personal incomes have deteriorated in recent years.

Tripoli

THE CLIMATE of Tripoli is Mediterranean with hot dry summers, cool winters and some modest rainfall. Weather can be variable, influenced by the Sahara Desert and the Mediterranean Sea which moderates daily temperature ranges.

INDICATORS *Alt* Sea level. The population of Greater Tripolitania is 2,014,200. District populations are Tripoli 1,083,100, Gharyan 204,300, Nikat Al-Khums (Homs) 196,000, Zaviyah 326,500 and Jabal Nafusa 204,300. Growth of population is 4.5% per year. Literacy in Tripoli is higher than the national average though official figures of M 95% F 90% seem too good to be true. The labour force comprises Libyans 300,000 and immigrants 250,000. The average income per head is US$5,310, with inflation at 10%. Although the official language is Arabic, Berber is also common in the hill lands of Tripolitania, and English, French and Italian are also spoken.

THE CAPITAL

Tripoli, or Tarabalus Al-Gharb (Tripoli of the W in Arabic), is the major city and de facto capital of Libya. The removal of many government secretariats and faculties of the Tripoli, Al-Fatah, university has not changed the reality of Tripoli as the real political centre of Libya. The People's Congress meets in Tripoli and Colonel Ghadhafi is for the most part resident there. Plans continue to be talked about in government circles for the construction of yet another new capital

which would be sited on neutral territory outside the two polarized traditional provinces of Tripolitania and Cyrenaica. Under King Idris Senussi, before the revolution of 1969, a new capital was set up at Al-Bayda in the Jabal Al-Akdar. It rooted itself well but political changes took away its role as capital. Colonel Ghadhafi and foreign consultants have

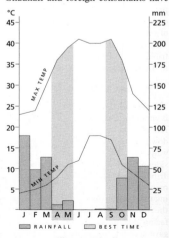

Climate: Tripoli

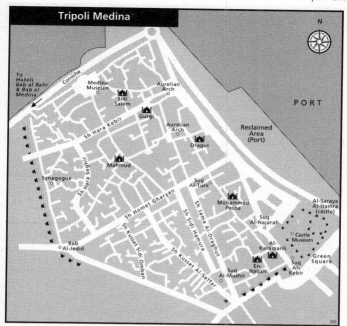

Tripoli Medina

To Hotels Bab el Bahr & Bab el Medina

Corniche

Medina Museum

Sidi Salem

Gurgi

Aurelian Arch

Aurelian Arch

Dragut

Sh Hara Kebir

Sh Hara Seghit

Mahmud

Synagogue

Sh Homet Gharyan

Sh Kusset Sidi Omban

Bab Al-Jedid

Sug Al-Turk

Sh Jama Al Draghut

Sh Sidi Hamura

Mohammad Pasha

Suq Al-Najarah

PORT

Reclaimed Area (Port)

Al-Saraya Al-Hamra (castle)

Castle Museum

Al-Karamanli

Sh Kusset Al-Seffar

En-Naqah

Suq Al-Mushir

Suq Al-Kebir

Green Square

N

205

proposed a new site for the capital on the coast of the Gulf of Sirte to act as a point of unity between the W and E regions. The fact that Colonel Ghadhafi has his tribal and close family links in Sirte adds to the attraction of this proposal.

PLACES OF INTEREST

The old walled city of Tripoli, the **medina**, is one of the classical sites of the Mediterranean. The basic street plan was laid down in the Roman period when the walls were constructed on the landward sides against attacks from the interior of Tripolitania. The high walls survived many invasions, each conqueror restoring the damage done. In the 8th century the Muslim ruler built a wall on the sea-facing side of the city. Three great gates gave access to the town, Bab Zanata on the W, Bab Hawara on the SE and Bab

Al-Bahr in the N wall. Constant rebuilding means that few ancient commercial buildings remain and even the oldest mosque, Al-Naqah, was reconstructed in 1610. The **castle**, Al-Saraya Al-Hamra, occupies a site known to be pre-Roman in the E quadrant of the city and still dominates the skyline of Tripoli. The castle is made up of many distinct sections, formerly public and private quarters of the ruling family. The women were kept in a harem and a number of beautiful courtyards lie segregated from the alleyways which run through the castle. The upper walls afford a fine view to the sea and across the town.

The old city itself was made up of a series of separate quarters, two major parts of which were Jewish (*hara* is the name designating the Jewish areas of Tripoli). Narrow streets criss-cross the

Ancient heritage is threatened

There is now a clear need for the advanced industrialized countries to understand the basis of Islamic science and technology. Not least this would help to bridge the growing cultural divide between themselves and their more numerous neighbours to the E. In particular, appreciation of the way in which Islamic culture has matured over the long-term is required so that the valuable skills and technologies of Tunisia and North Africa are not wastefully discarded for short-term commercial purposes. The erratic but now rapid pace of 20th century modernizations might precipitously sweep away all the remains and folk memories associated with traditional culture.

There is also a risk that the imposition of rapid technological change on developing countries such as Tunisia and Libya by the industrialized nations could lead to premature obsolescence and discarding of indigenous technology where it could still now and in the future be deployed with advantage. The modernization of the Japanese *mambo*, the equivalent of the Tunisian underground water channel, the *khattara*, is a case in point where improvement of traditional irrigation systems is seen, even in a society at the cutting edge of advanced technology, as useful. This Japanese view of continuity is one that has interesting implications for Tunisia and its older irrigation systems such as the *noria* water wheels in the Gafsa area and the *foggara* of El Guettar (see page 452).

The urgency of the problem of conservation or rescue of traditional Islamic technologies is acute. War and strife are depleting physical assets such as buildings and other works in Tunisia and Libya. Quite apart from man-made disasters, the processes weathering on mud brick, from which many Islamic traditional constructions are made, is considerable. The comparatively recent abandonment of traditional villages, old mosques and underground water cisterns in Tunisia and the entire old city of Tripoli, Libya, has exposed traditional technology/material culture to comprehensive destruction by neglect and natural erosion.

old city off which run blind alleys. While the piece-meal development of the city gave rise to the impasses and randomness to the street pattern the blind alleys were often ways of sealing off areas controlled by single or extended families or ethnic groups so that attackers or casual passers-by would not intrude on family life, especially the lives of women. The through alleys in Tripoli old city are generally unroofed but with buttresses at intervals which help to hold up the walls on either side of the alley and provide some shelter from the sun. Walls facing the public alleys are for the most part plain with few windows, a device to increase privacy and deter curiosity. Doorways to houses and interior courtyards are remarkably ornate in contrast to the tall plain walls around them. Massive arches are used, displaying Roman or Islamic decorations while the doors themselves are often high, studded and provided with ancient locks.

Individual houses in the old city still display their great cloistered courtyards and ornate tile, wood and plaster work. There are also several grand *serais* or *funduqs*, where merchants lodged their goods and animals around large courtyards. Generally less decorated than private houses, nonetheless they played an important role in the life of the city when the large traders organized and managed trans-Saharan caravans. The manufacturing and retail *suqs* of old Tripoli were carefully run by guilds of craftsmen and capitalists producing craft products for daily use. Pottery, metalwork, traditional clothing and jewellery were made

The immediate problems of the decline of the old medinas and some of the answers to them is illustrated by the struggle to protect the medinas of Tunis and of Tripoli. The Tripoli medina is one of the classical sites of the Mediterranean. Its street plan was laid down in the Roman period when the principal walls were built. The fortress walls survived many invasions, with each succeeding invader adding to the masonry of the defences.

The old city itself is made up of separate quarters, most parts Muslim and two districts Jewish *hara*. Narrow streets and impasses run through the medina. Individual houses in the old city have cloistered courtyards with ornate tile and plaster work. There are also less decorated commercial premises from which trans-Saharan caravans once set out.

Sadly, Libyan residents left the medina in 1951. Families moved to occupy houses and apartments in the new Italian-built city. Now the medina has declined materially. Many houses have fallen down. Despite attempts by the authorities to halt the deterioration of public buildings, little has been done to save the less prominent private housing or to bring back real life to the medina. Tripoli is thus a dead city and a stark warning of what happens when traditional economy and values are overwhelmed.

In Tunisia similar problems exist. The art of wood sculpture for doors, wall panels and the decoration of mosques such as the wooden *minbar* (pulpit) of the Aqba ibn Naffi Mosque in Kairouan is dying out. It is believed that, other than for the wood carvers of the Aïn Draham area of NW Tunisia, there are no skilled wood sculptors in the country.

There is thus a real threat that the existing stock of material examples of traditional North African and Islamic technology. Tunisia is currently less menaced than Libya but what remains of traditional material culture could vanish with little trace outside museums in less than a generation.

here. Some of the *suqs* still trade under vaulted brick ceilings, though very few goods are now manufactured in situ. Suq Al-Mushir is the popular tourist area of the old city situated immediately off Green Square adjacent to the castle. There are seven **mosques** in the old city, containing a wealth of indigenous architectural detail (see map, page 377).

There was an exodus of the traditional families from the old city after Independence in 1951. Families moved to occupy houses and apartments vacated by the departing Italians to take advantage of better sanitation, water supply and other facilities. By the mid 1970s the situation had deteriorated so badly that the majority of residents in the old city was immigrant workers from overseas. Neglect of the fragile buildings

enabled damp to get into their fabric and many fell to ruin. The Libyan authorities determined to halt the rot and established a group to undertake restoration of key buildings and to write up the history of the city. In addition to the establishment of a research workshop and library in the old city, the main mosques, synagogues and consular houses have been restored in excellent taste.

Any tour of the old city should begin at the **castle**, entered from the land side near Suq Al-Mushir, entrance free, closes at 1400. It houses a library and a well organized museum and has excellent views over the city from the walls. This is one of the two principal **museums** in Tripoli, the other being in the medina, approximately 500m away. The

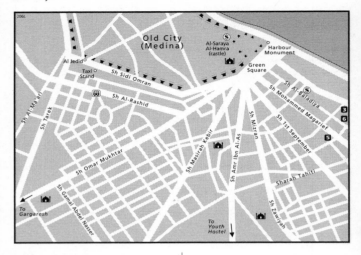

Castle Museum is essentially concerned with the archaeology and ancient history of Libya. It covers the Phoenician, Greek and Roman periods well and has an expanding collection of materials on the Islamic period. The top floor is devoted to Libyan modern history. Open weekdays 0800-1400, closed Fri. Entrance LD0.50. The main route through the old city runs from the castle towards the sea, with the old French and British consulates, the Medina Museum and the Aurelian Arch all worthy of close attention. The old city walls are still standing. The **Harbour Monument** stands at the gates of the old city on the edge of the former corniche road adjacent to the castle. There are a number of restored houses, consulates and a synagogue in the narrow streets. The **Medina Museum**, easily found as a renovated building standing all alone in a cleared section to the NW of the medina, has a library with illustrated displays and helpful staff with a great knowledge of the medina area. Open weekdays 0800-1400, closed Fri. Entry is free and is from Bab Al-Jedid on the W side of the city walls not

far from the taxi station. The main merchant quarter is entered from the gate at Suq Al-Mushir. There are many separate small *suqs* such as the Suq Al-Attar (medicinal drugs), Suq As-Siiaja (goldsmiths), the remnants of which still operate though without their former Jewish workers and owners.

There are a number of interesting mosques in the old town including the **Karamanli Mosque**, the **En-Naqah Mosque** and the **Gurgi Mosque**. The En-Naqah mosque, the oldest of the Tripoli mosques, is called the camel mosque because it is said that the citizens of Tripoli met the great Arab conqueror Amr Ibn Al-As with a camel-load of valuables to buy the survival of the city. Amr Ibn Al-As refused to accept this gift and instead asked that a mosque be built. The present mosque is of various dates, the last major rebuilding dating from 1610/11 when it was called the 'Great Mosque'. The plan of the mosque is slightly irregular and aligned on a NW axis. The sanctuary makes use of columns of varied sources, some Roman. There are 42 brick-built domes

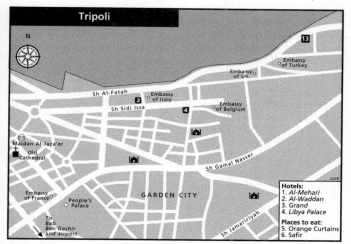

Tripoli

Hotels:
1. Al-Mehari
2. Al-Waddan
3. Grand
4. Libya Palace

Places to eat:
5. Orange Curtains
6. Safir

comprising the roof of the mosque. The *mihrab* (a niche in the wall indicating the direction of Mecca) is in the middle of the *qibla* wall. There is a *mimbar* (low pulpit). A square minaret has a spiral stairway of palm wood and plaster.

Another interesting mosque is that of **Dragut**, the well-known Islamic admiral and scourge of shipping in the Mediterranean. He died during the great siege of Malta and was returned and buried in Tripoli in the large Dragut mosque, which was damaged during WW2 but later restored. It has a square minaret and a small cemetery.

The **Al-Jami' Mosque**, the true 'Great Mosque' of Tripoli, contains interesting inscriptions to Othman Ra'is, who founded it in 1670 AD. The most magnificent mosque in Tripoli is the **Mosque of Ahmad Pasha Karamanli**, Governor of Tripoli in 1711 and founder of the Karamanli Dynasty. It is located a few metres from the castle near the main entrance to the *suq*. The mosque has an adjacent *medersa* in the W corner of the grounds, tombs and a cemetery. The centre point is a sanctuary with 25 domes as

a roof, the two domes over the fine *mihrab* being more elevated and carrying stucco work. The tombs of Ahmad Pasha and many of his family lie in a separate room with a large domed roof of spectacular design. The minaret is a very distinctive octagonal design in the Turkish style.

The best known of the Tripoli mosques is the **Gurgi Mosque** with its elegant architecture. It was built comparatively recently in 1833 by Yussef Gurgi (of Georgia in the Caucasus from which his family came) as an Islamic Hanifite establishment. It has a 16m square plan with nine columns and 16 small domes, of which four over the main structures such as the *mihrab* and the *mimbar* are elevated. There are many delicately decorated areas of the mosque, especially around the *mihrab*. The octagonal minaret with two balconies is the tallest of the old Tripoli mosques. If the traveller wishes to view just one of Tripoli's mosques, the Gurgi Mosque is the one to choose.

Modern Tripoli spilled out from the tight confines of the old city as early as the 18th century and possibly before that. It is known from the letters of the European consuls such as Tully, resident in Tripoli during Karamanli times, that a thriving community existed on the flat lands immediately outside the old city known as the Menshia. Here the troublesome members of the traditional military class lived with farmers, traders and other individuals. The entire area was redeveloped by the Italians in the first half of the 20th century as a colonial city for Italian residents. They created a set of administrative buildings, many of which stand today, together with official residences and general residential areas. The garden city is still the most affluent and pleasant area of Tripoli, situated adjacent to the People's Palace. Straight streets were constructed, radiating from Green Square in front of the castle, together with a cathedral and a financial district adjacent to the *suq*, along what is now Sharah Omar Mukhtar.

This pleasing colonial urban form was broken by the revolution of 1969. In an attempt to diminish the apparent colonial heritage and European influence, all street names were changed, the cathedral closed and signs not in Arabic removed. Far more influential in changing the character of Tripoli, there was massive population growth during the post-revolutionary years combined with an influx of Libyans to Tripoli. Tripoli City grew 5-fold in population size to stand at 600,000 by 1990. Extensive new suburbs grew up on all sides, many ill-planned so that Tripoli became a large metropolitan area in its own right spreading in all directions across the oases on its edge to reach out and encompass major satellite settlements such as Tajurah to the E and Zaviyah to the W.

The removal of some civil service personnel to other sites together with a fall in prosperity in the late 1980s eased some of the traffic congestion but expansion of the city continues, with people commuting 60-80 km into the city from outlying towns. At peak times, 0730-0900, 1330-1430 and 1800-1930, roads are choked and extra time must be allowed for travelling to appointments and particularly to the airport or bus station.

The main commercial streets lie in the centre. Most lead off Green Square in front of the castle. All street names are in Arabic but Libyans will assist in giving directions. The coast road, built over the former harbour area and adjacent to new wharves, is principally for vehicular traffic moving E. There are no buildings. The inner coast road from Green Square, Sharah Al-Fatah (originally Adrian Pelt, named after the UN official who sponsored Libyan Independence in 1951) is built up on its inland side with a number of public buildings and the main hotels. It travels on E along the corniche passing the major embassies of Italy, UK (currently operating as a 'British interests' section of the Italian embassy), Turkey and others. The road is planted with ornamental palms and has cafés and gardens along it. Sharah Mohammed Magarief, one of the capital's two main streets, runs from Green Square to the former cathedral. At its S end 500m S of the former cathedral is the People's Palace, built for the late King Idris and now in the service of the popular committees and the political activists supporting Colonel Ghadhafi. The French embassy faces it and on its NW corner is one of the oil company offices. The National Oil Company office is on Sharah Gamal Nasser, to the W side of the palace. Travelling up the E side of the palace leads to the Sharah Ben Ashur in the centre of a high class residential district, the garden city to the E and new properties to the W.

Walking around Tripoli centre is straightforward, though beyond the main business and shopping precincts there is little to see and walking, especially in the heat, is not recommended. For a **tour of the modern city** on foot begin in Green Square and travel W along Sharah Omar Mukhtar to see the private business district. Turn round at the Tripoli Fair building and return to Green Square from which go SE down Sharah Mohammed Magarief towards the post office and former cathedral, now used as a mosque. The rooms above the post office display pictures of Tripoli during the Italian and British occupation. From the post office square (Maidan Al-Jaza'er) either turn directly right to Sharah Tahiti and thence right again into one of the commercial thoroughfares with small Arab lock-up shops or go on past the post office towards the People's Palace and thence left to the harbour front and back towards the Green Square. This itinerary effectively shows the best of the modern city.

The cemetery for British and Italian Christians – Al Magbarah al Masihiyyah – lies between Sharah Gamal Nasser and Sharah Jamairiyah.

In Tripoli there are **war cemeteries** from WW2. The British and Commonwealth Cemetery is 2 km W of Tripoli and 364m S of the main road. There is also a British Military Cemetery.

LOCAL INFORMATION

Price guide

Hotels:			
AL	over US$75	D	US$20-40
A	US$75	E	US$10-20
B	US$60-75	F	under US$10
C	US$40-60		

Places to eat:		
♦♦♦	expensive	♦♦ average
♦	cheap	

● **Accommodation**

Tripoli is moderately endowed with hotels, adequate for a country with little development of commercial tourism but a large immigrant worker population. Business visitors are fairly well catered for with five or so luxury hotels in Tripoli centre. Cheaper accommodation is difficult to find when arriving in the evening, for example off the Benghazi bus, so book ahead. The newest hotel is the **A** *Al-Mehari*, Sharah Al-Fatah, overlooking the harbour, T 33 34091/6, Tx 22090, pool, best service in Tripoli, US$215 double room, must be paid in US

dollars, but not AL grade; **A** *Grand Hotel* (ask for *Funduq Al-Kebir*), also on Sharah Al-Fatah to the E, T 44 45940, F 45959 very close to the medina, central, two restaurants, good buffet, excellent café, car hire, tall building is good landmark, currently US$200 double room, must be in foreign exchange, but not AL grade, travel agency.

C *Bab al Bahr* and *Bab el Medina* side by side on sea front to W of medina, sea views, fair; **Al** *Waddan*, Sharah Sidi Issa at LD60 is not such a good deal as two mentioned above but better position in town.

D *Hotel Atlas*, top of Sharah Omar Mukhtar on a small square to the right, T 33 36815, simple but clean rooms with bath; **D** *Hotel Lula*, seafront to the E of the medina, T 33 31013, clean, many rooms with sea view, restaurant, café, room with bath, breakfast incl; **D** *Hotel White Sea*, off seafront E of the medina, T 606241, large, 200 rm, with bath, half a/c, roof terrace, clean but rather informal, breakfast incl; **D** *Libya Palace* (Qasr Libya), T 3331181, Sharah Sidi Issa, service and cleanliness of good standard, busy reception area, quiet rooms, travel agency, rec; *Hotel Tripoli*, Sharah Al Rached, T 4441095, just 200m from the central taxi station, clean rms, a bargain but eat elsewhere.

There are also small workers' hotels with shared facilities (category **E**) on the seafront beneath the walls of the medina, mainly clean but noisy. Outside Tripoli there are several tourist villages which can offer accommodation on request, but which are often very full in the vacation periods (see entries in Tripoli District section, pages 386).

Youth hostels: *Tripoli city* for camping and dormitory accommodation, 69 Sharah Amr Ibn Al-As, T 44 45171, kitchen, 120 beds, breakfast available, family rm, 2 km from Green Square. *Gergarish*, Sharah Gergarish, 5 km S of Tripoli, open 0700-2400, 200 beds, meals, family room, laundry, airport 20 km, harbour 2 km, T 74755. Booking recommended at both hostels.

● **Places to eat**

The main restaurants for western visitors are in the principal hotels, all of which are open to non-residents. Some hotels such as the *Grand* and the *Al-Mehari* have more than one restaurant. They are all 'dry' but adequate. Popular eating places for the large numbers of non-Libyan Arabs are to be found in the city centre on or just off Sharah Omar Mukhtar and on the main roads immediately leading off to the S from the Green Square. They are cheap and offer Arab cuisine tending towards the rough and ready but generally hygienic. ♦♦♦*Gazala*, T 4441079, Maidan Gazala nr main post office, open 1230-1530 and 1930-2230, fixed price menu of LD15, eat plenty of appetizers and soup before the one big fish course; *Grand Hotel* has excellent buffet, eat as much as you want for LD18, a real bargain; ♦♦*Safir Restaurant*, just behind *Grand Hotel* on Sharah al-Baladiya, fixed price menu LD13, serves very good Moroccan and Tunisian food; *Badwen*, 110-112 Sharah al-Baladiya, T 33 39995, in front of the public gardens, recognized by brown door and short queue at entrance, Lebanese owned, rec for tasty soup and meat; ♦Pizza Place and patisserie, in front of the main post office, excellent pizza and wide choice of cakes and pastries, take away only, open 1100-1400 and 1600-2000; *Orange Curtains* another fast food take away round the corner from *Safir* and *Badwen* recognized by orange curtains, tuna sandwiches, hamburgers, yoghourt and milkshakes.

Best coffee in town served in *Hotel Kebir* and the *Circolo Italiana* in Italian Consulate.

● **Banks & money changers**

As money can be changed elsewhere to greater advantage a bank may not be necessary.

Generally open 0800-1400, in the central shopping zone, with one conveniently on the roundabout adjacent to Green Square and others on the S main roads leaving the square. Go early for shorter queues. Al-Umma Bank, Sharah Omar Mukhtar, T 33 34031; Central Bank of Libya, Sharah Gamal Nasser, T 33 33591; Jamahiriya Bank, Sharah Mohammed Magarief, T 33 33553; Libyan National Arab Bank, Sharah 1st September, T 20751-2; National Commercial Bank, Green Square, T 33 37191; Sahara Bank, Sharah 1st September, T 33 32771; Wahhadah Bank, T 33 34016.

● **Embassies**

Tripoli is the diplomatic capital. UK citizens, for whom there is no embassy, should address themselves to the Italian embassy/consulate for assistance where there is a British affairs desk T 33 31191. Nationals of the USA, Venezuela and other countries suffer from periodic interruptions in diplomatic relations. Travel agents will have information on the current and constantly changing situation.

Algeria, 12 Sharah Kairouan, T 44 40025; Belgium, 1 Sharah Abu Obeidat Ibn Al-Jerah, T 33 37797; Chad, 25 Sharah Mohammed Sadeqi, T 44 43955; CIS, Sharah Mostafa Kamel, T 33 30545/6; Czechoslovakia, Sharah Ahmad Lotfi Al-Said, T 33 34959; France, Sharah Ahmad Lotfi Al-Said, T 33 33526-7; Germany, Sharah Hassan Al-Masha'i, T 33 30554; Greece, 18 Sharah Jellal Beyar, Tx 20409; India, 16 Sharah Mahmud Sheltut, T 44 41835-6; Iraq, Sharah Gurgi, T 70856; Italy, Sharah Wahran, POB 219, T 33 30742; Jordan, Sharah Ibn Oof, T 33 32707; Kuwait, Sharah Amar Ibn Yasr, T 44 40281-2; Lebanon, Sharah Amar Ibn Yasr, T 33 33733; Malta, 13 Sharah Abu Bin Ka'ab, T 33 38081-4; Mauritania, Sharah Issa Wukuak, T 44 43646; Morocco, Sharah Bashir Al-Ibrahimi, T 44 41346; Niger, Sharah Tantawi Jowheri, T 44 43104; Pakistan, Sharah Khatabi, T 44 40072; Saudi Arabia, 2 Sharah Kairouan, T 33 30485-6; Spain, Sharah Al-Jaza'er, T 33 35462; Syria, 4 Sharah Mohammed Rashid Rida, T 33 371955; Tunisia, Sharah Bashir Al-Ibrahimi, T 33 31051-2; Turkey, 36 Sharah Gamal Abdel Nasser, T 46528/9; UAE, Sharah Aljaza'er, T 44 44146-8; United Kingdom c/o Italian Embassy, T 33 31191, when open Sharah Al-Fatah, T 33 31195.

● **Hospitals & medical services**

Chemists: in all shopping areas are normally marked with a red crescent or green cross sign. Chemists have a duty rota which is normally reliable, but travellers with special needs are advised to bring their own stores.

Hospitals: there are several large, well-equipped hospitals. The central civil unit is on the main road out to Sidi Mesri near the inner ring road. A secondary hospital is at Al-Khadra (the old military hospital).

● **Post & telecommunications**

Area code: 021.

Post office: this is found on Maidan Al-Jaza'er opposite the former cathedral and has telecommunications facilities.

Telephone: 5 digit numbers beginning with 3 place 33 in front, beginning with 4 place 44 in front.

● **Shopping**

Sharah 1st September and Sharah Mohammed Magarief have shops with clothes and other consumer goods, travel agents, and an abundance of cafés. Two more streets fan out from Green Square and the adjacent traffic island.

Sharah Mizran and Sharah Amr Ibn Al-As carry small scale commercial activity, bakers, general goods shops, traders and others.

Joining these streets to Sharah 1st September and Al-Fatah area are cross links, the most important of which is Sharah Tahiti. Sharah Omar Mukhtar leads off Green Square directly to the SW. On the right is a red marble faced building, the Secretariat of Justice, with the rest of the street given over to trading houses, Arab restaurants, cafés and shops. On the right the street opens up on the site of the **Tripoli Fair ground** used for international exhibitions. Sharah Omar Mukhtar ultimately gives access to the main western suburbs such as **Gurgi** and the former European villa area of **Giorgim Poppoli** with its supermarkets, beach clubs and tourist centres. Sharah Ben Ashur has dry cleaning, a pharmacy, a bakery and grocery stores. Throughout the central business and inner residential districts there are excellent doctors' surgeries, chemist shops, food stores, general goods shops, bakeries and small cafés. There are some popular restaurants, though these are almost entirely confined to the streets off and adjacent to the streets fanning out of Green Square. The poorer residential suburbs have small scale facilities and often no doctors, though pharmacies are common. The larger suburbs with pre-existing commercial centres such as Gurgi have a full range of facilities.

Books: the main shop is *Fergiani's* nr the roundabout off Green Square on Sharah 1st September with a second shop in Sharah Al Jamaririyah nr Eliarmuk Square. Try also *Dar Al Hadara* close to *Fergiani's* at 90 Sharah 1st September, T 33 3975 for books in Arabic and English on scientific subjects. Books are otherwise available from official Libyan agencies which in the past acquired books exclusively by the state publishing organization. Most are in Arabic and/or are academic or somewhat propagandist.

● **Sports**

There is a state-sponsored football team and some local football played. Dates and times of games are advertised in the Arabic press. The main opening for sport for visitors to Tripoli is swimming, snorkelling and scuba-diving in the sea along the coastline. For medium to long stay travellers it is worth joining a beach club, most are on the Gurgia side of the city. Each club is marked with a large board which, though in Arabic, makes it quite clear that it is a sports centre. It is advised that enquiries are made personally at the gate, through a state agency or, most easily, through a travel agent.

● **Tour companies & travel agents**

These are in the shopping precincts in the main avenues leading from the Green Square. There are numerous travel agencies we recommend. *Libyan Travel & Tourist Co* on Mizran St headed by Salem Azzabi T 44 48005. Also *Libya Tours Co* in Libya Palace Hotel, T 33 31189, F 33 36688 where English and French are spoken. Ask for Mrs Hafida. *Libyan Arab Airlines* LAA main office opp Tripoli Fair ground, T 33 37500 open 0730-1630; best office is by Hotel Kebir.

● **Transport**

Local Bus: there are frequent, though in rush hour crowded, bus services across town on regular routes. The green/grey Tripoli service buses can be easily recognized with a destination board in Arabic but also a route number. The service can be rather erratic and breakdowns are common but the system is cheap. Buses run through the main bus terminal and other stops are clearly marked. There are no printed time tables and it is best to ask at your hotel before proceeding. **Taxis**: are very expensive with a price of LD5 for the shortest of trips but in the heat might be attractive to those with some distance to travel. Outlying parts of Tripoli can be reached by shared taxis at very reasonable rates. Otherwise, most travellers will be able to walk from point to point in the central area since the places to visit are concentrated around the city centre. Taxis leave from stands between Sharah Omar Mukhtar and the sea. They ply for hire on a shared basis but, with haggling over the price, can be hired by an individual or private group.

Air The main airport at Ben Ghashir/Suani Ben Yadim is some 24 km from the centre of Tripoli, but some planes leave from the smaller local airport just 4 km from the city on the beach. Always check! A bus service is available to/from the main hotels and the bus station. Passengers with a deal of luggage are advised to face a charge of some LD25 for a private taxi rather than try the alternative. Uncertainties over transport to and from the airport are such that travellers should check well before the date of their flight with the airline, hotel or travel agent. Note must be taken of difficulties caused by the UN embargo on international flights to Libya. It is now only possible to enter Libya by land and sea until the embargo is lifted. Most access under the embargo is by ferry from

Malta or overland through Tunisia. The Libyan Airlines central office is located on Sharah Haiti.

Internal flights to **Benghazi**, 3 daily flights at 1000, 1700 and 2200 with extra flights most days at 1300 or 1800. Takes 1 hr and costs LD28, LD56 return; to **Ghadames**, alternate Tues at 1230, cost LD20; to **Sabha**, Wed/Sat 1300, takes 1¼ hrs; to **Tobruk**, flights on 5 days each week, takes 1¾ hrs, costs LD44. There is no reserved seating and overbooking is very common.

Travellers are reminded that due to the shortage of spare parts caused by the embargo air journeys in Libya are not recommended.

Road Bus: the terminal is in the street adjacent to the international departure station approximately 1 km W from the medina. For international links (see page 434). Domestic timetables are very flexible. Departures from Tripoli leave early in the morning and passengers for small or distant Libyan settlements should be at the bus station not later than 0630 to be sure of a seat. Buses for the 12-hr journey to Benghazi cost LD10 for the public service and LD15 for the private service leaving daily at 0830 using air conditioned coaches. Internal bus routes cover all towns and cities. Small 10 seater private buses do the journey from/to **Ghadames**, leaving when full in the late afternoon. Cost LD7, with several stops for refreshment and police checks. Try the agency round the corner from the government ticket office, T 622090 or T501088.

TRIPOLI DISTRICT

Tripoli outside the city traditionally comprises the greater province and in this Handbook, the area defined by the Jefara Plain. The present administrative district of Tripoli is made up of the whole of the old province of Tripolitania taking in the Jabal Nafusa, Sirte and parts as far S as Jufra, Mizdah and Ghadames. The Great Jefara Plain covers the coastal lowlands from the Tunisian frontier in the W at Zuwarah to Misratah in the E and is bounded to the S by the line of the Jabal Nafusa as far as Al-Khums and thereafter as the 'Small Jefara' to Misratah in the E by a low range of hills. The district is a fertile and generally well watered zone except for the central area from Al-Assa to the S of Ajailat which is very arid. Rainfall comes in the winter months and causes flash flooding in the many *wadis*. Most water courses are now well controlled but it is wise to stay out of *wadi* beds in winter. Individuals may be carried away and drowned in flash floods.

The cultivated zone along the coastal strip is a narrow belt of palm oases. Cultivation here is very dense with multiple cropping in the spring and summer seasons. In its most sophisticated form, intercropping gives olives immediately below the palm canopy and other taller fruit trees, themselves standing clear of lower varieties such as pomegranates and apricot. Below the trees are tall vegetables such as peppers or maize and a final undercrop of wheat, barley or a vegetable such as broad beans. Cropping of this kind was labour-intensive but enabled a self-sufficient agriculture based on irrigation from shallow wells.

Animal herding is important on the Jefara Plain. Few black tents of the true nomads are now to be seen. Even the Sian nomads of the extreme W adjacent to Tunisia have become sedentary, but sheep and goats can be seen throughout Libya particularly in the Jefara where herds are exceptionally dense. The sheep are Barbary fat-tailed varieties for the most part, with an ability to survive heat and short periods of drought. The animals are very valuable, being much prized for eating by the Libyans, each sheep fetching US$300 or more, depending on the animal and the season. Most herds are looked after by a hired shepherd.

The Jefara Plain drops from the foot of the Jabal very evenly and gradually to reach the coast in an often rocky and shallow shelf though there are excellent beaches well away from Tripoli city. Zuwarah and the W coasts are open, sandy and generally deserted except on Fri when they are crowded with people from Tripoli. Inland from the Arab oases are the former Italian farms with their regularly laid out orchards spreading deep into the interior. The Jefara Plain narrows considerably E until the Jabal

reaches the coast in a low ridge at Al-Khums, separating the main Jefara from the limited coastal plain between Al-Khums and Misratah. The roads on the Jefara are wide, black topped and generally in good condition.

TRIPOLI TO AL-KHUMS AND MISRATAH

The main coastal highway runs from Tripoli to the E via Al-Khums and Misratah. The road links all the major coastal towns and passes through one of the richest agricultural zones of the country. The highlight of the route is Leptis Magna, the most imposing Roman ruin in North Africa.

This trip takes at least 1 hr. There is a choice of routes in the environs of Tripoli of either the old coast road or the modern highway. Buses and taxis leave Tripoli on the coastal main highway. A

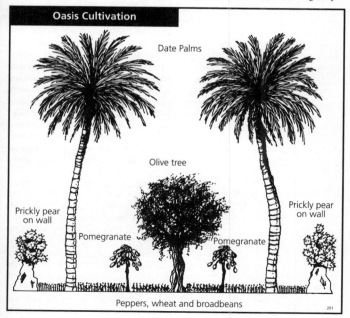

Oasis Cultivation

Date Palms

Olive tree

Prickly pear on wall

Pomegranate

Pomegranate

Prickly pear on wall

Peppers, wheat and broadbeans

dual carriageway leaves Tripoli city via Bab Ben Ghashir and travels through dense developments of villas and small houses, mainly expensive properties built on former oasis gardens. Architecturally the housing is very mixed – old square, single storey, whitewashed farmsteads interspersed with very modern villas of a slightly inferior finish. Occasional whitewashed small domed shrines, the tombs of *marabouts* or Islamic holy men, are visible, their titles being used for regional or topographical place names. **Accommodation E** *Madinah Siahiah Tajurah (Tajurah tourist village)* is located approximately 32 km E of Tripoli. Its surrounding beach is popular with Libyans on Fri but is otherwise clear for other tourists. Km 32 is its local name. The tourist village is an old development and open to all-comers.

Gasr Garabouli Km 60 from Tripoli lies on the old coast road and is now by-passed. Take the spur into town for petrol, police, shops and other services. There are small and mixed developments of shops, cafés and market places. The town area remains lightly wooded with some ex-Italian farms to be seen among dense, recent Libyan housing.

East from Gasr Garabouli there is open country with orchards and olives and almond plantations. At Gasr Khiar there are roadside shops on the main highway, cafés and petrol. Al-Khums is way-marked at Km 41. Along the main road other than in the smaller settlements there are plenty of roadside cafés. Small shacks of modern origin cater for travellers, especially on Fri and public holidays.

Telathin (literally Km 30 mark) is a tiny settlement providing chiefly a mosque, but with a shop and café adjacent. There is a fine area for swimming at the coast just N of the road. This is a highly recommended road in springtime when almond trees are flowering. In season succulent oranges are on sale at the roadside. A good black top road runs to it then goes on to a rocky seashore 2 km below. Al-Khums town lies approximately 20 km to the E over the forested ridge. **Accommodation D** *Funduq & Mat'am Al-Naqazzah*, clean, 15 beds, restaurant and café, cooler in summer than the surrounding plains, hotel and restaurant of good contemporary design but now run down, situated in an area of conifer trees just to the N of the main road.

AL-KHUMS

Al-Khums from the outside is not a very pretty sight. It contains low quality and incomplete dwellings in an apparently poor state of repair. The area has a very drab exterior with much accumulated rubbish around. The Al-Khums Fri market is held in the street leading to the old

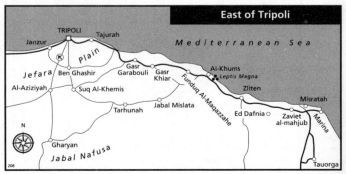

East of Tripoli

harbour. The main town has expanded considerably in recent years. Some Italian and British military and civilian landmarks are still to be found, with the army barracks as they were. The old market place next to the barracks is now the town taxi stand with transport available on a trip or day basis in private or shared taxi. There is an Arabic language cinema on the left of the street opposite the taxi ranks. Old Turkish houses have been demolished and replaced by a ghastly town

The Delu well – traditional well of Libya and North Africa

Water was always essential to life in North Africa. Given the scarcity of surface water, it was necessary for survival to lift water from underground. In traditional Libya – more or less until the 1960s – water was lifted from a shallow water table along the coast or from depressions in the desert by means of a device called a *delu*. The name is taken from the word for a goatskin, which is made into a bag, dipped into a well and drawn up full of water for both household and irrigation purposes.

The mechanism is simple and effective. A shallow one or 2m diameter well is hand dug to about 2 or 3m below the water table and lined with stone work or cement. Above ground an often ornate gantry is made of two upright stone or wooden pillars rising from the side of the wellhead. A cross beam between the top of the two pillars acts as an axle to a small pulley wheel which carries a rope tied to the mouth of the goatskin bag. The rope is drawn up or let down by the ingenious use of a ramp to ease the task of lifting water to the surface. An animal travels down the ramp when pulling up the goatskin from the bottom of the well and moves up the ramp to return the bag into the bottom of the well. Most *delu* wells have a secondary rope attached to the bottom of the goatskin bag which can be used when the full bag is at the top of the gantry to upend it and tip out the water.

The rate of water lifting by the *delu* method is obviously limited. The capacity of the bag is about 20 litres. Working from dawn to dusk, however, enough water could be raised to irrigate up to 3 or 4 ha of land – enough to feed a family and leave a small surplus for sale in the market. Most wells were equipped with a storage basin adjacent to the wellhead so that water could be raised and stored for household use and to give a reserve of water for irrigation.

The creak of the wooden pulley wheel of the *delu* was one of the characteristic sounds of the North African oases until the 1960s. After that time diesel and electric power pumps became available and the *delu* system fell into disuse. A few *delu* gantries remain as museum pieces and only the observant traveller in the deepest S of the Saharan oases will come across this splendid and environmentally friendly technology in day-to-day operation.

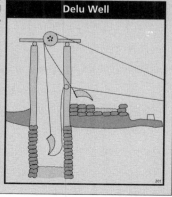

Delu Well

201

council building just below the cinema.

ACCESS Care is needed when driving at all times and especially on the outskirts of Al-Khums where slow moving vehicular and pedestrian traffic makes the main highway dangerous. Buses stop in the town centre near the taxi rank and on the main road at the *Al-Khums Hotel*.

● **Accommodation** Unfortunately the town's oldest hotel, *Funduq Al-Khums*, always fairly run down has now closed its doors. At the junction of the main coastal highway and the first black top road after the *Naqazzah Hotel*, turn off to the **E** *Funduq Kabir Al-Khums*, cheap but noisy from close-passing traffic, inc breakfast, and quantities of cockroaches; **F** *Funduq Al-Sherief* is cheaper. **Youth hostel**: *Sports City*, 3 km SW of centre, T (23) 20888, 160 beds, meals, kitchen, laundry, family rooms.

There is a vast extension to the town from the army barracks E along the coast towards Wadi Lebda and between the coast and the by-pass built up solidly with mainly poor quality housing areas with few services for the traveller. Chalets have been built along the sea shore towards Leptis Magna. The modern port is located on the W of the town. There is some industry including a cement plant. Shared taxi from Tripoli costs LD5 to Al-Khums and LD1 to the site, takes about 1½ hrs. Approximately 4 km W of Al-Khums is Villa Selena with fine mosaics. Permission obtained at entrance to Leptis at no extra charge.

LEPTIS MAGNA

Open daily 0800-1730, LD0.25 adult, LD0.1 child. Shared taxi from Tripoli costs LD5 to Al-Khums and LD1 to the site. With the new museum opened July 1995 (entrance LD0.5), café and telephone this is a busy site. There are warn-

The Roman Emperor from North Africa

Septimus Severus was born at Leptis Magna in Libya in 193 AD, the son of a Romanized Tripolitanian family and the only North African to become a Roman Emperor. He stayed loosely associated with his birthplace, directing investment into the city and its environs and making the North African province a substantial part of the Empire. Septimus Severus was known for his dislike of the corrupt politics of Rome and its Senate. He made his reputation initially as the head of the Roman army of the Danube which he used as a base to vie for total command of the Empire. His main rivals were ultimately defeated in battle thanks to the support of the Danubian legions and Septimus Severus went on to enforce a severe regime of control in Rome. He fought with moderate success in Mesopotamia (present-day Syria-Iraq) against the Parthians. He eventually travelled to Britain to command the legions in England against the invaders from the north. He died at York in 211.

The Empire he left was much changed from that which he inherited. The army was professionalized as an elite body and increased in size. Soldiers were better paid and given more opportunities for promotion. The management of the Empire was increasingly put into the hands of people from the provinces, especially the provinces in the E and North Africa. He left the Roman Empire to his son, Caracalla.

In North Africa, Septimus Severus did much good and was responsible for the widespread prosperity of the city merchants, especially those involved in the cereal trade. The large cities and towns of North Africa were expanded and rich merchants spent vast sums of money creating theatres and other civic amenities not least in Leptis Magna. Unfortunately his edict, preventing conversion to Christianity and Judaism, led to horrific persecution and produced many martyrs and it is more often for this he is remembered.

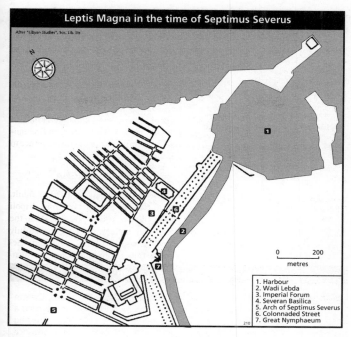

Leptis Magna in the time of Septimus Severus

After "Libyan Studies", Soc. Lib. Sts

N

0   200
metres

210

1. Harbour
2. Wadi Lebda
3. Imperial Forum
4. Severan Basilica
5. Arch of Septimus Severus
6. Colonnaded Street
7. Great Nymphaeum

ings that the ruins must not be touched nor artefacts taken away. These must be taken very seriously since successful prosecution can lead to imprisonment. The few sellers of items to be found on the site are operating illegally and should not be approached. There are guides available for a fee (LD5 seems to be a minimum) who speak the main European languages. Although Leptis Magna, designated by UNESCO as a World Heritage site, is an important archaeological site it is not complex since the best elements date from a fairly specific period. The information in this guide should enable most travellers to get a good overall view of the site. For specialists, an extended guided tour of the sites and the museum at Leptis Magna is recommended. Guidebooks, maps and postcards of this site and others in Libya are available here.

Leptis Magna is among the most complete and magnificent of the three towns (tripolis) of North Africa. It began as a Phoenician port of call on the trading route across the region, though it was ultimately administered in the 6th century BC, it is thought, from Carthage. The city grew up at the mouth of the Wadi Lebda where a small port was developed over the years, exporting important volumes of grain and olives. It joined Rome in 111 BC and enjoyed full rights as a *colonia* to Roman citizenship under the Emperor Trajan (98-117 AD).

The early Roman period saw the construction of basic harbour works and a forum close by the original Punic settlement. The city flourished under the rule and patronage of Septimus Severus (193-211 AD) who was born in Leptis

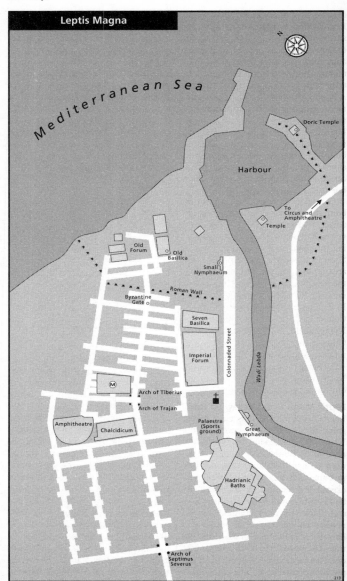

Leptis Magna

Mediterranean Sea

Harbour

Doric Temple

To Circus and Amphitheatre

Temple

Old Forum

Old Basilica

Small Nymphaeum

Roman Wall

Byzantine Gate

Seven Basilica

Imperial Forum

Colonnaded Street

Wadi Lebda

M

Arch of Tiberius

Arch of Trajan

Amphitheatre

Chalcidicum

Palaestra (Sports ground)

Great Nymphaeum

Hadrianic Baths

Arch of Septimus Severus

213

Magna. Most of the major buildings at Leptis date from his time. The city spread W along the coast and inland. All the important buildings can be reached adjacent to or just off the main paved monumental road from the present entrance through the new parts of the site. A full inspection of the wealth of monuments requires at least a full day and rather longer for visitors with a specialist interest since Leptis Magna is well preserved and has an unequalled range of buildings from the classical period. In summer the site is very hot and justice can be done only by a series of visits when the heat is less oppressive.

A minimum tour begins at the **harbour** at the original Punic site and the adjacent ruins of the **Old Forum**. The newer harbour works undertaken during the reign as Emperor of Septimus Severus are also on view in this same area. The **triumphal arch** together with the new quarter along the 410m monumental road also date from this period. In the new quarter the key sites are the Colonnaded Street, the semi circular **Nymphaeum**, the **Forum** and **Basilica**. Other areas to be seen include the magnificent **Amphitheatre** dating from 56 AD, among the most photogenic sites in North Africa, and the **baths** constructed during the time of the Emperor Hadrian.

Leptis Magna – an extended tour

Leptis Magna is a Roman city of great grandeur situated at the mouth of the Wadi Lebda immediately to the E of the town of Al-Khums. The origins of the town are not known with certainty. It is probable that a Berber settlement first existed at the site which was developed by Levantine trading groups from Tyre and Sidon that made use of the small natural harbour. Greeks also appear to have been at the site. In Carthaginian times the people at Lebda paid tribute of one talent per day, reflecting a certain prosperity based on a trading hinterland stretching deep into Tripolitania and

Sirte. By the time of the 3rd Punic War there were approximately 10,000-15,000 inhabitants in the city. In 107 AD Leptis set up formal relations with Rome and, despite the disruption caused by attacks from tribes from the desert interior, the city continued to develop.

The fortunes of Leptis Magna were greatly improved in 193 AD when Septimus Severus was made Emperor of Rome. He had been born at Leptis on Apr 11, 146 AD. He created a basilica at Leptis together with a great imperial forum as shown on the plan. The prosperity of the city was considerable and the population grew to 60,000-80,000 people. Leptis suffered later from a decline in the Saharan trade and the silting of the mouth of the river. Attacks from Asturian groups beginning in 363 AD brought great problems for the city. In 455 AD the Vandals arrived and took Leptis, leaving it eventually in the hands of the Berber Zenata tribe until 533 when the Byzantines under Belasarius restored Roman rule. The Byzantines were put under heavy pressure from all sides and in Libya from attacks by the Zenata and finally the Arab invasions of 643-644 AD. The later incursions of the Beni Hillal and Beni Sulaim led to the completed abandonment of Leptis Magna in the 11th century. Coastal sand dunes overwhelmed the site, preserving it from destruction during the succeeding centuries hence the site is below the present ground level with access via a steep flight of steps.

The first of the antiquities at the site is the **Arch of Septimus Severus** (1) which lies on the left at the end of a short avenue leading from the entrance. It has four facias. To the E of the arch is the **Hadrianic Baths** (2) (terme), an enormous construction covering with its ancilliary buildings approximately 3 ha and amongst the largest bath houses built outside Rome itself. The baths were put in place in 123-127 AD and improved and extended at various later dates. Excavations at the baths were begun in 1920 by Dr P Romanelli. The baths are best approached through the **Palaestra** (3), which is made up of a rectangular base with circular ends surrounded by a portico of 72 columns. There are five doorways into the baths, two on the N aspect leading from the Palestra. To the S two more doorways open onto a Corridor of 74.8m parallel to the fascia. Behind lies the Frigidarium a room of 30.35 x 15.40m. In the centre of the Frigidarium is a small monument dedicated to Septimus Severus, possibly commemorating the grant of full Roman rights to the city by that emperor. At the E and W sides of the Frigidarium are two highly decorated pools still showing their facings of black granite. Immediately S of the Frigidarium are two anterooms and connecting corridors together with a Tepidarium and its lateral pools. Further S lies the Calidarium in a room 22.15m x 19.90m. This room leads on by two doors to heated rooms,

the Stufe or Sudatorium. Along the E and W sides of this blocks of rooms are parallel salons which give access to the main baths.

The Severan **Nymphaeum** (4), high walls semicircular in shape and containing a fountain basin stands at the S end of the **Colonnaded Street** (5) which connects the Hadrianic Baths with the harbour. The street lies between the **Imperial Forum** (6) and the **Severan Basilica** (7) and the harbour. It has a broad, central section on either side of which stood covered porticoes. The supporting columns which carried arches stood on square raised pedestals. The **Imperial Forum** lies at the heart of Severan Leptis Magna. The Forum was constructed as a great wall of 92m backing on to the Basilica, with an inset arc. There is an entrance from the street on the SW side. It is a spectacular sight

Hadrianic Baths and Palaestra

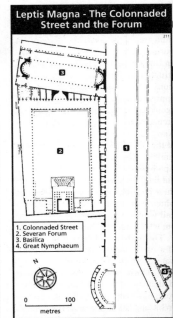

```
0                    50
        metres
```

1. Palaestra   5. Small pools
2. Frigidarium   6. Tepidarium
3. Corridor   7. Caldarium
4. Pool   8. Gymnasium

Leptis Magna - The Colonnaded Street and the Forum

1. Colonnaded Street
2. Severan Forum
3. Basilica
4. Great Nymphaeum

```
0                    100
        metres
```

despite the ravages of time and looters. It abuts onto the Basilica in the N and forms a great trapezoidal shape with maximum dimensions of 132m x 87m.

The **Old Basilica** (10) is 38m x 92m and built as a rectangle on the E side of the **Old Forum** (9). It has two semicircular recesses at its narrow ends. There are three lines of columns running the length of the church. The Basilica is surrounded by side galleries. Various dedications in Latin are found in the Basilica including an ornate inscription to Emperor Caesar Lucius Septimus. There is a great variety of sculptures and reliefs of mythical figures and animals.

The **amphitheatre** (8) at Leptis Magna is in excellent condition and commands views in all directions from the W side of the city. The theatre has a diameter of 70m and faces to the NE, heavily columned and with the stage and its entrances still clearly visible.

There is another set of baths at the site located close to the sea in the waterfront area of the city to the W of the Old Forum. These baths were never finished and are thought to have been under construction at the time of the Vandal invasions. The new baths are best approached from the E through a hexagonal domed hall, named by the British archaeologist Richard Goodchild the New Calidarium. Adjacent and to the N of the New Calidarium is a building of similar size which was used as an Apodyterium for an earlier bath system but later became disused. West again of these buildings is the New Frigidarium, which was constructed to be a vaulted hall with a plunge bath at each corner but which was not completed.

The **harbour** at Leptis is in the form of a basin open to the E and fed with water from the Wadi Lebda. There is a small **Doric temple** (18) at the site in Hellenistic style and a tower. The harbour has been studied by underwater archaeologists and some of the finds are shown in the main museum near the

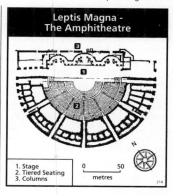

Leptis Magna - The Amphitheatre

1. Stage
2. Tiered Seating
3. Columns

0   50
metres

N

main site entrance. There are clear signs of severe silting, yet the historical record shows that Leptis port handled many thousands of tonnes of olive oil and food grain every year over many centuries as the centre of Rome's North African granary.

The **Circus** is on the extreme E side of the site, shaped as a great narrow horse shoe of 450m in length and 100m wide aligned parallel to the coastline. It is as yet not fully excavated but the starting gates are clearly to be seen at the city end, while the monumental arch and the circular terminus is at the E end. There are two tunnels at ground level carved apparently through solid rock. There are tiers of seats rising from the base around the arena. The **amphitheatre**, which lies immediately S of the Circus in the same complex, is thought to date from 56 AD and has been well excavated by Italian archaeologists. It is slightly elliptical in shape with circumferences of 100m x 80m.

Shortly after the time of Septimus Severus, the Roman Empire had increasing difficulties in maintaining law and order in its domains in North Africa. In 263 AD Leptis was overrun by the Asturians and, despite some attempts at reconstruction under Byzantine rule, it never again flourished. The Arab invaders of the 7th century brought a final extinction of urban life to the site. Most of the excavations at Leptis were undertaken in the Italian period when the monuments, preserved from damage by encroaching sands, were unearthed.

ACCESS Travelling E from Al-Khums and Leptis Magna take the old road through the palm oases. The road is a single black top carriageway, often built up above the adjacent gardens. Beware of local traffic emerging abruptly from side roads and of the road surface in wet weather when the black top becomes notoriously slippery and vehicles can slide off into the palmeries. For cyclists the steep road embankment through this narrow route also has its hazards since two cars can pass only with difficulty. The old single track road has constant small scale road works. Children walk on the road and there is much local traffic from side roads. Motorists and others wishing to avoid the oasis route can take the new road which passes 1 km further inland between the palmeries and the main area of the former Italian La Valdagno agricultural estate to Wadi Ki'am. Buildings come right up to the new road.

For those with time the oasis route is to be preferred. After Leptis, the oasis, here called the Sahel Al-Ahmad, has dense mainly modern farmhouses. Farming continues in *suani* (small walled irrigated traditional gardens) but little effort is put into farming at present. The principal spring field crops in the gardens are wheat, barley and broad beans. The crops are mainly thin but the palm canopy remains for most part in good trim, providing welcome shade.

At **Wadi Ki'am**, Tripolitania's only flowing river, the long-established agricultural estate spreads out on both sides of the road. The original farm was a mere 120 ha of 2 ha plots fed by irrigation from the impounded stream of a spring source in the Wadi Ki'am. There is now an extension of reclaimed land under orchards and trees from Wadi Ki'am W to join up with old Sahel Al-Ahmad oasis and ex-La Valdagno. (For route via Jabal to Tripoli, see page 411.)

ZLITEN

Zliten (37 km E of Al-Khums) is a thriving administrative and academic centre. Turn left into town for all main services. Zliten is surrounded by *marabout* tombs famous for their qualities of improving fertility, so inspiring pilgrimages. These tombs are best visited with a local inhabitant. Visit the *zawia* shrine of Sidi Abdesselam and the cemetery of his descendants. There is one hotel, *Des Gazelles*. **Accommodation Youth hostel** *Kashr House*, Zliten, 20 beds, breakfast, shop, kitchen.

MISRATAH

The highway E from Zliten passes through poor grade lands with a slightly less reliable rainfall than areas further W. The coastal strip was thinly populated in the past and had only small and very discontinuous Arab oases. The Italians seized much of the coastal strip to set up estates for Italian farmers. The largest was Ed-Dafnia where the orchard groves of olives and almonds cover what was originally a mainly thin pastureland. The Italian effort at land settlement was added to by the Libyan Government after Independence with new areas reclaimed and ex-Italian estates taken over by Libyan farmers. Close to Misratah in the Zaviet Al-Mahjub district, a former private estate developed by the pre-Fascist Governor of Tripolitania, General Volpi can be seen forming a fine garden and farmed area. However, the Italian farming estates which were so much the characteristic of Misratah oases have been reduced in importance by occupation by townsfolk who treat their holdings as amenity areas rather than as working farms.

The expansion of **Misratah** as an urban centre has also been prodigious. Population growth within the town has been much increased by mass migration from the rural areas. Misratah is the administrative and educational capital of E Tripolitania with most ministries having local offices. Schools, hospitals and colleges are located in the new town. Its layout is well organized and mainly rectangular. There seems to be less riotous self-build construction in progress than elsewhere.

Two events have strengthened the city. First, the construction of the two iron and steel mills in the settlement which have created employment and demand for local services so that there is a real sense in Misratah of growth and development. The power of the steel mill authorities is considerable and has helped to give a sense of unity to the town. Second, the old marina has been extensively redeveloped to take shipping coming to service the industrial plant with raw materials and other goods. The central business district provides a multitude of traditional shops, cafés and restaurants. A large number of immigrant managers and labourers live in the town and this is reflected in a fairly cosmopolitan atmosphere in the cafés. Many foreigners are housed on the steel mill residential site.

Places of interest The most interesting items are the sand dunes on the W side of the town, some of the tallest sea dunes in the world. There is also the steel mill and the port.

● **Accommodation** *Hotel Misratah* is large, modern and generally as well run as the larger hotels in Tripoli; booking is advised, rates as for those in the capital, large restaurant and other facilities. **Youth hostel**: 4 km W of centre, T 24855, open 0700-2300, 120 beds, family rooms, meals, kitchen, laundry, bus 400m, reservations rec May-Sep.

● **Places to eat** You can eat in Arab cafés in the central business district. For a western type menu use *Hotel Misratah*.

Tauorga, some 40 km S of Misratah, is situated in the middle of a swamp formed by the great Tauorga salt lake and was reputed to be a refuge for escaping slaves. The town is located on a set of springs which provides water for agriculture, including a modern farm settlement set up by the government. Travellers would be better basing themselves in Al-Khums so that they can more easily get access to Leptis Magna and the beautiful mountain countryside of the Jabal Mislata to its hinterland.

THE TUNISIAN-LIBYAN FRONTIER TO SABRATA AND TRIPOLI

There is a considerable flow of commercial heavy traffic as well as private cars and taxis through the border as a consequence of the UN air embargo and the easing by Libya of frontier controls. For Arabs there are only the slightest of restrictions on movements of goods and people but despite that the volume of traffic is such that large queues can build up on both sides.

Once through the frontier from Tunisia the road connects as a single carriageway highway along the coast from Farwa to Zuwarah. From Zuwarah travel E via the modern road to Zaviyah. It is however, narrow and still single carriageway and is known to be particularly dangerous since traffic is dense and undisciplined. Mists and coastal frets are a problem because local drivers tend to ignore these hazardous conditions.

From Zaviyah the road to the E becomes a dual carriageway through palmeries and orchards. Many commuters as well as large numbers of vehicles moving to the frontier or the chemical plants at Bu Kammash use this high speed road which can be exceptionally dangerous at rush hours and at major road junctions. The dual carriageway is nonetheless best taken by car, caravan and motorcycle drivers rather than the narrow and tortuous old single track coastal road

slightly to the N of it.

Tripoli has spread uncontrolled out to the W and is heavily built up with modern housing for many km before breaking out into open olive growing country. Travelling from the W gives sight of the famous antiquities of Sabrata to the left shortly after the settlement of Al-Ajailat.

Entry to the Tripoli suburbs and the city itself on this route is through the Gurgi district and the Sharah Omar Mukhtar, which leads directly to the Green Square and the sea front adjacent to the castle.

ACCESS Buses from Zaviyah and Zuwarah can be picked up or a shared taxi hired inside Libyan territory for those coming in from Tunisia. From Zuwarah both express luxury buses and ordinary interurban service buses can be caught to finish the journey to Tripoli. The border post has few facilities other than a petrol station and a small café on the Libyan side. *Fare*: shared taxi to Sabrata LD3, to Tripoli LD8. **Youth hostel** *Zaviyah*, 40 km W of Tripoli, T 24019, 80 beds, breakfast incl, other meals available, family rooms.

FARWA ISLAND

The island of Farwa lies just offshore adjacent to the coast at the border post. Access to the departure point for Farwa Island is by road, though there is an airstrip nearby that could be used if upgraded. The island is approached either by a rough causeway built at the time of the construction of the nearby Bu Kam-

West of Tripoli

Ras Ajdir · Farwa Island · Bu Kammash · *Mediterranean Sea* · TUNISIA · Zuwarah · Al-Jamil · Al-Ajailat · Sorman · Sabrata · Zaviyah · Abu Nawas · Janzur · TRIPOLI · Tajurah · N · *Jefara Plain*

209

mash petrochemical/refinery complex, or by ferry from a pier at Bu Kammash village to the W of the plant. The ferry, run by local fishermen, is an occasional rather than a regular service. There are sea police and customs officials at both the pier and the causeway to control movement and those at the pier can be helpful in retaining a boatman.

Places of interest

The island, 12 km long and 2 km at its widest, is basically flat with dunes giving a slight elevation. Some 4,000 palm trees exist and have been tidied up in the central section of the island to look attractive. There is perhaps to be a tourist complex built on the island. The sand is fine grained and silver coloured. Other than the view of the petrochemical plant, the site is absolutely first class.

Travelling back to Tripoli, take the old road and travel into the main settlements along the coast. The road is slower than the main highway and often crowded, especially in the Tripoli suburb of Gurgi.

ZUWARAH

This is an expanding town on the extreme W of the Tripolitanian coastal belt, approximately 100 km from Tripoli and 60 km from the border with Tunisia. The main employer is the petrochemical complex at Bu Kammash. Most commercial and municipal activity is concentrated in the centre of the town on the old road 1 km to the N of the new dual carriageway coastal highway. The town extends to the seashore. New villas mostly take up the coastal block.

Local information
● Accommodation
E *Zuwarah Esterah Siahiah* (*Zuwarah Tourist Resthouse*) in the middle of the town adjacent to the square, a cheap, small hotel used by Libyans.

Camp sites: no camping facilities are reported, though along the coast there are plenty of good camping sites in woodlands or on the coast. Ask permission if possible before setting up camp.

● Places to eat
Zuwarah Esterah Siahiah (*Zuwarah Tourist Resthouse*) is the best restaurant and café and is in the middle of the town adjacent to the square.

● Hospitals & medical services
First aid: the Red Crescent clinic is on the old road.

● Post & telecommunications
Post Office: this is near the clinic on the old road.

● Useful addresses
Petrol: there are two petrol stations to the E and W of town on the main highway.

● Transport
Road The shared taxi/bus services to E and W along the coast road are very frequent. Costs LD7 Zuwarah to Tunis. LD10 Tripoli to Tunis. Express buses with a/c on Tripoli to Tunis run can be stopped in Zuwarah.

Janzur is on the old road as is the **D** *Janzur Tourist Village*, right on the coast, mainly new, with a wide range of accommodation – bungalows and apartments, excellent facilities, sailing, tennis, cinema, well equipped children's play room, shops, clinic, signposted in Arabic as *Medina Siahiah Janzur*; **D** *Abu Nawas Village*, another beach village in the Giorgim Poppoli area, old but cheap and open to all-comers at LD7 per night, close to shops, chemists and restaurants sited on the main street of N Gurgi; **E** *Old Janzur Tourist Village*, is further in towards the Tripoli boundary, comparatively run down, but convenient for shopping and facilities of what was Giorgim Poppoli estate.

Booking at these tourist villages is not easy from a distance since they are run by state organizations and are not essentially commercial in design. Persistence in seeing the on-site manager might be the best way to get accommodation. Their big disadvantage is their isolation from the city though bus or shared taxi transport is available on the old coast road 500m S of the beach club sites. Charges per night vary with the season and the quality of the complex between LD5 and LD20.

The old coast road into Tripoli is very crowded with shopping traffic and local people and should be avoided in the rush hours. Tripoli centre is only 5 km away but it can take 30 mins or more to complete the journey across the Wadi Mejennin bridge and then via Sharah Omar Mukhtar.

SABRATA

This is a 2-part town, one a modern residential centre and the other the archaeological site. There is a café and other services, including shops and cold drinks available at many main roadside shops. Sabrata town is rapidly expanding and some new industry has been set up. Many large villas extend down from the old coastal road towards the ruins. A new Faculty of Arts of Zaviyah University has been set up here. Shared taxi to Sabrata LD2. Taxi from town to ruins LD1.

Places of interest

The Sabrata ruins (see page 401) are open all week. Entry for adults is 250 mills and children 100 mills. The main **Sabrata Museum** and new **Punic Museum** are open Wed-Mon 0800-1700. A café and shop are located outside the complex. The site is clean and well run.

Beach

At Telil there is a good sandy area with shallow water. It is popular with Libyan families. The beach is served by black top dual carriageway from the main road from junction W of Sabrata city.

Local information
● **Accommodation**

Funduq Sabrata on corner of main road only 100m from Tourist Information, very primitive but quite clean LD8 pp/night.

Camping: is banned in the woodlands around the archaeological site.

Youth hostel: 160 beds, kitchen, meals, family rooms, laundry, open 0700-2400, 1 km NW of town, T (24) 2821, booking rec May-Aug, LD5 pp.

● **Places to eat**

There is a major restaurant at the ruins at the side of the large car park immediately outside the archaeological compound, which is open 0800-2200 winter and summer. The restaurant caters

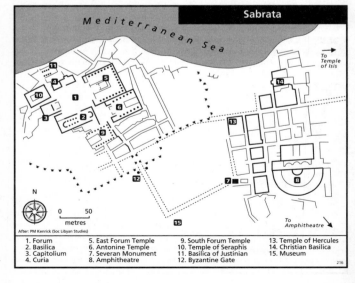

Sabrata

Mediterranean Sea

To Temple of Isis

To Amphitheatre

N

0   50
metres

After: PM Kenrick (Soc Libyan Studies)

1. Forum	5. East Forum Temple	9. South Forum Temple	13. Temple of Hercules
2. Basilica	6. Antonine Temple	10. Temple of Seraphis	14. Christian Basilica
3. Capitolium	7. Severan Monument	11. Basilica of Justinian	15. Museum
4. Curia	8. Amphitheatre	12. Byzantine Gate	

216

for Libyan and foreign visitors including large groups. The area offers a café and billiards. *Hotel Sabrata* in converted church on way to ruins is rec, good fish dishes with rice, spaghetti or couscous.

● **Useful addresses**

Petrol: there is a petrol station in the town and another at the road junction at Ajailat.

SABRATA RUINS

Like Leptis Magna, Sabrata began as a settlement to service the coastal trade of the Carthaginians. It was developed as a permanent site in the 4th century BC to act as a terminal for the trans-Saharan trade since it had a natural harbour on an otherwise long and unindented coastline. The site was later to become part of the three cities with Leptis and Oea (Tripoli). It was never favoured as much as Leptis Magna and has nothing to match its range and richness of buildings. Its coastal site is nonetheless impressive and Italian excavations and some reconstruction have made it well worth a visit. Access is from the main road in the new town towards the sea down a splendid avenue of old cypress trees. From Tripoli takes 50 mins in a black/white taxi, costs LD40.

The entrance is by the **museum** (15). Walk NW along the main thoroughfare, through the **Byzantine Gate** (12) in the walls down into the site. On the left is the **South Forum Temple** (9), 2nd century AD before the piazza is reached. This wider area has the **Antonine Temple** (5) up five steps on the right and the **Basilica** (2) on the left. The remains of the Basilica show that it has been much changed since the original building of the 1st century AD. The main monument is the **Amphitheatre** (8), used today as a theatre and concert hall. Further E are the remains of the **Temple of Isis**. There is a variety of public baths, temples and fountains, with many first class **mosaics** both on site and in the adjacent **museum**. Some Byzantine remains are on show to exemplify the revival after the Vandal invasions. The site was finally abandoned in the mid-7th century at the time of the Arab invasions. There appear to be no guides available but there are publications and artifacts on show at the museum. Entrance LD0.25, open from 0900-sunset daily, museums closed Tues. It is best to avoid visiting on Fri, other days are less crowded.

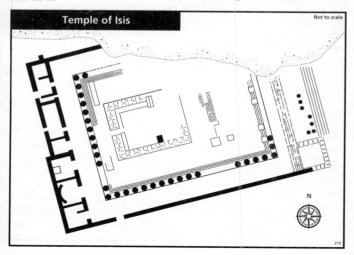

Temple of Isis

Not to scale

N

TRIPOLI TO THE JABAL NAFUSA AT GHARYAN

Directly S of Tripoli is the Gefara Plain, itself abutting the hills of the Jabal Nafusa. The Tripoli-Gharyan route gives an ideal cross-section of lands and climates through the Plain and the Jabal foothills.

Take the road S to Gharyan which now leads not only to the Jabal Nafusa but also from there to the deep SW at Ghadames and Ghat. The road is heavily built up in the long tentacles of the Tripoli suburbs. There are then dense farmstead settlements out to the Suani Ben Yadim turn off. The road is dual carriageway and busy with traffic, mostly local. After the Suani Ben Yadim and Ben Ghashir towns/oases, the highway runs through a countryside of trees and orchards. It is very green in spring, with uncultivated places forming rich pasture. The 2-lane highway is very fast from Suani Ben Yadim to Az-Zahra and onward to the main town of Al-Aziziyah.

Aziziyah has a petrol station, post office, hospital and several banks all situated on the main street or immediately adjacent in the few principal side roads. It is 221 km from Aziziyah to Nalut on the W end of Jabal Nafusa via the Wadi Hayyah route on the plain, via a single carriageway which is straight and fast.

AZIZIYAH TO GHARYAN

There are roadside stalls selling oranges in season. The wooded landscape thins rapidly with travel S. The road remains dual carriageway. The first sightings of the Jabal peaks can be had as the road approaches the scarp slope of the Jabal Nafusa. A few km S of Al-Aziziyah the landscape becomes open with very few trees. This is prime cereal-growing country in years of good rainfall. There is a large grain silo at Km 29 to Gharyan indicating this zone as a major contributor to Libyan wheat and barley production. At Km 25, the road begins the rise towards the Jabal. It is a slow climb through wooded terrain. There is a quarry for tile making materials on the right as the main road climbs into the scarp face, then at Km 18 the sharp rise into the scarp face begins. There is a café at its foot on the left hand side of the road. On climbing the scarp the old Italian road to the left can be seen. Though it is no longer maintained it is a good alternative route for walkers and the more adventurous cyclists. At the top of the slope the roadside is built up increasingly with houses. There are olive trees mainly around the Guassem area of Gharyan, 11 km from the town itself. Approximately an hour from Tripoli centre you arrive at Gharyan. (For travel in the Jabal (see page 403) – Jabal Nafusa and Ghadames.)

TRAVEL IN THE JABAL NAFUSA

The Jabal Nafusa, geologically complex, is a long plateau which runs in broken foothills from Al-Khums on the coast in the E to the start of the Jabal proper at Al-Qusbat, some 20 km to the SW of Al-Khums and then further W into S Tunisia. It forms a scarp slope between 600m and 900m above the Jefara Plain. It drops in altitude only gradually to the S into a set of rough basins, the largest of which lies around the town of Mizdah reputed to be the home of sorcerers, weavers of spells and holy men. The Hammadah Al-Hamra, a vast level-topped plateau, is reached after climbing another scarp to the S of Mizdah.

The Jabal has a climate quite different from the Jefara. Rains are slightly less reliable than the northern plains and diminish rapidly from the crest of the scarp to the S. Most places have over 250 mm of rain per year. Winters are quite cold and snow and frost can be experienced. Air temperatures throughout the year are lower than on the Jefara. Both winter dress and sleeping bags need to be heavier and windproof. The evenings and nights in the summer are far more comfortable than in the plains. **Gharyan** is the main town of the Jabal Nafusa.

The Jabal economy has proved remarkably versatile. Agriculture survives in most areas though it has become increasingly concentrated on growing cereals and rainfed orchard crops. Figs and apricots are famous on the Jabal and it is often the Berber groups who farm the rich grain land of the Jefara under the shadow of their mountain homes. The greatest source of funds for the Jabal groups is, however, remittance income from members of the family living elsewhere, usually in Tripoli or in other coastal towns. Even permanent residents of Tripoli have houses in their tribal territories and a great deal of investment flows back to the Jabal villages in this way.

BERBER HISTORY AND CULTURE

The culture of the Jabal Nafusa is for the most part Berber, though Arab tribes are interspersed within the main groups. Historically, the Berbers held the lands of the Jefara Plain with their main centre at Sabrata but they were driven back into the hills by the Arab invaders. The relative isolation of the Berber communities has meant not only a survival of their language and close kinship ties but also quite distinct urban forms and housing styles. In religion the Berbers are Muslim but follow the Ibadite branch of Islam, regarded by many Sunni Muslims as a heresy. The Berbers were aggressively separate from the Arabs on the Jabal Nafusa however much they intermarried with the Arab tribes elsewhere in Libya. The Berbers of the Jabal Nafusa participated in the revolts against Arab rule, the most ferocious of which took place in 896 AD.

More recently, the Berbers looked for the creation of a semi-autonomous Berber province. They had been a favoured group under the Italian occupation, making up important parts of the police forces in Tripolitania. On Independence it was hoped that Berber cultural separateness would be acknowledged and their language given equal status with Arabic. The rise of Arab nationalism at this time forestalled any chance that the small numbers of Berbers, less than an estimated 150,000 in all at that time, could make their voice heard. The revolution of 1969 set back Berber aspirations and for some time the government in Tripoli refused to admit there was any such group as the Berbers.

Despite the rapid economic changes that have taken place in Libya as a result of the spending of oil wealth, the Berbers still keep a sense of cultural separateness and even superiority.

BERBER ARCHITECTURE

A distinctive feature of the Jabal Nafusa is troglodyte architecture. Buildings are excavated into the earth and rock to give only a slight external built up area. Both houses and mosques were constructed in this fashion which made them warm in the often bitter winters experienced on the Jabal and cool in the heat of summer. At Mizdah the troglodyte way of life was pursued until the 1970s so that families could escape the extremes of heat experienced in ordinary houses.

There is a doubt about the origins of some of the great ruined **castles** on the Jabal such as those at **Sharwas** and **Wighu**. They were the centres of the original Berber societies which were set up after the Berbers were driven into the hills by the Arabs and became the focus of revolt against the invaders during the bitter struggles of the 9th century. There is evidence that internecine strife between powerful Berber clans at Sharwas and Wighu in the 11th century resulted in extensive damage to their fortresses. The castles were eventually abandoned, Sharwas as late as the 16th century, but stand as bleak but recognizable ruins on the peaks of the Jabal E of Yafran.

The castles are quite different from the fortified granaries seen at Nalut, Kabao and elsewhere in which small cells were created in the rock or built up one on top of another to accommodate stored grain and other items. These now mainly ruined buildings were surrounded by walls for reasons of defence. A third phase of abandoned dwellings can now be seen comprising the houses and quarters occupied until very recently in towns such as Jadu. The houses were built of loosely assembled stone with limited mortaring between joints and were clustered in tribal quarters and extended family dwellings incorporating areas for living, cooking and keeping the animals in safety at night. Prosperity in recent years has led many residents of the towns of the Jabal to move into villas style situated in the open fields around the old settlements. The old quarters have been abandoned and are crumbling into ruin. This situation is causing rapid deterioration in towns such as Jadu.

JABAL NAFUSA – GHARYAN TO NALUT

The Jabal Nafusa road is narrow and slow but offers the prospect of visits to a variety of Berber centres. There are apricot and fig orchards as well as traditional terraced farmland to be seen as the highway carries the traveller W and S along the top of the scarp slope.

GHARYAN

(*Pop* 100,000; *Alt* 900m) The centre of Gharyan shows signs of intensive rebuilding, reflecting the site's importance as a regional administrative centre. On climbing the scarp and traversing the olive groves where the road comes on to the summit of the Jabal, turn off right for Gharyan town, marked clearly but in Arabic script. Ask for '*al-markaz al-medinah*', the centre of the town. Note that the climate of Jabal is much cooler than the plain and even in spring can be several degrees colder on the ridge than on the Jefara. Petrol available here.

● **Accommodation** A *Hotel Rabta*, brand new, in excellent condition, clean, run in a business-like way, working lifts, 68 rm, for the business traveller are suites costing LD35 for single and LD45 for double, restaurant serves lunches and dinners at LD7.500 pp, modern café facing onto the street, film theatre, most modern facilities, owned by the Libyan Social Security Organization; D *Funduq Gharyan Siahiah (Gharyan Tourist Hotel)*, T 041 30105, very run down and seedy, 44 rm in use, smallest price for Libya, small restaurant and café, open all the year. **Youth hostel**: 120 beds, breakfast incl, family rooms, meals, laundry, kitchen and **camping** facilities in Gharyan at T (41) 31491, open 0700-2300, booking rec. Information at the City Hall.

Leave Gharyan and travel W via the dual carriageway, passing through olive groves in rolling uplands. Shortly there is a road on the left to **Tigrinnah**, a former tobacco-growing area and now with fairly dense villa housing straddling it. Good views are to be had to the

SW over broken country. The Jabal top is lightly wooded with olives and figs. After Tigrinnah, at a small settlement called Abuzeyan, the road divides with Mizdah 82 km and Sabha 700 km by road to the left.

After Tigrinnah the road on the top of the Jabal becomes a single carriageway. It passes through Assabah village with villas dispersed in farmlands. The village centre has a petrol station. Travel on 95 km to **Jadu**. The road traverses increasingly arid countryside with a light scrub covering to the hills. There are small occasional groups of houses such as Al-Gualith at Km 91 and Km 79. At Km 77 there is a mosque, a café and a petrol station. At Km 76 a turn to the right leads to **Kikla** 12 km away. On the main road, a green area under cultivation at Km 75-73 is an agricultural project run by the government. There are good places for picnics on sections of the old road visible from the new highway.

Turn right for **Yafran** off the main highway. This is classic old Berber town perched on the Jabal top and now much modernized but worth a visit. At Km 21

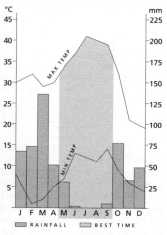

Climate: Gharyan

the black top road passes through fairly dense trees and cultivation. Note the good mainly reddish soils around Yafran. Reliable and heavy rains in late autumn and winter give the basis for a sound agriculture. There are fine views across the top of Jabal from the road towards Yafran. Also note the house decorations even on modern units, with complex ironwork doors, plaster work symbols such as butterflies and aircraft on house sides. Several small straggling villages lie along the roadside. A petrol station is located at **Qalah**, a village just before Yafran.

Yafran has been modernized. The old town and fortified grain storage towers and other ruins are still visible on the hilltops in the town. The new town spreads along the black top road. Cultivation is still undertaken sporadically on terraces and scarp-top fields. The town is very scattered around a one-way traffic system through narrow streets. A hotel is under construction but no hotel is currently in use. The town has all services, almost all clustered in the main square and the streets immediately adjacent to it. There is a **Youth hostel** in the city centre, T 0421 2394, 45 beds, meals available.

Leave Yafran and continue to **Al-Awenia** and **Aïn Rumia**. This road gives wide views across from the Jabal to the Jefara below. Some terraces cut into the Jabal face are still used for agriculture but many effectively have been abandoned. At Aïn Rumia there is a café open only in summer. The spring at the site is no longer running since the water is being used for the water supply to the town. But the gardens there are flourishing with palm trees in the cultivated valley. This spot can be crowded on Fri and public holidays. Return to the main road where a signpost at the junction gives 66 km to **Nalut** and 24 km to **Zintan**. Travel on the Zintan road to return to Tripoli. Otherwise continue W along the top of

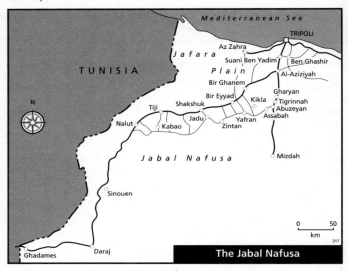

The Jabal Nafusa

the Jabal scarp. Pass through a further red soil zone with fruit tree cultivation. **Accommodation Youth hostel**: *Zintan*, T (44) 2191, 30 beds, breakfast provided, shop, central position.

Towards **Jadu** the rainfall decreases and the landscape is very arid, with few trees and little cultivation. At Km 10 turn right to Jadu. Arrive at Jadu passing through many new villas on the outskirts. The town gives the impression of a physical shambles since older communal and family stone constructed dwellings have been abandoned and new villas are randomly scattered across the landscape. In many ways Jadu has lost its old fashioned charm but is an important Berber town with notable tribes such as the Qabila Mizu there still. Berber is the main language in the households of the town. There is no hotel but petrol is available here. **Transport Road Bus**: services to both local and inter urban destinations run from just outside the town centre. **Taxi**: the taxi station is sited on the side of the main road at the entry to town.

Leave Jadu to head for **Shakshuk** at the foot of the scarp. There are two roads down the scarp, the newer one is better surfaced and better maintained. Both offer a breathtaking view N from the escarpment across the Jafara plain. Shakshuk is a small settlement with animal pens and houses sited a short distance off the road. At the junction with the Jefara highway from Nalut there is a petrol station and small general shop which sells drinks and grocery items.

The traveller can either go on the fast road along the Jefara W or return to the mountain road which leads on a winding route to Nalut. The mountain road passes through arid landscapes and enables rewarding visits to the Berber settlements at Tmizda, Kabao (petrol available here), Wighu, Sharwas and other sites. Those keen to see indigenous Berber architecture should perhaps take the slow road on the scarp. Those not prepared to accept the very considerable Berber charms of Nalut would find the Jefara road far quicker.

Nalut is a small town with all public

services near the centre. Work is proceeding to provide it with proper hotel facilities including a basic rest house for people coming up from Farwa on a desert tour. It is well provided with bus, taxi and other transport facilities, being the take off point for Ghadames and Ghat. It has petrol, car repair shops and garages. Expect work to be done slowly and at some considerable cost.

From Nalut and Jadu, as noted, there is access down the scarp to the Jefara single carriageway black top road returning to Tripoli. Roads off to the right lead back to the Jabal settlements at Kabao, Zintan, Yafran and most other settlements. There is a petrol station at Bir Eyyad and a roadside police control station. The control is not interested in tourists but have your passports ready in any case. At Bir Ghanem, the old stopping place on the Tripoli road, there is petrol, a café and shops. Carry on to the N passing through Sahel Jefara, again with a café and a small market. Another road to the left immediately after Sahel Jefara leads to Zaviyah, 78 km distant. Thereafter there is a slight increase in woodlands within government run agricultural projects and ex-Italian roadside trees. Some shifting grain cultivation is visible on the plain in spring. Increasingly dense cultivation indicates that **Al-Aziziyah** is being approached. Turn left at Al-Aziziyah (petrol available here) and Tripoli lies 38 km to the N.

GHADAMES

(*Pop* estimated 7,500; *Alt* 500m; *Rainfall* under 25 mm annually) Ghadames is a very beautiful small oasis town located where the international frontiers of Libya, Algeria and Tunisia join. The residential area is divided into the old and new towns. The old town is situated within the oasis whereas the new town has been built on the dry slopes above the oasis. Since 1986 all but one family have moved out of the old town. The old traditional houses are not easily adapted to the fast-changing contemporary lifestyles of the people of Ghadames. Fortunately, the old town has not been simply abandoned and still plays an important role in the life of the inhabitants. In effect, the old town is surrounded by small plots of farming land, still highly cultivated. In the high temperatures of the summer, the inhabitants of the new city return to their original town in search of coolness and protection. The old town with its Saharan architecture and great beauty is a uniquely preserved example of its kind.

History

The history of Ghadames is interesting. Paleolithic and Neolithic tools have been found in the surrounding region, but the first real documented information about Ghadames comes from the Romans who in 19 BC set up a garrison in what was then named Cydaus. Under the Byzantines, the town was set up to be an episcopate, under the tenure of a bishop, and some ruins from this period can be seen in the surrounding area. The Arab invasion in 667, led by Uqba Ibn Nefi, visited Ghadames before the Muslim forces con-

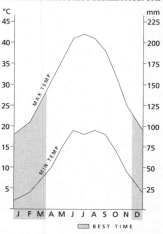

Climate: Ghadames

tinued on into Tunisia. By the 8th century, Ghadames was an important desert port of call for caravans and pilgrims but was also able to preserve its Independence. Until 1860, Ghadames was paying taxes to the Bey of Tunis. The second Turkish occupation of Libya in 1835 forced the town to recognize the authority of the Turkish Bey in Tripoli. When the Italians landed in Tripoli in 1911 it took them 3 years to reach Ghadames and even then their stay was of short duration. The Italians eventually returned on a permanent basis in 1924. They were great admirers of Ghadames and the area was treated sympathetically. New gardens were built and administrative offices set up there together with a small but pleasant hotel.

During WW2, Ghadames was occupied by the Free French Army led by General Leclerc and held under the Tunisian Protectorate until it was given up reluctantly at Libyan Independence in 1951. The last French troops left in 1955.

Ghadames suffered considerably with the development of less traditional sea-borne trade routes from West Africa. Situated in a very hostile environment even though there was water, trans-Saharan trade had been the main economic activity of the oasis. The people of Ghadames were trading and resident as far S as Timbuktu and on the Moroccan coast. The main trade consisted of caravans from the S bringing slaves, gold, leather and ivory in exchange for cotton, sugar and various products manufactured in Europe. By the start of the 19th century, trade had started to fall off due to the abolition of slavery. The decline was erratic and did not really end altogether until around 1910. Today, the inhabitants' only local sources of income are camel breeding and farming, the latter being very limited due to the lack of irrigation water and cultivable land, which is estimated at a mere 75 ha.

Architecture

The remarkable thing about Ghadames is the manner in which the people have been able to use all the resources available in a poor environment, together with their own traditions and architecture, to create perfect living conditions within this particular climate. The houses are built with mud, lime, palm tree trunks and fronds, the only available building materials. The result is impressive. Not only are the houses very elegant and beautiful, fitting perfectly into the environment, but they are also very practical. Built on two storeys, they have a central room on the first floor acting as a kind of courtyard with all the rooms leading out from it. The rooms are lit by an ingenious hole in the high ceiling, letting in sunlight that reflects off the white walls and provides quite sufficient illumination. The walls are made of mud and the upper floors are supported by palm tree trunks covered with fronds and mud. The interior of the house is decorated by the wife and tradition has it that this must be completed before the day of the marriage. The husband-to-be gives the key to his bride and she decorates their new home without his interference. The decorations are very simple, generally red patterns painted directly onto the white walls, with the addition of mirrors and a few small cabinets.

The roof is the domain of the women, the kitchen being on the roof. By tradition and due to the separation of sexes, the women were only permitted into the streets, either just after sunrise or just before sunset when the men are absent at the mosque for communal prayers. Otherwise in the old town they were confined to the house, especially the upper floors. However rather than hamper communication and freedom, this facilitated it, as most roofs touch and the women could easily move around from one roof to another. This is another remarkable feature of the architecture in Ghadames, possible because of the close intertwining of houses. All dwellings are physically linked together, to give shade

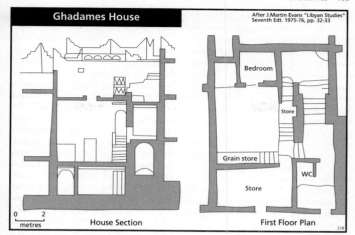

Ghadames House

After J.Martin Evans "Libyan Studies"
Seventh Edt. 1975-76, pp. 32-33

Bedroom

Store

Grain store

WC

Store

0 2
metres

House Section

First Floor Plan

218

from the sun and thus increasing the coolness of the settlement in the summer.

Within the houses there are some interesting features. One small room called the *koubba* is only used twice during the lifetime of the owners. First during the wedding ceremonies and second, if the husband dies, it is used by the widow to receive relatives and friends. The store room also has a clever system for preserving food. Due to climatic and other uncertainties, keeping a large stock of food was very important. Wheat would be stocked and a wall built with a small hole remaining open. A torch would be inserted in order to burn the oxygen and the hole quickly filled enabling wheat to be stored for years. When it was needed the walls would simply be demolished.

The streets also have charming characteristics. Small winding streets have covers for the most part, giving them a tunnel-like appearance and providing coolness with a few light wells between houses to illuminate the otherwise semi-dark streets. The roads lead to small public squares, some of which are covered. Most streets are lined with benches for the men to sit on.

Irrigation

An interesting feature of the oasis is the integration of the vegetation and cultivable land with the residential part of the town. The gardens are about 5m below normal street level in order to be closer to the water table. Within the village there are two artesian wells operating in addition to Aïn Fares, the spring of the horses. Aïn Fares is said to have been discovered by Oqba Ibn Nefi, but this seems unlikely since the oasis pre-dates the Muslim invasion by a very considerable period. The sense of coolness given by the running water and the shade of the palm trees makes the heat bearable in the summer months.

Places of interest

In the old town there is nothing specific to see because the beauty of the site is in the total harmony of the buildings and the small winding streets. In the old town situated behind the *Aïn Fares Hotel* there is a **House Museum**, a preserved Ghadames house. The interior is richly decorated with all the traditional furniture and implements of the oasis people. This is particularly interesting as it gives an insight into the traditional way of life in

Ghadames earlier this century.

There is another 'Popular' **museum** at the entrance to the new town with a collection covering the popular and traditional aspects of life throughout the region, with clothes, weapons, tools and even desert animals. On the main square of the new town there is a large **market** every Tues and a small market every other day.

Local information
● **Accommodation**
C *Hotel Luaha*, T (0484) 2569/70, 1 km or 10-min walk from town centre, currently clean and everything works, bargain at LD25 for double with sitting room, breakfast LD3 each. The **D** *Aïn Fares Hotel* used to be an old Italian colonial style hotel, wonderful location right by the old town but neglected and dirty and not very welcoming, at LD20 not a bargain.

Youth hostel: T 2023, 1 km SE of town centre, 120 beds, breakfast incl, family room, shop, laundry, open 0700-2300, booking rec Dec-Apr, kitchen. Its café is the young people's meeting point and gets very lively in the evenings.

● **Tour companies & travel agents**
The recently opened *Ghadames Travel and Tourism*, Sharah Saydi Aqba, T/F (0484) 2533 or *Cidamos Tours and Travel*, T/F (0484) 2596, Sharah Sidi Okba, manager Mr Bashir Hammoud will organize any trip in the surrounding area, including complete guided tours of the old town of Ghadames and trips into the desert down towards Ghat.

The best guide is Mr Ahmed Gassem Aoui, mayor of Ghadames for 40 years who delights in showing the old town and explaining the socio-economic system. If you ask for him by name you can avoid the Tourist agency upgrade of his fee.

● **Transport**
Air Flights to **Tripoli** every other Tues at 1230, costs LD20. Departure times change at short notice and travellers should check daily on the situation.

Road Bus: there are two buses a day to **Tripoli**. Officially they leave at 0700 and 1000, but in reality they leave when full. Be at the terminal at least 90 mins before the official time as this is when the bus is likely to leave. All buses to Tripoli go via **Nalut**. Small 10 seater private buses do the journey from/to Tripoli. Cost LD7, with several stops for refreshment and police checks. **Car**: the road surface from Ghadames to Nalut is good but attention must be given to the occasional small sand dunes across the road which can be dangerous even at moderate speeds.

To the W of the town, the small village of **Tunine** is very similar and still inhabited, though it is much smaller and less attractive. Some very primitive forms of water lifting *delu* systems are still standing (see box, page 389). Further along the road after Tunine there is a large number of sand dunes. It is particularly satisfying to walk up to the top of the dunes and watch the desert sunset.

To Algeria: in more settled times this is a border crossing to Algeria, currently **not** recommended.

AL-KHUMS TO TARHUNAH AND TRIPOLI

The Jabal road back to Tripoli from Al-Khums and Leptis Magna is well worth taking. The highway is occasionally narrow but this disadvantage is offset by a route through hill agriculture and breathtaking plantations of almond and olives.

The alternative to a direct route back to Tripoli from **Al-Khums** and **Leptis Magna** is to follow the road through the Jabal Nafusa via Tarhunah which takes about 2 hrs. From Al-Khums travel W on the main highway to Tripoli but take the Tarhunah road at the first left hand junction. It is 67 km to Tarhunah from this junction. The road follows more or less the line of old road but is a good width of carriageway now. Take care on this road as it is dangerous, with mixed traffic and many curves as the road rises towards the town of **Al-Qusbat**.

Al-Qusbat is the central place of the Jabal Mislata (a sub-region of the Jabal Nafusa) and has been much extended in an undistinguished way, spoiling the former charm of the place. There are most facilities including a post office, clinic,

petrol station and regional council office. A large hospital is being built. There is no hotel and travellers interested in walking across Mislata should stay in Al-Khums.

From Al-Qusbat take the road to Tarhunah. The road passes through scenic country in open landscape with ex-Italian olive and almond plantations at Al-Khadra and Qasr Dawn. Qasr Dawn has a hospital, police, school and shops.

At **Tarhunah** is the Faculty of Law of Al-Nasser University N of the town towards Shershara. Cinema, shops, Libyan Arab Airlines, an old hospital and a new one under construction are among the range of facilities in the town. This once beautiful town is now modernized to the detriment of its character. There was a hotel under construction but a dispute with the Turkish building firm has meant that it has been abandoned. The famous *Lady of Gharyan*, a wall painting on the barracks wall in the town painted by a US soldier in WW2, has sadly disappeared. Tarhunah's excellent wines are also no longer to be found on the open market. Leave Tarhunah towards Shershara. **Youth hostel**, c/o Education Department, Tarhunah, T 3379,

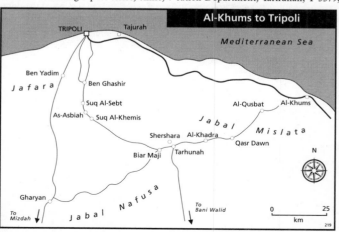

Al-Khums to Tripoli

TRIPOLI Tajurah

Mediterranean Sea

Ben Yadim

Jafara Ben Ghashir

Suq Al-Sebt

As-Asbiah Suq Al-Khemis Al-Qusbat Al-Khums

Shershara Al-Khadra *Jabal Mislata*

Biar Maji Tarhunah Qasr Dawn

N

Gharyan *Jabal Nafusa*

To Mizdah *To Bani Walid* 0   25   km

219

20 beds, breakfast available, kitchen.

Shershara The much-visited spring at Shershara has now stopped flowing as water has been diverted away and the local water table has fallen. A small stream now comes in through a narrow upper valley with dense trees. It flows under the road which acts as an Irish bridge and there is a tiny fall of water on rocks below the roadway. The lower valley is green but very dirty with plastic and other rubbish. What was a very beautiful area is now very disappointing. **Places to eat** The hotel at Shershara, *Funduq Shershara*, is in a poor state: the rooms are not now used, but it has a restaurant and café. The staff do their best but the general effect is not very good. The hotel has no water from time to time. Arabic tea and a selection of cold soft drinks are available. Open 0800 to 2100.

Take the main road from Tarhunah out to the NW. A dual carriageway leads down to Tripoli. An alternative road leads W to Gharyan. The Tripoli road is fast but winding. There is a junction slightly N of Tarhunah which permits a direct link from the petrol station at Biar Maji to Bani Walid approximately 85 km to the S, and a second junction to Qatamah, 32 km from Biar Maji. **Youth hostel** in former *Bani Walid hotel*, T (322) 2415, 30 beds, meals available, shop. It is a single carriageway road but good quality. Travellers can go directly via Mizdah to Sebha on black top without touching Tarhunah town. The road to Tripoli goes on to **Suq Al-Khemis**. Here there is a large roadside market, post office, police, shops and other basic facilities. At **As-Asbiah** is a junction with hospital, hospital-related housing but little else. Reaching **Suq Al-Sebt** there are more roadside shops, a petrol station and other services.

At **Ben Ghashir** the road leads off at a junction to the international airport link. Also from this point there is a dual carriageway to Tripoli. It is rather slow with lots of traffic. Roadside orange sellers are found in the spring season. Farm tractors and vehicles are plentiful on this dangerous road, mixing with fast airport and through traffic. Travellers can take the Tripoli-airport road with greater safety and speed.

Fezzan

FEZZAN is the third of the great historic provinces of Libya after Tripolitanian and Cyrenaica, the latter not in this volume. It is a region spreading over some 684,280 sq km of desert lands in the Southwest of the country. The bulk of Fezzan is made up of uninhabited sand seas and deserts interspersed with gravel and stone plains. In the North and the East of Fezzan there are extensive areas of stone desert called *hammada*. Sabha, the capital, is the hub of the transport system in Fezzan and travellers can move to all key sites from there.

SABHA

Within the desert areas are a number of great *wadis* which give human access and have a modest availability of underground water. The two main dry *wadi* beds are the Al-Shatti and the Al-Ajal (Al-Hayyah). A shallow topographic basin around Murzuq also gives access to sub-surface water at shallow depths.

There are dry salt lakes or *sabkhas* throughout the region, the greatest number being found in the Wadi Shatti and the Hofra-Sharqiya zone. The highest part of Fezzan lies in the Tibesti Mountain area, a huge uplifted massif in the Uzu region running to altitudes of 3,376m in the extreme SE of the system. Deeply incised *wadi* valleys are clearly vegetated and rich in animal and plant life. Lower elevations are reached in Jabal As-Soda, 840m and 1200m in the Jabal Al-Haruj Al-Aswad.

Climate

The climate of Fezzan is hot and dry. Everywhere is arid and desertic. Rainfall is slight and irregular at 8.3 mm per year,

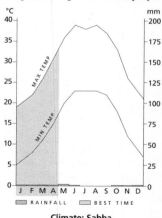

Climate: Sabha

often falling as an occasional heavy downpour. Heavy rain storms bring chaos to transport and can lead to extensive damage to property with flash floods and disintegrating walls of traditional buildings. Temperatures are high during the day with no cloud cover, allowing rapid cooling at night. Daily ranges in temperature of 40°C are possible. Temperatures are higher in the summer with the Jun mean monthly temperature at 30.6°C in the regional capital, Sabha. Spring and particularly Jan is a better time to travel when average temperatures fall to 11.6°C. Winds can be severe in the desert, with westerlies dominating the winter and easterly/northerlies the summer. Fezzan experiences the *ghibli* wind in the form of a very hot, dry and uncomfortable blast of several days' duration. Transport can be disrupted during the *ghibli*.

Population

Human settlement was possible only where water could be reached easily by primitive technology in the Wadis Ajal and Shatti and in the Murzuq basin. Even here the densities of human populations were thin and villages widely scattered. Recent economic development has, despite enormous expenditures of cash and effort, made little difference to this underlying pattern. In 1980 the population was estimated at 190,265 of which only 165,245 were Libyan nationals. The population was growing at 5.1% annually, mainly through inward migration by foreigners from countries such as Chad and Sudan. Non-Libyans represented 13% of the population of Fezzan at that time, a figure which has since gone up by at least 50%.

The indigenous peoples are dark-skinned but of Arab extraction. The Tibu and the Tuareg tribes have some Arab characteristics but are otherwise of separate origin. The Tuareg have their own, Berber-related, language of Tamashek. In recent years some have settled in towns. The Fezzanese are known as friendly and hospitable people. Only the Tibu, a tall and very dark group from the Tibesti, are unreliable in their treatment of strangers. A number of Europeans have been taken hostage in the Tibesti, though never within Libyan Tibesti. *Great care* is needed in travelling in Tibesti since it is isolated, difficult of access, bleakly inhospitable in its climate and unpoliced over very large areas.

Economy

The economy of Fezzan was traditionally dependent on oasis agriculture, some pastoral herding among the Tuareg and trans-Saharan trade. In recent years this has entirely changed as a result of oil revenues and the growing influence of the central authorities in Tripoli. Employment now depends on the state more than on traditional activities. No less than 80% of people rely on government generated services for a living. Agriculture employs a mere 7% and trade another 10%. Perhaps as much as 90% of all regional income comes from the government. The cause of the skew in the economy is directly related to the nature of oil income which is spent by the government. Investment by the government ran at US$7,000 per head of population in the region in the late 1970s and early 1980s, though it has since fallen significantly. Libyans have tended to give up active involvement in farming and employ foreigners. In services and construction foreigners make up over 80% of the work force.

Agriculture

This is known to have been practised in this region since the 5th century BC when the Garamantes used a form of irrigation in areas adjacent to Ghat. Agriculture was largely self-sufficient but was also designed to provide surpluses to feed passing caravan traffic. The main crops have always been barley and wheat in the winter and millet, sorghum and maize in the summer, together with vegetables and fruits in great variety. Forage crops were

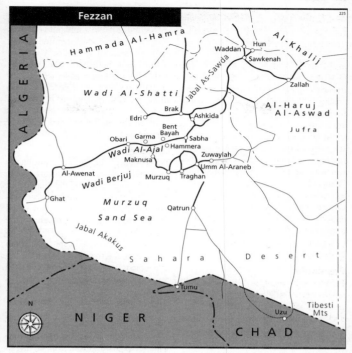

vital both for keeping animals on the farm and for providing food for the passing caravan trade. Farms are generally tiny and fragmented into small parcels. Including unused and unirrigated lands, average farm sizes at 7 ha were less than half of that for the rest of the country. Each irrigated plot is carefully levelled, provided with water and sheltered from the wind with palm frond hedges or mud walls. The main commercial field crops are tomatoes and onions, both of which are exported to the N. Fezzan produces more than two thirds of all dates in Libya at 86,523 tonnes per year from no less than 4,649,936 trees. Olives, grapes, figs and oranges are also grown among a vast range of fruits. Sheep and goats are the main animals kept, the richest grazing zone being the Wadi Shatti. The number

of camels (dromedaries) is falling rapidly as they are no longer used for transport or ploughing. Some development of cattle herding for milk production is underway.

Modern agricultural estates have sprung up throughout the region and are easily recognized by their straight boundaries and regularly laid out facilities. The biggest projects include those at Maknusa and Wadi Aril which are principally designed to produce grain and fodder. They are basically agribusinesses run with large amounts of capital but few employees. Occasionally they have attracted local herders who make use of the fodder for their livestock. A second category of development estates is the settlement farm where small farms are set up within large estates run initially by government agencies. Farmers are recruited to take over the farms. There has been friction from time to time as locals have resented incoming farmers. The presence of estates means fresh water, electricity and telephones but not necessarily accommodation for the traveller.

Industry

By definition, industry in Fezzan is poorly developed. The resource base is weak but there are some oil and natural gas deposits in the extreme W and some iron ores in the Wadi Shatti. But these resources are most easily used in the N and at best will represent primary exports. Small workshops have grown up in Fezzan but they are mainly concerned with servicing government activities and construction, with mechanical workshops, building materials and food processing jobs dominating the sector. For the traveller it will be worthwhile looking out for the *local glass making plant* at Brak, the *handicraft centre* at Ghat and the *leather factory* at Traghan.

Access and travel in the province

Access to Fezzan is limited by the few international entry points. Most travellers will have to come through Tripoli, though there is the chance to enter directly from Niger and Algeria. Similarly, the internal access points are either via the airports at Sabha and Ghat or along the main roads to Sabha from the N of the country.

There are two main lines of road entry to Fezzan. The first is the traditional route from the coast at Bu Grayn via the Jufra region to Sabha and the second is the new road from just outside Gharyan via Mizdah. Significant resources have been expended in Libya to improve the road system and the main highways are by and large in good condition and constantly being supplemented by new spurs. The road system in Fezzan (see below) covers the main economic and strategic axes.

Road system of the Fezzan

Key Routes	Journey	
	Length (km)	time (min)
Sabha – Traghan	128	100
Sabha – Obari	200	150
Edri – Brak – Ashkida	147	120
Murzuq – Zuwaylah	136	105
Obari – Ghat	370	300
Umm Al-Araneb – Qatrun	150	125

The main road system is fast and served by buses and taxis on regular scheduled/on demand routes. The buses are cheap but taxis can be expensive over long distances. The driving at times can be careless and even harrowing. Travel at cool times of day and use a/c buses when available. At present only the key routes between Sabha and Tripoli are served by super-express services. The bus services are important because the air link is crowded, infrequent and inconvenient. Buses give a cheap and easy way to continue a journey rather than put up with long stays in oasis towns.

The bus station in Sabha, the main transport hub for the area, is in the Jabeya district. Its facilities are very basic. Almost all long distance bus services run from Sabha usually on a once-a-day basis for major routes and alternate days or a lesser frequency for other services. The inter-urban taxi services are always

Brak						
671	Ghat					
833	544	Murzuq				
301	370	174	Obari			
939	570	183	200	Sabha		
939	1530	1143	1160	758	Tripoli	
317	920	533	550	350	610	Waddan

Fezzan: distances by road between major cities (Km)

available and are normally on, or adjacent to, the main street of each town.

Since travellers in Fezzan will find their lives dominated by the transport facilities, a distance matrix of main centres in the region is given below. The distances between centres are considerable and, even on the bus or in a taxi, you should take enough food, drink and clothing to manage through very hot and very cold conditions. A breakdown can cause long waits for which travellers should be well prepared, especially on some of the long inter-settlement roads in the S.

Places of interest

Topography Fezzan offers endless but varied desert landscapes. A good relief map is essential to make the best of this experience. Secondly, there are a few small sites to visit, some living oases, others archaeological monuments or remains. The oases are best grouped into areas for visiting. The smaller ones should be visited with a guide if unwelcome attention or suspicion is not to be aroused especially by male groups. In the Wadi Al-Ajal (Al-Hayyah) there are still comparatively unspoiled villages such as Bent Bayah to the W where magnificent forms of traditional architecture are still in use. In Ghat there are still strings of small traditional settlements worthy of a half day visit with a translator. Similar villages exist as populated or recently abandoned sites throughout the province. The further they are from the developed centres, the more interesting the villages become, though some, like Umm Al-Araneb, have undergone a total population change in recent times.

The **architecture** in Fezzan is highly individualistic. Houses are built of sundried mud bricks in most regions, though near rocky outcrops flat natural stone can be incorporated into the buildings with mud rendering on both sides. Most houses are single-storey. The flat roofs are constructed with palm wood cross members covered with palm fronds sealed with a beaten mud coating. Ornamentation is provided on the roof corners by a triangular motif in which two flat bricks are leaned against each other above a horizontal brick or stone. This emblem is used in a variety of forms either as a single unit or in combination along the top of a wall. Doorways can be highly decorated, often with calligraphic or symbolic representations above the main door to the house. Some houses carry horn-shaped fixtures above their entrances, thought to be against the effects of the evil eye. Painting is rare except to highlight a doorway and it is usually the religious buildings which carry white or blue washes. Variations of style are noticeable throughout Fezzan.

The minarets of mosques in Fezzan are also distinctive and worth looking out for. They are often square-shaped and only slightly raised above the level of single-storeyed mosques, usually painted white. A complex and beautiful three-tiered mosque of this kind exists at Obari. Other fine mosques can be found, and **Zuwaylah** is worth calling at to see its **mosque**, the ruins of an associated **fort** and the 12th century tombs of Beni El-Khattab, square constructions of mud bricks faced with stone. Some of the Turkish stone forts survive and the Murzuq fort can be seen in the centre of the new town.

The archaeological sites

Fezzan is rich in pre-historic sites where well-preserved cave paintings can be viewed. The main sites are: (1) **Akakus** and **Tashinat** where there are excellent wall carvings; (2) in the **Wadi Fuet** close to Ghat there are a number of coloured wall paintings; (3) **Zinkekra** in the W Garma area where there are rock carvings; (4) **Wadi Buzna**. The artwork depicting antelope, elephant and giraffe-like animals and human hunters dates from 6000-3000 BC.

Libya is famous for the **Garamantian**

civilization of the Wadi Al-Ajal. The centre was **Garma**, established about 2000 BC, and only rediscovered in the 1960s. A series of ruins and sites are open for visitors to the Wadi Al-Ajal. The city of Germa is a clear attraction, lying close to Obari just off the Sabha road. Nearby are the tombs of Saniat Jebril and Ben Howaidi. Other tombs and cemeteries include the tombs of Ahramat Al-Hatiyah, the royal cemetery to the S of Jarma, the cemeteries at Bent Bayah and Budrinnah, and Al-Khareyk, the latter W of Garagra. There are the remains of forts at Al-Abiad and Al-Gullah. The full range of urban life is not yet known since excavations at the site have not been finished.

All Libyan monuments are open 0800-1700 and are normally closed on Tues. In Fezzan there is a certain informality over working hours and even the guardianship of sites. Local guides will see that you review the full extent of the known ruins but often travellers will be on their own. Care is needed to treat the sites well and not to take artifacts. Urban monuments, especially mosques, need a low key approach with permission asked before entering. Again, having a local Fezzanese with you can make a great deal of difference to your reception. Housing of interest will either be a prepared tourist site without a family in residence as at Bent Bayah or must be approached with care if there are women resident. There are rarely facilities of any kind at the Fezzanese archaeological sites.

OBARI LAKES

A strange site, signposted off the only main road to the N and well worth travelling a short distance to see is that of the Obari lakes. About 13 small lakes exist in the Obari sand sea sited between the great dunes of the system. The main lakes are **Mandara** 200-300m diameter, lake **Umm Al-Ma'**, which usually has water throughout the year, **Bahar Al-Daud** 300m diameter, **Tademsha**, **Umm Al-Hassan**, **Neshnusha**, **Bahar Al-Trunia**, **Frejia** and **Oudnei**. They are fed by ground water from the sand sea when the water table builds up in the dune systems. Most are very shallow, less than a metre, and many dry up during the summer. The water is more brackish in the lakes but water drawn from the dunes can be used in irrigation and for human consumption. There is a myth in Libya that the lakes area was populated by people who were 'worm-eaters', a belief arising from the local custom of eating shrimps taken from the lakes. Not surprisingly, local people do not take kindly to the 'worm-eating' story!

Excursions

A first approach to an area as widespread but thinly populated as Fezzan is to take the major geographical axes along the excellent road system. The main elements can be taken in using the following routes: **(1) Brak – Edri** along the Wadi Al-Shatti giving access to the old town of Brak, the S rim of the Hammadah Al-Hamra and the small traditional settlements of the valley; **(2) Sabha to Obari** along the line of the Wadi Al-Ajal taking in the traditional villages and the Garamantian sites; **(3)** the **Murzuq – Zuwaylah** road with more Garamantian remains, the fort at Murzuq, the mosque at Zuwaylah and the old and new towns at Umm Al-Araneb and **(4)** either by road or air, a visit to **Ghat and the SW corner of Libya**, one of the most unspoiled and rewarding areas of the country for the traveller.

In addition to this overall travel scheme, some specific **organized excursions** are available through the travel agencies, the most active for Fezzan as a whole being in the *Akakus Tours*, see page 419.

Fezzan tour includes trips to the old villages of *Ghat* and down to the *Wadi Ayadar* and to *Takhakhori*. The visitor travels through the desert of the *Msak*

Mallat and *Msak Satafet* to look at the country and some ancient sites and also crosses one of the world's great sand seas, *Erg Murzuq*. The caravan then goes to the *Wadi Matkhandus* to look at wall engravings and to the *Wadi Berjuj* before arriving at *Murzuq city*. *Zuwaylah* and the sand dune lakes are visited. There is also a full scale visit to the ruins of *Garma* before returning via Al-Awenat to Ghat. The visit can be tailored to individual or group requirements to run between 7 nights to 13 nights under bivouac.

Teshuinat tour This takes the traveller in 4WD vehicles and under canvas through the *Akakus mountains*, and the immediately surrounding sand seas, to look in at *Ghat*, *Al-Awenat* and the extreme SW corner of Fezzan. The circuit lasts for between 3 and 5 nights and includes a visit to the cave painting sites of that region.

Discover Libya tour offers a very varied set of packages of as short as 3 nights and as long as 17 nights. Again, travel is in 4WD vehicles and accommodation mainly in tents. It begins in *Tripoli* then moves along the Mediterranean coast through *Leptis Magna* and then *Sabrata* to the W borders to track down through *Nalut* on the western Jabal to *Ghadames*, a long cross-desert run to *Sabha* and on to the principal sites in *Fezzan*.

Central Saharan expeditions Akakus have arranged with the authorities in Algeria and Niger to take visitors across the international border to visit all the major central *Saharan cave painting sites*. The excursion is imaginative and unusual, taking in *Ghat* and *Tumu* in Libya, *Djanet* in Algeria and *Madama* and *Bilma* and *Agadez* in Niger. This is an exciting chance to see this previously difficult region in a 21 night tour which enters via Libya and leaves via Niger or vice versa. A more limited route through Libya and Algeria takes to the sites in those two countries takes between 7 and 17 nights depending on how many sites are taken into the itinerary.

Given the costs and administrative difficulties of setting up desert visits to this part of the world, *Akakus Tours* offer of desert expeditions is extremely attractive. Other tour operators are being set up. The largest in Tripoli is the *Libyan Travel & Tourism Company*, T 21 48005/48011 F 21 43455. Their desert tours in Fezzan include a 15 day desert visit from Tripoli to the S flying from Tripoli to Sabha and thereafter by 4WD vehicle to Gabroun and Mandara sand dune lakes, and on to Garma and Wadi Berjuj. The itinerary goes to the Matkhandus prehistoric painting sites and then across the Murzuq sand sea to Gassi Ohabran, the Wadi Selfoufet in the Akakus and finally to Ghat, returning to Tripoli via Sabha by air.

Privately organized groups in 4WD vehicles or on desert motor cycles enjoy travelling this area. The more common itineraries are from Ghadames E to Darj, SE on the desert tracks to Idri and on to Brak perhaps returning N from here to the coast or else travelling S to Sabha then W to Obari and Ghat. From here the route is N adjacent to the Algerian border back to Ghadames. This last leg 450 km across the Hamadat al Hamrah plateau, windy, bleak and with extremes of temperature (-15°C at night) is not well defined and not to be undertaken lightly.

Local information
● **Accommodation**

The tourist potential of Fezzan has been neglected almost entirely. The obvious attractions of desert travel, of the unique nature of the less 'developed' oases and of the archaeological sites were overlooked. Few hotel facilities exist in general, and very few have been constructed with travellers from overseas in mind. There are only 400 or less hotel beds of a satisfactory kind available in the whole of Fezzan. The main hotels are in Sabha and include a new Social Insurance Tourist Centre, **B** *Hotel Al-Fatah*.

The **E** *Al-Galah Hotel*, rather run down, 57 rm, 114 beds; **E** *Mountain Hotel*, small, 19 rm, 38 beds. There are also rest houses in Sabha owned by official organizations to which access can only normally be obtained with the help of official letters of introduction from Tripoli. Other hotels include the new Hotel at Hun, where the old *Tourist Hotel* still functions, though parts of it seem to have been given over to foreign labourers. An 11-year-old hotel exists at Ghat and rest house facilities are available if not already occupied – ask for information at the Municipality building. It is best to telephone for a booking before arrival in Ghat to *Akakus Tours*, though they normally accommodate their guests in bivouacs. Small guest houses exist at Ghat, Traghan, Hun, Hammera and Garma but their facilities are limited and cannot be guaranteed to be available.

Camping: is unlimited in the desert, though the security services do not look kindly on wild camping by foreigners unless supervised by a Libyan agency. Individual campers should either be discreet in their overnight stops, providing all their needs from their own resources, or ask permission from tourist agencies/local authority *baladiyah* offices in the nearest town. Often school or college facilities can be used by travellers.

There is a growth industry in camping in the S though this is under official auspices. In the SW, *Akakus Tours*, T 0724 2804/2318, Tx 2938 Ghat, (General Manager, A Younis, home T 0724 2938) offers visits to the major archaeological sites of the region, especially Garma, under canvas. They will reserve travel to and from Libya, make hotel reservations in Libya, assist travel groups with handling arrangements on site. They offer a number of separate trips, one to Murzuq, Ghat, Obari, Al-Awenat over 8-13 nights, another through Teshuinat in the extreme SE of Ghat over 3-6 nights and another to a 21-night visit through the Libyan-Niger borderlands. These desert circuits are designed for fairly rich and very fit Europeans and are an excellent introduction to parts of the Sahara which have been virtually closed to all but a few specialists for the last 20 years.

Youth hostels: 1) *Sabha*, Gamal Abdel Nasser St, 3 km E of town centre, T 27337, 160 beds, family rooms, laundry, meals, kitchen, open 0700-2300. 2) *Ghat*, 40 beds, kitchen, meals, T (72) 32360. 3) *Hun*, 50 beds, kitchen, T (57) 3379. 4) *Waddan*, T (580) 2310, 160 beds, meals available, laundry, family rooms, booking rec Sep-Nov;. 5) *Murzuq*, T 62, former *Murzuq Tourist Hotel*, 30 beds, with breakfast, kitchen. 6) *Umm Al-Araneb*, T (72)

62228, 120 km from Sabha, 90 km from Murzuq, 30 beds, with breakfast, kitchen. 7) *Fejeaj*, People's Housing Project, 60 km from Sabah, 40 beds, meals, kitchen, T (71) 28323.

● **Places to eat**
Eating out in Fezzan is a rather limited experience because local Fezzanese rarely eat outside their own homes. Restaurants and cafeterias do exist adjacent to the hotels and guest houses. In Sabha, Brak and Obari, the range of facilities is acceptable, with two or three eating places available. Cooking is basic and to local or Arab tastes with either rice or macaroni as its basis except in the few new hotels where forms of international cuisine can be found. In the summer heat, cooking is scarcely worthwhile and there is cold or tinned food available from the small private shops at a comparatively high price. The tourist agencies normally provide their clients with food cooked by their own staff. Eating in private homes is to be encouraged where invitations are received. Here the food is varied, wholesome and often interesting.

● **Banks & money changers**
Few banking points in Fezzan deal with foreign exchange, especially any slightly unusual currency or TCs. Use the main banks in Sabha on the main street or, as a second and not always reliable best, the big hotels which usually have a small branch of a bank in-house.

● **Entertainment**
In Fezzan is limited to visiting friends' houses and having the occasional formal civic reception. Otherwise there are a few cafés and restaurants which stay open while customers remain. Most towns have a cinema with films in Arabic. Sports centres, nightclubs and other tourist attractions are altogether absent. For sport, the younger locals play volleyball and football.

● **Hospitals & medical services**
Chemists: most small settlements have pharmacies, but it is wise in Fezzan to travel with a comprehensive first aid kit and any personal medical drugs needed. Chemists shops are to be found in all centres and even small villages will have clinics of sorts with some medical drugs available. As elsewhere in Libya, people with special needs should ensure that they carry adequate supplies.

Hospitals: Fezzan is well served by health centres, clinics and dispensaries. Hospital facilities are spread thinly, not surprising in a landscape of very distant settlements and low population densities. There are principal hospitals at Murzuq, Obari, Sabha, Al-Shatti and Sawkenah, that is in each district. Some of the smaller hospitals have limited staffing and facilities. On average Fezzan has half the health provision that other parts of the country enjoy. The traveller is warned that, together with a road accident rate far higher than the rest of the country, the overall record of which is very bad in any case, health repatriation insurance is more than usually important.

● **Shopping**

In the Fezzan can be much more rewarding than in all other parts of Libya other than Ghadames. The leatherwork of the region, especially at Ghat, is excellent if at times quaintly crude in finish. The main traditional items are leather handled and sheathed knives, short spears/arrows and Arab slippers of ornate design. Woven date palm fronds are used to make a variety of matting products from fruit basins and rice trays to place mats. Tuareg and other ladies' ornaments are interesting and there is some glasswork. An attempt to resurrect the carpet industry is underway and some patterns are plain but effective.

● **Tour companies & travel agents**

There are many **LAA** offices in Tripoli for travelling to Fezzan. The head office at Sharah Haiti, POB 2555, Tripoli, Sales T 606833/36. In Fezzan, LAA has offices at Sabha T 071 23876, at Ghat T 0724 2035 and at Hun T 057 2456. In Ghat, **Akakus Tours**, T 0724 2804.

● **Transport**

Local Bus: within the larger towns access can either be by bus or taxi. Distances are very short since no town is large except Sabha. All the town centres or hotels and the airports are served by bus. **Car hire**: self-drive car hire is difficult though this can occasionally be arranged through a travel agent. More normally arrange for a car, preferably a 4WD vehicle if you are visiting sites off the road, with a driver. This can be expensive and rentals of LD100-LD200 per day are not uncommon. There are many mechanical workshops in the main towns which can repair and service vehicles. Some of the work is rough and ready but most makes of vehicle can be handled. Fuel is available in the main towns and most small villages. Drivers should always set off with a full tank and adequate spare fuel to reach the next large town rather than the next petrol station. Shortages of fuel do occur at individual stations from time to time. **Cycle hire**: hire of cycles and motorcycles is not normal though some repair shops will lease them, but not cheaply or readily. **Taxi**: this can be expensive and prices should be negotiated in advance where possible. (See also Access and travel, page 416.)

Air There are regional airports at **Sabha, Ghat, Hun** and **Uzu**, though only Sabha has facilities for international flights. The airport is on the fringe of the town next to the old Turkish fort area. It has been rebuilt as a regional/international airport. The passenger reception facilities are fair. Scheduled international air services to Sabha, when permitted, include flights from Accra, Alexandria, Casablanca, Damascus, Khartoum, and Ndjemena. Flights into **Sabha** are mainly by Libyan Arab Airlines. To **Tripoli** Wed and Sat at 1500, takes 1¼ hrs. Booking well in advance is essential. Due to the reduction in flights the airport at Ghat is currently closed.

Al-Khalij

AL-KHALIJ (THE GULF) takes its name from the Gulf of Sirte. The province is an artificial creation of recent years and includes the Sirteican coastal embayment together with the routes to and from the entire Southeast quadrant of the country down to the Egyptian border South of 28°N and the Sudanese border East of 16°30'E. The area of the province is estimated at 730,960 sq km. The province was intended in the period after the coup d'état of 1969 to unite the centre of the country and give a political bloc strong enough to offset the traditional domination of Tripolitania and Cyrenaica. In fact, it has remained as an enormous no man's land around the Gulf of Sirte with a long tail South into the desert, the oases of which retain their individuality from the coastlands to which they were attached.

Climate

In this region the climate is in general Saharan. There are still inadequate data to give precise definitions of microclimate over this very large region. Extreme temperatures run at well over 50°C and lows of well below freezing are experienced, especially at night. Rain is very rare but can come occasionally in downpours inducing flash floods and surface erosion over limited areas. The coast, especially around Sirte, gets a rainfall of more than 100 mm, though this is very erratic and rare wet years are followed by many years of drought.

Land

The Libyan Desert covers the territory between the 18° and 29° parallels N and the 18° and 28° meridians E. Its N limits are marked by the marginal settlement at Siwa in Egypt and Al-Jaghbub and Gialo in Libya. It comprises a vast sedimentary depression formed of limestones and marine origin clays. The area forms a flat platform with the strata tilted slightly to the N. The only high relief is in the Jabal Al-Awenat in the extreme SE where heights of 1,908m are attained at the Libyan-Egyptian-Sudanese border tripoint. The visible topography of the desert is dominated by sand, mainly in the form of dunes in the Jaghbub sand sea and elsewhere gravel desert such as the Serir Calanscio. Al-Khalij includes two other major sand seas, those of Calanscio, to the W of Serir Calanscio, and Rebiana, in the SW of Al-Khalij. The coast is also a desert, the Sirte desert made up of a low broken plateau.

The N coastlands are open to access from the sea and the sides. Southern Al-Khalij on the contrary has historically been, and still remains, difficult of entry from outside. Until the 1980s there was no permanent all-weather highway between the main settlement of the S, Al-Kufrah, and the N coast. Even now a single black top road acts as the link between the two very separate sections of the province, traversing 876 km from Ajdabiyah to Al-Kufrah.

Population

The Libyan population of Al-Khalij is very small, at best 175,000 and possibly as low as 165,000 in 1990 with a further 40,000-45,000 foreign migrant workers. These estimates are very imprecise. Growth rates for the area have generally fallen according to UN data to about 3% per year, with the exception of the main coastal urban site at Ben Jawad, where 5.5% growth prevails. Overall, it appears that the country and inland areas of Al-Khalij are approximately maintaining

their population size while losing many of their younger people to the coast and to the cities outside the region. The populations of the coastal sub-regions are very concentrated in the urban settlements. In the S the population is also clustered in small villages for security, except on modern farm estates where, incongruously, farms are laid out geometrically across the desert landscape in the teeth of regional social traditions.

Industry

The main towns of the province are the centres of the oil industry at Al-Brayqah, Ras Lanuf and Zuwetina. The only exceptions are Ajdabiyah and Sirte. The former is a route centre where the road from the S joins the coast. Ajdabiyah district contains approximately half the population of the Al-Khalij region, about 100,000 persons, by far the majority in the town area itself. Inland, the main towns are Al-Kufrah, Gialo-Awjilah and Tizerbu, all very small. The new coastal towns and the modern extensions to the S oases are dispersed and reliant on motor transport for communication between the different parts of the town. On the coast, the oil towns are well planned and the residential districts are made up of two areas, first the concentrated bungalow towns set up by foreign oil companies for their employees and second, modern

Climate: Al-Khalij

	Sirte	Ajdabiyah	Gialo	Al-Kufrah
Mean annual minimum °C	8.6	7.3	6.3	4.8
Extreme minimum °C	2.4	0.0	-2.0	-3.3
Mean annual maximum °C	31.0	33.7	37.8	38.9
Extreme maximum °C	46.7	46.7	49.1	46.0
Relative humidity %	51-84	45-82	26-61	11-61
Mean annual rainfall mm	180.8	126.9	9.2	1.9
Maximum monthly rainfall mm	215.7	102.6	26.2	11.2
Maximum annual rainfall mm	429.5	227.6	50.3	11.9
Minimum annual rainfall mm	6.7	3.4	1.0	0.0

Source: Speerplan

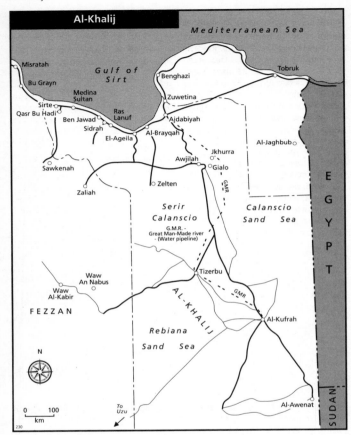

towns built by the Libyan authorities at great expense for civil servants and other services. The oil towns are strung along and adjacent to the coastal highway.

The local economy

In Al-Khalij, this comprises agriculture and government services. Approximately 25% of the work force is employed in agricultural pursuits and perhaps 30% in government services. Agriculture is, for Libyans, a part-time activity. The males in Al-Khalij work with a government agency and also labour or manage their own farms in their, often generous, spare time. There are 42,500 ha under cultivation, of which about 11,000 ha is irrigated. Most dryland cultivation and livestock herding is concentrated along the coast, where the rainfall is slightly better and more reliable than the interior.

Inland farming is oasis-based in small fields with associated palmeries. Modern sector large settlement projects have been developed at great expense, the Al-Kufrah project running into several billions of US$. The units are capital intensive, based on water lifted from deep within the Nubian sandstones. The deep wells fed 100 x 100 ha circles of land with water through an automated mobile-rotating arm sprinkler system. They were used first for growing fodder for sheep. The costs were unsupportable and the project was turned over to grain production. Technical and economic problems continued and the units were eventually run down and many abandoned with water switched to supply the Great Manmade River Scheme (GMR).

A settlement scheme was also devised for Al-Kufrah, comprising 5,500 ha of hexagons each made up of 16 farms. The history of the settlement scheme is sad and expensive. Libyans by and large ignored the project and costs ran out of control against a small return in agricultural produce. Other production projects of a comparable kind were put in hand further N at Serir and were also beset by environmental and economic problems. Settlement schemes at Gialo and Tizerbu were also attempted. The residual areas of cultivation can still be seen in these various sites.

Private sector commerce was always important in the province, tied into participation in trans-Saharan caravan traffic. In the period since liberalization of the economy there has been a return by Libyans to shopkeeping, commerce and small-scale manufacturing.

However it is **oil** and **natural gas** which dominate the economy of Al-Khalij. Oil and gas fields are located in the N section of the province, the materials being pumped to the coast where they are exported as crude hydrocarbons or refined. There are many oil-related industries in the region. There is a gas processing plant and oil refinery at Al-Brayqah and another old small refinery at Zuwetina. New refinery capacity has been added at Ras Lanuf, while petrochemical units have been set up at Al-

Brayqah, Ras Lanuf and Marada. Installations associated with the oil industry spread deep into the Sirteican embayment towards Waha, Mejid and Serir oilfields.

Al-Khalij's **water resources** are from three sources, groundwater, surface *wadi* flow and seawater desalination plants. The coastal zone has a limited and much depleted shallow aquifer. In the S there are very large deep aquifers in the Old Nubian sandstones within the 2 million sq km of the Al-Kufrah basin. The strength of these S reserves is uncertain and it is likely that extraction at present rates will be sustained for only 50 years or so. In the early 1980s it was decided to transfer water from the Al-Kufrah Basin to the N coastlands through a large diameter concrete pipeline, the Great Manmade River, costing some US$7bn or more. The GMR runs from the S water fields to the coast near to Ajdabiyah and from there along the coast towards Benghazi and Sirte. The object of the line is advertised as principally for agriculture but it is thought by many experts that the bulk of water will only be utilized economically in urban water supply and for industrial end use. The GMR has been the largest development project in Libya for the last decade and the future of Libyan agriculture will rest on how the water is put to use.

Zuwetina is a small, formerly agricultural, centre now overwhelmed by the growth of the oil industry in its vicinity and the influx of foreign workers. The old settlement is sited off the highway to the N, where there are still farmed gardens and some fishing.

The **oases of the S** were never heavily populated. They acted as stopover points for the trans-Saharan caravans. Al-Kufrah was in fact a set of scattered palm grove villages in a large low plain in which water seepages occurred. Recent changes have resulted in considerable building activity both for new agricultural estates on the perimeter of

Al-Jaghbub

Mediterranean Sea

Derna
Al-Bayda
Al-Marj
Benghazi   Tobruk
Jabal Al-Akhdar

Ajdabiyah

Al-Jaghbub

N

0   100
km

231   Awjilah

the settlements and administrative, military and other buildings, often rather unsympathetic in architecture.

Tizerbu (see also page 430), has recently been developed, formerly being no more than a fuelling and water point on the route from the S and W Sahara to Al-Kufrah and Ajdabiyah. It now has most services including garages, fuel and a chemist together with urban services such as telephones, piped water, clinics and electricity. It is of little other merit. The **Gialo group of oases** are scattered around water holes some 250 km from Ajdabiyah. Originally very pretty with traditional farms and well laid out palm groves, Gialo-Awjilah has had some development of settlement farms and administrative services. It has fuel, water and limited urban facilities and is well worth a visit (see Places of interest, page 428).

ACCESS Al-Khalij is reached mainly from adjacent provinces, though there are direct links in from Chad and Sudan, controlled by the military and not recommended both for that reason and because of the problem of finding safe transport overland. **Air** In normal times international flights come to Al-Khalij, mainly via Tripoli or Benghazi, although lateral entry is possible direct from Algiers or via Sabha or other airports when there are external links open for the entry of foreigners. On internal airlines, Sirte links directly with Tripoli, Benghazi and Sabha,

while Al-Kufrah links directly with Benghazi only. **Road** Access is from the N and still principally via the coastal highway coming in from Tripoli to the W. Ajdabiyah is then the gateway S to Al-Kufrah. New roads have been built across the Sirtican embayment to support the oil industry, some pastureland developments and military/ strategic objectives by providing a second land link between the two main parts of the country and reducing reliance of the exposed coast road. The main artery to the W comes in from Bu Grayn via Waddan and Zella through Marada eventually reaching Al-Brayqah and Gialo. A continuation of this road project continues E to Al-Jaghbub, hugging the N edge of the Libyan sand desert and thence leading N to Tobruk. The traveller should be aware that there are a number of roads leading S from the coastal highway at Sidrah, Ras Lanuf and through Bir Zelten. These are private roads run by the oil companies for servicing their oil fields and facilities. They should not be used except with specific permission as trespass might be misinterpreted as a threat to the security of the oil fields. **Sea** Theoretically, passengers from ships docking in the ports of Al-Khalij could enter by that route but, other than for sailors taking rare and limited shore leave, this is not open for most travellers.

Places of interest

The great deserts of Al-Khalij have an attraction of their own, though they are at least over large areas heavily visited by commercial activities connected with oil and water developments. Even the extreme S is no longer terra incognita in that a major war between Libya and Chad was fought across this region in the period 1980-90. The very light human settlement of the province in past centuries has meant that there is little of human interest by way of monuments to see. Rather, there is a limited number of small oasis sites with a certain charm. Only the dedicated and highly inquisitive traveller can be encouraged to traverse vast distances in Al-Khalij to visit them.

Local information
● Accommodation

Facilities for travellers and tourists in Al-Khalij are minimal. This, after all, is the country's oil producing area and there are deemed to be few sights that a bona fide tourist would wish to see. Even the official tours run by semi-state agencies steer clear of this area. Provisions are for oil workers, workers in the water industry and for service personnel. Most accommodation, transport and entertainment is dedicated to a specific company workforce. There are some hotels but very few that cater for travellers. Ajdabiyah has a number of rest houses and cheap hotels for migrant Arab workers. They are basic but can be serviceable. The traveller to Al-Khalij must be adaptable and willing to accept hospitality where he/she can find it or get official hospitality from a secretariat or other official agency before entering the region. The modest privatization of the economy is opening up better prospects for the availability of accommodation but the easiest way for travellers is to ask at the *baladiyah* (local council) offices for a room in the school dormitory or the youth hostel.

Camping: is possible but in the oilfield area this should be done discreetly and preferably with the permission of the owner or the authorities. Elsewhere, camping in the oases can only be undertaken with permission but this is unlikely to be withheld.

Youth hostel: *Sirte* on Sharah Sawadah, 2 km N of town centre, open 0700-2300, 120 beds, kitchen, meals provided, laundry, family groups, bus 1 km, airport 30 mins, T 2867, booking rec Mar-Apr.

● Places to eat

Eating out is difficult except in Ajdabiyah and Sirte where there are local cafeterias or restaurants providing often a limited service in range of meals and opening hours. Elsewhere, the coastal highway has small routestop cafés and cold drink stands where electricity is available. Catering is generally for institutions or households and the eating places are few and far between. Travellers should always have spare food and water, especially on the long inter-centre routes.

SIRTE – THE WESTERN ENTRY TO AL-KHALIJ

This small staging post on the coast road was used by the Italians as an administrative centre. It gained new life following the change of régime in 1969 since Colo-nel Ghadhafi came from the Ghadafha tribal area close by. Sirte was built up as a military centre and bastion for the government. Developments in communications, industry and agriculture there were given priority. The population of the town and its immediate hinterland is estimated at over 50,000. Development of the garrison and administrative centre has meant the emergence of a completely new, if not entirely well-integrated, town with all services but little of note for the visitor to see. Spreading from the town are a series of valleys and low hills where attempts have been made to develop agriculture, mainly orchards. Sirte has been connected by road to the Al-Jufra oases to the S by a good new 227 km black top road. Sirte has cafeterias, restaurants and hotel accommodation, *Hotel Mahari*, five star, T 60100, in addition to all services such as fuel, workshops, garages, PTT and medical facilities. Travellers should be careful when taking photographs not to include military installations.

Places of interest

Close by Sirte is the unmarked battlefield of **Qasr Bu Hadi** where in WW1 the Italians were beaten by the Libyans in a pitched battle. Along the coast is the site of **Medina Sultan** where the remains of a large mosque and Fatimid city have been discovered and partially excavated. Medina Sultan was set up at the point where a trans-Saharan route met the coast at a sheltered anchorage on the Gulf of Sirte coast. Fragments of pottery and inscriptions can be seen on the site.

Local information
● Transport

Air Air services support the government central administration in the S and there are two daily flights from **Tripoli**. Departures from **Benghazi** to Sirte are Mon, Wed, Fri 1745, Sat. Sirte also advertises direct flights internally to **Sabha** Tues, Thur and Sat. A direct flight to **Algiers** runs when the embargo is not in force.

Road By shared taxi or bus along the coast road.

AJDABIYAH AND THE ROAD TO GIALO AND AL-KUFRAH

Originally a small Arab town, Ajdabiyah has now been developed to the S of the coastal highway as a residential centre for foreign workers and some Libyan staff associated with the oil industry and government services in the Al-Khalij district. It is mainly new but badly maintained with little sense of civic pride. Its utilities including water, telephone, fuel and electricity are good but other services such as hospitals and clinics leave a lot to be desired by modern standards. The concentration of low paid temporary foreign workers, mainly Sudanese, Egyptian and undenominated central Africans has done nothing to enhance the position of the town and, compared with Ras Lanuf new town and Al Brayqah, it has little to recommend it. Shops, mosques and fuel are all available close to the coastal highway and the road is now dangerous for driving given the unplanned, encroaching shops and housing built close to it.

Places of interest

At Ajdabiyah there is a number of monuments worthy of a visit. A **10th century Fatimid mosque** existed here, highly regarded because of its external staircase and square block base originally carrying an octagonal minaret. The site is now in ruins. The mosque's courtyard is still visible. The sanctuary façade is composed of a series of niches and there is a single arcade surrounding the courtyard. There are small Roman remains in the form of rock-cut inscriptions, indicating that Ajdabiyah was a significant site long before the Arab invasion. Clearly, however, the Fatimid period was the one in which the city flourished.

Local information
● Accommodation

The run down *Ajdabiyah Travelling Hotel* is in the town centre. Early buses start from here because the driver sleeps in the hotel.

● Transport

Road Bus: there is an excellent de-luxe and a regular bus service from **Tripoli** as well as intermediate points on the coast road. Buses start their runs early in the morning covering 863 km from Tripoli. **Taxi**: shared taxis run from Tripoli and passengers can find their way to Misrath after having visited other Tripolitanian sites before catching the taxi or bus for the long run to Sirte (463 km from Tripoli and 561 km from Benghazi) and Ajdabiyah.

GIALO (JALU)

History

Gialo is a centre in the Gialo-Awjilah groups of oases with Jkhurra, Leskerre and Bir Buattifel. The site is some 30m above sea level and lies in a shallow 30 km depression in the desert. Water is available from wells and in Awjilah there was formerly an important spring source. Awjilah was the main trading oasis taking advantage of the routes S and to the coast. It had the largest and most productive palmeries with some 50,000 trees. Gialo has in recent times tended to be the main town of the group because of its prominence on the main N-S routeway and its central position within the oasis cluster. Gialo consists of a number of smaller villages, the main ones being Lebba and Al-Areg. Gialo is renowned for the quality of its dates. Limited accommodation available.

Places of interest

Outside Gialo itself, the area is thinly populated and consists mainly of palmeries owned by people living in Gialo, Awjilah or absentee from the district. The rural population of the groups of oases at Gialo is some 20,000, of which about 3,000 are non-Libyans. The Libyan population is almost entirely of Berber origin. There is a unique **mosque** at Awjilah, **Al-Jami Al-Atiq**, built of a series of beehive domes of clay bricks and mud. The building measures approximately 30m x 21m and has been abandoned as an active place of prayer. The minaret has collapsed. On the minaret gallery below there is an inscription in Arabic, 'The witness is here deposited till judgment day, I testify that there are no gods other than God and that Mohammed is His Prophet. May the blessing of God be upon him by Abd Allah Ibn Abdulahmid Al-Qadi 1178 H (1764 AD)'. This is situated about 3 km from the main road through the oasis.

Local information
● **Transport**
Road Buses and **shared taxi**: services run regularly to Gialo from the main station on the edge of Ajdabiyah or from the junction of the coast road with the S road to Al-Kufrah. The road to Al-Kufrah leaves on a clearly signposted road from the coastal highway at Ajdabiyah and cuts across the coastal hills and through a series of *wadis* and internal drainage basins to the settlement at Sahabi to Gialo at Km 250.

AL-KUFRAH

Al-Kufrah is a group of oases long isolated in the Libyan desert by its very distance from the N and lack of wells on the formidable route to it. The site is made up of five major clusters, the main one originally Busaimah, in an enormous elliptical desert depression around the Wadi Al-Kufrah. The basin is on a 50 km axis NE to SW, and a 20 km axis NW to SE. The centre of the oasis is at 475m above sea level. The main oases are Al-Jawf, with 5 km x 3 km of cultivated land in gardens and palmeries. To the E of Al-Jawf is Busaimah made up of two small oases and Ez-Zurgh a former slave settlement.

History
Al-Kufrah was a quiet and rarely visited Tibu settlement until 1840 when it was overwhelmed by the Zuwaya tribe from Awjilah who converted the people to follow the Senussiya movement. Al-Kufrah became the centre of the Senussiya when Sayyid Mohammed Ali Al-Senussi moved there in 1894 to escape the influence of the Turkish governor of Cyrenaica. The Senussi thrived at Al-Kufrah and spread their influence deep into the Sahara, developing trade and communications links as they went. Al-Kufrah took on a considerable prosperity. The site was unvisited by non-Muslims until the Saharan explorer Rohlfs called there in 1879. The period from 1911 when the Italians invaded N Libya to their occupation of Al-Kufrah in 1931 was a difficult one. Al-Kufrah's trading base was cut off and the war in the N depleted the resources of the Senussi.

In the modern period, the Italians made a rough motor road link between the oasis and the N and provided landing strips along its route. Al-Kufrah was a staging post within the Italian colonial system linking with its East African possessions. Modern facilities were set up including an airbase, a garrison, a school, hospital and other facilities. WW2 delivered a severe blow to Al-Kufrah. It was a base in early years for the Italians and then for the British Long Range Desert Group. The colonial subsidy was withdrawn. Trade never recovered and the place relapsed into a backwater until oil exploration began. The oil industry attracted the people of Al-Kufrah to act as guides and drivers in the desert and eventually a promise was made by Occidental Oil to assist in the development of the underground water at Al-Kufrah. Thus started a series of upheavals which entirely changed the oasis into a form of temporary boom town, overwhelmed local agriculture as a way of life and converted the site into a centre for military and civil government offices.

Places of interest
The settlement and production agricultural complexes are still there and can be visited with 4WD vehicles. The water gathering systems for the Great Manmade River are also visible. Otherwise there is nothing of lasting architectural and historical interest to see. Travel around the outlying oases is interesting

and some fragments of the original economy remain to be seen. **Al-Jawf** has all services, including guest houses. The *Hotel As Sudan* is superbly clean, a jewel in the desert, central, near bus station. *Hotel Al-Kufrah* is nearly as good, similar position. *Al Nahr As Sinai* is a guest house in Swedia the newest part of town. Hospitality is best gained from the town council offices if the traveller has not organized a family or official reservation in advance. The cattle and sheep market at the back of Suq al-Arab in Al-Jawf is recommended viewing.

Excursions

Jenzia 7 km S of Al-Kufrah, on the road to Sudan, has an interesting camel market. Taxi LD2. Buses from Jenzia (mini-buses) go 3 days a week to Al Fashir in Sudan (more frequently to Benghazi and Ajdabiyah). Service taxis go to Ajdabiyah.

Local information
● **Transport**

Air The airport is 7 km from Al-Jawf. There are internal flights to Al-Kufrah via Benghazi on Mon and the return the same day connects to Tripoli. There are no buses to/from the airport. A taxi costs LD2. **Road Bus**: the road to Al-Kufrah leaves directly S from Gialo as a well maintained black top highway some 625 km in length. Shared taxis and buses run from Ajdabiyah to Gialo regularly. Visits further S can be arranged but there are less frequent departures. For those travelling from Ajdabiyah to Al-Kufrah via the Gialo-Awjilah groups of oases it might be easier to pick up transport in Gialo for Al-Kufrah. An express bus service is promised on the Ajdabiyah-Al-Kufrah route.

OTHER DESERT OASES

In the S **Tizerbu** (see page 426), a palm grove oasis 600 km NW of Al-Kufrah is now served by black top road. Tizerbu is an elongated palmery almost 30 km long. It formerly had a tiny Tibu population the remains of whose fort, **Qasr Giranghedi**, can still be seen. Tizerbu has been modernized to manage agricultural development programmes in the oases and some settlement of Sudanese and

others has proceeded in recent years.

Al-Awenat lies in the extreme SE of Libya, 325 km from Al-Kufrah, to be distinguished from Al-Awenat in the SW. The town is small and a security point for the Libyan authorities on the frontier with Sudan and Egypt. A new road into Sudan is under debate but nothing has thus far been accomplished. The town has basic telephone, health and other services. Visitors to Al-Kufrah by air should ensure that they have return bookings though there is an LAA sales office in the town, T 28701. Flights elsewhere in the S of Al-Khalij are for oil company purposes and are normally available only to company personnel.

WARNING: TRAVEL IN AL-KHALIJ

Other than the detail given above on access and travel facilities in each of the small towns of the region, it must be emphasized that Al-Khalij is generally neutral or hostile to travellers and tourists. The desert is unforgiving to incompetence and bad planning. Very great distances separate the few settlements. The climate is increasingly extreme with travel S. Travellers should at all times stick to the black top roads. Off road travel is only for those with several all-terrain vehicles accompanied by a guide and with radio communication. Plenty of warm clothing, water and food should be carried. Travel in public transport during the cool but light hours of the day.

Al-Khalij is not tourist-friendly in other ways. As an oilfield and water source province of the country, it is run by either large commercial organizations, Libyan administrations or the military. The province is not structured for the normal traveller in either its transport or accommodation systems. To get round this, travellers should make arrangements to have their trip made 'official' by co-opting the help of the oil companies or a Libyan authority before arrival. If Libyan tourist companies offer passages through the area this should be used even by the hardened traveller since it will provide basic services from official sources. Local people can be friendly in this area and hospitality may be expected from the regional or town councils or individuals for a limited time.

There are very limited tourist facilities and guides to the area are few.

The Long Range Desert Group

During WW1 the British army in Egypt developed a light car patrol system using Model T Fords and Rolls Royce armoured cars to penetrate the Libyan desert to protect their western flanks against attacks from Senussi armed groups. This activity was the direct military predecessor of the Long Range Desert Group (LRDG) established in Jun 1940 as the Long Range Patrols attached to the British army command in Cairo. The organization was the brainchild of R A Bagnold, who gathered an initial team made up of men with great experience of pre-war travel in the desert to harry the Axis forces behind their lines in the Saharan regions of Libya. Early recruits to the team were taken from the New Zealand Command and it was New Zealanders who remained an essential part of the LRDG.

Each patrol was originally made up of two officers and some 30 men supported by 11 trucks, with heavy machine and anti-aircraft guns, though this complement was later halved. The basic skills of the men of the LRDG were in signalling, navigation and intelligence-gathering. Map-making and the determining of routes through the desert were also important activities for the men of the LRDG. The LRDG patrols went out from Siwa in Egypt to Al-Kufrah in Libya, usually in the early days of the war to bring information of enemy movements in Uwainat, Jalu, Agheila and Ain Dua. On 1 March, 1941, the Free French General Leclerc captured Al-Kufrah from the Italians and the LRDG thereafter used this oasis as their base for the war in Libya.

During 1942 the LRDG was used in association with Major David Stirling's parachute raiders and other commando groups to attack Axis airfields and aircraft behind enemy lines. Its personnel were important in monitoring General Rommel's troop movements in the period leading up to the battle of El-Alamein in late 1942. After the defeat of the Axis army in Egypt at El-Alamein, the LRGD was engaged in attempts to cut off German forces retreating to Tunisia. Once the North African campaign moved into central Tunisia in 1943, the role of the LRDG came to an end.

Information for travellers

● **General note**

Getting to Libya is not always easy. Visa allocation was carefully controlled and mainly confined to those with bona fide jobs in the country but circumstances have become relaxed and except for US or UK citizens obtaining a visa creates few problems. For a UK passport holder an invitation from a Libyan official agency or individual will perhaps assist the granting of a visa. Tourism is growing in importance for economic reasons and there is a gradual relaxation of controls on this score. The UN air embargo on international flights to Libya has added to the difficulties of all travellers.

BEFORE TRAVELLING

ENTRY REQUIREMENTS

● **Visas**

Travellers to Libya need a visa, normally issued at the People's Bureau, embassy or consulate overseas. Cost around US$50 (45DM + 16DM translation fee for German passport holders; £20 for UK nationals), valid for 3 months, must be used within 45 days of issue. Applications with a translation of passport details in Arabic, should be given 10 to 14 days in advance of travel since it is usual for the Libyan authorities overseas to check details with Tripoli before a visa is issued. It is possible to get a visa at the port of entry, though this carries risks of long delays or capricious acts by border officials. Those with Arab passports normally do not require visas. Non-Arabic passports must be stamped with an official Arabic translation of

the personal details of the individual's passport. In the UK the Passport Office 7-78 Petty France, London SW1, T 0171 279 3434 will do this as a matter of routine on presentation of the passport. Libyan embassy in Malta also provides visa and Arabic translation.

Visa extensions For extensions beyond the normal visa period, the immigration police should be informed and the fact noted in the passport. Tourists may extend the visa by 1 month, twice, at LD5 each time.

Registration Immigration and sometimes currency declaration forms are needed on arrival. The forms themselves are in Arabic but English translations are available from the airlines. Only the Arabic question form should be filled in with answers in English or French. Copies of the forms should be carefully retained since they will be requested on exit. Normally hotels register guests on arrival. Insist they do. The fee is LD5. If visitors are not staying in an official hotel, they should register themselves with the police otherwise they can be stopped and held. Worse, they can be delayed on departure, even missing flights if officials are convinced that malpractice rather than ignorance is the cause of the problem.

Departure There is no departure tax at land borders. Embarkation cards will be filled in with the help of attendants. There is also sometimes a currency control. Only small amounts of Libyan currency may be exported, preferably less than LD10. Any excess Libyan dinars should be changed back into hard currency.

Insurance For those travellers not already

equipped with travel or other insurance, there are facilities available in Libya directly through the Libyan Insurance Co or the Libya Travel and Tourist Co shop in Tripoli, T 36222.

● **Tourist information**

Libya is only now awakening to the potential of tourism. Facilities are few and far between. Local tourist offices exist but are generally understaffed and ill-informed. They rarely have useful information, maps or guides. At present the best sources of help and information are the new private travel agencies springing up across the country. They have enterprise and initiative and understand the needs of foreign travellers. In Tripoli contact the Libyan Travel and Tourist Co T 36222 which has an office in Sharah Mizran close by the LAA head office. Other area offices are mentioned in the regional sections within the Handbook.

Be warned that while private travel agencies can provide some information and perhaps transport some may imply that without the 'official' guides' which only they can provide, there may be problems with the police. Certainly this is not true.

WHEN TO GO

● **Best time to visit**

The coastal strips of Libya around Tripoli together with the Jabal Nafusah are all blessed with a Mediterranean climate which makes them pleasant in most seasons. The outstanding times to visit are in the spring after the rains when the ground is covered with flowers and other vegetation and the almond blossom is out. Autumn, too, can be most mild and attractive on the coast after the summer heat.

The ideal time to travel in the S is the period from Oct to Mar, when it is cooler. The summer in the S is absolutely to be avoided.

HEALTH

● **Staying healthy**

Certified vaccinations against smallpox are no longer required, but prudence demands that anti-cholera and tetanus injections are received before entry. Travellers expecting to travel into the Libyan S might feel that a voluntary, yellow fever injection is worthwhile. Walkers and cyclists would also be wise to take up any anti-rabies protection that is safely available.

● **Medical facilities**

Libyan hospitals are fairly well equipped but are under-resourced in some critical areas. Travellers must take into account that, with a UN air embargo in place, it is difficult to be airlifted out in case of emergency. There are hospitals and clinics in most towns of over 25,000 population and emergency para-medical services exist to service the main motor traffic routes. In theory treatment is free for all in public hospitals and clinics. In practice it is better to find private assistance if ill.

Most proprietary drugs are available over the counter in Libya and chemist shops are to be found in the main streets of all but the smallest of towns (see Chemist and Hospital sections for each of the regions).

● **Further health information**

See page 453, main health section.

MONEY

● **Credit cards**

Cards can be used only in a small number of big hotels and in some of the larger travel agents. Cash is the normal medium of exchange and most shops are not equipped to handle credit cards of any kind. Credit cards at hotels are best if not of US origin, though generics such as Visa and Mastercard are normally suitable.

● **Cost of living**

Libya is an oil economy and it mainly imports its necessities from abroad. Prices tend to be high reflecting this external reliance, some inefficiency in the distribution system and the high level of mark-up by the merchants. Specialist western foods and commodities like Libyan mutton are very expensive. Eating out is also far from cheap even in the small popular cafés if a full meal is taken. Otherwise fresh vegetables and fruit are moderately priced. Bread is very cheap and tasty. Pharmaceuticals, medical goods and imported high-tech items can be expensive. Personal services from plumbers to dry cleaners are expensive. Travel is comparatively cheap by air as well as land but hotels are few and the even fewer good quality hotels are very expensive. In general, assume that most things will be more expensive than in the USA or Western Europe, though this is offset by the generosity of the Libyans in rural areas in finding accommodation for visitors in public buildings.

● **Currency**

The Libyan dinar is the standard currency which is divided into 1,000 dirhams. Notes in circulation are LD10, 5, 1, 0.50, 0.25; coins LD0.10, and 0.05. There are banks at Tripoli airport. Principal banks will exchange TCs and currency notes at the official rate of exchange. There is also a black market in foreign currency in which a very variable rate is available but best rates are reported **inside** Libya itself, and even bank officials will recommend changing money on the street.

The Libyan Dinar is only convertible at the official rate inside Libya by official institutions. Travellers may have to fill in a currency form on arrival (cash and TCs) and present it together with receipts of monies exchanged on departure. The system is not watertight nor fully implemented but is perhaps best observed. Keep receipts from the banks. A sensible procedure is to make sure that you do not leave the country with either more than a few Libyan Dinars or more foreign currency than you arrived with.

For exchange rates at Jul 1996, see table on page 10.

● **Taxes**

Provided that travellers do not accept official employment in Libya, there are no direct taxes other than the LD3 exit tax payable at the airport before entering the departure gate. Indirect taxes are included in payments as you go.

GETTING THERE

● **Air**

Libyan Arab Airlines is the main carrier. Air services to and from Tripoli, the main entry port for the entire country, have been difficult for some years. An embargo on the transfer of arms and strategic materials to Libya by the USA for its alleged involvement in state terrorism in the early 1980s led to a depletion in the Libyan aircraft fleet, which is ageing and inefficient. A number of foreign airlines do not visit Tripoli for political or commercial reasons. In Apr 1992, the UN Security Council introduced a ban on air traffic to Libya as part of a campaign to bring to book alleged perpetrators of the Lockerbie air disaster of 1988. In normal conditions foreign visitors by air are advised to have reserved firm flights for departure since it is not always easy to get return flights booked inside Libya. It is advised that all entries to Libya while the embargo remains in force should be by land frontier or by sea.

International flights In normal circumstances flights to Tripoli via LAA or other regular scheduled services from Europe arrive from Amsterdam, Athens, Belgrade, Brussels, Budapest, Frankfurt, Larnaca, Madrid, Malta, Moscow, Paris, Prague, Rome, Sofia, Vienna, Warsaw and Zurich. Most of the above are only on a 1 day a week basis. Alitalia, Lufthansa, Malta Airlines and Swissair are among the most frequent carriers to Libya. There are no direct flights to Libya from the USA, Canada or UK at the present time even when the UN embargo is not operative. Flights to Libya from African points of origin include Accra, Alexandria, Algiers, Cairo, Casablanca, Khartoum, Ndjamena, Niamey, Nouakchott and Tunis. Most Middle Eastern airlines have flights to Tripoli with the main scheduled flights in from Amman, Damascus, Dubai, Istanbul and Jeddah. The other incoming flight in normal times is from Karachi.

Fares The fare structure for flights, when they are in operation, is polarized. Swissair, for example, runs business class only flights to Libya. LAA is also expensive and not easy to get discounts for. Cheapest access by air is via Air Malta. Air Malta or airlines serving the Tunisian S such as Liberté to Monastir or Tunis Air/UK Air to Sfax are amongst the cheapest carriers during the embargo.

● **Train**

Libya's railways were gradually dismantled after WW2 and there are no services within Libya. Libya can be approached by train from the Tunisian side from Tunis and the N as far S as Gabès from which travellers can go by bus or shared taxi to the Libyan frontier 188 km distant.

● **Road**

Bus These run from Tunis and all major E coast towns in Tunisia to the Libyan frontiers. Buses from further afield include direct services from Algiers and Casablanca. Passengers should cross the frontier on foot and then take advantage of Libyan domestic bus services (see Tunisia, page 343 for details of arrival at the Libyan border posts). Once in Libya, there are two main bus transport companies, one engaged principally in long-distance international services and the other plying between Libyan cities and towns.

When leaving Libya the traveller can use the Libyan International Bus Company which has an office behind the Tripoli medina off Sharah Omar Mukhtar to the W of the old citadel, in an area now being cleared of buildings and reconstructed. Buses tend to leave Tripoli very early in the morning, not later than 0800. Passengers should be at the bus station by at least 0700. The buses fill up rapidly, particularly while the air embargo is in operation and buses can leave as soon as all seats are taken.

Taxis Both local and international transport is as much in the hands of taxi drivers as the bus companies. In Tripoli, the taxis leave from large stands between Sharah Omar Mukhtar and the sea. They ply for hire normally on a shared basis but can be had for an individual or private group with suitable haggling over the price. On a shared basis they are normally cheaper than the luxury buses and far more frequent in their departures. Driving standards are variable among taxi drivers and good nerves are required of passengers! Travellers entering via land borders are advised that taking a shared taxi is easier and quicker than waiting for the bus. If a bus is preferred, take a shared taxi to the nearest town (Zuara) and take the bus from there in conditions of comfort.

Taxis to Djerba (Tunisia) leave from Sharah Al-Rashid nr the bus station, cost LD25-40 depending on number of passengers, takes 4-5 hrs, depending on border controls.

● **Sea**
Air travellers can bypass the UN air embargo on Libya by flying to an adjacent country – Malta or Tunisia and continuing their journeys by land, using buses or shared taxis or by sea on the regular ferry run from Malta.

Shipping services The overnight ferry from Valetta in Malta uses modern vessels, usually the *MV Garnata* of 3,672 dwt, with other passenger vessels, the *MV Toletela* of 3,671 dwt and the *MV Garyounis* of 3,423 dwt. Sailing times change monthly and travellers should check with the General National Maritime Transport Co, Sharah Al-Baladiya, T 33 34865 or via Seamalta in Malta on T 00356 25994212, Tx 1210 1321. Currently boat departs 1900 from Valletta and costs US$200 one-way, or 1800 from Tripoli in front of *Hotel Al-Mehari* costs LD63 one-way, LD102 return. Journey takes 12 hrs. There are agents for GNMTC in Tunisia, Morocco, Turkey, Italy, Germany, Belgium and Holland.

● **Customs**
Duty free goods are available at the main airport departure lounge at Tripoli airport for foreign currencies only. A range of cigarettes, cigars, perfumes, watches and travel goods can be found. No other tourist facilities of this kind

are available and offers elsewhere of duty free goods should be avoided as not worth the hassle.

Import-export bans Libya has a stringent ban on the import of alcohol of any kind. It is a pointless risk taking in beer, spirits, or indeed drugs. Severe penalties can be imposed and at the very least passengers can be incarcerated pending deportation. It is rather easier to carry books and newspapers into the country than formerly, though sensitivities remain and it is best not to carry literature which might be misunderstood or thought to be anti-Libyan. Firearms cannot be imported without special permission. Radio transmitters and electronic means of printing will attract official attention and should clearly be for personal use only.

On leaving Libya make sure that you have no antiquities. The Libyan authorities take unkindly to the illegal export of their ancient monuments and penalties for infringement can be ferocious.

ON ARRIVAL/DEPARTURE

● **Airport tax**
Is LD3 is payable on leaving Libya. Only Libyan currency is accepted. At Tripoli airport, from which the majority of flights leave Libya, there is a special counter for buying the exit stamp before passing through to the passport and customs formalities. Without a stamp you will be sent back to start the entire process again. (See Documents, page 432).

● **Clothing**
For general guidance, refer to the section on Travelling in Islamic countries on page 19.

There are three imperatives on clothing in Libya:
❑ Do not offend Muslim sentiment by wearing scanty clothing.
❑ Wear clothes which prevent sunstroke and sunburn;
❑ Wear clothes that enable you to keep your key documents on your person.

Libyan traditional workday dress, the *barakan*, is a vestige of the Roman toga made up in woven wool material of 5m length by 2m width which wraps round the head and body. This in a country with the world's highest recorded temperature! Scanty clothing is not regarded as sensible on grounds of either religion or practicality. Women should be careful not to leave arms and legs overly exposed. In a country where women dress well in public in both traditional and modern costume, to wear less could be seen as provocative or indicating moral slackness. In any case, outside the main hotels or private transport the need is to be sheltered from the sun, the sand and the glare. Desiccation problems effecting exposed areas of skin can come on quickly and harshly in the summer months for those who fail to look after themselves.

● **Electricity**

Libyan electricity services use a standard 240V system for power. Take an international adaptor plug as socket sizes can vary. Electric power is available in all but the most isolated of settlements.

● **Hours of business**

Working hours vary from summer 0700-1400 to winter 0800-1300 and 1600-1830 in private offices. Official agencies run on a basic day of 0800-1400, though it is always better to start communications with official offices and banks before 0900 since they can become busy or officials can be in meetings at later times. Shops open from approximately 0900-1400 and again from 1630-2030, depending on area and trade.

● **Official time**

GMT -1.

● **Photography**

The large sand deserts, arid rock formations and fine ruins of classical antiquity make photography in the excellent light conditions of Libya a great pleasure. Do not photograph military installations, and take care in photographing women: preferably if male do not photograph women at all. The camera still carries the feeling of intrusion and/or the evil eye in some areas. Film is generally available for 35 mm cameras and most other types of film can also be found in Tripoli. Kodak and Fuji brands are readily available in the capital. Check the 'sell by date'. For specialist and video film try to bring reserves from outside. Beyond Tripoli and Benghazi film supplies cannot be guaranteed.

● **Safety**

This is very good in Libya. Occasional violence causes more noise than damage and walking through the streets is generally safer than in Europe. After dark, and indeed at all times everywhere, in Libya foreign nationals are advised to carry their passports. Libyans are used to foreigners in their midst but their visitors are

almost exclusively male. European females need, therefore, to follow a sensible dress code and to act with suitable decorum, especially in Tripoli, to avoid arousing undue interest.

Women A woman travelling alone in Libya must appreciate that this is a totally segregated society, women sit apart and eat apart or after the men. On long distance buses the driver will organize space for the women. As no-one is prepared to speak it can be very lonely. The biggest problem is getting a room in a hotel without a male companion. The bus driver may feel obliged to introduce you to the hotel receptionist thereby giving some respectability, otherwise only the expensive hotels will accept women alone: take this into account when budgeting for a trip. One advantage of a woman being of no significance is the lack of problems at check points and compared with Egypt the lack of hassle. Travel alone in Libya by experienced female travellers can be recommended with the proviso that eventually the sheer masculinity of society and the feeling of isolation caused by the lack of communication makes leaving a welcome relief.

A special warning is necessary to travellers in the S Fezzan. This zone in the Uzu strip and to the S was a war zone until recently. There are risks off the road in Uzu of offending the Libyan security officials. Travel in this area should only be with official knowledge. Any abandoned or scattered armament or ammunition should not be touched.

● **Shopping**

Best buys Libya is more of a consumer society than a producer of goods for export other than petroleum. In the SW of the country, especially in Ghadames and Ghat, craft goods of value are available. Leatherwork, woven palm frond articles and small rugs all have an individual charm. Stamp collectors will find a vast range of interesting stamps available from the main post offices in Tripoli where some small attempt is made to cater for the philatelist.

● **Tipping**

Is not widespread in Libya and is only expected by those giving personal services in hotels, cafés and restaurants. The normal rate is 10%. For small services in hotels use quarter and half dinar notes. At the airport only use porters if you are heavily weighed down with luggage then tip at half a dinar per heavy bag. Taxi drivers should, unless there is actually a working meter and then perhaps in any case, give a price before starting the journey. Tips for Libyan drivers are not the rule but will be accepted. Foreign drivers in Libya employ tend to be more demanding of tips. Do not get drawn into bribing officials at any level since it is a sure way of bringing increasing difficulties and possibly severe delays.

● **Weights and measures**

Libya uses the metric system. See conversion table on page 14.

WHERE TO STAY

● **Hotels**

Libya is thinly provided with hotels, even in the populated N coastal area. This is mainly a result of years of state control when tourism was discouraged. The slow re-establishment of the private sector is making for a revival in the hotel trade at the bottom end of the market. Tripoli, the national capital, can boast few top quality international hotels (*Al-Mahari*, *Funduq Al-Kebir*, and *Waddan*) which despite their charges are not AL grade. Elsewhere standards are entirely variable and the regional comments on hotels should be read with care before setting out from the capital.

Hotel classifications

AL US$75+. International class luxury hotel. All facilities for business and leisure travellers are of the highest international standard.

A US$75. International hotel with air conditioned rooms with WC, bath/shower, TV, phone, mini-bar, daily clean linen. Choice of restaurants, coffee shop, shops, bank, travel agent, swimming pool, some sport and business facilities.

B US$60-75. As A but without the luxury, reduced number of restaurants, smaller rooms, limited range of shops and sport.

C US$40-60. Best rooms have air conditioning, own bath/shower and WC. Usually comfortable, bank, shop, pool.

D US$20-40. Best rooms may have own WC and bath/shower. Depending on management will have room service and choice of cuisine in restaurant.

E US$10-20. Simple provision. Perhaps fan cooler. May not have restaurant. Shared WC and showers with hot water (when available).

F under US$10. Very basic, shared toilet facilities, variable in cleanliness, noise, often in dubious locations.

On the coast there are a number of often well-provisioned beach clubs with residential facilities. They are designed to cater for groups of officially approved visitors but can in certain circumstances be open to all travellers. They are best approached through a Libyan travel agent or a Libyan state organization for sports, youth or scouts.

● **Youth hostels**

Libya has a remarkable number of youth hostel facilities. They are basic but often available when hotels are not! The locations, numbers of beds and telephone numbers of Libyan youth hostels are given in all regional sections. Opening hours 0600-1000 and 1400-2300 unless otherwise stated. In all there are 25 youth hostels in Libya. The minimum age is 14. Overnight fees for members are LD2 including sheets, breakfast LD0.5, lunch LD2.5 and dinner LD2. The Libyan Youth Hostel Association is at 69 Amr Ibn Al-As St POB 8886, Tripoli, T 45171, Tx 20420 LYHA. Additionally, it is possible to stay in the dormitories of secondary boarding schools during holiday periods. This is best arranged officially in advance, otherwise through the local *baladiyah* (municipality offices).

● **Camping**

Is moderately popular in Libya, though as a mass organized venture through the state. Private camping is less usual except near bathing places on the Mediterranean shore. Here there are picnic sites which double as camping areas. They are crowded on public holidays but otherwise little used. Certain areas near to military camps and oil company installations are closed to all camping and any indications to this end are best complied with. Do not camp close to private farms or housing without an invitation to do so. Whenever possible seek permission from local farmers or land owners before setting up camp.

FOOD AND DRINK

● **Food**

Outside the capital, eating is confined to the main hotel restaurants, their cafés or to popular eating houses which can be found near the centres of most provincial towns. Outside Tripoli, restaurant and popular café opening hours are limited. In the evening eat before 2100 or risk finding them closed. As Libyans prefer to eat at home, restaurants tend to be for foreigners and travellers. The exception is in the use of cafés in the towns where males, mainly

Restaurant classifications

Given the variations in price of food on any menu our restaurants are divided where possible into three simple grades:

◆◆◆ expensive, ◆◆ average and ◆ cheap.

younger males, gather for social purposes. On Fri and holidays, Libyans picnic and buy food from beachside stalls. Libyan cuisine is a Mediterranean mixture with a strong legacy of the Italian period with pastas very popular, particularly macaroni. Local dishes include *couscous*, with a bowl of boiled cereal as a base carrying large pieces of mutton and some potatoes. The best traditional forms of *couscous* in Libya use millet as a cereal though now most meals come with wheat. *Bazin* is a Libyan speciality – hard, paste-like food made of water, salt and barley and is really not recommended except to the gastronomically hardy. *'Aish* is a similar food from the same ingredients but slightly softer and prepared differently. *Sherba* (Libyan soup) is delicious but highly spiced. For the rest, the range of meals is quite sophisticated as in Tunisia, with Italian influences being greatest in Tripolitania and rather more Arab dishes (less macaroni!) in Cyrenaica (see Tunisia, Information for travellers, page 346). Family life is kept separate from public acquaintances, and invitations to dine in a Libyan home are rarely given. Any foreigner invited to a Libyan home

Alcohol-free Libya

Libya once had a wine industry producing some fair red wines in the Tarhuna district. There was also a brewery making rather heavy *Oea* beers. This is long gone. Libya is now officially 'dry' and it is very unwise either to attempt to smuggle in alcohol or to take advantage of what is known as Libya's second industry to oil – home brewing. As a foreigner the visitor is best to abide by Libyan rules, however much they are evaded by local people.

The only safe place for an alcoholic drink is in a non-Muslim country's embassy compound, if you should be so lucky as to be invited!

should thus feel very favoured.

The offerings in cafés and restaurants will be very limited and mainly made up of various hot meat, chicken and vegetable stews either with potatoes or macaroni. In the main hotels, cuisine is 'international' and very bland.

Good dates and excellent oranges can be bought cheaply. There are olives of a slightly sour taste, apricots, figs and almonds in season, all of which are good value. The smaller varieties of banana are available at increasingly competitive prices.

● **Drink**

It should be emphasized that alcoholic drinks are banned in Libya. Offers of illegal liquor should be avoided even in private houses unless its provenance is beyond doubt. Local brews or 'flash' can be of questionable quality while traditional brews of *bokha* (a form of arak), or *laghbi* (beer), made from the date palm are illegal and lead to abuse of the date palm. Otherwise, Libyans drink local bottled mineral waters, most of which are not always reliable copies of lemonades, colas and orange drinks available worldwide. Non-alcoholic beer is widely available in bottles and cans, price LD1.5-2, imported from Egypt, Tunisia, Germany, Switzerland and the Netherlands. In season, real orange juice can be bought from stalls on the streets. These drinks are cheap and widely available. Take a bottle opener since most drinks are in glass bottles. The local tap water throughout much of Libya is slightly brackish. For personal use, buy bottled water such as *moyyah Ben Ghashir* (Ben Ghashir water).

Beverages include Libyan tea, which is heavy boiled thick tea, often with mint or peanuts in a small glass. If ordinary tea is wanted ask for *shay kees* (tea from a teabag) *bil leben* (with milk). Coffees include Nescafé (ask for Nescafé) with or without milk and Turkish (sometimes called Arabic) coffee. With the latter, specify whether you want it *bil sukar* (sweet) or *bedoon sukar* (unsweetened).

GETTING AROUND

● **Air**

There are connecting flights to the main cities – easiest access is from Tripoli. See separate towns for details. Book in advance as all flights are very busy – overbooking is common so arrive early. **NB** the UK Foreign Office has advised travellers to Libya **not** to use internal airlines as a lack of spare parts prevents satisfactory safety standards.

● **Road**

Bus The bus service is excellent including good quality a/c intercity services and more interesting crowded local buses – see individual town entries.

Car hire Car hire for self-drive in Libya is not reliable. Vehicles on offer are often old and in only moderate condition. Whilst they are suitable for use in town, they should not be taken on long journeys without thorough pre-travel checks. Among the best hire locations are the main hotels, where agents have desks in the foyer. Hire rates for cars are high and variable, especially outside of Tripoli.

Cycling Travel by bicycle is unusual. Off the main track, cycling is extremely difficult in stony and sandy, albeit flat terrain. Cyclists are advised to be well marked in brightly coloured clothing. Puncture repair shops exist in the towns alongside the main roads at the point of entry, though they mainly deal with cars and light motorcycles rather than bicycles. In the countryside, repair of cycles will be difficult but the profusion of small pick-up trucks means that it is very easy to get a lift with a cycle into a settlement where repairs can be effected.

Hitchhiking Is used in Libya but not normally for a free ride except in emergencies. There are many shared taxis travelling the road and travellers usually make use of these on a paid basis. Private cars or pick-up trucks will act in the same capacity but will expect a small payment in the normal course. Foreign travellers might find themselves picked up for free by curiosity. In general hitchhiking is not to be encouraged since travellers in the S in particular will not be able to hitch reliably. Carry water and other safety supplies.

Motoring Great effort has gone into creating the road system and very few areas of the country are now inaccessible. Drive on the right of the road. Drivers are supposed to wear seat belts and these are checked by the police on entering and leaving Tripoli. Driving in Libya is poorly regulated and standards of driver training are very variable. The accident rate is high by international standards. Visitors should drive defensively for their own safety and to ensure that they are not involved in accidents, especially those involving injury to humans, for which they might be deemed culpable. Drivers can be held in jail for long periods and the settlement of law suits against drivers guilty of dangerous driving leading to death or injury of a third party can be protracted and difficult.

Care is needed in **off-road driving** since there are difficult sand dune areas and other regions where soft sand can quickly bog down other than 4WD vehicles. Even in far-flung parts of the Jefara Plain, the traffic is quite regular and people are never far away. In the central Jefara there are large areas of military installations which are best avoided. Petrol stations are fairly well distributed but only on the main through roads. Any off road travel should only be undertaken with a full tank and a spare petrol supply. Good practice is never to leave the black top road unless there are two vehicles available to the party. A reliable and generous water supply should also be taken. This is especially important in summer when exhaustion and dehydration can be major problems if vehicles need digging out of sand.

Fuel distribution is a monopoly of a state agency and there are petrol stations in every town and at most key road junctions. But, as noted in the regional sections of this Handbook, motorists should ensure that they fill up regularly rather than rely on stretching their fuel supply, since occasionally a station might be out of use for lack of deliveries or a cut in the electricity supply. Travel in the Saharan regions requires special precautions since running out of fuel can be fatal. There is no equivalent of Automobile Club services in Libya but passing motorists are normally very helpful. Drivers should always be aware of the enormous distances between settlements in S Libya and take defensive action to ensure fuel, water, food and clothing reserves at all times (see Surviving in the Desert, page 43). International driving licences are normally required though, in most cases, easily understood (English or Italian) foreign licences might be accepted.

Taxis Individual taxis are more expensive, more flexible and generally more comfortable over the same distance than the local bus. The taxis do have meters but these may not be in use. **Shared taxis** (larger) are a very popular mode of travel, leaving for a particular destination as soon as they are full. Be sure you have settled the price in advance. If in doubt check with the other passengers. These taxis look quite decrepit but generally get to their destination.

● **Walking**

In Libya other than for point to point travel, walking is not normal. Hiking is to be approached, therefore, in the knowledge that it may attract curiosity and possibly disbelief.

Maps of good scale for walking eg better than 1:50,000 are very rare and thus travel has to be by sight lines, compass work and common sense. In many areas of the Jefara sighting to topographic markers on the Jabal can be used or lines on the taller minarets in the small towns are distinctive guides. Dogs are not a general problem in Tripolitania except near large farms where they are used for security purposes. Carry a stout stick and have some stones for throwing at approaching aggressive dogs, which is how the Libyans deal with this problem.

● **Boat**
There are no rental facilities for boats and only a limited few individuals own boats for pleasure purposes. There are small boat marinas at Tripoli and Benghazi for sailors bringing their own boats into port. It is occasionally possible to hire small fishing boats with their owners for the hour or day. Visits to Farwa, for example, near Zuara are only feasible by this means. The opening of new watersport tourist sites for foreign tourists such as at Farwa Island will make boat hire easier in the future.

COMMUNICATIONS

● **Language**
Arabic is the official language throughout Libya. Given the Arab nationalist leanings of the government under Colonel Ghadhafi, Arabic is regarded with some pride as a cultural emblem. Immediately after the 1969 revolution or coup d'état, all foreign language signs were removed, including street names, shop names, signposts and indications on official buildings. The result is that it is difficult for non-Arabic speakers to make use of written signs. In normal circumstances Libyans are most helpful to foreigners and will point out routes and other destinations. Unfortunately, however, it is only the older generation who have colloquial English, French or Italian since the educational system is less good than formerly in teaching foreign languages and fewer Libyans travel abroad than previously. Tripoli City is the least difficult for the non-Arabic speaker. The answer to this problem, other than learning the Arabic script and some vocabulary before travelling, is to be very patient asking your way until help is volunteered by a source you can comprehend.

The private commercial sector is likely to be best aware of **English** and **Italian** since companies trade abroad so that calling in offices or agencies can locate assistance in an emergency. **French** is understood widely by the older generation in the SW of country in the areas of Ghadames and Ghat. Italian is still a used language in the Tripoli area. English is probably best used in Benghazi, Al-Khalij and the E where there are many oil industry workers who have rubbed shoulders with English speaking personnel. Language difficulties should not put off potential travellers to Libya since the Libyans themselves are helpful and patient. A few words or phrases in Arabic will ease the way considerably. (See key words and phrases, page 447.)

Berber is spoken as a first language in some rural areas, especially the Jabal Nafusah. Tamashek, related to Berber, is spoken by the few Tuaregs in the region of Ghadames. In the deep S around the Tibesti Mountains, the Tibu language is the lingua franca.

● **Postal services**
Independent Libya inherited a good postal system. Poste restante and post office box facilities are available in the main cities at the respective central post offices. The service to and from Europe, costing LD 350 for a letter, takes about 7 to 10 days in normal circumstances but, bearing in mind the international air embargo, long land transit for mail makes this a much longer and riskier process. Internal mail is cheap, and for in-city letters, fairly fast and efficient. Libya produces a great range of collectors' stamps and there is a philatelic counter in Tripoli main post office.

● **Telephone services**
PTT facilities exist in all towns and most villages. Internal calls are straightforward, though there can be some waiting time for a public line at the PTT office. International calls from all points can be difficult since there are restricted numbers of lines. The PTT offices in Tripoli are still quicker than trying international calls from private telephones. In-coming international calls, by contrast, are comparatively easy to get through. The **international code** for Libya is 218. Libya internal area codes are **Benghazi** 61, **Benina** 63, **Derna** 81, **Ghadames** 484, **Sabrata** 24, **Tobruk** 87, **Tripoli** 21, **Tripoli Int Airport** 22, **Zaviya** 23, **Zuarah** 25. Rates for calls are at standard international levels.

Fax and telex facilities are available from luxury hotels and the main PTT offices which are advertised as being open 24 hrs a day but suffer from the constraint on telephone lines. Late night automatic fax facilities in private offices are useful if available through friends of friends.

ENTERTAINMENT

● **Media**

Until very recently the Libyan media were powerfully controlled from the centre. This situation is changing only very slowly so that the media reflect the wishes of the régime. This does not make for good entertainment. Other than programmes in Arabic, which technically and in content leave so much to be desired that most Libyans watch videos or foreign stations via satellite especially CNN, not the regular local television, there is a news broadcast in French and English each evening for approximately half an hour each. There is an occasional sports programme, either Arab or international, shown on TV which is culturally neutral. The radio channel carries programmes of western music from time to time. The state produces daily broadsheets in French and English together with Arabic language newspapers. Foreign newspapers can be bought though they are often very out of date even when the air system is working normally. BBC World Service news and programmes can be picked up easily in Libya (see frequency chart, 17).

● **Sports**

Libya participates in the various Arab League sports tournaments but facilities for individuals are still very limited. Health centres exist for travellers at a few of the main hotels. Swimming is universally available in the Mediterranean or in the pools attached to the beach clubs in the main cities. Libyans themselves play volleyball for which there are plenty of facilities and football. Horse riding and trotting are also generally enjoyed. There is often a Tripoli Horse Show with international interest, now suspended. A Secretariat (ministry) of Sport exists but its activities are not given priority. The beach clubs near Tripoli have first class facilities for tennis, table tennis and canoeing and other sports. In the smaller towns the schools tend to be centres for sports while in industrial towns some of the companies have their own clubs with squash and tennis courts, for example.

HOLIDAYS AND FESTIVALS

Libya, as Muslim country, observes all the main Islamic festivals as holidays (see page 24 for details on Ramadan). Fridays are days of rest. In addition there are several national holidays.

2 Mar:	Declaration of the People's Authority
11 Jun:	Evacuation of foreign military bases
1 Sep:	Anniversary of the 1969 Revolution

Rounding up

ACKNOWLEDGEMENTS

TUNISIA

We wish to acknowledge the work done by Derek Alderton in the updating the chapters on Cap Bon and Tunis for his wide ranging contributions; Geoff Moss for the many new illustrations; Justin MacGuinness, our man in Tunis; Mohammed Ennaceur in El Djem; Emma Kay at the Tunisian National Tourist Office.

LIBYA

Thomas Tolk of Bonn and David Steinke of Deetz Havel, Germany.

FURTHER READING

TUNISIA

BOOKS

Anon, *Les Mosquées de Tunisie*, Tunis, 1973; Brett, M (ed), *Northern Africa, Islam and modernisation*, Cass, London, 1973; Brown, LC, *The Tunisia of Ahmed Bey*, University Press, Princeton, 1974; Douglas, N, *Fountains in the Sand*, 1985; Hopkins, M, *Tunisia to 1993*, London, 1989; Hopwood, D, *Habib Bourguiba of Tunisia – The tragedy of Longevity*, Macmillan, £45; Kassab, A, *Etudes Rurales en Tunisie*, Tunis, 1980; Knapp, W, *Tunisia*, Thames & Hudson, 1970; Latham, JD, *Towards a study of Andalusian immigration and its place in Tunisian history*, Cahiers de Tunisie, 1957; Lloyd, C, *English Corsairs on the Barbary Coast*, London, 1981; Messenger, C, *The Tunisian Campaign*, 1982; Sladen, D, *Carthage and Tunis*, London, 1906; Woodford, JS, *The City of Tunis*, Menas Press Ltd, Wisbech, 1990.

GUIDEBOOKS

Guide du Routard Tunisie, Algérie et Sahara edited by Hachette; *Guide Bleu Tunisie* edited by Hachette; *Stay Alive in the Desert*, KEM Melville, edited Roger Lascelles.

MAPS

The best map by far is Michelin 972, scale 1:million. Map of Tunisia by Kümmerly and Frey, scale 1:million gives geomorphological details and a pictorial view worth studying before the visit. World Map, Geo Centre International, Reise & Verkehrsverlag, Stuttgart, 1:800,000 gives clear information. The Tourist Office will give you their free map which is good enough to pinpoint the main places but lacks detail.

LIBYA

BOOKS AND MAPS

The best available maps are Michelin Carte Routière et Touristique, *Afrique Nord et Ouest* at 1/4,000,000 and Cartographia *Libya* at 1/2,000,000. Libyan maps of 1/50,000 are available for the main settled areas but are difficult to find except in the university library and the Secretariat of Planning. There are few contemporary guidebooks to Libya. A very useful book is the Arabic/English language *Atlas of Libya*, available at the Fergiani Book Stores, Sharah 1st September, Tripoli. The *Antiquities of Tripolitania* by DEL Hayes, pub Dept Antiquities, Tripoli 1981; *Cyrene and Apollonia an Historical guide*, by Richard Goodchild, Dept Antiquities, Tripoli 1963.

There are a few books on Libya which are not essentially political. Of these the best are J Davis's (1987) book *Libyan Politics: Tribe & Revolution*. On history J Wright's (1982) *Libya: A Modern History* is a good review while JA Allan's (1981) *Libya: The Experience of Oil* deals with oil and agricultural development. On the disputed areas of S Libya books include M Alawar, (1983) *Bibliography of Chad and the Libyan Borderlands* and J Wright, (1989) *Libya, Chad and the Central Sahara*.

Useful addresses

EMBASSIES AND CONSULATES

TUNISIA

Algeria
11 Rue de Bois de Boulogne, Algiers, T 601388

Austria
Chegastr 3, 1030 Vienna, T 786552

Belgium
278 Ave de Tervuesen, 1150 Brussels, T 7621448

Canada
515 O'Connor St, Ottawa, T 2370330, Tx 534161

Cuba
Ave Golfe Arab, T 714198

Denmark
Strandboulevarden 130, Copenhagen, T 01625010

Egypt
26 Rue el Jazirah, Zamalek, Cairo, T 3412379

France
27 Rue Barbet de Jouy, 75007 Paris, T 45559598

Germany
Godesberger Allee 103, 53 Bonn 2, T 228 376981

Italy
7 Via Asmara, Rome, T 8390748

Japan
292 Ichibabcho, Chiyoda-Ku, Tokyo 102, T 3534111, Tx 27146

Jordan
Ave el Aska, 4th Circle, Amman, T 674307

Libya
Rue Bèchir el Ibrahimi, Tripoli, T 30331

Malta
Dar Carthage, Qormi Rd, Attard, T 498853

Mauritania
BP 681, Nouakchott, T 52871

Morocco
Corner of 6 Ave du Fes & 1 Rue d'Ifrane, Rabat, T 30576

Senegal
Rue el Hadj Seydou, Nourou Tall, Dakar, T 31261

Spain
Plaza Alonzo-Martinez 3, Madrid, T 4473508

Sudan
Rue No 18, Baladia St, Khartoum, T 0024811/76538

Syria
6 Jaddet al-Chaffi, Damascus, T 660356

Switzerland
58 Rue de Moillebeau, 1029 Geneva, T 333023

UK
29 Princes Gate, London SW7, T 0171 5848117

USA
1515 Massachusetts Ave NW, Washington DC 20005, T 202 8621850, Tx 248377

LIBYA

Belgium
28 Ave Victoria, 1050 Brussels, T 02 6492113

France
Paris, T 45534070

Germany
Bonn, T 0228 820090

Italy
Rome, T 06 8414518

Malta
Dar Jamaharia Notabile Rd, Balzan, BZN 01, T 010 356 486347

Spain
Madrid, T 01 4571368

Tunisia
Tunis 48 bis rue du 1 Juin, T 283936

UK
London T 0171 486 8250/071 486 8387, F 0171 224 6349

TUNISIA NATIONAL TOURIST OFFICES OVERSEAS

Canada
1125 Blvd de Maisonneuve Ouest, Montreal, T 514 985 2586

France
32 Ave de l'Opera, Paris, T 75002

Germany
Dusseldorf Steinstrasse 23, 4000 Dusseldorf, T 84218

Italy
via Sardegna No 17, 00187 Rome, T 4821934

Netherlands, Muntplein 2111, 1012 WR Amsterdam, T 020224971

Saudi Arabia
BP 13582-Jeddah 21414, T 6534981, F 6534612

Spain
Plaza de Espana 18, Plaza de Madrid, Madrid 28008, T 2481435

Sweden
Engelbrektsgaten 19, 11432 Stockholm, T 00468 206773

UK
77A Wigmore St, London W1H 9LJ, T 0171 2245561

USA
contact embassy in Washington, T 2346644

SPECIALIST TOUR COMPANIES

TUNISIA

Martin Randall Travel
10 Barley Mow Passage, Chiswick, London W4 4PH, T 0181 994 6477 – Roman and Islamic Cities

Branta Holidays
7 Wingfield St, London SE15 4LN, T 0171 6344812 – birdwatching winter visitors on Lake Ichkeul and Tozeur

Andante Travel
Grange Cottage, Winterbourne Dauntsey, Salisbury, Wilts, SP4 6ER, T 01980 610555 – Art and Archaeology

Explore Worldwide
1 Frederick St, Aldershot, Hants, T 01252 319448, offer interesting excursions to the ancient sites and into the mountains

Prospect Music and Art Tours
454 Chiswick High Rd, London W4 5TT, T 0181 995 2151, accompanied tours with experts in art and art history, archaeology and architecture

Discovery Cruises
47 St Johns Wood High St, London NW8 7NJ, T 0171 5867191 – sailing from Athens

Medward Travel
304 Old Brompton Rd, London, SW5 9JF, T 0171 3734411, F 0171 2448174 for individual requirements

Regency Cruises
2 Telfords Yard, 6 The Highway, London E1 9BQ, T 01473 292222 – sailing from Nice

Wigmore Holidays
122 Wigmore St, London W1H 9FE, T 0171 4864425, F 0171 4863559, they specialize in Fly-Drive and Tailor-Made travel as well as breaks in Tunis and beach resorts, not cheap.

LIBYA

Arab Tours Ltd
60 Marylebone Lane, London, WIM 5FF, T 0171 9353273, F 0171 4864237, offer a 9-day tour of Libya's classical cities, via Tunisia, at £897 pp.

Language for travel

ARABIC It is impossible to indicate in the Latin script how Arabic should be pronounced so we have opted for a very simplified transliteration which will give the user a sporting chance of uttering something that can be understood by an Arab. An accent has been placed to show where the stress falls in each word of more than two syllables.

For French the gender of nouns has been given in brackets. In French the plural of both *le* (masculine) and *la* (feminine) is *les*. The final letter of the word pronounced unless accented as in *marché*.

NUMBERS

	Arabic	French
0	sífr	zéro
1	wáhad	un (m) une (f)
2	tnéen	deux
3	taláata	trois
4	árba	quatre
5	khámsa	cinq
6	sítta	six
7	sába	sept
8	tamánia	huit
9	tíssa	neuf
10	áshra	dix
11	ahdásh	onze
12	itnásh	douze
13	talatásh	treize
14	arbatásh	quatorze
15	khamstásh	quinze
16	sittásh	seize
17	sabatásh	dix-sept
18	tmantásh	dix-huit
19	tissatásh	dix-neuf

ARABIC NUMERALS

١	1	١٠	10	١٩	19	٨٠	80
٢	2	١١	11	٢٠	20	٩٠	90
٣	3	١٢	12	٢١	21	١٠٠	100
٤	4	١٣	13	٢٢	22	٢٠٠	200
٥	5	١٤	14	٣٠	30	٣٠٠	300
٦	6	١٥	15	٤٠	40	٤٠٠	400
٧	7	١٦	16	٥٠	50	١٠٠٠	1000
٨	8	١٧	17	٦٠	60		
٩	9	١٨	18	٧٠	70		

20	ishréen	vingt
30	tlaatéen	trente
40	arba'een	quarante
50	khamséen	cinquante
60	sittéen	soixante
70	saba'een	soixante-dix
80	tmanéen	quatre-vingts
90	tissa'een	quatre-vingt dix
100	mía	cent
200	miatéen	deux cents
300	tláata mia	trois cents
1,000	alf	mille

GREETINGS

Hello!
assálamu aláikum bonjour
How are you?
keef hálek? comment ça va?
Well!
kwáyes très bien
Good bye!
bisaláma au revoir
Go away!
ímshi, barra allez vous en!
God willing!
inshállah si Dieu le veut
Never mind
ma'lésh ne t'inquiète pas
Thank God!
hamdulilláh! Dieu merci!
Yes/no
naam, áiwa/la oui/non
Please
min fádlek s'il vous plaît
Thank you
shukran merci
OK
kwáyes d'accord
Excuse me
ismáh-lee excusez-moi

DAYS

Sunday
al-áhad dimanche
Monday
al-itnéen lundi
Tuesday
at-taláta mardi
Wednesday
al-árba mercredi
Thursday
al-khemées jeudi
Friday
al-júma vendredi
Saturday
as-sébt samedi

FOOD

banana
mouz banane (f)
beer
bírra bière (f)
bread
khubz pain (m)
breakfast
futóor petit déjeuner (m)
butter
zíbda beurre (m)
cheese
jíbna fromage (m)
coffee
qáhwa café (m)
dessert
hélwa dessert (m)
dinner
ásha dîner (m)
drink
mashróob boisson (f)
egg
baid oeuf (m)
fish
sámak poisson (m)
food
akl nourriture (f)
fruit
fawákih fruit (m)
lemonade
gazóoza limonade (f)
lunch
gháda déjeuner (m)
meat
láhma viande (f)
menu (fixed price)
ká'ima menu (à prix fixe)
milk
lában lait (m)
olive
zeitóon olive (f)
restaurant
restaurán restaurant (m)
salt
méleh sel (m)
soup
shórba potage (m)
sugar
súkar sucre (m)
tea (tea bag)
shay (shay kees) thé (m)
water (bottled)
móyyah (botri) l'eau (f) (en bouteille)
wine
khamr vin (m)

TRAVEL

airport
al-matár — aéroport (m)

arrival
wusóol — arrivée (f)

bicycle
bisiclét/darrája — vélo (m)

birth (date of)
youm al-meelád — date de naissance(f)

bus
autobées — autobus (m)

bus station
maháttat al- — gare routière (f)

car
sayára — voiture (f)

car hire
sayárat-ujra — location de voitures (f)

customs
júmruk/gúmruk — douane (f)

departure
khuróoj — départ

duty (excise)
daréebat — droit (m)

duty free
bidóon daréeba — hors-taxe

engine
motúr — moteur (m)

fare
ujrat as-safr — prix du billet (m)

ferry (boat)
má'diya — ferry/bac (m)

garage
garáge — garage (m)

here/there
héna/henák — ici/là

left/right
yesáar/yeméen — à gauche/droite

left luggage
máktab éeda al-afsh

map
kharéeta — carte (f)

oil (engine)
zeit — huile (f)

papers (documents)
watá'iq — papiers d'identité(m)

parking
máwkif as-sayyarát

passport
jawáz — passeport (m)

petrol
benzéen — essence (f)

port
méena — port (m)

puncture
tókob — crevaison (f)

quickly
sarée'an — vite

railway
as-sikka al-hadeedíya

road
trik — route (f)

slowly
shwai shwai — lentement

station
mahátta — gare (f)

straight on
alatóol — tout droit

surname
lákab — nom de famille (m)

taxi
taxi — taxi (m)

taxi rank
maháttat at-taxiyát

ticket
tázkara — billet (m)

ticket (return)
tázkara dhaháb — billet de retour (m)
wa-eeyáb

what time is it?
is-sa'a kam? — quelle heure est-il?

train
tren — train (m)

tyre
itár — pneu (m)

visa
fisa, ta'shéera — visa (m)

COMMON WORDS

after
bá'ad — après

afternoon
bá'ad az-zohr — après-midi

Algeria
Aljazáyer — Algérie (f)

America
Amréeka — Amérique (f)

and
wa — et

bank
bank — banque (f)

bath
hammám — bain (m)

beach
sháti al-bahr — plage (f)

bed
seréer — lit (m)

before
qabl — avant

Belgium
Belg — Belgique (f)

big
kebéer — grand

black
áswad — noir

blue
ázrag — bleu

camp site
mukháyyam — terrain de camping (m)

castle
kál'ah — château (m)

cheap
rakhées — bon marché

chemist shop
saidalíya — pharmacie (f)

church
kenéesa — église (f)

closed
múglaq — fermé

cold/hot
bárid/sukhna — froid/chaud

consulate
consulíya — consulat (m)

day/night
youm/lail — jour (m)/nuit (f)

desert
sahra — désert (m)

doctor
tebeeb — médecin (m)

Egypt
Masr — Egypte (f)

embassy
sifára — ambassade (f)

England
Ingiltérra — Angleterre (f)

enough
bás — assez

entrance
dukhóol — entrée (f)

evening
mássa — soir (m)

exchange (money)
tabdéel — change (m)

exit
khuróoj — sortie (f)

expensive (too)
kteer — cher (trop)

film
feelm — pellicule (f)

forbidden
mamnóoh — défendu

France
France/Francia — France (f)

full
melyán — complet

Germany
Almáni — Allemagne (f)

good (very good)
táyeb, kwáyes — bien (très bien)

great
ákbar — formidable

green
khádra — vert

he/she
húwa/híya — il/elle

house
mánzel — maison (f)

hospital
mustáshfa — hôpital (m)

hostel
bait ash-shebáb — auberge (f)

hotel
fúnduq/hotéel — hôtel (m)

how far to..?
kam kilometri... — ... est à combien de km?

how much?
bikám — c'est combien?

I/you
ána/inta — je/vous

information
malumát — renseignements (m)

is there/are there?
hinák — y a-t-il un ..?

Italy
Itálya — Italie (f)

key
miftáh — clef (m)

later
ba'déen — plus tard

Libya
Líbiya — Libye (f)

light
nour — lumière (f)

little
sghéer — petit

market
sook — marché (m)

me
ána — moi

money
flóos — argent (m)

more/less
áktar/akál — plus/moins

morning
sobh — matin

Morocco
al-Maghreb — Maroc

mosque
mesjéed — mosquée (f)

near
karéeb — près

Netherlands (Dutch)
Holánda — Pays-Bas (m) (hollandais)

newspaper
jaréeda — journal (m)

new
jedéed — nouveau

not
mush — ne...pas

now
al-án — maintenant

oil (heating)
naft · mazout (m)
open
maftooh · ouvert
pharmacy
(see chemist)
photography
taswéer · photographie (f)
police
bulées/shurta · gendarmerie (f)
post office
máktab al-baréed · poste
price
si'r · prix (m)
red
áhmar · rouge
river
wádi, wed · rivière (f),fleuve (m)
roof
sat'h · toit (m)
room
górfa · chambre (f)
sea
bahr · mer (f)
shop
dukkán · magasin (m)
shower
doosh · douche (f)
small
sghéer · petit
Spain
Espánya · Espagne (f)
square
maidán · place (f)
stamp
tábi' · timbre poste (m)
street
shári · rue (f)

Sudan
as-Sóodan · Soudan (m)
Switzerland
Esswízi · Suisse (f)
synagogue
kenées · synagogue (f)
telephone
teleefóon · téléphone (m)
today
al-yóom · aujourd'hui
toilet
tualét · toilette (f)
tomorrow
búkra · demain
tower
qasr · tour (f)
Tunisia
Toónis · Tunisie (f)
United States
al-wilayát al- · Etats-Unis (m) muttáhida
washbasin
tusht · évier (m)
water(hot)
móyya (sukhna) · eau (chaude)
week/year
usboo'/sána · semaine (f)/an (m)
what?
shenu? · quoi?
when?
ímta? · quand?
where (is)?
wain? · oú (est)?
white
ábyad · blanc
why
laih · pourquoi
yellow
ásfar · jaune
yesterday
ams · hier

Health

WITH THE FOLLOWING advice and precautions, you should keep as healthy as you do at home. Despite the countries being part of Africa where one expects to see much tropical disease this is not actually the case, although malaria remains a problem in some areas. Because much of the area is economically under-developed, infectious diseases still predominate in the same way as they did in the west some decades ago. There are obvious health differences between each of the countries of North Africa and in risks between the business traveller who tends to stay in international class hotels in large cities and the backpacker trekking through the rural areas. There are no hard and fast rules to follow; you will often have to make your own judgements on the healthiness or otherwise of your surroundings.

There are many well qualified doctors in the area, a large proportion of whom speak English or French but the quality and range of medical care is extremely variable from country to country and diminishes very rapidly away from big cities. In some countries, there are systems and traditions of medicine rather different from the Western model and you may be confronted with less usual modes of treatment. At least you can be reasonably sure that local practitioners have a lot of experience with the particular diseases of their region. If you are in a city it may be worthwhile calling on your Embassy to obtain a list of recommended doctors.

If you are a long way from medical help, a certain amount of self medication may be necessary and you will find that many of the drugs that are available have familiar names. However, always check the date stamping and buy from reputable pharmacists because the shelf life of some items, especially vaccines and antibiotics is markedly reduced in hot conditions. Unfortunately many locally produced drugs are not subjected to quality control procedures and can be unreliable. There have, in addition, been cases of substitution of inert materials for active drugs.

With the following precautions and advice you should keep as healthy as usual. Make local enquiries about health risks if you are apprehensive and take the general advice of European and North American families who have lived or are living in the area.

BEFORE YOU GO

Take out medical insurance. You should have a dental check up, obtain a spare glasses prescription and, if you suffer from a longstanding condition such as diabetes, high blood pressure, heart/lung disease or a nervous disorder, arrange for a check up with your doctor who can at the same time provide you with a letter explaining details of your disability (in English and French). Check the current practice for malaria prophylaxis (prevention) for the countries you intend to visit.

For a simple list of 'Health Kit' to take with you, see page 11.

INOCULATIONS

Smallpox vaccination is no longer required. Neither is cholera vaccination, despite the fact that the disease occurs in Tunisia. Yellow fever vaccination is not normally needed but in Libya, you may be asked for a certificate if you have been in an area (Sub-Saharan Africa for example) affected by yellow fever immediately before travelling to North Africa. Cholera vaccine is not effective which is the main reason for not recommending it but occasionally travellers from South America, where cholera is presently raging, or from parts of South Asia where the disease is endemic may be asked to provide evidence of vaccination. The following vaccinations are recommended:

Typhoid (*monovalent*): one dose followed by a booster in 1 month's time. Immunity from this course lasts 2-3 years. Other injectable types are now becoming available as are oral preparations marketed in some countries.

Poliomyelitis: this is a live vaccine, generally given orally and the full course consists of three doses with a booster in tropical regions every 3-5 years.

Tetanus: one dose should be given with a booster at 6 weeks and another at 6 months and 10 yearly boosters thereafter are recommended.

Children: should, in addition, be properly protected against diphtheria, whooping cough, mumps and measles. Teenage girls, if they have not yet had the disease, should be given rubella (German measles) vaccination. Consult your doctor for advice on BCG inoculation against tuberculosis. The disease is still common in the region. Tunisia and Libya lies mainly outside the meningitis belt and the disease is probably no more common than at home so vaccination is not indicated except during an epidemic.

INFECTIOUS HEPATITIS (JAUNDICE)

This is common throughout North Africa. It seems to be frequently caught by travellers probably because, coming from countries with higher standards of hygiene, they have not contracted the disease in childhood and are therefore not immune like the majority of adults in developing countries. The main symptoms are stomach pains, lack of appetite, nausea, lassitude and yellowness of the eyes and skin. Medically speaking there are two types: the less serious, but more common, is hepatitis A for which the best protection is careful preparation of food, the avoidance of contaminated drinking water and scrupulous attention to toilet hygiene. Human normal immunoglobulin (gammaglobulin) confers considerable protection against the disease and is particularly useful in epidemics. It should be obtained from a reputable source and is certainly recommended for travellers who intend to live rough. The injection should be given as close as possible to your departure and, as the dose depends on the likely time you are to spend in potentially infected areas, the manufacturer's instructions should be followed. A new vaccination against hepatitis A is now generally available and probably provides much better immunity for 10 years but is more expensive, being three separate injections.

The other more serious version is hepatitis B which is acquired as a sexually transmitted disease, from a blood transfusion or injection with an unclean needle or possibly by insect bites. The symptoms are the same as hepatitis A but the incubation period is much longer.

You may have had jaundice before or you may have had hepatitis of either type before without becoming jaundiced, in which case it is possible that you could be immune to either hepatitis A or B. This immunity can be tested for before you travel. If you are not immune to hepatitis B already, a vaccine is available (three shots over 6 months) and if you are not immune to hepatitis A already then you should consider vaccination (or gamma globulin if you are not going to be exposed for long).

MENINGITIS

This is a 'significant risk' in Mauritania. Protection against meningococcal meningitis A and C is conferred by a vaccine which is freely available.

AIDS

In North Africa AIDS is probably less common than in most of Europe and North America but is presumably increasing in its incidence, though not as rapidly as in Sub-Saharan Africa, South America or Southeast Asia. Having said that, the spread of the disease has not been well documented in the North African region; the real picture is unclear. The disease is possibly still mainly confined to the well known high risk sections of the population i.e. homosexual men, intravenous drug abusers, prostitutes and children of infected mothers. Whether heterosexual

transmission outside these groups is common or not, the main risk to travellers is from casual sex, heterosexual or homosexual. The same precautions should be taken as when encountering any sexually transmitted disease. In some of these countries there is widespread female prostitution and a higher proportion of this population is likely to be HIV antibody positive. In other parts, especially high class holiday resorts, intravenous drug abuse is prevalent and in certain cities, homosexual, transsexual and transvestite prostitution is common and again this part of the population is quite likely to harbour the HIV virus in large measure. The AIDS virus (HIV) can be passed via unsterile needles which have been previously used to inject an HIV positive patient but the risk of this is very small indeed. It would, however, be sensible to check that needles have been properly sterilized or disposable needles used. The chance of picking up hepatitis B in this way is much more of a danger. Be wary of carrying disposable needles yourself. Custom officials may find them suspicious. The risk of receiving a blood transfusion with blood infected with the HIV virus is greater than from dirty needles because of the amount of fluid exchanged. Supplies of blood for transfusion are now largely screened for HIV in all reputable hospitals so the risk must be very small indeed. Catching the AIDS virus does not necessarily produce an illness in itself; the only way to be sure if you feel you have been put at risk is to have a blood test for HIV antibodies on your return to a place where there are reliable laboratory facilities. The results may not be ready for many weeks.

COMMON PROBLEMS

ALTITUDE

Mountain sickness is hardly likely to occur Tunisia or Libya. A not-too-rapid ascent is the sure way to prevent it. Other problems experienced at moderate altitude are:

sunburn, excessively dry air causing skin cracking, sore eyes (it may be wise to leave your contact lenses out, especially in windy and dusty areas) and stuffy noses. Many travellers, as long as they are physically fit, enjoy travelling in the mountains where it is generally cooler and less humid and there are fewer insects.

HEAT AND COLD

Full acclimatisation to high temperatures takes about 2 weeks and during this period it is normal to feel a degree of apathy, especially if the relative humidity is high. Drink plenty of water (up to 15 litres a day are required when working physically hard in hot, dry conditions), use salt on your food and avoid extreme exertion. Tepid showers are more cooling than hot or cold ones. Large hats do not cool you down but prevent sunburn. Remember that, especially in the mountains, there can be a large and sudden drop in temperature between sun and shade and between night and day so dress accordingly. Clear desert nights can prove astoundingly cold with a rapid drop in temperature as the sun goes down. Loose fitting cotton clothes are still the best for hot weather; warm jackets and woollens are essential after dark in some desert areas, and especially at high altitude.

INSECTS

These can be a great nuisance. Some, of course, are carriers of serious diseases such as malaria and yellow fever. The best way of keeping insects away at night is to sleep off the ground with a mosquito net and to burn mosquito coils containing Pyrethrum. Aerosol sprays or a 'flit' gun may be effective as are insecticidal tablets which are heated on a mat which is plugged into the wall socket (if taking your, own check the voltage of the area you are visiting so that you can take an appliance that will work. Similarly check that your electrical adaptor is suitable for the repellent plug).

You can use personal insect repellent, the best of which contain a high concentration of Diethyltoluamide. Liquid is best for arms and face (take care around eyes and make sure you do not dissolve the plastic of your spectacles). Aerosol spray on clothes and ankles deters mites and ticks. Liquid DET suspended in water can be used to impregnate cotton clothes and mosquito nets. Wide mesh mosquito nets are now available impregnated with an insecticide called Permethrin and are generally more effective, lighter to carry and more comfortable to sleep in. If you are bitten, itching may be relieved by cool baths and anti-histamine tablets (care with alcohol or driving) corticosteroid creams (great care – never use if any hint of sepsis) or by judicious scratching. Calamine lotion and cream have limited effectiveness and anti-histamine creams have a tendency to cause skin allergies and are therefore not generally recommended. Bites which become infected (commonly in dirty and dusty places) should be treated with a local antiseptic or antibiotic cream such as Cetrimide as should infected scratches. Skin infestations with body lice, crabs and scabies are unfortunately easy to pick up. Use Gamma benzene hexachloride for lice and Benzyl benzoate for scabies. Crotamiton cream (Eurax) alleviates itching and also kills a number of skin parasites. Malathion lotion 5% is good for lice but avoid the highly toxic full strength Malathion used as an agricultural insecticide.

INTESTINAL UPSETS

Practically nobody escapes this one so be prepared for it. Some of these countries lead the world in their prevalence of diarrhoea. Most of the time intestinal upsets are due to the insanitary preparation of food. Do not eat uncooked fish or vegetables or meat, fruit with the skin on (always peel your fruit yourself) or food that is exposed to flies. Tap water is generally held to be unsafe or at least unreliable throughout the region. Filtered or bottled water is generally available. If your hotel has a central hot water supply this is safe to drink after cooling. Ice for drinks should be made from boiled water but rarely is, so stand your glass on the ice cubes, instead of putting them in the drink. Dirty water should first be strained through a filter bag (available from camping shops) and then boiled or treated. Bringing the water to a rolling boil at sea level is sufficient but at high altitude you have to boil the water for longer to ensure that all the microbes are killed. Various sterilising methods can be used and there are proprietary preparations containing chlorine or iodine compounds. Pasteurized or heat treated milk is now widely available as is ice cream and yoghurt produced by the same methods. Unpasteurized milk products including cheese and yoghurt are sources of tuberculosis, brucellosis, listeria and food poisoning germs. You can render fresh milk safe by heating it to 62°C for 30 mins followed by rapid cooling or by boiling it. Matured or processed cheeses are safer than fresh varieties.

Diarrhoea is usually the result of food poisoning, occasionally from contaminated water (including seawater when swimming near sewage outfalls). There are various causes – viruses, bacteria, protozoa (like amoeba) salmonella and cholera organisms. It may take one of several forms coming on suddenly, or rather slowly. It may be accompanied by vomiting or by severe abdominal pain and the passage of blood or mucus when it is called dysentery. How do you know which type you have and how do you treat it?

All kinds of diarrhoea, whether or not accompanied by vomiting, respond favourably to the replacement of water and salts taken as frequent small sips of some kind of rehydration solution. There are proprietary preparations consisting of sachets of powder which you dissolve

in water or you can make your own by adding half a teaspoonful of salt (3.5 grams) and four tablespoonfuls of sugar (40 grams) to a litre of boiled water. If you can time the onset of diarrhoea to the minute, then it is probably viral or bacterial and/or the onset of dysentery. The treatment, in addition to rehydration, is Ciprofloxacin 500 mgs every 12 hrs. The drug is now widely available as are various similar ones.

If the diarrhoea has come on slowly or intermittently, then it is more likely to be protozoal i.e. caused by amoeba or giardia and antibiotics will have no effect. These cases are best treated by a doctor, as is any outbreak of diarrhoea continuing for more than 3 days. If there are severe stomach cramps, the following drugs may help: Loperamide (Imodium, Arret) and Diphenoxylate with Atropine (Lomotil).

The lynchpins of treatment for diarrhoea are rest, fluid and salt replacement, antibiotics such as Ciprofloxacin for the bacterial types and special diagnostic tests and medical treatment for amoeba and giardia infections. Salmonella infections and cholera can be devastating diseases and it would be wise to get to a hospital as soon as possible if these were suspected. Fasting, peculiar diets and the consumption of large quantities of yoghourt have not been found useful in calming travellers diarrhoea or in rehabilitating inflamed bowels. Oral rehydration has on the other hand, especially in children, been a lifesaving technique. As there is some evidence that alcohol and milk might prolong diarrhoea, they should probably be avoided during and immediately after an attack. There are ways of preventing travellers diarrhoea for short periods of time when visiting these countries by taking antibiotics but these are ineffective against viruses and, to some extent, against protozoa, so this technique should not be used other than in exceptional circumstances. Some preventives such as Enterovioform can have serious side effects if taken for long periods.

MALARIA

This disease is not common in Tunisia. It is, however, common in Libya. Despite being nowhere near so common as in Sub-Saharan Africa, malaria remains a serious disease and you are advised to protect yourself against mosquito bites as described above and to take prophylactic (preventive) drugs where and when there is a risk. Start taking the tablets a few days before exposure and continue to take them 6 weeks after leaving the malarial zone. Remember to give the drugs to babies and children and pregnant women also.

The subject of malaria prevention is becoming more complex as the malaria parasite becomes immune to some of the older drugs. This phenomenon, at the time of writing, has not occurred in North African countries other than Mauritania and so the more traditional drugs can be taken with some confidence. Protection with Proguanil (Paludrine) two tablets per day, or Chloroquine two tablets per week will suffice and at this dose will not cause any side effects. You will have to find out locally the likelihood of malaria and perhaps be prepared to receive conflicting advice on how to prevent yourself from catching it. You can catch malaria even when taking prophylactic drugs, although it is unlikely. If you do develop symptoms (high fever, shivering, severe headache, sometimes diarrhoea) seek medical advice immediately. The risk of the disease is obviously greater the further you move from the cities into rural areas with limited facilities and standing water.

PSYCHOLOGICAL DISORDERS

First time exposure to countries where sections of the population live in extreme poverty or squalor and may even be starving can cause odd psychological reactions in visitors. So can the incessant pestering, especially of women which is unfortunately common in some of these countries. Simply be prepared for this and try not to over react.

SNAKE AND OTHER BITES & STINGS

If you are unlucky enough to be bitten by a venomous snake, spider, scorpion, lizard, centipede or sea creature try (within limits) to catch the animal for identification. The reactions to be expected are fright, swelling, pain and bruising around the bite, soreness of the regional lymph glands, nausea, vomiting and fever. If in addition any of the following symptoms supervene, get the victim to a doctor without delay: numbness, tingling of the face, muscular spasms, convulsions, shortness of breath or haemorrhage. Commercial snake bite or scorpion sting kits may be available but are only useful for the specific type of snake or scorpion for which they are designed. The serum has to be given intravenously, so is not much good unless you have had some practice in making injections into veins. If the bite is on a limb, immobilise it and apply a tight bandage between the bite and body, releasing it for 90 secs every 15 mins. Reassurance of the bitten person is very important because death by snake bite is in fact very rare. Do not slash the bite area and try and suck out the poison because this kind of heroism does more harm than good. Hospitals usually hold stocks of snake bite serum. Best precaution: do not walk in snake territory with bare feet, sandals or shorts.

If swimming in an area where there are poisonous fish such as stone or scorpion fish (also called by a variety of local names) or sea urchins on rocky coasts, tread carefully or wear plimsolls. The sting of such fish is intensely painful and this can be helped by immersing the stung part in water as hot as you can bear for as long as it remains painful. This is not always very practical and you must take care not to scald yourself but it does work. Avoid spiders and scorpions by keeping your bed away from the wall and look under lavatory seats and inside your shoes in the morning. In the rare event of being bitten, consult a doctor.

SUNBURN AND HEAT STROKE

The burning power of the sun is phenomenal, especially at high altitude. Always wear a wide-brimmed hat and use some form of sun cream or lotion on untanned skin. Normal temperate zone suntan lotions (protection factor up to seven) are not much good. You need to use the types designed specifically for the tropics or for mountaineers or skiers with a protection factor (against UVA) between seven and 15. Certain creams also protect against UVB and you should use these if you have a skin prone to burning. Glare from the sun can cause conjunctivitis so wear sunglasses, especially on the beach.

There are several varieties of heat stroke. The most common cause is severe dehydration. Avoid this by drinking lots of non-alcoholic fluid and adding some salt if you wish.

OTHER AFFLICTIONS

Athletes foot and other fungal infections are best treated by exposure to sunshine and a proprietary preparation such as Tolnaftate.

Intestinal worms do occur in insanitary areas and the more serious ones, such as hook-worm, can be contracted by walking bare foot on infested earth or beaches.

Leishmaniasis causing a skin ulcer which will not heal is also present in most of the North African countries. It is transmitted by sand flies.

Prickly heat is a common itchy rash avoided by frequent washing and by wearing loose clothing. It can be helped by the regular use of talcum powder to allow the skin to dry thoroughly after washing.

Schistosomiasis (bilharzia) can easily be avoided because it is transmitted by snails which live in fresh water lakes so do not swim in such places or in canals.

Rabies is endemic throughout North African countries. If you are bitten by a domestic animal try to have it captured for observation and see a doctor at once. Treatment with human diploid vaccine is now extremely effective and worth seeking out if the likelihood of having contracted rabies is high.

WHEN YOU RETURN HOME

Remember to take your anti-malarial tablets for 6 weeks. If you have had attacks of diarrhoea, it is worth having a stool specimen tested in case you have picked up amoebic dysentery. If you have been living rough, a blood test may be worthwhile to detect worms and other parasites.

FURTHER HEALTH INFORMATION

The following organizations give information regarding well-trained English speaking physicians throughout the world: International Association for Medical Assistance to Travellers, 745 Fifth Avenue, New York, 10022; Intermedic, 777 3rd Avenue, New York, 10017.

Information regarding country by country malaria risk can be obtained from the World Health Organisation (WHO) or the Ross Institute, The London School of Hygiene and Tropical Medicine, Keppel Street, London WCIE 7HT which publishes a strongly recommended book entitled *The Preservation of Personal Health in Warm Climates*. The organisation MASTA, (Medical-Advisory Service to Travellers Abroad), also based at The London School of Hygiene and Tropical Medicine, T 0171 6314408, F 0171 4365389, will provide country by country information on up-to-date health risks.

Further information on medical problems overseas can be obtained from Dawood, Richard (ed), *Travellers Health, How to Stay Healthy Abroad*, Oxford University Press, 1992, costing £7.99. We strongly recommend this revised and updated edition, especially to the intrepid traveller heading for the more out of the way places.

General advice is also available in *Health Advice for Travellers* published jointly by the Department of Health and the Central Office of Information (UK) and available free from your Travel Agent.

The above information has been prepared by Dr David Snashall, Senior Lecturer in Occupational Health, United Medical Schools of Guy's and St Thomas' Hospitals and Chief Medical Officer, Foreign and Commonwealth Office, London.

TEMPERATURE CONVERSION TABLE

°C	°F	°C	°F
1	34	26	79
2	36	27	81
3	38	28	82
4	39	29	84
5	41	30	86
6	43	31	88
7	45	32	90
8	46	33	92
9	48	34	93
10	50	35	95
11	52	36	97
12	54	37	99
13	56	38	100
14	57	39	102
15	59	40	104
16	61	41	106
17	63	42	108
18	64	43	109
19	66	44	111
20	68	45	113
21	70	46	115
22	72	47	117
23	74	48	118
24	75	49	120
25	77	50	122

The formula for converting °C to °F is:
°C x 9 ÷ 5 + 32 = °F

WEIGHTS AND MEASURES

Metric

Weight
1 Kilogram (Kg) = 2.205 pounds
1 metric ton = 1.102 short tons

Length
1 millimetre (mm)= 0.03937 inch
1 metre = 3.281 feet
1 kilometre (km) = 0.621 mile

Area
1 heactare = 2.471 acres
1 square km = 0.386 sq mile

Capacity
1 litre = 0.220 imperial gallon
    = 0.264 US gallon

Volume
1 cubic metre (m³) = 35.31 cubic feet
    = 1.31 cubic yards

British and US

Weight
1 pound (lb) = 454 grams
1 short ton (2,000lbs) = 0.907 m ton
1 long ton (2,240lbs) = 1.016 m tons

Length
1 inch = 25.417 millimetres
1 foot (ft) = 0.305 metre
1 mile = 1.609 kilometres

Area
1 acre = 0.405 hectare
1 sq mile = 2.590 sq kilometre

Capacity
1 imperial gallon = 4.546 litres
1 US gallon = 3.785 litres

Volume
1 cubic foot (cu ft) = 0.028 m³
1 cubic yard (cu yd) = 0.765 m³

NB 5 imperial gallons are approximately equal to 6 US gallons

Glossary

A

Abbasids
Muslim Dynasty ruled from Baghdad 750-1258
Affanes
Woollen slipper used by nomads
Aghlabid
Adjectival form of Aghlabite
Aghlabite
Orthodox Muslim Dynasty 800-909 AD
Agora
Market/meeting place
Aïd/Eïd
Religious Festival
Aïn
Spring
Almohads
Islamic Empire in North Africa 1130-1269
Amir
Mamluk military officer
Amulet
Object with magical power of protection
Ankh
Symbol of life
Apse
Semi-circular part of a room
Arabesque
Geometric pattern with flowers and foliage used in Islamic designs
Assif
see oued
Astrolabe
Instrument used to calculate latitude and altitude
Azib
Seasonal shelter (originally just animals)

B

Bab
City gate/door
Bâches
Converted pick-up truck
Bahri
North/northern
Bain Maure
see Hammam
Baladiyah
Municipality
Baksheesh
Money as alms, tip or bribe
Baraka
Blessing
Barakan
Woollen wrap 5m by 2m to cover entire body
Barbary
Name of North Africa 16th-19th centuries
Basha
see Pasha
Basilica
Imposing Roman building, with aisles, later used for worship
Bazaar
Market
Bedouin
Nomadic desert Arab
Beni
Sons of (tribe)
Berber
Indigenous tribe of North Africa
Bey
Governor (Ottoman) was title of heveditavy rulers in Tunisia until 1957
Bir
Well

Borj
Fort
Burnous
Man's cloak with hood – tradional wear

C

Caftan
Traditional 'cover all' garment worn by men and women
Caid
Official
Caldarium
hottest room in a Roman bath-house
Calèche
Horse drawn carriage
Calidarium
Hot room
Capital
Top section of a column
Caravanserai
Lodgings for travellers and animals around a courtyard
Cartouche
Oval ring containing a king's name in hieroglyphics
Cavea
Seating area in amphitheatre
Cella
Chamber of the divinity – chapel – sanctuary
Chechia
Man's small red felt hat
Chotts
Low-lying salt lakes
Colossus
Gigantic statue

D

Dar
House
Darj w ktaf
Carved geometric motif of intersecting arcs with super-imposed rectangles
Dayat
Lake
Decumanus
Roman road aligned E-W
Deglet Nur
High quality translucent date

Delu
Water lifting device at head of well
Dey
Commander (of janissaries)
Dikka
Raised platform in mosque for Koranic readings
Djebel
Mountain
Djemma
Main or Friday mosque
Djin
Spirit
Dólmenes
Prehistoric cave
Dour
Village settlement

E

Eïd
see Aïd
Eïn
see Aïn
Erg
Sand dune desert

F

Faqirs
Muslim who has taken a vow of poverty
Fatimids
Muslim dynasty 909-1171 AD claiming descent from Mohammed's daughter Fatimah
Felucca
Sailing boat on Nile
Fondouk/Funduq
Lodgings for goods and animals around a courtyard
Forum
Central open space in Roman town
Frigidarium
Cold room in a Roman bath-house
Ful/Fuul
Beans

G

Garrigue
Mediterranean scrubland – poor quality

Ghar
Grotto or cave
Ghibli
Hot dry wind from south
Ginan
Small garden or tree embayment
GP
Grand parcours (main road)
Gymnasium
Roman school for mind and body

H

Hafsids
Berber Dynasty 13th-16th century in present day Tunisia
Haik
Heavy cloak worn by Berber man
Hallal
Meat from animals killed ascending to Islamic law
Hamada
Stone desert
Hammam
Bath house
Harem
Women's quarters
Harira
Soup
Hypogeum
The part of the building below ground, underground chamber

I

Imam
Muslim religious leader
Izar
Long straight cotton wrap worn by Berber women over caftan

J

Jallabah
Outer garment with sleeves and a hood – often striped
Jami'
Mosque
Janissaries
Elite Ottoman soldiery
Jarapas
Rough cloth made with rags

Jihad
Holy war by Muslims against non-believers

K

Ka
Spirit
Khuttab
Korami school for young boys or orphans
Kilim
Woven carpet
Kif
Hashish
Kissaria
Covered market
Koran
Sacred book of the Moslems
Koubba
Dome on tomb of holy man
Koutab
Koranic school
Ksar (pl Ksour)
Fortified place – used also to mean fortified granary in South Tunisia
Kufic
Decorative Arabic script

L

Lintel
Piece of stone over a doorway, or arch
Liwan
Vaulted arcade
Loculus
Small compartment or cell, a recess

M

Mahboub
Coins worn as jewellery
Malekite
Section of Sunni Islam
Maquis
Mediterranean scrubland – often aromatic
Marabout
Muslim holy man/his tomb
Maristan
Hospital
Mashrabiyya
Wooden screen

Mashreq
Eastern Arab world
Mastaba
Tomb
Mausoleum
Large tomb building
Mechouar
Royal enclosure/meeting place
Medersa (pl Medressa)
School usually attached to a mosque
Medina
Old walled town, residential quarter
Mellah
Jewish quarter of old town
Menzel
House
Mihrab
Recess in wall of mosque indicating direction of Mecca
Minaret
Slender tower of mosque from which the muezzin calls the faithful to prayer
Minbar
Pulpit in a mosque
Monolithic
Column or pillar made out of one piece of stone
Mosque
Muslim place of worship
Moulid/Mouloud
Religious festival – Prophet's birthday
Moussem
Religious gathering
Muezzin
Priest who calls the faithful to prayer
Mullah
Muslim religious teacher
Murabtin
Dependent tribe

N

Necropolis
Cemetery

O

Oasis
Watered desert gardens
Obelisk
Tapering monolithic shaft of stone with pyramidal apex

Ottoman
Major Muslim Empire based in Turkey 13th-20th centuries
Oued
see Wadi
Ouled
Tribe
Outrepassé
Horse-shoe shaped arch

P

Palaestra
Exercise area associated with Roam bath-house
Pasha
Governor
Pediment
Triangular or circular ornament which crowns the fronts of buildings and serves as a finish to the tops of doors, porticoes, windows, etc
Peristyle
A central garden surrounded by portico
Phoenicians
Important trading nation based in eastern Mediterranean from 1100 BC
Pilaster
Square column partly built into, partly projecting from, the wall
Pisé
Sun-baked clay used for building
Piste
Unsurfaced road
Pylon
Gateway of Egyptian temple

Q

Qibla
Mosque wall in direction of Mecca

R

Rabbi
Head of Jewish community
Ramadan
Muslim month of fasting
Reg
Rock desert

Ribat
Fortified monastery
Riwaq
Arcaded aisle

S

Sabil
Public water fountain
Sabkha
Dry salt lake
Sahel
Coast/ coastal plain
Sahn
Courtyard
Salat
Worship
Saqiya
Water wheel
Sarcophagus
Decorated stone coffin
Sebkha
See Sabkha
Semi-columnar
Flat on one side and rounded on other
Serais
Lodging for men and animals
Serir
Sand desert
Shahada
Profession of faith
Shergui
Hot, dry desert wind
Sidi
Mr/Saint
Sifsari
Length of white fabric pulled over head and secured at waist worn by Tunisian women
Souq
Traditional market
Stalactite
An ornamental arrangement of multi-tiered niches, like a honeycomb, found in domes and portals
Stele
Inscribed pillar used as gravestone
Suani
Small walled irrigated traditional garden
Sufi

Muslim mystic
Sunni
Orthodox Muslims
Suq
see Souq

T

Tagine/Tajine
Stew
Taifa
Sub-tribe
Tariqa
Brotherhood/Order
Thòlos
Round building, dome, cupola
Torah
Parchment scrolls carying religious inscription important to the Jews
Triclinium
Dining room in Roman house with seating on three sides
Troglodyte
Underground dweller

V

Vandals
Empire in North Africa 429-534 AD
Visir
Governor

W

Wadi
Water course – usually dry
Waqf
Endowed land
Wikala
Merchants' hostel
Wilaya/Wilayat
Governorate/district

Z

Zaouia/Zawia/Zawiya
Shrine/Sennusi centre
Zellij
Geometrical mosaic pattern made from pieces of glazed tiles
Zeriba
House of straw/grass

Tinted boxes

LIBYA

Illustrations

Index

Maps

LIBYA

The Footprint list

SURPLUS

Andalucía Handbook
Cambodia Handbook
Caribbean Islands Handbook
Chile Handbook
East Africa Handbook
Ecuador Handbook
  with the Galápagos
Egypt Handbook
India Handbook
Indonesia Handbook
Laos Handbook
Malaysia & Singapore Handbook
Mexico & Central America Handbook
Morocco Handbook
  with Mauritania
Myanmar (Burma) Handbook
Namibia Handbook
Pakistan Handbook
Peru Handbook
South Africa Handbook
South American Handbook
Sri Lanka Handbook
Thailand Handbook
Tibet Handbook
Tunisia Handbook with Libya
Vietnam Handbook
Zimbabwe & Malawi Handbook
  with Botswana, Moçambique & Zambia

New in Autumn 1997
Israel Handbook
Nepal Handbook

In the pipeline
Argentina Handbook
Brazil Handbook
Colombia Handbook
Cuba Handbook
Jordan, Syria & Lebanon Handbook
Venezuela Handbook

Footprint T-shirt

The Footprint T-shirt is available in 100% cotton in various colours.

Mail Order

Footprint Handbooks are available worldwide in good bookstores. They can also be ordered directly from us in Bath (see below for address). Please contact us if you have difficulty finding a title.

The Footprint Handbook website will be coming to keep you up to date with all the latest news from us (http://www.footprint-handbooks.co.uk). For the most up-to-date information and to join our mailing list please contact us at:

Footprint Handbooks
6 Riverside Court
Lower Bristol Road
Bath BA2 3DZ, England
T +44(0)1225 469141
F +44(0)1225 469461
E Mail handbooks@footprint.cix.co.uk